Less managing. More teaching. Greater learning.

Q: INSTRUCTORS...

Would you like your **students** to show up for class **more prepared**?

(Let's face it, class is much more fun if everyone is engaged and prepared…)

Want an **easy way to assign** homework online and track student **progress**?

(Less time grading means more time teaching…)

Want an **instant view** of student or class performance?

(No more wondering if students understand…)

Need to **collect data and generate reports** required for administration or accreditation?

(Say goodbye to manually tracking student learning outcomes…)

Want to **record and post your lectures** for students to view online?

(The more students can see, hear, and experience class resources, the better they learn…)

A: With **McGraw-Hill's Connect,®**

INSTRUCTORS GET:

- Simple **assignment management**, allowing you to spend more time teaching.

- **Auto-graded** assignments, quizzes, and tests.

- **Detailed visual reporting** where student and section results can be viewed and analyzed.

- Sophisticated **online testing** capability.

- A **filtering and reporting** function that allows you to easily assign and report on materials that are correlated to learning objectives and Bloom's taxonomy.

- An easy-to-use **lecture capture** tool.

- The option to **upload course documents** for student access.

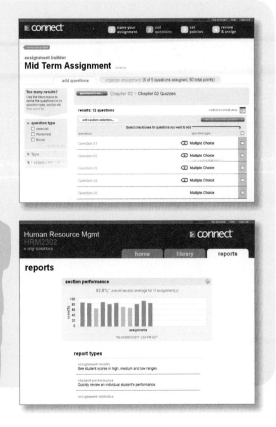

CANADIAN BUSINESS AND SOCIETY

Ethics, Responsibilities and Sustainability

Third Edition

ROBERT W. SEXTY

Professor Emeritus, Faculty of Business Administration
Memorial University of Newfoundland

Canadian Business and Society: Ethics, Responsibilities and Sustainability

Third Edition

Statistics Canada information is used with the permission of Statistics Canada. Users are forbidden to copy the data and redisseminate them, in an original or modified form, for commercial purposes, without permission from Statistics Canada. Information on the availability of the wide range of data from Statistics Canada can be obtained from Statistics Canada's Regional Offices, its World Wide Web site at www.statcan.gc.ca, and its toll-free access number 1-800-263-1136.

The Internet addresses listed in the text were accurate at the time of publication. The inclusion of a Web site does not indicate an endorsement by the authors or McGraw-Hill Ryerson, and McGraw-Hill Ryerson does not guarantee the accuracy of the information presented at these sites.

ISBN-13: 978-0-07-133885-1
ISBN-10: 0-07-133885-3

1 2 3 4 5 6 7 8 9 DOW 1 9 8 7 6 5 4 3

Printed and bound in the United States of America.

Care has been taken to trace ownership of copyright material contained in this text; however, the publisher will welcome any information that enables them to rectify any reference or credit for subsequent editions.

Director Product Management: *Rhondda McNabb*
Group Product Manager: *Kim Brewster*
Marketing Manager: *Cathie Lefebvre*
Product Developer: *Daphne Scriabin*
Senior Editorial Associate: *Christine Lomas*
Supervising Editor: *Stephanie Gay*
Photo/Permissions Research: *Alison Lloyd Baker*
Copy Editor: *Kelli Howey*
Plant Production Coordinator: *Tammy Mavroudi*
Manufacturing Production Coordinator: *Emily Hickey*
Cover Design: *Michelle Losier*
Cover Image: *Panoramic Images/Getty Images (RM)*
Interior Design: *Michelle Losier*
Page Layout: *Laserwords Private Limited*
Printer: *R.R. Donnelley/Willard*

Library and Archives Canada Cataloguing in Publication

Library and Archives Canada Cataloguing in Publication

Sexty, Robert W. (Robert William), 1942-,
   Canadian business and society : ethics, responsibility and sustainability / Robert W. Sexty.—Third edition.

Includes bibliographical references and index.
ISBN 978-0-07-133885-1 (pbk.)

   1. Business ethics—Canada—Textbooks. 2. Social responsibility of business—Textbooks. I. Title.

HF5387.5.C3S49 2013   174'.40971   C2013-904015-3

Dedication

To Suzanne, who has travelled with me through five books including many editions—and to more than 50 countries on seven continents!

About the Author

Dr. Robert Sexty was a Professor of Business Administration at the Faculty of Business Administration at Memorial University of Newfoundland for 39 years, and was awarded a *Professor Emeritus* title in 2008. He holds bachelor, masters, and doctoral degrees in Business Administration from the University of Alberta, Queen's University, and the University of Colorado, respectively. Sabbatical years have been spent at the Harvard Business School, Boston, and the University of Auckland, New Zealand. He was awarded one of the "2001–2002 Leaders in Management Education Awards" sponsored by the *National Post* and PricewaterhouseCoopers.

At Memorial, Robert Sexty taught Business Policy (Strategic Management), Introduction to Business, and Business and Society (Business Ethics) courses at the undergraduate and graduate levels. He developed, and has taught, the strategy and business and society courses in Athabasca University's Electronic MBA Program. He has taught numerous management development seminars and workshops on many management topics, including strategic management and the ethics of business.

Robert Sexty is the author of *Issues in Canadian Business,* the fourth edition of which was published in 1998 as *Canadian Business in the New Stakeholder Economy.* He is also the co-author of *Exploring Strategic Management,* published in 1989, and *Contemporary Management in Canada,* published in 1992, 1995, and 1998. A fourth book, *Canadian Business and Society: Understanding the Social and Ethical Challenges,* was published in January 1995.

Robert Sexty is a past President of the Administrative Sciences Association of Canada, and is a member of, and active in, many academic and professional associations. He consults in the area of strategic planning and management for business, government, and non-profit organizations, and acts as a facilitator in sessions for management groups and boards of directors. He has served on the Boards of Directors of the Egg Farmers of Canada, East Coast Trail Association, and Anglican Homes Inc.

Brief Contents

Contents

Preface

The Philosophy of the Book

Ethics is all the rage throughout society these days; the ethics of business is no exception. Today, integrity is important to business performance and acceptance by society. Society expects business's adherence to moral standards such as honesty, fairness, and justice. This book provides a broad overview of the Canadian business system and society's expectations of it.

The book's title emphasizes "business and society" in addition to three key words: ethics, responsibilities, and sustainability. The ethics of business refers to the rules, standards, codes, values, or principles that provide guidance for morally appropriate behaviour in managerial decision making relating to the operation of businesses and business's relationship with society. Business is accepted by society as long as it recognizes the responsibilities in its operations and considers the needs and desires of society. The result has been increasing obligations with business agreeing to do more. Sustainability represents a management approach that integrates economic, ethical, and environmental responsibilities into all management systems.

The corporation—the main business institution—accepts the necessity for integrity in business and recognizes the accompanying responsibilities. Throughout the book, the term *corporation* is used to represent business enterprises. The formal and legal entity of the corporation does not supply all the goods and services to society, but it is by far the principal business institution.

The ethics and responsibilities of business in society are connected to the concept of *stakeholders,* individuals or organizations that influence the corporation and/or that are influenced by the corporation. This concept will be described fully in the book and is key to the connection to or linkage between business and society.

Third Edition Changes

The most substantive change is a focus on corporate sustainability. Little agreement exists in the academic and practitioner literature on a definition of the concept. In this book, *corporate sustainability (CS)* refers to activities demonstrating the inclusion of social and environmental as well as economic responsibilities in business operations as they impact all stakeholders to ensure the long-term survival of the corporation. The term sustainability was first used in the context of environmental sustainability, but corporate sustainability has a wider meaning and includes economic, ethical, and social responsibilities as well. The difference from *corporate social responsibility (CSR)* is that the responsibilities are completely integrated into the structure, policies, and operations of the corporation. Corporate sustainability is referenced throughout the book, and Chapter 16 outlines sustainability strategy.

New topics introduced include social licence (Chapter 1); conscious capitalism and shared value (Chapter 2); crisis management (Chapter 3); unethical leadership (Chapter 6); the VBA model (value, balance, and accountability) (Chapter 7); the for-benefit or B Corporation and community bonds (Chapter 8); deregulation and the role of government in CSR (Chapter 10); workplace privacy (Chapter 12); and service learning (Chapter 16). More coverage is given to research findings about CSR and employees and consumers (Chapter 12). Additional materials are provided on supply chains (Chapter 12); non-governmental organizations (NGOs) and business partnerships (Chapter 13); and bribery and microfinance (Chapter 15). Other changes are identified in the following sections of this Preface.

Overview of the Book's Contents

The topics covered in the book represent a consensus on the current subjects making up the business and society field. This is confirmed by two references: the domain statement of the Academy of Management's Social Issues in Management Division, and a recently published article by Schwartz and Carroll that identifies, from an extensive literature review, the frameworks of the business and society field.

Business and the corporation operate within various societal environments,[1] and these environments provide a basis for the book's organization.

- **Business Environment**—The description of the business environment is given in Chapters 1, 2, and 16. Chapter 1, "The Relationship between Business and Society," provides an overview to the book and describes the concept of *business and society*. Other topics covered in this chapter include an outline of the Canadian business system, the role of the corporation, the stakeholders responsible for operating corporations, a brief introduction to ethical thinking, and society's acceptance of business. Chapter 2, "Ethics and Capitalism," describes the fundamentals of capitalism upon which the Canadian business system is based. It is important to understand these fundamentals, as the ethical implications associated with them reappear throughout the book. Finally, Chapter 16, "Sustainability Strategy," provides an overview to how corporations plan for and implement ethical programs and carry out their responsibilities. These chapters establish that corporations have economic responsibilities to meet if other responsibilities are to be undertaken.

- **Stakeholder Environment**—Chapters 3, 4, 11, 12, and 13 focus on stakeholders and their relationships with business and the corporation. Chapter 3, "Identifying Stakeholders and Issues," gives a detailed list of a corporation's stakeholders and the rationale for the stakeholder concept. The following chapter, "Stakeholder Relations and Analysis," advances the discussion of stakeholders by presenting approaches to the corporation's interrelationships with stakeholders. Although stakeholders are referred to throughout the textbook, some are studied in more detail: owners and directors in Chapter 11, "Ownership and Governance of the Corporation"; employees, consumers, competitors, and suppliers in Chapter 12, "Ethics and Responsibilities in the Workplace and Marketplace"; and non-governmental organizations, media, think tanks, religious organizations and education institutions in Chapter 13, "Civil Society Stakeholders."

- **Ethical Environment**—The ethical environment is addressed in two chapters: Chapter 5, "Ethics of Business: The Theoretical Basis," and Chapter 6, "Ethics of Business: Management and Leadership." The former chapter outlines several theoretical ethical principles that will assist in understanding and analyzing moral dilemmas and integrity issues confronting business and the corporation. The latter chapter takes a pragmatic approach to outlining the managerial techniques or methodologies of ethics programs in corporations.

- **Social Environment**—Similar to the approach taken with the ethical environment, the social environment is discussed from theoretical and practical perspectives. Chapter 7, "Corporate Social Responsibility: The Concept," describes the various theories of social responsibility that can be used when analyzing issues and cases throughout the book. In Chapter 8, "Corporate Social Responsibility: In Practice," the approaches taken by corporations to implement their social responsibilities are outlined.

- **Regulatory Environment**—Business and the corporation are accountable to stakeholders as they are influenced by them in various ways. In effect, this is a form of regulation of the corporation. Chapter 9, "Measuring, Reporting, and Communicating CSR," identifies auditing processes used by corporations in reporting how they respond to their economic, stakeholder, ethical, and social environments. Chapter 10, "Regulating

Business," identifies the range of regulation—from government legislation and policies through to self-regulation performed by industry associations and the corporation itself. Corporate governance is, in effect, the regulation or oversight of the corporation's activities provided by the board of directors. Corporate governance has been reformed in recent years, with emphasis placed on the corporation's ethics and responsibilities.

- **Ecological Environment**—The natural or ecological environment is considered in Chapter 14, "The Environment and Business Responsibilities." Ecology is a major issue involving many responsibilities and thus is discussed as a separate chapter.

- **International Environment**—The international environment, also referred to as globalization, involves many ethical issues and responsibilities. Chapter 15, "Globalization and Business Responsibilities," outlines how globalization is impacting almost every business and identifies how corporations are responding.

The business and society field can be described through the primary frameworks that are identified and discussed in an article by Schwartz and Carroll as:

- Corporate society responsibility
- Business ethics
- Stakeholder management
- Sustainability
- Corporate citizenship[2]

The frameworks are covered throughout the book and, with the environments described above, provide a comprehensive and contemporary view of the ethics, responsibilities, and sustainability of business.

Features and Benefits of the Book

- **A unique approach.** Each chapter offers unique materials or extensive descriptions of various topics as they relate to the ethics, responsibilities, and sustainability of business. Ethics refers to the fairness and integrity with which business functions in society, responsibilities refers to the increasing obligations that business is agreeing to undertake in society, and sustainability represents a management approach that integrates economic, ethical, and environmental responsibilities into all management systems. The text

  - considers academic integrity in business schools (Chapters 1, 9, and 16);
  - discusses the relationship of capitalism to ethics and responsibilities (Chapter 2);
  - provides a comprehensive view of the stakeholder concept (Chapter 3);
  - provides extensive discussion of approaches to understanding stakeholders, including matrix mapping, salience, collaboration, and social capital (Chapter 4);
  - presents a broader scope of ethical principles to guide behaviour (Chapter 5);
  - emphasizes compliance-based versus integrity-based approaches to ethics programs (Chapter 6);
  - discusses contemporary CSR approaches such as corporate sustainability, triple bottom line, and corporate citizenship (Chapter 7);
  - includes social venture philanthropy and social enterprise approaches to CSR (Chapter 8);
  - provides a separate chapter on measuring, reporting, and communicating CSR (Chapter 9);
  - views the regulation of business as a spectrum of approaches from total reliance on the market to complete government direction (Chapter 10);

- examines the influence of owners and directors on the ethics of business and their response to responsibilities expected by society, including the impact of social or responsible investing (Chapter 11);

- identifies and examines some of the ethical issues and responsibilities relating to employee, consumer, competitor, and supplier stakeholders (Chapter 12);

- introduces civil society stakeholders as a category, including extensive discussion of NGOs and the media (Chapter 13);

- discusses the possibility of a market-driven approach to solving environmental problems, including descriptions of emissions trading and offsets (Chapter 14);

- describes globalization as an economic, political, and social process (Chapter 15); and

- relates the ethics of business, corporate social responsibility, and the corporation's responsibilities to corporate sustainability, which is achieved through strategic management (Chapter 16).

- **A building approach.** The sequence of the chapters and the concepts covered enable students to learn about business and society incrementally. Thus, concepts relating to capitalism and the economic responsibilities of the corporation are introduced early, followed by the stakeholder concept. This body of knowledge is key to understanding the subsequent chapters. Similarly, theoretical material is followed by managerial practice in the social and ethical environments and becomes the basis for understanding the discussions in Parts IV and V.

- **A focus on Canadian content.** The material in the book emphasizes Canadian content; it is an indigenous manuscript rather than a conversion of an American or European text.

- **Business and managerial perspectives.** The book is written from the perspective of business and managers, as they have to cope with social, ethical, and environmental responsibilities while also having to meet economic responsibilities. The materials are not intended to make judgments about business behaviour, but instead to increase the understanding of businesspersons and managers of their influence on society and of society's influence on business. Both good and undesirable examples of business behaviour are presented.

- **Non-profit sector included.** Non-profit organizations also play a role in business and society. This sector is represented by stakeholders such as non-governmental organizations, educational institutions, religious groups, and charities. These stakeholders are important in social responsibility initiatives described throughout the book but particularly in Chapters 7, 8, and 9. Most of Chapter 13, "Civil Society Stakeholders," is devoted to non-profit stakeholders.

- **A student perspective.** Efforts have been made to present materials, vignettes, example inserts, and cases to which students can relate. Students are the future business leaders and managers and must understand the dynamic relationship between business and society and the ethics and responsibilities involved. More emphasis has been put on the ethics, responsibilities, and sustainability of students, in business programs, and at educational institutions.

- **"Learn more" boxes.** Readers who want to know more about certain topics are directed to "Go to Connect" where applicable.

Chapter 1
- Adam Smith
- The documentary *The Corporation*
- Changing attitudes toward business

Chapter 2
- The right to property
- Business fundamentals and the story of The Little Red Hen
- The pros and cons of capitalism

Chapter 3
- Accessing information about stakeholders
- Identifying and engaging stakeholders
- Approaches used to address issues

Chapter 4
- The principles of stakeholder management
- Matrix mapping
- Influence strategies

Chapter 5
- Ayn Rand
- Cowboy Style Ethics
- Your ethics

Chapter 6
- Giving voice to values
- A guide to practical ethics
- Business ethics by joining a blog

Chapter 7
- Sustainability
- *Corporate Knights*
- CSR jobs

Chapter 8
- Canadian social enterprises
- The Giving Pledge
- CSR and small business

Chapter 9
- Examples of the best CSR/sustainability reports
- Evaluating sustainability reports
- CSR in Canadian business

Chapter 10
- Your view of government regulation
- Lobbying government
- Ethics in government

Chapter 11
- What shareholders are demanding of corporations
- Facebook Inc.'s governance
- Responsible investing

Chapter 12
- Ethical practices in the workplace
- Ethical products and services
- Sustainable global supply chains

Chapter 13
- Digital protest movements
- "Watch" sites
- The efforts of OpenMedia.ca to keep the Internet affordable

Chapter 14
- "The tragedy of the commons"
- Calculating your carbon footprint
- Environmental Jobs

Chapter 15
- The international Principles of Responsible Investment
- Transparency International
- Defining the Canadian mining industry's social licence

Chapter 16
- Canadian corporations with comprehensive sustainability strategies
- Organizational culture and sustainability
- Sustainability and strategy

Encouraging Critical Thinking

Critical thinking is a higher-order intellectual, purposeful thought and action process. It integrates inquiry, reflection, and deliberation to facilitate more thorough and meaningful learning. This book enables students to accomplish this in several ways: by introducing new ideas and concepts, linking ideas to illustrations, addressing issues from different perspectives, and exposing readers to new sources of information. The concepts, theories, and illustrations allow students to use their skills to clarify facts, assess information, formulate and defend their own intellectual positions, and develop appropriate courses of action. The pedagogical approaches listed below encourage student critical thinking. The Instructor's Manual provides teachers with additional materials that will enhance this process.

Pedagogy: User Approach

- **Learning Outcomes.** At the beginning of each chapter, numbered Learning Outcomes are listed. These tie in with the numbered section headings in each chapter.

LEARNING OUTCOMES   *After studying this chapter, you will be able to:*

LO 9.1 Understand the background to measuring and reporting CSR performance.

LO 9.2 Define corporate reputation and understand its relationship to corporate social responsibility.

LO 9.3 Identify the stakeholders who influence CSR reporting.

LO 9.4 Describe the relationship between CSR and corporate profitability.

LO 9.5 Enumerate and discuss the types of criteria used in social auditing.

LO 9.6 Recognize the surveys that evaluate Canadian CSR reporting.

LO 9.7 Outline how CSR and sustainability results are communicated to stakeholders.

LO 9.8 Explain the role of business schools in CSR reporting.

LO 9.9 Discuss the future of CSR and CSR reporting.

- **In-depth examples.** Instead of inserting numerous but short one- or two-sentence examples in the text, this book takes a different approach. Lengthier boxed inserts allow for more discussion of the examples. The two types of boxes are Everyday Ethics and Responsibility for Ethics:

- **Everyday Ethics** boxes provide examples not only of best practices, but also of inappropriate or questionable practices. More than 27 new Everyday Ethics boxes have been included and all the remaining ones updated. Instructors are provided with additional information to facilitate classroom discussion in the Instructor's Manual and online.

Everyday Ethics
5.1

Business and Lance Armstrong's Virtues

Lance Armstrong was considered an outstanding athlete and had won the Tour de France cycling race seven times before retiring in 2011. He was a high-profile athlete and had sponsorships from sports shoe and apparel company Nike, brewer Anheuser-Busch, and bicycle manufacturer Trek. In 1996 he was diagnosed with testicular cancer and was admired for his fight to overcome it. The Lance Armstrong Foundation was established in 1997 to support cancer research, and Livestrong formed in 2003 to provide services and other support to cancer patients. There were various accusations during Armstrong's career that he used illegal performance-enhancing drugs, known as doping. He denied the accusations and was very critical of his accusers. Investigations were started but did not find evidence to support the accusations.

The release of a United States Anti-Doping Agency (USADA) report in October 2012 changed things. The comprehensive report was hundreds of pages long and contained eyewitness testimony from teammates, email correspondence, financial records, and laboratory analyses. The report accused Armstrong of running "the most sophisticated, professionalized and successful doping program that sport has ever seen." The doping included administration of testosterone, cortisone, human growth hormone, and blood booster erythropoietin (EPO). Armstrong was accused of having deep character flaws that included lying, bullying, cheating, and attacking people. As a result of the report, he was stripped of his seven Tour de France titles and barred for life from participating in Olympic sports. He later resigned from the board of Livestrong.

In January 2013, Armstrong confessed that he used drugs in interviews on the Oprah Winfrey Network. A common reaction to the interviews was that Armstrong did little to redeem himself, failed to convey a genuine sense of remorse, and lacked credibility. In a later media interview, he claimed that he was the fall guy for the cycling doping culture where cheating was common. Moreover, he claimed that doping existed in other endurance sports. It was felt that he did little to repair his tarnished reputation.

Armstrong still had admirers, as evidenced by support for Livestrong. After the USADA report, 16,000 donations averaging $97 were received, twice the usual number. On the other hand, his sponsors either cancelled or did not renew their sponsorship contracts, worth millions of dollars.

Sources: USADA, "Report on proceedings under the World Anti-Doping Code and the USADA Protocol: Reasoned decision of the United States Anti-Doping Agency on disqualification and ineligibility," http://d3epuodzu3wuis.cloudfront.net/ReasonedDecision.pdf; Mark Gollom, "Did Lance Armstrong redeem or incriminate himself? Armstrong did a poor job of rehabilitating his image, experts say," *CBC News*, January 18, 2013, http://www.cbc.ca/news/canada/story/2013/01/18/f-lance-armstrong-apology-reaction.html, accessed January 20, 2013; NBC News, "Lance Armstrong steps down from Livestrong, loses Nike, Bud contracts," http://www.nbcnews.com/business/lance-armstrong-steps-down-livestrong-loses-nike-bud-contracts-1C6512991, accessed January 20, 2013; Nick Hoult, "Lance Armstrong says he is 'fall guy' for cycling's problems, *The Telegraph*, http://www.telegraph.co.uk/sport/othersports/cycling/lancearmstrong/9838064/Lance-Armstrong-says-he-is-fall-guy-for-cyclings-problems.html, accessed January 20, 2013; and "Times Topics: Lance Armstrong," *The New York Times*, February 7, 2013, http://topics.nytimes.com/top/reference/timestopics/people/a/lance_armstrong/index.html, accessed February 20, 2013.

- **Responsibility for Ethics** boxes refer to or describe individuals, organizations, practices, or concepts that affect or influence the behaviour of business leaders, managers, or corporations. Most describe the roles or influence of stakeholders. Sixteen new Responsibility for Ethics boxes have been included and the remaining ones updated.

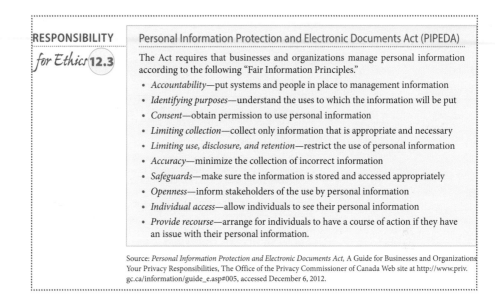

RESPONSIBILITY *for Ethics* **12.3**

Personal Information Protection and Electronic Documents Act (PIPEDA)

The Act requires that businesses and organizations manage personal information according to the following "Fair Information Principles."

- *Accountability*—put systems and people in place to management information
- *Identifying purposes*—understand the uses to which the information will be put
- *Consent*—obtain permission to use personal information
- *Limiting collection*—collect only information that is appropriate and necessary
- *Limiting use, disclosure, and retention*—restrict the use of personal information
- *Accuracy*—minimize the collection of incorrect information
- *Safeguards*—make sure the information is stored and accessed appropriately
- *Openness*—inform stakeholders of the use by personal information
- *Individual access*—allow individuals to see their personal information
- *Provide recourse*—arrange for individuals to have a course of action if they have an issue with their personal information.

Source: *Personal Information Protection and Electronic Documents Act,* A Guide for Businesses and Organizations Your Privacy Responsibilities, The Office of the Privacy Commissioner of Canada Web site at http://www.priv.gc.ca/information/guide_e.asp#005, accessed December 6, 2012.

- **Opening vignettes.** All vignettes are original and based on Canadian materials and examples. Each chapter begins with a real-world situation that introduces the chapter content. All require an individual to respond to an issue or dilemma. Six new vignettes are included in this edition and several others have been revised.

What would you do if . . . ?

Paul O'Doherty is the ethics officer for a medium-sized petroleum company; in this role he is responsible for the company's comprehensive ethics program. The program includes a code of business conduct that outlines the values to guide behaviour, identifies conflicts of interest, specifies appropriate and inappropriate practices, and provides an approach to reporting violations or suspected wrongdoing. One aspect of the reporting system is an employee hotline to which employees can contribute in written form, including by email, or orally by telephone or in person. Participants must identify themselves and all communications

go directly to Paul, who reports directly to the corporate secretary and legal counsel. The identity of the employee is not disclosed and confidentiality is maintained except in rare cases where legal action occurs.

Paul is a member of the Ethics Practitioners' Association of Canada (EPAC). According to EPAC, the skills of an ethics officer include "facilitating constructive dialogue on ethics-related issues, analyzing ethics issues and problems, and providing coherent, realistic solutions to ethical issues." Paul finds his job to be rewarding and his work has enabled the company to keep abreast of developments in the ethics

- **End-of-chapter cases.** Cases relevant to the chapter content can be found in the end-of-chapter material. The cases are of two types: descriptive of an issue in business and society to which management must respond and can be used as a basis for discussion, and decision making in that the student faces a dilemma that must be addressed. Ten new cases are included in this edition, and many others have been altered and updated.

4.2 *Walmart's Supplier Relationship*

Walmart is the world's largest retailer with a goal of keeping prices as low as possible to consumers. The corporation's management of its supply chain plays a Walmart and its suppliers.

- Due to its size Walmart can exert tremendous economic power over suppliers, not only in terms of prices but also in applying pressure on suppliers to reduce packaging and create environmentally friendly packaging.
- With its large market share for some products, it is possible for Walmart to reduce the price of a product so much that other retailers have difficulty matching it and the profit margin for the supplier is reduced.
- Walmart is reducing its use of procurement companies or intermediaries and purchasing directly from manufacturers or suppliers. Small suppliers will face greater challenges in coming to a face-to-face agreement with Walmart without the assistance of the procurement companies.

critical role in attaining this goal. Walmart's supply chain management involves four operational areas: adhering to customer demand, managing the relationship with price from suppliers. As suppliers will obtain fewer transportation economics of scale in deliveries to other customers, prices may increase to them.

Walmart has three basic beliefs: "respect for the individual, service to our customers, and striving for excellence." Some of the guiding principles associated with the beliefs are: "always act with integrity; lead with integrity, and expect others to work with integrity; follow the law at all times; and be honest and fair." Its Web site provides extensive information on how to become a supplier and offers of supplier training program.

Questions

1. Which stakeholders benefit and which are harmed by Walmart's approach to supply chain management?
2. What are the pros and cons of becoming a Walmart supplier? To answer this question, visit

---

- **NEW: "Learn more" boxes.** Boxed features directing readers who want to know more about certain chapter topics to "Go to Connect" are included where applicable.

---

connect   Want to learn more about **matrix mapping**? Go to CONNECT.

- **NEW: "Your Advice to . . ." boxes.** These boxes have been placed before each chapter summary and relate back to the chapter's opening vignette.

Your advice to Paul . . .

You are faced with a dilemma in advising Paul, because he faces difficulties no matter what he does. One possibility is to do nothing. This choice potentially harms co-workers, the supervisor involved, and perhaps customers and suppliers. Asking the violator to stop would be a sensitive matter; it may not be Paul's place to do it, and involving the supervisor and the human resources department involves confidentiality. The final possibility is to seek to change the policy or process. No clear alternative exists to the current approach to the hotline, and even if there were the same difficulties would likely be present.

- **Critical Thinking and Discussion Questions.** Every chapter ends with a set of questions that challenge the students to apply the concepts they have learned in each chapter. Some questions require students to think on their own to understand and evaluate concepts and, in some instances, to apply them appropriately. Other questions are designed to generate discussion and the articulation of different points of view.

CRITICAL THINKING AND DISCUSSION QUESTIONS

1. What is the strongest argument for business participating in corporate giving? What is the strongest argument for business not participating in corporate giving?

2. Why should corporations develop formal plans for implementing CSR?

3. How is the position that all corporate profits belong to the shareholders countered?

4. List guidelines that corporations might follow in developing and implementing a corporate giving program.

5. Why do some argue that corporate giving is now nothing more than corporate marketing or advertising?

6. Should a charity accept donations from tobacco, alcohol, or beer companies?

7. What are the drawbacks to corporate voluntarism?

8. What criteria should be used in selecting a charity for a corporate voluntary program?

9. What are the positive features of sponsorship programs? What are the drawbacks?

10. Should business be involved in social venture philanthropy? Is business better than government at addressing social ills?

11. From a business perspective, what are the positive features of social enterprises?

12. Why should small businesses become involved with CSR?

- **Ethics, Responsibilities and Sustainability Cases.** Longer cases are included that allow for more in-depth discussion of issues and dilemmas relating to the ethics, responsibilities and sustainability of business. The cases are of two types: descriptive of an issue in business and society to which management must respond and can be used as a basis for discussion of the issue, and decision making in that the student faces a dilemma that must be addressed. Four new cases are provided.

Ethics, Responsibilities, and Sustainability Cases

ZAPPING SALES AND TAXES[1]

Julia Hoben had graduated from a college business program with a major in accounting. She designed her program so that it enabled her to obtain a Certified General Accountant (CGA) designation within two years. She was employed as an accountant with a regional school board and she was enjoying the work.

Recently, her uncle asked if she was interested in doing some accounting for his restaurant. Julia first thought about this as moonlighting, of which her employer might not approve. She checked her employer's policy handbook and did not find any mention of moonlighting.

accounting designation. Julia concluded that there was no conflict between working for a school board and in the restaurant industry, and agreed to the offer. She did not feel it necessary to inform her employer.

During the first months, Julia experienced several complications in this part-time employment. Her first concern was prompted when her uncle paid her in cash for the first two weeks of work. At first, Julia did not think much about this, but upon further reflection she acknowledged that cash payments to employees or suppliers in the restaurant industry was a possible approach to avoiding taxes.

The book's contents have been developed and designed to make the study of Canadian business and society attractive and challenging. The capitalist business system exists in Canada and the ethics, responsibilities, and sustainability of business must be studied in this context. Ethical challenges do exist, and corporations should be held accountable for the responsibilities they have to Canadians. Increasingly, Canadian business is moving toward corporate sustainability strategies. It is hoped this book will increase students' understanding of Canadian business and society.

Supplements for Instructors

McGraw-Hill Connect McGraw-Hill Connect™ is a Web-based assignment and assessment platform that gives students the means to better connect with their coursework, with their instructors, and with the important concepts that they will need to know for success now and in the future.

With Connect, instructors can deliver assignments, quizzes, and tests online. Nearly all the questions from the text are presented in an auto-gradeable format and tied to the text's learning objectives. Instructors can edit existing questions and author entirely new problems. Track individual student performance—by question, assignment, or in relation to the class overall—with detailed grade reports. Integrate grade reports easily with Learning Management Systems (LMS) such as WebCT and Blackboard. And much more.

By choosing Connect, instructors are providing their students with a powerful tool for improving academic performance and truly mastering course material. Connect allows students to practise important skills at their own pace and on their own schedule. Importantly, students' assessment results and instructors' feedback are all saved online—so students can continually review their progress and plot their course to success.

Connect also provides 24/7 online access to an eBook—an online edition of the text—to aid them in successfully completing their work, wherever and whenever they choose.

KEY FEATURES

Simple Assignment Management

With Connect, creating assignments is easier than ever, so you can spend more time teaching and less time managing.

- Create and deliver assignments easily with selectable end-of-chapter questions and test bank material to assign online
- Streamline lesson planning, student progress reporting, and assignment grading to make classroom management more efficient than ever
- Go paperless with the eBook and online submission and grading of student assignments

Smart Grading

When it comes to studying, time is precious. Connect helps students learn more efficiently by providing feedback and practice material when they need it, where they need it.

- Automatically score assignments, giving students immediate feedback on their work and side-by-side comparisons with correct answers
- Access and review each response; manually change grades or leave comments for students to review
- Reinforce classroom concepts with practice tests and instant quizzes

Instructor Library

The Connect Instructor Library is your course creation hub. It provides all the critical resources you'll need to build your course, just how you want to teach it.

- Assign eBook readings and draw from a rich collection of textbook-specific assignments

- Access instructor resources, including ready-made PowerPoint presentations and media to use in your lectures
- View assignments and resources created for past sections
- Post your own resources for students to use

eBook

Connect reinvents the textbook learning experience for the modern student. Every Connect subject area is seamlessly integrated with Connect eBooks, which are designed to keep students focused on the concepts key to their success.

- Provide students with a Connect eBook, allowing for anytime, anywhere access to the textbook
- Merge media, animation, and assessments with the text's narrative to engage students and improve learning and retention
- Pinpoint and connect key concepts in a snap using the powerful eBook search engine
- Manage notes, highlights, and bookmarks in one place for simple, comprehensive review

INSTRUCTOR RESOURCES

- **Instructor's Manual:** Includes the "solution" to each chapter's opening vignette, material by section with the objective for each section, additional notes/materials/suggestions for instructors, responses to discussion questions, analysis of cases, additional resources such as references to case studies relevant for each chapter, video resources, and assignments/questions.

  The IM also provides additional information on the **Everyday Ethics** and **Responsibility for Ethics** boxes. The boxes are considered a key aspect of the text. Rather than give hundreds of one-line examples, the examples/illustrations in the boxes give more detailed information, and are constructed so that instructors can use them for discussion purposes or assignments. Features found throughout the boxes include:

  - Discussion questions
  - Additional information
  - Suggested assignments for students
  - Updated information
  - Internet links and related sites

- **Computerized Test Bank:** Developed as a ground-up, comprehensive Computerized Test Bank, McGraw-Hill Ryerson's EZ Test Online is a flexible and easy-to-use electronic testing program. The program allows instructors to create tests from book-specific items, accommodates a wide range of question types (including true/false, multiple-choice, and essay questions), and enables instructors to add their own questions. Multiple versions of the test can be created, and any test can be exported for use with WebCT, BlackBoard, or any other course management system. EZ Test Online is accessible to busy instructors virtually anywhere via the Web, and the program eliminates the need to install test software. EZ Test Online is supported at **www.mhhe.com/eztest**, where users can download a Quick Start Guide, access FAQs, or log a ticket for help with specific issues.

- **PowerPoint™ Presentation Slides:** These visually stimulating slides provide an overview using illustrations, definitions, and examples, focusing on the primary concepts in each chapter.

SUPERIOR LEARNING SOLUTIONS AND SUPPORT

The McGraw-Hill Ryerson team is ready to help you assess and integrate any of our products, technology, and services into your course for optimal teaching and learning performance. Whether it's helping your students improve their grades, or putting your entire course online, the McGraw-Hill Ryerson team is here to help you do it. Contact your *iLearning* Sales Specialist today to learn how to maximize all of McGraw-Hill Ryerson's resources! For more information on the latest technology and Learning Solutions offered by McGraw-Hill Ryerson and its partners, please visit us online: **www.mcgrawhill.ca/he/solutions**.

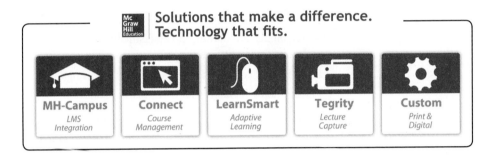

Acknowledgments

Review of an academic's work by peers is a well-established practice. Even with this being the case, an author never knows what to expect and often receives mixed advice. The reviewers for this book did a good job and set me straight on some things, and, even more importantly, provided me with insights and many good ideas. Thanks for being so helpful.

Reviewers

Katherine Chiste, University of Lethbridge

Peter Constantinou, York University

Cathy Driscoll, Saint Mary's University

Thomas Eng, Seneca College

William Holmes, Sheridan Institute of Technology

Brian Orend, University of Waterloo

Mark Schwartz, York University

Andrew Stark, University of Toronto, Scarborough

Doug Thibodeau, Nova Scotia Community College

Jaana Woiceshyn, University of Calgary

CHAPTER 1
The Relationship between Business and Society

LO 1.1 Describe the complexity of the interrelationships between business and society.

LO 1.2 Define the terminology relating to the integrity of business.

LO 1.3 Differentiate between the three main approaches to ethical thinking.

LO 1.4 Provide a brief description of the Canadian business system.

LO 1.5 Explain the role of the corporation as the main economic institution in the business system.

LO 1.6 Identify the three stakeholders mainly responsible for the operation of Canadian businesses.

LO 1.7 Summarize factors that influence society's attitudes toward business that lead to criticisms of the system.

LO 1.8 Recognize that business operates with the consent of society.

LO 1.9 Understand the relationship between business and academic integrity.

LO 1.10 Describe the integration of business and society.

What would you do if . . . ?

Angela Clegg was in the second month of her business program. She was enjoying the courses and interacting with her student colleagues. She was having a good time and felt that she had made a correct decision to enter the program.

When Angela announced that she was taking business, many of her friends questioned the wisdom of her choice by pointing out various business misdeeds. They said that the financial crisis in 2008–09, and the economic downturn that followed, was caused by the greed and mismanagement of bankers, particularly in the United States and Europe. Her friends pointed out that insult had been added to injury when taxpayers, through their governments, had to bail out some banks and automobile companies. Several other examples presented to her involved financial advisers who destroyed people's life savings with fraudulent Ponzi schemes; massive recalls of automobiles, especially Toyotas; environmental damage of the Alberta oil sands; excessive executive compensation schemes; and numerous plant closures throwing thousands out of work. Lastly, her friends said there is no ethics in business and that "business ethics" is an oxymoron.

These arguments did not discourage Angela. She was aware of ethics in business and society and of social responsibility from the extensive coverage they were receiving in the media. The media frequently carried stories about business ethics and social responsibility. An example was a feature in *BusinessWeek* entitled "Beyond the Green Corporation" that carried the tagline "Imagine a world in which eco-friendly and socially responsible practices help a company's bottom line. It's closer than you think." Many corporations even took out advertisements in newspapers, including Angela's campus newspaper, describing the contributions they were making to the community. Also, Angela had participated in the Junior Achievement program in high school and enjoyed developing and operating a small venture.

During a student society meeting, Angela heard about an interesting proposal—"The First Year Pledge of Social Justice, Economic Strength, and Environmental Responsibility":

I pledge that during my years in higher education I will explore and take into account the social, economic, and environmental consequences of my behaviour and that of my institution. I will learn about issues of environmentalism, social justice, and economic strength, and will try to promote a sustainable and just society both at my institution and in the wider world.

The pledge was developed in the United States but seemed applicable to Canadian business students. The purpose of the pledge was to increase awareness of social responsibility among students through teaching and by encouraging them to undertake social initiatives while in school. Examples given of such initiatives included counselling entrepreneurs on ethics, organizing recycling projects on campus, assisting Aboriginal business enterprises, and developing financial literacy programs for teens and seniors. It was argued that a business program would be given added meaning through participating in these initiatives rather than merely relying on the completion of courses.

Angela had some questions about the pledge proposal. Would it make any difference? In particular, would her friends view her goals to succeed in business any differently? Would anyone recognize or respect the pledge? What would be expected of her?

What is your advice to Angela?

Sources: North Carolina Campus Compact, *Digest,* April 2009, http://org.elon.edu/nccc/news/ResourcesApril09.html; and "Combining First-Year Engagement and Civic Engagement," *Inside Higher Ed,* January 28, 2008, http://www.insidehighered.com/news/2008/01/28/engage.

Ethical implications are present in all facets of life, and business and society is no exception. For this reason, students of business should learn about ethics in the relationship between business and society. This chapter gives some background on the setting for understanding the complexity of the relationship. The factors influencing morality in Canadian business are identified. The role of the corporation is outlined, as it is the principal institution in the business system along with the three main stakeholders in the governance and management of the corporation—owners, boards of directors, and managers. Society has expectations of business, and various factors influence society's attitudes toward business. The possible connection between academic integrity and the ethics of business is also discussed.

LO 1.1   The Complexity of Business and Society

Canadian business and society is a fascinating topic. It involves studying the history and background of the Canadian business system in addition to examining the contemporary issues confronting business. It is very important to obtain all the viewpoints that contribute, or should contribute, to what business's role will be in society. Canadian society comprises many institutions and groups that interact, including governments, labour unions, minority groups, environmentalists, consumers, the communications media, business organizations, and a variety of interest groups or non-governmental organizations. All have an important role to play, and all, in some way, influence business decision making. This book emphasizes several things about the Canadian business system, with certain goals in particular:

1. To increase awareness of the system by describing Canadian capitalism, the stakeholders involved, and society's attitudes toward business;

2. To identify business's response to its role in society by examining who owns and runs business corporations, how business has incorporated ethics and responsibilities into its operations, and how business manages its role;

3. To learn how business corporations have responded to many challenges in their environment; and

4. To address the above from the perspective of the manager or owner of a corporation to emphasize the dynamic nature of the environment in which they manage.

Rather than focusing on what is right or wrong beyond any doubt, the emphasis in this text is on the appropriate analysis of problems and issues using information from a variety of sources, including the conflicting and maybe erroneous perceptions of various parties as to the motives, strategies, and tactics of others. Since we are dealing with so many individuals and organizations, perceptions of business vary—from the very negative attitudes held by some political parties and non-governmental organizations to the very positive attitudes held by business-oriented groups.

The issues that arise as a result of these differing perceptions and points of view are not easily resolved. Solutions are not always straightforward or simple, and tend to be less than optimum for all involved. Trade-offs are a factor, and what is an appropriate solution for one group is not as appropriate for another. An optimum solution is still sought, but it is certainly realized that each group in society will not benefit to the maximum.

A shift has occurred in what society believes business responsibilities should be, and at the same time many corporations are recognizing that they must respond to this belief if they are to survive and continue to be profitable. Evidence of this shift is given in Everyday Ethics 1.1, and although the article is several years old, the points made are still relevant today. Most business academics and practitioners would agree that the business system is

---

Everyday Ethics

1.1

"Beyond the Green Corporation"

This was a headline in *BusinessWeek,* a leading American business periodical, and the subtitle was even more striking: "Imagine a world in which eco-friendly and socially responsible practices actually help a company's bottom line. It's closer than you think."

The following are some of the important points made in the article:

- Meeting humanity's needs without harming future generations has come to the top of many chief executive officers' agendas.
- The social responsibility or corporate sustainability reports being published by corporations move beyond the public relations exercises they may have been in the past.
- Increasing numbers of stakeholders are demanding that corporations have to account for more than economic responsibilities.
- Progressive and innovative responses to social, ethical, and environmental responsibilities constitute a valuable intangible asset.
- Executives must have the skills and competencies to manage these additional responsibilities successfully.
- Responses to these responsibilities will determine the corporations that will survive.

The article contained many examples of socially responsible and eco-friendly practices.

Source: Based on Pete Engardio, "Beyond the green corporation," *BusinessWeek,* January 29, 2007, 50–64.

progressing in the right direction. However, other stakeholders would suggest that business is changing too slowly or not at all. The next section, "Integrity in Business," discusses the appropriateness of the business relationship to society.

▰ LO 1.2 ▰   Integrity in Business

Integrity The appropriateness of a corporation's behaviour and its adherence to moral guidelines acceptable to society such as honesty, fairness, and justice.

In the business environment, **integrity** refers to the appropriateness of a corporation's behaviour and its adherence to moral guidelines acceptable to society such as honesty, fairness, and justice. Integrity is the same as acting ethically, but without the negative connotation, the moralizing tone, or the sense of naïveté. According to De George, "Acting with integrity means both acting in accordance with one's highest self-accepted norms of behaviour and imposing on oneself the norms demanded by ethics and morality."[1] Managing with integrity means that business leaders behave in a manner consistent with their own highest values and norms of behaviour, which are self-imposed but at the same time not arbitrary or self-serving. De George states behaviour need not be perfect either: "The imperative to act with integrity cannot insist on moral perfection. It can and does demand taking ethical considerations seriously."[2] Throughout this book, how business enterprises accomplish integrity is discussed and evaluated.

Some fundamental points are to be made about integrity in business. Ethics exist throughout society and are not unique to business. When referring to *business ethics*, what is meant is the ethics that apply to business. It does not mean there is a special kind of ethics peculiar to business and not applicable elsewhere in life. Thus, the phrase "ethics of business" is used in this book unless referring to another work or spokesperson.

Key terminologies relating to integrity in business are listed in Table 1.1. Many definitions for these terms exist; the table provides the basics to assist in understanding their

TABLE 1.1	*Key Terminology Relating to Integrity in Business*

Ethics of business: The rules, standards, codes, or principles that provide guidance for morally appropriate behaviour in managerial decision making relating to the operation of the business enterprise's and business's relationship with society. [Chapters 5 and 6] It is broadly defined to include corporate social responsibility (CSR), corporate sustainability (CS), triple bottom line, corporate citizenship, corporate governance, accountability, and environmental stewardship. [Chapters 7, 8, 9, 11, 14]

Stakeholder: An individual or group who can influence and/or is influenced by the achievement of an organization's purpose.* [Chapters 3 and 4]

Corporate social responsibility (CSR): The way a corporation achieves a balance among its economic, social, and environmental responsibilities in its operations so as to address stakeholder expectations. [Chapter 7]

Corporate sustainability (CS): Corporate activities demonstrating the inclusion of social and environmental as well as economic responsibilities in business operations as they impact all stakeholders to ensure the long-term survival of the corporation. The term sustainability was first used in the context of environmental sustainability, but corporate sustainability has the wider meaning and includes economic, ethical, and social responsibilities as well. The difference from CSR is that the responsibilities are completely integrated to the structure, policies, and operations of the corporation. [Chapters 7, 16]

Triple bottom line: The triple-E bottom line (3E) is the evaluation of a corporation's performance according to a summary of the economic, social or ethical, and environmental value the corporation adds or destroys. A variation is the triple-P bottom line (3P), which is an evaluation of the corporation's performance according to people, planet, and profits. [Chapter 7]

Corporate citizenship: A corporation demonstrating that it takes into account its role in and complete impact on society and the environment as well as its economic influence. [Chapter 7]

* This definition is based on the work of R. Edward Freeman in *Strategic Management: A Stakeholder Approach* (Boston: Pitman, 1984), 53.

usage prior to reading about them in more detail in the chapters identified within square brackets.

In this book, some assumptions are made about the integrity of business:

- Ethics apply to business in the same manner as they do in any other institution in society, for example public administration, politics, religious organizations, the professions, and the legal, health, and educational systems. There are no ethics unique to business; it is only the issues and settings that are different.

- The appropriateness of behaviour is examined in terms of the ethical implications of addressing issues or decisions and of the distribution of harms and benefits to the relevant stakeholders.

- Integrity results in the **responsible corporation**, a business undertaking that responds to social, ethical, and environmental responsibilities in addition to its economic obligations.

Responsible corporation A business undertaking that responds to social, ethical, and environmental responsibilities in addition to its economic obligations.

These assumptions do not mean that business is not involved in wrongdoing or in inappropriate behaviour, as will be pointed out throughout the book. The responses to the issues created relating to the ethics of business and society are usually complex, with implications for many stakeholders. Sometimes the actions, solutions, or outcomes are unsatisfactory to society, in which case business may be required to change its behaviour or may voluntarily change its behaviour. Everyday Ethics 1.2 makes the case that Walmart, a target of much criticism, could be given a Nobel Prize for the benefits it has brought to consumers.

Everyday Ethics 1.2   A Nobel Prize for Walmart?

It seems that Walmart is criticized by almost everyone. The list of criticisms is extensive and includes unfair labour practices, hostility to unions, low salaries, gender discrimination, use of government subsidies, domination of suppliers, destruction of local businesses, predatory pricing, pollution of the environment, elimination of domestic employment while creating sweatshop workplaces overseas, and bribery in countries such as Mexico.

There are a few Walmart defenders, one being Michael Strong, co-founder and chief executive officer (CEO) of FLOW. He states, "it is unlikely that there is any single organization on the planet that alleviates poverty so effectively for so many people." He claims that the wages paid to produce the goods Walmart sells are above the poverty level for millions of workers in developing countries. Furthermore, rural poverty in these countries is worse than that for sweatshop labour. He also states that low-income Americans save $263 billion per year as a result of Walmart's low prices.

In addition, Walmart has initiated several social responsibility programs in recent years. In Canada, it has received awards that include the following: GLOBE Award for Corporate Environmental Excellence; one of the 10 Most Admired Corporate Cultures by the *National Post;* Commitment to Care and Service Award; Food Logistics Golden Pallet Award for excellence in warehousing; and one of the Best Employers for 50-Plus Canadians by Workplace Institute.

Because Walmart is said to be reducing poverty and involved in other good works, should it receive the Nobel Prize for Peace?

Sources: John Tierney, "How about a Nobel Prize for Wal-Mart?" *National Post,* October 16, 2006, A22; Michael Strong, "Forget the World Bank, try Wal-Mart," *TCS Daily,* Tech Central Station, http://www.tcsdaily.com/article.aspx?id=082206D; Susan Berfield, "WalMart vs. Walmart," *BusinessWeek,* December 17–24, 2012, 54–60; FLOW, http://flowproject.org; and 2011 Awards and Recognition, Wal-Mart Stores Inc., http://www.walmartstores.com/sites/responsibility-report/2012/awardsRecognitions.aspx.

LO 1.3   Main Approaches to Ethical Thinking

Not everyone understands or interprets ethics in the same way, and thus disagreement exists as to the appropriate behaviour by business in society. Many decisions involving ethics are made automatically without thinking, based on individual value standards and judgments and not ethical principles. Unfortunately, automatic decisions cannot be relied upon. Different countries, cultures, and religions may define right and wrong differently. More complexity results in situations where no option is clearly right, giving rise to dilemmas where effort is required to sort out right versus wrong. For some dilemmas, the choice might be between what some would consider two wrongs. Sometimes, because of the challenges presented, it is preferable to have different views of what is right or wrong.

Throughout history, ethicists have described various theories and principles to help understand the ethics of decision making. The difficulty is that numerous theories exist and some even have multiple interpretations. This section describes the three dominant approaches to normative theories of ethics: deontological, teleological, and virtue ethics.

Deontological ethics An approach to ethics that determines goodness or rightness from examining the acts, rather than from the consequences of the acts.

In **deontological ethics**, or rule-based theories of ethics, actions are ethical if done for the sake of what is good without regard for the consequences of the act. Decisions are based upon duty and adherence to universal principles. In other words, individuals have a duty to do the right thing even if the consequences of another action are preferable. It is most important to act in a way in which one would like to see others act in the same or similar circumstances. A variation of deontology is broadened to the societal level, where individuals are born with natural rights possessed equally. But it is difficult to determine the rights to possess. Another variation is based on the principles of justice used to meet a "veil of ignorance" test. That is to say, a rule is just if everyone agrees to it if made ignorant of their position in society, thereby eliminating personal bias and guaranteeing fairness. A universal rule would result that could be used in similar circumstances and treating everyone with respect.

Teleological ethics An approach to ethics that focuses on outcomes, or results of actions.

Teleological ethics, or consequential theories of ethics, focus on the outcomes or results of actions. A well-known variation is utilitarianism, which is based on utility or usefulness. The approach looks to the end results and individuals make decisions based on the consequences of the action. The decision is believed to be good if the end result is good. A decision is to result in the greatest good or happiness for the greatest number, and allows for bad consequences or harms. This approach is used every day and in business to view the relative outcomes; that is, the distribution of harms and benefits. Thus, moral character depends upon the practical matter relating to the extent to which actions benefit or harm those involved.

Virtue ethics An approach to ethics that emphasizes the individual's character or identity, and focuses on being instead of doing.

The third approach is **virtue ethics**, which emphasizes the character or identity of the individual and focuses upon being rather than doing. Morality is based on the development of good character traits or virtues and assumes that a good person will perform ethically. There are dozens of desirable traits; nine were listed by Aristotle—wisdom, prudence, justice, fortitude, courage, liberality, magnificence, magnanimity, and temperance. In Responsibility for Ethics 1.1, some of today's ethicists argue that Aristotle was not anti-business or anti-profit. Virtue ethics acknowledges that absolute rules are unlikely to apply in all situations. Dozens of possible virtues exist, and the approach does not focus on which sorts of actions are morally permitted and which ones are not. An illustration is provided by responses to the question, "What virtues make a good businessperson or leader?" Possible answers include foresight, courage, commitment, compassion, respectfulness, and honesty. Table 1.2 compares the three approaches, all of which are applicable to the ethics of business as any other facet of life and society. In Chapter 5, these and other approaches to assessing ethical implications will be described.

RESPONSIBILITY
for Ethics **1.1**

Aristotle and the Ethics of Business

Aristotle was a Greek philosopher who lived from 384 to 322 BC and, according to some authors, provides guidance to modern businesspersons. He wrote on many topics, including physics, biology, zoology, theatre, poetry, logic, rhetoric, politics, and government. However, it is what he wrote in *Nicomachean Ethics* about leadership that is applicable today. He wrote that leadership was supposed to create opportunities for all to realize their potential, and not only to enhance a leader's power. In *Creating the Good Life* (Rodale, 2005), James O'Toole identified some ethical questions raised by Aristotle that apply to business:

- Am I behaving in a virtuous way?
- To what extent are there real opportunities for all employees to develop their talents and their potential?
- To what extent do employees participate in decisions that affect their work?

Denis Collins re-analyzed Aristotle's thought and concluded that it was not anti-business and anti-profit as interpreted by many modern philosophers. Aristotle would argue that the modern corporation is a natural entity, like the state, formed to meet certain needs of society. As Aristotle praised any attempt to help people toward their desired end, the corporation as an institution accomplishes this by fulfilling the needs of individuals and society. He would consider profits permissible if allowed by the state, and acceptable if corporations are fulfilling a proper function in society by supplying goods and services.

Sources: James O'Toole, "Advice from Aristotle," Markkula Center for Applied Ethics, Santa Clara University, http://www.scu.edu/ethics/publications/submitted/otoole/business-ethics-aristotle.html; and Denis Collins, "Aristotle and Business," *Journal of Business Ethics,* Vol. 6 (1987), 567–572.

TABLE 1.2	*Comparison of Approaches to Ethical Thinking*

Deontological or Rule-Based Theories	Teleological or Consequential Theories	Virtue Ethics
Description:	**Description:**	**Description:**
• Focus on moral obligations, duties, and rights	• Focus on goals, outcomes, or results	• Based on character of individual
• Rules should guide decision making and behaviour	• Emphasizes maximum benefit and minimum harm	• If individual has good traits or virtues, decisions will be good or ethical
• More individualistic focus, as individuals should be treated with respect and dignity	• Considers all stakeholders impacted	• Virtuous characteristics come into play when resolving ethical dilemmas
Limitation:	**Limitation:**	
• Allows individuals to avoid responsibility as they are following rules or orders	• Difficult to calculate benefits and harms and apply weights to each	**Limitation:**
Example: Categorical Imperative	**Example: Utilitarianism**	• Disagreement over what are virtues; that is, how a virtue is defined
• Respect for individuals, treating them as ends, not a means to ends	• Greatest good for the greatest number	**Ethicists:**
• Test: Would you do the same thing in similar circumstances?	• Aims to produce the most net utility; that is, benefits versus harms	• Plato
Ethicists:	• Provides a group or societal perspective	• Aristotle
• Immanuel Kant	**Ethicists:**	• Revived recently by several ethicists including Robert Solomon
• John Locke	• John Stuart Mill	
• John Rawls	• Jeremy Bentham	

This brief introduction to theoretical approaches to understanding ethics can be used to assess the behaviour of Canadian business, corporations, and managers. Ethical dilemmas often exist where the choice is between what those involved consider two right responses—or, put in the negative, two wrong responses. Different approaches can result in two responses where benefits are bestowed on some stakeholders and harms to others. Thus, no matter which choice is made, some stakeholders will consider it "wrong."

LO 1.4   The Canadian Business System

The Canadian business system produces, markets, distributes, and exchanges goods and services to satisfy society's needs and wants. The majority of goods and services demanded by Canadians are provided by a private-sector economic system. Most Canadians feel it is desirable to allow individual businesspersons and corporations—rather than some centralized government agency—to provide the goods and services they require. Business institutions have a history in Canada of more than 450 years, and their role in our economic and social development has been substantial. But, it is a role in a continuous state of change.

Terminology is a problem in discussing a business enterprise system. The following list provides definitions of some frequently mentioned terms:

- **Economic system**—An arrangement using land, labour, and capital to produce, distribute, and exchange goods and services to meet the needs and wants of people in society. The objective of an economic system is to use a society's resources to meet the society's needs.

- **Capitalism**—An economic system that allows for private ownership of the means of production (land, labour, and capital) and assumes that economic decision making is in the hands of individuals or enterprises who make decisions expecting to earn a profit. An early advocate of capitalism was Adam Smith, whose views are still influential as described in Responsibility for Ethics 1.2.

- **Free enterprise system**—An economic system characterized by ownership of private property by individuals and enterprises, the profit motive, a competitive market system, and a limited involvement by government. Also referred to as the *private enterprise system.*

- **Laissez-faire capitalism**—An economic system operating with absolute minimum interference by the government in the affairs of business. Government involvement is strictly limited to providing essential services such as police and fire protection. Laissez-faire stems from a French term that means "allow to do."

- **Responsible enterprise system**—An economic system operating as a free enterprise system but incorporating the element of accountability. This definition implies that business enterprises are responsible to society for their actions and are answerable or accountable for being the cause, agent, or source of something.

- **Stakeholder capitalism**—An economic system in which corporations accept broader obligations beyond financial ones for shareholders. Corporations are expected to balance the interests of shareholders with those of other stakeholders in the business system, for example employees, suppliers, customers, and the community at large. In stakeholder capitalism, corporations are expected to behave with greater social responsibility and be sensitive to the ethical consequences of their actions.

- **Clean capitalism**—*Corporate Knights* magazine uses this term to associate capitalism with social responsibility. The magazine defines clean capitalism as "an economic system that incorporates the social, economic and ecological costs (and benefits) into our marketplace activities and the prices we pay."[3]

RESPONSIBILITY
for Ethics (1.2)

Adam Smith, the "Father of Capitalism"

Adam Smith, 1723–90, was a Scottish philosopher and economist whose ideas have had a major impact on capitalist economic systems worldwide. He wrote extensively, but two books have been the most influential: *The Theory of Moral Sentiments*, published in 1759, and *An Inquiry into the Nature and Causes of the Wealth of Nations*, published in 1776.

Smith proposed a different view of morality than was prevalent at the time. One view was that moral principles could rationally identify right versus wrong, while the other view believed that governments and the laws they created established a standard of morality. Smith believed that people were born with a moral sense, or conscience, that told them what was right or wrong. For Smith, morality was a product of nature, not of reason. In any event, Smith believed that economic man and moral man had to co-exist.

The "invisible hand" concept was originated by Smith. He believed that well-functioning competitive markets efficiently distributed society's scarce resources without the guiding hand of government or economic planners. Pursuit of individual self-interest through consumption and the achievement of profits resulted in economic growth that benefited everyone.

Smith's writings continue to influence morality in capitalist economies, even though they are still being challenged by some in society.

connect   Want to learn more about **Adam Smith**? Go to CONNECT.

Our economic system has changed over time from a relatively "free" system with limited government involvement to one where government involvement was more intensive during most of the twentieth century. Although government involvement has declined recently, business is now expected to account to other stakeholders in society. Even with these changes, the economic system of Canada is still based on such fundamentals as individualism and economic freedom, the right to private property, the importance of competition, and the profit motive. Thus, the economic system is not laissez-faire, but is a capitalist system. The principal advantage of this business system is that it decentralizes decision making from a central authority to many individual enterprises. The system also provides freedom of choice to workers, consumers, and entrepreneurs. High productivity and a high standard of living have resulted.

Problems have occurred with the system, however. Business provided appalling working conditions for labour in the nineteenth century, and has sold unsafe products to consumers. Monopolistic behaviour has been evident in the operation of some business corporations, as witnessed by price fixing and supplier discrimination. Other problems include stock manipulation, misleading advertising, misrepresentation of financial information, and regional disparity. The impact on the environment is a concern to many, as discussed in Everyday Ethics 1.3. Business is blamed by some for failing to solve many social problems, for example inadequate housing and workplace discrimination against women and minorities.

Although capitalism is the economic system that provides most of the goods and services in society, two other sectors are involved: public and non-profit. The public or government sector is responsible for providing many services in society including the infrastructure that business uses. Government-owned corporations provide some transportation, insurance, pensions, and health and education systems. The non-profit

Everyday Ethics   Ethics and the Alberta Oil Sands Development

1.3   Dozens of companies are involved in developing the Alberta oil sands surrounding
Fort McMurray, including Suncor Energy Inc., Syncrude Canada Ltd., Shell Canada
Limited, and Husky Energy Inc. Several huge projects have been completed, with
others under construction.

The companies first focus on the economic or financial feasibility of a mega project.
Once the project is determined to be financially feasible, social and environmental
implications gain prominence. Some of the social and environmental implications
that must be considered in such projects are:
- The infrastructure necessary to attract employees to the area, for example housing,
  schools, and health care.
- The management of the pollution emissions generated by the processing plants,
  and the increasing number and size of tailings pools.
- The impact of the huge demand for natural gas to fuel the plants and the water
  needed in the process.
- The reclamation of the areas mined.
- The influence of the developments on the Aboriginal communities.
- The situation where some members of the U.S. Congress and legislators in sev-
  eral U.S. states consider the oil to be "dirty" and are proposing restrictions on its
  import. Greenpeace has produced the film *Petropolis: Aerial Perspectives on the
  Alberta Tar Sands* as a part of its "Stop the Tar Sands" campaign.

A review of the companies' annual reports or their Web sites will detail how they
report to be responding to the social and environmental impact of their projects. In
addition, the federal and Alberta governments are establishing new monitoring systems to track the impact of the oil sands development on the environment. Oil companies and the Canadian Association of Petroleum Producers appear to be increasing
efforts to inform all stakeholders of the various initiatives they have undertaken to
improve their social and environmental performance.

sector, also known as the third sector or plural sector, is a part of the economic system.
Examples of organizations in this sector are charities, cooperatives, and non-profit social
enterprises.

The result is a business system that has changed over time, and today is quite different
from 50 to 75 years ago. It is important to appreciate the fundamentals upon which the
system is based, and how the system has changed to accommodate the demands of society.
Chapter 2 examines in more detail how the business system works.

LO 1.5 ◀ The Corporation and the Business System

The Canadian business system comprises business enterprises varying from sole or single
proprietorships to partnerships and incorporated entities. A business can be established and
operated by an individual under very few legal requirements. Any individual may operate a
business provided he or she is capable of entering into a binding agreement, that the business activity is lawful, and that the individual respects the general legal principles governing
persons, property, and obligations. For larger undertakings, or where two or more persons
wish to share in ownership, a partnership is formed. In proprietorships or partnerships,

the business is identified only with the person or persons involved. The owners take all responsibility for success or failure, receive all profits and assume all losses, and can be held directly responsible for business wrongdoing. Today, most business enterprises are incorporated and so holding the owners, or shareholders, responsible is more complicated. Business enterprises are referred to as corporations in this book, but it is recognized that not all enterprises are incorporated, and that most businesses in Canada are small and medium sized enterprises.

The corporate form of business enterprise is quite unique. When a business incorporates, a separate legal entity is created. This entity is an "artificial being": invisible, intangible, existing only in contemplation of law, and with limited liability for owners.

Doctrines of Incorporation

The privilege of incorporation was traditionally viewed as a concession granted by the sovereign. The first corporations were granted by British sovereigns to nobility, allowing them to explore, colonize, or commercially exploit some geographical area. It is often suggested that the Hudson's Bay Company, with a charter granted in 1617, was one of the first corporations formed in this manner. The "concession" doctrine held that incorporation was conferred by public act and could not be generated merely by private agreements among several persons to associate together for business purposes. The concession was not followed to the letter, especially as monarchies lost their power to legislatures. There were obvious dangers to individual or group freedoms in the concession approach as the sovereign, and then the state, had the authority to grant the privilege of existence to a corporation. An alternative doctrine of incorporation evolved, and the relationship between business and society has changed.

The second doctrine of incorporation is based on the right to "freedom of association." The association of individuals coming together for some purpose is fundamental to forming a corporation. The argument is that it takes more than a formal agreement among incorporators, between the state and the corporation, and between the state and the shareholders to create and maintain a corporation. The entity, a "going concern," is given life by real people and exhibits collective behaviour unique to it and governed by rules of its own making. Thus, the corporation can be thought of as a "state within a state" and is the most highly developed and useful means of voluntary cooperation as it provides an easy way for people to join and leave. Therefore, incorporation is a right, not a privilege as it is in the "concession" doctrine.

These two doctrines, and others, underlie the statutes that determine how to incorporate a business activity, and who may do so. With the freedom of association doctrine, the privilege of incorporation is freely available with a minimum of special conditions and limitations being imposed by government. Legislative safeguards have been interposed at critical junctures where experience indicates difficulties may arise. These safeguards exist to protect investors and creditors, and to create and preserve the atmosphere of public confidence necessary for the legitimacy of the business system. In the past few decades, additional obligations have been placed on the modern corporation to function for the benefit of the broader society in addition to the benefit of investors, creditors, employees, and customers.

The modern corporation is not the state-created entity of the concession doctrine, nor the uncontrolled free association of owners. But it is more appropriately described by the freedom of association doctrine—and this requires greater responsibility and accountability to society. Today, corporations are studied to identify the best or most responsible, as described in Everyday Ethics 1.4.

Everyday Ethics   Canada's Best Corporate Citizens

1.4   Annually, *Corporate Knights* magazine identifies the 50 best corporate citizens in Canada. In 2012, the five top-ranking corporations were Desjardins Group (financial cooperative), Vancouver City Savings Credit Union, The Co-operators Group (insurance cooperative), Canadian National Railway Company, and Royal Bank of Canada.

The corporations are evaluated on several environmental, social, and governance indicators:

- Environmental: energy, carbon, and water productivity
- Social: ratio of highest-paid executive compensation to average employee pay; number of no-lost-time and lost-time incidents; average percentage of statutory taxes paid; funded status of benefit obligations under defined benefit pension plans
- Governance: existence of social responsibility or sustainability; board committees; existence of a link between sustainability criteria and a senior executive's compensation; percentage of women, Aboriginal, and visible minorities on the board of directors
- Transparency: existence of a Global Reporting Initiative evaluation; percentage of voluntary data points provided
- Relative core business impact: examination of relevant environmental and social impacts beyond strict resource use, for example sustainability-related assets under management (financial sector) and eco-social product differentiation (retail sector)

Source: "The 50 best corporate citizens," *Corporate Knights*, Summer 2012, Vol. 11.1, 28–39. A complete list of indicators is available at http://www.corporateknights.com/report/2012-best-corporate-citizens-canada/methodology.

> **LO 1.6**   **The People Who Run Canadian Business**

Three stakeholders are primarily responsible for the operation of Canadian business: owners, boards of directors, and managers. Each has some influence on the morality of the business system.

Owners

A variety of owners exist, categorized as direct and indirect. Direct individual owners are shareholders or investors and entrepreneurs. Also, sometimes employees participate in ownership through stock purchase and grant programs, and customers and producers participate in ownership through cooperatives. There are other direct owners, including corporations that own shares in other corporations, venture capitalists that finance growing businesses by purchasing shares, and governments that use corporations to deliver some goods and services to citizens.

A growing form of ownership is the indirect category, which occurs when consumers invest in mutual funds, or when employees contribute to pension plans. The managers of these funds have become much more active recently and now frequently are influencing corporate decisions.

Through direct and indirect ownership possibilities most Canadians participate in the ownership of business, a fact that is often overlooked. The influence of these owners varies and will be discussed in Chapter 11.

Boards of Directors

Owners are represented by a board of directors, which, according to section 97(1) of the *Canada Business Corporations Act,* "shall manage the business and affairs of a corporation"—a process referred to as corporate governance. The board members are elected by shareholders—that is, the direct owners—and are thus concerned with the shareholders' primary objective, return on investment, though in recent years there has been increasing interest in corporate social responsibility. The board's main tasks are to:

- Select, evaluate, and terminate employment of top management, including planning executive succession.
- Provide shareholders with financial statements and an external auditor's report on the financial affairs of the corporation presented in an annual corporate report.
- Direct and evaluate strategic planning including formulating plans, keeping management accountable for implementation, and assessing performance.
- Represent shareholders by participating in any major decisions impacting the corporation's operations relating to ownership, investments, acquisitions, divestments, takeovers, or insolvency.
- Fulfill the fiduciary and legal requirements as outlined in the *Canada Business Corporations Act.*

Recently, many boards have been active in overseeing the ethics of the corporation and its social and environmental responsibility, an example of which is given in Responsibility for Ethics 1.3. The role of the board will be examined in Chapter 11.

Managers

Managers require a variety of skills to oversee the operations of corporations in today's dynamic business environment. Managers must know how to direct the corporation's affairs

---

RESPONSIBILITY
for Ethics **1.3**

Nexen Board's Commitment to Ethics

The board of directors of Nexen, an energy company developing, producing, and marketing natural gas and power, is committed to addressing its responsibilities to society. The Board's Health, Safety, Environment, and Social Responsibility Committee has been given oversight responsibilities for the development and implementation of leading-edge practices in the management of the health, safety, environment, and social responsibility areas. The Committee's specific duties are to:

- Provide a leadership role in developing Nexen's approach to health, safety, environment, and social responsibility matters including monitoring performance, encouraging improvement in programs, and leading discussion of related issues.
- Review a health, safety, environmental, and social responsibility performance report and other applicable reports.
- Report to the board after each committee meeting about the corporation's performance in health, safety, environment, and social responsibilities.
- Monitor compliance with applicable laws and corporate policies.
- If necessary, make sure corrective measures are taken when issues arise.

Source: Nexen, Board Committees, Health, Safety, Environment, and Social Responsibility Committee, http://www.nexeninc.com/en/Governance/BoardCommittees/HSESR.aspx.

in an increasingly competitive environment and how to cope with large-scale change in their corporations. Technological developments and the globalization of business present additional challenges. In addition, managing relationships with stakeholders has become increasingly important, and knowledge of the ethics of business and social and environmental responsibility is necessary. Chapters 6 and 8 discuss the roles and responsibilities of managers in implementing morally acceptable behaviour and social responsibility in their corporations.

It has been argued that integrity is now at the top of the list of essential qualities of a good CEO. The operation of a business is about managing relationships with others, and the development of trust and credibility with stakeholders is necessary. Transparency is more important, and keeping hidden agendas or covering up information is more difficult. Relationships with others require a commitment to teamwork and partnerships, and managers must have the ability to build and sustain relationships. Finally, it must be remembered that managers are members of society and their behaviour is likely to reflect the standards of morality existing in society.[4]

All three of these stakeholders—owners, boards of directors, and managers—are more aware than ever of the ethics of business and the resulting implications. This awareness also includes monitoring society's attitudes toward business.

LO 1.7   Society's Attitudes toward Business

Occasionally, Canadians are surveyed about their attitudes toward business. A Hewlett-Packard (Canada) Co. survey of 1,506 Canadians found that 90 percent said the more socially and environmentally responsible they believe a corporation is, the more likely they are to purchase its goods and services.[5] Another survey commissioned by Canadian Business for Social Responsibility (CBSR), a coalition of Canadian companies, found that "three-quarters of 141 companies surveyed feel their companies are engaged in corporate social responsibility." In a survey of 1,000 consumers, only "5 per cent perceive Canadian business as being 'completely' involved in corporate social responsibility, and only 16 percent felt business is 'somewhat' involved."[6]

Factors Influencing Attitudes toward Business

Many factors influence these attitudes toward Canadian business. The following list discusses some of the more commonly identified factors that can lead to positive or negative attitudes.

Standard of living—A prominent argument used in justifying or supporting the business enterprise system is the standard of living that it provides. As living standards increase, it is more likely society will view business in a positive manner.

Decentralized decision making—Another factor of the business system considered desirable is the decentralized decision-making process involved. Millions of businesses make decisions independently of one another, ensuring that a wide variety of goods and services are available. This choice is viewed favourably by consumers.

Allocation of resources—Some argue that the efficient allocation of resources is more likely to occur with a business system, as allocation is based on the price and availability of resources. However, critics of the business system challenge the efficiency claim. They argue that enterprises control prices, for example in oligopolistic industries, or that business enterprises control the availability of resources, creating artificial scarcities.

Self-interest—In a business enterprise system, the individual can behave in his or her own self-interest. Self-interest acts as a motivator, and provides the drive for profit that encourages individuals to get things done. In a competitive business enterprise system, consumers choose among businesses that provide basically the same goods and services. Everyone working in his or her own self-interest provides a stimulus to the operation of the economy, even though it is referred to by some as greed. Positive self-interest is intended to produce intelligent and informed pursuit of wealth. However, some claim that self-interest sometimes becomes cruel and malicious—and, at other times, dumb and hysterical—and that this is appropriately referred to as greed. Self-interest appeals to many as a motivating force, but to others it is a source of negative attitudes toward the business system.

Inequities in society—Some critics of the business enterprise system claim that a system based on a capitalistic market leads to inequities. Supporters of the system say that inequities are inevitable and necessary in a dynamic economy to provide incentive and prevent the regimentation of equality. A problem arises when particular groups in society are discriminated against economically to an extent that cannot be tolerated. An example of an inequity being addressed by CEOs is given in Everyday Ethics 1.5.

Everyday Ethics

1.5

Calgary Business Cares about Poverty

Inequities in society are a concern for many businesspersons. The CEOs of companies such as TransAlta, Imperial Oil, CPR, and Suncor Energy, plus community leaders, have formed the Calgary Committee to End Homelessness (CCEH). In Canada, Calgary has the second largest number of homeless persons after Toronto. The CEOs were concerned that governments were not addressing the issue quickly enough and decided to do something themselves.

The homeless are mostly the working poor. It is estimated that more than 4,000 people and families sleep in shelters, under bridges, on the streets, or in their cars. Although not homeless, 58,000 families in Calgary spend more than 30 percent of their wages on rent. CCEH has developed a 10-year plan to reduce homelessness, and in January 2008 the Calgary Homeless Foundation began implementing the plan. The plan will identify affordable housing initiatives and the necessary facilities to help the homeless move from a state of dependence to one of independence. The plan is based on the principle that every person should have access to affordable, safe, and appropriate housing.

The plan appears to be working, as the number of people living in the streets had dropped 11.4 percent by 2012.

Sources: Deborah Yedlin, "Plight of homeless draws might of Calgary CEOs," *The Globe and Mail,* January 12, 2007, B2; Joseph Brean, "Calgary titans combine to fight poverty," *National Post,* January 11, 2007, A6; Kim Guttormson, "CEOs promise homeless solution," *Calgary Herald,* January 10, 2007, B1, B4; Judith Maxwell, "Forget government, hire a business leader if you've got social problems," *The Globe and Mail,* October 8, 2007, B2; Calgary Committee to End Homelessness, http://www.endinghomelessness.ca; and Dawn Walton, "Calgary turns 'bum heaven' into social success story," *The Globe and Mail,* February 7, 2012, A13.

Business cycle—Business cycles are natural in a market system, and probably are more accentuated in a business enterprise system than in a centralized economy. With periods of prosperity followed by recessions, the business enterprise system is vulnerable to criticisms because of the hardships imposed upon particular individuals and types of businesses at various times. The instability created by business cycles is resented by society.

Business wrongdoing—Corporate misdeeds also influence society's attitudes. Some of the most common examples of corporate wrongdoing are in the financial area, and include misleading financial statements, insider trading, stock manipulation, bid rigging, embezzlement, and bankruptcy fraud. Ponzi schemes are a common form of business wrongdoing where individuals posing as investment advisers obtain funds from unsuspecting or naïve investors who, in most cases, lose their money; Everyday Ethics 1.6 describes the Ponzi scheme. Members of society were particularly annoyed at bank and corporate bailouts in 2008–09, when governments loaned or gave corporations billions of dollars and executives still received high salaries. Some other recent criticism of business has related to workplace health and safety violations, bribery in international markets, weak or absent food safety practices, pollution of the environment, the plundering of natural resources, and excessively high profits and executive compensation.

Everyday Ethics

1.6

Ponzi Schemes Live On

One type of business wrongdoing is known as the Ponzi scheme. Such schemes promise high returns to investors. Instead of investors being paid from earnings, they are paid from the contributions made by new investors. A key to the success of the scheme is to continuously attract ever-increasing numbers of new investors to pay the previous ones. The schemes eventually collapse as the inflow of money cannot be sustained.

This type of scheme is considered fraudulent and is illegal in Canada. It is named after Charles K. Ponzi, who was born in Italy in 1882 and emigrated to the United States in 1903. He lived in Montreal for a short time but was charged with forgery and in 1910 returned to the United States to live in Boston, Massachusetts. In 1919–20, he started the investment scheme that would bear his name. He was charged with mail fraud and spent three and a half years in jail. Other charges for larceny and land scams followed in Massachusetts and Florida. Eventually he was deported to Italy as an undesirable alien as he had never obtained U.S. citizenship. He died in Rio de Janeiro, Brazil in 1949.

These schemes continue today, from some relatively small ones operating in a local area to international schemes involving billions of dollars. A record-breaking scheme exposed in 2008 was operated by Bernard Madoff, who created pyramid schemes that destroyed more than US$60 billion of his clients' money. In mid-2009, a Montreal financial adviser, Earl Jones, allegedly swindled investors out of an estimated $50 million in a Ponzi scheme.

Why do these schemes continue? A simple answer is greed and self-interest on the part of the instigators and the investors.

Sources: "Mr. Ponzi's dubious legacy," *The Globe and Mail*, December 17, 2008, B3; Paul Waldie, "Wall Street icon charged in fraud of 'epic' scope," *The Globe and Mail*, December 12, 2008, B1; "The Madoff affair: Con of the century," *The Economist*, December 20, 2008, 119–120; Graeme Hamilton, "Missing advisor surrenders to police," *National Post*, July 28, 2009, A1; and Mark C. Knutson, "The remarkable criminal financial career of Charles K. Ponzi," http://www.mark-knutson.com/.

Globalization—Business is being increasingly conducted on a worldwide or global scale. This trend applies to large as well as small businesses, and has led to several challenges. Increased competition comes from foreign producers, job loss occurs as production is outsourced to other countries, and businesses must respond to the demands of customers in other nations. Corporations operating globally are faced with ethical, social, and environmental issues relevant to local areas. As an example, Canadian mining corporations have had to respond to complaints about pollution and poor working conditions in their international operations. Chapter 15 will discuss the implications and challenges of globalization.

Unemployment—Employment is associated with a country's economic performance, business cycles, and productivity. How well the country's major industries are performing and the levels of consumer spending determine employment levels. Unemployment occurs when business lays off or fails to hire employees as business activity declines. Declining productivity of Canadian business may result in goods and services being provided from other countries.

Innovation—The business enterprise system is designed to constantly seek innovation. A large portion of technological development has been the result of the efforts of business enterprises. Some people criticize continuous and accelerating technology and social change, while conceding that technology has improved their material well-being. A problem associated with rapid technological change is alienation, particularly alienation in the workplace.

The Media—The popular media influence society's views of business. Books, magazines, newspapers, television, film documentaries, movies, and the Internet describe the activities of business and the implications for society. Some of the portrayals are positive, but many are negative and receive a lot of attention—for example, Michael Moore's documentaries *Roger & Me, The Big One,* and *Capitalism: A Love Story.* The extent to which the popular media influence attitudes toward business is not known for certain. As an example, the documentary *The Corporation* is very critical of business and presents a one-sided view of issues. The media as a stakeholder will be discussed further in Chapter 13.

connect Want to learn more about **the documentary *The Corporation*?** Go to CONNECT.

Government—Government is always involved in business and the relationship between business and society. Governments often identify what is unacceptable corporate behaviour and their influence is always changing, at times increasing while at other times declining. Government influence is described throughout the book, and particularly in Chapter 10.

At any time, one or a combination of the above factors influences attitudes. Even though the factors can be listed, it is unlikely consensus will occur on which factors are the most influential. Nevertheless, society's attitudes toward business change through time and businesspersons must always be aware of these changes. Monitoring attitudes toward business is important as it operates as the consent or permission of society.

connect Want to learn more about **changing attitudes toward business?** Go to CONNECT.

LO 1.8   Society's Permission for Business

Legitimacy The belief in the rightness of an institution, in this case the appropriateness of our business system to supply the goods and services wanted by Canadian society.

The business system, and corporations, do not function in isolation to society, and must receive some form of permission to operate. Two concepts that illustrate this relationship are legitimacy and social licence.

The attitudes toward business and the criticisms of it present challenges to its legitimacy as an economic system. **Legitimacy** is the belief in the rightness of an institution, in this case the appropriateness of our business system to supply the goods and services wanted by Canadian society. Society must believe in the business system, which involves trust and confidence and the perception that the system operates in the public interest.

The legitimacy of business is questioned by some in society who are suspicious of materialism and excessive consumption. They argue that there are nobler goals than the pursuit of wealth or material things in society. The hypocritical attitudes business has taken toward government lead society to question the legitimacy of the system. Businesses ask for government assistance in a great variety of ways—through tax concessions, grants, and tariff protection, for example—and have requested that the free enterprise system be rescued from particular difficulties in such areas as the automobile, textile, aircraft, and fishing industries. Although businesspersons speak highly of the free enterprise system and competition, many are reluctant to live in an unregulated competitive environment. Lastly, many in society simply do not understand how business works and are concerned by the poor examples set by some businesspeople.

The legitimacy of business is increasingly being shaped by a broader sense of values that includes the treatment of employees, respect for the environment, commitment to product safety and public health, perceived openness and honesty, enlightened recognition of all stakeholder interests, and overall contribution to community, society, and the quality of life. The conclusion is that, to be legitimate, the business enterprise system must respond to the changing values and expectations in society.

Two observations are important from the discussion of society's attitudes toward business: (1) the attitudes—in particular the criticisms—must be monitored by management, and (2) where justified and feasible, management should take actions to counter the negative views of business.

Social licence The privilege of operating in society with minimal formalized restrictions—that is, legislation, regulation, or market requirements—based on maintaining public trust by doing what is acceptable to stakeholders in the business and society relationship.

Social licence is the privilege of operating in society with minimal formalized restrictions—that is, legislation, regulation, or market requirements—based on maintaining public trust by doing what is acceptable to stakeholders in the business and society relationship. It has emerged as a concept to explain the relationship between business and society and is mentioned in several contexts, all attempting to explain the relationship between business and society in a general sense, between businesses or corporations and society within an industry, and between a corporation and society related to a particular project. The concept is sometimes referred to as a *social licence to operate*, which is particularly relevant to the latter relationship.[7]

In a general sense, social licence involves society's trust that the activities of business are legitimate and consistent with social expectations and the values of stakeholders. Social licence is based on ethics, values, expectations, and self-regulation being considered preferable to social or government control, which is based on regulation, legislation, litigation, and compliance. In practice, a balance exists between social licence and control, where the former is a proactive approach and the latter reactive. The balance can be shifted with intervention in the marketplace by government or the actions or demands of stakeholders—for example, through consumer boycotts.

Another variation on the concept applies to projects in resource industries and often is associated with environmental issues, a common occurrence in the Canadian economy. In this context, social licence to operate is often used and defined as existing when a project has ongoing approval within the local community and other stakeholders, ongoing approval or broad social acceptance, and, most frequently, ongoing acceptance.[8] A social licence is based upon the beliefs, perceptions, and opinions held by the stakeholders involved—for example, the community, residents, or government—and is in effect granted by those harmed or benefiting from the project. The life cycle of the project is involved, including a properly conducted environmental assessment, careful design of the project, effective operation practices, and a closure strategy.[9]

A social licence must be earned and maintained—it is non-permanent because society's beliefs, perceptions, and opinions change, as do the influential stakeholders. There must be an acceptance and approval of the project by stakeholders, which is accomplished when the corporation establishes its legitimacy and credibility and ultimately gains their trust.[10]

A key point to make is that a general or project social licence is not granted by a government, but instead by the acceptance received from the stakeholders involved. A social licence is one approach to describing the relationship between business and society.

LO 1.9 Business and Academic Integrity

This chapter has introduced the integrity of business, but the integrity of *future* business entrepreneurs, managers, and employees must also be examined while they are in academic programs. A *Maclean's* article provides some statistics that are of concern for the future integrity of business:

- 53 percent of students admit to cheating in written assignments
- 56 percent of business students admit to cheating
- 44 percent of professors said they didn't report students caught cheating[11]

At issue is whether the lack of academic integrity will have an influence on business integrity. College and university business programs are facing demands from society and the business community to better prepare their graduates to identify and address ethical implications in business. In business schools, ethics had been largely neglected until recently, with an emphasis on functional areas, some which have focused on the financial rather than the social responsibilities of business. Corporate corruption practices have increased awareness of ethical practice in business, and graduates who will be managers and businesspersons need a moral compass and sensitivity to acting consistently. In other words, graduates must be prepared to face the reality of moral dilemmas.

The focus must be not only on graduates and their future behaviour but also on the practices internal to business schools. Numerous ethical issues arise during the educational experience within the business school. These issues involve not only students, but also faculty members. The business school itself must become aware of and address moral dilemmas in the teaching and administrative processes. Processes must be put in place to detect moral deviation and to develop remedies. Many behaviours by students—for example, cheating on examinations, allowing others to cheat, plagiarism, false sources, signing attendance sheets for others, vandalizing school property, and failing to contribute appropriately to group work—have ethical implications; a list of ethical issues facing students is given in Table 1.3. Likewise, the behaviours of faculty members—for example, letting students get away with cheating, improper approaches to grading and examinations, favouritism and bias, one-sided presentation of concepts and theoretical materials, excessive workload, talking about students, and inappropriate relationships with students—have ethical implications.

LO 1.10 Integration of Business and Society

An article by Porter and Kramer made a good case for business and society needing each other. Business needs a healthy society in which education and health-care systems exist. There should be equal opportunity in the workforce and safe products for consumers. Carefully developed government policies increase the efficiency of business. This creates

TABLE 1.3	*Ethical Issues for Students*

Students are no different from any other group in society, and provide numerous examples of questionable behaviour or academic offences. Examples of such behaviour include:

- Plagiarism or copying without giving proper credit or acknowledgment from any printed or electronic source; in other words, theft of intellectual property.
- Copying from another student's paper or exam, or allowing another student to copy yours.
- Cheating on examinations or any other tests, assignments, and projects, including copying from another student's work.
- Bringing unauthorized materials or electronic devices into the classroom or examination room.
- Having communications or discussions with others during an examination, including through electronic means.
- Turning in the same work for two or more different courses, or turning in the work of others as your own.
- Giving false reasons for not attending class or handing in an assignment.
- Taking an examination for another student.
- Changing answers after a test or assignment has been graded and asking that it be graded again.
- Engaging in disrespectful and disruptive behaviour in class.
- Harassing others.
- Stealing or defacing the property of the school or others.

To test your academic integrity, access Carleton University's Academic Integrity Quiz at http://www1.carleton.ca/studentaffairs/academic-integrity/academic-integrity-quiz/ or York University's Academic Integrity Tutorial at http://www.yorku.ca/tutorial/academic_integrity.

demand for products and services, and corporations pursuing profits at the expense of society are naïve.

On the other hand, society needs successful companies. Business is needed to create jobs, wealth, and innovations that improve the standard of living for society. If business is weakened by governments and non-governmental organizations jobs disappear, competitiveness is lost, wages stagnate, and wealth declines.

In the past, too much focus has been placed on friction between society and business with not enough attention given to the interaction and integration between the two. There must be a shared value in which business and society both benefit. Illustrations of the benefits are provided throughout the book, although some of the frictions also are described. The direction of the ethics and responsibilities of business is toward reducing the frictions and increasing the benefits.[12]

Your advice to Angela . . .

Students of business face a similar situation to that confronting Angela. On the surface, pledges and oaths of this type appear to have little influence. But, they do remind students of business of their responsibility to society. Whether or not Angela can defend her choice depends upon the circumstances in which she finds herself. Today, most business students are interested in economic, social, and environmental sustainability. In a course focusing on business and society, an understanding of the ethics of business and the responsibilities involved prepares students to answer questions like those posed in the opening vignette.

SUMMARY

- The relationship between business and society is complex. To understand the relationship it is necessary to be knowledgeable of the business system and of capitalism in particular. There should also be an appreciation of the efforts being made by business to be responsive to society's expectations of its social and its economic responsibilities. (LO 1.1)

- Business integrity is the appropriateness of a corporation's behaviour and its adherence to moral guidelines acceptable to society such as honesty, fairness, and justice. The concepts used to describe the integrity of business are ethics of business, corporate social responsibility, corporate sustainability, the triple bottom line, and corporate citizenship. The integrity of business is no different from that of individuals or other institutions in society. (LO 1.2)

- The three main approaches to ethical thinking are deontological, teleological, and virtue ethics. (LO 1.3)

- The Canadian business system is referred to by various terms, but usually as a form of capitalism. The business system does have some defects, but it is constantly changing to reflect society's demands upon it. (LO 1.4)

- Several forms of business enterprise exist, but the most common is the incorporated enterprise referred to as the corporation. At one time, it was a privilege to form a corporation; that is, the monarch or government granted the right to incorporate. Today the corporation is viewed more as a free association of individuals who can incorporate as long as they are engaged in a legal activity. Thus, the modern corporation is accountable not only to the government, but also to society in general. (LO 1.5)

- Owners, boards of directors, and managers are the three most important stakeholders in the actual operation of the corporation. Each has a distinct role, and all influence the integrity of the corporation. (LO 1.6)

- Society's attitudes toward business vary over time, and its views are influenced by several factors. Corporate wrongdoing receives a lot of attention and creates negative views of business. (LO 1.7)

- Society allows business to function as a system to provide goods and services. Two concepts that help to understand this consent are legitimacy and social licence. (LO 1.8)

- Students and business academic programs are also challenged by issues of integrity. In particular, the behaviour of students has ethical implications, and they are no different than other stakeholders. (LO 1.9)

- Business needs society and society needs business. (LO 1.10)

KEY TERMS

Integrity	Responsible corporation	Laissez-faire capitalism
Ethics of business	Deontological ethics	Responsible enterprise system
Stakeholder	Teleological ethics	Stakeholder capitalism
Corporate social responsibility (CSR)	Virtue ethics	Clean capitalism
Corporate sustainability (CS)	Economic system	Legitimacy
Triple bottom line	Capitalism	Social licence
Corporate citizenship	Free enterprise system	

CRITICAL THINKING AND DISCUSSION QUESTIONS

1. Do most Canadians understand the workings of the Canadian business system or capitalism? Do you? Give reasons to support your answer.

2. Do you agree with the position that the frequency of business wrongdoing is about the same as for individuals or any other institutions in society?

3. Why do people disagree on what is morally appropriate behaviour? Which approach to ethical thinking do you practise?

4. How would you describe the Canadian business system?

5. Which two factors influence the integrity of Canadian business the most?

6. Should corporations be formed only with the permission of society as represented by government, or should they be allowed to form freely without much government oversight?

7. What is the connection between the type of approach to incorporation and society's expectations of the corporation?

8. Why should the members of the board of directors have any interest in the relationship between business and society?

9. What most influences your attitude toward business?

10. Should businesspersons be concerned about how they and business are portrayed in the popular media?

11. What are the ethical challenges you confront as a student?

CASES

1.1   The Pillaging of Pensions

Most Canadians expect employers to provide pensions as one benefit of the employment contract. The expectations include not only coverage but also adequate funds to maintain a desired retirement lifestyle and security for the longevity of the pension. Government officials and financial industry spokespersons are warning of a crisis in the pension system, especially pensions in the private or business sector. Some claim that the crisis in pensions will have a negative impact on overall economic efficiency.

The two most common types of pension plans are defined benefit and defined contribution. The defined benefit type is the most common, but this type is experiencing a major problem: there are insufficient assets to support the payment of pension obligations to retired employees. The deficits in the plans have resulted from lower interest rates reducing earnings, stricter standards imposed by government regulations, and higher costs or payouts.

Defined benefit plans guarantee a retirement payment based on income level and years of service. The risk of return and longevity is assumed by the employer; that is, the employer is responsible for deficits in the plan. Business employers have begun to collapse defined benefit plans or restrict new entrants, and have usually replaced them with defined contribution plans. In this type of plan, employees and employer make contributions in registered retirement savings plan (RRSP)–type accumulation accounts, with employees allocating the funds among investment alternatives. The risk of return and longevity is transferred to individuals, something with which Adam Smith would most likely agree. The difficulty is that individuals are less able to bear the risk of failures and they are less knowledgeable of investment

opportunities and dangers. Also, there is a possibility they will pay financial advisers too much to guide them in the investment process.

The process of switching from defined benefits to defined contributions has begun. IBM Canada stopped offering defined benefit plans to new employees in 1995. Some plans are reducing payments to retirees, and in some cases plans are unable to pay any pensions. When companies go bankrupt, pension plans are sometimes threatened. When the St. Anne Nackawic Pulp Company in New Brunswick ceased operations, younger employees were expected to lose pension benefits and older workers and retirees would experience cuts. Nortel retirees are uncertain of their pensions after the bankruptcy and dissolution of the company. A 2012 study of 45 publicly traded corporations with defined benefit plans found that their plans were underfunded by $18.8 billion.

While some employee pension plans are experiencing difficulties, others are flourishing. Some CEOs are negotiating and getting huge pensions while employees are having theirs reduced. Most politicians in Canada have pension plans that have superior benefits to those allowed to other citizens.

Questions

1. How is the integrity of business illustrated, or not illustrated, with pension plans?

2. Which approach to ethical thinking would aid decision making regarding this issue?

3. How do the difficulties and changes being experienced by pension plans influence society's attitudes toward business?

4. **What responsibility do corporations have to provide pension plans?**

5. **What responsibility do employees have to manage their own pension plans?**

Sources: Lana Payne, "Grasping a true pension solution," *The Telegram* (St. John's, NL), August 13, 2012, A19; "Paying pensions to a greying nation," *National Post,* December 22, 2011, A17; David Milstead, "Corporate Canada's pension hole," *The Globe and Mail,* October 11, 2012, B15; and Jack M. Mintz, "Tackle the pension crisis now," *National Post,* April 19, 2012, FP11.

1.2   *Detecting Plagiarism and Academic Integrity*

Students and faculty at colleges and universities are concerned about cheating in the academic environment. The reasons given for cheating include high expectations, pressures to succeed, students feeling they were unfairly treated in some way, and the belief that "everyone is doing it." There are many forms of cheating, but one that is receiving a lot of attention is plagiarism.

Studies indicate that about one in three students admit to plagiarizing at some time in their academic program. About 5 percent admit to purchasing an essay online and handing it in as their own. Business, engineering, journalism, and education students were found to be the most likely to plagiarize. There is no definitive reason why business students are the worst offenders, but there is speculation they have a "bottom-line" mentality toward getting things accomplished.

One approach to combat this problem is for educational institutions to use plagiarism detecting services such as Turnitin.com and Plagiarism.org. Essays are submitted directly by students or by faculty members. These services identify copied materials and issue a report to the instructor.

In some schools, the use of the detection systems has not been opposed by students or faculty. It is considered normal practice and is compared to the use of metal detectors at airports. The argument is made that it ensures the integrity of a degree and reduces the possibility of someone obtaining a degree by improper means. The point is made that detection also takes other forms, for example paid invigilators at examinations. Use of detection systems ensures everyone plays by the same rules and serves as a deterrent to improper behaviour. Faculty time is saved and the detection process is simplified, reducing the need for faculty to play police.

In other schools, the detection systems are criticized for several reasons. Students are often given no alternative but to submit their papers. Students resent the assumption of guilt and the impression that students are being hunted down for violations. Some argue that it is an infringement of their copyright, but legal experts refute this claim. The fact that private companies are making a profit at detection is considered inappropriate. The reliability of the systems is questioned, as they detect only about 50 percent of the actual plagiarism. Overall, an antagonistic atmosphere is created that does little to resolve the underlying causes of plagiarism.

Questions

1. **Academic integrity involves students, faculty members, and the universities. Who is served by the use of detection systems?**

2. **What responsibility should professors take to detect plagiarism?**

3. **When should disciplinary action be taken against a student?**

4. **What should be done about the problem of plagiarism other than using detection systems?**

5. **Is cheating in school through plagiarism a predictor of cheating in business careers?**

6. **Which approach to ethical thinking would increase understanding of behaviour regarding plagiarism?**

Sources: Léo Charbonneau, "The cheat checker," *University Affairs,* April 2004, 16–20; Sarah Schmidt, "Professors using in-class exams and essays to fight plagiarists," *National Post,* March 31, 2004, A1; and Heather Sokoloff, "One in three students plagiarize," *National Post,* August 30, 2003, A1.

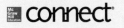 For more information on the resources available from McGraw-Hill Ryerson, go to www.mcgrawhill.ca/he/solutions.

CHAPTER 2
Ethics and Capitalism

LO 2.1 Enumerate and discuss the eight fundamentals of a capitalist business system.

LO 2.2 Define the right of private property and identify ethical implications associated with it.

LO 2.3 Explain individualism and economic freedom and the related ethical implications.

LO 2.4 Define equality of opportunity and elaborate upon the ethical implications for business.

LO 2.5 Describe the competition fundamental and link ethical implications to it.

LO 2.6 Understand profits and the associated ethical implications.

LO 2.7 Link the work ethic to ethical implications.

LO 2.8 Define consumer sovereignty and understand related ethical implications.

LO 2.9 Explain the role of government in a capitalist business system and what the ethical implications are.

LO 2.10 Define Canadian capitalism, and recognize that capitalism exists in different forms around the world.

LO 2.11 Link the fundamentals of a capitalist business system to social and ethical challenges in society, and describe a new view of capitalism.

What would you do if . . . ?

The Occupy movement was an international protest movement concerned with the perceived injustices of capitalism and the dysfunctional operations of government. The North American movement began with a protest demonstration at Zuccotti Park in New York City on September 17, 2011. This protest was called Occupy Wall Street, because it occurred on the tenth anniversary of the re-opening of Wall Street trading after the September 11, 2001 terrorist attacks. Over the next few months, protests were held in more than 900 cities in over 80 countries, including across Canada.

Those protesting had several grievances with the current economic, social, and political systems. The downturn in the economy, particularly in the United States, was causing hardships. It was believed that inequality existed in society and that powerful interests could no longer be trusted. Governments were viewed as not doing enough to address the problems and injustices in society.

The complaints were numerous. Income inequality was a major issue, with lower and middle income classes struggling while the higher class of millionaires (or the 1 percent of the population) gained a larger portion of the wealth. In other words, the gap between the rich and poor was widening, a belief supported by some economic studies. This was one of the reasons for the movement's slogan, "We are the 99 percent."

Many in the movement felt that governments were beholden to business lobbyists and industry special interests, with politicians favouring the rich and business. An example of this cronyism was the huge bailout of the American financial system in 2008, when Wall Street interests got help and the financial challenges faced by the lower and middle classes, including students, were ignored. Another annoyance was the high compensation of corporate executives even when their corporations were failing and receiving government assistance.

The remedies proposed were numerous, with a principal one being to tax the rich. Government spending should increase to create jobs and tax breaks given to the lower and middle classes. There was opposition to cuts in government spending, especially any that led to job reductions. However, there was no one unified message emerging from the protest, with many grievances identified and many solutions proposed. Critics claimed that it was not clear what those in the movement wanted. By November 2011, most public protest sites had been abandoned, with those involved forming loosely structured organizations to carry on the movement. Nevertheless, the movement continued to receive media attention.

Stephen Jacovich, a business college student, had been aware of the Occupy movement and could identify with some of the complaints. Students were accumulating substantial debts that would limit their ability to afford homes and automobiles after graduation. Also, the job prospects for some graduates were not encouraging, forcing them to take low-paying jobs. Stephen noted that *Maclean's* magazine had referred to this generation of young people as the new underclass.[1] During high school, Stephen had started volunteering to help others who were less fortunate. He assisted in a nursing home, participated in environmental cleanups, contributed to and worked at the local food bank, and helped teach the physically challenged to swim. One day Jennifer Koven, whom he had met while volunteering, invited him to attend a meeting to revitalize the local Occupy organization. As a business student, he viewed some of the grievances and proposed solutions as questionable, but he also believed that some others were legitimate.

What is your advice to Stephen?

LO 2.1   Introduction

The purpose of this chapter is to describe capitalism in Canada through the commonly accepted fundamentals of this economic system. This provides the context in which business operates and identifies the ethical implications of a capitalist system.

The assumption made is that the Canadian economic system has been, and still is, largely comprised of business enterprises operating in a market system. The majority of goods and services wanted by Canadians are provided by the market system, which coordinates and organizes economic activity (see Everyday Ethics 2.1). Most Canadians accept that an economic responsibility of business is to make a profit in providing goods and services. It is argued that this private system is less cumbersome and less costly to run than a centralized, government-operated system, and that it is more responsive to society's needs because it allows individuals and business corporations to be more innovative.

Everyday Ethics
2.1

How Business Works for You

Think about the following goods and services you encounter on a typical day as a student. The cereal, fruit, and milk you eat for breakfast. The vehicle you use to get to classes. The iPod you listen to music on. The coffee you purchase. The textbook you use in a course. The laptop computer you carry all day. The pens, pencils, and paper you use. The pizza you have for lunch. The video game you play to relax. The cell phone you use constantly. The Aspirin you take for a headache. The newspaper, magazine, or comic book you read during break. The clothing you wear. The fried chicken you eat for dinner at home. The television programs or movies you watch in the evening. The bed you go to sleep in.

Business enterprises are responsible for providing most of these goods and services. Most are provided without a problem, but sometimes there are issues about this responsibility that relate to the fundamentals of capitalism. This is how the business system works for you.

The theory of capitalism can be described by examining some of the fundamental elements of such a system. In reality, it is more difficult to explain how the business system works. The ideal operation of the system is not expected, and much of the theory of the classical capitalist system is based on the philosophical underpinnings of the American system and may never have been applicable in Canada. These fundamental elements exist in different forms in various countries, and they are important to examine as they provide a basis for explaining some of the ethics and responsibilities of business that exist today.

Eight fundamentals are described, and some ethical implications of each are identified. Capitalism requires a strong system of ethical behaviour, as without it the government and the justice system will intervene. The business system's approach to addressing economic, social, and ethical challenges is influenced by the form of capitalism in practice. The issues confronting managers today are assessed in the context of these fundamentals.[2]

LO 2.2   The Right of Private Property

The Fundamental

Right of private property The legal right to own and use economic goods, for example land and buildings.

The right to ownership of property by individuals and enterprises is fundamental to the business system. The **right of private property** is the legal right to own and use economic goods, for example land and buildings. Property is not owned by the state, and individuals may own property and use it as they see fit. Individuals are allowed to accumulate property and other forms of capital and wealth without restriction. This accumulation of privately owned property allows individuals to control their own destiny and not have decisions affecting them made by others. Other rationales for the right to private property are that the pride taken in ownership results in better care of property; the ownership of private property gives a sense of security and a feeling of satisfaction from participation in society; and private ownership develops respect for the property of others.

Ethical Implications

Individuals and enterprises have been allowed to accumulate capital wealth, but there is an uneven distribution of wealth among members of society. This has led to demands for a more equable distribution, usually achieved by government actions or abridgements to the right of private property. The government has "eminent domain" over property and can expropriate after payment of a fair price. Governments have even nationalized corporations and whole industries in some countries.

Taxation is one method of redistributing wealth. Despite this taxation, business retains some advantages because corporations are allowed to consolidate financial statements, to average taxable income over several years, to depreciate fixed assets, and to receive tax concessions. The government controls property through zoning regulations and restrictions on foreign ownership of property in some provinces. Most of the natural resources of Canada are still owned by the federal or provincial governments. Also, in the modern knowledge economy, the protection of another type of property—intellectual— is becoming increasingly important. **Intellectual property** is an umbrella term for patents, copyrights, trademarks, industrial designs, integrated circuit topographies, and plant breeders' rights.

> **Intellectual property** Umbrella term for patents, copyrights, trademarks, industrial designs, integrated circuit topographies, and plant breeders' rights.

 Want to learn more about **the right to intellectual property**? Go to CONNECT.

In theory, property rights guarantee an individual's security and freedom. Today, membership rights, such as those offered by labour unions, cooperatives, trade associations, and professional societies, are for some a preferred basis for security and freedom. This leads to the discussion of the desirability of having property in private hands versus held by governments or some form of collective. An example of the issues involved with property rights in a particular culture are described in Everyday Ethics 2.2.

LO 2.3   Individualism and Economic Freedom

The Fundamental

> **Individualism** The view that the individual, and not society or a collective, is the paramount decision maker in society; assumes that the individual is inherently decent and rational.

Individualism is the view that the individual, and not society or a collective, is the paramount decision maker in society and assumes that the individual is inherently decent and rational. Individuals should have the privilege of determining their own course of action; that is, of behaving in their own self-interest with the minimum of authority being exercised over them. The privilege of determining for oneself what actions to take encourages individual initiative and self-interest.

Individualism is linked to freedom, and this has provided a connection between the business system in Canada and a democratic form of government. In general terms, freedoms are identified as the capability to have and control property, freedom of association, freedom of information, and freedom of movement. **Economic freedoms** exist when the business system operates with few restrictions on its activities. Examples of economic freedom include the freedom of individuals to enter business; to locate anywhere; to enter contracts; to choose among competing goods and services; to choose an occupation; to access consumer and output markets; and to develop their own economic ends and the means to attain these ends by choosing and utilizing resources as they see fit. This approach encourages entrepreneurial talent and innovation.

> **Economic freedoms** Exist when the business system operates with few restrictions on its activities.

Individualism and economic freedoms were based on the division of labour, or specialization. Individuals did things that naturally contributed to the production of the goods and services required by society. Likewise, each corporation performed some functions in the productive system, but several corporations were involved in the realization of the final product. The production system was based on specialization and was fragmented, but the idea was that if attention were paid to the parts of the system, the whole would take care of itself. Responsibility for Ethics 2.1 gives another description of economic freedoms.

Ethical Implications

Many in society consider the emphasis on individuals inappropriate and believe that communitarianism is more important in society as individuals seek to join and identify with some type of community organization. Status is achieved by working with others

---

Everyday Ethics
2.2

First Nations and Property Rights

Most native peoples are denied individual property rights, one of the basic freedoms of individuals and a fundamental of business. However, granting property rights on First Nations lands has been discussed as a way to encourage economic prosperity. Currently the lands are owned by the federal government in trust for native peoples living on them. This is a collective arrangement leading to an absence of a sense of ownership and belonging fostering dependence on the federal and native governments (band councils). An example of the consequence of collective ownership is that some native peoples neglect their homes, allowing them to become uninhabitable.

It is proposed that full property rights be granted to individual native peoples to buy, sell, mortgage, lease, and develop property. A benefit of this approach is that it creates an ownership culture leading to more productive use of the land. Privately owned property provides collateral for mortgages and capital for business enterprises. Overall, this will create wealth on native lands, lead to increased economic activity, and improve living conditions. In other words, native peoples would have control over their economic destiny.

There are difficulties with granting individual property rights. The concept of individual property rights is contrary to the traditional way of life of native peoples and their attachment to land in general. There would be some difficulties in allocating property among present band members, and whether or not members who had left but previously resided on the reserve had a right to some property. There is fear that a class system based on property may emerge. Another issue is whether or not individuals could sell their acquired property to non-native peoples. Some chiefs oppose the individual property rights as it will limit their power over the bands.

Property rights in some form do exist on a few First Peoples nations and various possibilities are being considered. A land tenure system has to reflect a nation's culture and traditions by maintaining a sense of community and collective interest. The federal government is considering allowing property rights on native lands, but it is feared that the proposed approach will not be in the best interests of all First Nations. Property rights was one of the issues highlighted in the early-2013 Idle No More protests by native peoples across the country.

Sources: Richard Truscott, "Property rights are the key to Indian prosperity," Canadian Taxpayers Federation Web site at http://taxpayer.com/commentary/property-rights-are-key-indian-prosperity, accessed August 20, 2012; Christopher Alcantara, "Individual property rights on Canadian Indian reserves: The historical emergence and jurisprudence of certificates of possession," available at http://www2.brandonu.ca/library/cjns/23.2/cjnsv23no2_pg391–424.pdf; Tom Flanagan, Christopher Alcantara, and Andre Le Dressay, *Beyond the Indian Act: Restoring Aboriginal Property Rights,* Montreal: McGill-Queen's University Press, 2010; and Tom Flanagan and Christopher Alcantara, "Individual property rights on Canadian Indian reserves," Fraser Institute, 2002, available at http://www.fraserinstitute.org/publicationdisplay.aspx?id=12290&terms=property+rights+indian.

RESPONSIBILITY
for Ethics **2.1**

Economic Freedoms

In recent years, conservative-oriented research organizations have developed indices of economic freedom. Two examples are The Heritage Institute and The Fraser Institute (in conjunction with several other institutes in the Economic Freedom of the World project). How individuals view these economic freedoms has an effect on their ethical behaviour.

The following is a list of some factors that are considered when identifying and measuring economic freedoms:

- *Property rights*—This factor relates to the ability to accumulate property, and the extent to which government protects private property. Private property should be safe from expropriation, and a rule of law ensures an efficient court system to enforce contracts.

- *Taxation*—All taxes are considered harmful to economic activity, whether income, capital gains, value-added, or payroll. The greater the taxation burden, the greater the disincentive to carry out economic activity, as taxes can slow economic growth.

- *Government intervention*—Greater economic freedom exists when the level of government expenditures as a percentage of the economy is low and when there is no government ownership of business enterprises and industries. Economic output produced by the government restricts individuals from being involved.

- *Regulation*—Any government regulations should be straightforward and applied uniformly to all businesses. Regulatory requirements should not be a burden on businesses, licensing requirements should be at a minimum, and there should be no corruption within the bureaucracy.

- *International exchange*—There should be no restrictions on the movement of goods, services, or money between nations. Tariff rates should be low (if in place at all), non-tariff barriers should be minimized, and there should be no corruption in the customs service. There should be few, if any, restrictions on capital flows, and no difference between an official or market exchange rate and a black market one.

- *Foreign investment*—There are few, if any, limits on the extent of foreign investment. All industries are open to foreign investors, and there are no restrictions and performance requirements on foreign companies. Foreigners are allowed to own land and receive equal treatment under the law.

- *Money and inflation*—The government maintains a tight monetary policy where the supply of currency does not exceed the demand. Monetary policy is measured by analyzing the inflation rate over a period.

- *Wage and price controls*—A free economy allows corporations to set the prices on the goods and services they require and to establish the wages they pay workers. Restrictions on economic freedom would include minimum-wage laws, government price controls, and government subsidies that affect prices.

- *Corruption*—Corruption in the economy, as represented by a black market, should not exist. There should be no smuggling and piracy of intellectual property. The operation of a black market suggests too many government restrictions exist for a free market economy.

For each of these factors, grading scales have been developed. After scoring the factors, a total score is ascertained by country and countries ranked. In recent years, Canada has been one of the top 10 countries on such economic freedom indices.

rather than by struggling alone. Unions and cooperatives are examples of such organizations, as are the recent developments in industrial democracy and social enterprise.

It is argued that a systematic societal approach is preferable to the atomistic thinking of individualism. The whole society is viewed, rather than its parts, and understanding the interrelationships among the parts is favoured over a highly specialized, subdivided view of society.

The issue arises as to the extent individuals are responsible for their economic well-being versus governments or some form of collective organization. Governments operate many social programs for various members of society, and individualism and economic freedom become less important than social well-being, distribution of income, health, and education. Although most of the economic freedoms mentioned in the previous section exist to some extent, there have been abridgments to these freedoms. All business enterprises now require some form of licensing prior to commencing business, and if an enterprise wishes to incorporate, it must be registered with the government. Also, the freedoms of employees are restricted by the corporations that employ them (dress codes, required purchase of firm's products) and by membership in unions (compulsory membership, allocation of work).

Recently, economic freedoms have been defined by various research organizations and national economies have been evaluated according to the extent that the freedoms exist. Ethical implications are present as the issue arises about the desirability of individual versus collective action, and about the extent to which economic freedoms should exist.

LO 2.4   Equality of Opportunity

The Fundamental

> **Equality of opportunity** The assumption that all individuals or groups have an even chance at responding to some condition in society.

Equality of opportunity is the assumption that all individuals or groups have an even chance at responding to some condition in society. Many of those involved in Canadian business in the nineteenth and twentieth centuries were attracted to Canada because there was less influence exerted by nobility, landed gentry, and a rigid class system in North America than in Europe. There was less established wealth, and the "frontier" environment allowed individuals the opportunity to create their own wealth no matter what their background. This type of environment was appropriate for business: everyone was more likely to start the economic challenge of establishing and operating a corporation on about the same terms, and to have about an equal chance of succeeding. The opportunity existed to make one's own way by establishing a new business with minimum government intervention, and it was possible to pull up stakes and move to another part of the frontier.

Ethical Implications

In reality, equality of opportunity is challenging to achieve in a capitalist system. It is a societal issue because lack of equality of opportunity leads to economic or income inequality, which often is blamed on business. Many examples stem from income distribution, for example wages that are stagnant while profits increase, the gap between the poor and the rich (among individuals within an organization or a country and among countries), and male versus female income disparity. Everyday Ethics 2.3 discusses unequal distribution of income or wealth and in particular the ethical implications of excessively high executive compensation.

In place of equality of opportunity has come the call for equality of results, such as the desire for an adequate income, quality health care, good education, and retirement security. In other words, a more equalitarian society and a move away from opportunity,

Everyday Ethics

2.3

Executive Compensation

A survey by *The Globe and Mail* found that the five highest paid Canadian chief executives in 2011 were:

- J. Michael Pearson, Valeant Pharmaceuticals International Inc., $36,318,841
- Bradley Shaw, Shaw Communications Inc., $15,851,336
- Donald Walker, Magna International Inc., $14,841,085
- Gerald Schwartz, Onex Corporation, $14,137,644
- Peter Marrone, Yamana Gold Inc., $12,420,462

These figures represent total compensation including salary, bonus, shares, and options.

It is argued that chief executive officers (CEOs) of Canadian corporations are earning a disproportionate share of the wealth. According to a study by the Canadian Centre for Policy Alternatives, average compensation of the 100 best-paid CEOs was $8.38 million in 2011, while the average wage and salary earnings of Canadians was $44,436 (in 2010). The study found that the 100 highest-paid corporate executives earn an average Canadian's annual salary by noon on January 3. Several ethical implications result from this practice:

- Some executive compensation packages are so large they can affect the returns of shareholders, including employee pension plans.
- Compensation often increases when the performance of the corporation declines.
- Employees feel unfairly treated when layoffs occur while the CEO's salary increases.
- Often the compensation packages are not disclosed or properly accounted for.
- Stock options are exercised before performance is achieved, and sometimes at share prices beyond the market price.
- The highly paid executives are able to hire the best expert tax accountants to avoid paying taxes.

Several initiatives are proposed to counter the trend toward high compensation packages, including placing restrictions on the exercising of options, limiting severance benefits, delaying payment of bonuses until performance is clear, requiring shareholder approval of preferential pensions, and implementing the complete disclosure of all costs associated with compensation. Some governments, including those in the United States and United Kingdom, are regulating executive compensation in industries to which they have provided financial support.

Sources: "Executive compensation: 40 top-earning CEOs, *The Globe and Mail,* June 11, 2012, B4; and Hugh Mackenzie, "Canada's CEO elite 100: The 0.01%," Toronto: Canadian Centre for Policy Alternatives, January 2012.

individualism, and personal freedom toward social, economic, and cultural levelling has been sought. Equality was redefined to be an equality of result, with all persons in society having nearly equal incomes, status, and power. The new equality was to be achieved through government involvement. The result has been a conflict between the motivational incentive provided by a competitive system and a system advocating equal reward to all despite the extent of effort or contribution.

Inequality is inevitable with a capitalistic system and has ethical implications. As economic growth occurs, the wealth created is not distributed equally and a debate centres on the relationship between growth and equality. Does faster growth necessarily cause greater inequality? Or, does greater inequality cause faster growth? If growth results in everyone being better off, most people are satisfied. But if the rich get richer and the poor get poorer, a problem arises in that social instability might occur. Another outcome might be demands for an engineered egalitarian society attempted through government initiatives such as affirmative action in employment and education, hiring quotas, and pay equity.

As it is not possible to achieve equality of opportunities or results, an alternative is to think in terms of increasing equity or fairness in the business system. This approach would have the corporation striving to achieve greater perceived fairness in the distribution of economic wealth and in its treatment of stakeholder interests. Equity would involve fairness in the opening up of economic opportunity, fairness in the way stakeholders are treated by the corporation, and fairness in the way the economic pie is divided. Examples of inequities would be sudden and drastic layoffs, large drops in living standards, excessively high executive salaries, and fortunes for some while the bargaining power of others is reduced. Although it is difficult to define what is fair, it is easier to achieve equity than equality.

LO 2.5 ‹ Competition

The Fundamental

Competition The condition in a market system in which many rival sellers seek to provide goods and services to many buyers.

Competition is the condition in a market system in which many rival sellers seek to provide goods and services to many buyers. It is believed that competition is natural and desirable: it ensures that corporations provide the goods and services desired by society. The survival of the corporation is at stake as it exists in rivalry with others to provide goods and services to consumers who usually have alternative sources of supply. No one corporation, or seller, can influence the market by its behaviour—a multitude of sellers ensures competition, thus preventing concentration of economic power. The advantages of competition are that it ensures goods and services are provided at lowest costs; reduces waste and inefficiency and holds profits to a minimum; widens the choice of goods and services available to consumers; and regulates prices. Competition is the invisible hand that is responsible for the orderly operation of the market. Society rewards the most competent firms, and only the fittest survive.

Ethical Implications

Oligopoly A type of competition where the few sellers in an industry behave similarly.

The circumstances described in the previous paragraph represent perfect competition—which seldom exists today, as illustrated in Everyday Ethics 2.4. The pricing system is sometimes controlled or influenced by business or government actions. An **oligopoly**, where the few sellers in an industry behave similarly, exists in many industries, and even monopolies exist in others. Some business enterprises have become very large and have diversified into many industries. Government regulates prices in some industries such as utilities, and in oligopolies there is a tendency for price leadership by one of the larger enterprises. Some industries, such as real estate and insurance, tend to charge identical commissions or establish premiums from rate books available to all enterprises in the industry. The professions have suggested price ranges for their services. Governments control or influence prices through direct control over wages and profits (as during the Second World War, or the period from 1975 to 1978), taxation, direct regulation, provincial barriers to trade, and tariffs.

No longer is it possible for corporations to easily enter some industries, as barriers to entry exist in the form of the size of plant necessary to achieve economies of scale, the domination of the market by one or a few corporations through advertising, or the inability to obtain the necessary technology. The ideal situation of perfect competition no longer exists, if it ever did. The invisible hand of a free market is now sometimes replaced by the visible hand of government.

The nature of competition in an industry influences behaviour between the corporation and various other stakeholders, including other corporations in the industry, consumers,

Everyday Ethics

2.4

Consequences of Restricted Competition

Many in society believe business practices that restrict competition are unfair to consumers by reducing choice and increasing prices. Entry to the industry also is often restricted, preventing competition. The following points provide some examples of such practices:

Pharmaceuticals for pets—Some veterinarians are refusing to give out prescriptions for drugs, forcing clients to purchase from their own pharmacy. This prevents comparison shopping and reduces competition. Some drug companies sell only through a veterinary purchasing company and do not make the drugs available to other vendors.

Dairy prices—Wholesale milk prices are controlled by a marketing board that, for the past few years, has increased prices despite declining demand. Canadian producers are protected by restricting entry and high tariffs on imports, which has reduced consumer choice. A similar situation exists in the poultry industry.

Rail monopoly—In many parts of Canada, Canadian National and Canadian Pacific operate as monopolies. To overcome this practice, railways should be required to offer "running rights" where other companies are able to use the tracks for a fee. Such a practice is already the case in telecom, cable television, and electricity and gas distribution.

Public company auditing in Ontario—Only chartered accountants (CAs) can audit publicly traded corporations in Ontario. In other provinces, certified general accountants (CGAs) are allowed to do this type of auditing.

Ticket sales—Ticketmaster has a monopoly on ticket sales to many concerts and sports events. The prices are increased by various convenience and service fees, facility fees, and delivery charges. It is argued that alternate ticket sellers are necessary to make the ticket market work efficiently.

Telecommunications, transportation, and banking industries—All are regulated by governments, resulting in some form of restrictions on entry to the industry including restrictions on foreign ownership, which limits new entrants and therefore choice for consumers. In particular, competition in wireless communications—cell phones and smartphones—is limited by entry restrictions and similar market behaviours by the few competitors that exist, for example through very complicated cell phone contracts. Some practices in these industries illustrate oligopolistic market behaviour.

and suppliers. There are ethical implications of competitive behaviour, and governments in developed economies have attempted to influence this behaviour to protect various stakeholder interests.

LO 2.6 ▸ Profits

The Fundamental

Profits The excess of revenues over expenses; closely associated with competition.

Profits are the excess of revenues over expenses and are closely associated with competition. The pursuit of profits spurs people into action and provides the drive and desire to do things. Corporations compete for profits, yet competition ensures that if excessive profits are made, others will be attracted to the industry. Profits are not only a regulator of efficiency, but also a measure of effectiveness. They can be retained in the business as a source of funds, and provide both an incentive to develop new products and technology and a reward for risk taking.

Ethical Implications

Many in society view profits with disdain, and some even consider them immoral. Many consider earning a profit to be appropriate, but attempts at maximizing profits through reducing competition to be not appropriate. As corporations have become larger and fewer in number in some industries, and more prices are government- or self-regulated, the role of profits as envisioned in classical theory has altered. Profits do not act as a "regulator" for many reasons. The introduction of taxation, especially income taxation, and the rates of inflation redistribute profits. The barriers to entry existing in many industries and the need for increasing size to achieve efficiency may have led to profits higher than normal under perfect competition. Competition not only is reflected by the number of corporations operating in an industry, but also is impacted by the services offered, advertising, brand loyalty, and image or reputation. Profits are controversial, as illustrated in Everyday Ethics 2.5.

Everyday Ethics
2.5

Petroleum Industry Profits—Reasonable or Excessive?

The year 2011 was a good one for corporations in the petroleum industry. The following list gives an indication of the industry's profitability or net earnings in 2011; the profits of all corporations increased over those of 2010.

- Suncor Energy Inc.—$4.3 billion
- Imperial Oil Ltd.—$3.4 billion
- Husky Energy Inc.—$2.2 billion
- Cenovus Energy Inc.—$1.5 billion
- Canadian Natural Resources Limited—$2.6 billion

Note that the word "profits" was not used by the corporations in the presentation of these financial data. Are these profits reasonable at a time when consumers are paying high prices for gasoline and home heating fuel oil? Should the excessive profits be taxed by the government? Should the pricing practices in the industry be investigated? These questions raise issues with ethical implications for the petroleum corporations, consumers, and government.

LO 2.7   The Work Ethic

The Fundamental

> **Work ethic** A code of values, or a body of moral principles, claiming that work is desirable, that work is a natural activity, and that work is good in and of itself.

The **work ethic** is a code of values, or a body of moral principles, claiming that work is desirable, it is a natural activity, and it is good in and of itself. It has been assumed that work is the purpose of one's life and that unemployment is only a temporary misfortune. Individuals in society are assumed to be willing to support themselves and the members of their family. Work in itself is worthy, admirable, and both personally and socially valuable. The Protestant ethic reinforced the work ethic by claiming that hard work, diligence, thrift, and "busyness" were desirable for religious reasons; that is, to serve as an earthly expression of God's will.

Ethical Implications

It is argued that individuals' attitudes toward work have changed as a result of government programs and society's expectations. Government programs now support the less fortunate, and the effects of unemployment have been reduced by Employment Insurance payments. These programs may not have a socially desirable impact, as sometimes labour markets are distorted—actually causing unemployment. Individuals now expect that more will be done for them, usually by governments but also by business enterprises by way of working conditions, fringe benefits, and salaries—as illustrated, for example, in Responsibility for Ethics 2.2. The tendency toward government handouts and a somewhat more paternal attitude by employers has resulted in less need to work hard—or, as some argue, to work at all. The traditional form of the work ethic encouraged thrift and saving. In modern society, the desire to consume is a driving force, and individuals work hard to acquire material possessions. The resulting consumption ethic relates to the next fundamental, consumer sovereignty.

RESPONSIBILITY
for Ethics **2.2**

Work Ethic of the Millennials

If you are between 10 and 30 years old, you are most likely a "Millennial." Millennials, also known as Generation Y or the Net Generation, were born during the 1980s and 1990s and are now entering the workplace. Some describe them as spoiled, narcissistic layabouts who spend too much time with social networking; a lot of time and effort is spent downloading audio and video materials, often illegally, and they have a tendency to plagiarize. They are considered to be overly self-confident and treat work as a way to personal fulfillment. Managers say that they are difficult to manage, requiring precise direction and more feedback, particularly praise. They grew up in good times and believe that they are entitled to a particular lifestyle and workplace environment. Unreasonable demands are put on employers as they think work should be not only fulfilling but also fun, with flexible hours, good salaries, and ample vacations.

Not everyone holds this view of the Millennials' work ethic. They are computer-literate multi-taskers who are good at online collaboration, making them natural team players. Some say they are smarter, quicker, and more tolerant of diversity. They care about society's problems, believe in justice, value innovation, and insist on integrity. Also, the economic downturn has imposed some reality to their work ethic as obtaining jobs and job hopping has become more difficult.

Sources: Steve Maich, "Is this the future? Don't bet on it," *Maclean's*, December 1, 2008, 42; Lianne George, "Dude, where's my job," *Maclean's*, January 19, 2009, 48–49; Geoff Gloeckler, "Here come the Millennials," *BusinessWeek*, November 24, 2008, 047–050; "Managing the Facebookers," *The Economist*, January 3, 2009, 10; "Generation Y goes to work," *The Economist*, January 3, 2009, 47–48; and Don Tapscott, *Grown Up Digital: How the New Generation Is Changing Your World* (New York: McGraw-Hill, 2009).

LO 2.8   **Consumer Sovereignty**

The Fundamental

Consumer sovereignty
The assumption existing in an economy that consumers have and exercise power over producers through the decisions they make in purchasing the goods and services provided by corporations.

Consumer sovereignty is the assumption existing in an economy that consumers have and exercise power over producers through the decisions they make in purchasing the goods and services provided by corporations. It is assumed that consumption is the end purpose of production. Consumers, by "voting" for a product when they purchase it, dictate the types, styles, and quality of goods and services provided by business. It is the consumers' evaluation and acceptance or rejection that determines the success of a business. It is clear that the producer is servant to the consumer and is to obey the instruction of the consumer, who commands and directs. Consumer sovereignty is a fundamental part of any competitive system, and generally the more competitive the market the stronger the power of the consumer.

Ethical Implications

Consumers often face challenges in exercising their sovereignty. Sometimes consumers are not aware of all alternatives available to them and sometimes they are not capable of understanding the technical complexities of many goods and services. With some goods and services there is less choice, or no choice, available to the consumer. Giant corporations are said to mould consumers' tastes and preferences through persuasive advertising. It is argued that producers have the power to ignore some consumer wishes, something necessary for mass production. On the other hand, it is suggested that there are too many products, or brands, with too little difference. Trivial product differentiation and artificial product obsolescence have encouraged this proliferation of products.

Canadian governments have passed legislation relating to consumer matters that has imposed many regulations, standards, and approvals prior to the introduction of a product. Governments influence or regulate in the "public interest," which frequently is more in the "producer interest." Monopolistic institutions are tolerated or created by the government, such as agricultural marketing organizations or professional associations. Tariffs and quotas on imported goods create contrived scarcities, increasing the prices paid by consumers. It is doubtful that consumers have much influence on the market compared to the impact of organizations of large corporations, government agencies, organized labour, or minority producer groups such as farmers. Responsibility for Ethics 2.3 illustrates how even one consumer can change the way a corporation conducts its business.

RESPONSIBILITY
for Ethics **2.3**

One Consumer Influences Facebook

Harley Finkelstein was concerned about the personal details being collected about his 14-year-old sister when she used Facebook. Harley and Jordon Plener, both law student interns at the Canadian Internet Policy and Public Interest Clinic (CIPPIC) at the University of Ottawa, decided to investigate the issue. Their research eventually led to a complaint being filed with the Privacy Commissioner of Canada under the *Personal Information Protection and Electronic Documents Act* (PIPEDA).

The Privacy Commissioner determined that many of the complaints identified were well founded, including the following:

- The sharing of information with third-party developers
- A lack of distinction between account deactivation, where personal data are held in storage, versus deletion, where data are actually erased
- The inadequate protection of the privacy of non-users who are invited to join the site
- The treatment of the accounts of deceased users

Facebook responded to the complaints by altering its policies. It agreed to retrofit its application platform to prevent the use of information unless express consent is given. It agreed to make clear to users the option of deleting versus deactivating their account. More information would be provided in Facebook's terms of use statement, and wording included in its privacy policy to explain what will happen in the event of a user's death.

The changes applied to Facebook's estimated 2 million users in Canada and, more importantly, to its more than a quarter of a billion users around the world.

Sources: Office of the Privacy Commissioner of Canada, Elizabeth Denham, "Report of findings into the complaint filed by the Canadian Internet Policy and Public Interest Clinic (CIPPIC) against Facebook Inc. under the *Personal Information Protection and Electronic Documents Act*," July 16, 2009, http://www.priv.gc.ca/cf-dc/2009/2009_008_0716_e.cfm#sect1; Office of the Privacy Commissioner of Canada, News Release, "Facebook agrees to address Privacy Commissioner's concerns," August 27, 2009, http://www.priv.gc.ca/media/nr-c/2009/nr-c_090827_e.cfm; and Matt Hartley, "How a kid sister changed Facebook," *National Post*, August 28, 2009, A1, A2.

> ## LO 2.9   The Role of Government

The Fundamental

Government's role is to be kept to a minimum and is frequently expressed as a laissez-faire approach: "leave us alone." Although minimum government involvement is advocated, government is to provide for such things as national security, internal law and order, and a system of currency and measures. Government also provides the mechanisms for individuals to associate with others for a common, lawful purpose by evolving a body of law relating to contracts between individuals, which provides a basis for individual behaviour and expectations with respect to contractual arrangements. Government intervention in the business system for other than these types of activities is considered to lessen efficiency as the movement of resources is restricted and market pricing is interfered with.

Ethical Implications

Instead of the modest intended role of government, the government now is an influential stakeholder in the business system. Government involvement in the economy has always been greater in Canada than in the United States. Government was involved in building or financing transportation facilities very early in Canadian history. The National Policy of the 1890s, involving the imposition of tariffs to protect domestic manufacturers, has been a major intervention in the economy. Governments are now extensively involved in the economy through subsidies, taxation, tariffs, regulations and legislation, loans and grants programs, and ownership. Government is not only a monitor of business activity, but also an active participant in the system.

connect

Want to learn about **business fundamentals and the story of The Little Red Hen?** Go to CONNECT.

Governments restrict capital movements and natural resource sales, impose product standards, and in some cases even prevent businesses from shutting down plants when they want. Legislation governs how employees are treated and regulates the types of contracts that can be made with customers. Competition legislation makes some types of trade practices illegal and attempts to prevent monopolization. Responsibility for Ethics 2.4 describes an example of government's regulation of advertising.

These eight fundamentals are not isolated from one another but are linked to become the basis for the capitalist market system. Private property is the basis of individualism and economic freedom; competition regulates profits; profits motivate individuals and reinforce the work ethic; the work ethic is rewarded by profits and the accumulation of property; individualism is critical for competition and consistent with the work ethic; and consumer sovereignty is related to economic freedom, competition, and profits. The fundamentals are the basis of capitalism, but capitalism takes different forms around the world and at different times.

> ## LO 2.10   The Fundamentals and Various Forms of Capitalism

Capitalism is an economic system that allows for private ownership of the means of production (land, labour, and capital) and assumes that economic decision making is in the hands of individuals or enterprises that make decisions expecting to earn a profit. Canadian capitalism satisfies this definition to some degree, but not all means of production are privately owned, not all economic decision making is in the hands of individuals, and many economic decisions are made where profit is not the motive.

Restricting Freedom of Commercial Expression

The advertising of tobacco products has been regulated for some time, with the most recent legislation being the 1997 *Tobacco Act*. It prohibited tobacco company sponsorship of events and mandated larger, graphic warnings on packages. The tobacco industry has challenged advertising bans, and this act was no exception. The industry claimed that the act was vague and did not clearly indicate what was acceptable and that it restricted advertising, or freedom of commercial expression.

In February 2007, the challenge ended up in the Supreme Court of Canada, with the three tobacco companies—Imperial Tobacco Canada, JTI-Macdonald Corp., and Rothmans, Benson and Hedges Inc.—on one side, and the federal and six provincial governments plus the Canadian Cancer Society on the other.

The governments and the Cancer Society argued that the advertising restriction was justified to protect Canadian society, in particular youth. They claimed that there was evidence to support the harmful effects of tobacco use and pointed to the fact that 45,000 Canadians died every year from tobacco use. Furthermore, the Canadian government was one of 144 countries that signed a World Health Organization treaty in 2005 that bans all tobacco advertising and sponsorship as long as it was constitutionally possible.

The governments claim that tobacco products do not deserve the free speech protection, while the corporations argue that their advertising is a constitutionally protected form of freedom of expression.

Sources: Based on Sue Bailey, "Tobacco case makes it to top court," *The Telegram* (St. John's, NL), February 19, 2007, A7; and Kirk Makin, "B.C. aims to choke tobacco industry," *The Globe and Mail*, February 19, 2007, A5.

Canada does not have a pure free-enterprise system, but instead a complex, "patched up" one. This patched system is the best that can be expected given human limitations; that is, no system can be perfect if it is to operate democratically. Moreover, the system is an integrated and complex one, making the separation of fundamental elements difficult. Government involvement has increased as the underlying assumptions of capitalism have become less valid in practice. Some would argue that laissez-faire capitalism was a myth in the first place and never really operational.

While capitalism takes one form in Canada, different forms or versions are in existence around the world. Also, the form of capitalism within a country can change. Canadian managers and entrepreneurs must recognize this phenomenon.

The following list outlines some of the more common forms of capitalism.[5]

Consumer capitalism—This form of capitalism is also referred to as liberal market capitalism and is practised in the United States, Britain, Canada, and Australia. Government involvement in the economic system is limited, there are open borders, and a profit mentality exists. Consumers have considerable influence over the market and producers respond to their wishes. Potential problems with this form are income inequity, low savings rate, and weak central governments.

Producer capitalism—This form emphasizes production, employment, and statist policies; that is, the concentration of economic controls and planning in the hands of a centralized government. As practised in Germany, it is referred to as a social market economy and is a regulated capitalist market with generous social welfare. Input is sought from other stakeholders, particularly employees or labour, a practice referred to as co-determination. Other forms of producer capitalism are practised in France, Japan, and Mexico. Potential problems with this form are that the social safety nets fray, innovation is slowed, and consumer dissatisfaction often occurs.

Family capitalism—Also referred to as crony and Confucian capitalism, this form is found in eastern Asian countries such as Taiwan, Malaysia, Thailand, and Indonesia. In some economies, extended clans dominate business activities and control capital flows. In many countries, the clans or families are created by Chinese descendants scattered throughout the region. In Japan, the form is based on the implicit belief in social balance and harmony or domestic peace. An emotional attachment is formed with groups, family, households, working teams, and nature, with an embracing of belongingness. This view differs from the Western beliefs in objectivity, equal treatment, and the "level playing field." Under this form, outsiders are not considered equal, modern corporate organizations are less likely to be formed, and money markets are restricted.

Frontier capitalism—Russia and China are examples of frontier capitalism, suggesting that capitalism is in its beginning stages. The fundamentals of business are being introduced as the government pursues for-profit business activities and an entrepreneurial class sprouts. The fundamentals are in various stages of being made operational. The role of government changes with the need to develop commercial law and regulation. The rule of law is not clearly established, and criminal activity often fills the void. Barriers to trade with other economies have to be removed. Mechanisms and institutions have to be developed that will facilitate a transition to consumer or producer capitalism.

In addition, other phrases are often used: "employee capitalism," when workers own shares in the corporation; "democratic capitalism," when shareholders have the right to vote on major initiatives; and "people's capitalism," when ownership of corporations is widely distributed. Recently, the phrase "stakeholder capitalism" has even been used to describe some forms of producer capitalism, such as that practised in Germany.

Various forms of capitalism are advocated as a result of changes in society's view of business. Three examples currently receiving attention are conscious capitalism, creative capitalism, and state capitalism.

Conscious capitalism is the reorientation of business from a single focus on profits to emphasis being placed on integrity, higher standards of corporate behaviour, and inclusion of all stakeholders. A higher social purpose is pursued and assumes that the fundamentals of business must change if society is to thrive. Business must have a stakeholder orientation where conscious leadership should involve and consult those influenced. The culture of business must embody values, principles, and practices incorporating social responsibilities.[4]

Creative capitalism is a new form of capitalism that places the resolution of social needs as a primary goal of economic activity, rather than as secondary consequence of economic activity and performance. It was described initially by Bill Gates of Microsoft, who was concerned by the inequities between the world's rich and poor peoples. He asserts that non-creative capitalism does not have to concern itself directly with the well-being of people. It took for granted its benefits to all, through its mechanisms of social Darwinism, competition, and evolutionary success of the fittest. Creative capitalism would discover new, innovative ways to solve the problems of the poorest by combining self-interest (or individualism) and caring for others.[5] An alternative form has emerged from the 2008 financial crisis and resulting recession.

A different type of capitalism being sought by some involves a greater role of government directly in the business system through the ownership of corporations. **State capitalism** is "an economic system in which governments manipulate market outcomes for political and social purposes." The financial crisis and economic downturn of 2009 shook the fundamentals of free markets, spurring countries to take control of property and financial resources within a country. The stimulus packages offered by governments included expenditures of goods and services and refinancing corporations, in particular in the banking and

Conscious capitalism The reorientation of business from a single focus on profits to emphasis being placed on integrity, higher standards of corporate behaviour, and inclusion of all stakeholders.

Creative capitalism Places the resolution of social needs as primary, instead of secondary to economic activity and performance.

State capitalism An economic system in which governments manipulate market outcomes for political and social purposes.

automobile industries, in which governments became a part owner. Many economists fear that government involvement in business for political or economic purposes will not result in the most efficient use of resources.[6]

The discussion of capitalist fundamentals and the differing forms of capitalism explains the lack of clarity surrounding the description given to the economic systems operating in particular countries. Students of business should appreciate that different forms of capitalism exist in different economies and that the form changes over time in the same economy. All this complicates the relationship between business and society.

LO 2.11   The Challenges, the Ethics, and a New View of Capitalism

The Challenges

Capitalism is a controversial economic system: many stakeholders advocate the benefits of the system, and many oppose or are critical of it. This has been the case with the recent financial crisis, economic downturn, and occurrences of corporate crime. The following discussion examines some of the challenges.

Greed—Humans act in their own self-interest to some extent; that is, they desire to improve their situation. **Greed** is an excessive and selfish form of self-interest where individuals desire more of something than what is needed or fair. Of course, what is needed and fair is open to interpretation. Self-interest is harmful if channelled improperly through deceit, corruption, force, fraud, and theft; an example is given in Everyday Ethics 2.6. Some say capitalism is only about greed, but this is unfair as it is also about creativity, innovation, and entrepreneurship, which provide society with employment and goods and services.

Greed The excessive desire to acquire or possess more, especially more material wealth, than one needs or deserves.

Everyday Ethics
2.6

Gordon Gekko's "Greed Is Good"

Michael Douglas played Gordon Gekko, a ruthless businessman who symbolized greed and corruption, in the 1987 movie *Wall Street.* In the movie, Gekko made an often-quoted reference to greed:

> The point is, ladies and gentleman, that greed—for lack of a better word—is good. Greed is right. Greed works. Greed clarifies, cuts through, and captures the essence of the evolutionary spirit. Greed, in all of its forms—greed for life, for money, for love, knowledge—has marked the upward surge of mankind.

In 2009, a sequel to the film came out with Michael Douglas again playing Gekko. In *Wall Street: Money Never Sleeps,* Gekko is back in business after being in jail for 20 years for insider trading—this time, though, he has a seemingly different view of morality.

Sources: "'Greed is good,' again," *The Telegram* (St. John's, NL), April 29, 2009, B4; "Recession won't make Gekko blush in sequel," *National Post,* April 30, 2009, A1; and Terence Corcoran, "In Hollywood, war and Wall St. are both hell," *National Post,* March 23, 2010, FP15.

Mistrust—Trust is important in all relationships, including between business and society. It should not be taken for granted or assumed to exist. It is dynamic and involves reputation and integrity. After corporate failures when people have lost jobs and investments, there is likely to be less trust of business. The 2009 Edelman Trust Barometer found that two-thirds of Canadian respondents trusted corporations less than the year before, 45 percent did not trust business to do what is right, and only about 20 percent agreed that information provided by CEOs was credible.[7] Business must build trust with internal stakeholders, such as employees and lenders, and with external stakeholders such as consumers, governments, and non-governmental organizations.

Economic downturns—Economic cycles are a feature of capitalism. Because capitalism is based on a market system, there will be swings between prosperous times and recessions or even depressions. An example is the 2008 collapse of financial institutions in the United States and Europe. Several investment banks failed, followed by many banks in other parts of the world, resulting in a credit squeeze and fall in value of financial assets. This was attributed to the lack of government regulation and oversight plus business practices such as the focus on share value and incentive-based executive compensation. But markets are dynamic and correct themselves eventually. Responsibility for Ethics 2.5 identifies some stakeholders that have been blamed for the 2008 financial crisis and economic downturn.

Business failures—Another aspect of capitalism is failure that disposes of weak corporations and shifts resources to new or stronger ones. Thus, bankruptcy laws need to work well to transfer resources efficiently from the less productive to more productive uses. Governments could become involved and bail out or prop up these corporations. This involvement is expensive, and the selection of which corporations to support is not easy. Nevertheless, those who have lost jobs and investments do pay a price for failure.

RESPONSIBILITY
for Ethics (**2.5**)

Placing Blame for the Financial Crisis

During the 2008 financial crisis and economic downturn there was much speculation about what was to blame. The following are some stakeholders that were blamed:

- *Lenders or bankers*—They offered initial low interest and other inducements to sell mortgages, sometimes to individuals who could not afford them.

- *Boards of directors/management*—Their focus on share value and incentive-based compensation led to risk taking.

- *Investment dealers*—Dealers repackaged mortgages as so-called asset-backed commercial paper (ABCP) to other financial institutions.

- *Regulators*—The regulators did insufficient monitoring and policing of the financial industry.

- *Government*—Governments deregulated the financial industry and facilitated a low-interest-rate economy.

- *Consumers*—Consumers took on mortgages for which they had insufficient incomes to finance in their desire, or greed, to own homes that were more expensive than they could actually afford.

    Or, capitalism could be blamed—namely the greedy pursuit of profits and the lack of regulation.

Corporate crime and wrongdoing—Crime and wrongdoing exists in all societal institutions. As mentioned in Chapter 1, corporate crime and wrongdoing comes in many forms and often receives considerable publicity and damages the reputations of businesses.

 **connect**   Want to learn more about **the pros and cons of capitalism**? Go to CONNECT.

The Ethics

Given these challenges, many in society wonder whether capitalism operates with *any* ethics, while others argue that capitalism does not prevent the pursuit of what is good for society. An assumption exists that moral individuals operate the business system and that they are in the majority. For capitalism to operate effectively, a strong system of moral behaviour and integrity is necessary. Aspects of this include the need to be honest and truthful, to operate by the rules of society and government, to keep one's word, to be responsible for actions, and to treat others as you would like them to treat you, including with compassion and forgiveness. Most corporations behave ethically, because if they behave inconsistently with the values of society and its stakeholders this behaviour would be corrected in various ways. For example, employees would leave, customers would be lost, and governments would legislate appropriate behaviour. Integrity in business makes sense, and many contend that a more ethically minded business culture is emerging. Many demonstrations of this culture will be examined throughout this book.

The fundamentals of capitalism are to be viewed in light of ethically minded corporate developments such as social responsibility, business ethics, corporate citizenship, and stakeholder management. More importantly, how these fundamentals are interpreted in society influences the values held by businesspersons and managers. If capitalism is to be accepted as the economic system in society, businesspersons and managers must somehow take into account the ethical implications resulting from the workings of the fundamentals.

A New View

New forms of capitalism are always being proposed. An article that is receiving attention is "Creating Shared Value: How to reinvent capitalism—and unleash a wave of innovation and growth" by Michael E. Porter and Mark R. Kramer.[8] According to the authors, "Capitalism is under siege." It is blamed for many of society's economic, social, and environmental problems with the legitimacy of business and trust in business being questioned.

Corporations must think beyond social responsibility, philanthropy, and sustainability to what the authors refer to as "shared value," which is a new way to achieve success. Capitalism is unparalleled in meeting human needs, improving efficiency, creating jobs, and building wealth, but it has not achieved its full potential to meet society's challenges. There should not be a business versus society approach. Instead, shared wealth involves expanding the total pool of economic and social value, not the redistribution of existing wealth. Business should look at decisions and opportunities in terms of sharing value, which will lead to new approaches generating greater innovation and growth, and greater benefits to society.[9]

Shared value | The idea that economic value to companies can be obtained by creating social value.

Shared value is defined as "policies and operating practices that enhance the competitiveness of a company while simultaneously advancing the economic and social conditions in the communities in which it operates."[10] Economic value to companies can be obtained by creating social value. This can be achieved in three ways. The first way is by re-conceiving products and markets by responding to society's needs for health, better housing, improved nutrition, help for the aging, and less damage to the environment. A second approach is by redefining productivity in the value chain by addressing such things as energy use and logistics, procurement policies, distribution approaches, and employee productivity. Lastly, social value is achieved by enabling local cluster development of related businesses, suppliers, service providers, and logistical infrastructure. These three reinforce one another.[11]

Government has a role to play by providing the right type and approach to regulation—by setting clear and measurable social goals, by setting performance standards, by defining practical phase-in periods, by putting in universal measurement and reporting systems and collecting the necessary data, and by reporting results in an efficient and timely manner.

Profits must involve a social purpose, which will result in a higher form of capitalism advancing society and allowing companies to grow more.[12]

The authors believe that creating shared value (CSV) should supersede corporate social responsibility (CSR). In some cases, CSR focuses on programs to build reputation that have limited connection to the business. CSV is key to profitability and leverages resources and expertise to create economic value by creating social value.[13] Finally, it is proposed that capitalism will evolve if there is a focus on the right kind of profits and that a more sophisticated capitalism will be imbued with a social purpose.[14] In its coverage of the article *The Economist* was critical of the idea, stating that it was not well developed and will have little impact.[15]

Other models or forms of capitalism are being proposed, and all incorporate the fundamentals in some way. Various stakeholders of the business system are impacted by how the fundamentals are interrupted or applied. It should be noted that many business organizations, businesspeople, and corporations are advocating greater responsibility and sensitivity to society and stakeholders. The following chapters will provide illustrations of these business initiatives.

Your advice to Stephen . . .

Different forms of capitalism exist and the application of the fundamentals varies in each. There are always some stakeholders in society who believe that there should be improvements to how capitalism works; that is, how it harms or benefits various stakeholders. This is the view of those involved in the Occupy movement. One problem with the movement was that it did not identify very clearly what should be done to improve capitalism. For the most part, there were complaints about capitalism with few suggestions for ways to change it. Stephen must decide whether he wishes to become involved in such an organization. If one believes there should be some changes to how capitalism works, it is very difficult to influence change as an individual. In society today, many suggestions relate to *why* capitalism should be changed, but few specify *what* should be changed.

SUMMARY

- Most goods and services needed by Canadians are supplied by business enterprises operating in a capitalist system. Many ethical implications arise as a result.

- Eight fundamental elements of Canadian capitalism were identified: the right of private property; equality of opportunity; competition; individualism and economic freedom; profits; the work ethic; consumer sovereignty; and the role of government. The elements represent values that must be held to some extent by a society in order for capitalism to operate effectively as an economic system. (LO 2.1)

- The right of private property facilitates the operation of business, but some in society resent a few acquiring large amounts. (LO 2.2)

- For capitalism to be acceptable to most Canadians, it must allow for equality of opportunity to share in economic well-being even though the results are not the same for everyone. (LO 2.3)

- To ensure that capitalism is regulated in the best interests of stakeholders, competitive rivalry must exist between sellers of goods and services, providing buyers with choice. The difficulty is that even in Canada's form of capitalism competitive markets do not exist. (LO 2.4)

- Individualism encourages people to participate in a capitalistic system, because they are free to make economic decisions in providing goods and services in a marketplace. Some Canadians resent the focus on individuals and believe the economy should be directed more by governments. (LO 2.5)

- In theory, when profits become too high in an industry, more businesses are attracted. Due to market imperfections such as barriers of entry, this sometimes does not occur. (LO 2.6)

- How employees and employers view the work ethic influences the ethics and responsibilities of a corporation. (LO 2.7)

- The goods and services produced by capitalism should be determined by consumers as they make purchase decisions. Unfortunately, consumer choice is restricted by various business practices and some government regulations. (LO 2.8)

- Government has a role in a capitalistic system, but its involvement should be only to protect the interests of stakeholders unable to defend themselves and to provide the infrastructure for the market system to operate effectively. (LO 2.9)

- The fundamentals were described as together they form the basis of Canadian capitalism. These elements give rise to many social or ethical issues that present challenges for Canadian businesspersons and managers. Therefore, the fundamentals discussed will provide a basis for an understanding of economic, social, or ethical responsibilities and of the relationships between business and its various stakeholders.

- Capitalism exists in several forms around the world. The functioning of capitalism faces changes, but does operate most of the time with moral standards. New forms of capitalism are always being proposed to make business more responsive to society's needs. (LO 2.10)

- Throughout this book, the fundamentals of capitalism are to be viewed in light of developments in corporate social responsibility, business ethics, sustainability, corporate citizenship, and stakeholder management. (LO 2.11)

KEY TERMS

Right of private property	Competition	Conscious capitalism
Intellectual property	Oligopoly	Creative capitalism
Individualism	Profits	State capitalism
Economic freedoms	Work ethic	Greed
Equality of opportunity	Consumer sovereignty	Shared value

CRITICAL THINKING AND DISCUSSION QUESTIONS

1. Identify the intellectual property you use in your studies. Have you always respected the rights of the owners of this type of private property?

2. Should equality of opportunity equal equality of results? What are the implications for business of the inequalities that result from capitalism?

3. Why doesn't competition exist in some industries, and what are the ethical implications?

4. Assess the amount of economic freedom that exists in Canada today. How does this freedom, or lack thereof, influence Canadian businesses?

5. What is the connection between competition and profits?

6. Do you believe that employees no longer possess a genuine work ethic?

7. In Canadian business, is the consumer sovereign?

8. Is government's role in the Canadian business system increasing or decreasing?

9. What individual and societal values are involved with each of the fundamentals? Values are defined as core beliefs or desires that guide or motivate attitudes and actions.

10. Does capitalism or the free market system erode moral character?

CASES

2.1   *Accepting a Job in the Payday Loan Industry*

Matthew Simmons was agonizing about whether or not to accept a management job in the payday loan industry. Matthew had graduated from a college business program and had received three job offers, the best of which in terms of salary was as a management trainee with a payday loan company.

Payday loans are small, unsecured loans against the customer's next paycheque. This type of lending began in the mid-1990s and today has about two million customers in Canada. There are about 1,400 stores, some of which are open seven days a week, 24 hours a day. It is estimated that the industry does about $2 billion a year in business.

The operation of these stores has become an informal banking system for a segment of the population. The loans are made and covered by a post-dated cheque cashed on the next payday. The average loan is about $280 and made for 10 days. The service offered is convenient, but high interest rates are charged and fees are levied. It is even alleged by some consumer advocates that the payday loan business is illegal and a form of loan-sharking. The industry responds that their lending practices are better than the alternatives available to some in society who would have to resort to using pawnshops or unscrupulous lenders.

The payday loan industry is responding to a consumer need for short-term, unsecured loans. The chartered banks and credit unions are unwilling and/or unable to provide the service. In fact, it is argued that the banks have encouraged the industry by closing so many branches. The banks say they have overdraft and credit card loans available. Some critics have determined that the payday loan stores are increasingly being set up near banks.

Some consider the industry to be a scam against poor and financially illiterate consumers that traps many into a never-ending spiral of debt. Industry observers counter that there is a business case for the payday loans. First of all, there is a huge demand, suggesting a need. Flexibility is provided to consumers in managing their financial affairs and other services are provided such as cheque cashing and money transfer. The loans may be used to pay off other loans with even higher interest rates, such as those on some credit cards. The high interest rates and fees are justified as there is a high default rate, and there are high administrative costs involved with small loans. The industry is mostly unregulated as there are jurisdictional complications, with the federal government being responsible for interest rates and the provinces for consumer protection.

An industry association, the Canadian Payday Loan Association (CPLA), is attempting to clean up the industry's reputation and supports regulation by government. Its mandate is "to work with governments toward a national regulatory framework that will allow for a viable industry and protect consumers." Of the 1,400 retail outlets in Canada, about 760 are CPLA members. The members must adhere to a "Code of Best Business Practices" that covers such things as rollovers (businesses are not allowed to grant another loan to pay off a previous one), collection practices, privacy protection, advertising, and responding to consumer complaints.

From a career perspective, the payday loan industry appeared promising. The company was expanding rapidly by adding locations in smaller communities and adding financial services such as insurance, mortgage referrals, foreign exchange, and tax preparation. Matthew's offer stated that he would start with a six-week training course followed by an intern period in a branch under the supervision of a manager. There was a good possibility of being a branch manager in less than a year and a division manager a few years afterwards.

Questions

1. What fundamentals of capitalism are relevant to this case?

2. Which stakeholders benefit from the payday loan industry, and which ones are harmed?

3. What are the economic, social, and ethical implications or issues in the industry?

4. Should Matthew take the job?

Sources: This case was prepared from public sources to provide material for classroom discussion, and it is not intended to illustrate either effective or ineffective response to a business and society managerial situation.

2.2   *Two-Faced Capitalism: Unmasking Corporate Social Responsibility*

Christian Aid is a non-governmental organization (NGO) dedicated "to supporting those which work among unreached peoples where hitherto our Lord has had no people for his Name." The organization has more than 90,000 native missionaries in the field, establishes more than 52,000 churches a year, and conducts evangelistic campaigns through print and broadcast media. It was established more than 50 years ago and provides assistance to victims of persecution, diseases, and disasters.

In 2004 the organization published the report *Behind the Mask: The Real Face of Corporate Social Responsibility*. The report states that corporations make loud, public commitments to principles of ethical behaviour and undertake "good works" in the communities in which they operate. On the surface, this looks like selfless philanthropy and might even be motivated by a genuine wish to help communities. These initiatives have resulted in some benefits, but at times have merely been to defend operations or counter public criticism. According to Christian Aid, CSR reporting is merely the use of fine words and lofty statements to describe initiatives that usually do not benefit those who need help.

The report contains case studies to illustrate the failure of CSR to deliver on what corporations have promised. Among the allegations are the following:

- *Shell in Nigeria:* It promised to be a better corporate citizen, but fails to clean up oil spills and runs community development projects that are ineffective.

- *British American Tobacco:* It claims to be upholding high standards of employee health and safety, but contract farmers in Kenya and Brazil claim they suffer from chronic ill health related to growing tobacco.

- *Coca-Cola:* It emphasizes using natural resources responsibly, but a subsidiary in India is accused of depleting the water supply in local communities.

The NGO no longer trusts corporations and wants governments to be responsible for the ethical operations of corporations. It recommends that the UK government adopt new laws to make corporate and social environmental reporting and disclosure mandatory, frame new responsibilities for company directors, and change the law to enable people harmed by British companies' overseas operations to seek redress in UK courts.

Questions

1. What are the implications of this report for the fundamentals of capitalism?

2. Should government regulate the CSR reporting of corporations?

3. How should the corporations identified in the report respond?

4. Will this report change the practices of the corporations mentioned?

Sources: "Corporate social responsibility: Two-faced capitalism," *The Economist*, January 24, 2004, 53–54; Christian Aid, "Behind the mask: The real face of corporate social responsibility," http://www.christianaid.org.uk/; and Christian Aid, http://www.christianaid.org/.

connect For more information on the resources available from McGraw-Hill Ryerson, go to www.mcgrawhill.ca/he/solutions.

CHAPTER 3
Identifying Stakeholders and Issues

LO 3.1 Recognize business as one institution in society and understand that its activities are influenced by other institutions and individuals referred to as stakeholders.

LO 3.2 Define and identify the corporation's stakeholders generally and the stakeholders relating to particular issues confronting the corporation.

LO 3.3 Understand the dynamic nature of stakeholder influence and that stakeholders have different goals and influence.

LO 3.4 Recognize the role of managers in relation to stakeholders.

LO 3.5 Formulate arguments supporting and opposing the stakeholder concept.

LO 3.6 Define an issue and describe issues management.

LO 3.7 List the purposes and benefits of issues management.

LO 3.8 Describe an issue life cycle.

LO 3.9 Understand the stages in the issues management process.

LO 3.10 Learn the importance of managing issues that become crises.

What would you do if . . . ?

Tom Carroll operated a small construction business building new homes and renovating older ones. He had been in business for 20 years and had a good reputation for quality work completed on time. His company employed six workers year-round, but the number increased to about 20 between May and October when outside construction was viable. He operated his business "by the book" and attempted to be fair in dealings with employees and customers. In addition, he made a point of dealing with the Canada Revenue Agency fairly and did not avoid or evade taxes. He believed that this was not the case with many of his competitors.

Tom felt that some of his competitors were simply greedy. In chatting with them about evading taxes, they said that they were unlikely to get caught and customers did not care. Furthermore, they felt that it was necessary sometimes to survive and that entrepreneurs deserved the extra compensation for working hard and long hours. Although they believed that evading large amounts in taxes was a crime, evading small amounts was okay. There was a common feeling that small business pays too much tax, the government wastes money, and large businesses get more tax breaks than small businesses.

The two main areas where the contractors evaded paying taxes were paying workers off the books and hiding income. The downsides of paying off the books were the always-present chance of being caught, the inability to declare the labour costs as an expense, the liability in the event of worker injury, and the risk of worker disclosure. Income was more likely to be hidden when the business was struggling financially, the owner had close control of operations, the business's objectives were short-term, and workers were paid off the books. Hiding income was facilitated by customers paying cash, sometimes in exchange for a lower price.

Hearing all this got Tom to thinking. There were certainly opportunities to evade taxes with slight chances of being caught. It was clear that his competitors were benefiting from the evasion practices while he paid all his taxes. He asked his wife about it, and she said he should not follow the same practice. Despite this, he started considering the possibility.

What is your advice to Tom?

This chapter introduces three topics that enable managers to assess the overall business environment—that is, to understand the economic, ethical, and environmental circumstances in which a corporation finds itself. The first topic describes the stakeholder concept, lists the corporation's stakeholders, and examines the pros and cons of the concept. The second topic is the identification of the issues confronting the corporation. Another topic will be the managing of crises. The three topics are closely related, as issues always involve stakeholders, and issues sometimes become crises. The identification of the corporation's relevant and salient stakeholders along with the issues is one approach to scanning the environment and will assist in understanding the corporation's circumstances.

LO 3.1   The Stakeholder Concept and Business

The business enterprise system impacts the lives of all citizens. In Canada, and in other democracies with private enterprise systems, business operates in a pluralistic social system where a variety of groups and institutions use power or influence to represent the interests of particular groups of citizens. The business corporation is one of many institutions in a pluralistic society, but its influence is widespread.

Pluralistic society One where influence or power is decentralized by dispersing it among a variety of institutions.

A **pluralistic society** is one where influence or power is decentralized by dispersing it among a variety of institutions. No one institution is completely independent of others, but each institution does possess some autonomy to pursue its own interests. With power diffused in this way, society is somewhat protected from the dominance of one group or one institution. Business is subject to the influence of other institutions in society and must respond to the various participants in society. In this book, these participants are referred to as stakeholders.

LO 3.2   Defining and Identifying Stakeholders

A stakeholder is an individual, or group, who can influence and/or is influenced by the achievement of an organization's purpose.[1] Stakeholders may also be referred to as claimants, influencers, publics, or constituencies. Although all these terms have their merits, the term "stakeholder" is preferable as it provides the most general identification of the parties to which business is responsible or accountable.

It is important for managers to identify the complete array of stakeholders for two reasons: (1) to obtain resources, business has to recognize the groups that control scarce resources, and (2) the support of other groups is required to maintain the legitimacy of business as an institution in society. Freeman argues that the use of the word "stakeholder" and the stakeholder concept is important for the following reason:

> By using "stakeholder," managers and theorists alike will come to see these groups as having a "stake." "Stakeholder" connotes "legitimacy," and while managers may not think that certain groups are "legitimate" in the sense that their demands on the firm are inappropriate, they had better give "legitimacy" to these groups in terms of their ability to affect the direction of the firm. Hence, "legitimacy" can be understood in a managerial sense implying that it is "legitimate to spend time and resources" on stakeholders, regardless of the appropriateness of their demand.[2]

Freeman points out that managers must seek out stakeholders, and argues that if "you want to manage effectively, then you must take your stakeholders into account in a systematic fashion."[3] Furthermore, the corporation should undertake on its own to identify and to satisfy key stakeholders before a solution is imposed, often by government or the courts. It is important that corporations develop managers with the expertise to deal with stakeholders.

All stakeholders have expectations, such as reasonably priced and good-quality products, adequate wage levels, good working conditions, and a clean, safe environment. Business must understand the preferences and expectations of the various stakeholder groups. Managers cannot look only inward to the needs of owners; in order to be successful managers must behave in a manner compatible with the beliefs and values of their stakeholders.

The complexity of business is often due to changing relationships between a corporation and its stakeholders. It should be remembered that the relationships are two-way. Corporations must understand how their activities influence stakeholders and also how stakeholders can influence their activities. Another approach to viewing these relationships is in terms of ethics and responsibilities. The corporation must consider the ethical implications of its behaviour toward stakeholders as must stakeholders toward the corporation. Corporations have responsibilities to stakeholders, depending on the situation and issue. Likewise, stakeholders must consider their responsibilities to the corporation depending on the circumstances of the relationship.

Identifying Stakeholders (19)

The first step for business is to identify the stakeholders that influence the corporation and/or that are influenced by the corporation. The following is a generic listing (that is, a list that applies to most corporations) of a corporation's stakeholders. This list is not intended to be in any particular order of importance.

Owners

Owners Those individuals or groups who have invested in a corporation in the form of equity or shares; usually referred to as shareholders.

Owners of the corporation, usually referred to as shareholders, are those individuals or groups who have invested in the form of equity, or shares. Shareholders can number in the hundreds of thousands for large corporations, or be a single individual in the case of an unincorporated business. Large institutions, such as trust or pension funds, may hold shares in corporations, as may a government. A corporation may be a shareholder in one or several other corporations. The influence shareholders have on business varies. One generalization is based on the number of shareholders: where there are thousands of investors, each holding a small number of shares, the individual shareholder's influence is usually minimal. But, where ownership is concentrated in the hands of a few shareholders, they usually exert significant influence over the corporation. In recent years mutual and pension funds, which in the past did not exercise their influence despite substantial holdings, have become more active in influencing major corporate decisions. Owners are stakeholders fundamental to the corporation and will be discussed in detail in Chapter 11.

Directors

Directors are elected by shareholders to represent their interests. They vary in number but are usually fewer than 20, and comprise a board that meets to decide on issues confronting the corporation. Directors can be from inside or from outside the corporation, in which case they are usually executives, managers, or owners of other corporations. The purpose of a board of directors is to determine the corporation's strategic direction, monitor and review the corporation's performance, and hire and fire the top executives. In theory, the ultimate responsibility for the corporation rests with the directors, but in reality, their influence varies. If the board comprises mainly insiders—that is, management—its influence on the corporation is substantial. Often boards comprising outsiders are mainly token bodies that rubber-stamp management's decisions. However, the board of directors has the potential to be a very powerful body. The influence of directors will be examined in Chapter 11.

It should be noted that small, unincorporated business enterprises do not have directors. In these enterprises the owners are also the operators and/or managers, and no board of directors exists. However, even small enterprises can be incorporated, and the owner/manager often is the principal shareholder and serves on the small board of directors, which operates on an informal basis.

Employees

Employees are individuals who work for the corporation and are categorized in several different ways. Managers are employees involved in supervising tasks at low, middle, and top levels in the corporation. Workers may be thought of as blue- versus white-collar. Blue-collar workers are involved in manufacturing, production, or servicing tasks, while white-collar workers are office employees. A corporation employs several professional groups, such as engineers, lawyers, and accountants. Employees may be hired on a part-time or full-time basis, with part-time employment becoming more prevalent recently. Labour unions often represent some employees, especially blue-collar workers. One issue relating to unions is dealing with the corporate trend to seek wage and benefit concessions from employees during a period of economic downturn.

Retired employees, either managers or workers, have a stake in the corporation where company pension plans exist. Recently, more attention has been focused on the employment of disadvantaged groups, including women, minorities, and persons with exceptionalities. Employees are considered among the most obvious and, perhaps, most important stakeholders. They have considerable influence for the simple reason that they are critical for the operation of the corporation. The ethics and responsibilities relating to employees will be discussed in Chapter 12.

Customers or Consumers

A corporation's customers may be members of the public, usually referred to as consumers; other corporations, referred to as industrial (or business-to-business) customers; or governments or government agencies. Customers are the source of revenue for the corporation and should be treated carefully. However, where a corporation is a monopoly, or where there is a lack of competition in the market, customers can be taken for granted. It is argued that the needs of individual consumers are ignored by large corporations that, through persuasive promotional practices, manipulate consumers. Instead of consumers influencing production decisions, producers influence or determine what consumers will purchase. Today, consumers are influencing the ethics of corporations, as described in Responsibility for Ethics 3.1. The ethics and responsibilities relating to consumers will be discussed in Chapter 12.

Ethical Consumers

Consumers are influencing corporations to offer goods and services that they consider to be "ethical" or "socially responsible." Also, many businesses have taken the initiative and are responding to these "ethical" consumers. Consumers can also exert influence on corporations through boycotts.

- *Whole Foods Market*—This Austin, Texas, company claims to be the world's leading natural and organic food supermarket, with 340 stores throughout North America and the United Kingdom, including several in the Vancouver and Toronto areas. It is publicly traded on the NASDAQ.

- *Fairtrade products*—This involves the identification of products such as coffee, cocoa, sugar, and flowers that have been produced under conditions where human rights, good working conditions, and the environment are respected.

- *Product Red brand*—Corporations are allowed to license this brand, with a percentage of the profits going to The Global Fund to provide sustainable funding for programs to fight AIDS, tuberculosis, and malaria in developing countries.

- *Boycott*—Organized boycotts of products or particular corporations are increasing in number. These efforts have been made easier and more successful because of the Internet.

Lenders and Creditors

Different types of individuals or groups lend corporations money. Some lend for long terms by purchasing bonds or debentures, while others advance funds for short periods, as with trade creditors. The lenders may be individuals or other corporations, usually financial intermediaries that exist to lend money. This stakeholder has substantial influence: if the lender is not paid as agreed upon in the contract, the corporation's assets can often be seized. Mortgagees, lenders, and creditors have a prior claim on the assets of a corporation if it ceases operations or goes bankrupt.

Suppliers

Suppliers are usually other corporations that provide raw materials, component parts, or finished materials used in the manufacture or provision of the corporation's goods and services. The influence of suppliers varies. If a supplier is the only source of a particular material or component, then more of the corporation's attention must be devoted to this supplier. If the material component is available from several suppliers, the corporation has alternative sources and is not dependent upon a sole source. Sometimes, a corporation may, for a variety of reasons, own its supplier. The ethics and responsibilities relating to suppliers will be discussed in Chapter 12.

Service Professionals

Service professionals are individuals who are not employees of the corporation but provide services on a fee-for-service basis. Included in this type of stakeholder are lawyers, accountants, engineers, and management consultants. Their influence is in the form of the advice they provide the corporation. It is in their own interest to see that the advice is reliable, as they are then more likely to be rehired. Corporations rely on service professionals as it is often too expensive to employ such expertise on a permanent basis.

Dealers, Distributors, and Franchisees

In some types of business, many other corporations distribute a firm's product to customers along a distribution or supply chain. A good example is the automobile industry, where hundreds of dealers form a distribution system. Wholesalers are also this type of stakeholder. Some corporations allow others to sell their product or service through a franchising system. The arrangement under which distributors or franchisees operate varies, but can be complex, especially in the case of franchising. The extent and complexity of these arrangements determine the influence a corporation has over the distributors or franchisees. But this influence is not one-sided, as the corporation depends on these types of businesses to get its products to the customers. If the corporation in question is a dealer, distributor, or franchise, the operations of the business will be impacted substantially by the agreement under which it operates. Everyday Ethics 3.1 is an example of a franchiser distributing environmentally responsible products.

Everyday Ethics

3.1

Lord & Partners: "Protecting the Environment for Tomorrow"

Lord & Partners is a Canadian manufacturer and supplier of environmentally responsible solvents, cleaners, degreasers, and specialty products used in a variety of settings including automotive, aviation, government, industry, institutions, marine, mining, pulp and paper, oil exploration, and transportation. The company's Environmental Management System is registered as meeting the requirements of ISO 14001:2004. All Ecologo products are certified by Environment Canada's Environmental Choice Program and are naturally derived, rapidly biodegradable, non-toxic, non–Workplace Hazardous Materials Information System (WHMIS), and non–Système d'information sur les matières dangereuses utilisées au travail (SIMDUT).

Lord & Partners has developed a franchise system to support local and national accounts and is looking for individuals who are interested in establishing environmental businesses in various Canadian locations. Their franchise agreement operates in accordance with the *Arthur Wishart Act* (Franchise Disclosure Regulation, Ontario Government's Bill 33) and the Canadian Franchise Association's Code of Ethics; Lord & Partners has served as a member since December 2005.

Source: LORD & PARTNERS™ and "Protecting the environment for tomorrow"™ are trade marks of Lord & Partners Holdings Ltd. and are used under license.

Business Organizations

Corporations join together to form hundreds of organizations to represent their interests. An example of such an organization representing large business corporations is the Canadian Council of Chief Executives, a group comprising the executives of Canada's largest 150 corporations. Chambers of Commerce or Boards of Trade exist in thousands of communities, and a national coordinating organization operates as the Canadian Chamber of Commerce.

There are organizations representing small businesses, including the Canadian Federation of Independent Business and the Association of Chinese Canadian Entrepreneurs. Trade associations represent corporations operating within particular industries, for example the Forest Products Association of Canada or the Canadian Manufacturers & Exporters. Business also forms self-regulating agencies such as the Advertising Standards Council, which monitors advertising practices. In some areas, or industries, corporations are represented by employer associations usually dealing with industrial relations matters.

The impact of these types of organizations varies, but by uniting to speak as one they are bound to have more influence than by acting individually. Often it is difficult to obtain consensus within these groups, as not all businesspersons think the same way. The effectiveness of voluntary, self-regulating agencies has been questioned.

Competitors

Competitors are those firms that sell the same products. However, competitors should be viewed more broadly. Corporations producing substitute products should be identified and ~~also~~ monitored. Not only should existing competitors be considered, but potential future competitors should be identified. With rapid technological advances, new products and services are constantly being researched and developed. Competitors should not be restricted to those from the domestic environment: those from foreign countries should also be considered. The ethics and responsibilities relating to competitors will be discussed in Chapter 12.

Joint-Venture Participants

Joint-venture participants are partners cooperating in a particular enterprise or project. Usually, written agreements outline the relationships between the corporation and its partners. Several other terms are also used to describe this cooperation, including alliances, consortia, networks, and partnerships. The word "strategic" is often used in conjunction with these terms, for example strategic alliances, cooperative strategies, and strategic partnerships.

Non-Governmental Organizations (NGOs)

Non-governmental organization (NGO) Any group outside of the public and private sectors that holds shared values or attitudes about an issue confronting society.

A **non-governmental organization (NGO)** is any group outside of the public and private sectors that holds shared values or attitudes about an issue confronting society. Such organizations, previously known as interest groups, operate on a non-profit basis with volunteer members or networks, with many having paid employees. They are numerous, but their impact on the corporation varies. Examples of groups currently having considerable impact on the corporation are environmental, women's, and neighbourhood (community) groups. Chapter 13 will examine this stakeholder in detail.

Society at Large

This stakeholder represents the general public; that is, the views of society. The views of this stakeholder can be difficult to determine, making it difficult to ascertain this stakeholder's influence. In opinion surveys, members of society will express concern for energy conservation but continue to purchase high-gasoline-consumption vehicles or choose to live long distances from where they work. Communities in which businesses are located fall into this category, but their views are often made explicit to the corporation.

Educational Institutions

Schools, colleges, and universities educate not only employees but also the general public. Business relies on these institutions to provide it with educated and skilled employees.

These institutions also educate the public about economic systems and the role of business in society. Universities, in particular, are relied upon to perform basic research that is often applied to industrial situations. Educational institutions, although mainly government funded, are now seeking financial and other support from business, giving rise to the issue of commercialization involving corporate advertising on campus, research funding, and naming buildings after major donors. The student is also a stakeholder of the corporation in several ways including as a consumer of goods, as employees with part-time jobs while in school, and as potential employees in the future. The topic of educational institutions as stakeholders is discussed in Chapter 13.

Religious Groups

Churches often speak out on issues related to business. Religious leaders occasionally speak of concerns with capitalism and the dangers of the free market and profits.[4] Business-persons are individually influenced by the values and beliefs upheld by religious groups. The influence of this stakeholder will be described in Chapter 13. There is even a patron saint of business, described in Responsibility for Ethics 3.2, who was an early practitioner of corporate social responsibility.

RESPONSIBILITY
for Ethics **3.2**

The Patron Saint of Business

The patron saint most closely related to business is Homobonus, who was a successful merchant and tailor, and acknowledged for his good works in the community. Saint Homobonus (meaning "good man") is listed as the patron to merchants, cloth workers, tailors, and shoemakers. In addition, he is also recognized as the patron saint of businesspeople, the only saint recognized as such.

Homobonus Tucingo was born sometime during the first half of the twelfth century in Cremona, Italy, the son of a wealthy tailor and merchant. He never attended school but his father taught him the trade and how to conduct business diligently and honestly. He successfully operated the business after his father's death, and viewed it as an employment given him by God and as a means of serving both his family and the wider society of which he was a member.

He is described as an industrious and thrifty businessman, yet exhibiting boundless charity. His business prospered in spite of his generous charity to the poor. There is a claim that the more he gave away, the more prosperous he became. He died on November 13, 1197, and was canonized in 1199. It was unusual to canonize a layman, especially one in business, and to do it within two years after his death. An invocation or prayer to Saint Homobonus is:

> St. Homobonus, you merited the favour of both God and man by being a doer of the Word, and not just a hearer. You have shown us that it is possible to live a Christian life in the world, for you, yourself were a prosperous businessman—yet you loved God with all your heart, and you loved your neighbour as yourself. We bring to you our petition [specifically mention here] and ask you to intercede before the Father on our behalf.

Source: Robert W. Sexty, "Recognizing saintly business: Lessons from Saint Homobonus," *New Academy Review,* Autumn 2003, Vol. 2, No. 3, 55–56.

Charities

Charitable organizations receive some of their funding from corporations, and in return the business donors expect careful stewardship of the funding. In addition, some corporations have a direct involvement in charitable activities. Charities are a part of the non-profit sector and some operate commercial enterprises.

Service, Fraternal, Cultural, and Ethnic Associations

Employees of business corporations join numerous service/fraternal/cultural/ethnic associations, such as Rotary and Lions Clubs, Parents for French, and the Association of Ukrainian Businessmen. These memberships often involve volunteerism through the donation of employee time and efforts, and association with such organizations is often viewed as a source of business contacts. Responsibility for Ethics 3.3 is an example of a service organization attempting to influence the behaviour of its members.

RESPONSIBILITY
for Ethics **3.3**

Rotary's Guiding Principles

Business networks and social organizations are involved in activities for the betterment of the communities in which they exist. Pledges, codes, and principles of these organizations impact the behaviour of members, most of whom are businesspersons. An example is Rotary International's Guiding Principles, part of which is highlighted below:

The Four-Way Test
The test, which has been translated into more than 100 languages, asks the following questions:
Of the things we think, say or do
1. Is it the TRUTH?
2. Is it FAIR to all concerned?
3. Will it build GOODWILL and BETTER FRIENDSHIPS?
4. Will it be BENEFICIAL to all concerned?

Source: Rotary International, "Guiding principles," http://www.rotary.org/en/AboutUs/RotaryInternational/GuidingPrinciples/Pages/ridefault.aspx.

The Media

The media cover events associated with business. Managers are interviewed and quoted on a corporation's plans or business issues. Media publicity about the practices of a particular corporation or the quality of its products or services can have a substantial positive or negative impact on a corporation's sales. On some occasions, the corporation attempts to influence media coverage through media releases and public relations initiatives. Chapter 13 will discuss this stakeholder further.

Government

It is important to recognize that government is not a monolith. Instead, government has several dimensions. In Canada, there are three levels of government: local, provincial/territorial, and federal. Governments are formed by politicians and staffed by civil servants. Business must consider the impact of both of these groups. Governments are organized by departments, and the influence of these departments on business varies by industry and by specific corporation. Governments have agencies that impact business operations, including regulatory bodies such as the Canadian Transport Commission, the Canadian Radio-television and Telecommunications Commission, and provincial public utility boards. Governments own many business enterprises, wholly or in part, and many government-owned financial institutions lend money to business corporations. Even foreign governments may have an impact by influencing sales in other countries.

Two other institutions are associated with governments: political parties and the legal system. Political parties play a role in business, and business supports these parties financially. The legal system is established and maintained by governments, and court decisions impact business corporations. Government is an influential stakeholder in the business system; its role is mentioned frequently in this book and discussed in Chapter 10.

Some stakeholder theorists argue that the environment should be a stakeholder. Their main point is that this would give the natural environment prominence—or make it a priority—with management and stakeholders. Others disagree, saying that stakeholders must have a voice; that is, the capability to speak for themselves. The natural environment is unable to do this, but its well-being is certainly the concern of others. Furthermore, the environment does not meet the definition of a stakeholder upon which the theory is based. In this book, the natural environment is considered and taken into account, but not as a stakeholder.

connect | Want to learn more about **assessing information about stakeholders**? Go to CONNECT.

LO 3.3 | The Dynamics of Stakeholder Influence

Traditionally, the principal stakeholders or power groups were identified as owners, government, and labour (employees). This list is too simplistic: many others have a stake, and the enlarged view illustrated in the previous section is becoming more widely accepted. In effect, these stakeholders act as a system of checks and balances and business cannot act alone without considering the possible actions, and impacts, of groups other than government and labour.

All of these groups, or stakeholders, influence business decision making in a pluralistic society. However, this list is not exhaustive or definitive. It is not possible to list all stakeholders, and they vary by industry and corporation. A corporation's stakeholders may be defined differently for several reasons.

Each of the above stakeholder categories can be broken down further in a manner appropriate to a particular corporation. There are differing perceptions of stakeholders, and their power—or stake—varies depending upon one's point of view. One corporation may consider the influence of stakeholder groups not considered "legitimate" by another corporation, as the two have vastly different values—for example terrorist groups, which some corporations must take into account (see Everyday Ethics 3.2). The perceived relevance of stakeholders also varies with level of management and functional area. Middle managers conceptualize a different set of stakeholders as being more influential than do chief executives.

When identifying stakeholders it is important to know the corporation's relevant stakeholders, in particular those that have a moral claim. Some stakeholders have a limited or non-evident moral claim on the corporation. This varies with industries and corporations and over time. These factors add to the dynamics of stakeholder influence.

Categorizing Stakeholders

No attempt has been made here to categorize the stakeholders as other writers do. Frederick, Davis, and Post[5] categorize the corporation's interactions with society as primary or secondary. Primary interactions are with employees (unions), shareholders, creditors,

Everyday Ethics

3.2

Industrial Terrorist

Occasions occur when unusual stakeholders exert influence over the corporation. An example is Encana's experience with industrial sabotage that took the form of drastic action in an attempt to influence the corporation.

In October 2008, a community newspaper in Chetwynd, B.C. received a warning note demanding that Encana cease its natural gas operations and leave the area. The corporation had extensive operations in the area including the Steeprock gas plant at Kelly Lake, built in 2006 at a cost of $60 million. The threat focused on the issue of sour gas, natural gas that contains hydrogen sulphide. Sour gas causes headaches, respiratory problems, loss of balance, and loss of consciousness. If inhaled in any amount, it can kill humans and animals within minutes. The production of sour gas had been a concern to residents in the Peace River area of British Columbia and Alberta for some time. Many residents were concerned about accidental leaks from production wells and pipeline facilities near their homes and farm operations. Landowners also expressed frustration at the treatment they received from Encana, claiming that the company did not respect their rights.

The first bombing of an Encana pipeline occurred on October 11, followed by four more over the next few months. Police forces and Encana employees attempted to locate or capture the bomber(s), and a $500,000 reward was offered. In July 2009 there were two more pipeline bombings. On July 15, 2009, another letter was sent to the *Dawson Creek Daily News* demanding Encana leave within three months or things would get worse for the company. Encana increased its reward to $1 million.

In 2012, the federal government established a counterterrorism unit in Alberta whose main function would be to protect the energy industry from attacks.

Sources: Andrew Nikiforuk, "Under attack: EnCana is again the target of a mysterious saboteur opposed to development," *Canadian Business,* August 17, 2009, 34–35; Nathan Vanderklippe, "Pipeline blasts put B.C. town on edge," *The Globe and Mail,* July 6, 2009, A3; Nathan Vanderklippe and Wendy Stueck, "Bomber's second letter taunts EnCana, RCMP," *The Globe and Mail,* July 17, 2009, A2; and John Cotter, "RCMP to shield oil patch from attack," *National Post,* June 7, 2012, FP1.

suppliers, customers, competitors, and wholesalers or retailers, while secondary interactions are with local communities, governments, social activist groups, media, business support groups, and the general public. The difficulty with such a categorization is that stakeholders' involvement and influence shift over time and vary among corporations. It is difficult to ascertain who should be on each list; for example, government is listed as secondary, whereas in Canada it is primary in regulated or protected industries.

Stakeholders are sometimes categorized as being external versus internal to the corporation. Mintzberg's external influencers are owners, associates, employee associations, the public, and directors, while internal influencers are the chief executive officers, line managers, operators, analysts of the technostructure, support staff, and ideology. This categorization serves Mintzberg well for conceptualizing power in and around organizations, but is not sufficiently detailed to identify all stakeholder groups in society. Problems also occur in identifying influencers as internal or external. Mintzberg considers owners to be external, but it might be argued that they are internal; directors might be considered to fit in between the two categories.[6]

Phillips identifies two types of stakeholders, making a useful distinction. Normative stakeholders are those to whom the organization has an obligation and stakeholders from whom the corporation has voluntarily accepted benefits. Examples are financers, employees, consumers, suppliers, and the local community. In contrast, derivative stakeholders are those from whom the corporation has not accepted benefits, but they hold power over the corporation and may exert either a beneficial or harmful influence. Two examples are NGOs and competitors.

Differing Goals and Power

Conflict may exist among stakeholders. The goals of the various groups differ and may or may not be compatible with those of the corporation. This is natural, as all are in effect sharing from one pot and benefits to one most likely represent losses to another. Corporation managers must be aware of this fact and, if necessary, negotiate an accommodation. The interaction between the corporation and stakeholders is very much a balancing act. If priority is given to profits for shareholders at the expense of benefits to employees or consumers, then these stakeholders will react. They may reduce the quantity or quality of their contribution (effort or purchases) until they receive what they perceive as a return commensurate with their contribution. Ultimately, such action can jeopardize returns on capital to shareholders.

It should be recognized that some stakeholders have more power or influence than others. There may be a shifting of power among the groups at various times, or coalitions may form to counterbalance a powerful group exerting too much influence. Business management may even attempt to co-opt an interest group's or regulatory agency's influence. When some stakeholders become too influential, other stakeholders may somehow counterbalance the power. An example is provided by a corporation's actions to exert control over its suppliers or purchasers: government may impose competition legislation or other laws to counter such restrictive trade practices. It is also argued that there is a managerial elite, comprising managers of larger businesses plus politicians and senior civil servants, that controls business within a nation, resulting in most important business decisions being made by a few. Hopefully, if such elite control is the case, other stakeholders will point this out (media) or initiate action (non-governmental organizations).

Just because a stakeholder is out of the limelight does not mean it is not exerting influence on business. Some stakeholders are just more evident than others; for example, the demands of unions, employees, and shareholders are usually known, while the demands of others are emerging. Also, the influence of stakeholders varies over time. Consumer interest groups were influential in the 1960s and 1970s but declined in the 1980s as government and public support was reduced. The reverse was the case with environmental interest groups. It is the task of managers to identify the most influential stakeholders; that is, those groups that make a difference to the well-being of the corporation.

LO 3.4   The Manager: A Special Stakeholder

The managers of Canadian business enterprises are also stakeholders, of course: they can be employees, and may be shareholders as well. The uniqueness of managers is that they are in charge of enterprises; that is, they are very influential in dealing with other stakeholders. Managers, and chief executive officers (CEOs) in particular, determine the corporation's social responsibility initiatives—as illustrated in Everyday Ethics 3.3, where the stakeholders supported are identified.

Managers are responsible for carefully identifying and analyzing the stakeholders influencing the enterprise and the stakeholders influenced by the enterprise. They are also responsible for responding to stakeholders. This managerial responsibility might be outlined as follows:

- Identify stakeholders influenced by, or having an influence on, the corporation.
- Understand how the corporation currently views the stakeholders.

Everyday Ethics

3.3

Canada's Outstanding CEO of the Year

Each year, an outstanding CEO is identified based on several criteria: corporate performance, vision and leadership, global competitiveness, innovation, and social responsibility. The social responsibility criterion is based upon how a CEO "uses his or her private sector skills and creativity to help the community overcome social or environmental problems."

The 2012 award winner was Alain Bouchard, President and CEO of Alimentation Couche-Tard Inc. The corporation operates 5,800 convenience stores under the Couche-Tard, Mac's, and Circle K brands. The company commits at least one percent of its net earnings to the support of youth, health, welfare, and humanitarian causes. A commitment to the communities in which it operates is important, and Couche-Tard supports dozens of organizations—from national ones such as the Red Cross and United Way to a local centre for homeless children.

In the community, Mr. Bouchard supports several social, humanitarian, and cultural causes, and with his wife, Sandra, maintains a foundation to help children.

Sources: Canada's Outstanding CEO of the Year™ Web site at http://www.ceoaward.ca/home, accessed October 17, 2012; and Social Engagement, Couche-Tard Inc. Web site at http://www.couche-tard.com/corporate/social-engagement.html, accessed October 17, 2012.

- Examine how each stakeholder will or might influence the corporation.
- Assess opportunities or threats, and the magnitude of their influence on the stakeholder.
- Rank stakeholders by influence.
- Prepare programs or policies detailing how to deal or cope with stakeholders.

The first step in this approach is usually the development of a diagram or map that visually presents the corporation's stakeholders. Usually the corporation is represented in the centre of the map, with stakeholders surrounding it. Elaborate maps include arrows that indicate the direction of the influence, line thickness that represents the importance or amount of influence, and box sizes that represent the importance of stakeholders. The next chapter will outline various ways managers can develop and maintain relationships with stakeholders.

LO 3.5 Arguing the Stakeholder Concept

The Argument against the Stakeholder Concept

Although the stakeholder concept has been widely accepted, some opposition does exist. The case against the concept can be summarized by four main points: problems of categorization, challenges in meeting expectations, dilution of top management focus, and the impracticality of shared governance.

Opponents argue that the list of stakeholders is extensive and diverse and the stakeholders often have contrary objectives. Furthermore, there is no agreement on the priority or importance of the stakeholders. In fact, it has been pointed out that there is not even agreement on the number of stakeholders.

Meeting the expectations of all stakeholders is an impossible challenge. There is no clear statement of stakeholder expectations except for shareholders. It is difficult to determine the "share" each stakeholder should claim (or be entitled to claim). There are complex trade-offs among the stakeholders, making it impossible to operate for the benefit of all.

To meet the objectives of the corporation, managers need a clear, unequivocal corporate purpose. The "social market" as represented by the communist and socialist economic systems has failed for the most part. The social goals of many stakeholders divert management attention from the measurable results necessary to judge corporate performance.

The corporation's governance structure does not accommodate multiple stakeholders, and efforts to do so have failed. It is challenging to have competing and conflicting interests attempting to govern the corporation. The corporation as it functions today is designed to confer advantages to one set of stakeholders, the shareholders.[8]

The Argument for the Stakeholder Concept

Advocates of the stakeholder concept argue that the opponents do not understand the basis for the concept. They argue that an appreciation for stakeholders is fundamental to understanding how to make money. Recognition of stakeholder interests does not promote equity, and certainly not equality. Responding to stakeholders is simply good business, as they are often capable of adversely impacting the performance of the corporation.

It is necessary not only to recognize the interests of all stakeholders but also to promote the loyalty of other individuals and groups. Shareholders are a principal stakeholder, but ignoring others—for example, employees, customers, and lenders—can have substantial economic consequences. Even interest groups or NGOs can prevent the corporation from accomplishing its goals. Stakeholder thinking identifies the full range of individuals and groups from whom loyalty is needed (or, in some cases, is not needed).

The purpose of the corporation in today's society is a complex combination of desires and expectations. The stakeholder concept is a systematic approach to recognizing these expectations and deciding whether to respond. Through an assessment of each stakeholder, the value of each to the corporation can be ascertained to suit the stakeholder and to suit the corporation's purpose.[9]

A topic related to the stakeholder concept is the process of issues management, which involves the identification of issues that confront business or the corporation as well as the development of appropriate responses. The following section describes issues and their management.

---

connect — Want to learn more about **identifying and engaging stakeholders**? Go to CONNECT.

> **LO 3.6**   ## Issues Management

Issue A point in question or a matter that is in dispute where different views are held of what is or what ought to be corporate performance–based management or stakeholder expectations.

Issues arise from the relationships between business corporations and their stakeholders. In the context of business and society, an **issue** is a point in question or a matter that is in dispute where different views are held of what is or what ought to be corporate performance–based management or stakeholder expectations. Everyday Ethics 3.4 identifies some issues in selected industries.

Wartick and Mahon expanded the definition of a corporate issue by identifying the following:

a. a controversial inconsistency based on one or more expectation gaps,

b. involving management perceptions of changing legitimacy and other stakeholder perceptions of changing cost/benefit positions,

c. that occur with or between views of what is and/or what ought to be corporate performance or stakeholder perceptions of corporate performance, and

d. imply an actual or anticipated resolution that creates significant, identifiable present or future impact on the organization.[10]

These definitions will assist in identifying economic, ethical, social, and environmental issues important to the study of business's relationship to society. They are the first step in establishing an issues management process.

Everyday Ethics
3.4

Main Issues in Selected Canadian Industries

	Industry				
	Automotive	**Telecommunications**	**Mining**	**Banking**	**Pharmaceutical**
Main Issues	Green manufacturing	Restrictions on competition	Community relations	Executive compensation	Product safety
	Emissions	Complicated contracts	Health and safety	International financial crisis	Pricing
	Union wage concessions	Health and safety risk of using devices	Corruption in developing countries	Government regulation	Marketing practices
	Electric cars	Construction of cell phone towers	Waste and discharges	Credit card charges	Competition from generics
	Production overcapacity	Higher fees than in other countries	Environmental legacy	Service charges	Responding to pandemics
	Shift to smaller cars less profitable				

Issues management
A systematic process by which the corporation can identify, evaluate, and respond to those economic, social, and environmental issues that may impact significantly upon it.

Issues management is a systematic process by which the corporation can identify, evaluate, and respond to those economic, social, and environmental issues that may impact significantly upon it.[11] The definition suggests that corporations can manage the issues confronting them. The term "issues management" is considered a misnomer, as no corporation can manage or influence events to attain a desired outcome on a particular issue in all situations at all times. Issues management does not mean the corporation can create social change, or can control or manipulate society. Instead, the term refers to the process by which the corporation responds to economic, social, and environmental issues.

LO 3.7   **The Purposes and Benefits of Issues Management**

One purpose of issues management is to minimize surprises relating to events or trends in society by serving as an early warning system. Also, it prompts managers to be more systematic in coping with issues and stakeholder concerns by using foresight to anticipate change, and by participating in the resolution of existing issues. Issues management attempts to fill a void by providing a framework for assessing matters confronting the corporation that otherwise may be overlooked. It also provides the mechanism for coordinating and integrating management of issues that might confront several departments or units throughout the corporation.

There are several benefits to practising issues management: corporations are more likely to maintain a competitive advantage over rivals; corporate behaviour is more likely to be consistent with societal expectations; and the corporation is less likely to make a serious social or ethical mistake. Issues management enables the corporation to detect issues earlier and develop appropriate responses much sooner, sometimes even when the issues are emerging. The corporation's vulnerability is reduced and its credibility enhanced.

Like any other management methodology or technique, issues management does not just happen and appropriate conditions must exist for success. Top management must support it and be involved. There must be broad participation at the operating and staff levels. The approach must adapt to the culture and the management dynamics of the corporation. The issues management approach should be implemented gradually, making sure that it is supported by operating units. It is important to stress output (position papers, ideas, and interpretation of data) over process (the techniques and mechanisms used for issues identification, issues evaluation, and response development). Decisions must be made, and analysis cannot go on forever.[12]

> **LO 3.8** < ## Issue Life Cycles

Issue life cycles are similar in concept to the marketing product life cycle. The purpose of this discussion is only to introduce them. Issues can be viewed in two dimensions, over time and by degree of awareness. In Figure 3.1 the degrees of awareness at various stages of the cycle are identified as (none or little, increasing, prominent, peak, and declining) Issues are often present that receive little or no attention (T1). It is also possible for an issue not to be evident at all. Managers should be aware of these possibilities, particularly when facing the early stages of a new issue or the re-emergence of an old issue.

According to Coates, Coates, Jarratt, and Heinz,[13] early identification, in period T1, of an emerging issue having any of six characteristics is important. These characteristics are as follows.

1. The terms of the debate cannot yet be clearly defined.
2. One of the actors (stakeholders) will define the emerging issue and make it a current issue.
3. It deals with matters of conflicting values and interest.
4. It is not a problem that expert knowledge will automatically be able to resolve.
5. It is stated in value-laden terms.
6. Trade-offs are possible.

This list indicates that an emerging issue may not be easy to resolve in the short term.

In period T2 the awareness of the issue increases—for example, as the issue receives some media attention. It is unlikely that all corporations have formulated a response by this time. In period T3, the issue is very prominent and cannot be ignored. Responses or solutions are widely discussed, and most corporations have taken a stance. The issue peaks at some point (T4), and then declines. The challenge for managers is to be sensitive to the degrees of issue awareness of society or a significant number of stakeholders. The decline stage should not necessarily be viewed with relief, because issue awareness may not decline, as indicated in Figure 3.1. The issue may re-emerge and awareness increase, or awareness may remain constant.

FIGURE 3.1   *Issue Life Cycle*

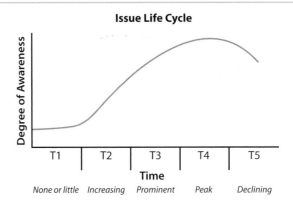

LO 3.9   The Issues Management Process

The following discussion is an outline of a typical issues management process, broken into six steps: identification, analysis, ranking, response formulation, implementation, and monitoring and evaluating. The description is a general one and is based on the steps outlined by Carroll and Bryson.[14]

There may be variations in the overall process used, and different methodologies or techniques may be used in the steps. This description is meant to serve as a general description of the issues management process.

1. ***Identification of issues***—This step involves the formulation of issues in many ways, including social forecasting, futures research, environmental scanning, and public issues scanning.

2. ***Analysis of issues***—In this step issues are described and evaluated, usually in writing, so that a consensus is achieved among managers. All stakeholders who are influenced and/or can influence the issue should be identified. Everyday Ethics 3.5 identifies a major issue confronting the telecommunications industry and the relevant stakeholders.

Everyday Ethics
3.5

Stakeholders and Cell Phone Towers

In order to provide cell phone service to larger geographic areas or to improve reception quality, a telecommunications corporation must erect towers. If the tower height is more than 15 metres, the corporation must consult with residents. However, if the tower is less than 15 metres, the corporation is allowed to erect the tower without consulting residents or even informing them. The industry is erecting towers 14.9 metres high in many cities without consultation.

The issue: How can telecommunications corporations erect needed cell phone towers in a socially responsible manner?

The stakeholders:

- *Cell phone users:* Consumers who have cell phones demand good service, and are unhappy when reception is not available or of poor quality. They put pressure on the corporations for better service.

- *Community residents:* People living near the cell phone towers are concerned about the effect they will have on property values and the health hazards associated with the radio frequency fields they give off.

- *The federal government:* Industry Canada regulates the erection of towers and has final say as to where they are placed.

- *Local governments:* Municipal governments receive complaints from residents, but have limited, if any, power to control the erection of the towers.

- *Competitors:* All telecommunications corporations are confronted by the issue.

- *Health professionals:* Health risks have been studied extensively and are believed to be low, although some European studies have found a risk. However, many persons living near the towers are not convinced that a risk does not exist.

- *Churches:* Towers are placed on church properties or structures as a source of revenue; neighbours often are annoyed.

- *Shareholders:* Most are concerned about profitability and dividends and thus want cell phone revenues to increase.

- *Media:* National and local media have given extensive coverage to the issue, making more people aware of it.

3. *Ranking or prioritizing of issues*—The purpose of this step is to establish the importance of the issues identified, which should be possible after the description of each issue has been agreed to in step 2.

4. *Formulating issue response*—The choices available to the corporation are identified and evaluated. It is important to identify all response alternatives that may be pursued to address the issue.

5. *Implementing issue response*—At this stage, specific plans are formulated to implement the response selected. A work plan is developed to ensure the implementation of the response.

6. *Monitoring and evaluating issue response*—The status of the issue and the response is reviewed on a regular basis.

This process ensures that the most salient or critical issues are addressed. The remaining issues are not dropped, but are maintained in a list of issues that is reformulated on a regular basis.

Managers must identify and recognize all the relevant stakeholders for their corporation and also those that have influence on particular issues relating to the corporation's operations. From a managerial perspective, the next consideration is how to influence the stakeholders. Issues can be dealt with in a variety of ways, for example lobbying to influence the government, improving media relations, improving ethics programs, and consulting or engaging stakeholder groups such as NGOs. Some issues appear suddenly and require immediate and comprehensive responses; crisis management is required in these situations. The following section discusses crisis issues requiring special management skills.

connect Want to learn more about **approaches used to address issues**? Go to CONNECT.

> **LO 3.10** **Crisis Management**

Sometimes an issue will become a crisis for management. Crises could arise from issues such as industrial accidents, product failure or tampering, product recalls, product safety, technology failure, executive kidnapping, malicious rumours or media leaks, natural disasters, environmental problems, labour disputes, and government regulatory actions. Issues that become crises can be addressed through approaches to crisis management. Everyday Ethics 3.6 describes an example of a crisis and the responses from various stakeholders.

Fink's "Anatomy of a Crisis"

Crisis A turning point, a crucial time, and a situation that has reached a critical point.

Crisis management An approach involving planning and removing much of the risk and uncertainty, allowing the corporation to achieve more control over events.

Many discussions of crisis management make reference to Fink's "anatomy of a crisis."[15] A **crisis** is defined as a turning point, a crucial time, and a situation that has reached a critical point. Fink states that a crisis is an unstable time but the outcome may not necessarily be bad, and that there can be positive outcomes. He defines **crisis management** as an approach involving planning and removing much of the risk and uncertainty, allowing the corporation to achieve more control over events.[16]

Fink proposed that there were four stages to any crisis: prodromal, acute, chronic, and resolution, which are shown diagrammatically in Figure 3.2. The prodromal, or pre-crisis, stage is one where the corporation receives some warning or some symptoms appear, even if subtle. This stage represents a turning point that if recognized should not be ignored, because an anticipated crisis is much easier to manage at this stage. Situations exist where management, even if aware of a crisis, may not be able to do anything in advance.

Everyday Ethics

3.6

The Outbreak of Escherichia Coli O157.H7 at XL Foods Inc.

XL Foods operates one of the three largest beef processing plants in Canada at Brooks, Alberta. On September 4, 2012, a U.S. food safety agency found evidence of the bacterium *Escherichia Coli (E. coli)* in beef crossing the border. It was not until later in the day that Canada's food safety agency, the Canadian Food Inspection Agency (CFIA), found the same *E. coli.* The CFIA continued to investigate the incident but believed that a recall was not necessary because harmful products had not reached Canadian consumers. The CFIA allowed the plant to continue operating but recalled some products on September 16. On September 27, the plant was closed.

Many issues surfaced as a result of this incident. The company, the government through the Minister of Agriculture, and the CFIA were all slow in providing information, and it was often incomplete. XL Foods took responsibility for the outbreak, but offered no apology. Only brief messages were provided on the company's telephone system or Web site, and managers made only brief statements. The government assured consumers that the Canadian food safety system was protecting Canadians. The CFIA allowed the plant to operate for two days before closing it. Eventually, about 1,800 products were recalled from 33 retail chains.

There are serious consequences for many stakeholders. It was confirmed that an estimated 18 consumers became sick from the XL Foods products. The cattle industry was concerned about its future, because consumers may purchase less beef and there may be damage to international markets. Many questioned Canada's food safety system and the way the CFIA operated. Some believed that too much reliance was placed on industry self-regulation, because it was disclosed that XL Foods had not followed its own *E. coli* protocols. Employees became very concerned as layoffs occurred and the union called for a public inquiry.

Many stakeholders questioned whether the crisis in food safety was handled properly.

Source: Adapted from Canadian Food Inspection Agency, "Timeline of events: CFIA investigation into XL Foods Inc. (*E. coli* O157:H7)," http://www.inspection.gc.ca/food/consumer-centre/food-safety-investigations/xl-foods/timeline/eng/1349149063487/1349149874246.

FIGURE 3.2   *Fink's Anatomy of a Crisis*

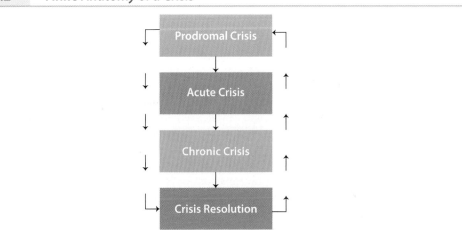

Source: Based on description in Chapter 3 of Steven Fink, *Crisis Management: Planning for the Inevitable* (New York: AMACOM, 1986), 20–28.

The acute crisis stage is the point at which the crisis has occurred and the damage has resulted. If the corporation is prepared it is easier to control the response, but this stage often is one where there are rapid developments that may be hard to control. The cleanup or post-mortem phase is referred to as the chronic crisis stage. This is a stage for recovery, investigations, audits, and self-analysis, as well as for further development of crisis management approaches. It is a stage that can linger for some time. The final stage is crisis resolution, when the corporation has recovered from the damage of a crisis.

Fink points out that all four stages may not be present, they may overlap, and their duration and intensity varies. Ideally, he says, the prodromal stage should be followed immediately by resolution, as shown by the arrows on the left side of the figure. The arrows on the right side indicate a learning process is possible so that previous stages of future crises can be dealt with more effectively.[17]

Augustine's Six Stages of Crisis Management

An alternative to Fink's anatomy is the six stages of crisis management formulated by Augustine.[18] From his experience, he distinguished six stages that would prevent crisis mismanagement—although he admits that the desired outcome cannot be guaranteed:

- *Stage 1—Avoiding the Crisis:* This stage is often skipped, even though it is the least costly and the simplest way to control crises that corporations are bound to experience.
- *Stage 2—Preparing to Manage the Crisis:* Managers tend to ignore the planning necessary to manage a future crisis because they are busy with day-to-day operations. Preparations for a crisis include establishing a crisis centre, making contingency plans, selecting members of a crisis response team, and testing communication approaches.
- *Stage 3—Recognizing the Crisis:* An event or trend may be misclassified and not recognized as a crisis. It is important to understand what others perceive as a crisis. Independent observers or investigators can help in crisis recognition.
- *Stage 4—Containing the Crisis:* This stage is to contain the damage being done. Decisiveness is critical and responses must be timely. Caution is necessary, because conflicting advice may be present—for example, from lawyers warning of liability. Augustine recommends erring on the side of overdisclosure even if there is harm to the legal position. CEOs must communicate that they care and are accountable.
- *Stage 5—Resolving the Crisis:* Speed is critical and resources must be mobilized.
- *Stage 6—Profiting from the Crisis:* Often an opportunity exists to recoup some of the loss experienced and to repair reputation.[19]

Crisis management always includes a discussion on communications. All the relevant or key stakeholders must be identified and contacted including the media, those affected, and governments. Internal stakeholders such as employees should be fully informed of the situation. Transparency is stressed, where the corporation tells everything it knows, what it does not know, and what it would like to know. There should be answers to all questions and the media should be provided with accurate and timely information.

A key ingredient is honesty. Telling the truth is viewed as the only policy as it is the ethical and practical thing to do. Incomplete information to guard against possible legal actions should be avoided. The correct facts should be stated clearly without media spin. Above all, there should be empathy for the victims. The spokesperson should be carefully selected and possess effective communication skills. Arm's-length advisers should be engaged to objectively assess the corporation's communications approach.[20]

The following chapter will discuss the approaches to influencing or engaging stakeholders, and the approaches or tactics that stakeholders use to influence the corporation.

Your advice to Tom . . .

What Tom is facing is a common dilemma that involves numerous rationalizations: taxes are too high and he pays too much, it is necessary to survive in a competitive business, and everyone is doing it. Several stakeholders influence Tom. Many of his competitors are doing it, so the government collects less tax revenue, which in turn places a larger burden on those who do pay taxes. Some customers are attracted by a lower price and will not care even though they may be liable for accidents on their property—and employees who are not covered by workers' compensation schemes have little recourse if injured. Tom would be wise to consult another person!

SUMMARY

- This chapter defines and identifies the stakeholders in the business system and describes the management of issues that arise in the system. A stakeholder is an individual, or group, that has some share, interest, or "stake" in the business system and the activities of corporations. (LO 3.1) Nineteen types of stakeholders are listed and described, but several things should be remembered about the list:

  - The list is not necessarily complete but it includes the most commonly acknowledged stakeholders and comprises generic or general labels. The stakeholder names or participants have to be customized for each corporation. (LO 3.2)

  - Although some stakeholders—for example, employees, shareholders, and customers—are important to all corporations, the dynamic nature of the relationships between business and stakeholders means that the importance of other stakeholders will vary by corporation and over time. Because of this variability, the list is not categorized in any way so the reader is less likely to predetermine the influence of particular stakeholders. (LO 3.3)

  - Each stakeholder has different goals and expectations of the corporation. Sometimes conflict exists among stakeholders and/or the interests of stakeholders. Overseeing the various stakeholder interests is an important aspect of the modern manager's job. Stakeholders, and their influence, are referred to constantly throughout the book, as is the influence managers have over stakeholders. (LO 3.4)

  - Despite the widespread use of the stakeholder concept in business organizations, it is not universally accepted as legitimate. However, today most managers believe that the stakeholder concept is a systematic approach to understanding and responding to various influences in the corporation's environment. (LO 3.5)

- Also described was the identification and management of economic, ethical, and environmental issues that may confront the corporation. Issues always involve stakeholders, and their appropriate identification and management is important. (LO 3.6)

- Issue management is defined and its components and different perspectives are described. (LO 3.7)

- Understanding issue life cycles is important to identifying issues and to implementing a response. (LO 3.8)

- Management should use some systematic response to the issues it is confronting, and a process involving identifying, analyzing, ranking, responding, implementing, monitoring, and evaluating is described. (LO 3.9)

- Some issues lead to crises and the response must be timely and comprehensive. Crises in business have been described and crisis management frameworks developed that enable the corporation to take appropriate actions in such situations. (LO 3.10)

- The use of the stakeholder concept and issue and crisis management provide good frameworks for examining the economic, ethical, and environmental responsibilities of the corporation. The next chapter will explore how relationships among stakeholders, the relevant issues, and the corporation can be monitored and managed.

KEY TERMS

Pluralistic society	Issue	Crisis
Owners	Issues management	Crisis management
Non-governmental organization (NGO)		

CRITICAL THINKING AND DISCUSSION QUESTIONS

1. List the stakeholders that have influence and/or are influenced in the opening vignette of this chapter. What are the economic, social, and ethical issues involved?

2. How can all stakeholders be satisfied? Should a corporation be accountable to stakeholders, or take into account stakeholders?

3. Why can different stakeholders have more influence at one time and less at another time?

4. Access the Web sites of three large corporations and list the members of the board of directors by occupation. What are your conclusions about the type of people who serve on boards?

5. Discuss the influence that business corporations and businesspersons have on your educational institution.

6. Monitor the media's coverage of Canadian business in newspapers or on radio and television. Identify whether the coverage is positive or negative.

7. Why do some businesspeople still oppose the stakeholder concept despite its widespread adoption?

8. Identify the three main issues confronting business in Canada today.

9. Where in their life cycle are the following business and society issues?
   - Consumption of bottled water (past increasing)
   - Climate change (peak)
   - Obesity (prominent)
   - Excessive executive compensation (prominent)
   - Global outsourcing (prominent)
   - Privatization of health care (increasing)

For additional study tools and interactive ways to learn about ethics, visit **www.mcgrawhillconnect.ca**

CASES

3.1   *"Boondocking" at Walmart*

Ted McAfee owns the Blue Spruce RV Park on the outskirts of Prince George, B.C.—and he has a problem. Business has declined substantially in recent years as recreational vehicle (RV) owners are parking (or camping) in Walmart store parking lots for free.

The RV owners are allowed by the stores to park for free, but no facilities are provided such as electricity, fresh water, or wastewater disposal. In RV slang this practice is known as "boondocking." The practice is also made possible as many of the RVs are self-contained with their own electrical systems and with water supplies for several days.

Parking in the Walmart lots has become more appealing to owners as the prices at RV parks have risen and the cost of gasoline increased. The lots provide a safe location as they are lighted all night and monitored by security cameras. Also, the stores are a convenient source for supplies and services such as pharmacies.

The Walmart stores have an RV-friendly policy although it is not an official one. A Rand McNally atlas sold at Walmart gives directions to every store, and RV owners can purchase a store locator from the RV Web site rvtravel.com.

In Prince George and many other communities, the practice of staying overnight in a store parking lot is not allowed by local city regulations. Prince George city authorities had Walmart put up signs informing RV owners of the regulations. But it is difficult to enforce the regulations, especially as Walmart does not care about the practice. In addition, there is a threat from RV owners who are organized, and in the U.S. communities that enforced the local regulations were boycotted.

Meanwhile, Ted McAfee and other park owners are losing business and may close down.

Questions

1. **List the stakeholders involved and their influence. Identify any fundamentals of business or capitalism involved.**

2. **What are the issues for Walmart and stakeholders?**

3. **What can or should RV park operators like Ted McAfee do?**

Sources: Based on Eric Moskowitz, "On the road: A paved, well-lighted campsite," *Business Week,* October 11, 2004, 18; Chris Wattie, "In Newfoundland, camping is yet again controversial," *National Post,* September 21, 2004, A1, A9; and Jonathan Woodward, "The world of the RV: A Wal-Mart atlas and freeloading in B.C.," *The Globe and Mail,* July 19, 2005, A1, A6.

3.2 *A Union Strikes and a Small Business Is Challenged*

Nick Bartiromo operated a restaurant and takeout service next to a Toronto subway station. Nick had started the business 10 years ago; the business had done quite well, and had a steady clientele for its breakfast and lunch meals. The business had five full-time and 15 part-time employees even though it was only open five days a week, 6:00 a.m. to 3:00 p.m. Nick believed in paying his employees a decent salary, which was above the average rate for the hospitality industry.

In summer 2009, the 24,000 City of Toronto inside and outside workers represented by the Canadian Union of Public Employees went on strike. Nick had some understanding of industrial relations and knew that the workers had the right to strike and to picket their workplaces. The strike created a major inconvenience for Nick; the garbage from his restaurant was no longer picked up. The garbage was mostly food leftovers, which began to rot in the heat. The City had established several sites where citizens could drop off garbage, but they were some distance away and he had to hire a truck to haul the garbage. A bigger problem arose when he got to the site—the picketers delayed each person making a delivery and it took him hours to complete the task. The picketers were illegally stopping each person for 15 minutes and the City did not stop them. As he was restricted to three bags, he had to make the trip daily. Also, the stench of rotting food was almost unbearable and the sites were bound to attract pests such as rats and mice.

As the strike went on, his resentment for the municipal workers grew. The 1,100 garbage workers were paid well, an average of $25.00 per hour. Furthermore, their benefits were generous—they received six weeks of vacation and were allowed to bank 18 sick days per year and cash in six months' worth at retirement. This created an unfunded liability of over $150 million for the City. They had the right of permanent employment and their contract imposed strict work rules that increased costs of garbage collection. Nick read in the newspaper that it cost the City of Toronto $317 per dwelling to collect garbage, about 65 percent higher than the average for Canadian cities.

Nick was not impressed with the City politicians. They agreed to generous employee contracts to obtain labour peace, appearing unwilling to stand up to the unions. Between 2003 and 2008, City employee salaries had increased 32 percent. At the same time, taxes were increasing. The union had a monopoly on garbage collection, and knew how to use it. Some of Nick's customers complained that the strikers were fortunate to have such well-paying jobs especially during a period of higher unemployment.

Nick got to thinking about what could be done to reduce this imbalance in influence that some unions had in society. Two solutions were evident: declare garbage collection an essential service, and introduce competition. If made an essential service, the workers would lose the right to strike, a fundamental feature of industrial contracts. It was unlikely that the City could introduce this without a prolonged labour conflict.

The newspapers and his customers talked about outsourcing, or contracting out, the collection of garbage, as was done in Etobicoke. That municipality had been absorbed into Toronto but its private garbage collection contract remained in force. The Canadian Taxpayers Federation advocated the privatization of waste management to introduce competition in awarding contracts for providing the service. It estimated that Winnipeg had saved $5.7 million per year when it privatized collection.

If a monopoly exists in a particular industry, it either is ruled illegal under the *Competition Act* or other legislation, or is tightly regulated. Garbage collection in most cities is a monopoly of local governments and they lacked the incentives to reduce costs and introduce innovations as aggressively as private business. In effect, taxpayers were held hostage by a system with rigid work rules that prohibited rewarding superior performance. Furthermore, there was no threat to driving the City out of business. The usual result was higher taxes, and Toronto was no exception. In fact, taxes had increased so much that the Canadian Federation of Independent Business claimed that many businesses had already left the city due to high taxation.

Nick paid a lot in taxes, and expected good service in return. For the most part, he felt that the City was providing many services for these taxes. But, he felt that garbage collection was an exception. He believed that he was being held hostage by greedy municipal workers and politicians who were unable to confront the monopoly power of unions. He believed that it was time to do something about the union's monopoly.

Questions

1. Who are the stakeholders and what is their influence?

2. What issues associated with the business fundamentals as described in Chapter 2 are illustrated in the case?

3. What can or should Nick do?

4. What should be done about the union's monopoly?

Sources: Charlie Gillis and Fate Lunau, "Toronto stinks," *Maclean's,* July 27, 2009, 22–25; Gwyn Morgan, "Enough with this union monopoly of the public sector: Time to contract out," *The Globe and Mail,* July 20, 2009, B2; Katherine Laidlaw, "Councillor backs bid to hire waste haulers," *National Post,* July 23, 2009, A1, A10; and Howard Levitt, "It is up to employers to thwart strikes," *National Post,* July 22, 2009, FP11.

This case was prepared from public sources to provide material for classroom discussion, and it is not intended to illustrate either effective or ineffective response to a business and society managerial situation. Nick Bartiromo is a fictional character.

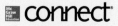 For more information on the resources available from McGraw-Hill Ryerson, go to www.mcgrawhill.ca/he/solutions.

CHAPTER 4
Stakeholder Relations and Analysis

| LEARNING OUTCOMES | *After studying this chapter, you will be able to:* |

LO 4.1 Explain stakeholder analysis in an organization.

LO 4.2 Describe stakeholder management capability.

LO 4.3 Understand stakeholder matrix mapping.

LO 4.4 Discuss the diagnostic typology of organizational stakeholders.

LO 4.5 Apply the stakeholder identification and salience typology.

LO 4.6 Explain the application of stakeholder influence strategies.

LO 4.7 Identify the use of stakeholder collaboration approaches.

LO 4.8 Define social capital and understand its relationship to stakeholder theory.

What would you do if . . . ?

Carol Duggan had recently been promoted to manager of The Coffeepot, one of several coffee shops owned by her boss, who had delegated responsibility for day-to-day management of the shop to her. It was a new shop and in addition to serving coffee and other beverages offered a light food menu including sandwiches and desserts.

Carol was interested in the shop doing well, because in addition to her salary she was to receive bonuses based on the shop's financial performance. Things were going quite well but she was always on the lookout for ways to increase business. Since she had become manager, she observed that some customers occupied tables and lounges for extended periods of time. She felt that many customers

viewed the shop as a way to get out of the house or as a place to get away from other distractions.

Internet connections were provided free through a Wi-Fi service, and many customers sat for hours surfing the net. The shop also offered students a discount on purchases to encourage their patronage. Post secondary students would purchase a coffee and then do their studying or assignments with books and computers spread out at the tables.

At the same time, she noticed that other customers could not find a table or a place to sit. Some students did give up their tables, but others did not. Several customers complained to Carol about the monopolization of tables by students. As a result, she decided to monitor the offenders and began to maintain a record of their behaviour. She found that some were staying three to four hours three or four nights a week despite the signs posted at the counter and on the walls requesting that table occupancy be limited to one hour.

The next step was to decide what to do. Carol faced a dilemma involving balancing profitability with a social service to the community. She was reluctant to address the offending individuals verbally, as this might lead to a confrontation or embarrassment. Instead, she slipped a small orange-coloured note to offending customers that stated "Your time is up. Please make this table available for other customers. Thanks." This action was taken only when the shop was busy and customers were seeking tables.

The reaction was immediate. Customers went online (some from within the shop!) on Facebook and Twitter to share their thoughts about this new practice with hundreds of contacts. Within 24 hours, various student leaders were proposing a boycott of The Coffeepot. A writing group announced that it would no longer meet there. Some students claimed that they paid for their food and drinks and were entitled to stay as long as they wanted. Others stated that they realized that the shop was a business and had to make profits. The incident became a feature story in the local media. Responses to Carol and the shop owner were split about 50/50 between negative and supportive.

What is your advice to Carol?

This chapter reviews a variety of approaches to understanding the relationships between the corporation and its stakeholders. Figure 4.1 outlines these approaches, which range from the basic listing and mapping to more complicated concepts such as stakeholder collaboration and social capital. The phrase "stakeholder management" is used for some approaches because this represents how managers perceive stakeholders; that is, as individuals or groups that could be "managed," suggesting that stakeholders could be controlled or even manipulated. Recently, stakeholder-theory academics and researchers have developed other approaches to understanding stakeholders, particularly those with a moral claim. Today, many enlightened corporations are using these approaches to enhance their understanding of stakeholder relations, referred to as **stakeholder engagement**—any efforts by a corporation to understand and involve relevant individuals, groups, or organizations by considering their moral concerns in strategic and operational initiatives.

> **Stakeholder engagement** Efforts by a corporation to understand and involve relevant individuals, groups, or organizations by considering their moral concerns in strategic and operational initiatives.

LO 4.1   Basic Stakeholder Analysis

All corporations should involve themselves in stakeholder management, even at a preliminary level. If nothing else, corporations should identify and attempt to understand the stakeholders that influence and are influenced by the corporation. At the least, the corporation should prepare a stakeholder map of its stakeholders.

The corporation can increase its understanding of these stakeholders by answering the following questions, which will capture the essential information needed for effective stakeholder management:

1. Who are our stakeholders?
2. What are their stakes?
3. What opportunities and challenges are presented to our firm?
4. What responsibilities (economic, legal, ethical, and philanthropic) does our firm have to all its stakeholders?
5. What strategies or actions should our firm take to best deal with stakeholder challenges and opportunities?[1]

FIGURE 4.1   *Approaches to Stakeholder Relations and Analysis*

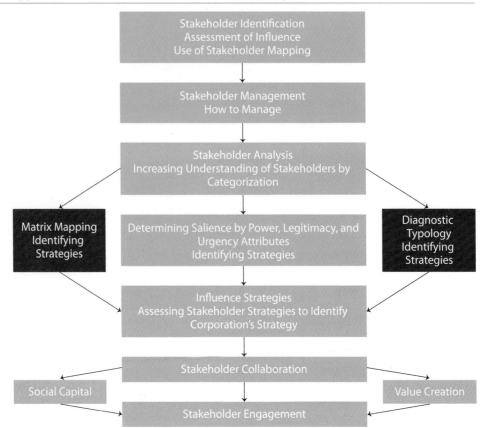

A similar approach is to complete a stakeholder analysis worksheet for each stakeholder, like the one in Table 4.1. Note that two parts exist in the lower portion of the worksheet, for stakeholders that influence the organization and for those that are influenced by the organization. Some stakeholders are one or the other, while others may be both.

Basic stakeholder analysis may include a map or diagram of the stakeholders arrayed around the corporation. Such diagrams are of value in appreciating the extent of stakeholders influencing the corporation and that are influenced. Lines connecting the stakeholders to the corporation can include arrows to indicate the direction of influence. The thickness or colour of the lines can also be indications of influence. The main value of such diagrams is to gain an appreciation for the number of stakeholders and an understanding of real and possible influences. Figure 4.2 is an example of a stakeholder map for a Tim Hortons restaurant. This is the beginning of an analysis, as the nature of the influence—the direction and extent of the influence—would have to be ascertained.

LO 4.2   Freeman's Stakeholder Management Capability

According to Freeman,[2] the process an organization uses to manage relationships with its stakeholder groups involves three levels: (1) identifying the organization's stakeholders and their perceived stakes according to the rational perspective; (2) determining the organizational processes used to manage relationships with stakeholders and fitting these processes with the

TABLE 4.1   *Stakeholder Analysis Worksheet*

Definition

Stakeholder—An individual or group who can influence, or is influenced by, the operations (or activities) of an organization.

Stakeholder Identification

Stakeholder _____

Sub-categories _____

Stakeholder Analysis

Influences the organization _____

How? _____

Organization's response _____

How satisfactory is the response? _____

Influenced by the organization _____

How? _____

Stakeholder's response _____

How successful is this influence? _____

FIGURE 4.2   *Stakeholder Map for Tim Hortons Restaurant*

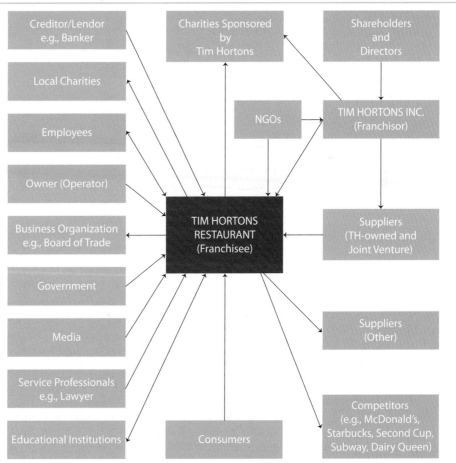

stakeholder map of the organization; and (3) understanding the set of transactions or bargains between the organization and its stakeholders and deciding whether these negotiations fit the map and the processes. Thus, Freeman defines **stakeholder management capability** as the ability of managers to identify stakeholders and their influence, to develop the organizational practices to understand stakeholders, and to undertake direct contact with stakeholders.[3]

> **Stakeholder management capability**
> The ability of managers to identify stakeholders and their influence, to develop the organizational practices to understand stakeholders, and to undertake direct contact with stakeholders.

The rational level involves preparing a stakeholder map that identifies specific stakeholders. For example, the stakeholder map should include the names of non-governmental organizations (NGOs) influencing the corporation, or the government agencies with which the corporation is involved. A problem arises in that membership among groups may overlap; for example, someone can be an employee but also a shareholder through stock purchase plans. There also may be networks or coalitions among stakeholders, and these should be indicated somehow. An attempt must be made to ascertain the "stake" of each group and the power it has, keeping in mind that different perceptions of stake and power exist.[4]

The second level, process, identifies the procedures used to assess stakeholders. Freeman mentions some possible procedures—including portfolio analysis, which he believes applies to some stakeholders but is too financially oriented, and strategic management, which applies if stakeholder questions are included in each component.[5] In some corporations, specific managers are responsible for stakeholder relations, as described in Responsibility for Ethics 4.1.

RESPONSIBILITY for Ethics 4.1

Jobs in Stakeholder Relations

The following is a sample of stakeholder relations job opportunities. The posting of these jobs indicates the importance corporations are placing on stakeholder relations. Note that these listings are not the complete job descriptions.

- Manager, Sustainability and Stakeholder Communications Western Canada, COCA-COLA, Coquitlam, BC. Position involves responsibility for stakeholder and community relations including monitoring and engaging with priority stakeholder organizations, identifying and managing community investment and partnership activities.

- Manager, Stakeholder Relations & Communications, Atomic Energy of Canada, Port Hope, ON. Among other things, the manager is responsible for analyzing and evaluating issues for senior management, advising them on actions, defining the formal and informal stakeholder liaison channels, and ensuring that those involved are briefed on key messages and issues.

- Stakeholder & Aboriginal Relations Administrator, ENMAX Corporation, Calgary, AB. The activities include assisting in editing and producing informational materials, maintaining project documentation, and assisting in coordinating project logistics for internal and external project team meetings and other events.

- Stakeholder Relations Administrator, Canadian Natural Resources Limited, Calgary, AB. The administrator is responsible for supporting the Stakeholder Relations team. Among the tasks are supporting the community investment and consultation processes, organizing meetings and events, monitoring agreements, and tracking agreement expenses.

- Stakeholder Engagement Planner, AltaLink Management Ltd., Edmonton, AB. The planner will manage stakeholder consultation strategies for major electric transmission projects and consult directly with stakeholders.

Source: Compiled from Careerjet, Workopolis, and Simply Hired Web sites, accessed October 17, 2012.

The "transactional" level deals with the actual interaction with stakeholders. It is important to employ managers with the appropriate value set to deal with particular stakeholders if the relationship is to be an effective one. An obvious example is dealing with the media. Some executives are not comfortable dealing with the media, and such contact should be assigned to someone with skills in that area.[6]

 **connect** Want to learn more about the **principles of stakeholder management**? Go to CONNECT.

Freeman's work is the basis upon which other approaches to understanding stakeholders were formulated.

> **LO 4.3**   ## Stakeholder Matrix Mapping

The identification of stakeholders is an important first step, but the interpretation of the relationships between the organization and the stakeholders is important. Stakeholder theory has progressed substantially in recent years, and several methodologies or models now exist that can be used to understand or interpret the influence stakeholders have on the organization and/or the influence the organization has on the stakeholders.

Matrix mapping
A technique of categorizing an organization's stakeholders by their influence according to two variables; usually involves plotting them on a two-by-two matrix.

Matrix mapping is a technique of categorizing an organization's stakeholders by their influence according to two variables, and usually involves plotting them on a two-by-two matrix. Managers need such a methodology for assessing the importance or power of stakeholders to achieve their demands and whether they have the means or resources to influence. Through a mapping process, management can ascertain the likely impact of stakeholder demands on the corporation's strategies and identify appropriate courses of action to counter or influence these demands.

The matrix in Figure 4.3 illustrates one methodology in which stakeholders are categorized according to their position on a particular issue or proposal and their importance. On the

FIGURE 4.3   *The Position/Importance Matrix*

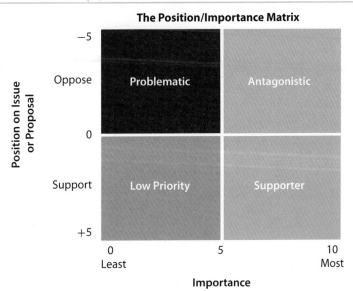

Sources: Based on Paul C. Nutt and Robert W. Backoff, *Strategic Management of Public and Third Sector Organizations: A Handbook for Leaders* (San Francisco: Jossey-Bass Publishers, 1992), 191; and John M. Bryson, *Strategic Planning for Public and Nonprofit Organizations: A Guide to Strengthening and Sustaining Organizational Achievement,* revised edition (San Francisco: Jossey-Bass Publishers, 1995), 284.

vertical axis, the stakeholders are identified and assessed on whether they oppose the corporation on the issue or support it. A numerical value of 0 to −5 is assigned to those stakeholders opposing, and a value of 0 to +5 is assigned to those supporting. The importance of stakeholders is measured on a horizontal axis and varies from least, at a value of 0, to most, at a value of 10. After the two values are agreed upon, the location of the stakeholder is plotted on the matrix.

Four categories of stakeholders result from this analysis:

- *Problematic stakeholders*—those who would oppose the organization's course of action and are relatively unimportant to the organization.
- *Antagonistic stakeholders*—those who would oppose or be hostile to the organization's course of action and are very important to the organization.

RESPONSIBILITY
for Ethics **4.2**

Stakeholders and Large Retail Development

An ethical issue arises when large retailers such as Walmart or Canadian Tire enter smaller communities and compete against local, small businesses. From the perspective of the large retailer, the stakeholders involved with the issue are plotted on a position/importance matrix.

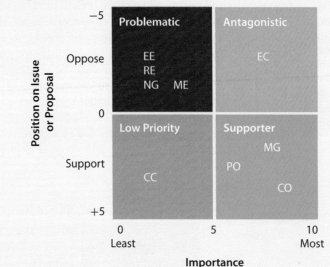

Stakeholders:
- Existing competitors (EC), including small businesses
- Municipal government (MG), mostly likely supporter; considers development desirable
- Consumers (CO), most likely supporter as prices lower and selection increases
- Chamber of Commerce (CC), supporter but some members may oppose
- Residents (RE) in area of the development
- NGOs (NG), especially environmental ones, would oppose
- Possible employees (PO) in development view as opportunity
- Employees (EE) of existing retailers
- Media (ME) would outline both positions

After all stakeholders are identified, the large retailer can develop strategies to influence some stakeholders and to counter the influence of other stakeholders.

- *Low priority stakeholders*—those who support the organization's course of action and are relatively unimportant to the organization.
- *Supporter stakeholders*—those who would support the organization's course of action and are important to the organization.[7]

An example of stakeholder categorization is given in Responsibility for Ethics 4.2 relating to the issue of a large retailer entering a small community.

After the categorization is completed, managers can develop tactics or strategies to most appropriately deal with each stakeholder. The following are examples:

- *Strategies for problematic stakeholders*—Target moderate stakeholders with educational programs, adjust corporate plans to accommodate stakeholders, and prepare defensive plans if coalitions of stakeholders form.
- *Strategies for antagonistic stakeholders*—Identify potential coalitions and take defensive action, prepare for undermining of supporters, anticipate nature of objections and develop counter-arguments, engage selected stakeholders in bargaining, and determine plan changes to gain support.
- *Strategies for low priority stakeholders*—Provide educational programs and promote involvement with supporters.
- *Strategies for supporter stakeholders*—Provide information to reinforce position, and ask supporters to influence indifferent stakeholders.[8]

This stakeholder matrix mapping uses two variables relating to position and importance. Other matrices could use variables such as power/dynamism, or power/interest. Regardless of the variables used, the importance of the technique is a systematic analysis of stakeholders and their influence.

connect   Want to learn more about **matrix mapping**? Go to CONNECT.

LO 4.4   The Diagnostic Typology of Organizational Stakeholders

One methodology for assessing and managing stakeholders is outlined by Savage, Nix, Whitehead, and Blair[9] and appears to be based on Freeman's generic stakeholder strategies.[10] The authors claim that a stakeholder's significance or influence depends on the situation and the issues involved, and as a result managers must use the appropriate methods to deal with various stakeholders. Two assessments are considered critical: the assessments of stakeholders' potential to threaten the organization, and of their potential to cooperate with it.

Diagnosing the potential for threat involves ascertaining the stakeholder's power to disrupt the organization's accomplishment of its objectives. Diagnosing the potential for cooperation allows the organization to move beyond defensive and offensive strategies against a threat to a situation in which cooperation with stakeholders allows the organization to accomplish its objectives.

The stakeholder's potential for threat or cooperation becomes the basis for categorizing, on a matrix, the types of stakeholders. Figure 4.4 indicates that stakeholders can be classified into four types—supportive, marginal, nonsupportive, and mixed blessing—and that different strategies exist for responding to each type. The following is a brief description of each stakeholder type and corresponding strategy.

- *Type 1: Supportive stakeholder and strategy*—This is the ideal stakeholder, providing support by being a low threat and high on potential for cooperation. Examples are boards of directors, managers, employees, parent companies, and possibly suppliers

| FIGURE 4.4 | *Diagnostic Typology of Organizational Stakeholders* |

Source: Grant T. Savage et al. "Strategies for assessing and managing organizational stakeholders," *Academy of Management Executive,* 5(2) (1991): 65. This work is protected by copyright and it is being used with the permission of Access Copyright. Any alteration of its content or further copying in any form whatsoever is strictly prohibited.

and service providers. The strategy for managing this type of stakeholder is to encourage the cooperative potential and not ignore them or take them for granted.

- *Type 2: The marginal stakeholder and strategy*—These stakeholders are neither highly threatening nor especially cooperative. They potentially have a stake, but it varies by issue or is limited to particular issues. Examples are consumer groups, shareholders, and professional associations for employees. The strategy for managing stakeholders of this type is to monitor them closely while recognizing that their interests are narrow and issue-specific.

- *Type 3: The nonsupportive stakeholder and strategy*—These stakeholders have a high threat potential, but low cooperation potential. Because of this, they are the most challenging to manage. Examples for, say, a manufacturing firm are competing firms, employee unions, government, and perhaps the media. The strategy to follow with this type of stakeholder is defensive, attempting to reduce the organization's dependence on the stakeholder.

- *Type 4: The mixed blessing stakeholder and strategy*—These stakeholders play a major role in the organization as their threat and cooperation potential are high. Examples are employees who are in short supply, important clients, and organizations with complementary products or services. The two arrows in Figure 4.4 represent the two possibilities for such stakeholders: to become supportive or nonsupportive. The strategy to deal with this type of stakeholder is collaboration of some sort, for example joint ventures, alliances, or mergers.

Savage et al. outline a stakeholder management process based on this typology. The first step is to identify the key organizational stakeholders by considering factors such as relative power, the specific context and history of the relationship, and specific issues that may be salient. Next, managers diagnose stakeholders according to critical dimensions of potential for threat or cooperation. Following this step, appropriate strategies are formulated to enhance or change current relationships with the key stakeholders. Finally, the strategies must be effectively implemented, including the possibility of transforming the stakeholder relationship from a less favourable to a more favourable one if appropriate. Strategies should attempt to satisfy the needs of marginal stakeholders minimally and to satisfy the needs of supportive and mixed blessing stakeholders maximally. Savage et al. recommend that managers develop objectives for the organization's relationship with current and possible stakeholders as part of an ongoing strategic management process. Responsibility for Ethics 4.3 analyzes the issue of bank automated teller machine (ATM) fees using this typology.

RESPONSIBILITY
for Ethics **4.3**

Bank ATM Fees, Stakeholders, and Strategies

From December 2006 into winter 2007, the issue of fees charged by banks for ATM services was contentious. Critics said the banks were not being responsible in that consumers were being charged high fees for withdrawing their money. The following is an analysis of this issue, the stakeholders involved, and possible strategies from the perspective of one Canadian bank.

Stakeholder Type 4—Mixed Blessing/Collaborate Strategy

- Government: non-interventionist, but could make election issue
- Minister of Finance: has power to regulate, but prefers not
- Competing banks: have same fee structure, but one may decide to go for lower or no fee
- Media: balanced reporting of issue, but do give voice to critics; also cover banks' views on issue

Stakeholder Type 1—Supportive/Involve Strategy

- Canadian Bankers Association: preparing case in support of existing fee structure
- University finance professors: view fees as "user pay"; research indicates fees reasonable
- Shareholders: keep informed and more concerned with dividends
- White-label ATM providers: may be concerned with future revenue and connections with banks

Stakeholder Type 2—Marginal/Monitor Strategy

- Consumers: 75 percent are not charged for service (i.e., use their own bank); no concern
- Consumer groups: given 75 percent of consumers do not view as issue, unlikely to do anything
- Credit unions: some do not charge customers fees; may decide to promote this feature

Stakeholder Type 3—Nonsupportive/Defend Strategy

- New Democratic Party (NDP) raised the issue
- House of Commons Finance Committee: may force government to take action
- Consumers: 25 percent who are charged feel disadvantaged and overcharged
- Some media, for example *Toronto Star:* very critical of banks
- Society at large: general mistrust and dislike of banks due to high profits and poor service.

Sources: Based on Steven Case, "Flaherty to talk fees with banks," *The Globe and Mail,* December 12, 2006, B2; Sinclair Stewart and Steven Case, "On fees: Banks to give Flaherty a 'win,'" *The Globe and Mail,* February 22, 2007, B1, B10; and Paul Vieira, "Politics runs deep in ATM attack," *National Post,* February 27, 2007, FP1.

LO 4.5   ## Stakeholder Identification and Salience

Salience The degree to which managers give priority to competing stakeholder claims.

Power A relationship among social actors in which one social actor, A, can get another social actor, B, to do something that B would not otherwise do.

Legitimacy A generalized perception or assumption that the actions of an entity are desirable, proper, or appropriate within some socially constructed system of norms, values, beliefs, and definition that is based on the individual, the organization, or society.

Urgency The degree to which the stakeholder's claim or relationship calls for immediate attention; exists when a claim or relationship is of a time-sensitive nature and when that claim or relationship is important or critical to the stakeholder.

Despite the popularity of the stakeholder concept, little consensus exists on who (or what) the stakeholders of the firm are and to whom (or what) managers pay attention. Mitchell, Agle, and Wood[11] developed a theory of stakeholder identification and salience based upon stakeholder possession of one or more of three attributes: power, legitimacy, and urgency. **Salience** is the degree to which managers give priority to competing stakeholder claims.

The authors provide an extensive review of stakeholder theory, develop a typology of stakeholders, formulate propositions concerning their salience to managers, and discuss research and management implications. Only the stakeholder attributes and the typology will be reviewed here.

Mitchell, Agle, and Wood define the three attributes as follows:

- **Power** is exercising a relationship among social actors in which one social actor, A, can get another social actor, B, to do something that B would not otherwise do. Power can be based upon force or threat, incentives, or symbolic influences.

- **Legitimacy** is a generalized perception or assumption that the actions of an entity are desirable, proper, or appropriate within some socially constructed system of norms, values, beliefs, and definition that is based on the individual, the organization, or society.

- **Urgency** is the degree to which the stakeholder's claim or relationship calls for immediate attention, and exists when a claim or relationship is of a time-sensitive nature and when that claim or relationship is important or critical to the stakeholder.[12]

Additional features make the stakeholder attributes dynamic: the attributes are variable—that is, they do not exist in a steady state; the attributes are socially constructed—not objective; and the consciousness and wilful exercise of the attributes may or may not be present.

It is assumed that managers who wish to achieve a particular end will pay attention to the various classes of stakeholders, and that managers' perceptions dictate stakeholder salience. In addition, the various classes of stakeholders might be identified based upon the possession of one, two, or all three of the attributes power, legitimacy, and urgency. The stakeholder classes resulting from possessing the attributes are illustrated in Figure 4.5. The authors

FIGURE 4.5   *Stakeholder Typology: One, Two, or Three Attributes Present*

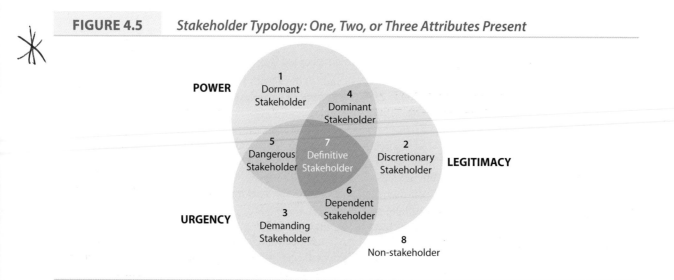

Source: Ronald K. Mitchell, Bradley R. Agle, and Donna J. Wood, "Toward a theory of stakeholder identification and salience: Defining the principle of who and what really counts," *Academy of Management Review,* Vol. 22, No. 4 (1997): 874. This work is protected by copyright and it is being used with the permission of Access Copyright. Any alteration of its content or further copying in any form whatsoever is strictly prohibited.

TABLE 4.2	*Definitions and Examples of Stakeholder Types*

Latent Stakeholders → 1 attribute

- Managers may not recognize the existence of these stakeholders or may not give them any attention. There are three types:
  - Dormant—Possess power and should receive attention, as in the case of a fired or laid-off employee speaking out against the firm or filing wrongful dismissal suit (area 1).
  - Discretionary—Possess legitimacy, as would the recipients of discretionary corporate social responsibility (area 2).
  - Demanding—Possess urgency, as with a lone picketer opposing actions of the corporation who gets passing attention as he/she is troublesome but not dangerous (area 3).

Expectant Stakeholders → 2 attributes

- Expectant stakeholders possess two attributes, are more salient, and require more attention from management. There are three types:
  - Dominant—Have legitimate claims and have power to act upon the claims (area 4). An example is shareholders and creditors who expect to receive management's attention.
  - Dangerous—Possess power and urgency attributes but lack legitimacy; will be coercive and possibly violent thus making the stakeholder dangerous (area 5). This is illustrated when employees are involved in wildcat strikes or sabotage, or by interest group terrorism or blockages.
  - Dependent—Stakeholders who lack power but have urgent legitimate claims and often depend on others for power (area 6). Examples are local residents of the environment who depend on a dominant stakeholder, often the government.

Definitive → 3 attributes

- Management must address the claims of stakeholders immediately and give priority as they possess all three attributes (area 7). An example is shareholders voting to replace management.

Non-stakeholder → 0 attributes

- Non or Potential—Individuals or entities possessing none of the attributes.

Source: Compiled based on Ronald K. Mitchell, Bradley R. Agle, and Donna J. Wood, "Toward a theory of stakeholder identification and salience: Defining the principle of who and what really counts," *Academy of Management Review,* Vol. 22, No. 4 (1997): 299–304.

group the stakeholders into the following classes: (a) those with one attribute are latent or warrant low salience (areas 1, 2, and 3); (b) those with two attributes are expectant or moderately salient (areas 4, 5, and 6); and (c) those with three attributes are definitive or highly salient (area 7). Individuals or entities possessing none of the attributes are non or potential stakeholders (area 8). Table 4.2 provides examples of each type of stakeholder.

The authors acknowledge that the typology they have developed may require refinement, further development, and testing. Its advantage not only is that stakeholders are identified, but also that their salience is assessed and the dynamic nature of stakeholder relationships emphasized. By acquiring a missing attribute or attributes, or by losing an existing attribute, the salience of the stakeholder changes. Managers must be aware of such changes and adjust their responses.

The typology presented incorporates the three attributes of power, legitimacy, and urgency that previously had been used in developing various stakeholder theories. It enables managers to perform a systematic categorization of stakeholder–management relationships, and allows them to deal with multiple stakeholder influences. The result is more dynamic, and comprehensive theory will assist managers to more effectively deal with the corporation's stakeholders. The salience of one stakeholder is described in Responsibility for Ethics 4.4.

RESPONSIBILITY
for Ethics (4.4)

PETA's Milk Campaign and the Three Salience Attributes

Many businesses are confronted by the activities of People for the Ethical Treatment of Animals (PETA), an animal rights NGO. One of PETA's campaigns is to discourage the consumption of milk and, if possible, ban it. PETA's criticisms of milk include the following: it is produced on factory farms by inhumanely treated animals, it is an inefficient food source placing demand on the environment, and it is linked to various health problems such as allergies, constipation, obesity, heart disease, and cancer. PETA's ultimate goal is to convert people to vegetarianism.

This campaign concerns the dairy industry. The following is an example of how PETA, as a stakeholder in the dairy industry, can be evaluated according to the three salience attributes.

Stakeholder	Attribute		
	Power	Legitimacy	Urgency
PETA's "Milk Sucks" campaign	Through the media and the Internet there is some influence on consumers. To date, it appears that PETA lacks power to change the minds of many consumers. It uses celebrities to support its position.	PETA quotes medical studies and health researchers on the dangers of consuming milk. All this evidence can be countered by other scientists and health organizations.	The campaign should be monitored but other immediate action is not necessary. The industry would continue its advertising messages on the benefits of milk.
	Conclusion: Low	**Conclusion: Low**	**Conclusion: Medium**

Although the salience is relatively low when the attributes are considered together, the campaign cannot be ignored. Thus, there is some salience based on urgency, and PETA is therefore a "demanding" stakeholder.

LO 4.6   Stakeholder Influence Strategies

Frooman[13] takes another approach to understanding the relationship between the corporation and its stakeholders. He states that in developing responses to stakeholders three general questions must be answered: who are they (that is, what are their attributes), what do they want, and how are they going to try to get it? He suggests that the first two questions have been addressed by researchers while the third has been neglected.   *gets neglected*

Frooman was interested in determining how stakeholders try to act to influence the organization's decision making and behaviour. In his research, he sought to answer two questions: What are the different types of influence strategies? and What are the determinants of the choice of influence strategy?

He chose resource dependence theory as a framework for answering these questions, as organizations are usually dependent on stakeholders for some of their resources. **Resource dependence** exists when a stakeholder is supplying a resource and can exert some form of control over it. For example, this control could be based on the amount of the resource controlled, the non-substitutability of the resource, or the essentiality of the resource.

Types of resource control and the types of influence pathways determine the influence strategies available to stakeholders. There are two general means of control over an organization: withholding strategies and usage strategies. **Withholding strategies** are those where

Resource dependence Exists when a stakeholder is supplying a resource and can exert some form of control over it.

Withholding strategies An approach where the stakeholder discontinues providing a resource to an organization with the intention of changing a certain behaviour.

Usage strategies
An approach in which the stakeholder continues to supply a resource but specifies how it will be used.

Influence pathway Occurs where withholding and usage strategies could be performed by an ally of the stakeholder with whom the organization has a resource dependence.

the stakeholder discontinues providing a resource to an organization with the intention of changing a certain behaviour. **Usage strategies** are those in which the stakeholder continues to supply a resource but specifies how it will be used—that is, it attaches conditions to the use of the resource. Both strategies could be credible threats to an organization.[14]

A second source of power or influence involves the resource dependence that arises from relationships between stakeholders. An **influence pathway** occurs where withholding and usage strategies could be performed by an ally of the stakeholder with whom the organization has a resource dependence. Direct strategies are those in which the stakeholder itself manipulates the flow of resources by withholding or through usage conditions. Indirect strategies are those where the stakeholder works through an ally by having the ally manipulate the flow of resources by withholding or through usage conditions. Indirect strategies require substantial communication and cooperation between stakeholders and are difficult to sustain.[15]

The influence strategies available to stakeholders were summarized by Frooman in a typology of influence strategies such as the one presented in Table 4.3. The table generated is based upon two questions: Is the stakeholder dependent on the corporation? and Is the corporation dependent on the stakeholder? In the four cell possibilities created, the resource dependence is identified and the applicable influence strategies specified. The influence strategies chosen will be determined by who is dependent upon whom and by how much.

TABLE 4.3   *Typology of Influence Strategies*

		Is the stakeholder dependent on the corporation?	
		No	**Yes**
Is the corporation dependent on the stakeholder?	**No**	Indirect/withholding (low interdependence)	Indirect/usage (firm power)
	Yes	Direct/withholding (stakeholder power)	Direct/usage (high interdependence)

Source: Jeff Frooman, "Stakeholder influence strategies," *Academy of Management Review,* Vol. 24, No. 2 (1999): 200. This work is protected by copyright and it is being used with the permission of Access Copyright. Any alteration of its content or further copying in any form whatsoever is strictly prohibited.

Of the four cells, indirect/usage represents no difficulties for the firm, but the other three do. Indirect/withholding exists where the stakeholder, for example an NGO, encourages a customer of the corporation to withhold its business unless the corporation supplied goods in a particular form or condition. The corporation has no influence over the NGO, but the customer has influence over the corporation. British Columbia timber producers faced this situation when environmental groups convinced European customers to boycott original-growth timber resources. The direct/withholding cell is illustrated by a consumer boycott, and if successful, the stakeholder has the power. The fourth cell, direct/usage, is more complicated. An example is KFC restaurants directing suppliers to provide chickens that were produced under specified humane conditions. These types of influence strategies have become more common and are more challenging for managers.

Managers can gain an understanding of stakeholders and their influence by utilizing this typology. If managers can forecast the influence strategies to be used, they can counter the influence strategy likely to occur. Instead of formulating their own strategies to influence stakeholders, it may be more appropriate for managers first to anticipate and understand the possible influence strategies available to stakeholders. Responsibility for Ethics 4.5 illustrates the use of influence strategies in the Canadian mining industry.

connect Want to learn more about **influence strategies**? Go to CONNECT.

RESPONSIBILITY
for Ethics **4.5**

Stakeholders and Their Influence in the Canadian Mining Industry

This is a typology of influence strategy for corporations operating in the Canadian mining industry in general. Particular corporations and issues would result in a different allocation of stakeholders.

		Is the stakeholder dependent on the corporation?	
		No	**Yes**
Is the corporation dependent on the stakeholder?	**No**	*Low Interdependence* Stakeholders: • Environmental NGOs • Aboriginal groups • Religious organizations • Educational institutions ↓ *Indirect/Withholding Influence Strategy*	*Firm Power* Stakeholders: • Suppliers • Employees • Service professionals • Charities ↓ *Indirect/Usage Influence Strategy*
	Yes	*Stakeholder Power* Stakeholders: • Government regulators • Customers • Media • Local communities • Activist shareholders ↓ *Direct/Withholding Influence Strategy*	*High Interdependence* Stakeholders: • Owners/investors • Business organizations • Local communities • Suppliers • Competitors ↓ *Indirect/Usage Influence Strategy*

Note: The allocation of stakeholders could be challenged. It could be argued that environmental NGOs and Aboriginal groups currently have power over companies. Local communities are in two categories, as operations may depend on whether it was a single industry community. The influence of suppliers and competitors would depend on the nature of the market.

LO 4.7 **Stakeholder Collaboration**

Recent research and consulting efforts focus on changing the relationship between the corporation and its stakeholders from "management" to "collaboration." Stakeholder management emphasized mechanisms of how an organization identified, monitored, and responded to its stakeholders. The mechanisms included issue analysis, consultation, strategic communication, and formal contacts. The impression was created that managers could direct and control the interactions with stakeholders, and that the main purpose was to buffer the organization from negative or challenging stakeholder activities. In the corporation, the responsibility for stakeholder management was assigned to functional departments rather than being a top-management task.

Collaboration A meta-capability to establish and maintain relationships that allows the organization to tap into a powerful source of creative energy, a large pool of innovative ideas, and a wider network.

The recent approach focuses on building stakeholder relationships that are reciprocal, evolving, and mutually defined, and that are a source of opportunity and competitive advantage. **Collaboration** is a meta-capability to establish and maintain relationships that allows the organization to tap into a powerful source of creative energy, a large pool of innovative ideas, and a wider network.[16] The goal is to increase the organization's environmental stability and to enhance control over changing circumstances. The approach would be more integrated and company-wide, with responsibility for stakeholder collaboration assigned to a senior executive.[17] Stakeholder collaboration is also referred to as stakeholder engagement in the academic literature and in corporate reports. A summary of the approach is given in Table 4.4.

TABLE 4.4   *Characteristics of Old and New Approaches to Corporate–Stakeholder Relations*

Stakeholder Management	Stakeholder Collaboration
Fragmented among various departments	Integrated management approach
Focus on managing relationships	Focus on building relationships
Emphasis on buffering the organization	Emphasis on creating opportunities and mutual benefits
Linked to short-term business goals	Linked to long-term business goals
Idiosyncratic implementation dependent on division interests and personal style of manager	Coherent approach driven by business goals, mission, values, and corporate strategies

Source: Reprinted with permission of the publisher. From *The Stakeholder Strategy*, copyright © 1998 by Ann Svendsen, Berrett-Koehler Publishers, Inc., San Francisco, CA. All rights reserved. www.bkconnection.com.

Svendsen provides a framework or guide for organizations that wish to develop collaborative stakeholder relationships. The framework, identified as FOSTERing stakeholder relationships, involves six steps:

- *Creating a foundation*—The beginning stage involves relationship building in a strategic mode by incorporating it into corporate missions, values, and ethics guidelines.
- *Organizational alignment*—The organization's internal systems and structures need to be aligned—that is, put in a state of readiness—to support the development of collaborative relationships including dialogue with stakeholders to obtain a clear understanding of their comments and perceptions.
- *Strategy development*—A strategy is necessary to forge new stakeholder relationships.
- *Trust building*—Trust is essential for stable social relationships as it promotes cooperation and understanding.
- *Evaluation*—The effectiveness of the relationship-building effort must be assessed and improvements identified.
- *Repeat the process*—The process is repeated to further improve social performance.[18]

Svendsen outlines the various tasks necessary at each stage, describes the tools and methodologies to be used, and identifies results to be expected. Stakeholder collaboration moves beyond the stakeholder management approach to a new level of stakeholder analysis and understanding. Many corporations consider stakeholder relations an important management function. Everyday Ethics 4.1 describes the approaches to stakeholder collaboration or engagement at one corporation.

4.1

Stakeholder Engagement at Bombardier Inc.

Bombardier Inc., headquartered in Montreal, manufactures aircraft and rail transportation equipment with 71,700 employees at 80 production and engineering sites in 26 countries. The company takes corporate social responsibility seriously and has extensive programs of implementation. One such program is its approach to stakeholder engagement.

Bombardier began to develop an organization-wide strategy and process for engaging with its stakeholders in 2010 and prioritizing them based upon their interests and influence or impact. The main stakeholders identified and some of the approaches to engaging them are:

- *Employees*—employee engagement surveys, union–management forums, and work council consultations.
- *Customers*—advisory committees, focus groups, and customer satisfaction surveys.
- *Shareholders, investors, and financial analysts*—annual meetings of shareholders and quarterly conference calls, one-on-one meetings.
- *Suppliers*—forums, supplier development programs, and recognition programs.
- *Communities*—community investments through donations and sponsorships, and employee volunteering.
- *Academia*—research projects, scientific committees, internships, and lectures.
- *Industry partnerships and associations*—memberships, participation in committees and working groups, technical support on regulatory and policy issues, and involvement in standard setting.
- *Non-government organizations*—meetings and conference calls, donations and sponsorships, events, and conferences.
- *Government and regulatory authorities*—meetings and briefings, regulatory filings, and technical support on regulatory and policy issues.

Source: "Stakeholder Engagement," Bombardier Inc. corporate web site at http://csr.bombardier.com/en/our-approach/stakeholder-engagement accessed on October 18, 2012. © 1997–2011, Bombardier Inc. All rights reserved.

> ### LO 4.8   Stakeholders and Social Capital

The concept of social capital is used by a growing number of sociologists, political scientists, economists, and organizational theorists to improve the understanding of social relationships among individuals, organizations, and within and between societies.[19] Stakeholder concept researchers are beginning to use social capital as another approach to understanding the relationships between the corporation and its stakeholders.

As social capital is a broad concept and can be used in understanding many different types of relationships, many definitions and perspectives of the concept exist. This discussion examines social capital as it applies to understanding corporate stakeholder relationships.

Social capital Any aspect of a corporation's organizational arrangements that creates value and facilitates the actions of stakeholders within and external to the corporation.

Social capital is any aspect of a corporation's organizational arrangements that creates value and facilitates the actions of stakeholders within and external to the corporation. Social capital is created when the relations between stakeholders and the corporation change in ways that facilitate increased understanding, cooperation, and coordination. In effect, the corporation's stakeholders are a network; that is, a pattern of ties linking the corporation with those it influences and those that can influence it.[20]

Another perspective views social capital as the trust or goodwill existing between the corporation and its stakeholders. This is a valuable resource to the corporation and its source is in the relationships established with stakeholders and the nature of these relationships. The more trust and goodwill the better off the corporation is because it works more efficiently with stakeholders. Corporations benefit from social capital because it facilitates cooperation and coordination that minimizes transaction costs, such as boycotts, legal actions, negotiations, and disruptions in production. More effective and efficient relations with stakeholders may provide a competitive edge over corporations that possess less social capital.

A research report prepared for the Canadian Institute of Chartered Accountants[21] outlined how value is created through social capital obtained from stakeholder relationships. The report identified three levels of organizational culture that explain how corporations orient themselves toward stakeholders. Level 1 is a compliance culture that preserves the value of stakeholder relationships as established by laws and norms and seeks to avoid unacceptable destruction of value. Level 2 is referred to as a relationship management culture where value is created but often is traded off, usually after the demands of the shareholders are satisfied. Maximum value is created at Level 3, a sustainable organizational culture. This culture maximizes the creation of value simultaneously in economic, ethical, and environmental terms.[22] The research focused on corporations at Levels 2 and 3.

From the research, a model of social capital and business value creation was developed; it is shown in Figure 4.6.

| FIGURE 4.6 | *Model of Social Capital and Business Value Creation* |

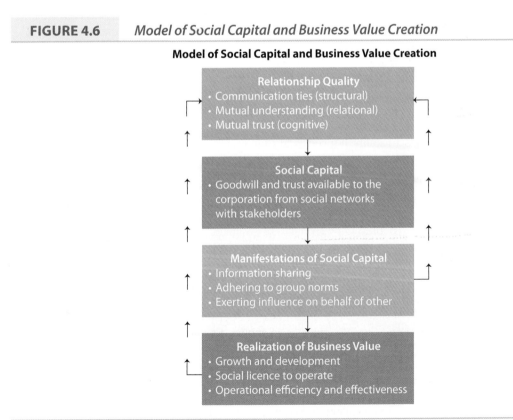

Model of Social Capital and Business Value Creation

Relationship Quality
• Communication ties (structural)
• Mutual understanding (relational)
• Mutual trust (cognitive)

Social Capital
• Goodwill and trust available to the corporation from social networks with stakeholders

Manifestations of Social Capital
• Information sharing
• Adhering to group norms
• Exerting influence on behalf of other

Realization of Business Value
• Growth and development
• Social licence to operate
• Operational efficiency and effectiveness

Source: Ann Svendsen, Robert G. Boutilier, and David Wheeler (2003). *Stakeholder Relationships, Social Capital, and Business Value Creation* (Toronto: The Canadian Institute of Chartered Accountants, 12 [with modifications]).

Svendsen, Boutilier, and Wheeler summarize the source of social capital as three dimensions or attributes: *structural,* represented by the networks in which the relationships are embedded; *relational,* referring to trust and reciprocity; and *cognitive,* involving mutual understanding. Three manifest benefits of social capital were identified:

- Willingness to share information.
- Willingness to exert one's influence or power to benefit the other where influence also means control and power.
- Solidarity/norm adherence referring to group cohesiveness.[23]

The researchers identified the potential business value created by the benefits of social capital. The following are some examples:

- Information allows employees to access new ideas from external networks.
- Information and norm adherence enables employees to share information and work collaboratively.
- Norm adherence establishes a strong emotional connection between the corporation and its customers.
- Influence can be obtained by making a valuable contribution to the community.
- Influence and norm adherence allows the corporation and union to have reciprocal debts to each other that merge their interests in each other's success.[24]

The concept of social capital is an additional approach to understanding stakeholder relationships and illustrates the sophistication possible in the analysis of stakeholder relationships. The argument that business value is created will most likely encourage other corporations to become involved with methodologies to increase their understanding of stakeholders.

Various approaches to stakeholder relations and analysis have been presented leading to the most comprehensive and inclusive approach, which is now referred to as stakeholder engagement. A corporation establishes many relationship networks with stakeholders through analysis, communications, consultation, participation, collaboration, and partnership. Stakeholder engagement is an integral aspect of corporate social responsibility or corporate sustainability. It involves creating value for all stakeholders and an honest, open, and respectful engagement of stakeholders vital to corporate strategy.

Your advice to Carol . . .

Stakeholder relations or engagement exists in all types of business and not just in large corporations, as this vignette illustrates. Large corporations often have a manager or even a department devoted to stakeholder relations. In smaller business, stakeholder relations are looked after by operational managers already responsible for other business functions. Carol must be sensitive not only to who the coffee shop's stakeholders are, but also to the influence that these stakeholders have on her and the influence she might have on them. For example, Millennials may expect different amenities from a coffee shop than senior citizens would. It is important for Carol, like all managers, to think through the consequences of a decision for various stakeholders before acting.

SUMMARY

- The appropriate identification of stakeholders is very important to business corporations as one approach to understanding the environment in which they operate. Identification should be only the first step, as managers must analyze the nature of the relationships between the corporation and its stakeholders. (LO 4.1)

- Freeman's stakeholder management capability provides a good starting point for understanding stakeholder relationships. Although he stresses the importance of proper identification of stakeholders, he also appreciates that appropriate organizational arrangements must be in place to understand the relationships and ultimately to interact with stakeholders. (LO 4.2)

- The various stakeholder matrix mapping methodologies give managers a practical approach to assessing the influence of stakeholders. Matrices can be based on a variety of dimensions and designed to suit the corporation's purpose in stakeholder understanding. The variables illustrated were position on an issue and importance of the issue to the stakeholder. (LO 4.3)

- The diagnostic typology of organizational stakeholders attempts to understand stakeholder influence by

assessing the potential threat or potential for cooperation. (LO 4.4)

- The salience stakeholder typology increases the complexity of analysis by using three attributes to assess stakeholder importance: power, legitimacy, and urgency. (LO 4.5)

- Frooman's influence strategies provide another perspective on understanding stakeholders. He argues that managers should appreciate that stakeholders can influence one another and the corporation in direct and indirect ways and by withholding or specifying usage conditions. Understanding influence strategies further enhances managers' understanding of stakeholder actions. (LO 4.6)

- The most sophisticated approach to understanding stakeholders is through collaboration and the application of the concept of social capital. Collaboration changes the approach from managing stakeholders to dialoguing with them. (LO 4.7)

- The social capital concept identifies that business value can be created from meaningful and sincere stakeholder relations. Few managers or corporations have reached this level of sophistication in their understanding of stakeholder relationships. (LO 4.8)

KEY TERMS

Stakeholder engagement	Power	Usage strategies
Stakeholder management capability	Legitimacy	Influence pathway
Matrix mapping	Urgency	Collaboration
Salience	Resource dependence	Social capital
	Withholding strategies	

CRITICAL THINKING AND DISCUSSION QUESTIONS

1. Complete the stakeholder analysis worksheet for three stakeholders of a local business, or for your business program at a university or college.

2. How do corporations develop "stakeholder management capability"?

3. Write a job description for a "manager of stakeholder relations."

4. Why should corporations develop "stakeholder management capability"?

5. How does stakeholder matrix mapping help managers?

6. Can stakeholders be managed? If yes, why should they? If no, what can management do to influence stakeholders?

7. Some stakeholders are more important, or salient, than others. How do the concepts of power, legitimacy, and urgency assist managers in assessing stakeholder salience?

8. Explain how stakeholder influence strategies impact the corporation.

9. How is value added to the corporation's business by understanding stakeholder social capital?

10. Freeman identified three levels of "stakeholder management capability": identification, organization processes for understanding stakeholders, and establishing relations. Which of these levels are illustrated by the following:

- Stakeholder analysis worksheet
- A stakeholder manager position
- Stakeholder matrix mapping
- The stakeholder typology based on salience
- Stakeholder influence strategies
- Stakeholder collaboration
- Social capital

CASES

4.1   Stakeholders and the One-Industry Town

Butte Manufacturing Company produces fertilizers from potash, phosphates, and nitrogen at several plants in North America and Europe. The company does not produce the raw materials but instead purchases them on the open market. It then refines the raw materials and sells the fertilizer product to a variety of vendors. In terms of operations, the greatest challenge is in finding a location for a plant as the manufacturing process can harm the environment and requires access to a large supply of electricity.

One location being considered is on the south coast of Newfoundland near the small town of Harbour Breton. The plant is to be located on an isolated piece of land and a deep-water inlet. The raw materials used in the plant will be brought in by bulk carriers and processed at the site. A hydro-electricity plant would be built to provide energy and various waterways dammed to provide the large amounts of water necessary in the process. The finished product would be shipped out by ocean transport.

The main issue confronting the company is its approach to developing the site and surrounding area. The plant will employ 300 and is located 20 km from the town of Harbour Breton. This community is experiencing high levels of unemployment due to the closure of its local fish plant. There are some other small towns in the area accessible by car, including Hermitage and St. Alban's as well as the Conne River Indian Reservation.

The villages of Gaultois and Bay L'Argent are in close proximity by boat.

This is the first time the company would be operating in an area where it would most likely be the sole employer. There are insufficient eligible workers in the immediate area and workers would have to be attracted from other communities. The company has to decide whether to establish a town site near the plant, transport workers to the plant by boat and provide accommodations, or build a road to the site. These alternatives present challenges. The company is not sure it wishes to become involved in a "company town" with the infrastructure necessary. On-site accommodations are feasible, but shift work would involve constant transportation of employees back and forth to the nearest highway. It would be expensive to build and maintain a road, because of the rugged terrain.

Questions

1. Identify the stakeholders that influence and/or that are influenced by the company's decision.

2. Use the stakeholder mapping matrix to plot the stakeholders based upon their support or opposition to the plant and their importance to the decision.

3. Make recommendations to management on how they should establish relationships with various stakeholders.

4.2   Walmart's Supplier Relationship

Walmart is the world's largest retailer with a goal of keeping prices as low as possible to consumers. The corporation's management of its supply chain plays a critical role in attaining this goal. Walmart's supply chain management involves four operational areas: adhering to customer demand, managing the relationship with suppliers, ensuring there is an efficient logistics and distribution system, and implementing a comprehensive supply chain management information system.

When implementing this supply chain management, several economic and ethical issues arise between Walmart and its suppliers.

- Due to its size Walmart can exert tremendous economic power over suppliers, not only in terms of prices but also in applying pressure on suppliers to reduce packaging and create environmentally friendly packaging.

- With its large market share for some products, it is possible for Walmart to reduce the price of a product so much that other retailers have difficulty matching it and the profit margin for the supplier is reduced.

- Walmart is reducing its use of procurement companies or intermediaries and purchasing directly from manufacturers or suppliers. Small suppliers will face greater challenges in coming to a face-to-face agreement with Walmart without the assistance of the procurement companies.

- In the effort to reduce prices, some suppliers are forced to manufacture goods overseas. This in turn reduces employment in Canada.

- In an attempt to reduce distribution costs, Walmart now wants to handle the distribution of goods from some suppliers. It believes that by arranging deliveries itself, it can be more efficient and lower transportation costs. In return, Walmart expects a lower price from suppliers. As suppliers will obtain fewer transportation economics of scale in deliveries to other customers, prices may increase to them.

Walmart has three basic beliefs: "respect for the individual, service to our customers, and striving for excellence." Some of the guiding principles associated with the beliefs are: "always act with integrity; lead with integrity, and expect others to work with integrity; follow the law at all times; and be honest and fair." Its Web site provides extensive information on how to become a supplier and offers of supplier training program.

Questions

1. **Which stakeholders benefit and which are harmed by Walmart's approach to supply chain management?**

2. **What are the pros and cons of becoming a Walmart supplier? To answer this question, visit http://walmartstores.com/Suppliers.**

3. **Is Walmart "leading with integrity" in its dealing with suppliers? Is Walmart engaging its suppliers?**

Sources: "Become a supplier," Walmart corporate Web site at http://walmartstores.com/Suppliers/252.aspx; Emily Schmitt, "The profits and perils of supplying to Wal-Mart," *BloombergBusinessweek,* July 14, 2009 online edition at http://www.businessweek.com/smallbiz/content/jul2009/sb20090714_270767.htm; Jason Kirby, "How to drive down prices," *Maclean's,* June 10, 2010, 41; "Why Wal-Mart wants to take the driver's seat," *BloombergBusinessweek,* May 31–June 6, 2010, 17–18; Steve Hall, "How will suppliers handle Wal-Mart now?" Procurementblog at http://blog.procurementleaders.com/procurement-blog/2010/1/7/how-will-suppliers-handle-wal-mart-now.html; and "Personal relationships with suppliers," Statement of Ethics, Walmart corporate Web site at http://ethics.walmartstores.com/IntegrityIntheWorkplace/Personalrelbuysupply.aspx.

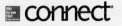

CHAPTER 5
Ethics of Business: The Theoretical Basis

LEARNING OUTCOMES — *After studying this chapter, you will be able to:*

LO 5.1 Define the ethics of business.

LO 5.2 Understand the different approaches managers and businesspersons take to assessing the ethical implications of their decisions.

LO 5.3 Identify the influences on ethical behaviour and define ethical relativism.

LO 5.4 Describe the seven common theoretical bases for ethical conduct.

LO 5.5 Outline a sequence of moral reasoning.

LO 5.6 Appreciate the challenges of ethics in business.

What would you do if . . . ?

Jonathan Devereaux graduated with his Bachelor of Commerce but could not find the type of job he wanted and that matched his qualifications. He was competing for jobs not only with other recent graduates, but also with people who had been recently laid off because of the economic downturn. He had school loans that had to be repaid—and, because he no longer lived at home, he had living expenses to cover. After two months of rejections, Jonathan was getting desperate and somehow had to earn a living. He decided to apply for jobs for which he was overqualified in order to improve his financial situation until he could get his desired job. He applied for several positions, but was turned down because he was considered too qualified. Jonathan decided to overcome this hurdle by customizing—or "stripping"—his résumé. When applying for some jobs, he omitted his degree. When applying for others, he deleted information about academic awards received in high school and university. He altered his résumé to reflect the skills he thought were relevant to each specific job. He found this ironic as he had been enhancing his résumé in an attempt to impress potential employers. His conscience bothered him and it presented him with a dilemma, but he felt that he had no other alternative. One job he applied for was to work as a cook in a fast food outlet.

Rosemary Lynch was the manager of the fast food outlet to which Jonathan had applied. She found him to be very personable and enthusiastic. She glanced over his résumé quickly and did not notice anything unusual. Few skills were necessary to be a cook in the fast food outlet and she thought he could be trained very quickly. She was about to call to offer him the job when one of the staff approached and asked to have a word with her. The staff member said that she had seen Jonathan around the university and thought that he had graduated last year. This information presented Rosemary with a dilemma and caused her to rethink the job offer.

What is your advice to Jonathan and Rosemary?

Business ethics: Isn't that an oxymoron? Many stakeholders in society believe that business simply has no ethics. This position is unfair, and most likely reflects a lack of understanding of business—and of ethics. Ethics are involved in all aspects of human interaction and ethical implications exist in religious institutions, government, policing organizations, family life, and union organizations. As illustrated above, students are also confronted by ethical issues. It is no different for business enterprises, and so the phrase "ethics of business" is used instead of "business ethics."

This chapter presents materials that will enable you to better understand the ethical implications of business, so that you will be better able to respond to this "oxymoron" argument. The *ethics of business* phrase is defined, and the influence on moral behaviour is identified. The most common ethical principles are described, and moral reasoning is explained.

LO 5.1   Introducing the Ethics of Business

Ethics has always been a concern for society and its various institutions. Business corporations and their managers are no different, despite the view held by many that businesspersons are somehow less ethical than others. To some extent this has been the result of the traditional view of the free enterprise system, alleging that profits are the only motivating force for business, business activity requires and rewards deception, business evades the law, businesspersons and managers manipulate others, and business activity leads to materialism.

At times, business ethics became a focus for discussion in society and among managers, as in the latter half of the 1980s and the first years of the twenty-first century. The ethics of business is constantly in the media, especially after the financial crisis and economic downturn since 2008.

Many definitions of business ethics exist. The definitions include terms such as moral principles, morality of human actions, standards of conduct, rights and wrongs, truth, honesty and fairness, values, customs, the Golden Rule, and philosophy. One researcher, Philip Lewis, developed a definition that synthesizes what he found to be the four most mentioned concepts in existing definitions: "**Business ethics** is the rules, standards, codes or principles which provide guidelines for morally right behaviour and truthfulness in specific situations."[1] Lewis and others argue that business ethics is difficult to define as it apparently means different things to different managers.

In this book, the preference is to use the term "ethics of business," which in Chapter 1 was defined as the rules, standards, codes, or principles that provide guidance for morally appropriate behaviour in managerial decision making relating to the operation of the corporation and business's relationship with society.

Business ethics The rules, standards, codes, or principles that provide guidelines for morally right behaviour and truthfulness in specific situations.

LO 5.2 **Assessment of Ethical Implications in Business Decisions**

Figure 5.1 illustrates how managers consider the ethical implications of business decisions or actions. Three levels of assessing ethical implications are identified: awareness, assessment based upon influences, and assessment based upon ethical principles.

FIGURE 5.1 *Levels of Ethical Assessment*

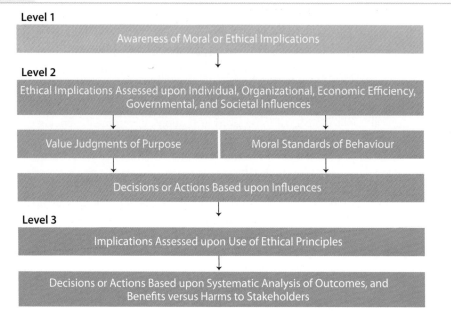

Level 1

Awareness of Moral or Ethical Implications

Level 2

Ethical Implications Assessed upon Individual, Organizational, Economic Efficiency, Governmental, and Societal Influences

Value Judgments of Purpose | Moral Standards of Behaviour

Decisions or Actions Based upon Influences

Level 3

Implications Assessed upon Use of Ethical Principles

Decisions or Actions Based upon Systematic Analysis of Outcomes, and Benefits versus Harms to Stakeholders

Level 1 assumes an awareness of moral or ethical implications of business decisions or actions. This may not be the case, as some managers behave in an amoral manner. Managers with an amoral approach to ethics disregard all moral responsibilities when making decisions. In order to assess ethical implications there must be an awareness of ethics.

The ethical implications of business decisions or actions can be assessed by individual and/or societal influences that are described as value judgments of purpose and moral standards of behaviour. **Value judgments** are subjective evaluations of what is considered important and are based on how managers intuitively feel about the goodness or rightness of various goals.[2] **Moral standards** are defined as the means by which individuals judge their actions and the actions of others based upon accepted behaviour in society.[3] Both types of influences can vary by culture, country, and time. Level 2 is the one most commonly used by managers, and most individuals.

Level 3 represents a more systematic analysis or assessment of ethical implications. The assessment is based on the use of fundamental ethical principles to evaluate the outcomes from decisions or corporate actions. A conscious effort is made to identify and analyze the distribution of benefits and harms to all stakeholders affected.

Levels 2 and 3 are described in the following sections.

Value judgments Subjective evaluations of what is considered important; based on how managers intuitively feel about the goodness or rightness of various goals.

Moral standards The means by which individuals judge their actions and the actions of others based upon accepted behaviour in society.

LO 5.3 **Influences on Ethical Behaviour**

No definitive factor can explain ethical behaviour, but many influences can provide an understanding of behaviour. These influences become the bases for an individual's value judgments and moral standards that determine behaviour. For many individuals, value judgments and moral standards are used in making a Level 2 ethical-related decision. The action resulting is certainly better than a Level 1 assessment, and may not be inappropriate or even wrong. Furthermore, the assessment is not as comprehensive as it might have been if a Level 3 assessment were used.

The influences on ethical behaviour are summarized in five categories: influences on individuals, corporate or organizational influences, economic efficiency influences, government and the legal system influences, and societal influences.

Influences on Individuals

Managers often make ethical decisions based on the morals they acquire while growing up. The family or home environment is a major influence, making the personal convictions of individual managers a source of ethical standards. For some managers, religious upbringing and contact with religious organizations as an adult provide a basis for assessing and analyzing ethical decisions. The moral standards set by other businesspersons may become the basis on which an individual manager considers ethical issues. The educational process that a manager is exposed to may become a reference point. Ethical matters in general are examined in schools, and some managers may be influenced by university-level education in ethics or philosophy.

Corporate or Organizational Influences

The culture of a corporation or organization influences how a manager behaves. In other words, the behaviour of superiors and colleagues sets the tone or standard by which ethical decisions are made. Many corporations develop mission, vision, and values statements that identify the values that are held by the organization and reflected in the corporate culture. As described in Chapter 8, many corporations and organizations have codes of conduct and ethics. Corporate social responsibility objectives emphasize values or moral considerations to be considered when operating in society.

Many business or industry organizations encourage members to act ethically. One of the most widely known is the Better Business Bureau (BBB), described in Responsibility for Ethics 5.1. Business employs professionals such as lawyers, architects, engineers, and

---

RESPONSIBILITY *for Ethics* **5.1**

The Better Business Bureau's (BBB) Ethical Marketplace

Vision: An ethical marketplace where buyers and sellers can trust each other.

Mission: BBB's mission is to be the leader in advancing marketplace trust. BBB accomplishes this mission by:

- Creating a community of trustworthy businesses
- Setting standards for marketplace trust
- Encouraging and supporting best practices
- Celebrating marketplace role models, and
- Denouncing substandard marketplace behaviour

One BBB value is integrity by being honest and ethical in all business activities. Another is trust, and its standards for trust include the following: advertise honestly, tell the truth, be transparent, honour promises, be responsive, safeguard privacy, and embody integrity.

Sources: Canadian Council of Better Business Bureaus, "Vision, mission and values," http://www.bbb.org/canada/mission-and-values; and Canadian Council of Better Business Bureaus, "BBB standards for trust," http://www.bbb.org/canada/bbb-standards-for-trust.

doctors. Ethical codes or guidelines have been developed by their respective professional associations and must be adhered to by their members. In some associations the codes are rigorously enforced, and expulsion from the profession is possible.

Economic Efficiency Influences

The capitalist economic system was discussed in Chapter 2 and the implications for the ethics of business were identified.

Some managers assess the moral implications of a decision by its economic consequences, and a moral justification is based on the workings of a market system. They believe it is necessary to maximize output as it is in society's interests to provide the essentials of food, clothing, and shelter. Adam Smith's *Wealth of Nations*[4] is held up as the foundation for this focus on economic efficiency whereby managers and corporations may appear to take selfish actions and be motivated by personal gains in business dealings. Self-interested actions in the marketplace are justified as they contribute to the efficient operation of the economy, which in turn results in prosperity and the optimum use of society's resources. Profits are maximized but are subject to market and legal constraints, and the role of the state is minimized.

The corporation's success is measured by its economic efficiency and competitive effectiveness, which leads to social betterment. Society benefits, or the public good is increased, when there is an improved use of scarce resources. This does not mean cutting corners and producing poor-quality products or providing unsafe working conditions for employees. But it does involve the substitution of capital for labour and making use of the economies of scale, scope, and experience. Abuses will be avoided if effective markets exist, and economic efficiency differs from self-interest in that business must operate within market constraints.

There are some difficulties with economic efficiency influences. Often non-competitive markets exist resulting in market domination and excessive profits. Economic efficiency leads to some stakeholders not participating fully, and inequalities will result. Those who oppose capitalism and those who advocate for alleviation of the perceived abuses of business frequently criticize this influence.

Government and the Legal System Influences

In order to maintain fair competition, fair treatment of stakeholders, and a set of laws governing business transactions, there has to be a central authority that has the power to enforce basic rules of conduct. In a democratic society, this authority is the government that enacts legislation and regulations; that is, a code of laws. Government legislation does influence business decisions. The *Competition Act* makes some questionable market practices illegal and thus discourages some managers from becoming involved in such practices. Government regulations require the disclosure of information to protect the interests of stakeholders—for example, when selling shares to the public, a corporation must clearly state certain information about its finances and operations.

The legal system makes certain behaviour illegal, and most managers are sensitive to behaving within the law. Many laws at one time were moral standards and became laws because practice showed it was necessary to control some behaviours. Businesspersons often argue that it is better to self-regulate or to self-police than to encourage legislation or regulations. This is one of the main arguments for corporations to practise social responsibility.

The minimal moral standard for some managers and corporations is to take actions that do not violate the law—that is, "It's legal so it's okay." This approach to ascertain what is right has some drawbacks. Morality is more than just what is legal versus illegal, and laws cannot cover everything. Laws or government regulations can be arbitrary and designed to further the interests of particular individuals or organizations in society. Nevertheless, for many in business the law does represent the minimal moral standards. Chapter 10 examines the ethics implications of government's regulation of the business system.

Societal Influences

Members of society form social relationships with those of similar interests, customs, beliefs, or values. These relationships can be based on the views of a particular community—for example, a town's reaction to a plant closure. Views of appropriate ethical behaviour may be influenced by a dominant culture, political views, and economic status. Some stakeholders of business represent societal views including volunteer, charitable, religious, service, fraternal, cultural, and ethnic organizations. The cultural traditions of a country or an ethnic group influence how managers view society and business practices especially for Canadian managers operating in a foreign country.

One test of ethical behaviour is whether the manager can defend the decision if it becomes known through the media. The numerous activist or advocacy groups in society known as NGOs (non-governmental organizations) can have an impact on business decisions. An example is the pressure NGOs applied to Talisman Energy for its alleged role in Sudanese genocide, eventually causing the company to divest its petroleum interests in that country.

Together these influences on ethical standards affect the decisions of managers and how they view moral dilemmas. But, by themselves, these influences do not ensure any type of standardized or uniform behaviour. These influences result in individual value judgments and moral standards that affect the assessment of ethical implications by managers.

Most of these influences are not based on any theoretical basis of ethical assessment. As a result, the degree of assessment of ethical implications is most likely not complete or thorough. Proper and acceptable decisions may be made, but to perform a more systematic assessment of business decisions or actions managers should consider a Level 3 analysis, as described in the following section.

Ethical relativism
The belief that ethical answers depend on the situation and no universal standards or rules exist to guide or evaluate morality.

The reliance on a variety of influences illustrates **ethical relativism**, the belief that ethical answers depend on the situation and no universal standards or rules exist to guide or evaluate morality. In other words, ethics is relative and people set their own standards for judging their behaviour. One example of ethical relativism occurs when consideration is given only to one's self-interest and values with the assumption that different people have different beliefs. Another example is cultural relativism, where various societies have different customs and belief systems. What is considered morally appropriate in one society may not be so in another, and outsiders should be careful about condemning behaviours within a society. There are problems with ethical relativism. It is considered a lazy way to approach ethics as it lacks a rigorous analysis of the circumstances and consequences. Also, it contradicts everyday behaviour where individuals seek differing views and opinions. On the other hand, it is dangerous when individuals become moral absolutists, believing that they alone know what is acceptable in society.

Table 5.1 distinguishes among value judgments and moral standards as discussed in this section, and ethical principles as described in the next section. The principles described offer some guidance for managers when confronted with decisions that have ethical implications. These principles by no means describe the only approaches to making such decisions.

TABLE 5.1	*Distinguishing among Values, Morals, and Ethics*	
Value Judgments	**Moral Standards**	**Ethical Principles**
Managers use value judgments when they must decide what is right or wrong	Managers turn to moral standards of behaviour in decision making	Managers can examine standards of behaviour and choice of goals by using the fundamental logic of ethical principles of analysis
Subjective evaluations of what managers think is important; based upon a manager's own values	Represent the expectations of society and the means by which managers judge their actions	Ethics is the study of what is good or right in human beings
The way managers intuitively feel about right or wrong	Vary with individuals and by culture, country, organization, and time	Ethics is a way of thinking about morality in a logical and systematic manner
Can be thought of as priorities or preferences and are variable	Are subjective gauges of conduct, and are the way managers bring intuitive feelings about right or good into decision making	Do not differ between people and remain the same
Used along with moral standards when confronted with a complex managerial dilemma	Are not objective, consistent, or timeless, as are ethical principles	Are the foundation of moral philosophy
		Are the fundamental rules by which moral standards and value judgments can be examined

Source: Summarized from Larue Tone Hosmer, "Strategic planning as if ethics mattered," *Strategic Management Journal*, Vol. 15 (1994): 22–24.

LO 5.4   The Theoretical Basis for Ethical Conduct

Businesspeople do incorporate morality into decision making, but it is commonly based on value judgments and moral standards. Formal ethics principles exist, but they are often described in very theoretical, abstract, and complex language. The same principle is sometimes broken down into several categories that can be confusing for individuals without ethics education. Many businesspeople simply do not know how to apply ethics principles to business circumstances.

Hosmer claims that it is no longer necessary to recognize all the distinctions in ethical theories for them to be useful.[5] Moral problems should be defined as resulting in harms to some and benefits to others. This introduces more realism in the business context—for example, it takes into account the effects of competition. Some management actions have to be taken despite the harms to some stakeholders in order to maintain or enlarge the benefits to other stakeholders.

To enable businesspeople to apply ethical principles, the seven most cited principles of ethical analysis are described in more detail: self-interest, personal virtues, caring, utilitarian benefits, universal rules, individual rights, and justice. These ethical principles are applied the same way in any context. Ethical principles are not subjective measures that vary with cultural, social, and economic conditions. Instead, they are objective statements that transcend countries, religions, cultures, and times.

Self-Interest Ethic (Ethical Egoism)

Self-interest ethic Individuals or corporations set their own standards for judging the ethical implications of their actions; only the individual's values and standards are the basis for actions.

The **self-interest ethic** means that individuals or corporations set their own standards for judging the ethical implications of their actions; that is, only the individual's values and standards are the basis for actions. Most individuals are influenced by their own interests and have a tendency to do what is right for them. Self-interest is always present and cannot be ignored, even though many moralists have a low opinion of it as a basis of behaviour. Self-interest is extended to organizations, and in particular to corporations, that are criticized for profit maximization.

There are problems associated with the self-interest ethic. Carried to the extreme, self-interest is not desirable as an ethic. It is considered an easy way out and implies laziness because the person is relying on his or her own beliefs without a more complicated analysis. In the short term self-interest is viewed as selfish behaviour even though the long-term results of a self-interested action may be beneficial. Individuals relying on this ethic may become absolutists who consider only what they think is right and fail to take into consideration the interests of others. Few in society practise extreme self-interest or egoism.

Yet, many observers fail to recognize that some degree of self-interest can be reconciled with morality and does include the consideration of others. Maitland claims that many people confuse self-interest with selfishness, self-absorption, disregard for the rights and interests of others, money-making, greed, materialism, hedonism, and profit maximization.[6] He argues that many people do not distinguish between morally acceptable and unacceptable expressions of self-interest.

Kaler admits that the line between self-interest and concern for others is blurred, but has attempted to make the distinction through the gradations of self-interest and morality presented in Figure 5.2. At the two extremes are complete altruism and egoism. The goals of altruists are to account for and be sensitive to the interests of others to the point where their own interests are sacrificed or neglected (ultra-moral). Egoism, or extreme self-interest, is excessive interest in oneself, ignoring completely the interests of others.[7]

| FIGURE 5.2 | *Kaler's Gradations of Self-Interest and Morality* |

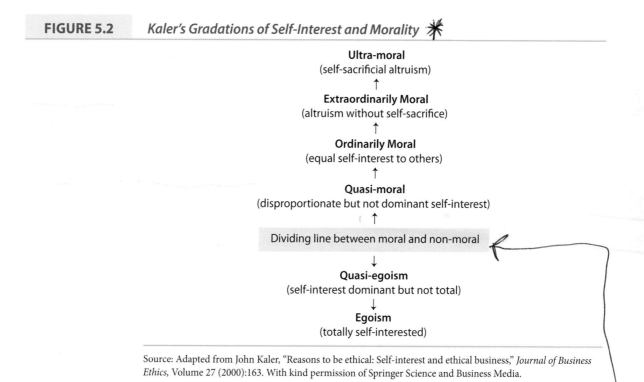

Ultra-moral
(self-sacrificial altruism)
↑
Extraordinarily Moral
(altruism without self-sacrifice)
↑
Ordinarily Moral
(equal self-interest to others)
↑
Quasi-moral
(disproportionate but not dominant self-interest)
↑
Dividing line between moral and non-moral
↓
Quasi-egoism
(self-interest dominant but not total)
↓
Egoism
(totally self-interested)

Source: Adapted from John Kaler, "Reasons to be ethical: Self-interest and ethical business," *Journal of Business Ethics,* Volume 27 (2000):163. With kind permission of Springer Science and Business Media.

In between these extremes are degrees or gradations of self-interest. In Figure 5.2, the shaded area represents the blurred distinction between the appropriate consideration of others and consideration only of oneself. Quasi-egoism and complete egoism could be considered unacceptable approaches to morality. However, the gradations above the box could be considered acceptable.

Many people find no fault with reasonable, measured, and proportionate self-interest, and it is acceptable for an individual to be appropriately self-concerned as long as the interests of others are considered. Maitland argues that it is in an individual's interests to not be too self-concerned. An appropriate gradation of self-interest draws the egoist into relations with others who are required to assist or enable the accomplishment of his or her self-interest. Thus, the enlightened egoist will be attentive to the needs of others, and self-interest provides an incentive to restrain one's self-interest. Maitland counters the various attacks on self-interest and argues that it is not the same as money-making, greed, and hedonism. Maximization of profits is acceptable in society as long as the interests of all relevant stakeholders have been considered and the corporation stays within the rules of operation provided in society through government.[8] An advocate of self-interest was Ayn Rand, who provides an explanation of the relationship between self-interest and ethics in Responsibility for Ethics 5.2.

RESPONSIBILITY
for Ethics (**5.2**)

Ayn Rand's Views on Ethics and Self-Interest

Ayn Rand (1902–82) was a philosopher whose writings have influenced many including the advocates of capitalism; she still has a substantial following. Rand developed a theory of objectivism that involved the concepts of reality of nature, reason, self-interest, and capitalism. She described her philosophy in the best-selling novels and films *The Fountainhead* (1943) and *Atlas Shrugged* (1957), in plays and short stories, and also in nonfiction writings.

She believed that rationality was an individual's basic virtue and rested on three fundamental values: reason, purpose, and self-esteem. For individuals, reason was the judge of values and the only guide to action, and the proper standard for ethics was man's survival.

Self-interest was to be discovered and achieved in individuals though a rational process instead of by a random means. The individual was an end in him- or herself but was not the means to the ends of others. Individuals were to behave in their own rational self-interest, not sacrificing themselves to others—this did not mean a right to sacrifice others in the pursuit of their self-interest. An individual's pursuit of rational self-interest and happiness was the highest moral purpose in life.

Sources: The Ayn Rand Institute, http://www.aynrand.org/site/PageServer?pagename=index; and The Ayn Rand Institute Canada, http://aynrandinstitute.ca, accessed June 28, 2012.

 Want to learn more about **Ayn Rand**? Go to CONNECT.

The self-interest ethic has been described in some detail because it is so pervasive in society (despite denials), it is often cited by critics of business as the only ethic businesspersons use, and it is widely misunderstood.

Personal Virtues Ethic

Personal virtues ethic An individual's or corporation's behaviour is based upon being a good person or corporate citizen with traits such as courage, honesty, wisdom, temperance, courage, fidelity, integrity, and generosity.

The application of self-interest, especially in the short term, may not result in the fair and courteous treatment of others. The lack of forceful interference is not enough even if the long-term result is good. The **personal virtues ethic** means that an individual's or corporation's behaviour is based upon being a good person or corporate citizen with traits such as courage, honesty, wisdom, temperance, courage, fidelity, integrity, and generosity. People should act in ways to convey a sense of honour, pride, and self-worth. The moral decisions made are not necessarily based on being kind and compassionate, and are not necessarily concerned about rights or benefits. Instead, the decision maker is concerned about the character of his or her own actions. An illustration of undesirable virtues is given in Everyday Ethics 5.1. In this example, the lack of virtue traits can harm a person's reputation and be expensive.

Everyday Ethics   Business and Lance Armstrong's Virtues

5.1   Lance Armstrong was considered an outstanding athlete and had won the Tour de France cycling race seven times before retiring in 2011. He was a high-profile athlete and had sponsorships from sports shoe and apparel company Nike, brewer Anheuser-Busch, and bicycle manufacturer Trek. In 1996 he was diagnosed with testicular cancer and was admired for his fight to overcome it. The Lance Armstrong Foundation was established in 1997 to support cancer research, and Livestrong formed in 2003 to provide services and other support to cancer patients. There were various accusations during Armstrong's career that he used illegal performance-enhancing drugs, known as doping. He denied the accusations and was very critical of his accusers. Investigations were started but did not find evidence to support the accusations.

The release of a United States Anti-Doping Agency (USADA) report in October 2012 changed things. The comprehensive report was hundreds of pages long and contained eyewitness testimony from teammates, email correspondence, financial records, and laboratory analyses. The report accused Armstrong of running "the most sophisticated, professionalized and successful doping program that sport has ever seen." The doping included administration of testosterone, cortisone, human growth hormone, and blood booster erythropoietin (EPO). Armstrong was accused of having deep character flaws that included lying, bullying, cheating, and attacking people. As a result of the report, he was stripped of his seven Tour de France titles and barred for life from participating in Olympic sports. He later resigned from the board of Livestrong.

In January 2013, Armstrong confessed that he used drugs in interviews on the Oprah Winfrey Network. A common reaction to the interviews was that Armstrong did little to redeem himself, failed to convey a genuine sense of remorse, and lacked credibility. In a later media interview, he claimed that he was the fall guy for the cycling doping culture where cheating was common. Moreover, he claimed that doping existed in other endurance sports. It was felt that he did little to repair his tarnished reputation.

Armstrong still had admirers, as evidenced by support for Livestrong. After the USADA report, 16,000 donations averaging $97 were received, twice the usual number. On the other hand, his sponsors either cancelled or did not renew their sponsorship contracts, worth millions of dollars.

Sources: USADA, "Report on proceedings under the World Anti-Doping Code and the USADA Protocol: Reasoned decision of the United States Anti-Doping Agency on disqualification and ineligibility," http://d3epuodzu3wuis.cloudfront.net/ReasonedDecision.pdf; Mark Gollom, "Did Lance Armstrong redeem or incriminate himself? Armstrong did a poor job of rehabilitating his image, experts say," *CBC News,* January 18, 2013, http://www.cbc.ca/news/canada/story/2013/01/18/f-lance-armstrong-apology-reaction.html, accessed January 20, 2013; NBC News, "Lance Armstrong steps down from Livestrong, loses Nike, Bud contracts," http://www.nbcnews.com/business/lance-armstrong-steps-down-livestrong-loses-nike-bud-contracts-1C6512991, accessed January 20, 2013; Nick Hoult, "Lance Armstrong says he is 'fall guy' for cycling's problems, *The Telegraph,* http://www.telegraph.co.uk/sport/othersports/cycling/lancearmstrong/9838064/Lance-Armstrong-says-he-is-fall-guy-for-cyclings-problems.html, accessed January 20, 2013; and "Times Topics: Lance Armstrong," *The New York Times,* February 7, 2013, http://topics.nytimes.com/top/reference/timestopics/people/a/lance_armstrong/index.html, accessed February 20, 2013.

Managers and corporations must be honest, open, and truthful and should be proud of their actions. Standards of behaviour toward others reflect fair and courteous treatment of one another—or, in the case of business, the treatment of its stakeholders. Managers should ask themselves how they would feel if the bases and details of a moral action became known. Managers should ask, "Would I feel comfortable explaining to a national television audience why a particular decision was made?" The disclosure audience can be colleagues, friends, partners, family, or the public. The application of this principle in this manner is referred to as the "TV test" or "light of day test" by some ethicists (e.g., Pagano[9]). The personal virtues of managers and businesspersons do provide a basis for deciding what is the right thing to do in business.

Ethic of Caring

Managers should consider what is truly good for society. Honesty, truthfulness, and temperance are not enough, and there has to be some degree of caring, compassion, and kindness toward others. The **ethic of caring** gives attention to specific individuals or stakeholders harmed or disadvantaged and their particular circumstances. There should be some sense of responsibility for reducing the harm or suffering of others, and solutions are designed to respond to the needs of particular individuals or stakeholders. Decision makers will be concerned with equity, or what is appropriate in the circumstances. Exceptions to universal application are fine when they will relieve suffering and harm. Stated another way, this ethic assumes there should be a sense of responsibility to reduce actual harm to or suffering of particular stakeholders.

Managers and corporations should act toward others in a way they would expect others to act toward them. The moral decision should be examined from the perspective of other parties or stakeholders involved or affected to try to determine what response the other stakeholders see as the most ethical. This principle is referred to as the Golden Rule: "Do unto others as you would have them do unto you." Managers would take actions that would be caring and work toward building a sense of community. In the corporation, this would include developing people, recognizing effort, considering family responsibilities, responding to a community problem, and accommodating disadvantaged groups.

The advantage of this ethic is that it is responsive to immediate suffering or harm. It allows for flexibility, enabling the manager to respond quickly to changing circumstances, and precedents are not a concern. There are downsides to the use of this ethic in decision making. The consideration of individual stakeholder problems might result in losing sight of the bigger picture and thus unintentionally harming some other stakeholder. Quite often the caring actions rely on subjective criteria or gut responses that limit the understanding of all the factors involved. If used to the extreme, this ethic can result in decisions that appear subjective and arbitrary.

In business organizations, the ethic of caring is exemplified by developing employees, responding to family or community problems, and participating in affirmative programs for disadvantaged groups—an example of which is given in Everyday Ethics 5.2.

Utilitarian Ethic

The **utilitarian ethic** focuses on the distribution of benefits and harms to all stakeholders with the view to maximizing benefits. One approach to this ethic is that managers and corporations should make moral decisions that do "the greatest good for the greatest number." When managers make decisions, they should consider whether the harm in an action is outweighed by the good—that is, a cost–benefit analysis is conducted. If the action maximizes benefits, then it is the optimum course to take among alternatives that provide fewer

Ethic of caring Gives attention to specific individuals or stakeholders harmed or disadvantaged and their particular circumstances.

Utilitarian ethic Focuses on the distribution of benefits and harms to all stakeholders with the view to maximizing benefits.

Everyday Ethics
5.2

Shoppers Drug Mart Cares about the Community

Shoppers Drug Mart founder Murray Koffler instilled a strong sense of community spirit in the first stores he opened 50 years ago. The company states that this commitment continues in the hundreds of communities in which there are stores today. In particular, the company focuses on the health care needs of the communities in which it operates.

The Tree of Life campaign is an illustration of the commitment to the community. Since its inception in 2002, customers and employees have donated over $17 million to support a local health charity. In 2012, 450 local women's health charities were selected to benefit from the campaign. The health charity changes each year.

Under its partnership programs the company also supports the Canadian Breast Cancer Foundation, WomensHealthMatters.ca, Motherisk, and Facing Cancer Together.

Source: Shoppers Drug Mart, "Corporate responsibility: Community investment," http://www1. shoppersdrugmart.ca/en/women/tol.aspx.

benefits. Ethicists have described many variations of the utilitarian ethic, but this description is the most appropriate for business. It is particularly appropriate when managers are attempting to understand the impact of an action on society and its various stakeholders. Some ethicists prefer the utilitarian ethic instead of relying on government legislation and policies as those associated with government, such as politicians and civil servants, also have their self-interests.

As with other ethical theories, there are difficulties. The utilitarian ethic does not account for what is just. Also, there is a question of what is maximized to result in the community's happiness. There is no accepted means to accurately measure some costs and benefits, and even if there were, there is a risk of miscalculating them. Finally, there is no method for distributing the costs or benefits. Despite these difficulties, managers often make a moral decision based on what they perceive to be the greatest good for the greatest number.

Universal Rules Ethic

Universal rules ethic Ensures that managers or corporations have the same moral obligations in morally similar situations.

The determination of the net social benefit is good in theory, but it is difficult to apply, especially in business situations. It is challenging to distribute benefits and allocate harms fairly, as it is not possible to eliminate the self-interest of the person who decides. The **universal rules ethic** ensures that managers or corporations have the same moral obligations in morally similar situations. Managers should behave in such a way that the action they take under the circumstances can be an appropriate decision or rule of behaviour for others in a similar situation. One way to express this principle is, "What individuals believe is right for themselves, they should believe is right for all others." Persons should be treated as an end in themselves, worthy of dignity and respect and never as a means to one's own ends. An advantage of the ethic is that it eliminates self-interest.

The ethic indicates there should be rules and morals in society that should be fair to everyone, that they should universally apply, and that they should apply over time. This principle is also referred to as categorical imperative ethics—that is, it is complete in itself without reference to any other ends. This means that a manager acts only if he or she were willing to have the decision become a universal law.

There are drawbacks to this approach to moral decision making. It is questionable whether it is possible to always work to universal rules, as exceptions usually exist. The ethic provides no scale between actions that are considered to be morally right or wrong.

Individual Rights Ethic

Individual rights ethic Relies on a list of agreed-upon rights for everyone that will be upheld by everyone and that becomes the basis for deciding what is right, just, or fair.

Given human nature, it is difficult—if not impossible—to eliminate self-interest. The **individual rights ethic** relies on a list of agreed-upon rights for everyone that will be upheld by everyone and that becomes the basis for deciding what is right, just, or fair. Examples of such rights are guarantees against arbitrary actions of government, the reinforcement of freedom of speech and religion, security against seizure of property, access to due process, and protection of privacy. Governments identify rights in constitutions, and the United Nations has published a *Universal Declaration of Human Rights*. The advantage of this ethic is that there is no need to determine the greatest good or to establish a universal duty.

Problems exist in determining and agreeing upon the list of rights. Often rights are in conflict with one another, or there is a conflict between the holders of those rights, creating dilemmas that are not easily resolved. In business, stakeholders have various rights, some of which are supported by laws. Employees have a right to privacy, and shareholders to disclosure of information that will affect their investments. Responsibility for Ethics 5.3 identifies where the legal rights of Canadians are explicitly stated in laws.

RESPONSIBILITY *for Ethics* **5.3**

Rights and Responsibilities of Canadians

The legal rights of Canadians are based on the unwritten constitution of Great Britain, legislation by Canadian governments, English common law, the *Canadian Charter of Rights and Freedoms,* and the Constitution of Canada. These rights include the following:

- Freedom of conscience and religion
- Freedom of expression, including freedom of speech and of the press
- Freedom of peaceful assembly
- Freedom of association
- Mobility rights; that is, the choice of where to live within Canada and whether to enter and leave the country
- Aboriginal peoples' rights
- Official language rights and minority language educational rights
- Multiculturalism as a fundamental characteristic of Canadian heritage and identity.

With rights come responsibilities, including the following:

- Obeying the law
- Respecting the rights and freedoms of others
- Taking responsibility for oneself and one's family
- Serving on a jury
- Participating in democracy, for example by voting in elections
- Helping others in the community
- Protecting and enjoying heritage and environment

Source: "Rights and Responsibilities of Citizenship," Citizenship and Immigration Canada web site at http://www.cic.gc.ca/english/resources/publications/discover/section-04.asp. accessed July 3, 2012.

Ethic of Justice

Ethic of justice Considers that moral decisions are based on the primacy of a single value: justice.

The **ethic of justice** considers that moral decisions are based on the primacy of a single value: justice. It is preferred by those who view ethical dilemmas as involving a conflict among rights that can be resolved by the impartial application of some general principle. Thus, the fairness of the process is important, but so is the equitable (but not necessarily equal) distribution of results. Each stakeholder has rights relating to the distribution of benefits or harms from an action or decision. In the equitable treatment of stakeholders, precedents should be avoided. There is a need to ensure that no stakeholders are left out, and an implicit social contract exists in society that the poor, uneducated, and unemployed should not be made worse off, in particular by any actions of business.

Ethicists have identified several forms of justice.

- *Procedural*—This involves the impartial application of rules or procedures.
- *Corrective*—Stakeholders are compensated appropriately for wrongs that are suffered.
- *Retributive*—This form is concerned that punishment should fit the offence.
- *Distributive*—There is concern for how all stakeholders are treated. This form of justice is often applicable in business situations.

The advantage to using this ethic is that it attempts to look at a dilemma logically and impartially. This ethic is appealing, as all are perceived to have an equal right to equitable treatment. A disadvantage is that it is difficult to decide, outside of the law, who has the moral authority to reward or punish whom. Ensuring that benefits are distributed fairly to everyone is challenging, and there may be arbitrariness in deciding which rules to apply. Persons relying on this ethic may unintentionally ride roughshod over some stakeholders in favour of some abstract ideal. The immediate interests of particular stakeholders may be overlooked, and the ethic is perceived as being impersonal, inflexible, cold, and uncaring. Persons who prefer this ethic may tolerate harms to some stakeholders in the name of justice or some right. Discriminatory behaviour is acceptable as long as the relative inputs of those affected are considered.

With this ethic, managers should act to ensure a more equitable distribution of benefits so that all individuals are better off. But markets are unjust in the distribution of resources, resulting in poverty, some poorly educated citizens, and unemployment. Justice is reflected in the following business practices: the development of outstanding goods and services, employee skill and competency development, the use of teams, and fair and honest treatment of all stakeholders. Responsibility for Ethics 5.4 is an example of how one industry attempts to resolve customer grievances in a just manner.

RESPONSIBILITY
for Ethics (5.4)

CAMVAP: The Canadian Motor Vehicle Arbitration Plan

The Canadian automobile industry was concerned about the increasing number of customers who were frustrated by not having an accessible way to resolve disputes involving new-car warranties. In 1994, the industry created the Canadian Motor Vehicle Arbitration Plan (CAMVAP), which provides consumers with recourse to justice without going to court.

CAMVAP is an arbitration program for resolving disputes with an automobile manufacturer. In a dispute, the consumer and the manufacturer agree to accept the decision of an impartial person, or arbitrator, who hears both sides of the case, considers the evidence, and makes a final decision binding on both parties. Sixteen manufacturers participate in the plan and CAMVAP claims several advantages including "fair, fast, free, friendly, and final."

Source: Based on the Canadian Motor Vehicle Arbitration Plan, "Your guide to CAMVAP," http://www.camvap.ca/.

The seven principles represent a wide range of ethical philosophy. The assessment of the appropriateness of behaviour would vary substantially among these principles. This is one reason why there is such a deviance of views regarding whether particular actions are correct. Managers and corporations can use these principles to become better informed of the consequences of their decisions.

Mc Graw Hill Education connect   Want to learn about **ethics "cowboy" style**? Go to CONNECT.

LO 5.5   Moral Reasoning

Moral reasoning
A systematic approach to thinking or reasoning through the implications of a moral problem or issue.

Moral reasoning is a systematic approach to thinking or reasoning through the implications of a moral problem or issue. In general terms, an approach to moral decision making includes the following steps, although variations to the sequence do exist:

- Define the moral issue or decision
- Gather all relevant information
- Identify the stakeholders involved
- Develop possible alternative solutions
- Consider the applicable value judgments, moral standards, and ethical principles
- Identify the distribution of harms and benefits to the stakeholders by each alternative with each ethical principle used
- Determine any practical constraints that might apply
- Decide on the action or decision to be taken that can be supported, explained, and defended if necessary

Hosmer argues that one or more of the ethical principles should be used to analyze a moral dilemma. For each principle the distribution of harms and benefits to the relevant stakeholders is identified. Because the principles represent a wide range of perspectives, and no one principle is necessarily consistent with the others, the conclusions reached through the use of each principle will vary. By using a range of perspectives, managers can increase their understanding of the various ethical implications of their decisions. It is unlikely that any single ethical principle can ensure a satisfactory analysis to every business decision or to a complex decision. The use of several principles provides a broad-based range of options to the manager, and identification of harms and benefits to stakeholders enables the manager to better understand the consequences of an ethical decision.

According to Hosmer, managers confuse ethics, morals, and values. Whereas ethics remain the same and do not differ among people, cultures, or countries, morals and values do. Decisions involving moral considerations are often based upon moral standards of society and value judgments held by individuals. It is important that managers use ethics principles as the basis of analysis and do not rely solely on morals and values. The moral standards and value judgments are partly determined by the influences mentioned above.[10]

Many managers rely solely on moral standards and value judgments, but this approach may not provide a sufficient analysis of the situation or result in the most satisfactory course of action. The ethical principles offer a form of analysis that systematically allocates the benefits and harms in a manner that recognizes the interests and rights of each stakeholder. This is more likely to result in an accommodation of stakeholders that will lead to more confidence and trust in the corporation.

Table 5.2 summarizes the approaches managers might take to consider the ethical implications of business decisions. Approach 1 is to ignore the ethical implications and not consider them, an approach increasingly considered unacceptable in today's society. Approach 2 represents Level 2 of ethical assessment, where value judgments and moral standards

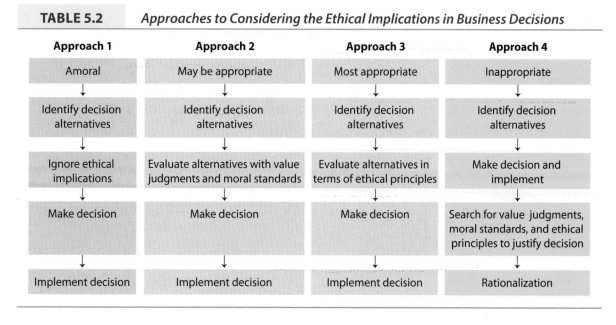

| TABLE 5.2 | *Approaches to Considering the Ethical Implications in Business Decisions* |

Approach 1	**Approach 2**	**Approach 3**	**Approach 4**
Amoral	May be appropriate	Most appropriate	Inappropriate
↓	↓	↓	↓
Identify decision alternatives	Identify decision alternatives	Identify decision alternatives	Identify decision alternatives
↓	↓	↓	↓
Ignore ethical implications	Evaluate alternatives with value judgments and moral standards	Evaluate alternatives in terms of ethical principles	Make decision and implement
↓	↓	↓	↓
Make decision	Make decision	Make decision	Search for value judgments, moral standards, and ethical principles to justify decision
↓	↓	↓	↓
Implement decision	Implement decision	Implement decision	Rationalization

are considered. Depending upon the values and morals identified, this approach might be acceptable and result in a satisfactory consideration of ethical implications. Approach 3 involves the systematic evaluation of business decisions through the use of ethical principles. This approach would most likely result in a more satisfactory decision, because the distribution of harms and benefits among stakeholders is analyzed from different ethical perspectives and is viewed as being the most appropriate method.

In approaches 2 and 3, consideration of ethical implications is performed prior to making the decision. Approach 4 is thought to be inappropriate, as the decision is made without any consideration of ethics but value judgments, moral standards, and ethical principles are searched for after the fact as justification of the decision. Such an approach would not be considered acceptable given today's sensitivity to social responsibility and ethics.

Kohlberg's Stages of Moral Development

How managers assess ethical issues and challenges varies greatly; one explanation is provided in this reading. Another commonly referred-to theory of moral reasoning was developed by Kohlberg, and speculates that individuals have identifiable cognitive skill levels that they use in resolving moral dilemmas.[11] These skills are developed over time as a result of educational experience and the socialization processes in maturing from childhood to adulthood. Table 5.3 summarizes Kohlberg's six stages of moral development in three levels. He has also proposed a seventh stage, "Beyond morality and justice," which is not described.[12]

Kohlberg's work has been criticized on theoretical and methodological grounds but is often described in relation to the ethics of business. It is another approach to explaining how managers behave morally, and it is believed that most managers use stages 3 and 4. The stages of moral development suggest that managers learn through experience and training to consider the ethical implications of decisions differently over time and in different situations.

How can managers and businesspersons be moved toward approach 3 identified in Table 5.2, and the post-conventional level in Table 5.3? Several things can be suggested in general terms. Managers should be encouraged to view situations from various points of view or from the perspectives of relevant stakeholders. They should be introduced to moral reasoning

TABLE 5.3	*Kohlberg's Stages of Moral Development*

PRE-CONVENTIONAL LEVEL

At this level, individuals are focused on themselves and awareness of others is virtually non-existent. What is right is determined by self-interest.

Stage 1—Punishment and obedience orientation. There is obedience to rules and authority and concern for possible punishment if caught. Good or bad is decided in terms of the power to determine the rules. Authority is exercised and fear used as an influencer.

Stage 2—Individual instrumental purpose and exchange orientation. The individual focuses on what he or she will get out of an exchange; that is, the reward involved or "what is in it for me." What is right is defined in terms of whether something serves one's own needs. The situation is evaluated on the basis of fairness to one's self or self-satisfaction.

CONVENTIONAL LEVEL

The individual is more aware of others at this level, and is group- or organization-focused. Individuals take into account the expectations and overall welfare of society and therefore are responding to notions of fairness and justice as outlined in laws, rules, and codes.

Stage 3—Mutual interpersonal expectations, relationships, and conformity orientation. Individuals are concerned with being a good person. The well being of, and fairness to, others is considered. Group norms are followed and loyalty and belonging are important.

Stage 4—Law and order orientation. Laws are viewed as promoting societal welfare and thus observed. What is right is determined by a sense of duty to society.

POST-CONVENTIONAL LEVEL

Involves universal and humankind orientation. Concepts of rights and justice are considered when determining what is right. There is an increased capacity to consciously use principled judgment; that is, ethical principles. Rules and laws are questioned as the only basis for making moral decisions.

Stage 5—Social contract orientation. Laws and morals may be in conflict, and another basis more appropriate for determining what is considered right is necessary. Societal standards apply that are established through consensus.

Stage 6—Universal ethical principles orientation. Ethical principles are chosen as a basis for what is considered right regardless of society's views. Decisions are based upon one's conscience, and logical ethical principles are used.

Sources: Based on Lawrence Kohlberg, "Stage and sequence: The cognitive development approach to socialization," in *Handbook of Socialization Theory and Research,* D.A. Goslin, ed. (Chicago: Rand McNally, 1969), 347–480; Lawrence Kohlberg, "The claim of moral adequacy of a highest stage of moral judgment," *The Journal of Philosophy,* Vol. LXX (1973), 630–646; and Lawrence Kohlberg, *Essays on Moral Development Vol. 1: The Philosophy of Moral Development* (New York: Harper and Row, 1981).

processes and engage in logical thinking or a reasoned argument. In addition, they should be exposed to moral controversy, through training or by example. Resource persons more experienced in moral reasoning should be available to advise managers and businesspeople.

LO 5.6   Ethics in Business: Some Challenges

Everyone is confronted by moral dilemmas and faced with difficult moral decisions, whether in one's personal life, the workplace, or management. Ethical breaches can never be eliminated, and it is idealistic or naïve to think otherwise. But there should be some approach to keeping wrongs or harms to a minimum. Most individuals and organizations strive toward increasing the likelihood of "getting it right" through some systematic and thoughtful approach to resolve ethical dilemmas. Thus, there are challenges to ethics in business including simplistic approaches, myths, and lack of awareness.

Quite often the expression "just do the right thing" is proposed as a guide or standard for determining acceptable moral behaviour. This is not satisfactory because it is too open-ended and leads to many interpretations. What is "right" is in the eyes of the beholder and can have many meanings. Accountability is not achieved with this approach because no standard exists to measure or judge against. Instead, accountability is achieved by organizational processes and structures that will be examined in Chapter 6.

Treviño and Brown identified several myths pertaining to business ethics, three of which are applicable to this chapter. The first myth is *It's easy to be ethical.* Ethical decisions and theories are complex even when discussed in applied situations. They state that moral awareness—that is, ethical recognition and ethical sensitivity—is necessary as a first step in moral reasoning. Usually ethical decision making is a complex, multi-stage process and the organizational context creates additional pressures and complexity.

Another myth is *Unethical behaviour in business is simply the result of "bad apples."* The first reaction is to look for a culprit who can be punished and removed. Most people are followers when it comes to ethics, and they engage in unethical conduct when directed by a boss. Ethics can be taught and the behaviour of adults influenced. Finally, it is a myth that *People are less ethical than they used to be.* Ethical behaviour today is not that different than in the past. The tendency is to remember recent unethical behaviour or events and forget those of the past.[13]

Another challenge relates to an individual's perception of his or her own morality. Most people believe that they behave ethically toward others, but self-perception often falls short. People are not objective in self-assessment; there are sources of unintended, unethical decision making that are an unconscious, implicit bias of which they are unaware. Banaji, Bazerman, and Chugh identified four biases: prejudice, favouritism, overclaiming credit, and conflict of interest.[14]

Implicit prejudice is a bias that emerges from unconscious beliefs such as stereotyping. Associations are made that may not always be valid. In-group favouritism is a bias that favours a group to which a person belongs or is associated. Such groups can be based on friendship, sharing a nationality, religion, social class, race, or educational affiliation. Extra credit is given for group membership leading to discrimination in favour of someone instead of against. Overclaiming credit is a bias that favours one's self. Many people hold positive views of themselves and believe that they are entitled to more than they deserve. Finally, conflict of interest is a bias that favours those who benefit the individual. Such conflicts lead honest, ethical persons to make decisions that are neither sound nor ethical.

A discussion of an individual's perception of his or her morality leads to the challenge of how to learn about one's own ethics. Table 5.4 contains some checklists and tests for assessing one's ethics, which assist an individual in understanding the basis for his or her ethical decision making.

connect   Want to learn more about **your ethics**? Go to CONNECT.

This chapter identifies why business morality is complex and challenging. Managers can rely on intuitive approaches based on value judgments and moral standards to identify what they consider proper. This is not a reliable approach, as it may not consider the distribution of harms and benefits among all stakeholders. A more systematic approach is necessary, as frequently dilemmas exist and it is not possible to avoid harms. Ethics principles are relied upon to provide a more thorough approach.

Naturally, conflicts occur among the corporation's economic, legal, and social responsibilities. As discussed in Chapter 2, the market-based business system involves certain fundamentals, the application of which involves ethical implications. In addition, the corporation has legal responsibilities that must be obeyed, but the application of government requirements does not address all economic and ethical responsibilities. Chapters 7, 8,

TABLE 5.4	*Learning about One's Own Ethics*

Checklists and tests are useful approaches to translating ethical principles into practical terminology that is more easily understood. Some checklists or quizzes are available at:

- Bill Frey and Chuck Huff, "Ethics Tests," ComputingCases.org. This is a good source of "applied" or common language tests. http://computingcases.org/general_tools/teaching_with_cases/ethics_tests/ethics_test_intro.html
- Lander University, "Ethics: Sample Quizzes." http://philosophy.lander.edu/ethics/quizzes.html
- Institute for Global Ethics, "Business Ethical Dilemmas." Read the business dilemmas, decide what you would do, and then check the provided solutions against your decision. http://www.globalethics.org/dilemmas.php
- World Bank Institute, "Self-Test: For Course on Legislative Ethics and Codes of Conduct." http://siteresources.worldbank.org/PSGLP/Resources/ethicsselftest.pdf
- San Diego State University, Survey of Ethical Theoretical Aptitudes, "Business Ethics and Social Issues Exercise." http://www-rohan.sdsu.edu/faculty/dunnweb/exer.bradyinstrument.html
- Loyola Marymount University, Center for Ethics and Business, "Ethics Toolbox" for handling ethical dilemmas. http://cba.lmu.edu/academicprogramscenters/centers/centerforethicsandbusiness/toolbox/
- Back to B-School, "Test Yourself: Would You Act Unethically on the Job?" http://www.cbsnews.com/8301-505125_162-31041330/test-yourself-would-you-act-unethically-on-the-job/?tag=bnetdomain

and 9 examine the ethical responsibilities—social and environmental—of business in its relationship to society. The next chapter describes how the ethics of business can be managed within the corporation.

Your advice to Jonathan and Rosemary . . .

Several issues and stakeholders are involved in this situation. For Jonathan, it appears that self-interest is the primary motivator, but the personal virtues ethic also is evident. When considering other stakeholders, the utilitarian and universal rules ethics come into play. What about the consequences for other applicants who have the appropriate qualifications? What are the implications for employers? How do Jonathan's fellow employees feel about his being hired? If Jonathan thinks about the ethics of this situation at all, he is bound to be faced with a dilemma—but a different one from that facing Rosemary.

SUMMARY

- The topic of business ethics has been "in" for the past decade and has been discussed extensively in the literature, the media, and the classroom as well as on the Internet. Ethical behaviour as it relates to a variety of contexts has been examined, for example as it relates to public administration and government, the environment, multinational corporations, banking, competitiveness, and industrial relations. An extensive examination of ethical behaviour has occurred not only as it relates to business and the corporation but also as it impacts the various interrelationships among business, society, and stakeholders. (LO 5.1)

- The operations of any business involve the potential that decisions will have ethical implications for managers and stakeholders. The preferred phrase "ethics of business" is defined as the rules, standards, codes, or principles that provide guidance for morally appropriate behaviour in managerial decision making relating to the operation of the corporation and business's relationship with society. (LO 5.1)

- The three levels of ethical assessment are (1) awareness of moral or ethical implications, (2) ethical implications assessed upon individual, organizational, economic efficiency, governmental, and societal influences, described as value judgments and moral standards, and (3) implications assessed upon use of ethical principles. (LO 5.2)

- The multitude of influences on ethical behaviour range from educational and religious backgrounds to professional organizations and governments. These influences lead to ethical relativism, the belief that ethical answers depend on the situation and that no universal standards or rules guide or evaluate morality. (LO 5.3)

- Seven theoretical bases, or ethics, for understanding ethical conduct are described: self-interest, personal virtues, caring, utilitarian, universal rules, individual rights, and justice. (LO 5.4)

- The process of moral reasoning is described. In particular, Kohlberg's theory of the stages of moral development is outlined in regard to its application to the ethics of business. The pre-conventional, conventional, and post-conventional levels and the six stages illustrate the attitude that managers may have toward assessing the implications of ethics in the business environment. (LO 5.5)

- The consideration of the ethical implications of the responsibilities of business is prevalent in what corporations do. The theoretical basis for ethics has been outlined and sets the stage for further examination of the ethics and responsibilities of business. But, there are several challenges to ethical behaviour in corporations. (LO 5.6)

KEY TERMS

Business ethics	Self-interest ethic	Universal rules ethic
Value judgments	Personal virtues ethic	Individual rights ethic
Moral standards	Ethic of caring	Ethic of justice
Ethical relativism	Utilitarian ethic	Moral reasoning

CRITICAL THINKING AND DISCUSSION QUESTIONS

1. Why should managers consider ethical relativism when doing business in a foreign country?

2. How is an ethical principle different from a moral standard?

3. Why can the self-interest ethic not be avoided when studying the ethics of business?

4. Which personal virtues are most important in the operation of a corporation?

5. Under what circumstances would a manager or a corporation use the ethic of caring in assessing the ethical implications of a decision?

6. What is attractive about the utilitarian ethic when analyzing business decisions?

7. How do corporate managers apply the universal rules ethic?

8. What are the rights of a corporation?

9. In what situations would it be appropriate to use the economic efficiency ethic in assessing ethical implications?

10. Is the ethic of justice applicable to capitalism?

11. Why is a system of moral reasoning important for managers?

> **CASES**

5.1 *Working Overtime*

It was 9:05 p.m. and Tyler Simms was facing a dilemma. He was at the office working late, again, completing a report that his boss asked him to have ready for the next morning. She had received the draft report ten days earlier but waited until 4:33 p.m. that afternoon to return it for revision. Tyler felt that there was no excuse for the rushed revision because there had been plenty of time for his boss to give the feedback necessary to prepare the final draft. Tyler was becoming increasingly annoyed at having to work overtime under these circumstances. She had done this to him six times in the last month, and the practice was disrupting his family life. Other than for this annoyance, he liked his job, it paid well, and there were career opportunities. His dilemma was what he could do about this situation without risking his career.

The telephone rang. It was his wife, who was experiencing a problem of her own. She had been helping their six-year-old daughter with a school project and was missing some supplies to complete it. It was getting late and she did not think she could get to any stores in time. Furthermore, she would have to get their one-year-old twin boys out of bed to go to the store with her. She said that she needed poster board, coloured markers, and tape. Given where his office was located, Tyler did not think he had time to get to a store stocking these supplies. He knew that the supplies were in the stationery cabinet in the outer office, to which he had access. He also knew that there was an explicit company policy not to use stationery for personal reasons. While on the phone, he wondered whether he should mention to his wife the existence of the supplies in his office. He also pondered whether he should immediately leave and go to a store to buy supplies. If he did, there was a risk of not completing the report. Thus, a second dilemma emerged.

Questions

1. What are the issues involved with these dilemmas?

2. Who are the stakeholders?

3. What ethical principles could be applied to this situation?

4. What should Tyler do? Justify your choice using ethical reasoning.

5.2 *Ethical Responsibility on Mount Everest*

Many mountain climbers dream of scaling the highest mountain on Earth. It is a dangerous venture and some of them die in pursuit of this dream every year, including a 33-year-old Canadian woman in May 2012. The following describes one situation involving the ethics and responsibilities of climbers toward one another.

In May 2006, several climbing parties passed by David Sharp, 34, who was near death at 28,000 feet on Mount Everest. He later died alone, without companionship in his final hours. He was one of 11 who perished during the 2006 climbing season and one of more than 200 who have died attempting to climb the mountain.

One climber to leave Sharp was Mark Inglis, 47, a New Zealander who was climbing the mountain on artificial legs. He and his party stopped to consider Sharp's situation. He was in poor condition and near death, but was given oxygen. Rescue was not feasible as helicopters cannot operate at that altitude. The lives of Inglis's party would likely have been endangered trying to move Sharp to a base camp.

It was disclosed that Sharp's group was loosely organized without a leader. The members of the group appeared to be functioning independently according to an expedition outfitter. The outfitter said that Sharp's group did not have sufficient oxygen and climbed without a Sherpa guide.

Discussion of the incident was extensive. One position presented was that climbers do not endanger themselves to save another. Furthermore, looking after another climber may jeopardize one's own chance at climbing the mountain. Sir Edmund Hillary, who with his Sherpa became the first to reach the summit of Mount Everest, said that human life is more important than conquering mountains. Others suggested that the incident was an example of a lack of sense of responsibility and caring for one another.

Questions

1. What ethical principles are involved in this situation?
2. Why blame Inglis?
3. Who is responsible?
4. Should the climbing of Mount Everest be regulated?

Sources: Thomas Ball, "Amputee defends decision to let climber die on Everest," *National Post,* May 23, 2006, A2; Oliver Moore, "Left to die at 28,000 feet," *The Globe and Mail,* May 25, 2006, A1, A9; Paul Chapman, "Saving life more important than peak," *National Post,* May 25, 2006, A2; and "No heroes in thin air," *National Post,* May 26, 2006, A16.

 For more information on the resources available from McGraw-Hill Ryerson, go to www.mcgrawhill.ca/he/solutions.

For additional study tools and interactive ways to learn about ethics, visit **www.mcgrawhillconnect.ca**

CHAPTER 6
Ethics of Business: Management and Leadership

LO 6.1 Define and describe the pros and cons of a statement of values.

LO 6.2 Make the distinction between codes of conduct and codes of ethics.

LO 6.3 Appreciate the purpose of ethics training in an organization.

LO 6.4 Define an ethics audit.

LO 6.5 Explain the role of ethics officers and ethics committees.

LO 6.6 Understand how ethics reporting systems work and define whistleblowing.

LO 6.7 Know who is responsible for managing the ethics of business.

LO 6.8 Identify the approaches to ethics programs.

LO 6.9 Evaluate ethics programs and list their benefits.

LO 6.10 Recognize that ethical misbehaviour may occur despite management efforts and the implementation of ethics programs.

What would you do if . . . ?

Paul O'Doherty is the ethics officer for a medium-sized petroleum company; in this role he is responsible for the company's comprehensive ethics program. The program includes a code of business conduct that outlines the values to guide behaviour, identifies conflicts of interest, specifies appropriate and inappropriate practices, and provides an approach to reporting violations or suspected wrongdoing. One aspect of the reporting system is an employee hotline to which employees can contribute in written form, including by email, or orally by telephone or in person. Participants must identify themselves and all communications

go directly to Paul, who reports directly to the corporate secretary and legal counsel. The identity of the employee is not disclosed and confidentiality is maintained except in rare cases where legal action occurs.

Paul is a member of the Ethics Practitioners' Association of Canada (EPAC). According to EPAC, the skills of an ethics officer include "facilitating constructive dialogue on ethics-related issues, analyzing ethics issues and problems, and providing coherent, realistic solutions to ethical issues." Paul finds his job to be rewarding and his work has enabled the company to keep abreast of developments in the ethics area. The company has received awards for its ethics program, and is recognized as a leader in corporate ethics.

Recently, Paul has experienced a problem with the hotline component of the ethics program. An employee has been making numerous complaints to the hotline, almost weekly. The complaints cover many aspects of the employee's department: a supervisor is giving unfair treatment, co-workers are stealing office supplies, management is exercising favouritism in assigning holidays, a fellow employee is moonlighting, and co-workers are providing a poor quality of service to customers. All of the complaints have been investigated according to the procedures outlined in the corporation's reporting guidelines. The investigations have been costly, both monetarily and in time. None of the complaints have been determined to be justified, and many lack credibility. Paul has reluctantly concluded that the employee is a whiner or troublemaker, but he cannot state this to others. It also appears that the employee's reporting practices have been damaging to department morale. Paul's challenge now is to decide what should be done about the situation.

What is your advice to Paul?

Source: Information on the skills of an ethics officer was obtained from Ethics Practitioners' Association of Canada (EPAC), "Competency profile of ethics practitioners," http://www.epac-apec.ca/competency-profile-ethics-practitioners, accessed October 21, 2012.

Business has responded to the increased concern surrounding ethics. Various initiatives have been taken to institutionalize ethics; that is, to implement policies or programs that increase the awareness of ethics in the organization. Every organization has an ethics program, whether it knows it or not. In organizations there is a set of factors both implicit and explicit that communicate corporate values, define parameters of decision making, establish general rules for behaviour, and provide mechanisms for analysis.

Many initiatives can be taken, and several of these are described in this chapter. In the beginning sections, the explicit aspects of ethics programs are outlined. Toward the end of the chapter, the more implicit aspects of programs are described, including ethical leadership.

Corporate ethics programs Some combination of a statement of values, code of conduct and/or ethics, ethics training, ethics audits and consulting services, ethics officers and committees, and ethics reporting systems.

The approaches of ethics programs are categorized and their evaluation discussed. Several components might comprise an ethics program, whether on a formal or informal basis. No model or standard program has emerged, and programs vary by business enterprise. **Corporate ethics programs** comprise some combination of the following: a statement of values, code of conduct and/or ethics, ethics training, ethics audits and consulting services, ethics officers and committees, and ethics reporting systems.

LO 6.1 | Statement of Values

Statement of values A description of the beliefs, principles, and basic assumptions about what is desirable or worth striving for in an organization.

A **statement of values** contains a description of the beliefs, principles, and basic assumptions about what is desirable or worth striving for in an organization. Many corporations have articulated their values in such statements, also referred to as creeds and statements of philosophy. A statement of values also becomes the basis for a code of ethics. An example is provided in Everyday Ethics 6.1.

Most business enterprises are concerned to some extent about ethical behaviour, integrity, employee health and safety, the environment, quality, and service. Such concerns are a part of corporate life today. A study of 15 Canadian multinational corporations found the top ten corporate values to be integrity, honesty, justice, equality, objectivity (impartiality), loyalty, devotion, respect, prudence, and tolerance.[1]

Everyday Ethics

6.1

Values at Cameco Corporation

Cameco, the world's largest producer of uranium, has identified the following values that will guide its behaviour:

"*Safety and Environment*—The safety of people and protection of the environment are the foundations of our work. All of us share in the responsibility of continually improving the safety of our workplace and the quality of our environment.

People—We value the contribution of every employee and we treat people fairly by demonstrating our respect for individual dignity, creativity and cultural diversity. By being open and honest we achieve the strong relationships we seek.

Integrity—Through personal and professional integrity, we lead by example, earn trust, honour our commitments and conduct our business ethically.

Excellence—We pursue excellence in all that we do. Through leadership, collaboration and innovation, we strive to achieve our full potential and inspire others to reach theirs."

Source: Cameco Corporation, "Cameco value statement," http://www.cameco.com/about/vision.

There is no uniformity in content or format in these statements. Kooten found that a value statement may contain any combination of components, such as:

- the key interests to be satisfied and balanced; for example, the public or community interest, owners, employers, and suppliers;

- an emphasis on quality and/or excellence in relation to product and service, employees, and technology;

- efficiency as indicated by low cost, high productivity, and value for money or investment;

- the atmosphere or climate of enterprise; for example, a good place to work, an emphasis on teamwork, managers' support of staff, and development of employees;

- the observance of codes of conduct to enhance integrity and to ensure fairness in all dealings.[2]

By using a statement of values, managers are recognizing that individual and corporate actions are caused, in part, by the values that the individuals and the corporation have in common. Values need to be shared by everyone, at least to some degree, so that the values are reinforced and widely accepted. It is important that everyone in the corporation is able to identify the shared values and describe their rationale.

The values the organization wishes to operate with in the future are not necessarily the values implicit at the present. It is important to identify the organizational values desired, to compare them to individual values, and to ascertain how they can be reinforced. Value statements should be developed with the involvement, over time, of as many employees as possible. Although the production of a statement is the desired end result, the process used to accomplish that end is an important learning process.

What happens in practice is often quite different. The statements usually express the beliefs of the chief executive or top-level management and little, if any, effort is made to communicate or explain the values. In other cases, value statements, creeds, or philosophies are designed to improve the public image of the corporation and are only cited in advertisements, press releases, and newsletters. As a result, they are not taken seriously. A related problem is that no effort is made to instill the values throughout the corporation. In effect, the values are not shared and do not become a part of daily life—the ideals expressed are not reflected in reality, the meaning of the values is unclear, and employees and others do not understand the process.

Despite these problems, it is argued that management should be value-driven; that is, all plans, decisions, actions, and rewards are governed by a value focus. Thus, values have influence on organizational objectives, corporate plans, individual accountability, standards of performance, and reward systems.[3] This type of thinking is necessary if values are to influence corporate operations. Values must be identified, defined, prioritized, and then communicated throughout the enterprise, including corporate training programs and employee meetings. Whether the desired values are being practised should be measured within the organization and with customers or clients. In particular, current management practices must be monitored to ascertain the extent to which values are supported and incorporated into decision making, which may necessitate modifying leadership styles and management systems. Finally, values must be reinforced, including through the reward system.

connect   Want to learn more about **giving voice to values**? Go to CONNECT.

LO 6.2   Codes of Conduct and Codes of Ethics

Code of conduct Explicitly states what appropriate behaviour is by identifying what is acceptable and unacceptable.

Code of ethics A statement of principles or values that guide behaviour by describing the general value system within which a corporation attempts to operate in a given environment.

A **code of conduct** explicitly states what appropriate behaviour is by identifying what is acceptable and unacceptable. A **code of ethics** is a statement of principles or values that guide behaviour by describing the general value system within which a corporation attempts to operate in a given environment. A distinction should be made between a code of ethics and a code of conduct even though academics and practitioners often do not do so; these differences are described in Table 6.1. As there is little consistency in the contents of the codes in practice, the following discussion refers to codes generally. Codes are referred to by a variety of titles, including "Standards of Practice," "Code of Behaviour," and "Standards of Professional Conduct," and can be 20 or more pages in length. Corporations often develop codes that are a mix of conduct behaviour and ethics guides.

TABLE 6.1	*Distinction between Codes of Conduct and Codes of Ethics*
Codes of Conduct	**Codes of Ethics**
Enforced by an external power and authority; convey rules that tell people what they must or must not do. Members of organizations must obey or face penalties for failing to do so.	Voluntary codes of ethics suggest guidelines to follow and empower individuals to act according to their consciences. Penalties are not imposed and writers emphasize the qualities they think members should have.
Key characteristics: • Imposed by others • What must be done or what must not be done • Rules	Key characteristics: • Self-imposed • Who we are • What we stand for • Guidelines or guiding principles

Source: About Manulife, "Corporate Culture" accessed at http://www.manulife.com/public/about/index/0,,lang=en&navId=610009,00.html on October 19, 2012.

Codes have been developed at different levels in the business system, and they all contribute to the managing of ethics:

- *Corporate or business enterprise*—Individual corporations prepare codes for their own use (see Everyday Ethics 6.2).

- *Professional organizations*—Professions such as lawyers, accountants, and architects have been early users of codes and are influenced by them when employed by business enterprises.

- *Industry and sector*—Industry associations formulate codes that enterprises in the industry or sector may voluntarily follow. Also referred to as voluntary codes; sometimes are developed in conjunction with government agencies. Everyday Ethics 6.3 outlines the principles that must be followed in order to become a Certified Financial Planner (CFP®).

Everyday Ethics

6.2

Manulife Financial's Code of Business Conduct and Ethics

"The Manulife Financial Code of Business Conduct and Ethics (the "Code") reaffirms the Company's commitment to ethical conduct and its practice of complying with all applicable laws and avoiding potential or actual conflicts of interest. We should all be thoroughly familiar with its provisions and conduct ourselves according to both the letter and the spirit of the Code. With a long tradition of uncompromising dedication to the highest standards of business conduct, Manulife enjoys a reputation of unquestioned integrity and honesty. This reputation is among our most valuable assets and we must protect it."

The Code is organized into the following sections:

I. Why Ethics Matter—Outlines the purpose of the code and how it is applied.

II. Living Manulife Financial's Values—Lists corporate values, which guide operations.

III. Ethics in the Workplace—Articulates workplace principles, fairness, professionalism, and safety.

IV. Ethics in Your Business Relationships—Includes fairness and honesty toward customers, compliance with laws, gifts to government officials, lobbying and campaign finance issues, and handling of media inquiries.

V. Conflicts of Interest—Identifies possible conflicts and indicates how to avoid them.

VI. Handling Information—Discusses appropriate information disclosure to ensure privacy of stakeholders, including that of employees, policyholders, and investors.

VII. Ethics and the Law—Stresses the need to be knowledgeable of appropriate laws and the duty to report inappropriate behaviour.

VIII. A Final Word—Reinforces the importance of employee conduct and good judgment as it impacts Manulife's reputation.

IX. Disclosure Policy—Helps to ensure Manulife makes required disclosures clearly, completely, and in a timely manner.

Each of the sections is described in more detail. A sample *Code of Business Conduct and Ethics Certification and Conflict of Interest Disclosure Statement* is included.

Source: Manulife, "About Manulife, corporate culture," http://www.manulife.com/public/about/index/0,,lang=en&navId=610009,00.html, accessed October 19, 2012.

Everyday Ethics
6.3

FPSC® Code of Ethics—Synopsis of the Principles

Financial Planning Standards Council (FPSC®) continually strives to ensure all standards for CERTIFIED FINANCIAL PLANNER®/CFP® professionals and FPSC Registered Candidates are relevant and rigorous. It is critical that standards evolve with the needs of the public and the profession, to ensure the public is well served.

The FPSC® Code of Ethics, as found in the *Standards of Professional Responsibility for CFP® Professionals and FPSC® Registered Candidates,* outlines the eight principles guiding the conduct of CFP professionals and FPSC Registered Candidates in all professional activities.

The following [is] a synopsis of the Principles embodied in the FPSC Code of Ethics to which all CFP professionals and FPSC Registered Candidates must adhere. Principles are statements, expressing in general terms, the ethical and professional ideals of financial planning professionals. Additional guidance on the interpretation of the principles can be found at www.fpsc.ca.

- *Principle 1: Client First*—A CFP professional shall always place the client's interests first.
- *Principle 2: Integrity*—A CFP professional shall always act with integrity.
- *Principle 3: Objectivity*—A CFP professional shall be objective when providing advice and/or services to clients.
- *Principle 4: Competence*—A CFP professional shall develop and maintain the abilities, skills and knowledge necessary to competently provide advice and/or services to clients.
- *Principle 5: Fairness*–A CFP professional shall be fair and open in all professional relationships.
- *Principle 6: Confidentiality*—A CFP professional shall maintain confidentiality of all client information.
- *Principle 7: Diligence*—A CFP professional shall act diligently when providing advice and/or services to clients.
- *Principle 8: Professionalism*—A CFP professional shall act in a manner that reflects positively upon the profession.

Source: Reprinted from "Code of Ethics for Financial Planners," https://www.fpsc.ca/files/documents/CodeofEthicsJan2010.pdf.

- *Single issue*—Non-governmental organizations (NGOs) or business associations develop codes applicable to a particular issue, for example sweatshop labour in developing countries.
- *Codes from national and international bodies*—International NGOs or agencies such as the United Nations or the Organisation for Economic Co-operation and Development (OECD) prepare codes.

Codes are the most common approach to institutionalizing ethical behaviour, and aid in understanding relationships with stakeholders. They can improve customer confidence in the quality of a product or the level of service, and also help ensure ethical and fair treatment of customers. The reputation of the business enterprise or organization that develops codes is improved and attracts high-calibre employees and customers. Codes simplify the detection of unethical behaviour in competitors and employees by standardizing norms of behaviour. Lastly, codes provide for self-regulation, which is preferable to external control.

Overall, codes increase awareness, discourage ethical apathy, facilitate ethical decision making, and make it easier to refuse an unethical request. The content of codes varies, but Table 6.2 identifies commonly found items.

TABLE 6.2	*Content of Codes of Conduct and Codes of Ethics*

A general statement of ethics, values, or philosophies

Criteria for decision making and compliance with laws

Responsibility toward employees, including items such as health and safety, non-discrimination, and privacy

Conflicts of interest, their identification, and how to handle them

Protection of corporate assets, including accurate accounting, security or property, and insider information

Appropriate business practices, including honesty, fairness, obeying the law, and information disclosure

Appropriate conduct on behalf of the corporation; for example, relationships with customers, suppliers, competitors, creditors, and government

Responsibilities to society at large, including contribution to political parties, responses to media, treatment of communities, and concern for environmental protection

Implementation procedures, including familiarity with the code, reporting of violations, refusing unethical requests, and seeking help on ethical matters

Specification of enforcement/compliance procedures and the penalties for inappropriate or illegal behaviour.

Content

The content of codes has evolved over time and through five generations. The *first generation* focused on conflict of interest, involving the protection of company interests from employees, and was concerned with the shareholder interest and mostly excluded the public interest. Commercial conduct was emphasized in the *second generation,* including such things as bribery of foreign officials and arranging for kickbacks. It was argued that ethical practices protected the corporation's interest and reputation, as there was a relationship between ethical behaviour and profitability. The *third generation* focused on employee rights and the motivation of the workforce along with relationships with customers and suppliers. Ethical consumerism emerged with renewed mention of the importance of satisfying the customer. During this generation of codes, the exploration of child labour also emerged. A wider responsibility was assumed in the *fourth generation* of codes, with attention to the protection of the environment and respect for communities in which corporations operated. Corporations wished to reduce legal liabilities as well as maintain their image. Finally, the *fifth generation* extended coverage to international concerns, for example countries whose governments ignored human rights, the rule of law, and labour conditions in developing countries.[4]

The development and implementation of codes has not been a static process. Corporations have been challenged by societal demands to address different social responsibilities. As a result, codes have become more challenging not only to develop but also to implement.

Criticisms

Some critics claim that codes of ethics or conduct are at best a minimal but unenforceable standard and at worst a hollow pretence. An implication of this claim is that most corporations and professions operate at an ethical level above that specified in the codes. It is for only the less scrupulous that the codes are intended, but the guidelines may not be very effective with this group. It is, therefore, difficult to enforce the codes and, even if they are enforced, the penalties may be insignificant. Those following a code may also be placed in a disadvantageous position because those who don't adhere to the code are not restricted in their actions. As a result, convincing everyone to comply is not easy. In corporations, codes are sometimes pointed to with pride but ignored in practice. Frequently, the codes are idealistic or written in meaningless generalities.

Sometimes, codes of ethics are developed merely to control competitive conduct among business corporations or individuals. They specify conduct that is considered unprofessional, such as pricing practices in some industries. In these cases the code of conduct is really designed to reduce competition, and this kind of self-regulation is sometimes a stop-gap measure of questionable intent designed merely to prevent government legislation and serve as a response to public criticism.

Nevertheless, the use of codes and their reasons for existing are no longer issues for many corporations. Codes are important devices for communicating and controlling employees' behaviour within the corporation, and the behaviour of corporations and industries in society. Codes can be made more effective through improving their content, increasing commitment to the codes, and creating mechanisms that encourage employees to embrace the codes and live by them on a daily basis.

LO 6.3 ▸ Ethics Training

Ethics training involves teaching employees about the values and policies on ethics they should follow in their decision making. The teaching sessions involve an orientation on values or ethics and related policies and deal with reputation and legal risks. A code of ethics or statement of values may be used in this teaching process, in addition to handbooks or policy statements. Such teaching can be done by managers or outside consultants and addressed to all levels of employees, but more emphasis has been placed on management levels.

Larger corporations have developed online exercises to increase awareness of ethical implications. Employees complete such exercises at their computers, with appropriate responses presented or a scoring of the employee's ethical awareness given. Such training programs are established not only to develop employee awareness of ethics in business but also to draw attention to the ethical issues to which an employee may be exposed.

Training involves giving participants practical checklists and tests to evaluate their actions. Training usually also includes a description of conflict of interest, something that inevitably arises in a discussion of ethics.

Checklists and Tests

Lists of questions, moral standards, and tests have been developed to assist managers in making ethical decisions. Writing in the *Harvard Business Review,* Nash argues that plainly worded questions, such as the following, should be used by managers when examining the ethics of a business decision:

1. Have you defined the problem accurately?
2. How would you define the problem if you stood on the other side of the fence?
3. How did this situation occur in the first place?

4. To whom and to what do you give your loyalty as a person and as a member of the corporation?

5. What is your intention in making this decision?

6. How does this intention compare with the probable results?

7. Whom could your decision or action injure?

8. Can you discuss the problem with the affected parties before you make your decision?

9. Are you confident that your position will be as valid over a long period of time as it seems now?

10. Could you disclose without qualm your decision or action to your boss, your CEO, the board of directors, your family, society as a whole?

11. What is the symbolic potential of your action if understood? If misunderstood?

12. Under what conditions would you allow exceptions to your stand?[5]

Nash refers to this approach as the "good puppy" theory, as it allows corporate morality to be defined and explored halfway between the rigorous moral analogy of the corporation being the "good person" and the purely amoral definition of good. According to Nash,

> *Moral capacity is perceived as present, but its potential is limited. A moral evaluation of the good puppy is possible but exists largely on concrete terms: we do not need to identify the puppy's intentions as utilitarian to understand and agree that its "ethical" fulfillment of the social contract consists of not soiling the carpet or biting the baby.[6]*

A second example is the Pagano model, which uses six clear questions that serve as several tests of the ethics of a particular action. Pagano identifies six tests that he feels provide useful insights into the ethics of a business's actions. The tests are as follows:

1. *Is it legal?*—This is a core starting point.

2. *The benefit–cost test*—This test employs the utilitarian perspective of the greatest good for the greatest number.

3. *The categorical imperative*—Do you want this action to be a universal standard? This test takes the view that if it's good for the goose, it's good for the gander.

4. *The light of day test*—What if your actions appeared on TV? Would you be proud?

5. *Do unto others*—This test uses the Golden Rule. Do you want the same to happen to you?

6. *The ventilation test*—Get a second opinion from a wise friend with no investment in the outcome.[7]

The author feels that this approach has the advantages of being compact and simple. Note that most of the questions represent the principles discussed in Chapter 5; Table 5.4 lists Web sites to consult in order to learn about your own ethics.

Understanding Conflicts of Interest

Conflict of interest
A situation in which an individual has a private or personal interest that is sufficient to appear to influence the objective exercise of that individual's duties.

A conflict of interest occurs when there is a clash between the interests of an individual—that is, a manager or employee—and the organization that employs the individual. A **conflict of interest** is a situation in which an individual has a private or personal interest that is sufficient to appear to influence the objective exercise of that individual's duties.[8] The personal interest usually involves a financial gain or a promised future promotion or gift obtained by the individual or his or her immediate family. "Duties" refers to the responsibilities the individual was hired to perform in good faith and loyalty. Common conflicts are listed in Table 6.3.

TABLE 6.3	*Common Conflicts of Interest*

Self-dealing—Exists where a manager or employee takes an action in an official capacity that involves dealing with oneself in a private capacity and that confers a benefit to oneself. Today this extends to one's spouse, family members, and business partners.

Accepting gifts or benefits—Involves the acceptance of some benefit.

Influence peddling—The practice of soliciting some form of benefit; for example, asking for a kickback or gift from a supplier if a purchase is made.

Using employer's property—The inappropriate use of an employer's property; for example, taking office supplies for home use.

Using confidential information—The use for personal or private purposes of confidential information obtained from some other source, for example customers or suppliers, to gain some benefit.

Outside employment or moonlighting—The work or activity in which an employee engages outside normal working hours for additional remuneration.

Post-employment—Subsequent or future employment where information or contacts obtained during employment results in some benefit.

Personal conduct—The situation where an employee's behaviour in private life may reflect adversely on the employer.

Sources: Kenneth Kernaghan and John W. Langford, "Conflict of interest," Chapter 6 in *The Responsible Public Servant* (Halifax: The Institute for Research on Public Policy and The Institute of Public Administration of Canada, 1990), 133–155; and Michael McDonald, "Ethics and conflict of interest," The W. Maurice Young Centre of Applied Ethics, University of British Columbia, http://www.ethics.ubc.ca/people/mcdonald/conflict.htm.

Several complications exist in defining a manager's or employee's involvement in a conflict of interest. There are many variations of conflict of interest, from "influence peddling" to the improper use of company property. Interpretation of conflict of interest varies from one organization to another, from one department to another, and from one individual to another. Some conflicts of interest are defined in laws or regulations, but it is not possible to prohibit all possible business arrangements. Finally, it is difficult to distinguish among the types of conflict of interest.

The following are brief explanations of the three types of conflict:

- *Real*—A situation in which a manager or employee has knowledge of a private economic interest, or any kind of private or personal gain, that is sufficient to influence the exercise of his or her duties and responsibilities. Conflict occurs when there is an existence of a private interest, when it is known to the employee, and when there is a connection with the employer's duties or responsibilities that is sufficient to influence the exercise of those duties or responsibilities.

- *Apparent*—A situation where a conflict of interest can be deduced from appearances; exists when there is a reasonable apprehension that a well-informed person could make the connection.

- *Potential*—A situation that may develop into an actual conflict; exists when an employee can foresee that he or she has a private interest that may be sufficient to influence a duty or responsibility.[9]

Managers or employees must be aware of and concerned about all types and categories of conflict, and many corporations have statements describing potential conflicts. They must be familiar with any conflict of interest rules that exist, and also be able to recognize unidentified potential conflicts. Managers and employees must be continuously sensitive to conflicts of interest, as their reputation and the corporation's is at stake. Responsibility for Ethics 6.1 is an example of a corporation's conflict of interest policy.

RESPONSIBILITY

for Ethics (6.1)

> ### Husky Energy Inc.'s Conflict of Interest Policy
>
> Husky Energy Inc.'s Code of Conduct includes a substantial section on conflict of interest. In general it states that all employees and directors are to avoid all situations in which their personal interests conflict with their duties or the interests of the company. The conflict of interest definition states that it arises when an employee (including family members and acquaintances) will benefit at the expense of Husky or will interfere with the employee's objectivity or effectiveness on the job.
>
> Examples of conflict of interest include outside employment, use of Husky's resources for outside work, activities that reflect negatively on Husky's reputation, and holding a financial interest in a company doing business with Husky. Guidelines are listed for the implementation of the policy and detailed descriptions of possible violations are provided. Potential conflicts of interest must be immediately disclosed to the employee's supervisor. New employees must disclose any potential conflict of interest prior to accepting employment. If a violation of the policy is considered serious, disciplinary action will be taken, including possible termination of employment.

Source: Summarized from Husky Energy Inc. Code of Business Conduct, Conflict of Interest Section, pages 4-6 available at http://www.huskyenergy.com/downloads/abouthusky/coporategovernance/Code-of-Business-Conduct-Sept2011.pdf © 2002-2013 Husky Energy Inc.

LO 6.4   Ethics Audits and Consultants

Ethics audit A systematic effort to discover actual or potential unethical behaviour in an organization.

An **ethics audit** is a systematic effort to discover actual or potential unethical behaviour in an organization. It is designed not only to uncover unethical behaviour, but also to identify the opportunities for unethical behaviour that exist. There is a preventive as well as a remedial purpose. Audits are particularly useful when used in conjunction with a code of ethics, as the code can be the basis for comparison to establish how well or poorly the organization is doing. Regular audits foster ethical practice.

In recent years, several ethics audits or ethics accountability measures have been developed. These will be discussed in Chapter 9.

Consultants knowledgeable in the area of ethics advise management on how to put "integrity" into enterprise culture. Ethics audits or surveys can be conducted by consultants to ascertain compliance to ethical standards, and consultants may be involved in training and code development. The consultants are usually persons external to the organization who have some education and experience in ethics management. The Ethics Practitioners' Association of Canada (described in Responsibility for Ethics 6.2) is attempting to improve the quality of ethics advice.

LO 6.5   The Role of Ethics Officers and Ethics Committees

Ethics officer An independent manager, reporting to the board of directors or CEO, who reviews complaints or information from anyone in the organization or any stakeholder, studies the situation, and recommends action if necessary.

Some corporations have gone beyond implementing codes, training, audits, and the use of consultants and established ethics officers, indicating that ethical issues are being treated seriously. An **ethics officer** is an independent manager, reporting to the board of directors or CEO, who reviews complaints or information from anyone in the organization or any stakeholder, studies the situation, and recommends action if necessary. Sometimes this role is performed by an ombudsperson or advocate, who also must be independent to ensure the trust of stakeholders. Such officers can alert the organization to ethical problems or issues before they become public knowledge, allowing time to prepare a defence or to take remedial actions.

RESPONSIBILITY
for Ethics **6.2**

Ethics Practitioners' Association of Canada

The Ethics Practitioners' Association of Canada was formed in 1996 "to maintain a community of individuals promoting ethical behaviour in organizations in Canada." Its members include ethics officers, consultants, educators, students, and others interested in applied ethics for any type of organization. The Association has developed ethical standards for its members, a competency profile that describes functions a practitioner in the field of organizational ethics carries out, and a list of skills that such a practitioner should possess. Its activities are designed to encourage members to operate in an exemplary ethical and social manner locally and internationally.

Source: Based on Ethics Practitioners' Association of Canada, http://www.epac-apec.ca.

In larger American corporations, the position of chief ethics officer is responsible for the ethics program. Increasingly, the title of compliance officer is appearing in the executive ranks of corporations. This person makes sure that all legal requirements are followed, in particular those originating in government legislation and regulation. This position might also include responsibility for other aspects of an ethics program. In Canada, the corporate secretary quite often performs this role.

> **Ethics committee** A group, comprising directors, managers, or staff, formed to monitor ethical standards and behaviour.

An **ethics committee** is a group comprising directors, managers, or staff formed to monitor ethical standards and behaviour. The formation of such a committee, sometimes referred to as a business conduct committee, injects ethics at the highest level in the organization, and is a signal to all stakeholders of the company's commitment to ethical practice. This type of committee is involved in developing an ethics program and may monitor management and employee behaviour for ethical issues.

Ethics committees comprising management, employees, and outside stakeholders can also exist within the organization. Present practice appears to be that ethics committees are top-management focused. Such committees may also be called corporate ethics and responsibility committees, or advisory boards or councils, which usually comprise a variety of stakeholders.

LO 6.6   Ethics Reporting Systems and Whistleblowing

Corporations have established reporting systems so that they can become aware of issues and concerns relating to corporate ethical conduct or irregularities. The reporting systems are known by various names, the most common being "hotlines." Codes of ethics or conduct usually contain sections outlining the reporting system, and outside service providers are hired to process the reports. An example of one corporation's compliance and reporting system is outlined in Everyday Ethics 6.4. Corporations believe that such systems alert them to problems before they become public and allow time for remedial action. The system also reinforces the importance being placed on the corporation's code of ethics or business conduct. The systems are a secure forum to report problems and enable individuals to be anonymous without fear of retaliation.

> **Whistleblowing** An act of voluntary disclosure of inappropriate behaviour or decisions to persons in positions of authority in an organization.

The practice of reporting alleged wrongdoing, code violations, and irregularities in corporate operations is commonly referred to as whistleblowing. **Whistleblowing** is an act of voluntary disclosure of inappropriate behaviour or decisions to persons in positions of authority in the organization. The term may have originated from the practice of English police officers blowing whistles to get someone's attention, or from the use of whistles by sports referees. The most frequent form of whistleblowing occurs in the workplace where

Everyday Ethics
6.4

Compliance and Reporting at Barrick Gold Corporation

Corporate codes of ethics or conduct usually include a mechanism to identify issues arising from the codes, and to prevent and identify violations. This enables employees to seek guidance on these matters and allows the corporation to act prior to them becoming problems.

Barrick Gold has an extensive "Compliance and Reporting" section in its Code of Business Conduct and Ethics, which includes the following topics:

* Employees and directors have a duty to report suspected code violations to the appropriate management level.
* "Formal reporting channels" are identified.
* The matters that must be reported through the "formal reporting channels" are specified; for example alleged misstatement of financial statements, or known or suspected fraud.
* A compliance hotline is available and is operated by an outside service provider.
* The process for handling reports of alleged issue or concern is outlined.
* A statement is made about the confidentiality of any reports and there will be no retaliatory action against the individual raising the concern.

Source: Based on Barrick Gold Corporation, "Code of business conduct & ethics," http://www.barrick.com/files/governance/Barrick-Code-of-Business-Conduct-and-Ethics.pdf.

employees, managers, or directors are concerned about some matter. Whistleblowers are also referred to as do-gooders, bell-ringers, lighthouse keepers, people's witnesses, snitches, rats, tattletales, and squealers.

Several issues relating to whistleblowing have ethical implications for whistleblowers and managers:

* The whistleblower is faced with the choices of silence, quitting, and disclosing when he or she becomes aware of the inappropriate behaviour. All these choices can be uncomfortable and involve risk.
* The range of concerns may go from clearly illegal, to maybe illegal, to an issue of morality, all of which may be difficult to define.
* The whistleblower is faced with several moral obligations to self and to professional, corporate, or industry codes. There most likely is an obligation to an employer due to a legal duty, loyalty, or confidentiality agreement. There may be an obligation to society at large.
* The whistleblower faces a credibility issue: Will he/she be believed? Will the disclosure be taken seriously? Is the matter important enough? Will the matter be addressed anyway?
* Concern also exists about the perception of others toward the whistleblower: noble, honourable, ethical hero, or snitch, mole, traitor?
* When to tell and whom to tell are often problems. The whistleblower must decide how far to let the concern continue before disclosure and then has the challenge of deciding whom to tell, particularly in organizations without reporting systems.
* The whistleblower must be concerned about his/her self-interest. There are costs and risks, consequences for personal and professional lives, and the possibility of retaliation to consider.

- Anonymity encourages reporting, but it might result in trivial claims that are a nuisance and unfounded.

Although this discussion has focused on workplace stakeholders—employees, managers, and directors—other stakeholders may be whistleblowers. Suppliers and consumers may disclose inappropriate corporate practices to the corporation's reporting system, the legal system, government regulators, or the general public. The media often are whistleblowers, as are non-governmental organizations (NGOs). The movie industry also may depict whistleblowing (see Everyday Ethics 6.5).

Everyday Ethics
6.5

Whistleblowing in the Movies

The ethics of business is the topic of many popular movies. The following is a list of some movies with a focus on whistleblowing:

Boiler Room (2000)—The story of a stockbroker operation using aggressive selling techniques to the disadvantage of clients. An employee discloses the abuses.

A Civil Action (1998)—Story of the disclosure of industrial pollution contaminating drinking water in New England.

Erin Brockovich (2000)—A small law firm discovers that a chemical company is polluting and discloses the cover-up.

The Informant! (2009)—The story of a corporate executive who blows the whistle on price fixing in the large agri-business corporation where he works.

The Insider (1999)—Detailed account of an employee who discloses the misleading practices in the tobacco industry.

The Rainmaker (1997)—Disclosure of the insurance industry's denial of health care payments to a dying client.

Silkwood (1983)—An employee tries to disclose that she and others have been exposed to radiation in the workplace. Based on a real story and widely considered the best movie on whistleblowing.

In addition to corporate disclosure or reporting policies, several government whistleblowing regulations impact on a corporation's reporting system. All are designed to facilitate regulation and enforcement in particular areas and may require employees to disclose corporate practices.

- *Canadian federal and provincial/territorial governments*—Whistleblowing provisions exist in many regulatory areas including environmental protection, health and safety, competition, and industrial relations. There is no comprehensive whistleblowing legislation except in New Brunswick. The federal government has passed regulations relating to whistleblowing within the public service.[10]

- *United States governments*—U.S. legislation impacts on Canadian corporations with operations in that country. There is extensive legislation requiring disclosure and protecting whistleblowers, and the *Whistleblower Protection Act* applies to federal government employees. The *Sarbanes-Oxley Act* of 2002 contained several whistleblowing provisions, including prohibition against employment discrimination and the acceptance of social responsibility complaints.[11]

An ethics reporting system is challenging to administer and involves risks for the corporation and the discloser, but recently it has become an important component of a corporate ethics program.

LO 6.7   Ethics—Who Is Responsible?

A simple answer to the question "Who is responsible for ethics?" is "Everyone." But in a corporation it is argued that the responsibility for recognizing the importance of ethical behaviour in business and doing something about it has to start at the top—that is, with the board of directors.

Board of Directors Responsibility

Bavaria claims that directors have been remiss in this area, especially the docile outside directors who have the independence to monitor ethical behaviour.[12] Gillies states that directors have two tasks in relation to ethics: to collectively identify values that determine acceptable behaviour in the firm, and to put in place a process that ensures values are reflected in action. Merely acting on the basis of one's own values is not sufficient, and it is necessary to deliberately consider the implications of unethical behaviour. Not all directors agree with this position, and the arguments for and against it reflect the general discussion of whether or not business has any social responsibility.[13]

The reasons given for the board's responsibility for ethical or moral behaviour include the point that it is simply good management to develop an appropriate culture that is sensitive to ethics issues. In addition, the board itself is involved in ethical questions such as conflicts of interest, compensation schemes, management buyouts, the rights of minority shareholders, and changes in management. Finally, it is easier to make decisions if the fundamental principles or values of the corporation are known and can serve as a reference point. In the past, and maybe the present, directors often were not aware that ethics were involved in a decision. They must be aware that values change over time and that their own values may not have altered. Because directors are the ultimate decision makers in corporations, they must demand that decisions made by management and all employees be based on ethical standards acceptable to society. Chapter 11 will also discuss the role of the board of directors in a corporation's social responsibility program.

Management Responsibility

The success of any ethics program depends on the commitment of top management. Managers must announce the program, champion its development and implementation, and always aspire to lead in an ethical manner. They must provide moral leadership as opposed to immoral or amoral leadership. Table 6.4 distinguishes the three models of moral management and leadership.

Carroll, in an article that summarized his views on moral leadership, identified seven attributes of a moral leader: having a passion to "do right," being morally proactive, considering stakeholder inclusiveness, having a strong ethical character, being obsessed with fairness, practising principled decision making, and integrating ethics wisdom with management wisdom.[14]

Inside the organization, managers are responsible for developing and supporting a variety of policies and procedures to ensure the ethical implications of decision making are considered. An ethics manual should be available, maybe even online. A values statement and codes would be included. Such a manual would include policies regarding such things as whistleblowing protection, guidelines for offering or accepting gifts, and the privacy of employee records. Codes of conduct or ethics would be supported through training, the appointment of an ethics ombudsperson, the establishment of an ethics hotline, and regular consultation with employees. Corporate publications or newsletters would feature articles on ethics, and consideration of ethics would be integrated into corporate planning, recruitment, and performance appraisals.

TABLE 6.4	*Management and Leadership Models*	
Immoral	**Amoral**	**Moral**
A posture or approach that is devoid of ethical principles and actively opposed to what is moral	A posture or approach that is without ethics, but not actively immoral	Conform to high standards of ethical behaviour or professional standards
Management's motives are selfish and it cares only about the individual's or the organization's gains	Two types: intentionally or unintentionally amoral	Aspire to succeed only within confines of ethical principles; for example fairness, justice, and due process
Management to some degree knows right from wrong and chooses to do wrong	Intentionally amoral leaders do not consider ethics, as they believe business activity lies outside of moral judgments; neither moral nor immoral, as different rules apply to business	Concerned with letter and spirit of the law
May be motivated by greed and profitability, and organizational (or personal) success is the goal to be achieved at any price	Unintentionally amoral leaders are morally careless, unaware of or inattentive to impact of their decisions on others	Prefer standards that are higher than the minimum set by the law
Do not care about claims or expectations of others	They lack ethical perception, sensitivity, or awareness	Assume leadership when ethical dilemmas arise
The law is regarded as a barrier to be overcome and will circumvent if it will achieve their ends	May be well-intentioned but unaware of harms from their actions	Make ethics a driving force of the organization
Do not make good corporate citizens	"Ethical gears in neutral"	
	Use letter of the law instead of spirit	
	Cannot make good corporate citizens	

Source: Based on and summarized from Archie B. Carroll, "The moral leader: Essential for successful corporate citizenship," in Jorg Andriof and Malcolm McIntosh, *Perspectives on Corporate Citizenship* (London: Greenleaf Publishing, 2002), 142–145.

Managers not only must be supportive of ethics programs within the organization, but also must advocate for ethical approaches to management with external stakeholders. Executive speech making provides an example. Speeches should inform certain stakeholders that the business enterprise and its management are concerned about ethics and are responding to society's interest in the matter. It is not always clear to which stakeholders the speeches are directed, but they most likely address society at large, NGOs, business groups, students, and possibly even shareholders.

The next section outlines approaches to ethics programs.

LO 6.8 ► Ethics Programs: Approaches

From the materials presented, corporations can design a variety of programs to provide ethics leadership in an organization. The resulting programs are classified as formal, monological, and dialogical,[15] and as being compliance-based versus values-based.

Classification of Programs

A *formal approach* is based on organizational norms that are written as a code of conduct. This approach focuses on unacceptable practices or behaviour and emphasizes compliance and penalties. Usually the approach is top-down, as codes are imposed from top management. The advantages of such programs are that they provide clear guidance for decision making and that their fulfillment is measurable. The rights ethical principle is likely to be used in this approach. The disadvantages are that employees may resist the necessary coercion and indoctrination.[16]

The *monological approach* allows organizational members, for example managers and employees, to determine for themselves what is right or wrong. Codes of values, philosophies, and ethics would facilitate this approach. Organizational members are encouraged to reflect on the appropriateness of their behaviour by considering their own values, the circumstances of the incident or issue, and the alternative choices for resolution. This approach focuses on argument and reflection but leaves room to act upon specific circumstances. The justice ethic is the principle most likely to be used. On the other hand, performance is difficult to measure and the possibility exists that it will lead to differences in behaviour.[17]

The *dialogical approach* emphasizes communication before decisions are made and implemented. The stakeholders influenced or that can influence are consulted and an appeal is made for input. The approach is similar to that advocated in the collaborative view of stakeholder relations, and the values and opinions of all stakeholders involved are included. It seeks inclusive solutions and attention is given to the social dynamic side of ethical issues, usually based on the ethic of caring. The monitoring of these programs is more challenging, as it is based on the process and not on outcomes. There is a danger of ethical relativism, which may lead to differences in behaviour by the stakeholders involved.

The formal approach is the most commonly used and the least dialogical. Larger organizations most likely use a combination of approaches, especially formal and monological. Nijhof, Fisscher, and Looise state that it is challenging to combine the approaches, and suggest that it might be more appropriate to use different approaches in different circumstances.[18] Although conscientious programs have been discussed, it is possible that corporations will have informal, unwritten programs that are implemented implicitly instead of explicitly and without a structured, deliberate approach.

Compliance-based versus Values-based Programs

Increasingly in the literature and in practice a distinction is made between compliance-based versus values-based approaches to managing the ethics of business. Table 6.5 summarizes the differences between the two approaches.

TABLE 6.5   *Compliance-based versus Values-based Approaches*

Compliance-based	Values-based
Rules, laws, policies	Values, ethics, guiding principles
Conformity with externally imposed standards	Self-governance to chosen standards; self-imposed
Prevent criminal misconduct	Enable responsible conduct
Lawyer-driven	Management-driven
Educational approach: policies and rules, legalistic	Educational approach: policies and rules, but also guidelines and awareness through leadership
Employee discretion: limited	Employee discretion: increased
Control: auditing, penalties	Control: accountability, organizational systems, and decision processes
Code of Conduct: • Specific • Prescriptions/directives • Uniformity • Enforceable statements of specific behaviour	Code of Ethics: • General • Values/principles • Judgment • "Empowering" and "aspiration"

The compliance-based approach focuses on adherence to legal and regulatory requirements and to corporate policies. Clear rules guide ethics and the rules are clearly communicated, limiting an individual's discretion. These rules are enforced and sanctions are imposed for violating them. In contrast, the values-based approach is defined by organizational values and ethical standards, which are to be applied to decision making. This approach increases awareness of ethical issues through dialogue, training, and fostering an ethical corporate climate. It is the preferred approach, as many people do not like rules that cannot cover all the circumstances that are encountered.

Integrity management An ethics program that combines a compliance-based and a values-based approach.

The trend is to incorporate both approaches, because it is recognized that one alone cannot yield results. It is necessary to recognize compliance to rules or policies on the one hand, but also the positive effects of values on the other. A compliance-based approach has reduced misconduct, but a values-based approach is a more powerful influence on attitudes and behaviour. Combining the two approaches is referred to as **integrity management.** The codes of many corporations now follow this approach.[19]

 Want to learn about **a guide to practical ethics**? Go to CONNECT.

LO 6.9   Ethics Programs: Evaluation and Benefits

The components of a corporate ethics program have been outlined. Just because a corporation is not involved in the components mentioned does not mean that it does not have an ethics program, according to Max Clarkson, the founding Director of the Centre for Corporate Social Performance and Ethics. He argued that all corporations have programs, but that some of them were implicit. The implicit ethics programs were implemented through such things as the organization's culture, reward systems, valued behaviour, promotion policies, management example, general practice, and performance measures.[20]

Clarkson identified criteria for evaluating the effectiveness of an ethics program: visibility, ownership, fit, and balance. The components of an ethics program were clearly evident in statements such as codes, which should be widely distributed and communicated in a variety of formats. There was evidence of a commitment to the ethics program, as demonstrated by awareness and usage of the initiatives, and by their integration into the organizational culture. Initiatives should be appropriate to the circumstances of the corporation; that is, programs should be complementary with the type of business or industry. Lastly, there should be a balance in the programs among rules, redress, and principles, or a balance between "imposed control" and "self-control." Clarkson also identified criteria for evaluation of the program's implementation. Such criteria were the extent of resource commitment to the program, the CEO's involvement, the extent of communication about the program, and the training and education carried out.[21]

Business ethics is identified as an "in" topic, yet it has been discussed seriously for four decades. Much of the earlier material on ethics is still applicable. An article by Laczniak contains some ethical propositions that are still appropriate and can serve as criteria for justifying the formulation and implementation of ethics programs.

- Ethical conflicts and choices are inherent in business decision making.
- Proper ethical behaviour exists on a plane above the law. The law merely specifies the lowest common denominator of acceptable behaviour.
- There is no single satisfactory standard of ethical action agreeable to everyone that a manager can use to make specific operational decisions.
- Managers should be familiar with a wide variety of ethical standards.

- The discussion of business cases or of situations having ethical implications can make managers more ethically sensitive.
- There are diverse and sometimes conflicting determinants of ethical action. These stem primarily from the individual, the organization, professional norms, and the values of society.
- Individual values are the final standard, although not necessarily the determining reason for ethical behaviour.
- Consensus regarding what constitutes proper ethical behaviour in a decision-making situation diminishes as the level of analysis proceeds from abstract to specific.
- The moral tone of an organization is set by top management.
- The lower the organizational level of a manager, the greater the perceived pressure to act unethically.
- Individual managers perceive themselves as more ethical than their colleagues.
- Effective codes of ethics should contain meaningful and clearly stated provisions, along with enforced sanctions for noncompliance.
- Employees must have a non-punitive, fail-safe mechanism for reporting ethical abuses in the organization.
- Every organization should appoint a top-level manager or director to be responsible for acting as an ethical advocate in the organization.[22]

The propositions summarize many of the components described in this chapter. They also indicate that, within the corporation, directors and managers are all responsible for ethical behaviour, with top management assuming leadership. Despite being compiled more than two decades ago, these propositions provide practical guidance to the institutionalization of ethical behaviour in corporations.

It is not known how many business enterprises have formally organized programs, but there is no doubt that many are consciously attempting to increase awareness of ethical behaviour even though it may be done in an informal manner. Some benefits of programs to manage ethics are listed below.

- Many improvements in business practices and benefits to society have occurred as a result of attention paid to ethics in the past. Some practices are no longer considered acceptable, for example misleading advertising, child labour, and price fixing.
- Turbulent times have increased the awareness of ethics, and business leaders need a moral compass and to be sensitive to acting consistently.
- Ethics programs align corporate behaviour, especially that of managers and employees, with the principal ethical values preferred by the leaders of the business enterprise.
- Employees are prepared to face the reality of moral dilemmas; that is, to be sensitive to what might be considered good or bad.
- A focus on ethics sensitizes managers and employees to the legal requirements in a moral dilemma.
- Criminal acts are more likely to be avoided, as such behaviour is likely to be detected earlier and violations caught within the organization.
- Awareness of ethics helps managers to integrate values with quality management practices and strategic management.

- The implications or influence of management decisions on various stakeholders is more likely recognized.
- A more favourable public image is created for the business organization.[23]

The components of an ethics program can be evaluated by their focus. Some components are values-based, providing guidelines to influence behaviour with fewer specific rules or directions.

A concluding note to this chapter is supplied by Treviño and Brown. They argued it is a myth that "ethics can be managed through formal ethics codes and programs." Compliance-based approaches including codes alone cannot address ethical behaviour and values-based approaches are also needed. It is necessary to reinforce an ethical culture every day. Another myth focuses on leadership: "Ethical leadership is mostly about leader integrity." Managers must lead others to behave ethically, not just be ethical themselves. Not all leaders are capable of this. Four types of executive ethical leadership were identified:

- hypocritical leader = strong moral manager and weak moral person
- unethical leader = weak moral manager and weak moral person
- ethical leader = strong moral manager and strong moral person
- ethically silent leader = weak moral manager and either a weak or strong moral person

Unfortunately, not all corporations are led by ethical leaders. The authors concluded their article by indicating what executives can do to provide ethical leadership. Their guidelines for effective ethics management are:

"First: Understand the Existing Ethical Culture
Second: Communicate the Importance of Ethical Standards
Third: Focus on the Reward System
Fourth: Promote Ethical Leadership Throughout the Firm."[24]

LO 6.10 ▸ Why Ethical Leadership and Programs Fail

There are frequent examples in the media of executives, managers, or corporations engaging in unethical behaviours such as accounting fraud, bribery, insider trading, price fixing, and Ponzi schemes. Sometimes these behaviours are portrayed as being a modern phenomenon, but in reality ethical mistakes have occurred throughout history, they are inevitable, and they come in waves or cycles. It is important to increase understanding of why unethical decisions are made by business managers and corporations even though the unethical behaviour occurs in other professions and institutions in society.

The issues of unethical leadership and failed ethics programs are not easy to explain. Conduct that is illegal, like the behaviours mentioned above, is relatively easy to condemn because laws or regulations are violated. Other conduct may be unethical or immoral but not illegal, in which case right versus wrong is often difficult to ascertain. Also, the literature on this topic presents contradictory findings and conclusions are often difficult.[25] The following discussion provides some explanations or answers from the literature.

Managers are morally imperfect—With well-designed systems and policies such as the organization's culture, governance system, and ethical programs plus the existence of government regulations to influence behaviour, it could be assumed that unethical behaviour is unlikely. But some individuals are morally imperfect and will take advantage when systems and regulations fail, and at the same time there is a good possibility of not being caught. Managers with moral commitment are less likely to be unethical. Note that personality screening for unethical predispositions is not an exact science and is unlikely to prevent bad behaviour.

Self-interest—Managers may do something wrong simply because they will benefit and they will get away with it. Self-interest also influences managers not to be unethical because of the possibility of being caught and the fear of punishment.

Rationalization and self-delusion—If managers observe others getting away with inappropriate behaviour, they are more likely to become involved in similar activities. When others are cheating and getting away with it, individuals feel that it is only fair that they should also. This is a form of rationalization, and may even be self-delusion.

Threat of formal sanctions—When managers perceive that the threat of legal action and the imposition of sanctions are high, they may avoid unethical conduct. Unethical conduct is more likely when the sanctions are not imposed quickly, not highly likely to occur, and not punitive. Some research has found that the threat of formal sanctions or punishment does not deter unethical behaviour.

Threat of informal sanctions: An informal sanction such as social disapproval by colleagues, family, or society in general may be sufficient to discourage unethical behaviour.

Tolerance to risk-taking behaviour: Those managers who accept high risk taking are more likely to be involved in unethical behaviour.

Pressure in particular situations: Managers may be willing or forced to compromise their personal values when pressured to do so by superiors or a particular situation or requirement. Thus, bad behaviour may be exhibited by an otherwise good manager. An example of a situational pressure may be investor expectations to achieve returns, which may result in illegal activities such as price fixing, overcharging customers, or inappropriately polluting the environment.

Despite designing and implementing comprehensive ethics programs and an active role by management in emphasizing ethical behaviour, misbehaviour will still occur. When misbehaviour does occur, an issue arises relating to how much responsibility management, particularly top management, should assume for the misdeeds. The issue is complicated in large corporations when top management does not even know about the misbehaviour, and by the fact that he or she could not reasonably be expected to be aware of the circumstances.

connect | Want to learn more about **business ethics by joining a blog**? Go to CONNECT.

Your advice to Paul . . .

You are faced with a dilemma in advising Paul, because he faces difficulties no matter what he does. One possibility is to do nothing. This choice potentially harms co-workers, the supervisor involved, and perhaps customers and suppliers. Asking the violator to stop would be a sensitive matter; it may not be Paul's place to do it, and involving the supervisor and the human resources department involves confidentiality. The final possibility is to seek to change the policy or process. No clear alternative exists to the current approach to the hotline, and even if there were the same difficulties would likely be present.

SUMMARY

- As emphasized in Chapter 5, increasing sensitivity to the ethical implications of managerial actions in general is a start. In addition, corporations must take deliberate actions to reinforce the importance by considering ethical implications in decision making. The components of a corporation's ethics program to accomplish this are described in the chapter. The initial stage should be a statement of values or the equivalent that states in general terms the behaviours expected. These values become the foundation for the corporation's ethics program. (LO 6.1)

- A code of ethics reflects the values of an organization. A distinction should be made from a code of conduct, which focuses on compliance to rules or regulations instead of values. The contents of codes are outlined and drawbacks are presented. (LO 6.2)

- Today, corporations are not leaving an understanding of morality to chance and are engaged in a variety of training for everyone in the organization. (LO 6.3)

- Ethics audits are becoming more common as an approach to assessing the ethical implications of a corporation's practices. Usually such audits are conducted by outside consultants, who can also provide a range of advice about ethics programs. (LO 6.4)

- In larger corporations, there is a trend toward an ethics officer of some type being responsible for all aspects of compliance and morality in the organization. Ethics committees in many corporations facilitate the implementation of ethics programs. (LO 6.5)

- Ethics reporting systems are being established. Closely associated with such systems is the practice of whistleblowing. Several complicated issues are associated with whistleblowing and whistleblowers. Managers must carefully monitor the practice to make sure its benefits outweigh the drawbacks. (LO 6.6)

- Someone must take responsibility for the development and implementation of ethics programs. The board of directors and top management must signal their commitment to any program if it is to be successful. A "moral" leadership model is necessary to achieve this. (LO 6.7)

- Approaches to ethics programs are described. The formal approach is most common; the dialogical the least. Most corporations have programs that are a combination of these approaches. Also, the components of programs can be identified as being compliance-based versus values-based. (LO 6.8)

- Ethics programs should be evaluated on a regular basis and the benefits clearly identified. The programs can be justified on several bases ranging from economics to doing the right thing. The components of an ethics program are either compliance-based, following rules and requiring conformance, or values-based, emphasizing values as a way to influence behaviour. In most corporations today, a combination of these approaches is used and referred to as integrity management. (LO 6.9)

- There are several explanations for why ethical leadership and programs fail despite the best efforts and intentions of the corporation and its managers. (LO 6.10)

KEY TERMS

Corporate ethics programs	Conflict of interest	Ethics committee
Statement of values	Ethics audit	Whistleblowing
Code of conduct	Ethics officer	Integrity management
Code of ethics		

CRITICAL THINKING AND DISCUSSION QUESTIONS

1. What values do you think corporations and their managers should observe in business? Which ones do you think they really follow?

2. How would the stakeholders of a corporation be influenced by codes of ethics or conduct?

3. What are the drawbacks to codes of ethics or conduct?

4. Is it possible or feasible to train managers in ethics?

5. Why is it becoming necessary to have one manager to coordinate corporate ethics programs?

6. What are the benefits of ethics reporting systems?

7. What are the positive aspects of whistleblowing? What are some downsides?

8. How are governments involved in whistleblowing?

9. Why should responsibility for ethics programs rest with top management?

10. Should ethics programs rely on compliance-based or integrity-based approaches?

11. What is the justification for corporate ethics programs?

12. In your experiences in the workplace or educational institution, have you been provided with appropriate ethical leadership?

CASES

6.1 Citizen's Arrest: The Law and Ethics

David Chen was very frustrated by the theft of goods from his store, particularly one individual's repeated stealing. David operated the Lucky Moose convenience store in Toronto's Chinatown, and the thievery not only was annoying but also impacted on profits. This was a problem for most retailers and is referred to as shoplifting.

It is estimated that shoplifting costs Canadian retailers about $3.5 billion a year. About 90 percent of small independent retailers like David reported being victims of crime, and lost about $1,000 a month. Shoplifting was done by individuals and by organized crime groups posing as customers. Employees may also steal from their employers.

After noticing the theft on a surveillance system, David decided to pursue the individual and located him about an hour later. David and two employees caught him, tied him up, and threw him in their van. After returning to the store David called police.

The shoplifter was charged, but so was David—with assault and forcible confinement. In court, the shoplifter stated that he feared for his life when arrested by David. The *Criminal Code* states that a property owner ". . . may

arrest without warrant a person whom he finds committing a criminal offence on or in relation to that property." In David's case, it was alleged that the arrest was not made within a reasonable time.

The situation received extensive media coverage, especially on radio talk shows, and David became known as the "vigilante grocer." Public opinion was that David should be considered a hero for capturing the shoplifter, and not punished with a criminal record. Local Members of Parliament agreed, and even Prime Minister Harper visited David at his store and expressed agreement with David's actions.

Questions

1. **What are the ethical issues involved?**

2. **Did David do the right thing in arresting the shoplifter?**

3. **What rights do business owners have to protect their property?**

4. **What are the dangers of taking the law into your own hands; that is, becoming a vigilante?**

Sources: Library of Parliament Research Publication, "Legislative summary of Bill C-26: The *Citizen's Arrest and Self-Defence Act*," http://www.parl.gc.ca/About/Parliament/LegislativeSummaries/bills_ls.asp?Language=E&ls=c26&Parl=41&Ses=1&source=library_prb, accessed May 3, 2012; CBC Documentaries, "Fact sheet: Shoplifting," http://www.cbc.ca/documentaries/doczone/2009/shoplifting/factsheet.html, accessed July 13, 2012; "Taking the law into our own hands," *National Post*, April 26, 2012, A14; and "Trial begins for shopkeeper David Chen, charged in citizen's arrest case," CP24 Canadian Press Online, October 6, 2010.

6.2 Heidi Heise, Sub Samaritan

On June 3, 2010, a fire broke out in Heidi Heise's Dartmouth, N.S., apartment building. Several tenants had to find other accommodations, but fortunately Heidi's apartment was not damaged and she did not have to move out. Two of her neighbours were affected and,

feeling sorry for them, Heidi offered them the use of her apartment while they looked for other accommodations.

Heidi had worked at three Subway fast-food restaurants during the previous three years, most recently including ten months full time at one outlet. After the fire

the neighbours to whom she had lent her apartment came to the restaurant to thank her. Because they were hungry and had no money, Heidi prepared two six-inch subs for them. As an employee working over her lunch period she was entitled to one free 12-inch sub, but decided to forgo it and gave it away. Store policy required that she record her consumption of the sub, but she forgot to do this.

A restaurant manager observed Heidi giving away the subs on a surveillance camera a few days later, and fired her. Heidi was not impressed to have been fired for helping someone in need. She also believed that she had been a good employee, never receiving warnings or punishments related to her job. Several people intervened on Heidi's behalf, including her direct supervisor, but the general manager insisted on the firing. One of the neighbours and the apartment building manager also appealed to Subway in favour of Heidi.

A representative of Atlantic Subway Ltd. commented that the incident was unfortunate. Subway Restaurants Canada issued a statement saying that it was concerned, but personnel matters were the responsibility of the franchise owner. Calls by the media to Subway were not answered, but the incident received nationwide coverage. Reader comments to a Halifax *Chronicle Herald* story stated the following opinions:

- Subway had missed an opportunity to recognize an employee doing a good or right thing.
- The incident may have a negative impact on the morale of other employees.
- Subway should be boycotted.

About a week later, Heidi was offered a job by Subway competitor Quiznos, which also decided to donate $2 from the sale of subs to the victims of the fire.

Questions

1. **What are the issues involved in this incident?**
2. **What ethical theories can be applied to analyze this incident?**
3. **Was Subway justified in firing Heidi?**
4. **As a manager, how would you have handled this incident? What aspects of an ethics program would have assisted you?**

Sources: "Subway worker fired for feeding fire victims," Cnews, canoe.ca, June 11, 2010, http://cnews.canoe.ca/CNEWS/Canada/2010/06/11/14355351.html?cid=rssnewscanada, accessed February 23, 2012; *CTV News,* June 10, 2010, http://www.ctv.ca/CTVNews/TopStories/20100610/ns-subway-firing-100610, accessed February 23, 2012; "Fired Subway worker doesn't want to work there anymore," *CTV News,* June 11, 2010, http://www.ctv.ca/CTVNews/TopStories/20100611/subway-firing-folo-100611, accessed February 23, 2012; "Nova Scotia Quiznos offers job to submarine Samaritan fired by rival chain," *National Post,* June 12, 2010, A12; Roger Taylor, "Fired sandwich artist back on job with competitor," *The ChronicleHerald.ca,* June 12, 2010, http://thechronicleherald.ca/Business/1186991.html, accessed June 21, 2010; and Mark Harden, "Quiznos franchisee rescues Canada's hoagie hero," *Denver Business Journal,* June 15, 2010, http://www.bizjournals.com/denver/blog/broadway_17th/2010/06/quiznos_franchisee_helps_out_canadas_hoagie_hero.html, accessed February 23, 2010.

CHAPTER 7
Corporate Social Responsibility: The Concept

What would you do if . . . ?

Louis Richard graduated from a college business program and started work for a mid-sized Canadian cosmetics company. During the first few months, he was rotated among various departments so that he could become familiar with the company. The appraisals of his performance must have been good, as the chief executive officer (CEO) asked him to work in her office as an assistant for a year with a focus on special projects.

The CEO had attended a recent Conference Board of Canada seminar and learned about corporate social responsibility (CSR), corporate sustainability, reputation management, social impact management, triple bottom line (TBL), and corporate citizenship. The conference and the supporting materials provided a lot of background on the concepts, and she learned a lot from other executive participants.

In the interview for the job, the CEO asked if Louis had been exposed to business ethics and CSR in any of his college courses. He had taken a course in "Business and Society," which covered these topics, and many other courses had touched upon them. This must have satisfied the CEO, as she offered Louis the job.

The CEO admitted to Louis that, despite having attended the seminar and having read some papers on the subject, she was still not clear on the concepts and approaches involved. She was confused by the terminology and had difficulty distinguishing

among all the variations on corporate social responsibility. In addition, she was not clear what CSR would look like in the cosmetics industry. As a first assignment, she asked Louis to prepare a concise position paper outlining what this whole area means to the company and what course(s) of action should be followed. Louis left the office wondering where to start.

What is your advice to Louis?

This chapter defines social responsibility, reviews the case for business social involvement, reviews the arguments against involvement, and describes recent theories and approaches to corporate social responsibility including corporate citizenship.

LO 7.1   Describing Corporate Social Responsibility

Corporate social responsibility (CSR)   The way a corporation achieves a balance among its economic, social, and environmental responsibilities in its operations so as to address shareholder and other stakeholder expectations.

Corporate social responsibility (CSR) has had many definitions to date; one of these is the way a corporation achieves a balance among its economic, social, and environmental responsibilities in its operations so as to address shareholder and other stakeholder expectations. CSR is known by many names, including corporate responsibility, corporate accountability, corporate ethics, corporate citizenship, sustainability, stewardship, and the triple-E bottom line (economical, ethical, and environmental). CSR is a general management concern; that is, it is important to all aspects of business, and it is integrated into a corporation's operations through its values, culture, decision making, strategy, and reporting mechanisms.

A definition receiving some attention is the one developed by the International Organization for Standardization (ISO). This standards-setting organization already has formulated standards for risk, quality, environmental, and energy management. Its ISO 26000 standard defined social responsibility as the responsibility of an organization for the impacts of its decisions and activities on society and the environment, through transparent and ethical behaviour that:

- contributes to sustainable development, including health and the welfare of society;
- takes into account the expectations of stakeholders;
- is in compliance with applicable law and consistent with international norms of behaviour; and
- is integrated throughout the organization and practised in its relationships[1]

Rather than use a definitive definition, researchers have identified the elements or topics that might be included. Buchholz identified five key elements found in most, if not all, definitions:

- Corporations have responsibilities that go beyond the production of goods and services at a profit.
- These responsibilities involve helping to solve important social problems, especially those they have helped create.
- Corporations have a broader constituency than shareholders alone.
- Corporations have impacts that go beyond simple marketplace transactions.
- Corporations serve a wider range of human values than can be captured by a sole focus on economic values.[2]

In another example of this approach, Dahlsrud examined 37 definitions through content analysis and found that five dimensions of CSR existed:

- Environmental: the natural environment
- Social: the relationship between business and society
- Economic: socio-economic and financial aspects
- Stakeholder: stakeholders and stakeholder groups
- Voluntariness: actions not prescribed by law

He concluded that existing definitions were largely congruent and that "the confusion is not so much about how CSR is defined, as about how CSR is socially constructed in a specific context."[3]

According to Wood, the "basic idea of corporate social responsibility is that business and society are interwoven rather than distinct entities" and that expectations are placed on business due to its three roles: as an institution in society, as a particular corporation or organization in society, and as individual managers who are moral actors within the corporation. These roles result in three levels of analysis—institutional, organizational, and individual—and can be expressed in terms of three principles of corporate social responsibility: legitimacy, public responsibility, and managerial discretion.[4]

The principle of *legitimacy* refers to society's granting of legitimacy and power to business, and business's appropriate use of that power and the possibility of losing that power. Corporate social responsibility defines the institutional relationship between business and society that is expected of any corporation. Society has the right to grant this power, to impose a balance of power among its institutions, and to define their legitimate functions. The focus is on business's obligations as a social institution, and society takes away power or imposes some sort of sanction on business if expectations are not met.

The principle of *public responsibility* means that business is responsible for outcomes related to its areas of involvement with society. The level of application is organizational—that is, the corporation—and confines business's responsibility to those problems related to a firm's activities and interests. This principle includes the view that corporations are responsible for solving the problems they create. The nature of social responsibility will vary from corporation to corporation as each corporation impacts society's resources in different ways or creates different problems. The principle involves emphasizing each corporation's relationship to its specific social, ethical, and political environment.

Last, the principle of *managerial discretion* refers to managers as moral actors who are obliged to exercise such discretion as is available to them to achieve socially responsible outcomes. Discretion is involved because the actions of managers are not totally prescribed by corporate procedures. The level of application is the individual who has the choices, opportunities, and personal responsibility to achieve the corporation's social responsibility.[5] Table 7.1 summarizes the three principles.

The many elements of corporate social responsibility have been introduced so that the concept's complexity is appreciated. A later section of this chapter will present a unified framework of corporate social responsibility as it relates to business and society.

The Importance of Corporate Social Responsibility

CSR is important because the business system is the mechanism selected by society to produce and distribute goods and services. Originally, people felt that a business enterprise had fulfilled its social responsibility by surviving and realizing the maximum

| TABLE 7.1 | *Wood's Principles of Corporate Social Responsibility* |

Principle of Legitimacy	Principle of Public Responsibility	Principle of Managerial Discretion
• External focus on expectations of society	• Beyond general expectations of society, that is, at the corporation level	• Involves individual choice or managerial discretion
• Society grants the right to business to operate	• Determined by uniqueness for circumstances of the corporation	• Individual decision makers or managers determine
• Adherence to social norms of society	• Resource dependence determines	• Relates to latitude of action possible by management
• Pressures particularly strong on some corporations, e.g. large ones or consumer products	• Involves managing relationships with immediate environment	• Focuses on range of strategic options available to management

Source: Compiled from Christine Shropshire and Amy J. Hillman, "A longitudinal study of significant change in stakeholder management," *Business & Society,* Volume 46, Number 1, March 2007, 68–74.

profit possible. The resources of society could be used by the corporation to make profits as long as the corporation complied with the few rules imposed by governments to check abusive practices. The market system provided the regulation necessary to police the system, and profits provided incentive and ensured efficiency. The work ethic and self-interest were the guiding principles of the system. By making a profit, corporations contributed to a growing, healthy economic system that provided employment and adequate incomes for all. In other words, corporate social responsibility was to operate profitably, and the corporation could not survive without profits, much less play a social role.

More recently, there has been a belief that business exists for more than profits (or economic goals), with the public expecting something else from business. As a result, the original concept of social responsibility involving the maximization of profits has been modified. Although profits are to be made, social goals are also to receive attention. Society depends on business to achieve social as well as economic goals—that is, social responsibilities are placed on business.

The issue of social responsibility cannot be easily resolved. To illustrate, consider the following questions: How should corporate performance in society be judged apart from traditional economic standards? Are there goals and measures that individuals inside and outside the corporation can use for guidance? Given the relationship between the corporation and its social environment, what is the scope of managerial responsibility? To what extent should the corporation involve itself in social concerns? How do corporations typically respond to social involvement issues? Is there a common process that will enhance the corporation's understanding of corporate social performance?

It must be appreciated that corporate social responsibility and a corporation's social performance are two of many factors in an extremely complex business environment in which the corporate manager is called upon to operate the business. Various stakeholders are constantly seeking a different role for business in society. Government continues to influence the business system and to change the forms and manner of this influence. Technological change is occurring at a very rapid pace. The media advise citizens quickly of events in the business world, allowing for quick public reaction.

The discussion of definitions and meanings of corporate social responsibility could be extensive, but the purpose is to provide an introduction to and appreciation for social responsibility. Further understanding of the concept, its origins, and its interpretations is achieved by summarizing some of the debate surrounding social responsibility.

LO 7.2   The Corporate Social Responsibility Debate

The discussion of the appropriateness and meaning of social responsibility continues. This debate is treated in two ways in this chapter: through a listing of the arguments for and against social responsibility, and through a summary of the theories used to represent the variety of views toward social responsibility.

The Case for Involvement

Many arguments support the involvement of business in society; that is, they support the social responsibility or social responsiveness of business.

Business must realize that society is a "system" of which corporations are a part, and that the system is interdependent. Therefore, if business institutions interact with others in society, the need for social involvement along with increasing interdependence brings the need to participate in the complex system that exists in society. There are many mutual involvements among individuals, groups, and organizations in society, or among subsectors of society. Business is vulnerable to the actions or events that occur in other subsectors. As a result, business should operate in such a way as to fulfill society's needs or expectations. It should do so for a very pragmatic reason: it is believed in some quarters that business functions by the consent of society and therefore must be sure to satisfy the needs of society. In other words, the existence of the business system depends on its acceptance by society. If business is to prevent criticisms or mutinous behaviour, it must be receptive to what is happening in society and respond in some way.

Corporations must be concerned with the public image and the goodwill generated by responsible social actions. A social responsibility role should be undertaken in order to prevent some public criticism and discourage further government involvement or regulation. This is a defensive approach designed to offset possible government action against those in the business system who use their power irresponsibly. Preventing is better than curing. It is better to take a proactive stance than a reactive one.

Social responsibility is in the shareholder's interest; that is, corporate virtue is good for profits, especially in the long term. A poor social responsibility role on the part of the corporation means poor management to some investors. They view failure to perform in society's interests in much the same way as they view the corporation's failure to perform in financial matters. Similarly, investors and consumers are showing increasing interest in and support for responsible business practices (see Responsibility for Ethics 7.1).

RESPONSIBILITY
for Ethics **7.1**

Ethical Investment Funds

Pension and mutual funds are one type of owner of Canadian corporations. These funds manage the contributions of employees/employers to pension funds and the mutual funds purchased by consumers. The managers of some of these funds explicitly state their intention to consider the social and environmental performance as well as the economic performance of a corporation when investing.

Fund managers influence corporations in two ways. One approach is that they can decide not to purchase shares or bonds in corporations they consider not socially responsible. Criteria for undesirable corporations, for example those that sell tobacco products or that manufacture military weapons, are excluded by a "negative" screen. Corporations considered socially responsible are selected on the basis of a "positive" screen. A second approach is that they can purchase shares in corporations that are not socially responsible and attempt to get management to change their operations. Some mutual funds are even marketed as containing only corporations that are ethically, socially, or environmentally responsible. Ethical investing is discussed further in Chapter 11.

Business must realize that social problems can become opportunities, or can lead to profits, lower costs, and reduced risks. Expenditures on pollution abatement may result in the retrieval of materials that were formerly disposed of as waste, or may allow for equipment to operate more efficiently, thereby generating more profits on future operations. Also with regard to social responsibility matters, business should take a long-run as opposed to a short-run view. Profits may increase in the long run as a result of actions taken at the present time. Judging the benefits of social responsibility becomes a simple matter of ascertaining whether it is in the corporation's longest-term self-interest to be conscious of social responsibility matters by reducing risk. Finally, some corporations have built their competitive advantage on social responsibility initiatives or strategies that set them apart from competitors.

Business should be given an opportunity to solve some social problems. The logic behind this argument is that business can solve problems as well as government can and that it certainly cannot do any worse than government has in the past. Business possesses the expertise, in its managers and executives, to develop plans to overcome social problems. As government is reducing its efforts to address some social problems, business needs to fill the gap. Businesspeople are also concerned citizens and humans; it is not appropriate for them to ignore social matters.

The Counterargument to the Case for Involvement

Although several arguments can be made for social involvement by business corporations, there also are many arguments *against* business social involvement.

Profit maximization is the primary purpose of business, and to have any other purpose is not socially responsible (as argued in Responsibility for Ethics 7.2). To have anything other than a profit-maximizing goal is to sabotage the market mechanism and distort the allocation of resources. Generally, then, it is contrary to the basic function of business to become involved in social matters. It should not be forgotten that business is an economic institution, not a social one, and its only responsibility is to manage efficiently within the law. The corporation would be irresponsible if it did not pursue profits and operate in the efficient market.

RESPONSIBILITY

| Milton Friedman |

Milton Friedman, a Nobel Prize winner in economics, is often quoted as saying the only social responsibility of business is to make profits. Here is the quotation this refers to:

> *The view has been gaining widespread acceptance that corporate officials and labor leaders have a "social responsibility" that goes beyond serving the interest of their stockholders or their members. This view shows a fundamental misconception of the character and nature of a free economy. In such an economy, there is one and only one social responsibility of business—to use its resources and engage in activities designed to increase its profits so long as it stays within the rules of the game, which is to say, engages in open and free competition, without deception or fraud. Similarly, the "social responsibility" of labor leaders is to serve the interests of the members of their unions.*

Source: Based on Milton Friedman, *Capitalism and Freedom: A Leading Economist's View of the Proper Role of Competitive Capitalism* (Chicago: The University of Chicago Press, 1962), 133.

Business corporations are responsible to the shareholders and, in effect, have no authority to operate in the social area. When a corporation becomes involved in social matters, there is a question of legitimacy. Even if corporations are sufficiently competent and powerful to bring about social changes in matters considered beyond the range of their immediate involvement, there is a real question as to whether such endeavours are appropriate. Managers should let shareholders decide whether or not they wish to become involved in social issues.

Social policy is the jurisdiction of governments, not business. Business lacks training in social issues, and lacks social skills necessary to carry out social programs. In other words, business is not competent to undertake social responsibility tasks. Furthermore, social responsibility is viewed by some as another excuse to let big business increase its power. The increase in power comes as a result of business becoming involved in social as well as economic matters. Imposing business values on social issues may lead to inappropriate domination: business already has sufficient power, and it would be inappropriate to extend that power to other matters.

Business involvement in social matters increases costs—not only costs to the organization, but also possibly even social costs—instead of decreasing them. This in turn may lead to business failures. There is no acknowledged source of reliable guidance or policy for business in social responsibility questions, and it is not easy to make the choice between responsible and selfish action in social issues. Social responsibility is an elusive concept for which few standards are available to evaluate and control the actions of corporations.

As institutions in society, business corporations cannot be held accountable for their actions in a way sufficient to satisfy demands for social involvement. Institutions involved in social matters should be accountable to society for that involvement. At the present time, few mechanisms are available to ensure that business corporations are accountable for their social actions.

There is divided support in the business community for social involvement, and as a result there is unlikely to be a very satisfactory treatment of social issues by business.

Critiquing CSR

Explanations and critiques of corporate social responsibility appear regularly in the media and academic literature (some examples are provided in Responsibility for Ethics 7.3). Many of these discussions are repetitious, but one that added to the analysis of the concept was a special section in *The Economist,* "The good company: A survey of corporate responsibility."[6] The thesis of the section was that the corporate social responsibility movement dominates most management thinking, and that this is unfortunate because it is not necessary if the functioning of capitalism is understood. Furthermore, CSR is practised in many different ways, creating confusion regarding what it really means.

The article argues that there is no need to impose CSR on corporations, because they are acting in a responsible manner already. The point is made that capitalism has been the driving force behind unparalleled economic and social progress, but unfortunately it is still suspected, feared, and deplored. Two reasons are given for this fear of capitalism: the idea that profit is inconsistent with the public or social good, and the belief that in their pursuit of private gain corporations are placing crippling burdens on society and the environment. *The Economist*'s article does not consider either of these reasons to be appropriate.[7]

The Economist article says that enlightened self-interest and ethical conduct work well together. But, two values must be understood in relation to the proper good of the

RESPONSIBILITY
for Ethics (7.3)

Critical Comments on CSR

Despite widespread acceptance of corporate social responsibility, there are those who are critical of it. The following quotations from the business press illustrate the criticism.

"Business ethics has become not so much about honesty and fair dealing as about the additional burdens companies should be taking on the name of infinitely expansive corporate social responsibility and getting out in front of environmental issues."—Peter Foster, "Trading honesty for 'social responsibility'," *National Post,* April 17, 2009, FP11.

"When corporations take on a social role, often at the urging of elected officials themselves, it relieves governments of their responsibilities to mediate social demands. It removes policy-making from its proper forum. Put plainly, CSR is undemocratic."—Konrad Yakabuski, "The kindness of corporations," *Report on Business Magazine,* July/August 2008, 68.

"Under the label of Corporate Social Responsibility, firms are to take on a non-wealth-producing agenda of goals: profits will be lowered to safeguard labour rights, human health, civil liberties, environmental quality, sexual equality, and social justice. The fact that the corporation already plays its most effective role in these areas by profit maximization is little understood by CSR advocates."—Steve Forbes, "Welcome to market socialism," *National Post,* January 15, 2005, FP11.

"Corporate Social Responsibility is a proposition with which it is allegedly impossible to argue. If you question its multiplying meanings or its murky metrics, you are accused of espousing 'irresponsibility,' of wanting to outlaw philanthropy and trash the environment, of being a blinkered ideologue who believes employees, suppliers and local communities should be treated with contempt. This is all, to put it bluntly, baloney."—Peter Foster, "The bottomless pit of CSR policies," *National Post,* March 2, 2005, FP23.

corporation, and without these two values business is not possible. The first value is ordinary decency—that is, being just, honest, and fair. The second value involves distributive justice, where the benefits within the corporation are aligned to the contribution made in adhering to the aims of the corporation—for example, pay is linked to performance and promotion to merit. With regard to stakeholders, corporations should take them into account without being accountable to them.[8]

This critique generated substantial response, including several letters to the editor in subsequent issues—the majority of which disagreed with the thesis of the survey. An invited contributor to *The Economist* responded with a countering view. Ian Davis, worldwide managing director of McKinsey & Company, stated that business leaders should not fear greater advocacy of the contract between business and society and that the role of business is changing.[9] *Corporate Knights* did an analysis of the survey, pointing out that the complete separation of government and society from the private sector was no longer a reasonable assumption to hold.[10] Most commentators thought that to be successful the modern corporation must consider the interests of stakeholders in addition to shareholders.

The Economist published a follow-up report in January 2008, "Just good business: A special report on corporate social responsibility."[11] An accompanying editorial was entitled "Ethical capitalism: How good should your business be?"[12] The tone of the second report was somewhat different from the first one. The first report questioned the legitimacy of CSR, while the second report focused on how CSR was being accomplished. An observation from the second report was that CSR has gained considerable momentum and, rather than being a sideshow, is now seen as mainstream. Few corporations are doing it well and it has some limitations. The report concluded that CSR is just good business.

The arguments for and against CSR have been made. Various forms of CSR are widely practised and knowledge of the concept is essential for effective management in today's environment. The following section also addresses this debate but from a different perspective, summarizing the varying corporate social responsibility theories that exist. The existence of these theories helps explain why so many interpretations are associated with the concept.

LO 7.3   ## Social Responsibility Theories

Klonoski[13] sets out to address a fundamental question: "Does business and the corporation have a social nature, or not?" The answer given by any stakeholder can be associated with a theory of corporate social responsibility, and these theories fall into three categories: amoral, personal, and social.

The Amoral View

This category represents a traditional view of business and the role of the corporation; that is, the corporation is seen as a "highly individualized rights bearing economic entity designed for profit making and legitimatized by the laws governing incorporated businesses."[14] Free market defenders and legal recognition theorists are among those holding this view, including some who believe there is no such thing as corporate social responsibility. Over the years many theories have advocated this view of social responsibility; these are listed in Table 7.2. The amoral view is still held by some in the business community.

TABLE 7.2   *Examples of Amoral-View Theories of Social Responsibility*

Fundamentalism—The corporation has no or very little social responsibility.

Legal recognition—The corporation is an autonomous entry and not the creation of society.

Individual agreement—Corporations can be socially responsible, but only within the limits of a prior contractual agreement with shareholders.

Traditional shareholders model—Beyond individual agreements, corporations are not ethically required to be socially responsible; they are responsible only to monies and to maximize profits (as so famously stated by Milton Friedman).

Source: Summarized from Richard J. Klonoski, "Foundational considerations in the corporate social responsibility debate," *Business Horizons* (July/August 1991): 9–18.

The "amoral" view should be carefully defined and not confused with an "immoral" view. Amoral refers to an activity without a moral quality; that is, something that is neither moral nor immoral: moral standards, restraints, or principles do not exist. This is quite different from immoral, which denotes activities that are not moral and do not conform to usually accepted or established patterns of conduct. Amoral means lacking in morals, good or bad, while immoral connotes evil or licentious behaviour. Although in some contexts being amoral is considered as reprehensible as being immoral, that is not the position taken by most advocates of the theories listed in this category.

The Personal View

This view discusses the nature of the corporation in ascertaining whether it can be held accountable. The question involved is whether corporations are "moral agents" or "full fledged" moral persons. Corporations are viewed as collectives that act as individuals; they exist as legal persons and can be held responsible for their actions. This question has been extensively discussed in the literature.

Those arguing that corporations are persons claim that corporations are responsible for their actions in a way comparable to the actions taken by natural persons or individuals. Therefore, the corporation can be morally blamed in a way that is identical or very similar to natural persons. A strong counterargument in the literature claims that corporations are not persons. Supporters of this view argue that it is not possible to impose moral sanctions or punishments on corporations as corporations. It is possible to blame or punish the people who work for or manage the corporation, but not the corporation itself. Some punishments, such as fines, are in effect paid by shareholders or passed on as costs to consumers.

The debate over whether the corporation can be seen as a moral person does not provide an answer as to whether the corporation is a social institution. Those who claim the corporation is a person believe that it is socially responsible for its impact on society, and that it can be held morally accountable for its actions in the social sphere. Those who do not consider the corporation to be a person say that claims against the corporation by society need a different basis than that provided by the moral person or agency theory. The "personal" view represents a middle position between the amoral and social views.

The personal view leaves the debate unresolved. However, the arguments favouring the treatment of corporations as persons lead to the next theoretical view of corporate social responsibility: the social view.

The Social View

This view holds that the activities of corporations occur within an interpersonal and, most likely, social context. The corporation is considered a social institution in society, with social responsibilities. The social nature of business can rest in many different theories, some of which are listed in Table 7.3. The extent of corporate social responsibility depends on the theoretical foundation used to support the view.

It is argued that the corporation should be considered a social institution, as it exists because individuals come together to achieve some objective related to the provision of goods and services. Today, corporations exist because society implicitly sanctions them to operate in that form. Many in society believe that corporations now operate within the "social" view of corporate social responsibility despite the continuing claims of those who argue the "amoral" view, with its incomplete vision of the corporation operating as a private institution with a solely economic purpose.

Many theories and frameworks have been presented to describe corporate social responsibility. Some of them overlap and some parallel the arguments for and against

TABLE 7.3	*Examples of Social-View Theories of Social Responsibility*

Social contract—An implicit social agreement exists between business and society that determines the social nature of the corporation, identifies its duties and rights, and is considered to be an evolving document.

Ideological/historical—Society evolves and history gives rise to new social needs, societal demands, and changes in social values to which business is expected to contribute.

Stakeholder—There is a social responsibility function of the interrelationships developed by the corporation with groups that have a stake. This approach was also referred to as "constituency theory." This theory is one of the main underpinnings of this book.

Legal creator—The corporation is a creature of law, existing only in contemplation of law, and is thus made by society for the common good of society.

Social permission—Society can legitimately demand the corporation do certain kinds of activities and, if the corporation is harming the public good, can restrict or eliminate its activities.

Corporate citizenship—With the charter, the corporation becomes a legal entity with standing as a citizen similar to that of the individual and has duties as well as rights and privileges.

Social impact—Business has the power to change society and must consider social responsibilities.

Social interpenetration—Business is so intertwined with society that it cannot avoid social responsibilities.

Moral gratitude/reciprocity—As business operates within a social system, it should be socially responsible out of "gratitude" or have a moral responsibility to "reciprocate." Corporations benefit from and thus owe society.

Utilitarian—It is to the benefit of society or for the greatest good for the greatest number of people that corporations are socially responsible; social responsibility is in business's best interest.

Virtue-based—This view focuses on the development of good or morally virtuous people instead of principles or contracts. A morally responsible business is one in which good people make decisions based on generally developed moral character, self-discipline, moderation, hard work, courage, creativity, good humour, and intelligence.

Source: Summarized from Richard J. Klonoski, "Foundational considerations in the corporate social responsibility debate," *Business Horizons* (July/August 1991): 9–18.

corporate social involvement. The existence of numerous theories supporting corporate social responsibility makes it difficult to find a comprehensive and definitive definition, as mentioned in the previous section about describing social responsibility.

Despite the numerous views of corporate social responsibility, many business-supported organizations advocate it; some of these are listed in Responsibility for Ethics 7.4. The literature contains numerous models of social responsibility, and one has been selected for presentation. Carroll's pyramid of corporate social responsibility is a practical framework for managers that incorporates economic, legal, social, and ethical responsibilities.

LO 7.4 ⟩ The Pyramid of Corporate Social Responsibility

One way to view corporate social responsibility is through Carroll's[15] pyramid, which he claims presents the concept such that social responsibility will be accepted by a conscientious businessperson. There are four kinds of social responsibility—economic, legal, ethical, and philanthropic—which can be depicted in a pyramid, as presented in Figure 7.1. Carroll contends that all of these responsibilities have always existed to some degree, but ethical and philanthropic responsibilities have become significant only in recent years.

Economic responsibilities relate to business's provision of goods and services of value to society. Profits result from this activity and are necessary for any other responsibilities to be carried out. It is assumed that corporations will be as profitable as possible, maintain

RESPONSIBILITY

for Ethics **7.4**

Business-Supported Organizations Working on CSR

Several organizations are promoting CSR with support from Canadian businesses:

Canadian Business for Social Responsibility—Founded in 1995, CBSR is a business-led, non-profit CSR consultancy and peer-to-peer learning organization that provides its members with candid counsel and customized advisory services as they formulate powerful business decisions that improve performance and contribute to a better world.

Conference Board of Canada—The Conference Board of Canada is an independent source of insights for business leaders. CSR is considered relevant to business, a key determinant of a corporation's relationship to the world. It conducts and publishes research, and disseminates knowledge to its members by conducting and publishing research and sponsoring conferences and seminars.

Corporate Knights—Founded in 2002, Corporate Knights Inc. is an independent Canadian-based media company that publishes the world's largest-circulation magazine with an explicit focus on corporate responsibility.

Canadian Centre for Ethics and Corporate Policy (EthicsCentre.ca)—EthicsCentre.ca is a registered charity and independent ethics centre formed to champion the application of ethical values in the decision-making process of business and other organizations.

Canadian Centre for Ethics in Public Affairs—CCEPA facilitates critical thinking, public discussion, and research into current ethical challenges in society. It promotes the public good through research into and dissemination of knowledge of ethical issues, which helps generate new insights, provide greater awareness, and heal misunderstandings.

Ethics in Action Awards Society—This non-profit organization is incorporated in British Columbia and governed by a volunteer board of directors. Its main purpose is to recognize leaders and businesses that go beyond the financial bottom line in balancing social principles with profits. The Society partners with the local Better Business Bureau (BBB) to offer the awards. The Atlantic Provinces BBB has a similar award, the Atlantic Business Ethics Awards.

Imagine Canada—Imagine Canada is a non-profit organization that helps charities and non-profit organizations fulfill their missions, champions corporate citizenship, and helps businesses partner in the community. It accomplishes this through research, developing public policy, promoting public awareness, and encouraging businesses to become better corporate citizens.

a strong competitive position, and maintain a high level of operating efficiency. These are responsibilities that the corporation "must do" and the key stakeholders are shareholders, creditors, and consumers.

Society expects business to conform to laws and regulations formulated by governments that act as the ground rules under which business must operate. Corporations are expected

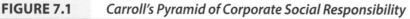

FIGURE 7.1   *Carroll's Pyramid of Corporate Social Responsibility*

Source: Archie Carroll, "The pyramid of corporate social responsibility," p. 42 in *Business Horizons* journal, July/August 1991. Copyright Elsevier & Kelley School of Business, Indiana University.

to pursue profits within the framework of the law, which establishes what are considered fair operations. Society expects that all goods and services and relationships with stakeholders will meet at least minimal legal requirements.

Ethical responsibilities include those activities that are not expected or prohibited by society as economic or legal responsibilities. Standards, norms, or expectations that reflect concern for select stakeholder input are fair, just, or in keeping with their moral rights. Ethics or values may be reflected in laws or regulations, but ethical responsibilities are seen as embracing the emerging values and norms that society expects of business even if not currently required by law. These responsibilities can be thought of as things the corporation "should do." These responsibilities are more difficult for business to deal with as they are often ill-defined or under continual public debate. Ethical responsibilities also involve the fundamental ethical principles of moral philosophy, such as justice, human rights, and utilitarianism. The changing or emerging ethical responsibilities are constantly pushing legal responsibilities to broaden or expand, while at the same time expecting business's ethical behaviour to go beyond mere compliance with laws and regulations.

Philanthropic responsibilities involve being a good corporate citizen and include active participation in acts or programs to promote human welfare or goodwill. Examples are contributions to the arts, charities, and education. Such responsibilities are not expected in an ethical or moral sense, making philanthropy more discretionary or voluntary on the part of business even though society may have such expectations of business. Few in society expect corporations to have these responsibilities, and they can be thought of as things corporations "might do."

Carroll views the pyramid as a basic building-block structure, with economic performance as the foundation. At the same time, business is expected to obey the law, behave ethically, and be a good corporate citizen. Although the responsibilities are portrayed as separate elements, in practice they are not mutually exclusive; however, the separation aids managers to appreciate the different obligations that are in a constant but dynamic tension with one another. For example, there are particular tensions between economic and ethical responsibilities. In summary, Carroll views the total social responsibility of business as involving the simultaneous fulfillment of the four responsibilities—which, stated in pragmatic terms, means that the corporation should strive to make a profit, obey the law, be ethical, and be a good corporate citizen.[16]

Carroll's pyramid represents one of the earliest attempts to integrate the economic and social responsibilities of the corporation. Evidence is accumulating that supports consideration of economic (tangible) and social (intangible) responsibilities:

- Economic (profits) and social responsibilities (ethics) are not mutually exclusive.
- Research shows that economic and social responsibilities are often inseparable.
- Corporations that consider social responsibilities seriously tend to outperform solely profit-seeking corporations.

Resistance to this convergence of economic and social responsibilities does occur. Managers who incorporate social responsibilities into decision making are sometimes labelled as "do-gooders" who are ignoring profits. There are segments of society that suggest there is nothing good about business and that it cannot be ethical or concerned about social issues. It is argued that business should stay out of social responsibilities, as it is often difficult to judge what is right or wrong and managers are not prepared to make such decisions.

An outcome of this shift toward integrating economic, social, and environmental responsibilities has been the emergence of new concepts, several of which are discussed in the following section.

LO 7.5   Contemporary CSR Concepts

Corporate social responsibility is the terminology still widely used to represent business's social responsibilities. However, other terms have appeared that incorporate the consideration of economic responsibilities as well, including corporate sustainability, reputation management, social impact management, triple bottom line (TBL), and corporate citizenship. The first four terms will be briefly described here; corporate citizenship is a more prominent term and will be discussed in detail in the following section.

Corporate Sustainability

> **Corporate sustainability (CS)** Corporate activities demonstrating the inclusion of social and environmental as well as economic responsibilities in business operations as they impact all stakeholders.

As with the definition of CSR, academics, consultants, and practitioners have formulated many definitions of corporate sustainability, some of which are similar to those for CSR. **Corporate sustainability (CS)** refers to corporate activities demonstrating the inclusion of social and environmental as well as economic responsibilities in business operations as they impact all stakeholders. Marrewijk identified five levels of CS that are similar to how CSR could be viewed:

- *Compliance-driven CS*—Involves following government regulations and responding to charity and stewardship considerations considered appropriate by society.
- *Profit-driven CS*—Consideration is given to the social, ethical, and environmental aspects of business operations provided they contribute to the financial bottom line.
- *Caring CS*—CS initiatives go beyond legal compliance and profit considerations where economic, social, and environmental concerns are balanced, as it is the right thing to do.

- *Synergistic CS*—Well-balanced and functional solutions are sought that create value in the economic, social, and environmental areas, as it is a winning approach for all stakeholders.

- *Holistic CS*—CS is fully integrated and embedded in every aspect of the corporation's activities, as this is important to the quality and continuation of life on this planet.[17]

Corporate sustainability has been recognized by the financial markets because it creates long-term shareholder value by embracing opportunities and managing risks as the result of economic, social, and environmental developments. This idea is illustrated in Responsibility for Ethics 7.5.

McGraw Hill Education connect Want to learn more about **sustainability**? Go to CONNECT.

RESPONSIBILITY *for Ethics* **7.5**

The Dow Jones Sustainability Indexes

Dow Jones states that corporate sustainability is important to long-term shareholder value, which is achieved by embracing opportunities and management risks from economic, social, and environmental developments. Launched in 1999, the Dow Jones Sustainability Indexes (DJSI) track the financial performance of the leading sustainability-driven companies worldwide. Based on the cooperation of Dow Jones Indexes, STOXX Limited, and SAM Group, the indexes provide asset managers with reliable and objective benchmarks to manage sustainability portfolios. The DJSI family currently includes indexes covering global, European, North American, Asian, and U.S. benchmarks.

The DJSI North America index surveys the 600 largest corporations of which several are Canadian, including Suncor Energy, TransAlta, TransCanada Corp., Royal Bank of Canada, Bank of Nova Scotia, Canadian Imperial Bank of Commerce, and Bombardier Inc. The corporations included in the index vary from year to year.

Source: Dow Jones Sustainability Indexes, http://www.sustainability-index.com/.

Reputation Management

> **Reputation management** Any effort to enhance the corporation's image and good name; in the past, the focus of these efforts was on media and public relations and, to some extent, crisis management.

Reputation management is any effort to enhance the corporation's image and good name. In the past, the focus of these efforts was on media and public relations and, to some extent, crisis management. Today, reputation management is being extended to relations with all stakeholders. Many managers believe that reputation management enhances financial performance, improves competitive positions, and increases public approval of corporate activities, and studies support this view.[18]

A successful process to implement reputation management involves several stages: the identification of a desired perception of the corporation, the recognition of the significance of image with all stakeholders, an awareness of the influence of interactions with stakeholders on the corporation's reputation, and continuous efforts at maintaining relationships with stakeholders.

Reputations take a long time to establish and can be destroyed quickly. As a result, a reputation can be an asset but at times a liability. Managers must understand all the factors that encompass a reputation and be aware of the measures used to differentiate a good reputation from a bad one. Examples are provided by surveys appearing in the media, including the "Canada's Most Respected Corporations" survey in *The Globe and Mail,* sponsored by KPMG and conducted by Ipsos-Reid; the "Canada's Best Managed Companies" survey in the *National Post,* sponsored by Deloitte, CIBC, and the Queen's School of Business; and the "Best Corporate Citizens in Canada" survey by *Corporate Knights: The Magazine for Clean Capitalism.* The purpose in describing these surveys is to establish that public measures assessing a corporation's reputation are available. It also establishes the importance of reputation and the need for managers to consciously monitor it.

connect Want to learn more about *Corporate Knights*? Go to CONNECT.

Social Impact Management

Social impact management Defined by the Aspen Institute as "the field of inquiry at the intersection of business needs and wider societal concerns that reflects and respects the complex interdependency between the two."

One of the main advocates of social impact management is the Aspen Institute. The Institute defines **social impact management** as "the field of inquiry at the intersection of business needs and wider societal concerns that reflects and respects the complex interdependency between the two."[19] This is very much a "business and society" approach, stressing the need for contemporary business to recognize and understand this interdependency if business and the society in which it operates wish to thrive. The Institute argues that this understanding is becoming increasingly important as corporations take on a bigger role and society increases pressure for corporations to address more essential social and environmental concerns.

The approach stresses the intersection of traditional business concerns (i.e., for financial or economic matters) and society's concerns for the consequences of the impact of the corporation (i.e., the social impact of business). Thus, social impact management is two-directional: society's influence on corporations, and the corporations' influence on the social and environmental concerns of society.

The Institute believes that "social impact management, as a way of thinking about business activities, explicitly considers and evaluates three aspects of a business:

1. Purpose: What is the purpose—in both societal and business terms—of a business or business activity?

2. Social Context: Are the legitimate rights and responsibilities of multiple stakeholders considered? Is a proposed strategy evaluated not only in terms of predicted business outcomes, but also in terms of its broader impacts—for example, on quality of life, the wider economy of a region, and security and safety?

3. Metrics: How is performance and profitability measured? What is being counted and what is not being counted? Are impacts and results measured across both short and long term time frames?"[20]

Triple Bottom Line (TBL)

Triple-E (economic, ethical, and environmental) bottom line Evaluates a corporation's performance according to a summary of the economic, social, and environmental value the corporation adds or destroys.

The **triple-E (economic, ethical, and environmental) bottom line** evaluates a corporation's performance according to a summary of the economic, social, and environmental value the corporation adds or destroys. A variation of the term is the triple-P bottom line: people, planet, profit. The narrowest meaning of the term is a framework for measuring and reporting corporate performance against economic, social, and environmental indicators. Recently, a broader meaning has been attributed to the term in that the concept is used to capture a whole set of values, issues, and processes that corporations must address in order to minimize any harm resulting from their value-adding or destroying activities. This includes clarifying the corporation's purpose and taking into consideration all stakeholders. The triple bottom line approach is often the basis for corporate reporting of economic, ethical, and environmental responsibilities. Everyday Ethics 7.1 is an example of TBL at Novex Couriers.

Everyday Ethics

7.1

Triple Bottom Line at Novex Couriers

Novex Couriers, Richmond, B.C., has "gone green" over the past ten years through the use of its hybrid, natural gas, biodiesel, and electric vehicles fleet, which minimizes the company's carbon footprint. The company has a real-time triple bottom line report, known as SEE-IT (Social-Environmental-Economic Integration Tool), available on its Web site.

SEE-IT enables all stakeholders, including employees, clients, suppliers, and the public, to monitor the progress and status of the company's TBL initiatives. The company views SEE-IT as not only a presentation of results but also a way of communication and education about sustainability.

In addition to using emission-reducing vehicles, Novex has several other initiatives in the area of the environment. It is reducing waste and energy in its office, educating through environmental awareness campaigns, and purchasing from sustainable suppliers. It is the first courier service in North America to become carbon neutral.

Novex is engaging its employees by supporting a diversity program, rewarding employees for their personal and organizational performance, and offering a training benefits program. In the community, the company and its employees support and assist in fundraising for a variety of social causes and community events including Big Brothers of Vancouver, Juvenile Diabetes, United Way, breast cancer research, Boys and Girls Clubs of Vancouver, and the Canadian Cancer Society. The company also holds a contest where participants are invited to submit an idea on addressing a social and environmental challenge. The winner receives a monetary prize.

Sources: Novex Couriers, "Sustainability," http:www.novex.c/sustainability; and Novex Couriers, http://www.novex.ca/see-it-how-novex-manages, accessed October 27, 2012.

The triple bottom line approach has been criticized as being of limited value and even misleading. Norman and MacDonald argue that conceptually and practically the approach is not helping the discussion of CSR. According to these scholars, the claims made are difficult to assess and amount to misleading rhetoric. The authors claim that the use of the triple bottom line may be providing a smokescreen behind which corporations can avoid ethical and environmental responsibilities and reporting.[21]

LO 7.6 ▸ Views on Corporate and Business Citizenship

Corporate citizenship Occurs when a corporation demonstrates that it takes into account its complete impact on society and the environment as well as its economic influence.

Corporate citizenship has recently become a commonly used term to describe the role of business in society. The term appears in the academic literature and business media and is used by corporations to describe their activities. Consulting firms promote their version of corporate citizenship and sell services to assist corporations in establishing and describing their citizenship activities. University research centres have been established on the topic, numerous books describe the concept, and there is a *Journal of Corporate Citizenship.*

Despite the common usage of the term, definitions vary. **Corporate citizenship** occurs when a corporation demonstrates that it takes into account its complete impact on society and the environment as well as its economic influence. It concerns the economic, ethical or social, and environmental responsibilities to all stakeholders involved, with consideration given to inputs from various stakeholders and the practices of corporations to develop relationships with stakeholders.

Many justifications for corporate citizenship exist, with one of the most frequently referenced being the "Business Case for Corporate Citizenship" that was posted on the World Economic Forum Web site.[22] According to this report, good corporate citizenship can provide business benefits in eight areas:

XBOXONE

- *Reputation management*—A corporate reputation is built and maintained by fulfilling the expectations of multiple stakeholders.

- *Risk profile and risk management*—Risk is reduced when corporations understand stakeholder concerns.

- *Employee recruitment, motivation, and retention*—Obtaining and keeping employees is made easier for companies known as good corporate citizens.

- *Investor relations and access to capital*—Many investors are interested in non-financial as well as financial performance, and there is a proven link between good corporate citizenship and good financial performance.

- *Learning and innovation*—Corporate citizenship objectives can encourage creativity and innovation.

- *Competitiveness and market positioning*—Increasingly, consumers are inquiring about the corporate citizenship performance of companies and tend to be loyal to those with a good record.

- *Operational efficiency*—A focus on corporate citizenship can lead to direct improvements to the bottom line.

- *Licence to operate*—Companies with a good record of corporate citizenship are given greater leeway when problems occur and are less subject to unfair criticism.

This list illustrates the broad scope of activities and stakeholders that are impacted by corporate citizenship practices, including on a global scale. The report concluded that increasing corporate citizenship was an integral part of good business management. Everyday Ethics 7.2 is an example of how one corporation defines citizenship.

Everyday Ethics   Corporate Citizenship at Imperial Oil
7.2

Many corporations are utilizing the concept of corporate citizenship to outline their relationship with society. Imperial Oil's "Corporate Citizenship Report" contains information such as:
- an outline of the company's approach to corporate citizenship;
- an overview of key citizenship performance data;
- a listing of environmental performance;
- information on a major undertaking, the Kearl oil sands project;
- details of community initiatives including economic development, community investment, stakeholder engagement, and Aboriginal relations;
- a review of safety management and practices;
- a statement on the approach to governance; and
- an evaluation of their corporate citizenship using independent indexes.

Source: Imperial Oil Limited, "2011 corporate citizenship report," http://www.imperialoil.ca/Canada-English/Files/Imperial_Oil_CCR_Report_2011.pdf.

The quantity and diversity of the literature on corporate citizenship makes it difficult to concisely review. The following discussion attempts to organize the views that are held regarding corporate citizenship (inappropriate, limited, equivalent, extended, and business). The final section argues that a more appropriate term is "business citizenship."

The Inappropriate View

Many have posed the questions, "Can the corporation be a citizen?" and "Is a corporate citizen the same as an individual citizen?" The nature of citizenship has its roots in political theory, philosophy, law, sociology, and psychology and is a complex phenomenon that has been discussed and debated for centuries. Individual citizenship involves the relationship of the person to the state, the rights and duties of citizens, and the national and cultural identity involved.[23]

Any attempt to extend the individual's role as a citizen to that of a corporation is thought by many to be completely inappropriate. A corporation is not an individual citizen, as it does not possess the attributes or characteristics of a person. Any attempt to project the qualities of a person to the corporation is false and meaningless. Given the prominence of corporate citizenship in the academic and practitioner spheres, this view is not widely held, although it does have its advocates.

The Limited, Equivalent, and Extended Views

Matten and Crane[24] described three views of corporate citizenship: limited, equivalent, and extended. These views will form the categories of how corporate citizenship is considered. These three views are summarized in Table 7.4, which is followed by an explanation of why "corporate" citizenship would be more appropriately viewed as "business" citizenship.

TABLE 7.4	*Three Views of Corporate Citizenship*	
Limited	**Equivalent**	**Extended**
Corporate giving or philanthropic responsibility was the focus	Citizenship is defined as what society expects are responsibilities of business	Citizenship is defined as a set of individual, social, civil, and political rights
Reasoning is that something should be given back to the community	Emphasis on sustainability, the stewardship role of business, and the stakeholder approach	Social rights provide the individual with the freedom to participate in society, for example the right to education
Considered to be enlightened self-interest	Considered to be rebranding or re-launching existing ideas and concepts of business–society relations	Civil rights provide freedom from abuses and interference by third parties, for example the right to own property
		Political rights extend beyond the protection of the individual and involve the individual's participation in society, for example the rights to hold office and to vote

Source: Compiled based on Dirk Matten and Andrew Crane, "Corporate citizenship: Towards an extended theoretical conceptualization," *Academy of Management Review* 30, No. 1 (2005): 168–170.

Approach to Corporate Citizenship

Building on the "extended" view that citizenship is based on the shared understanding of basic social, civil, and political rights, a different way of considering corporate citizenship emerges. However, it is questionable whether social and political rights can be regarded as rights of the corporation. Instead, the corporations could be viewed as powerful actors that have a responsibility to respect individual rights.

Globalization has shifted responsibility for protecting citizenship rights away from governments, as seen by the activism of non-governmental organizations (NGOs). Instead of seeking from governments a solution to corporate misdeeds, NGOs pressure corporations directly or indirectly through stakeholders such as consumers and the media. The result is that many social changes are taking place beyond the power and influence of the nation-state. The absence of government initiatives has caused a gap in providing these rights, and corporations are increasingly filling this gap as they are principal actors in society and drivers of globalization.

Matten and Crane[25] cited some examples of change that have resulted as governments ceased to be the only guarantor of citizenship. There are areas where governments cease to administer citizenship rights, and corporations may step in or their role may become more pronounced, as illustrated in privatization and welfare reform. Another occurs where governments have not yet administered citizenship, for example in the regulation of sweatshop working conditions. Lastly, there are areas where the administration of citizenship rights may be beyond the nation-state or government, for example the creation of transnational institutions and global codes of conduct.

In this context, corporate citizenship is described as the role the corporation plays in administering citizenship rights for individuals, moving away from considering the corporation a citizen toward a view where the corporation administers some rights. Corporations would take on this role for altruistic, enlightened self-interest and pure self-interest motivations. This extended role of the corporation is represented in the following diagram:

Social role of the corporation in administering citizenship rights

↓

Social rights: The corporation as a *provider*

+

Civil rights: The corporation as an *enabler*

+

Political rights: The corporation as a *channel*[26]

This view describes the role of the corporation as being involved with administering citizenship rights for individuals rather than as a "citizen" as such. Matten and Crane's summary argument is that:

> We have identified citizenship as an arena where two parties are involved: (1) the state (originally) as the party administering rights of citizenship and (2) the private citizen as the receiver of those rights. We have then argued that corporations have become major actors in this arena. Our extended conceptualization locates CC [corporate citizenship] in the administration of citizenship rights, which, in the liberal view, is clearly an aspect of citizenship. Of course, this does not mean that corporations "are" citizens or that they "have" citizenship, but they are certainly active in citizenship behaviors.[27]

Corporate citizenship is considered at a different level; that is, not at the same level as for a private citizen. This view of corporate citizenship implies that corporations have replaced some of the functions of government as they administer citizenship. Corporations enter this different level on a discretionary or voluntary basis and accountability becomes an issue. The adequacy of such accountability will be discussed later.

The Business View

Wood and Logsdon[28] argue that the term "business citizenship" may better incorporate the broader perspective on business rights and duties, stakeholder relationships, and responses to the opportunities and challenges that accompany the global socio-economy of the twenty-first century. **Business citizenship** includes the responsibilities of corporate citizenship on a local and national basis and extends it to a global or universal scope.

The authors explain the status of citizenship for individuals and then compare this reasoning to the business organization or the corporation. Thus, the individual as citizen is local, community, and national in scope and the relationship of the individual is with the state and involves rights and duties. Today, the individual as citizen is global or universal in scope and concerned with common humanity, interdependence, and universalism, which are less grounded on fixed rules or laws.

Further, the corporation as citizen can be considered as either a "corporate" citizen or a "business" citizen. As a corporate citizen, corporations are a responsible player in local environments, involved with volunteerism, charity, and rights and duties in and for the community. Today, thinking in terms of being a corporate citizen associated with corporate–community relations may be too narrow to represent the depth and variety of business–society relationships. Thus, a "business citizen" would be responsible not only for local actions—that is, concerned with organizations' rights and societies within and across national and/or cultural borders—but also for global or universal actions. Wood and Logsdon provide the rationale for moving from individual citizenship to corporate citizenship by outlining the similarities and differences, and then moving the corporate citizen on a local, community, and national scope to the global or universal scope.[29]

The following quotation summarizes Wood and Logsdon's argument for using "business" instead of "corporate" citizenship:

> *"Business citizenship," . . ., provides an overarching rationale for corporate social performance, for the study of ethics in business, for stakeholder theory and issues management, for business-government relations and for concerns over major social, political and human issues such as labour rights and environmental protection. Business citizenship can be one of the conceptual balance beams of the long-standing paradox of self-interest and other interest, of individual versus collective outcomes.*[30]

This presentation has provided background on the views of corporate and business citizenship in the literature and in practice. Currently, the more widely accepted term is corporate citizenship, but the use of business citizenship is considered more appropriate as it avoids the problematic discussion of whether or not the corporation is a citizen. It is also more inclusive as it incorporates the complete business system, including the global nature of business.

LO 7.7 The VBA Model: An Integration of CSR Concepts

Schwartz and Carroll developed a model of the business and society field that integrated and unified five frameworks in common usage by academics and managers: corporate social responsibility (CSR), business ethics (BE), stakeholder management (SM), sustainability (SUS), and corporate citizenship (CC). They named their framework the VBA model and believed that it would reduce the confusion resulting from the existence of the various frameworks. Three core concepts were identified as being common, to some degree, in all frameworks: value, balance, and accountability.[31]

The generation of value to business and society was found to be a fundamental element of all the frameworks. Value results "when business meets society's needs by producing goods and services in an efficient manner while avoiding unnecessary negative externalities."[32] A degree of balance occurs when some effort is made in "addressing and appropriately responding to potentially conflicting stakeholder interests and/or moral standards." Other similar concepts are respect, weigh, trade-off, and satisfy.[33] Accountability is present in all frameworks, meaning that while attempting to fulfill its economic, legal, and ethical responsibilities, business "must acknowledge responsibility for [its] actions and decisions and take steps to rectify failure and prevent them from happening again in the future."[34] The authors note that the three core concepts receive different emphasis in the frameworks, but they are present to some degree.

The VBA model integrating the frameworks is represented by the equation:

$$\text{Value} + \text{Balance} + \text{Accountability} = \text{Proper Role of Business in Society}$$

Schwartz and Carroll set forth the following normative proposition relating to their VBA model:

> *All organizations and individuals operating within a business context have a responsibility (CSR) as good corporate citizens (CC) to (a) contribute to sustainable societal value and (SUS), (b) appropriately balance stakeholder interests (SM), including shareholders or owners and/or moral standards (BE), while (c) demonstrating sufficient accountability.*[35]

The integration of the five frameworks and three core concepts in the VBA model is portrayed in Figure 7.2. The authors argue that by focusing on three core elements of the five

FIGURE 7.2 *The VBA Model: Five Business and Society Frameworks and Their Three Core Concepts*

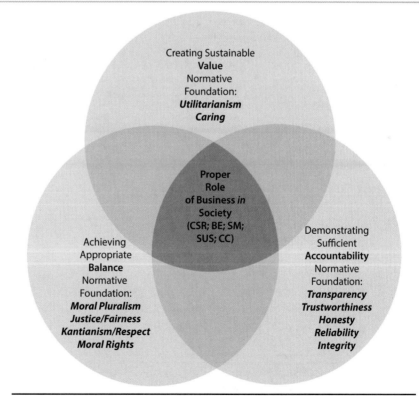

Note: VBA = value, balance, accountability; CSR = corporate social responsibility; BE = business ethics; SM = stakeholder management; SUS = sustainability; CC = corporate citizenship.

Source: Mark S. Schwartz and Archie B. Carroll, "Integrating and Unifying Competing and Complementary Frameworks: The Search For a Common Core in the Business and Society Field," *Business and Society,* Volume 47, Number 2, June 2008, 175.

frameworks, the VBA model integrates the shareholder theory and emphasizes the importance of others in managerial decision making while maintaining relevance for managers and ensuring a long-term global prospective.

The VBA model clarifies the relationships among the various frameworks of corporate social responsibility presented in this chapter. In doing so, the confusion over the terminology should be reduced. The theoretical basis for social responsibility has been outlined, and the following chapters will discuss approaches used by corporations to implement or apply it and the methodologies used to evaluate it.

connect | Want to learn more about **CSR jobs**? Go to CONNECT.

Your advice to Louis . . .

You can understand why Louis and his boss were confused! Corporate social responsibility academics or practitioners have not reached a consensus on the definitive meaning of various terms and concepts. As a result, to some the concepts of CSR and sustainability mean the same thing, while others distinguish between them. The only thing Louis and his boss can do is attempt to understand how people using the terms describe the concepts. Likewise, when they formulate social responsibility plans, policies, or programs for their company, they should describe their interpretation of the concepts used.

SUMMARY

- Rather than provide one definition of social responsibility, the chapter identifies the elements found in the majority of definitions. Corporate social responsibility is a reflection of the fact that business and society are interwoven and can be expressed in terms of three principles: legitimacy, public responsibility, and managerial discretion. The principle of legitimacy refers to society's granting of legitimacy and authority to business, along with business's appropriate use of that power; the principle of public responsibility means business is responsible for outcomes related to its areas of involvement with society; and the principle of managerial discretion refers to managers as moral actors who are obligated to exercise such discretion as is available to them to achieve socially responsible outcomes. (LO 7.1)

- The debate as to whether social responsibility is an appropriate concept is summarized in arguments for and against corporate social involvement. (LO 7.2)

- These arguments are reflected in Klonoski's summary of social responsibility theories, categorized according to three alternative views of the corporation as amoral, personal, and social. The arguments and theories are presented not to provide a definitive answer to the question of corporate social responsibility but to review the background to the debate. In fact, the debate has not been resolved to date, as evidenced by the critique of CSR in a leading business magazine. (LO 7.3)

- A pyramid of corporate social responsibilities is presented, based on economic, legal, ethical, and philanthropic responsibilities. A hierarchy of responsibilities exists; economic and legal obligations are primary and basic. In recent years, the ethical and philanthropic responsibilities have received more attention. (LO 7.4)

- Social responsibility has evolved and today other terminology is being used to describe the concept, including *corporate sustainability, reputation management, social impact management, triple bottom line*, and *corporate citizenship*. Definitions are provided so that a distinction can be made among the terms. (LO 7.5)

- Corporate citizenship is another term used interchangeably with CSR. It is an inclusive term to capture the economic, social, and environmental responsibilities of the corporation and relies on stakeholder theory. As with CSR various interpretations are given to the term, and it is argued that the term *business citizenship* would be even more inclusive as it is global or universal in scope. (LO 7.6)

- The VBA model is an attempt at unifying and integrating the various frameworks within CSR around three core concepts: value, balance, and accountability. This model reduces the confusion resulting from the various terminology used in the business and society and CSR field. (LO 7.7)

KEY TERMS

Corporate social responsibility (CSR)	Social impact management	Corporate citizenship
Corporate sustainability (CS)	Triple-E (economic, ethical, and	Business citizenship
Reputation management	environmental) bottom line	

CRITICAL THINKING AND DISCUSSION QUESTIONS

1. Why should corporations and their management be concerned with corporate social responsibility?

2. Distinguish among Wood's three principles of corporate responsibility: legitimacy, public responsibility, and managerial discretion.

3. Why do some corporations and their management oppose corporate social responsibility?

4. Is there any legitimacy to the argument put forth by Milton Friedman and *The Economist*'s article on corporate social responsibility?

5. Social responsibility is interpreted in many ways. State your understanding of corporate social responsibility.

6. List the 10 stakeholders you think have the greatest influence on a corporation's social responsibility.

7. Can the corporation have a conscience?

8. Do you agree that "economic responsibilities" are a component of corporate social responsibility?

9. What does a corporation have to do to have a "good" reputation?

10. Is the corporation a "citizen" of society?

CASES

7.1   *Would You Like to Donate . . . ?*

Suzanne Valentine had been noticing an increasing number of businesses asking their customers to donate to charities when they make a purchase. One example was the Shoppers Drug Mart "Tree of Life" campaign, which encourages customers to purchase a leaf for $1, a maple leaf for $5, or an apple for $50. All proceeds go directly to the women's health charity organization chosen by the Associate-owner of that particular store. In 2009, 249 community women's health charities benefited from the campaign.

Loblaws has a similar approach. Customers are asked to contribute to charity at the checkout through the "Give a Little Help a Lot" campaign. The Canada Post Foundation for Mental Health supports mental health organizations through sales of special commemorative postage stamp booklets and donations directly at post office sales counters.

Suzanne was directly affected by this type of corporate social responsibility fundraising. She worked part-time as a cashier at her neighbourhood grocery store where the owner established a donation scheme, "Pennies for Pets." The owner was a strong supporter of animal causes and the donations were to support the local animal shelter. All cashiers were instructed to ask customers if they wanted to donate $1 or $2 to the shelter.

Suzanne followed instructions but she had several reservations about the scheme. She felt awkward asking customers for the donation, particularly those who looked like they could not afford it. Some customers might be intimidated by the request and she did not believe that they should be put on the spot to say yes or no. Some customers may not wish to support this particular charity. As well, she was not convinced that the particular shelter deserved funding, as there had been some articles in the media about its poor management and treatment of animals. Lastly, she was not sure how much of the money collected was forwarded to the charity, and whether or not the owner matched the customer donations.

Questions

1. **What are the ethical implications in this example of corporate social responsibility?**

2. **What information should the company provide to Suzanne and its customers?**

3. **Carroll has identified four corporate social responsibilities: economic, legal, ethical, and philanthropic. Which responsibilities are involved in "Pennies for Pets" or similar fundraising schemes?**

4. **How should Suzanne resolve her personal ethical dilemma?**

Sources: Shoppers Drug Mart Inc., "Community investment, 2009 Tree of Life campaign," http://www.shoppersdrugmart.ca/english/corporate_information/about_us/community_investment/local_community_support/tree_of_life.html; and Canada Post, "Canada Post Foundation for Mental Health," http://www.canadapost.ca/cpo/mc/aboutus/cpfoundation/default.jsf.

7.2   *Magna's "The Next Great Prime Minister" Award Competition*

Magna International Inc. is the most diversified automotive supplier in the world; it designs and produces parts and components in 22 countries on four continents. The company was started in 1957 by Frank Stronach in a Toronto garage as a one-man tool and die shop called Multimatic. First-year sales were C$13,000,

and in 2005 total sales were US$22.8 billion with a net income of US$636 million.

Stronach is still the Chairman of the corporation and is active in its management, with a special interest in corporate social responsibility. Magna's Corporate Constitution is considered a very progressive statement of how a corporation will conduct its business. The Constitution contains a provision that Magna will allocate a maximum of two percent of pre-tax profits to support charitable and non-profit organizations in health, culture, education, sports, and politics.

Of particular interest to Stronach is the "Next Great Prime Minister" competition, which he originated in 1995. Up until 2004, young Canadians were asked to prepare essays describing their vision for Canada. The competition now requires young persons aged 18 to 25 to submit videotapes of three- to five-minute speeches outlining what they would do if they were prime minister. The submissions of the top five contestants are aired on a one-hour televised final, where finalists participate in challenges and debates to determine the winner. The winner receives a prize of $50,000 and a six-month paid internship to a maximum compensation of

$30,000 equally split among corporate, government, and non-governmental organizations. The remaining four contenders receive $5,000 and a three-month internship to a maximum compensation of $9,000 equally divided among the three employment sectors.

Questions

1. **What are the ethical implications in this example of corporate social responsibility?**

2. **Does the sponsorship of this competition make Magna a good corporate citizen? Why or why not?**

3. **Carroll has identified four corporate social responsibilities: economic, legal, ethical, and philanthropic. Which responsibilities are involved in the "Next Great Prime Minister" award competition?**

Sources: Based on Magna International Inc., http://www.magnaint.com/magna/en/; and The Next Great Prime Minister, http://www.thenextgreatprimeminister.ca/Home/.

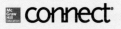 For more information on the resources available from McGraw-Hill Ryerson, go to www.mcgrawhill.ca/he/solutions.

CHAPTER 8
Corporate Social Responsibility: In Practice

What would you do if . . . ?

Walter Zuberek once read a quote from Warren Buffett: "Giving money away is easy. Giving money away well is fiendishly difficult." He was learning just what Buffett meant.

Walter has just stepped down as CEO of York and Smith Limited after being associated with the company for 50 years. Walter came to Canada from Europe in the 1950s and went to work as an engineer for a small construction company known as York Construction. Over the years, the company expanded and acquired a building materials company from the Smith family, which led to the name change to York and Smith. Walter started as a site foreman, but steadily rose in the company as the owners recognized his managerial abilities. In the mid-1960s, the owners decided to sell the business and Walter was able to purchase it with financial assistance from a venture capitalist.

York and Smith grew into a $200 million a year business that manufactured and distributed building products for North American construction markets. The company served four construction market sectors: residential (both new construction and renovations), non-residential, agricultural and industrial storage, and infrastructure. The company believed in operating in a socially and ethically responsible manner and in providing the broadest possible opportunity for personal and professional development for its employees. The company also believed in giving back to the community and supported hospital and university capital fund campaigns, literacy programs, sports programs for the disabled, and school lunch programs.

Walter's two sons now run the business, but Walter provides some oversight as chair of the board of directors. Because he is not as closely associated with the day-to-day operations, Walter has time to pay more attention to things that are of interest to him. He considers himself fortunate to have worked for York and Smith and to have been able to acquire the business. He is grateful for the opportunities provided in Canada, and appreciates the support he has received from various stakeholders over the years.

York and Smith Limited is experiencing good financial returns, with some discretionary funds available for social responsibility endeavours. Walter himself has accumulated a small fortune and wonders what to do with the money beyond leaving some to family members. He thought maybe it was appropriate to give something back to society.

Now that Walter is retired, a reassessment of the company's social contributions would be a good job for him, and at the same time he could investigate what he could do with his fortune. He wants to make sure the company's—and his—contributions to society are used in the most effective and efficient manner. This is a challenge, as Charity Intelligence Canada points out. There are issues about which charities to select, how the charities will spend the donation, and what the charities will achieve. Alternatively, Walter could set up a new charity for a cause that he and his family support.

What is your advice to Walter?

This chapter describes the various forms or approaches to practising or implementing corporate social responsibility (CSR) or corporate sustainability (CS) in corporations. Corporate social responsibility and the related concepts described in Chapter 7 have resulted in a range of activities. Large corporations have CSR or equivalent departments, with staff trained in the area that oversees the implementation of CSR initiatives. Corporate Web sites often contain details of all CSR activities. Professional associations provide advice to corporations, as do various newsletters. In addition, numerous consultant services are available to assist with CSR activities.

Figure 8.1 illustrates a range of approaches to social responsibility practices; these approaches are described in this chapter. Corporations have moved from expressing CSR through corporate philanthropy in the form of donations to other approaches involving some form of direct community involvement or investment. Corporate giving, or donations, is the most traditional approach and is still practised. Many corporations now view writing a cheque to be insufficient or inappropriate to demonstrate their commitment to the community.

FIGURE 8.1   *Approaches to Corporate Social Responsibility*

Corporations are now involved in voluntarism programs and corporate sponsorship in addition to donations. Recently, as corporations seek more effective approaches to contributing to the community, two forms of CSR have emerged: social venture philanthropy and social enterprise. Today, many corporations are involved in more than one of these approaches to CSR, with corporate philanthropy being the most common. In addition, the final section of this chapter will discuss CSR in small business as a separate topic. It should be noted that the corporation's CSR toward the environment is not dealt with in this chapter but is the focus in Chapter 14.

LO 8.1   The Responses to Corporate Social Responsibility

Despite the widespread acceptance and practise of CSR, business enterprises are responding to it in different ways. Table 8.1 identifies business responses to CSR, beginning with high acceptance and declining to little or none.

TABLE 8.1   *Responses to CSR*

Response	Explanation	Acceptance of CSR
Social enterprise—social return	Organizations that operate with a social mission without the intention of operating to make profits with all earnings committed to social causes or projects. Example: Habitat for Humanity, Goodwill	High
Social enterprise—mixed return	Organizations that operate with a social mission but with the intention of making a profit. "Doing well by doing good" (social paradigm). A portion of profits are committed to social causes or projects with the remainder reinvested or returned to owners. Examples: Whole Foods Market Inc. and Value Village	High
CSR recognition or embracers	CSR and sustainability placed high on corporate agenda. Often are larger corporations and traded on stock exchanges. Corporate giving and citizenship are involved. Publish "social reports" of their initiatives. "Doing good by doing well" (economic paradigm).	Above average
Cautious CSR adaptors	Recognize CSR and sustainability but focus on savings from environmental projects, energy cost reductions, material efficiency, and risk reduction.	Some recognition
Tokenism or greenwashing	Corporations are not serious about CSR, but believe they should respond. Might be forced into initiatives by non-governmental organizations (NGOs), the media, or competitors. NGOs allege many multi-national corporations are responding this way.	Low commitment
Amoral	Corporations, and their managers, simply ignore CSR, intentionally or unintentionally. Difficult to identify and measure numbers.	Very little, by chance or legal requirement
Anti-CSR	As CSR is widely accepted and practised, it is unlikely that these corporations will identify themselves as being anti-CSR. Difficult to identify numbers.	Very little, most likely as required by law
Unknown	Businesses about which not much is known regarding CSR initiatives, including small business enterprises and privately held companies. There is a modest literature on CSR in these types of enterprises.	Low, but not documented

The businesses most committed to CSR are social enterprises, which will be defined in a later section. Such businesses practise the *social paradigm,* which can be described as "Doing well by doing good." This means that the corporation will undertake socially desirable activities that will result in its doing well economically. There appear to be an increasing number of businesses responding to CSR in this manner. This approach is the highest level of CSR acceptance.

Many businesses are recognizing CSR as an essential aspect of management. Usually, these businesses audit their activities and report them to relevant stakeholders. This response is based on the *economic paradigm,* which can be described as "Doing good by doing well." This means that the corporation will do well economically and then undertake to do good socially.

The tokenism response is the one alleged by some non-governmental organizations (NGOs) when they evaluate CSR programs. An example is the report published by Christian Aid, an agency of churches in the United Kingdom and Ireland, entitled *Behind the Mask: The Real Face of Corporate Social Responsibility.* This report challenges the effectiveness of CSR efforts by multinational companies. It claims to have revealed the true face of CSR—a false image and public relations. The following quotation is an illustration of the argument:

> *In simple terms, companies make loud, public commitments to principles of ethical behaviour and undertake "good works" in the communities in which they operate. It sounds and looks like a modern version of selfless philanthropy and no doubt in many individual cases is motivated by a genuine wish to help and has led to some benefits. What's different is that companies frequently use such initiatives to defend operations or ways of working which come in for public criticism.[1]*

An amoral response is illustrated by several views of CSR. Managers believe that a corporation has no or very little social responsibility, or that the corporation is an autonomous entity and not the creation of society. Others believe that the corporation is socially responsible only within the limits of a prior contractual agreement with shareholders. Finally, the traditional shareholder model argues that corporations are not ethically required to be socially responsible and their only responsibility is to maximize profits. This view is closely related to the fourth response, anti-CSR. Since CSR is a widely accepted conventional wisdom, those opposing it are unlikely to be vocal.

Lastly, the CSR response "unknown" has not been widely studied. Two examples are privately held corporations and small businesses. Small business will be discussed later in the chapter.

Not responding to society's demands for CSR can be risky. Several of these risks are listed in Table 8.2, emphasizing the need for corporations to plan their CSR initiatives.

When corporations are involved with CSR in some manner, there is a need to establish a planning process if the effort is to be most effective. To start with, there must be commitment from top management, including the board of directors. Without this commitment, any CSR efforts are unlikely to be as successful as they might be. Small as well as large businesses can plan for CSR although there is media coverage of large corporation activities. CSR also involves many stakeholders both internal and external to the corporation that should be involved in the process. The following sections describe some of the CSR approaches that are being undertaken by businesses.

TABLE 8.2	*Risks of Not Practising CSR*

The risks associated with not practising CSR include:

Damaged reputation

- Negative media coverage
- Consumer boycotts
- Lost sales and revenues
- Labour disruptions
- Blockages, attacks against assets
- Decrease in share value
- More onerous financing or insurance terms

Increased spending to remedy past damage for core activities

- Increased shareholder activism
- Failure to attract and retain quality employees
- Civil lawsuits, including class action initiatives
- Criminal and regulatory prosecution

Suspended operating permits

- Liability for the conduct of subsidiaries and arm's-length affiliates, for example suppliers
- Increased and onerous government regulation

Source: Compiled from the December 2003 issue of Canadian Business for Social Responsibility's *Good Company Newsletter,* and other sources.

LO 8.2 ▸ Corporate Philanthropy

Corporate philanthropy The effort of business to contribute to society socially; manifested by donations of money or goods and services in kind, voluntarism (where corporate employees work for social causes), and sponsorship of events that contribute to society.

Corporate philanthropy is the effort of business to contribute to society socially and is manifested by donations of money or goods and services in kind; voluntarism, where corporate employees work for social causes; and sponsorship of events that contribute to society. Also referred to as corporate giving, philanthropy takes many forms. Three of these forms are discussed here: corporate giving, or the making of donations; support for employee voluntarism; and sponsorship of social events and causes.

Donations

Canadian business corporations donate to a variety of causes and organizations, including health and welfare agencies, educational institutions, community services, service clubs, civic projects, arts and culture groups, athletic organizations, and environmental groups. Some corporations spread contributions across a variety of causes, while others are more focused in their giving. In addition to the donation of money, corporate giving or philanthropy can involve the donation of goods and services. Imagine Canada gives some idea of the magnitude of corporate giving; more than $2.3 billion was given in charitable donations by corporations that claimed it on their tax returns.[2] The industries that gave the most were finance and insurance, and manufacturing. The majority of the support went to three non-profit sectors: sports and recreation; grant making, fundraising, and voluntarism; and arts and culture.

Most Canadians believe corporations have a responsibility to provide support to charities and non-profit organizations, as illustrated in Everyday Ethics 8.1. This section provides arguments for and against corporate giving, examines how the decision to donate is made, and indicates trends in corporate giving.

Everyday Ethics
8.1

Corporate Donations: Cameco Corporation

Cameco is one of the world's largest uranium producers, accounting for 16 percent of world production from its mines in Canada and the United States. Its target is to donate 1 percent of after-tax net earnings. The corporation supports dozens of community projects, large and small, and believes that it makes a difference. Although Cameco's community investment takes several forms, the list below identifies the focuses on its donations to the community.

- *Youth*—Supports youth projects from preschool to high school.
- *Education and Literacy*—Provides support because education and literacy benefit society.
- *Health and Wellness*—Supports projects that improve access to health services.
- *Community Development*—Helps to build sustainable communities by contributing to their prosperity and quality of life.

Source: Cameco Corporation, "Community investment," http://www.cameco.com/responsibility/community_investment/, accessed November 1, 2012.

Arguments For and Against Corporate Giving

The arguments for and against corporate giving are similar to those for social responsibility. Corporate giving is a widely used and acceptable approach to express social responsibility to the community and to show that business is not just concerned with society as a market for its good and services. The act of corporate giving promotes an image of good citizenship and creates goodwill. This is important for the acceptance of business by society either in terms of legitimacy or a social licence to operate. Most businesspersons recognize that the volunteer sector provides some services very efficiently, and that even business enterprises benefit from such services—as, for example, when employees belong to Alcoholics Anonymous.

Corporations receive significant benefits from a corporate community investment program in terms of employee commitment, corporate reputation, marketing visibility, and relationships with customers, suppliers, neighbours, and governments. It is argued that a corporation's success is tightly linked with economic health and social conditions in the community in which it operates, and thus a corporation should invest in the organizations that underpin community vitality.

Not everyone accepts the argument that business should be involved with corporate giving. It is argued that the funds given actually belong to shareholders, and it is presumptuous first for management to make the decision to give the funds, and then to choose particular recipients. Some claim that business corporations should not become involved with social welfare because that is the job of governments. Support for social causes could give business even more power in society at a time when many feel that it already has too much. By supporting any cause or charitable organization the corporation might become accountable for the actions taken by the charity, or adverse publicity could damage the corporation's image or reputation. Usually there are no guidelines, no standards to measure against, and no evaluation process for making decisions and monitoring corporate giving. The benefits of corporate giving are seldom measurable or directly related to the corporation.

Despite the arguments against corporate giving, most businesses, including small ones, are involved with corporate giving in some way.

Making Corporate Giving Decisions

In earlier times, corporate giving decisions were made by individual executives who often were members of the family at the helm of a corporation—the Eatons, Woodwards, Burtons, Molsons, and Labatts. This is still the case today as many wealthy individuals contribute large amounts to society, exemplified by the "Giving Pledge" challenge described in Everyday Ethics 8.2.

Everyday Ethics

8.2

The Giving Pledge

Bill Gates and Warren Buffett issued a "Giving Pledge" challenge to billionaires in June 2010, urging them to give away more than half of their fortunes. By August 4, 2010, 40 U.S. billionaires had pledged US$160 billion. The Giving Pledge Web site states:

> *The Giving Pledge is an effort to invite the wealthiest individuals and families in America to commit to giving the majority of their wealth to the philanthropic causes and charitable organizations of their choice either during their lifetime or after their death.*

Over 100 billionaires have made pledges, available for perusal on Givingpledge .org. Canadians who have participated include Jeff Skoll (born in Montreal and the first president of eBay) and Charles and Edgar Bronfman (whose family established Seagrams).

Domestic and international causes will receive funding. Each donor decides how his or her money is to be allocated and there is no central agency to distribute the funds. The process will work on an honour system; that is, the pledge is non-binding and represents a moral commitment rather than a legal one. The donors will meet once a year to review progress. The approach has been criticized as the lack of collaboration and coordination may result in duplication of effort. This is countered by the view that individual decision making is preferred over a groupthink approach that may result from a centralized process. A concern has been expressed that most of the funds will go to universities, colleges, medical centres, and arts and culture organizations instead of focusing on the poor or minorities.

Source: The Giving Pledge Web site at http://givingpledge.org; accessed November 1, 2012. © 2010–2013 Giving Pledge LLC and its licensors and suppliers.

connect   Want to learn more about **the Giving Pledge**? Go to CONNECT.

On the other hand, many large corporations make donation decisions by committee consensus where the process is more complicated. In the most formalized processes, decisions relating to corporate giving are made in head offices by chief executives and boards of directors with assistance from a committee. The first decision relates to the donations budget. Budgets are set as a percentage of expected pre-tax profit, increased an arbitrary amount from the previous year, set in relation to industry norms or in comparison to peers, or set upon a formula based on number of employees. Assistance is available from several organizations, including the ones listed in Responsibility for Ethics 8.1. These organizations provide advice to individual executives and corporations including evaluations of a charity's efficiency and use of funds.

RESPONSIBILITY
for Ethics **8.1**

Organizations Assisting in Corporate Philanthropy

Organizations outside the corporation that provide advice on corporate giving or donations include:

Imagine Canada (formerly the Canadian Centre for Philanthropy)—Established in 1980, the centre's mission is to promote the generous application of charitable time and funds, and to strengthen the philanthropic community of Canada through research and training. The centre initiated the IMAGINE program, a Canada-wide corporate and individual awareness program, to increase support for charitable non-profit organizations.

MoneySense—Each year this magazine and Web site evaluates the 100 largest charities in Canada on efficiency and where the money is spent.

Charity Intelligence Canada—This organization provides advice to donors and helps them identify which charities should receive money, how the donations are spent, and what the charities achieve.

Better Business Bureau (BBB) Canada—Corporations wishing to donate can check out charities to ascertain whether they comply with the BBB's Wise Giving Alliance *Charitable Accountability Standards*. Information provided about the charity includes how it is governed, how the money is spent, the truthfulness of their representatives, and their willingness to disclose information to the public.

Some corporations carefully establish the objectives for giving so that some guidelines are available to ascertain how much money is given and to whom. Criteria for evaluating requests are formulated and used by in-house staff or consultants in making decisions. Some givers perform cost–benefit analyses of the grant, while others require that social performance programs be proactive. Grants given in one year are evaluated prior to another grant being made. Some corporate givers, such as Imperial Oil Ltd. and John Labatt Ltd., have managers to supervise the process. Despite the formalization suggested above, the single most important influence in the decision-making process is still often the chair of the board or the chief executive officer (CEO).

Either through formal or ad hoc processes, decisions are made to fund—or to reject—requests. A request is typically rejected when policy excludes a particular type of project or charity; there are not enough funds; a donation has already been made to an organization with parallel services; the organization is located outside the corporation's community; there is no Canada Revenue Agency registration number; there are inadequate financial statements; no new approaches are being accepted; the size of the request is too large; or the corporation receives too many requests.

Another form of rejection is the decision to cease giving to a particular organization. Such a decision may have serious consequences, including the failure of the organization. Many causes are rejected because they are somehow controversial. For example, many corporations are reluctant to support Planned Parenthood organizations because of possible backlash from pro-life groups. There is without doubt a tendency to seek out "safe" causes on the part of those who make the donating decision.

Trends and Concerns in Corporate Giving

A number of trends and concerns have occurred that have impacted upon corporate giving. Large requests from institutions such as universities and hospitals have resulted in a higher portion of the donation budget being committed to five-year programs. This doesn't leave much opportunity to fund new causes or groups.

Business corporations in Canada are supporting a wide variety of charities, and this support has become much more important as government grants have declined. For those corporations that donate on a regular basis, philanthropy is a responsibility, a part of the cost of doing business. For other corporations, it is a frill. Some corporations support charities while they are experiencing good financial performance but in economic downturns or recessions reduce or stop corporate giving. It appears that some corporations are willing to give, but are becoming more selective and will have to be convinced to part with their money.

Some businesses or their owners choose to set up charitable foundations to handle corporate philanthropy. A **charitable foundation** is defined as a corporation or trust that is constituted and operated exclusively for charitable purposes. They are established by families of successful entrepreneurs, corporations, communities, special interest groups such as schools and hospitals, and governments. There are about 3,000 grant-making foundations in Canada that donate about $1.3 billion to a wide variety of causes including education, health, environment, community development, and arts and culture (see the examples provided in Everyday Ethics 8.3).

> **Charitable foundation** A corporation or trust that is constituted and operated exclusively for charitable purposes.

Everyday Ethics
8.3

Philanthropy through Charitable Foundations

Philanthropic Foundations Canada (PFC) is a national membership organization for Canada's independent grant-making foundations and is a registered charity. There are about 3,000 private foundations in Canada that give away about $1.5 billion per year. Examples of foundations established by businesspersons are:

- The J.W. McConnell Family Foundation (various businesses including newspapers): The Foundation is a private family foundation funding programs to foster a more inclusive, sustainable, and resilient society. Its grants are intended to alleviate poverty and support hospitals and other charities.
- The Birks Family Foundation (jewellery retailing): The mission of the Birks Family Foundation is to contribute to a higher standard of living and quality of life for all Canadians. It funds programs in the arts, education, and health sectors. The Foundation also provides bursaries for deserving post-secondary students at Canadian universities.
- Donner Canadian Foundation (petroleum): The Donner Canadian Foundation funds public policy research and supports environmental, international development, and social service projects. Every year, the Donner Book Prize honours the best book on Canadian public policy.

Sources: Philanthropic Foundations Canada, http://www.pfc.ca/cms_en/; The J.W. McConnell Family Foundation, http://www.mcconnellfoundation.ca/en/about; The Birks Family Foundation, http://www.birksfamilyfoundation.ca/Index.htm; and the Donner Canadian Foundation, http://www.donnerfoundation.org/.

Some of the strongest supporters of charitable organizations in Canada produce products that are not considered socially desirable by some—for example, tobacco, beer, and liquor. At issue is whether a group should be associated with the consumption of these products. Society might even find such support unacceptable. For example, in 1987 the federal government proposed legislation to prohibit the advertising and promotion of tobacco products. Yet corporations in the tobacco industry have been innovative and imaginative in their support of the arts. Groups that received support from the tobacco industry may find it difficult to obtain other sources of funding.

The trend to "marketing" and "business" orientations in supporting charities has raised concern. Marketing can be viewed as being "too commercial," as products or services are being directly promoted. Also, conditions can be placed on support, which is considered a threat to artistic or administrative freedom. Support may be given to activities and events where a marketing tie-in is possible, while other activities are neglected.

Some corporate giving is conditional on non-profit organizations becoming more efficient. The argument is that since corporations are tightening their belts, charitable organizations must also become more efficient. Included in this request for efficiency are demands that organizations share resources, avoid duplication, and reduce administrative costs. Charities must develop strategic plans, information and control systems, and generally improve their administrative systems.

Thus, pressure is on charities to produce returns, to be more accountable, and to ensure high visibility for their corporate supporters. Managers of charities argue that this restricts their activities and might prevent them from achieving their objectives. Corporations are also focusing their support on particular programs, projects, or events and are reluctant to provide support for basic operating expenses, placing even more pressure on the charitable organizations.

> **Cause-related marketing** The purchase of a particular product results in a donation being made by a corporation to a non-profit organization's program.

Another trend is toward **cause-related marketing**, where the purchase of a particular product results in a donation being made by the corporation to a non-profit organization's program. For example, the purchase of a particular brand of frozen vegetables results in a contribution to a food bank, or the purchase of a cake mix helps to fund a health cause. There are several criticisms of this approach, as it pushes philanthropy past even the marketing aspect of sponsorship.

Cause-related marketing is considered another way of making a profit, and there are fears that it will replace philanthropy by reducing the amount of no-strings corporate giving. The selection of causes is problematic. Safe, non-controversial causes are selected that will sell, and some companies base their selection of charities on opinion polls conducted to ascertain the most popular causes.

This approach to corporate giving is likely to continue as government funding declines, making commercial tie-ins inviting to managers of non-profit organizations. For business, it makes their product stand out, and if they can associate with the correct "hot" causes sales performance improves. Target audiences are chosen and promotional strategies are selected, making corporate giving "like selling soap suds," according to some critics. These critics question whether self-interested charitable investment or strategic giving is not becoming self-serving commercial activity.

> **Strategic giving** An attempt to rationalize the shareholder interest with corporate philanthropy where the corporation benefits directly from the funds given.

Overall, these trends or concerns have given rise to **strategic giving**, an attempt to rationalize the shareholder interest with corporate philanthropy where the corporation benefits directly from the funds given. Some believe it is really shareholders' money that is being given away. To avoid complaints from shareholders, management should act in enlightened self-interest as a counterargument to the profit maximization position of shareholders. Thus, strategic giving is donating with an eye to the corporation's eventual best interests.[3]

Strategic giving leads corporations to make contributions within their own areas of interest. For example, funding of educational programs would be considered appropriate, as would support for a park facility that could be used by employees and their families. This enlightened self-interest, however, may not lead to support for women's shelters or housing for the poor, where the benefits to the corporation are not as evident. Although strategic giving is a way of justifying philanthropy consistent with shareholder interests, it would require managers to walk an ethical tightrope when rationalizing their proposals for support of particular charities.

Corporate Voluntarism

Corporate voluntarism The time and talent employees commit to community organizations with support and/or consent from employers who recognize the value of such efforts to society.

Corporate voluntarism is the time and talent employees commit to community organizations with support and/or consent from employers who recognize the value of such efforts to society. Corporations view voluntarism as giving something back to the community and society beyond monetary donations. In addition to employees, corporations now support the voluntary activities of retirees. An example of voluntarism is given in Everyday Ethics 8.4.

Everyday Ethics
8.4

Volunteerism at TELUS Corporation

As a part of its commitment to corporate citizenship, TELUS encourages employees and retirees to donate their time to personal causes and community volunteer work. Volunteerism activities include:

- When an employee completes a minimum of 50 hours of volunteer service, a $200 donation is made to the registered Canadian charity of their choice. If 200 volunteer hours is accumulated by four or more employees together, a $1,000 donation is made to a registered Canadian charity of their choice.
- An annual TELUS Day of Service where employees, retirees, and their families volunteer and undertake a project to improve the communities where they live and work.
- TELUS Community Ambassadors participate in volunteer activities that are of service to the community. Examples of the activities are providing comfort kits with personal hygiene items for homeless or displaced families, backpacks of school supplies for less fortunate children, and heart and lung pillows for patients after surgery.

Source: TELUS Corporation, TELUS Community Annual Report, "We give where we live," http://about.telus.com/community/en/community_report/, accessed November 1, 2012.

The principle of voluntarism is well established in society, and there is a continuing need to recruit and motivate members of society to support the many voluntary organizations. Employee voluntarism has become more important for two reasons: the decline of the professional volunteer of the past, the homemaker who did not work outside the home; and the increasing need for volunteers to serve. The former point results from more women working, and the latter refers to the increasing load on volunteers during cutbacks in government support and greater demand from an aging population.

There are benefits to employers, employees, and, of course, the non-profit organizations involved. But there also can be drawbacks, especially for employers and employees. Many of these benefits and drawbacks for the parties are summarized in Table 8.3.

The general benefits for employers include the creation of a better community environment, and opportunities for employee team building and corporate image building. For employees, general benefits are that the personal involvement improves the quality of life in the community; that contacts are made with community members, especially helpful to new employees in an area; and that an educational and broadening experience is received.

Organizations Supported and Forms of Support

A majority of corporations support voluntary activities and encourage employees to become involved in the community. Voluntary activities that are encouraged involve organizations such as the United Way, professional associations, business and trade associations, the

TABLE 8.3	*Employee Voluntarism: Advantages and Disadvantages*

ADVANTAGES

- Benefits employee morale by enhancing professional skill development, providing a learning experience, and providing a personal experience
- Good for the community
- Good for the organizations supported
- Improves the corporation's local and national image or profile
- Good for the overall environment in which employees, customers, and the corporation must operate
- Can contribute to corporate team building, employee involvement initiatives, and employee retention
- Sets a good example
- Helps employees integrate with the community, provides a source of contacts or a network, and encourages a sense of community commitment

DISADVANTAGES

- Possible employee resentment at perceived coercion to participate
- Possible distractions from the job, corporate objectives
- Cost in dollars and time
- Implication of picking "winners" or "losers" from among community organizations; that is, deciding which to support
- Possibility of controversy over objectives of some voluntary organization reflecting adversely on the corporation
- Some employees may overcommit themselves, impacting upon job performance
- A controversy involving the efforts of an employee volunteer may reflect unfavourably on the corporation

Sources: Based on Peter M. Brophey, "Corporate voluntarism: Putting something back," *Canadian Business Review* (Spring 1987); Julie Traves, "What goes around . . . corporate volunteering boosts the bottom line," *Canadian Business*, January 31–February 13, 2005, 67–68; and Shirley Won, "Doing good helps you do well at work," *The Globe and Mail*, January 19, 2005, C1.

Chamber of Commerce, service clubs, Junior Achievement, and community athletic groups. Several voluntary activities are usually excluded from employer support, for example working for trade unions (not in collective agreement), political parties, religious groups, and special interest advocacy groups.

The forms of support given to voluntary activities include providing facilities, allowing time off or schedule adjustments, assisting with personal expenses incurred while undertaking voluntary activities, extending special recognition to employees exhibiting outstanding performances, and issuing letters of thanks. Many corporations do not consider support and recognition for volunteer work to be an element in the regular performance review process. However, many corporate recruiters consider voluntary experience when assessing a candidate for employment.

Corporate Policies Regarding Voluntarism

Many corporations do not allow employee voluntarism to just exist without some policies formulated to serve as guidelines in the activity. Some corporate actions that would encourage involvement in the voluntary section:

- providing information for new employees on available volunteer organizations and opportunities;
- providing recognition or awards to employees who volunteer in order to spur additional employee involvement;

- encouraging employees to volunteer via corporate-sponsored loaned executive and paid leave programs (a recent practice in this area is described in Everyday Ethics 8.5);
- supporting programs for retirees; and
- establishing formal programs and designating someone to give administrative support.

Everyday Ethics

8.5

Corporate Service Corps

A recent form of voluntarism is "corporate service corps" set up by some corporations where employees donate their time to working on development projects in various countries. The IBM Corporate Service Corps was launched in 2007 as a corporate version of the Peace Corps, and by February 2011 had involved 1,000 employees in projects. It is viewed as a form of training for global employees in addition to providing assistance in developing countries. IBM cooperates with various non-governmental organizations (NGOs) to place its volunteers, and placements are usually for only a few weeks. Other corporations with similar programs include Novartis Pharmaceuticals Corporation, Dow Corning Corporation, and FedEx.

A Canadian initiative is "Leave for Change" operated by the Uniterra Program, a joint effort of the Centre for International Studies and Cooperation (CECI) and the World University Service of Canada (WUSC) and financially supported by the Canadian International Development Agency (CIDA). It is a corporate volunteering initiative that enables employees to spend a three- or four-week vacation period on assignment in a developing country. Employers support the programs by investing in their human resources and because it demonstrates their social responsibility. Canadian corporations that have participated in the program include Transat, SAHARA Communications, Deloitte & Touche, Abbott Laboratories, and The Co-operators.

Benefits are afforded to communities, employees, and the corporation. Communities receive pro bono help in solving problems confronting them economically, socially, and environmentally. Having the volunteers work in the communities increases international understanding. Benefits for the employee volunteers include gaining leadership training, experience in emerging countries, an opportunity to develop new knowledge and skills, and possibly increased job satisfaction. Corporations obtain insights into potential markets, and their employees obtain new skills and knowledge of developing countries.

It is questioned whether these volunteer placements of only a few weeks can accomplish much. Communities may be overwhelmed by enthusiastic volunteers promoting North American approaches to local problems. Projects may fail, creating ill will and not solving the problems of the communities.

Sources: IBM, "Corporate service corps," https://www-146.ibm.com/corporateservicecorps/; YouTube: search "corporate service corps" and "IBM corporate service corps"; Blog: https://www-146.ibm.com/corporateservicecorps/blog; and Uniterra, Leave for Change®, http://www.uniterra.ca/become-an-international-volunteer/leave-for-change-sup-sup.

Policies on voluntarism are of three types: encouraging, enabling, and promoting. Encouraging policy statements set the tone or position of the corporation relating to employee voluntarism, and are positive statements about the value of volunteer activities. Enabling policies provide guidelines to managers and employees regarding the implementation of the positive policy. They often set the boundaries and establish procedures relating to voluntarism; for example, the policy relating to a leave of absence to work for a voluntary organization. Overall, enabling policies facilitate the participation of employees in voluntary activity. The third policy category promotes participation in voluntary activity. These promoting policies recognize and reward employee achievement in voluntary activities. Taken together, these types of policies encourage employee voluntarism in Canada.

Employee voluntarism is most successful where top management, especially the chief executive officer, indicate it is a worthy and commendable activity. Top management support is vital for the corporate volunteer program to succeed. Employee voluntarism has endured even through the difficulties created by the economic downturns and will continue to be a significant way in which corporations contribute to the communities where they operate.

LO 8.4 | Corporate Sponsorship

Corporate sponsorship A partnership between a business sponsor and an event or a non-profit organization that is established for mutual benefit.

Corporate sponsorship is defined as "a partnership, which has been established for mutual benefit between a business sponsor and an event or a non-profit."[4] A distinction should be made between corporate donations and sponsorship. A donation is a gift that goes one way, from a corporation to a charity, while a sponsorship, whether a single event or a series of events, confers benefits on both parties.

Sponsorship covers a wide range of sport, cultural, and educational events. There are also examples of extending corporate sponsorship programs to such social concerns as literacy, race relations, drug abuse, and environmental issues. Sponsorship provides a definite link between business and social issues.

Charity or Marketing?

Some acknowledge that corporate sponsorship has little to do with charity, donations, or philanthropy but instead is a business or marketing arrangement. Yet companies often mention sponsorships in "Involvement in or Contribution to the Community" sections of their annual or social reports. The trend toward sponsorships has been found to be attractive for a variety of reasons:

- favourable media exposure or publicity
- opportunity to entertain clients
- building a company/product presence
- reaching select market segments
- business-to-business networking[5]

Sponsorship is one way to increase corporate awareness, as broad exposure of a name or logo increases recognition and may result in a purchase decision. It is considered a positive and low-cost image-building approach and allows targeting; that is, the sponsorship can be directed at specific audiences or potential customers. An example is given in Everyday Ethics 8.6.

Everyday Ethics

8.6

Sponsorship at Bell Aliant

Bell Aliant is one of North America's largest regional communications providers. Its sponsorship marketing program may take the form of providing financial support, value in kind, or other resources that assist in making a project a reality. It focuses on extending support to events and projects in two areas:

Sports—Company support of sports includes the Canada Games, and youth sport including pee wee hockey and soccer.

Culture and Festivals—Support is given to programs and events such as the Confederation Centre for the Arts, the East Coast Music Awards, the Harvest Jazz and Blues Festival, and Charlottetown SummerFest.

Source: Bell Aliant, "Sponsorships," http://bellaliant.ca/english/about/cr_sponsorship_02.shtml.

The corporate sponsor looks for a charitable situation that satisfies the company's marketing ambitions and that coincides with the needs of the charity group. There must be some common ground so that both parties benefit. To accomplish this, the sponsorship agreement should define clearly the role and needs of each partner. For the corporation, the sponsorship must fit into the marketing scheme, while the charity's integrity must not be threatened. A well-defined plan is necessary to avoid failure and disagreements. Many now consider corporate sponsorship to be a form of advertising.

Sponsorship is now so common that it has lost its novelty, and thus its capability to attract attention. The public may be cynical about cause-related sponsorships, or simply may not understand the linkage. Many question the appropriateness of the support given by alcohol companies to the arts and sports. The government might question whether some sponsorship violates advertising regulations.

Corporations may find it difficult to keep their hands off the event after the initial agreement is reached, and the relationship may turn sour. The return from a sponsorship is seldom precisely known, and it might be difficult to withdraw support without attracting attention. For example, the sponsorship of the Canadian equestrian team became awkward for some corporate sponsors when the sport experienced problems with drugs and dishonesty. But the withdrawal of support becomes a problem, as without corporate sponsorship many programs fail.

New approaches are being used by business to address social ills beyond giving money, social venture philanthropy, and social enterprises. Both assume that it is appropriate for business to solve social problems such as jobs in communities, training programs, and housing. The purpose of these approaches is to give the underprivileged the tools to create new opportunities by creating their own wealth instead of it being transferred to them.

▶ LO 8.5 ◀   Social Venture Philanthropy

Social venture philanthropy The investment of human and financial resources by corporations in non-profit community development agencies to generate a social return instead of only a financial one.

Social venture philanthropy is the investment of human and financial resources by corporations in non-profit community development agencies to generate a social return instead of only a financial one. This approach is also known as social venturing, the new philanthropy, and high-engagement philanthropy. Sometimes it is used interchangeably with social enterprise, but there is a distinction that is explained in the next section.

Social venture philanthropy applies venture capital management practices to social responsibility. Investments are made, but a social return is expected rather than a financial one. There is a high engagement with the non-profit agency that provides leadership, bold ideas to address social problems, and strong teams with an active board involvement. Whereas venture capitalists plan an exit strategy, the social venture capitalist focuses on long-term funding and sustainability of the recipient.

Several examples of social venture philanthropy organizations exist in Canada, including Social Venture Partners (described in Everyday Ethics 8.7), B.C. Technology Social Venture Partners, Social Capital Partners, the Tides Foundation, and the Enterprising Non-Profits Program Vancouver.[6]

▶ LO 8.6 ◀   Social Enterprise and Social Entrepreneurship

Social enterprise A model of business operation where some or all profits are deliberately used to further social aims.

A **social enterprise** is a model of business operation where some or all profits are deliberately used to further social aims. There are two types: non-profit enterprises that contribute all profits to social initiatives, for example the St. John's Bakery described in Everyday Ethics 8.8, and for-profit enterprises that divide profits between social initiatives and shareholders, such as The Body Shop. Social enterprises are dynamic business operations capable of

Everyday Ethics
8.7

Social Venture Philanthropy and Social Venture Partners Calgary

Social Venture Partners Calgary's mission is to stimulate positive social change in Calgary. It is a partnership among generous individuals, businesspersons, and others, and needy not-for-profits to create a new model of giving. Social Venture Partners Calgary combines the time, expertise, financial, and physical resources of its partners and turns them into a powerful tool of positive change for cash-strapped, advice-ready, and resource-constrained not-for-profits. These organizations get not only the commitment of money and resources over a number of years, but also the professional advice that leads to more successful outcomes. Examples of the investments made include the following:

The Calgary Youth Justice Society—Support to this organization contributes to the success of Youth Justice Committees by providing fundamental support through public awareness, resources, training, and guidance.

Connections Counselling and Consulting—This grant recipient empowers individuals by providing ongoing education, programs, and advocacy; ongoing family support to parents with an intellectual disability and their children; and counselling to persons with an intellectual disability.

EvenStart for Children Foundation—The organization gives "at-risk" children who are economically disadvantaged the educational, therapeutic, nutritional, and nurturing support necessary to gain an "even start" in their lives.

Source: Based on Social Ventures Partners Calgary, http://www.svpcalgary.org/, accessed November 1, 2012.

improving the well-being of citizens while making money, but are distinct from charities and from private-sector companies that practise social responsibility. Although the idea has received attention recently, it has existed for some time, for example in the cooperatives of the 1800s. Social enterprises take various forms including community enterprises, credit unions, commercial operations of charities, employee-owned businesses, co-operatives, development trusts, housing associations, and companies operating under "fair trade" principles.

Everyday Ethics
8.8

St. John's Bakery

The St. John's Bakery in Toronto is operated by the St. John's Mission "to provide our customers with outstanding artisan breads and sweets" and "to be and to build an inclusive community through the gifts and the needs that each of us brings."

The bakery sells a variety of organic breads and sweets to consumers, retailers, cafés and restaurants, farmers' markets, and wholesale customers. It is sponsored by the St. John the Compassionate Mission, a non-profit organization of the Carpatho-Russian Orthodox, with support from other orthodox churches in the Greater Toronto Area. It employs refugees, persons suffering addictions or mental illness, and those struggling with poverty.

Green Living magazine refers to the operation as an artisanal bakery in which its employees "handcraft breads and sweets from locally sourced ingredients and 100 percent organic, stone-ground unbleached flour."

Sources: St. John's Bakery, http://www.stjohnsbakery.com; St. John the Compassionate Mission, http://www.stjohnsmission.org; and Green Living™, http://www.greenlivingonline.com/guide/st-johns-bakery.

Although social enterprises take various forms, there are some common characteristics. They have an enterprise orientation; that is, they are involved in the production of goods or provision of services to a market, with the intention that revenues will exceed costs. They have social aims, such as providing employment, training, and investment funding. There is a commitment of local capacity building, and they are accountable to their members and community stakeholders. They are autonomous organizations with governance and ownership structures based on participation by stakeholder groups such as users and local community groups or shareholders. Profits are distributed to stakeholders or used for the benefit of the community.[7]

Want to learn more about **Canadian social enterprises**? Go to CONNECT.

> **Social entrepreneurship** The activities undertaken to enhance social wealth in some innovative way.
>
> **Social entrepreneur** An innovative, visionary leader of a non-profit or for-profit business with real-world problem-solving creativity and a high awareness for ethical, social, and environmental considerations.

Social entrepreneurship involves the activities undertaken to enhance social wealth in some innovative way. A **social entrepreneur** is an innovative, visionary leader of a non-profit or for-profit business with real-world problem-solving creativity and a high awareness for ethical, social, and environmental considerations. Social entrepreneurs seek out innovative approaches to social issues in the community and use business skills to achieve social objectives. They also have the ability to meet community needs while being financially self-sufficient and paying attention to market forces. Successful social entrepreneurs do not believe that capitalism and profits are societal evils, but instead believe that business enterprises can be operated to enhance social aims.

Several centres focus on social enterprises and entrepreneurship; these are usually associated with universities, and sometimes are in association with regular entrepreneurial studies. In Canada, colleges and universities offer programs or courses that focus on social entrepreneurship, and many business graduates are seeking employment in social enterprises where they apply their business and managerial skills.[8] In order to gain experience in social entrepreneurship and social enterprises, university and college students can participate in Enactus groups or teams as described in Responsibility for Ethics 8.2.

RESPONSIBILITY *for Ethics* **8.2**

Enactus

Enactus, formerly Students in Free Enterprise (SIFE), is a student-run organization whose purpose is to create community empowerment projects with the assistance of academics and business leaders. Each project can be considered a social enterprise that uses the power of entrepreneurial spirit and skill to transform lives and shape a better, more sustainable world.

It is an international non-profit organization with groups around the world including more than 60 teams at Canadian universities and colleges. Student participation in Enactus provides an opportunity for students to develop talents and skills necessary for leadership roles in business. The values encouraged are imagination, courage, determination, partnership, accountability, and curiosity.

Source: Enactus, http://enactus.org/; and http://enactus.org/country/canada/.

> **Philanthrocapitalism** Draws upon modern business practices and an entrepreneurial spirit to get more from corporate social responsibility.

The Economist refers to the new approaches such as social venture philanthropy and social enterprise as philanthrocapitalism. **Philanthrocapitalism** draws upon modern business practices and an entrepreneurial spirit to get more from corporate social responsibility.[9]

For-benefit corporation Operates to make profits but also has a strong commitment to addressing social and environmental problems.

A recent variation on the social enterprise is the **for-benefit corporation**, which operates to make profits but also has a strong commitment to addressing social and environmental problems. For-benefit corporations are expected to have a material impact on society and to consider how their actions affect stakeholders. Accountability and transparency are requirements, and they are expected to publicly report their social and environmental performance using recognized third-party standards.[10] These corporations are also known as B Corporations; a certification process is required in order to be eligible to receive this designation. In Canada the certification is performed by the non-profit MaRS Centre for Impact Investing, Toronto.[11] In the United States, several states have passed legislation allowing for the incorporation of for-benefit corporations, giving them legal status. According to the Certified B Corporation Web site, more than 600 B Corporations exist in 15 countries and 60 industries as of November 2012.[12] Thirty-nine of these are in Canada; some examples are given in Everyday Ethics 8.9. No for-benefit incorporation legislation has been passed in Canada as it is considered unnecessary. The requirements for certification are making amendments to corporate documents—for example, bylaws—to permit boards of directors to consider other stakeholders, and meeting rigorous and independent standards of social and environment accountability and transparency.

Everyday Ethics   Examples of Canadian B Corporations

8.9

Bullfrog Power, Toronto, ON—A green energy provider to homes and businesses through renewable energy solutions that reduce the impact on the environment.
Salt Spring Coffee, Richmond, B.C.—Coffee roasters that have formed farmer partnerships with a vision to be at the leading edge of coffee in quality, sustainability, pioneering, and origin.
PeaceWorks Technology Solutions, Waterloo, ON—Provides technology solutions that enable organizations to achieve their mission with increased ease and efficiency.
Enviro-Stewards, Elmira, ON—A company of engineers and scientists helping clients conserve their resources and effectively address their environmental liabilities.
The Sustainability Advantage, Whitby, ON—Author and consultant on corporate sustainability.

Sources: Corporate Web sites at http://www.bullfrogpower.com/about/about.cfm; http://www.saltspringcoffee.com/; http://www.peaceworks.ca/; http://www.enviro-stewards.com/; and http://sustainabilityadvantage.com/index.php.

LO 8.7   Small Business and CSR

CSR has a lower profile in small business enterprises, but it is practised sometimes without entrepreneurs recognizing it. There are challenges to implementing CSR in small businesses. Entrepreneurs do not have time to devote to it as they are confronting the daily demands of their business. The expenses associated with obtaining the resources necessary, including consultants and employee time, may be beyond the means of a small business.[13] There is likely a lack of knowledge of CSR planning and monitoring methodologies, as resources relevant to small businesses are not readily available.[14]

The understanding of CSR that does exist is strongly influenced by the personal values of the entrepreneur. Small businesses must confront most of the social and ethical issues experienced by large business. But some issues are associated more with small business: entrepreneurs are more likely to participate in the underground economy, misleading advertising and financial reporting, improper gift giving and receiving, and tax evasion. In addition, human resource abuses are more common as entrepreneurs ignore or are unaware of workplace regulations. Entrepreneurs are sometimes accused of nepotism in the hiring and promotion of family members instead of employees.[15] Research has found differences between CSR practice in large versus small businesses; the findings are summarized in Table 8.4.[16]

TABLE 8.4	*Differences in CSR in Large Corporations versus Small Businesses*
Large Corporations	**Small Businesses**
• Accountable to a large number of stakeholders	• Accountable to fewer stakeholders
• Responsible to society at large	• Responsible to local communities
• Concerned with brand image and reputation	• Concerned about retaining business
• Shareholder pressure; ethical investing	• Pressure from lenders
• Based on corporate values	• Based on owner values
• Formal planning for CSR	• Unlikely to be formal planning
• Emphasis on standards and indices	• Emphasis on intuition and ad hoc processes
• Involvement of CSR professionals	• No dedicated personnel
• Prominent campaign; for example, cause-related marketing	• Small scale activities; for example, sponsoring local sports teams
• Awareness through CSR reporting, publicity	• Often unrecognized as CSR activities

Source: Compiled and adapted from Heledd Jenkins, "A critique of conventional CSR theory: An SME perspective," *Journal of General Management*, Vol. 29, No 4, Summer 2004, Table 3: Divergence in CSR Theory for Large and Small Organizations, page 51. Braybrooke Press.

The Network for Business Sustainability has developed a guide for small business involvement with local communities. A community comprises individuals or groups by issues, interactions, geography, or a sense of identity, and includes residents, community associations, sports leagues, online networks, parent–teacher associations, environmental activists, and religious groups. Examples of typical community concerns could be the hiring or laying off of local people, problems created such as pollution, and the construction of facilities. Working with community groups improves management decision making, creates legitimacy or social licence, and makes recruitment easier.[17] Table 8.5 outlines the three strategies for working with communities. Small business owners must carefully identify the relevant community groups, prioritize them, and then pick the best engagement strategy.

Although this guide is based on 200 studies of small business involvement in communities, it can be used by larger corporations at a local level, for example when building a plant in a community. Other assistance with CSR is available for entrepreneurs from industry associations, for example accessing the Canadian Federation of Independent Business, completing self-assessment checklists available on the Internet, cooperating with local non-profit organizations, and referring to the limited literature.[18] Although not receiving the attention for their CSR practices that large corporations do, most small businesses and their owners do contribute to local communities. Small business entrepreneurs make donations to local charities, sponsor area sports teams and cultural activities, and volunteer in community organizations. An example of a small business practising CSR is given in Everyday Ethics 8.10.

TABLE 8.5	*Three Strategies for Working with Communities*		
	Investment	**Involvement**	**Integration**
Company perspective	"Giving Back"	"Building Bridges"	"Changing Society"
Description	The company provides information or resources to the community	The company uses community input to shape its actions	The company and the community jointly manage projects
Communication	One-way	Two-way	Two-way
Number of partners	Many	Many	Few
Interaction	Occasional	Repeated	Frequent
Information/knowledge	Goes from company to community	Goes from community to company	Is jointly generated
Control over process	Company	Company	Company and community
Tools and techniques	Advertisements; information kiosks; press releases; newsletters; door-to-door visits; information sessions; charitable donations; employee volunteering	Surveys; studies; interviews; consultative committees; interactive websites; public hearings; neutral forums	Strategic local or regional partnerships; sector discussion groups; joint brainstorming; conflict resolution; work groups

Source: Network for Business Sustainability, *Working with Community Groups: A Guide for Small Business,* November 5, 2012. Available at http://nbs.net/wp-content/uploads/SME-Resource-Community-Engagement.pdf.

connect Want to learn more about **CSR and small business**? Go to CONNECT.

Everyday Ethics — CSR at a Small Business

8.10

In 1998, David Van Seters established a small business based on social responsibility—a food delivery company named SPUD: Sustainable Produce Urban Delivery. Based in Vancouver and serving five other urban areas, SPUD markets produce that is certified either organic or local, and sustainably produced including Fairtrade products. About 50 percent is locally produced, creating local jobs and reducing transportation emissions.

SPUD illustrates social responsibility by partnering with local NGOs by collecting donations of clothing, toiletries, household items, and children's toys when making deliveries. The NGOs involved include the Children's Hospital, The Food Bank, SPCA, and the Women's Transition House.

Source: SPUD: Sustainable Produce Urban Delivery, https://www.spud.ca/index.cfm.

LO 8.8   Trends and Issues in Contemporary CSR

Substantial wealth has been generated by businesspersons and entrepreneurs, and much of this is being devoted to CSR. CSR is increasingly viewed as being appropriate to ease social problems in society, but the approaches have changed. There is a trend to corporations placing money into foundations and other types of non-profit agencies instead of distributing money directly through donations. In addition, the givers are using entrepreneurial practices, demanding more efficiency from non-profit organizations, requesting greater accountability, and becoming more directly involved in the projects.

As mentioned, these CSR approaches can be described by terminology including *strategic giving, market conscious, knowledge-based, entrepreneurial,* and *leveraging of donor funding.* CSR projects are concentrating on areas where government has failed, or has withdrawn. The motivations for contemporary CSR contributions include making a difference and giving something to society. For others the rationale is based on religious principles, personal experience or preferences, or self-interest as represented by tax incentives and recognition.[19]

Community investment has become another trend in CSR. It is defined as the efforts of a corporation to help develop a community and create economic opportunities through a variety of means from donations to direct involvement in commercial undertakings. According to Business for Social Responsibility, "corporate community investment bridges traditional areas of philanthropy and volunteerism with commercial-community relationships in sourcing, workforce, financial investments, site selection, and the development and delivery of products and services."[20] The purpose of community investment is to develop CSR strategies in relation to corporate community–related issues and to link economic responsibilities with the social needs of the community.

Rather than making an equity investment in socially responsible corporations, an initiative exists to lend capital through a **community bond**, which is a debt instrument issued by a social enterprise to a network of supporters and used to finance or advance a specific proposal. It is a mortgage-backed investment that is interest bearing and used to fund infrastructure projects.[21] The March 2012 federal budget stated that the government "will explore social finance instruments," and social impact bonds are cited as holding promise "as a tool to further encourage the development of government-community partnerships."[22]

A multitude of awards and recognition are designated for effective CSR or corporate sustainability programs. Examples of such awards are the *Corporate Knights* Best 50 Corporate Citizens in Canada, the *Maclean's* Top 50 Socially Responsible Corporations in Canada, and the Global 100 Most Sustainable Corporations in the World. These awards are displayed on the corporation's Web site and in CSR or sustainability reports, and are mentioned in this book. Imagine Canada recognizes the best CSR programs with its Caring Company Program, described in Responsibility for Ethics 8.3.

Community investment The efforts of a corporation to help develop a community and create economic opportunities through a variety of means, from donations to direct involvement in commercial undertakings.

Community bond A debt instrument issued by a social enterprise to a network of supporters and used to finance or advance a specific proposal.

RESPONSIBILITY
for Ethics **8.3**

Imagine Canada's Caring Company Program

Imagine Canada describes a Caring Company as one that is a good corporate citizen, drives social innovation, and invests money, ideas, and time in communities. It considers the Caring Company Program to be Canada's leading corporate citizenship initiative, and more than 100 businesses are members. Membership assures stakeholders that the company is committed to investing in the community.

Commitments necessary to join include:

- Donate one percent of pre-tax profits to the community,
- Develop one community project supported by senior management, and
- Publish a brief annual report on the company's activities.

Large or small corporations can become members once they agree to the principles of corporate citizenship and the benchmarks for community investment established by Imagine Canada.

Source: Imagine Canada, "Caring Company Program," http://www.imaginecanada.ca/node/18, accessed October 30, 2012.

Lastly, there is concern that CSR will receive less attention during an economic downturn. An article in *The Guardian* examined the possibility that CSR might be less of a priority with corporations as turbulent economic conditions refocus attention to the bottom line.[23] The advocates of sustainability or CSR feared that it may not receive as much attention by management and boards of directors, and that it would not be viewed seriously. Examples were given where corporations did not mention CSR in their annual strategy statements to the financial market. At the World Economic Forum in February 2009, the discussion of climate change was overshadowed by the credit crunch in the United States.

Evidence to the contrary comes from consultants who claim that CSR has been temporarily derailed before and re-emerged in a revised form. It is pointed out that commitment to CSR in times of economic turndown is even more important for corporations as it differentiates them from competitors. Furthermore, CSR has moved into the mainstream because of climate change, financial scandals, and alleged human rights and environmental abuses. Corporations will continue commitment to CSR as they want to avoid government regulation being demanded by NGOs while others argue that regulation is necessary—a voluntary approach does not work. As discussed in Chapter 7, a major critic of CSR, *The Economist,* has softened its position: a 2005 supplement was skeptical, but a 2008 supplement considered CSR just good business and illustrated how corporations were implementing it.

Even with the doubts, the approaches discussed in this chapter illustrate an increasing belief that business should be investing in CSR or sustainability with the goal of a social return, and that business-type practices will be used in its implementation.

Your advice to Walter . . .

There are thousands of charities in Canada, and selecting which among them to support is a challenging task. For businesspersons with considerable funds they wish to give back to society it is an even greater challenge. Walter might consider the Giving Pledge, but this is not appropriate to everyone. If Walter is thinking of giving to a charity, Charity Intelligence Canada might be of help. It evaluates charities on various criteria and recommends a list of the most efficient and effective. Walter does have access to some resources to address his challenge.

SUMMARY

- A spectrum of corporate social responsibility and corporate sustainability approaches are described: corporate giving or donations, voluntarism, sponsorship, social venture philanthropy, and social enterprise. Most corporations practise one or more of these approaches as they seek the most effective way to practise CSR. (LO 8.1)

- There are arguments for and against corporate donations; in particular, the issue of whether such activity is in the best interests of the corporation and its shareholders has not been resolved. Once the corporation decides to become involved in corporate giving, another challenge emerges—how to manage the process. A decision-making process involving committees or foundations should be established if the corporation wants to be consistent and perceived to be treating all requests fairly. Although something positive can be gained from donations, there is the possibility of negative outcomes when requests are rejected. Rejections must be handled as professionally as successful requests. Philanthropic decision making is even more challenging given the increasing demands for corporate support and the limited amount of funds available. In addition, there is a trend toward tying giving to economic gains, an issue that re-emerges throughout the chapter. (LO 8.2)

- Voluntarism is receiving more attention as an approach to corporate philanthropy. Employees and retirees of corporations make contributions to charitable organizations, often with the encouragement of managers. Many corporations have well-defined policies relating to employee volunteer activities to avoid conflicts with work obligations or to protect the reputation of the corporation. Although voluntarism is usually encouraged, it is not without challenges for management. (LO 8.3)

- Sponsorship has grown as a form of philanthropy. Discussion continues as to whether such an activity is in support of a charity or an aspect of marketing. Corporations are pressured for greater return on donation funds, and tying support to sponsorship of projects or events appears to result. The discussion of sponsorship is a logical lead-in to the examination of the trend toward corporations seeking to satisfy economic as well as social objectives with corporate philanthropic initiatives. Corporate management is demanding more efficiency and accountability from non-profit charities, and receivers of support from corporations in "sin industries" are being challenged for accepting it. (LO 8.4)

- Social venture philanthropy is a newer approach to CSR where donors believe their funds should be invested rather than merely handed over as a cheque. The approach also involves more engagement with the recipient organization to encourage the use of entrepreneurial and managerial approaches. (LO 8.5)

- Social enterprises can be viewed as two types. One type is as a commercial enterprise operated by a non-profit organization with the goal of making profits, which are devoted completely to social purposes. Another for-profit type distributes its earnings to social causes and to shareholders. Both types are committed to contributing to the alleviation of social problems in society. The for-benefit corporation is another approach to the social enterprise that has emerged recently. (LO 8.6)

- Small businesses are involved in CSR but receive less recognition than large corporations. CSR decisions are driven by the entrepreneur and focus on local community social issues. (LO 8.7)

- Corporate philanthropy appears to be a relatively straightforward matter. But in practice this is not the case, and managers must plan and establish policies to implement initiatives to support charitable endeavours. Observers of CSR are monitoring the impact of the economic downturn on CSR. (LO 8.8)

KEY TERMS

Corporate philanthropy	Corporate sponsorship	Philanthrocapitalism
Charitable foundation	Social venture philanthropy	For-benefit corporation
Cause-related marketing	Social enterprise	Community investment
Strategic giving	Social entrepreneurship	Community bond
Corporate voluntarism	Social entrepreneur	

CRITICAL THINKING AND DISCUSSION QUESTIONS

1. What is the strongest argument for business participating in corporate giving? What is the strongest argument for business not participating in corporate giving?

2. Why should corporations develop formal plans for implementing CSR?

3. How is the position that all corporate profits belong to the shareholders countered?

4. List guidelines that corporations might follow in developing and implementing a corporate giving program.

5. Why do some argue that corporate giving is now nothing more than corporate marketing or advertising?

6. Should a charity accept donations from tobacco, alcohol, or beer companies?

7. What are the drawbacks to corporate voluntarism?

8. What criteria should be used in selecting a charity for a corporate voluntary program?

9. What are the positive features of sponsorship programs? What are the drawbacks?

10. Should business be involved in social venture philanthropy? Is business better than government at addressing social ills?

11. From a business perspective, what are the positive features of social enterprises?

12. Why should small businesses become involved with CSR?

CASES

8.1   *Walmart's Responsible Store*

Walmart has been criticized for virtually every aspect of its operation including the impact of its stores on the environment. The list of issues is long: water quality violations, improper construction site cleanup, pollution from improper storage of pesticides, and the increase in greenhouse gas emissions due to just-in-time deliveries. In addition, it has been accused of increasing traffic as the locations of their stores are dependent on car transportation.

In 2001, Walmart Canada began the process of planning a store in the southeast section of Vancouver. It was to be its first store in Vancouver, although it had several in the areas immediately surrounding the city. A change in zoning was necessary before the store could be built. The zoning, and thus the store, were opposed for various reasons, but the environmental impact was a main one. In addition, many city councillors opposed Walmart, accusing it of being anti-union, paying low wages, and engaging in unfair labour practices, domination of suppliers, and predatory pricing. As the application slowly worked its way through the city bureaucracy and political process, increasing demands were placed on Walmart to address the environmental issues. The store hired the architectural firm Busby Perkins and Will to design a store that would respond to the demands. Peter Busby, who headed up the project, was a well-known environmentally conscious architect.

Over the years various environmental requirements were placed on the Walmart application, to which Busby's design responded. In 2005, the design was likely the most environmentally friendly big-box store, with the following features: rainwater collected on the roof was to be recycled for toilets, heating and cooling was to be done using geothermal wells and wind power, the parking lot was to be covered with absorbent asphalt to reduce runoff, skylights would provide natural light, and large shade trees would be placed in the parking lot to reduce "heat island" effect. The store would use 48 percent less water, energy use would be reduced by 36 percent, and carbon dioxide emissions reduced by 40 percent.

The redesigned store would cost $30 million instead of the normal $15 million to build. Walmart was willing to seek Leadership in Energy and Environmental Design (LEED) certification, an accepted benchmark environmental design, for the project. The store would be one-of-a-kind and a benchmark in the revolutionary development of big-box stores. Even after this innovative design critics complained about the store, saying it would cause traffic congestion and air pollution, and that it would drive small retailers out of business. On the other hand, the store would create employment in the area, reduce the number of consumers travelling to surrounding cities to shop at a Walmart, and allow local residents to take advantage of lower prices.

Questions

1. Which stakeholders influenced and/or are influencing Walmart's attempt to open a store in Vancouver?

2. What are the issues for business and society in dealing with zoning regulations that prevent the opening of a new business?

3. What fundamentals of capitalism are in possible conflict with zoning regulations?

4. Was Walmart being socially and environmentally responsible?

5. Should the store be allowed?

Sources: Various documents from the City of Vancouver, including by-laws, reports, studies, and Council Meeting Minutes; John Greenwood, "Wal-mart goes green to appease opponents," *National Post,* February 2, 2005, FP6; John Greenwood, "Wal-Mart backs away from first Vancouver store," *National Post,* December 17, 2002, FP1, FP9; and Gary Mason, "Vancouver's green-friendly Wal-Mart could become envy of North America," *The Globe and Mail,* June 28, 2005, A10.

8.2   *Having to Give at the Office*

Roxanne Kampf was an accounts payable clerk for a large corporation. She enjoyed the job and was generally happy with her workplace. Her employer had an extensive corporate giving program and supported employee voluntarism, in which she participated. For example, Roxanne volunteered to participate in the cleanup of a park near the office. It was an enjoyable activity and involved social interaction with many colleagues. Overall, she was pleased to be working for a corporation that was socially responsible.

Roxanne had reservations about the corporate giving program—in particular, about the annual United Way campaign. Firstly, she did not agree with the purposes of some of the charities covered by United Way. Secondly, she preferred to contribute directly to the charities she supported and whose aims she endorsed. Lastly, she felt pressure from supervisors and peers to contribute. This last reservation caused Roxanne some anxiety.

She had been reading in the newspaper about workplace charity drives. A poll of readers of *The Globe and Mail* found that 51 percent liked to support charity drives, 36 percent preferred to make their donations privately, and 13 percent felt pressured to contribute. Obviously Roxanne was not alone in her concern.

Roxanne felt very uneasy about her direct supervisor heading up the campaign in her department. Although the actual canvassing was done by peers, she still felt pressure and anxiety. She was not sure how to say no or what excuse to make. She wondered if anyone would believe a statement that she had already used up her "charitable budget." Also, she was not sure how others would feel when she stated that she should be able to give to the charities she preferred and in private. Even more troublesome was her concern about how saying no would impact her career.

The campaign made her very uncomfortable and she was even feeling guilty. Fun campaign activities were organized in the office and it was obvious to all when she did not attend. Also, the office had a goal to raise $5,000 and she was not contributing as expected of team members. Roxanne faced a dilemma and did not know what to do.

Questions

1. What are the pros and cons of workplace charity drives? What are the issues involved?

2. Does Roxanne have an ethical dilemma? State what it is.

3. What ethical principles (from Chapter 5) might she use to analyze the dilemma?

4. What should Roxanne do?

Sources: Marjorie Polycarpe, "Re-examining workplace giving programs," http://onphilanthropy.com; Tara Weiss, "Giving at the office without going broke," *Forbes,* June 22, 2006, http://www.forbes.com; David Aston, "'Tis the season to be inundated," *The Globe and Mail,* November 14, 2007, C1–C2; and Jennifer Myers, "Giving spirit untarnished by recession," *The Globe and Mail,* November 28, 2009, B17.

connect

For more information on the resources available from McGraw-Hill Ryerson, go to www.mcgrawhill.ca/he/solutions.

CHAPTER 9
Measuring, Reporting, and Communicating CSR

LEARNING OUTCOMES   *After studying this chapter, you will be able to:*

LO 9.1 Understand the background to measuring and reporting CSR performance.

LO 9.2 Define corporate reputation and understand its relationship to corporate social responsibility.

LO 9.3 Identify the stakeholders who influence CSR reporting.

LO 9.4 Describe the relationship between CSR and corporate profitability.

LO 9.5 Enumerate and discuss the types of criteria used in social auditing.

LO 9.6 Recognize the surveys that evaluate Canadian CSR reporting.

LO 9.7 Outline how CSR and sustainability results are communicated to stakeholders.

LO 9.8 Explain the role of business schools in CSR reporting.

LO 9.9 Discuss the future of CSR and CSR reporting.

What would you do if . . . ?

Clare O'Neill was confused. She had been introduced to the ethics of business and corporate social responsibility (CSR) in a university business course. She had become very interested in business and in particular how corporations were responding to social and environmental issues. Her instructor had used various corporate Web sites and had reviewed several corporate responsibility or sustainability reports in class, and also had recommended that students who were interested in the topic should subscribe to *Corporate Knights*—described as "the magazine for clean capitalism."

Clare's confusion began when she received the Spring 2012 issue, which featured a list titled "The 2012 Best 50 Corporate Citizens in Canada." The list contained some prominent corporations that she recognized as socially and environmentally responsible, such as Mountain Equipment Co-op, Vancouver City Savings Credit Union, and Desjardins Group. But also on the list were several industries that Clare did not feel were the most responsible, and she did not understand why they were represented. Popular media coverage was not always positive, and a series of documentaries she viewed at the college had been particularly critical.

The industries and corporations that Clare found doubtful included the following:

• *Chemicals:* Agrium Inc. Clare felt this industry extensively polluted the environment, and produced chemicals used in the mass production of food and home/beauty products with potentially negative impacts.

• *Petroleum:* Encana Corp., Enbridge Inc., Suncor Energy Inc., Husky Energy Inc., Talisman Energy Inc., and Nexen Inc. Clare viewed the petroleum industry as being irresponsible toward the environment, especially the operations in the Alberta oil sands. Recent reports had confirmed a significant increase in pollution in Alberta due to the oil sands developments.

• *Mining:* Cameco Corp., Barrick Gold Corp., IAMGOLD Corp., Inmet Mining Corp., Kinross Gold Corp., and Teck Resources Ltd. Claire knew that Cameco was in the uranium business, which supplied the nuclear energy industry. She believed many mine properties were polluters and harmed the environment and local communities, especially when operating in developing countries.

• *Forestry:* Domtar Corp., Catalyst Paper Corp., Canfor Corp., and Cascades Inc. In Clare's view, forestry corporations were not doing enough reforestation nor making sufficient efforts to prevent harm to the environment. They also had closed many plants and laid off thousands of workers, many of whom had inadequate pensions.

Clare looked up the CSR reports for the corporations mentioned, and found that indeed they were involved with many significant socially responsible programs. She still viewed the industries as problematic in their responsibility to society. Also, she wondered if the corporations were reporting only good news and overlooking less favourable situations.

Clare wondered if she should cancel her subscription to the magazine. She also thought about writing a letter to the editor. She considered the possibility that she had misunderstood the CSR and corporate citizenship concepts. She was disappointed and confused.

What is your advice to Clare?

This chapter reviews how CSR and sustainability performance is measured, reported, and communicated in Canada by:

- Establishing the existence of this reporting and examining why it is taking place.
- Evaluating the quality of the reporting in terms of the reliability of the information.
- Reviewing the verification or assurance mechanisms used to enhance the credibility of the reporting.
- Identifying the efforts made by corporations to communicate the reports to stakeholders.[1]

Two other sections examine related topics: CSR education in business courses, and the future of corporate social responsibility and CSR reporting.

The terms CSR and sustainability are used interchangeably in this chapter.

LO 9.1   Measuring and Reporting CSR

Social auditing A systematic assessment that identifies, measures, evaluates, reports, and monitors the effects an enterprise has on society that are not covered in the traditional financial reports.

The first step in the measurement of CSR or sustainability performance involves some type of auditing. **Social auditing** is a systematic assessment that identifies, measures, evaluates, reports, and monitors the effects an enterprise has on society that are not covered in the traditional financial reports. The purpose of social auditing is to provide information to management and to various stakeholders about the impact of the enterprise on society, and to provide a basis of accountability for the social consequences of corporate activities. Such audits can be used to assess existing performance, to evaluate the performance of managers in relation to social objectives, to provide an information base for planning, and to serve as a measure for assessing future performance.

There are many social auditing approaches. The main ones are:

- *Inventory*—a listing of social activities without any evaluation.

- *Program management*—a statement describing particular programs or initiatives, including an indication of the resources committed.

- *Process*—a more elaborate approach incorporating the inventory and program management approaches. It includes an assessment of how each social program came into being, a statement of each program's objectives and the rationales behind each activity, and a description of what has been accomplished.

- *Cost or outlay*—a social-economic operating statement that tabulates the expenditures an enterprise makes on social objectives less the negative costs for social objectives not addressed. The approach is to measure the total social impact, positive and negative.

- *Social responsibility accounting*—a system of accounting that tabulates social costs and benefits with the objective of the best social return for the social investment made.

- *Social indicators*—an audit of the community is conducted using social indicators to provide data on the most pressing needs. Corporate social performances are compared or related to community or social indicators.

Corporations have moved beyond the social auditing approaches listed above. The following is a representation of the trend to the more sophisticated social auditing necessary for sustainability reporting:

- *Social objective setting*—In addition to economic objectives, corporations are establishing social and environmental objectives and reporting on their accomplishments in corporate annual reports.

- *Triple bottom line reporting*—Corporations prepare and publicize reports outlining economic, social, and environmental criteria and the extent to which they have been satisfied. Examples of such bottom lines are economic, ethical and environmental, and people, planet, and prosperity.

- *Social reports*—Quite often the objectives and triple bottom line criteria are presented in comprehensive social reports prepared by the corporations themselves.

- *Sustainable guidelines*—Comprehensive sets of economic, social, and environmental criteria and performance indicators are being developed by organizations independent of corporations such as business research institutes, consultants, and nongovernmental organizations (NGOs). These criteria and indicators are also referred to as guidelines or benchmarks and are being used in the preparation of social reports.

- *Externally verified social reports*—The corporations are using outside, independent organizations not only to develop the guidelines, but also to verify the corporation's performance relating to the guidelines. This independent verification is a major turning point in social reporting, or sustainability reporting. Although this practice is not widespread, it is gaining acceptance.

- *Consultation with stakeholders*—Some corporations are consulting stakeholders on the preparation of CSR or sustainability reports. Such consultation obtains the views of relevant stakeholders and is another approach to evaluating the corporation's CSR program.

Corporate social responsibility (CSR) reporting (sustainability reporting) A management function that documents the corporation's economic, ethical/social, and environmental responsibilities and initiatives, and communicates this information to relevant stakeholders.

The results of this auditing process become the basis for social reporting. **Corporate social responsibility (CSR) reporting** is a management function that documents the corporation's economic, ethical/social, and environmental responsibilities and initiatives, and communicates this information to relevant stakeholders. It is also known as *sustainability reporting*.

Managers and businesspersons must now be familiar with this trend and its implications. Traditionally they worried about financial audits, but now many corporations are performing audits or developing reporting mechanisms that measure how well the corporation is achieving its social responsibilities as well as its economic responsibilities. The formats and organization of these reports differ among corporations, with some being innovative and creative. Several of these reports are referenced in this chapter.

connect

Want to learn about examples of **the best CSR/sustainability reports**? Go to CONNECT.

Three reasons why reporting is necessary are to maintain the corporation's reputation, to meet the demands of stakeholders, and to sustain corporate profitability.

LO 9.2 Corporate Reputation and CSR

Corporate reputation As defined by Fombrun, "a perceptual representation of a corporation's past actions and future prospects that describes the corporation's overall appeal to all of its key constituents [stakeholders] when compared with other leading rivals."

Corporate reputation is "a perceptual representation of a corporation's past actions and future prospects that describes the corporation's overall appeal to all of its key constituents [stakeholders] when compared with other leading rivals."[2] It is often associated with corporate image, especially as promoted through public relations. The problem is that a corporate image has a temporary effect and is not an enduring solution to the relationship between business and society. Today corporate reputation is related more to the "character" of the corporation and involves corporate credibility, trust, and responsibility.

Corporate reputation is an asset, though an intangible one. It is difficult to measure, although surveys attempt it[3] (see Everyday Ethics 9.1 for examples). Reputation is measured by being able to do the right thing, and through CSR reporting corporations hope to convince stakeholders that they are indeed behaving this way.

A distinction should be made between CSR and corporate reputation. CSR involves the way in which a corporation interacts with its stakeholders (as discussed in Chapters 4 and 8), whereas corporate reputation focuses on the perceptions that stakeholders have about the corporation as a result of the interactions. Thus, stakeholders' impressions are most often formed by a corporation's CSR performance. The drivers of corporate reputation include customer service, ethical conduct, community involvement, employee relations, quality of products and services, innovativeness, and environmental stewardship.[4]

A connection exists not only between corporate reputation and stakeholders but also to issues management and strategy.[5] Stakeholders determine the issues that affect reputation, and managers must address stakeholders and the issues that concern them. Because reputation is good for business it is the responsibility of all managers, starting with the chief executive officer (CEO). A corporate reputation builds trust with stakeholders, might enable the corporation to command higher prices, attracts qualified people, and minimizes the risk of damage from a crisis. Corporate reputation rather than image has become a key to a successful corporate strategy.

Researchers have found a relationship between corporate reputation and social responsibility, particularly when the corporation experiences a crisis or event that damages its image or reputation. A study by Minor and Morgan found that corporations with higher CSR ratings are more successful at overcoming setbacks.[6] Another study found that CSR created a layer of protection, and corporations known for social responsibility experienced less decline in stock prices when a crisis occurred.[7] Other researchers examined the influence that socially responsible images or reputations have on consumers. A commitment to ethics statements such as a values statement or code of ethics creates a reputation of responsibility that legitimizes a corporation in the eyes of consumers. They also found that consumers expect financially successful corporations to contribute to society. A corporation's reputation decreases consumer perception of purchase risk and increases consumer loyalty.[8]

Everyday Ethics
9.1

CSR and Reputation and Trust of Canadian Business

The three examples in this vignette illustrate the reputation of Canadian corporations and the trust placed in them. In the 2012 *Marketing*/Leger Corporate Reputation Survey, 1,500 Canadians were asked which corporations they considered to be the most reputable in Canada. The survey identified 202 corporations in 33 industries and found that the ten most reputable companies were Heinz, Google, Kellogg, Sony, Kraft, Tim Hortons, Campbell, Canadian Tire, Subway, and Staples. All the companies were involved in doing good deeds in their communities. The following were among the tips for achieving a good reputation:

- Have a strong set of corporate values,
- Behave in an ethical manner,
- Be socially and environmentally responsible,
- Deal with customers and communities in an honest, transparent way.

Edelman, a public relations firm, surveys the trust that the public has in various institutions, including business. In its 2012 survey, the technology, food and beverage, and brewing and spirits industries were the most trusted in Canada while the pharmaceutical, media, and energy industries were trusted the least. Business leaders were trusted more than government leaders, but business was not meeting the public's expectations.

The School of Public Policy, University of Calgary, surveyed 1,508 Canadians about their knowledge of energy. As part of the survey, respondents were asked which individuals or organizations they trusted relating to energy matters. The most trusted were academics and economics experts and least trusted were oil and gas companies, energy company executives, and the Canadian Association of Petroleum Producers. The image or reputation of the energy industry is a serious problem for corporations, especially because of the existence of several major industry issues such as the Alberta oil sands and pipeline construction.

Sources: Rebecca Harris, "Best brand reputations 2012," *Marketing Magazine,* May 10, 2012, http://www.marketingmag.ca/news/marketer-news/best-brand-reputations-2012-52296#methodology, accessed November 6, 2012; "2012 Edelman Trust Barometer Canada and global results," http://www.slideshare.net/EdelmanTO/2012-edelman-trust-barometer-canada-and-global-results, accessed November 6, 2012; and The School of Policy, University of Calgary, "Energy literacy in Canada," SPP Research Papers, volume 5, issue 32, October 2012, http://policyschool.ucalgary.ca/sites/default/files/research/energy-literacy-survey.pdf, accessed November 7, 2012.

Corporate reputations are hard to build and easy to lose. Corporate social responsibility or sustainability can help build a corporation's reputation—and can help preserve it when an ethical crisis occurs.

LO 9.3   Stakeholders Expect CSR Accountability

Several stakeholders are expecting—or even demanding—corporations to be accountable for their economic, social, and environmental responsibilities. The following is a list of the most influential stakeholders.

- *Shareholders and financial institutions*—Institutional investors and individual shareholders interested in ethical or social investing require additional information on CSR. Financial indexes have been formulated to guide investors, for example the Jantzi Social Index[9] in Canada and the Dow Jones Sustainability Index[10] in the United States. Responsibility for Ethics 9.1 describes the Jantzi Social Index.

RESPONSIBILITY
for Ethics (9.1)

> ## The Jantzi Social Index
>
> The Jantzi Social Index (JSI) is a socially screened, common stock index modelled on the S&P/TSX 60 of 60 corporations that have passed a set of broadly based environmental, social, and governance rating criteria. Criteria have been developed to evaluate issue areas such as Aboriginal relations, community involvement, corporate governance, employee and customer relations, environment, and human rights. Some indicators may exclude corporations with significant involvement in the production of nuclear power; the provision of pornography, tobacco, and gaming products; the use of genetic engineering; and weapons-related contracting.
>
> The index measures how a market for the selected corporations has changed over time. A benchmark is also established against which the success of the process is measured. Thus, the JSI provides a process against which institutional investors—for example, pension and mutual funds—can measure the performance of their socially screened stock portfolios. Also, the Jantzi–Sustainalytics Canadian Social Investment Database provides a comprehensive analysis of approximately 300 companies and income trusts, including all constituents of the S&P/TSX Composite Index.

Source: Jantzi–Sustainalytics Web site at http://www.sustainalytics.com/indexes, accessed November 2, 2012.

- *Employees*—Informing employees of the corporation's CSR initiatives results in intangible benefits such as increasing employee satisfaction and reducing turnover. In a recent survey, about 80 percent of employees agreed with the statement that the more socially responsible their employer was the more motivated and loyal the employees became.[11]

- *Consumers*—Consumers are concerned about aspects of the goods and services they purchase including, for example, such things as the conditions under which they were produced, genetic modifications, environmental harm, and treatment of employees.

- *Society at large*—Local communities are interested in social and environmental issues confronting them. Corporate reporting is now addressing this by presenting materials by facility and community. Even students are seeking more information on corporate reporting, either for personal use or for use in classroom discussions or assignments.

- *Service professionals*—The professional accounting associations are recommending more elaborate CSR and sustainability reporting. An example is the Canadian Institute of Chartered Accountants' efforts encouraging corporations to enhance sustainability disclosure in the Management Discussion and Analysis (MD&A) filing. Other professions also encourage increased disclosure.

- *Non-governmental organizations*—NGOs are constantly seeking information on corporations. In many cases, it is questionable how they use the information. For this reason, CSR reporting should be scrutinized and verified prior to release. This stakeholder will be discussed more in Chapter 13.

- *Charities*—CSR reporting informs the public of the corporation's philanthropic efforts. In addition, many social reports identify the corporation's giving policies, including areas of interest, and provide application information.

- *Media*—Journalists are constantly seeking story ideas or information to complete a story. The availability of CSR reports, especially online, is one quick source for them.

- *Government*—Numerous government acts and regulations require disclosure. On the other hand, governments are also interested in corporate self-disclosure because it avoids the need for legislation. Chapter 10 examines the association between ethics and government's role in society and its involvement with business.

Although this is not a complete list, it does indicate that many stakeholders are demanding or expecting increasing amounts of CSR or sustainability disclosure—one good reason why corporations should be serious about considering this type of disclosure.

> **LO 9.4** ## CSR and Profitability

It is generally accepted that the blind pursuit of maximum profits would be socially irresponsible. It is also believed that most enterprises have multiple objectives, some of which are social in nature. If these statements are accurate, it is interesting to speculate about the relationship between the extent of socially responsible actions of an enterprise and its level of profitability.

The relationship between profitability and CSR has been extensively studied, with mixed conclusions that can be summarized as follows:

- expenditures on social responsibility initiatives do not contribute to profits
- expenditures on social responsibility initiatives do contribute to profits
- expenditures on social responsibility initiatives might contribute to profits.

A study by Laffer, Coors, and Winegarden found that CSR is not positively correlated with business profitability. Furthermore, the authors found some evidence that CSR activities lead to decreased profitability.[12] Another study found that up to some point, increased expenditures in social responsibility are associated with higher profits but further increases are associated with lower profit levels.[13]

An example of a study supporting the position that a positive relationship exists between CSR and profitability was a mega-analysis of 52 previous studies on the impact of CSR on profits by Orlitzky et al. Their findings confirmed that social responsibility and, to a lesser extent, environmental responsibility do have a measurable positive impact on profits. They concluded that their analysis established a greater degree of certainty with respect to the corporate social responsibility and corporate financial performance relationship than was assumed to exist by many business academics.[14]

On the other hand, a study by Margolis and Walsh expressed doubt about research methodologies used in examining the relationship. They examined the 30-year quest for an empirical relationship between a corporation's social initiatives and its financial performance—127 studies were analyzed, almost half of which pointed to a positive relationship between CSR and financial results. The other half reported a negative relationship, a non-significant relationship, or a mixed relationship. The authors argue that a definite link between CSR and profits may be more illusory than the research results suggest. Serious questions are raised about methodological difficulties, including problems with the sample used, concerns about reliability and validity of the measures used, and influence of moderating conditions.[15]

The research and debate on the relationship will continue, most likely without a definitive conclusion, for some time. However, the Network for Business Sustainability (NBS) has taken another view of the CSR and profitability relationship. It points out that 63 percent of the studies on CSR and profitability have found a positive relationship, 15 percent a negative one, and 22 percent a mixed or neutral one. NBS suggests calculating the return of investment of CSR by thinking in terms of creating value. Corporations have financial management systems and financial metrics or measures, but few metrics relating to CSR or sustainability. Initiatives can result in positive impacts, and the social and environmental benefits fall into one of three categories:

- *Firm processes*—The value created can be identified by readily available measures. The costs and savings of an energy conservation program can be measured, most likely with savings exceeding costs.

- *Firm outcomes*—The value created is less obvious and as a result may not be measured—but it should be. An example is provided by a conservation program that may improve employee satisfaction and increase productivity.
- *External outcomes*—The value created is in the more positive perceptions of external stakeholders, such as consumers who may view the corporation more favourably and increase their loyalty, thus increasing sales of the corporation's products.

Some of this value may have been overlooked in the past. NBS has identified three categories of metrics that business should use to capture this value. Financial metrics are the easiest to measure; for example, stock price or return on investment. Valuing CSR at this stage is relatively easy. The second metric is operational, which measures the direct bottom-line impacts of CSR activities and represents the direct costs and revenues associated with an activity. Lastly, strategic metrics are those that result in the corporation improving its strategic position. The metrics are less tangible but are value created from improved employee motivation, the creation of a culture of innovation, and greater brand loyalty.[16]

Now that reasons have been given for CSR reporting, the criteria used in evaluating such reports are discussed.

> **LO 9.5**   ## Social Auditing and Reporting Criteria

The contents of corporate social reports reflect the criteria used in social audits. Several surveys or guidelines are examined to provide illustrations of the criteria used to assess the ethics of business and identify socially responsible initiatives.

Canadian Business for Social Responsibility (CBSR) is a business-supported, non-profit CSR consultancy that assists Canadian businesses in their social reporting. Responsibility for Ethics 9.2 gives more information on the organization.

RESPONSIBILITY
for Ethics **9.2**

Canadian Business for Social Responsibility

Canadian Business for Social Responsibility (CBSR) is a membership-led, non-profit organization that assists Canadian corporations in formulating decisions that improve performance and contribute to a better world. It believes that corporate responsibility and business success go hand-in-hand, and supports its business members on their CSR agendas. Its vision is "Better Business: Better World," and its mission is "Changing the Way Business Does Business."

CBSR's values indicate how it operates:

- To lead in the definition of responsible business practice.
- To change the way business does business with practical and high-impact management tools.
- To anticipate and translate CSR trends and opportunities.
- To engage members and others to deliver high-impact results.
- To respect and value members' interests.

Membership provides advice on CSR issues, access to various CSR tools and research, and entry to the leading network of CSR companies, executives, and practitioners in Canada. Members learn from networking events including working groups, seminars, and dialogue on emerging issues. CBSR also offers a consulting service.

Source: Canadian Business for Social Responsibility, http://www.cbsr.ca.

CBSR has developed a checklist of criteria it calls *GoodCompany Guidelines for Corporate Social Performance.* The guidelines are useful for all businesses, but some of the items may not be applicable to small and medium-sized businesses. The seven checklists are community (9 criteria), employee (19 criteria), customer (7 criteria), supplier (9 criteria), environment (6 criteria), shareholder (6 criteria), and international operations (4 criteria). Each criterion has six assessment items: accountability/transparency, stakeholder involvement, program evaluation and measurement, program, policy, and commitment.[17]

Other resources on CSR are available to Canadian businesspersons and managers. The Conference Board of Canada has a "Corporate Responsibility Assessment Tool" to help members better understand how to effectively manage and integrate CSR.[18] The Canadian Centre for Ethics and Corporate Policy operates EthicsCentre CA, an independent ethics centre promoting an ethical orientation to Canadian organizations. It operates as a registered charity governed by volunteers and supported by corporations and individuals, sponsors speaker events for members, and publishes a newsletter, *Management Ethics.*[19] Finally, The Accountability Project is an initiative to improve CSR and sustainability reporting among business leaders and managers.[20]

Everyday Ethics 9.2 describes one corporation's approach to CSR reporting.

Everyday Ethics
9.2

Corporate Responsibility Reporting at RBC

Royal Bank of Canada (RBC) uses a comprehensive approach to sustainability reporting that includes the following components:

- A 131-page corporate responsibility report and public accountability statement
- A Global Reporting Initiative (GRI) report of RBC's performance
- A listing of investments in the community and their impact
- A statement of RBC's commitment to the environment
- Responsible business practices in the areas of workplace, access to banking, economic impact, and corporate integrity
- Social finance initiative in support of social enterprises

Sources: RBC, "Community and sustainability," http://www.rbc.com/community-sustainability/index.html; "Reporting and performance," http://www.rbc.com/community-sustainability/reporting-performance.html; and "Corporate responsibility report & public accountability statement," http://www.rbc.com/community-sustainability/_assets-custom/pdf/RBC-CRR-Report-e.pdf, accessed November 2, 2012.

Global Reporting Initiative (GRI) A non-profit organization that works toward a sustainable global economy by providing guidance in sustainability reporting.

An example of an international undertaking to establish reporting criteria is the **Global Reporting Initiative (GRI)**, a non-profit organization that works toward a sustainable global economy by providing guidance in sustainability reporting. Its vision is for a sustainable global economy where organizations manage their economic, environmental, social, and governance performance impacts responsibly and report them transparently.[21]

Among GRI's principles are those intended to define report content: materiality, stakeholder inclusiveness, sustainability context, and completeness, and those intended to define report quality: balance, comparability, accuracy, timeliness, reliability, and clarity.[22] Corporations using the GRI *Sustainability Reporting Guidelines* are expected to include the following standard disclosures:

- Strategy and Profile
  - Strategy and Analysis
  - Organizational Profile
  - Report Parameters

- Governance, Commitments, and Engagement
- Management Approach and Performance Indicators
- Economic
- Environmental
- Social
  - Labour Practices and Decent Work
  - Human Rights
  - Society
  - Product Responsibility[23]

The organization states that GRI reports can be used for three purposes, among others: (1) benchmarking and assessing sustainability performance with respect to laws, norms, codes, performance standards, and voluntary initiatives; (2) understanding how the organization influences and is influenced by expectations about sustainable development; and (3) comparing performance within an organization and between different organizations over time.[24]

A third version of the *Sustainability Reporting Guidelines* was released in March 2006 for public consultation. The development of these guidelines is a continuing process; the current version is 3.1. Many corporations utilize the *Guidelines* in their CSR reporting.

There are numerous other guidelines and indicators, some of which are listed in Responsibility for Ethics 9.3. These and other indicators will be discussed in Chapter 11, "Ownership and Governance of the Corporation," Chapter 14, "The Environment and Business Responsibilities," and Chapter 15, "Globalization and Business Responsibilities."

RESPONSIBILITY
for Ethics **9.3**

Global Corporate Reporting Guidelines

Several international comprehensive indicators exist in addition to the ones mentioned in the text. Some examples include the following:

- *OECD Guidelines for Multinational Enterprises*—recommendations to multinational corporations operating in or from an adhering country.
- *UN Global Compact*—an initiative to bring together UN agencies, labour, and civil society to support universal environmental and social principles.
- *Caux Round Table Principles for Business*—an international network of principled business leaders working to promote a moral capitalism.
- *International Code of Ethics for Canadian Business*—a statement of the beliefs, values, and principles Canadian corporations should follow in global business operations.
- *ISO 26000 CSR Standard*—The International Organization for Standardization (ISO) has developed a guidance standard for corporate social responsibility that relates to CSR reporting. The 14000 standards apply to the environment.

LO 9.6   Evaluating Canadian CSR Reporting

CSR and sustainability reports cover the corporation's economic, social, and environmental responsibility initiatives as identified in the auditing process. At this time in Canada, CSR reporting is voluntary. Several surveys evaluate the reporting of Canadian corporations and are listed in Responsibility for Ethics 9.4. The assessment criteria vary among the surveys, but all refer to those identified in the previous section.

RESPONSIBILITY
for Ethics (9.4)

Surveys of Canadian Social Responsibility and Sustainability Reporting

- Corporate Knights *magazine's "Best 50 Corporate Citizens in Canada"*—The corporations are selected on several environmental, social, and governance indicators found in the public domain.
- Maclean's *magazine's "Top 50 Socially Responsible Corporations"*—Maclean's, in cooperation with Jantzi Research, selects the corporations on the basis of several social, environmental, and governance indicators.
- *The Canadian Institute of Chartered Accountants (CICA) "Corporate Reporting Awards"*—This survey recognizes leaders in the areas of financial reporting, electronic disclosure, corporate governance disclosure, and sustainable development reporting.
- *Best Practices in Canadian Corporate Sustainability Reporting*—Stratos Inc. reports on CSR in Canada. The report presents the results of research on the uptake of and approaches to sustainability reporting and reviews the sustainability reporting at seven leading Canadian companies.

Sources: "Best 50 corporate citizens," *Corporate Knights,* Spring 2012, volume 11, issue 1, 28–36; "The top 50 socially responsible corporations," *Maclean's,* June 25, 2012, 37–50; Corporate Reporting Award, Canadian Institute of Chartered Accountants, http://www.cica.ca; and Stratos Inc., *Best Practices in Canadian Corporate Sustainability Reporting,* http://www.stratos-sts.com/resources/insights/reporting-communication.html.

Questioning the Rankings and What Makes a Good Report

Dozens of codes and standards rank or evaluate corporations on every aspect of CSR. Corporations are confronted with lengthy forms and are required to meet various compliance practices. An issue that exists involves whether or not the standards and codes are valid measures of the numerous aspects of CSR. The information supplied by management may be manipulated to the corporation's advantage. Some corporations ignore all requests as there are too many, and too much work is needed to complete the surveys.[25]

Chatterji and Levine make several recommendations for improving the process:

- The codes or standards should be more transparent.
- The measures should be better explained and the source of weightings justified.
- Efforts should be made to reduce compliance costs by better designed forms and measures.
- The data used should be improved, with less reliance on information being supplied by management and more being sought from stakeholders.
- Financial performance measurement uses sophisticated methodology which should be incorporated into the measurement of social indicators.[26]

As indicated in Responsibility for Ethics 9.4, CSR reports are analyzed by several stakeholders. The analysis has identified best practices that corporations should consider when preparing a CSR report. These include:

- Identify the stakeholders to the target audience.
- Describe trends, risks, challenges, and opportunities facing the industry and the corporation. Give an outlook for the future.
- Identify issues, indicating which are priorities so the report has a focus.
- Identify major stakeholders and the approaches used to engage them. Report negative feedback as well as positive.

- Describe the reporting guidelines or standards used; for example, the Global Reporting Initiative. Consider having an external auditor verify the measures.

- Include objectives for the future and report on objective accomplishments from previous years.

- Use visuals such as photographs, illustrations, and graphs to effectively enhance appearance and readability.

- Identify the managers responsible for CSR in the corporation.[27]

connect Want to learn more about **evaluating sustainability reports**? Go to CONNECT.

Another aspect of CSR reporting is understanding how the report should be communicated to stakeholders.

LO 9.7 Communicating CSR and Sustainability Results

The reports themselves are a form of communication that will enhance reputation, but the production of a report in itself is not sufficient. Efforts must be made to communicate it to stakeholders.

Within the corporation, various communications activities will inform employees: articles in newsletters, information on the employee intranet, agenda items at regular meetings, and corporate reputation committees. The integration of reporting with any performance measures is key so that employees are reminded constantly of CSR reporting.[28]

Communication with other stakeholders can be with the complete CSR report, or with brochures or mini-reports that mention only the highlights. These summaries can be inserted in customer invoices or billings, or other correspondence. Corporate Web sites should include electronic versions of the report that are easily accessed. Reporting is being segmented by audience to match messages with stakeholders, for example reports by facility site or community. Also, reporting should be communicated to those who are ready for it, or who are demanding it.

Managers should be aware that newspaper and magazine articles and television news programs are important sources of information for many stakeholders. Corporations must "manage the message," being honest in all communications and informing stakeholders how the corporation has promptly responded to issues or crises. Word of mouth should not be forgotten, as it is a form of communication among some stakeholders. Stakeholders who are influencers or opinion leaders should be identified and communications designed specially to reach them. Finally, communicating CSR and sustainability information is a continuous process, as is the practice of CSR.

In a corporation, one manager or department should be made responsible for the reporting process. Responsibility for Ethics 9.5 describes whom this person might be. Everyday Ethics 9.3 describes Catalyst Paper Corp.'s efforts at auditing, reporting, and communicating its CSR.

An emphasis on CSR auditing, reporting, and communication will be part of the education received by future entrepreneurs and managers. Business programs are initiating changes to incorporate the ethics and responsibilities of business topics into their programs.

connect Want to learn more about **CSR in Canadian business**? Go to CONNECT.

RESPONSIBILITY
for Ethics **9.5**

Corporate Responsibility Officer (CRO)

Some manager should be responsible for preparing and communicating CSR or sustainability reports; it is a function unto itself that requires managerial leadership. The manager responsible for this is now being referred to as the corporate responsibility officer (CRO), a title being advocated by a membership-based organization by the same name.

Today, various management positions are responsible for this function, including chief compliance officer, chief ethics officer, director or VP of corporate social responsibility, general counsel, corporate secretary, and executive vice-president for human resources or investor relations. The new position consolidates such activities as compliance management, corporate communications and public relations, environmental sustainability, government relations and lobbying, investor relations, socially responsible investing, and workforce diversity.

CRO members receive information on current trends, success stories, best practices, methodologies, and navigational tools. Membership includes subscriptions to *CRO Magazine* and *Business Ethics Magazine* as well as newsletters, access to TheCRO.com Web site, and information on conferences.

LO 9.8   Business Schools and Sustainability Reporting

Very few business schools are preparing their own CSR or sustainability reports, but they are being evaluated on their response to the ethics of business and corporate social responsibility. They are facing demands from society and the business community to better prepare their graduates to identify and address ethical implications in business. In business schools ethics and social responsibility have received attention only recently, as the emphasis has been on functional areas—some of which have focused on financial rather than social responsibilities. Corporate corruption practices have increased awareness of ethical practice in business, and graduates who will be managers and businesspersons need a moral compass and sensitivity to acting consistently. In other words, graduates must be prepared to face the reality of moral dilemmas.

Corporations are increasingly using accountability audits to develop social responsibility reports for various stakeholders. Although very few business schools publish CSR reports on themselves, they are being held accountable for the integration of ethics of business and social responsibility topics into courses and programs. An example of a business school that has prepared a sustainability report is provided in Everyday Ethics 9.4.

The best known surveys evaluating the social and environmental performance of business schools are the American survey "Beyond Grey Pinstripes" and the Canadian survey "Knight Schools: The Annual Knight School Guide to Business Education"; both are described in Responsibility for Ethics 9.6. It is not clear whether these surveys will influence business school behaviour, but social audits have had an impact on corporations.

The Association to Advance Collegiate Schools of Business (AACSB International)[29] does not require stand-alone courses in the ethics of business, assuming that the treatment of ethics is infused into other courses. Some controversy in the business and society academic community exists regarding this standard, with many arguing for stand-alone courses in addition to infusion. Accredited schools must monitor AACSB International's

Everyday Ethics

9.3

Measuring, Reporting, and Communicating Sustainability at Catalyst Paper

Catalyst Paper Corporation manufactures a broad range of high-quality paper products and is one of the largest producers of mechanical printing paper. It is recognized for its sustainable business practices.

Its 2011 sustainability report "Moving Forward . . ." illustrates the efforts that corporations go to in measuring, reporting, and communicating their sustainability performance. The 46-page report includes the following sections on various aspects of the corporation's operations:

- Stakeholder engagement
- Governance and management systems
- Worker engagement and development, and workplace safety
- Compensation and representation
- Economic footprint
- Communities and taxation

- First Nations
- Customers
- Wood fibre
- Environmental impact: water use, greenhouse gases, particulate emissions, and solid waste
- Production procurement

Extensive data are given on each and reported according to the United Nations Global Compact principles and the Global Reporting Initiative Index outlined below:

United Nations Global Compact Principles	Global Reporting Initiative Indicators
• Human rights	• Strategy and analysis
• Labour standards	• Organizational profile
• Environment	• Report parameters
• Anti-corruption	• Governance
	• Economic
	• Environmental
	• Labour relations
	• Human rights
	• Society
	• Product sustainability

Source: Catalyst Paper 2011 Sustainability Report, "Moving forward. . . ," http://www.catalystpaper.com/investors/sustainability-reports/moving-forward, accessed November 5, 2012.

position on ethics and be prepared for possible revisions. In fact, the following was included in the *Eligibility Procedures and Standards for Business Accreditation*:

> *E. The institution or the business programs of the institution must establish expectations for ethical behaviour by administrators, faculty, and students.*

> *INTERPRETATION: AACSB believes that ethical behaviour is paramount to the delivery of quality business education. Schools are encouraged to develop "codes of conduct" to indicate the importance of proper behaviour of administrators, faculty, and students in their professional and personal actions. Schools also may foster ethical behaviour through procedures such as disciplinary systems to manage inappropriate behaviour and through honour codes.*[30]

Everyday Ethics   Sustainability at the Haskayne School of Business, University of Calgary

9.4   The Haskayne School of Business embraces "the values of building a strong community infrastructure and giving back where we can." Its "Business and Community" report comprises the following:

- *Outreach activities*—In cooperation with others, sponsors the Distinguished Leader Award and three of the Calgary Youth Services Awards.
- *Community partnerships*—Hosting events and information sessions in cooperation with the Calgary Chamber of Commerce, staging events and promotions with Calgary Economic Development, and sponsoring the Calgary Philharmonic Orchestra.
- *Business partnerships*—Supporting development of a strategic plan where the vision includes ethical leadership, entrepreneurship, and energy.
- *Support for charities*—Providing support by faculty and students to charities including the United Way, Ronald McDonald House, Children's Wish Foundation, "Spicing up Spaces," which renovates a house for a deserving family, and "Top Gun," which fundraises for breast cancer research.
- *Management consulting*—Providing advice to local non-profits.
- *Enbridge Centre for Corporate Sustainability*—Implementing a research and education initiative promoting the advance of the triple bottom line: people, planet, prosperity.

Source: Haskayne School of Business, University of Calgary, "Business and community," http://haskayne. ucalgary.ca/business-and-community, accessed November 5, 2012.

Finally, a comprehensive ethics program for a business school will create a more favourable public image—within universities, the business community, and society. An ethics program will enable business schools to align their behaviour more closely with that demanded by society. Given the trends in society and in the field of business and management education, business schools need to prepare themselves for possible demands relating to the ethics of business and the implications of ethics on the business programs and schools as well.

LO 9.9   The Future of CSR and Social Reporting

To understand the form CSR reporting will take, it is necessary to speculate on the future of CSR itself. The following are two views of what might happen with CSR.

In a report for VanCity Credit Union, Strandberg interviewed 47 CSR thought leaders about the future and a variety of views emerged. It is agreed that CSR is an aspect of the paradigm shift from industrial to sustainability capitalism. The progress on CSR has been slow, but it appears to be moving into the mainstream of business.[31]

Some of the interviewees felt corporations will lose interest in CSR and it will not move beyond a token baseline. Others thought CSR would develop quickly, especially if driven by high-profile wrongdoing. Continuous improvement would occur in CSR but it would be inconsistent across industry sectors. It was felt by some that CSR was part of a search for a new social contract between business and society. Despite the differences in views of the social impact and degree of corporate commitment, the majority agreed that:

5–10 years from now CSR will nonetheless become increasingly mainstream within business, even if not with the public consciousness. CSR tools, resources, language—all will

Social Responsibility Assessment of Business Schools

"Beyond Grey Pinstripes"

This survey of MBA programs is an independent, biennial business sustainability survey by the Aspen Institute's Business and Society Program. "Beyond Grey Pinstripes" highlights the most innovative MBA programs and faculty infusing environmental and social impact management into business school curriculum. Participating business schools are ranked on the extent to which they have incorporated environmental and social impact management using the following criteria:

- **Availability of Relevant Courses** counts the number of courses offered that contain social, environmental, or ethical content.

- **Student Exposure** measures teaching hours and student enrolment in these courses to understand to what extent students are actually exposed to such content.

- **Relevant Courses to Impact Business** is a simple count of the number of courses that not only demonstrate their relevance to the survey, but specifically address the intersection of social and environmental issues in mainstream, for-profit business.

- **Faculty Research** counts the number of scholarly articles containing some degree of social, environmental, or ethical content being published in peer-reviewed business journals.

"Knight Schools"

The "Knight Schools" survey is conducted for and published in *Corporate Knights,* a magazine for Canadian corporate responsibility. The survey is carried out on an annual basis and covers graduate programs. It is similar to the "Beyond Grey Pinstripes" report but involves different criteria and weightings. Details of the criteria used include the following:

- **Institutional Support**—guest speakers, orientation, internship programs, scholarships, competitions, endowed chairs, institutes and centres, and faculty research.

- **Student-led Initiatives**—student groups and their activities.

- **Coursework**—core and elective courses, joint degrees, and specializations.

Sources: Based on Aspen Institute, "Beyond grey pinstripes," http://www.beyondgreypinstripes.org/; and "9th annual ranking Knight Schools," *Corporate Knights,* volume 11, issue 2, Summer 2012, 42–47.

become more aligned with business norms and systems. CSR standards—to greater or lesser effect—will be part of business basics and not an add-on.[32]

Strandberg identified a continuum of CSR possibilities, from "CSR Lite" to "Deep CSR"; these are presented in Table 9.1.

Some other main findings by Strandberg are that:

- The role of stakeholders will become more important and consultation will become a core competency for managers. The relationship with NGOs will become more challenging and CSR will extend along the corporation's supply chain. Ethical consumers will be more powerful, and employees and investors will place more demands on the corporation.

TABLE 9.1	*Continuum of Future Commitment to CSR*

Possible Future CSR	Corporate Commitment
CSR Lite	Superficial and marginal, may be required by law
	Concerned mainly about responsiveness to complaints
	May use indicators such as GRI and think they are in compliance
CSR Compliant	Voluntarily take on environmental and social obligations to maintain licence to operate
	Keep abreast of emerging standards and norms of CSR
CSR Strategic	Become compliant with standards and then create niches in areas more strategic to the corporation
	May use CSR as key to survival by providing goods and services acceptable to society
CSR Integrated	Believe the need to take social and environmental impacts and opportunities into account.
	Comprehensive CSR policies and operationalizing CSR principles through rigorous standards and objectives
Deep CSR	Business model where mission is to improve social or environmental conditions
	Move to addressing trade-offs between different elements of triple bottom line

Source: Based on Coro Strandberg, *The Future of Corporate Social Responsibility* (Vancouver: VanCity Credit Union, September 2002), 6. Available at the Canadian Business for Social Responsibility Web site at http://www.cbsr.ca/cbsrsupport/reportpapers.htm.

- The top CSR issues will be the environment, reduction of poverty, governance, and accountability.
- There will be a new focus on CSR measurement and reporting with increased standardization.
- Governments may impose mandatory reporting.
- Corporations will be expected to play a greater role in social change.[33]

Overall, most participants in the study agreed that "CSR progress will be slow over the next ten years, but will become increasingly mainstreamed by business."[34] This observation is for the most part still applicable and the only finding that has not occurred is the imposition of mandatory reporting.

In another study, White developed three scenarios of the future of CSR: fade, integrate, or transform. Each of these is described briefly.

- *Fad-and-fade scenario*—Awareness and practise of CSR will decline significantly. This is the result of external trends or events beyond the control of the corporation. Government regulation emerges, replacing the self-regulatory purpose of CSR. The failure to address social, ethical, and governance challenges is also blamed.
- *Embed-and-integrate scenario*—CSR is accepted and the case for it no longer has to be made. Continuous enhancement of CSR approaches and practices occurs, and managers demonstrate a strong sense of moral and ethical commitment.
- *Transition-and-transformation*—Incremental changes to CSR are insufficient and stakeholders demand a redesign of the corporation. This will alter the nature and

purpose of the corporation and broaden its social function. There is a challenge to the prevailing wisdom relating to the rights and obligations of the corporation. This became necessary as the public lost confidence in the corporation.[35]

Implications for reporting and communication exist depending what the future holds for CSR. Assuming that CSR becomes "CSR integrated" or "deep CSR," as argued by Strandberg, or that it follows the "embed-and-integrate" or "transition-and-transformation" scenarios proposed by White, the following are considerations. A multiplicity of standards or guidelines exist, and at this time there does not appear to be any convergence around one. The willingness of corporations to make the extensive disclosures necessary and the reliability of information provided are issues. The process of independent verification has not become routine or formalized.

Management must continue to consciously reinforce the CSR measuring, reporting, and communicating process within corporations. Acceptance of CSR reporting has been relatively slow, with only a small number of publicly listed corporations—usually in consumer products and resource industries—making the effort. It is clear that CSR initiatives must be sincere and benefit society, and this is not achieved by merely reporting token actions or approaching it as a public relations tactic.

Your advice to Clare . . .

This chapter identified some of the difficulties with CSR reports that would help explain Clare's confusion. You advise her to check out the methodology used when she is looking at any of the rankings or lists of the "best" corporations; the criteria that were considered in selecting the corporations will be identified and should explain how a particular corporation made the list. Some criteria or measures are better than others. Clare also should keep in mind that corporations often "self-report," which may not be reliable. Furthermore, with any set of criteria, a corporation's good attributes may outweigh its (real or alleged) bad attributes.

SUMMARY

- Corporate reporting of social responsibility and sustainability has become a management function in many organizations. Social auditing is performed and the results become the basis for social reporting. Today, economic, ethical, and environmental standards or measures are being developed and used by corporations. The ultimate in social reporting is to evaluate the corporation's performance on these standards and to have the results externally verified. (LO 9.1)

- An important reason for social reporting is to sustain the corporation's reputation; that is, the stakeholders' perceived views of the corporation. There are connections among reputation, the corporation's stakeholders, the management of the issues they raise, and the approach to strategic management. Today, corporate reputation rather than image has become important to a successful corporate strategy. (LO 9.2)

- Today, CSR reporting is expected or demanded by several stakeholders, in particular shareholders, employees, consumers, society at large, service professionals, NGOs, charities, the media, and government. Too many stakeholders are interested in the corporation's social and environmental initiatives for reporting to be ignored by management. (LO 9.3)

- The relationship between CSR and profitability has been extensively studied. A majority of studies have found a positive relationship, but the research approaches and techniques used are being questioned. (LO 9.4)

- Several organizations are establishing criteria to be used in social auditing, which in turn determine the contents of CSR reports. Organizations assisting managers in this area include Canadian Business for Social Responsibility, the Conference Board of Canada, the Accountability Project, and the Global Reporting Initiative. The latter is the most prominent, and its indicators are utilized by many corporations in their CSR reports. (LO 9.5)

- The CSR reports produced by Canadian corporations are evaluated by newspapers, magazines, consulting firms, and professional organizations. This evaluation provides best-practice examples for corporations beginning to develop CSR reports. (LO 9.6)

- The act of producing the CSR report is a good learning exercise for the corporation, but it is necessary to communicate the results to stakeholders in various formats and delivery modes. (LO 9.7)

- Few business schools produce a CSR report on themselves. But they are being evaluated in terms of how they are integrating corporate social responsibility and the ethics of business into programs, courses, faculty activities, and student initiatives. (LO 9.8)

- The future of CSR and reporting is not certain. It is thought that it will become a required management function with a minimum baseline standard being established. What happens to CSR will determine the changes in social measuring, reporting, and communicating approaches. (LO 9.9)

KEY TERMS

Social auditing
Corporate social responsibility
  (CSR) reporting (sustainability
  reporting)

Corporate reputation
Global Reporting Initiative (GRI)

CRITICAL THINKING AND DISCUSSION QUESTIONS

1. Why should CSR measuring or auditing be externally verified?

2. What are the interrelationships among stakeholders, issues management, social responsibility, and corporate reputation?

3. Why are shareholders interested in social auditing and CSR reporting?

4. Why will the debate about the relationship between CSR and profitability not be resolved soon?

5. Why is transparency important in CSR reporting?

6. Why would a corporation use GRI's *Sustainability Reporting Guidelines* in its CSR reporting?

7. What kind of influence do the surveys of Canadian business's social responsibility and sustainability have on management?

8. What advice would you give to a manager responsible for preparing and communicating a CSR report?

9. What influence will business schools have on social auditing and reporting?

10. What is the future of CSR and corporate social reporting?

CASES

9.1   *Philanthropy and Academic Freedom*

A fundamental principle of any university or college is the concept of academic freedom. The Canadian Association of University Teachers (CAUT) defines academic freedom as "the right to teach, learn, study and publish free of orthodoxy or threat of reprisal and discrimination." It allows academics to criticize the university and comment on issues that affect their academic activities. Academic freedom applies in many areas, but a particular issue of concern in recent years has occurred when a businessperson donates funds to the university for a certain purpose, for example the funding of a building, research, scholarships, or research centres. Often the donor's name is associated in some way with the area funded. Many business schools or programs are named after prominent businesspersons who have provided funding.

These collaborations between universities and businesspersons are usually welcomed, because universities are insufficiently funded by governments. The CAUT has developed *Guiding Principles for University Collaborations,* which require the protection of academic freedom, university autonomy, and academic integrity in all activities; a commitment of free and open exchange of ideas and research results; the disclosure of real, potential, or perceived conflicts of interest; and the assurance of transparency. The Association of Universities and Colleges of Canada (AUCC) has also recently issued a "Statement of Academic Freedom" that included "ensuring that funding and other partnerships do not interfere with autonomy in deciding what is studied and how."

An example of the issues related to business funding was illustrated by a project to establish an international law studies program at York University. Jim Balsillie, co-founder of RIM, established an independent, nonpartisan think tank on international governance, the Centre for International Innovation (CIGI), to support research activities at Canadian universities. The Balsillie School of International Affairs had been established by a partnership among CIGI, Wilfrid Laurier University, and the University of Waterloo. In early 2012, he proposed establishing an international law studies program at York that included 10 research chairs and 20 graduate scholarships. He planned to donate $30 million, which would be matched by the province.

Faculty, particularly those in the law school, opposed the plan even though York's administration had supported the proposal. The faculty argued that the proposal had too many strings attached, including rights over hiring, renewal and termination of faculty, influence over curriculum and research, and veto over the program's budget. CAUT opposed the program, but it was accused of spreading misleading information about the program.

Questions

1. What are the issues involved in business philanthropy to universities?

2. Who are the stakeholders influencing these issues and/or those influenced by them?

3. What role does business have in funding universities and colleges? How will the York incident influence business support for universities?

Sources: Canadian Association of University Teachers (CAUT), "Academic freedom," http://www.caut.ca/pages.asp?page=140, accessed July 24, 2012; "CAUT guiding principles for university collaborations," April 2012, http://www.caut.ca/uploads/GuidingPrinc_UCollaboration.pdf, accessed July 24, 2012; Media Release, Association of Universities and Colleges of Canada, "Canada's universities adopt new Statement on Academic Freedom," October 25, 2011, http://www.aucc.ca/media-room/news-and-commentary/canadas-universities-adopt-new-statement-on-academic-freedom, accessed July 24, 2012; Centre for International Innovation, "About CIGI," http://www.cigionline.org/about; Tristin Hopper, "York U rejects RIM founder's $60M deal," *National Post* online edition, April 3, 2012, p. A2; Joseph Brean, "The academy vs. Jim Balsillie," *National Post* online edition, April 4, 2012, pp. A1, A6; and "Professors happy to keep Balsillie's hand off York," *National Post* online edition, April 5, 2012, p. A13.

9.2   *Ethics of Oil*

The phrase "ethical oil" has been popularized through the publication of Ezra Levant's book *Ethical Oil: The Case for Canada's Oil Sands* and is frequently used by politicians, including the prime minister and the federal minister of the environment.

Those who use the phrase argue that the oil sands petroleum has been unfairly demonized and they wish to downplay the negatives. They claim that petroleum from the oil sands is "ethical" compared to that from some other sources. Oil purchased from dictatorships and kleptocracies has been problematic because in those countries human rights, worker welfare, and social programs may be ignored. Corruption also has occurred in situations where leaders siphon off wealth for themselves and their friends. Saudi Arabia, Venezuela, Iran, and Libya have been mentioned as examples.

It also has been pointed out that oil produced in Canada must meet higher environmental standards than that produced in many countries. Alberta oil could be considered a morally superior resource because Canada has a democratically elected government, is concerned with peace, and maintains social programs for its citizens. Supporters claim that "ethical oil" is comparable to fair trade products such as coffee and certified non–conflict diamonds.

Critics state that it is inappropriate to use the phrase because ethics involves rules, standards, codes, or principles that provide guidance for morally appropriate behaviour in decision making. Others believe that the ethical question is really whether consumers should be consuming oil at all. In contrast to "ethical oil," environmental NGOs and some U.S. and European Union politicians have labelled petroleum from the oil sands as "dirty oil."

Critics claim that oil from the Alberta sands should be considered unethical or dirty oil because it is an unsustainable product, produces high emissions per barrel, lacks environmental monitoring, threatens wildlife (with the use of tailings pools), pollutes lakes, soils, and groundwater, has health consequences for local residents, and causes deforestation. Some U.S. politicians and government agencies have proposed that petroleum from the Alberta oil sands be banned, but California has been the only jurisdiction to impose restrictions to March 2011. European Union agencies have considered sanctions against oil sands production. The delay of the Keystone XL pipeline was linked to the branding of Alberta oil sands; this $7.0 billion project would carry oil sands bitumen across the Midwestern states, including Nebraska, to surplus refining capacity on the U.S. Gulf Coast.

According to some, the use of the phrases "ethical oil" and "dirty oil" is merely a rhetorical device or a way to spin the issue to get people to think of the positives or forget the negatives associated with oil sands production. Environmental NGOs argue that comparisons among oil producers are distractions and do nothing to make oil from any source a better product.

Questions

1. Is there such a thing as "ethical oil"?
2. **Who are the stakeholders involved in the discussion of this issue?**
3. **How does the use of terms like "ethical oil" and "dirty oil" contribute to the discussion of the issue? Are they merely a rhetorical device or method for spin intended to distract?**
4. **Does using the term "ethical oil" change how stakeholders view oil from the oil sands?**
5. **What are the implications for CSR measuring, reporting, and communicating?**

Sources: Ezra Levant, *Ethical Oil: The Case for Canada's Oil Sands* (Toronto: McClelland & Stewart, 2010); Ethical Oil Web site at http://www.ethicaloil.org; Garnet Barlow, "Spinning Alberta's oil sands disaster," *National Post,* January 15, 2011, FP19; Adam McDowell, "Alberta tar sands praised as 'ethical oil,'" *National Post* online edition, September 22, 2010; "Ethical oil: A debate," Small Dead Animals Web site at http://www.smalldeadanimals.com/archives/015431.html; "Rant: Ethical oil. . .really?" Rantrave Web site at http://wwwrantrave.com/Rant/Ethical-Oil-Really.aspx; Andrew Nikiforuk, "The fallacy of 'ethical oil,'" The Tyee Web site at http://thetyee.ca/Opinion/2010/09/22/EthicalOilFallacy; Steven Chase, "Peter Kent's plan to clean up the oil sands' dirty reputation," *The Globe and Mail,* January 7, 2011, A8–A9; and Jane Taber, "Meet the Prime Minister's oil-sands muse," *The Globe and Mail,* January 15, 2011, A12.

CHAPTER 10
Regulating Business

LO 10.1 Understand that business is regulated by a variety of approaches.

LO 10.2 Explain the eight forms of market regulation, self-regulation, and government regulation.

LO 10.3 Describe the scope of government's involvement in business.

LO 10.4 Describe government initiatives to encourage corporate social responsibility and accountability.

LO 10.5 Acknowledge the involvement of business in politics.

LO 10.6 Define lobbying and explain the process.

LO 10.7 Explain the role of corporate public affairs departments, and define corporate agenda and corporate welfare.

LO 10.8 Discuss the consequences of changing government involvement in business.

LO 10.9 Understand the ethical implications of business–government relationships.

LO 10.10 Realize that governments also have ethics programs.

What would you do if . . . ?

Luke Boychuk was in the kitchen reading the newspaper as his mother prepared dinner. He had graduated from a business program at the local college but was still living at home as he attempted to pay off his student loans. He said to his mother, "Here's another story about the federal government assistance to business. I really resent those big companies not paying back all their loans when I have no choice but to pay back my student loans with interest. They are nothing but corporate welfare bums."

Luke's annoyance was prompted by a story he had recently seen in the newspaper, detailing how between 1982 and 2012 the federal Department of Industry made loans totalling $7.4 billion that were intended to be repaid. However, only $2.1 billion had been repaid to taxpayers. Furthermore, only $9 million had been collected in interest by the department on all the loans made. In addition, the government had given business $6 billion in grants with no repayment required.

Defenders of the program argued that such assistance is necessary for high-technology companies to survive in Canada because other countries are providing similar aid. Because the corporations remain in Canada employment has been created, although exact figures were not known. Furthermore, a long time is required to research, develop, and market the innovations and returns should not yet be expected. On the other hand, the Canada Student Loans Program requires students to start paying interest immediately upon graduation, and to start repaying their loans six months after graduation.

Luke's mother, a chartered accountant, stopped her dinner preparations and turned to him. "But aren't *you* some kind of a welfare bum? The government paid the interest on your loans while you were in school. Besides, while you were a student, you were eligible for the GST/HST tax credit, could deduct tuition and education expenses, and, when you moved, you could also deduct those expenses.

Now you can deduct the interest paid on your loans. I don't recall you paying any income tax while you were in college. Today, students get an even better deal as they receive tax credits for transit passes and textbooks, and don't pay income tax on any scholarship, fellowship, or bursary income."

This information took Luke by surprise as he realized that individuals as well as corporations receive subsidies from the government. He thought he should reconsider the appropriateness of government programs to assist business.

What is your advice to Luke?

Sources: Human Resources and Social Development Canada (HRSDC), "Canada student loans program," http://www.hrsdc.gc.ca/eng/learning/canada_student_loan/index.shtml; Canada Revenue Agency, "Students and income tax," http://www.cra-arc.gc.ca/E/pub/tg/p105/p105-e.html; Government of Canada, "Technology partnerships Canada," http://www.ic.gc.ca/eic/site/ito-oti.nsf/eng/h_00154.html; and Mark Milke, "Corporate welfare bums at Industry Canada," Fraser Alert, Fraser Institute, September 2012.

Governments are a significant stakeholder in the relationship between business and society as they regulate, in a variety of ways, the activities of corporations. However, governments are not the sole regulator of business activity. The purpose of this chapter is to identify a spectrum of regulation, from self-regulation to government-formulated regulation.

>LO 10.1< The Spectrum of Regulation

When considering the regulation of business, most think immediately of government regulation. This section lists types of regulation that influence corporations based on (1) market forces, (2) self-regulation, and (3) government. Figure 10.1 identifies the range of regulation. No economies rely on market forces exclusively, and only a few socialist countries rely totally on government regulation.[1]

Self-regulation
Regulation imposed by the corporation or industry and not by the government or market forces.

A brief review of the pros and cons of self-regulation versus government regulation will establish the context for the discussion. **Self-regulation** is that imposed by the corporation or industry and not by the government or market forces. Businesspersons advocating this type of regulation claim that it is faster, cheaper, and more efficient and effective than government regulation. It is more likely to be accepted because it is voluntarily developed and adapted. It improves the relationship between business and consumers, and allows government to focus on other priorities.

Self-regulation is criticized because it impairs business competition and innovation due to self-serving restraint by industry participants. It may result in lower standards than those imposed by government, and it is ineffective whenever competition and other laws forbid compulsory membership necessary to ensure the worst offenders are involved. Its administration presents challenges, including the lack of adequate penalties for those who violate the regulations; insufficient financing, publicity, and promotion; and lack of public or consumer representation.

By contrast, it is argued that government regulation is necessary because society cannot trust business to regulate itself. Government provides a countervailing power to business by reflecting society's concerns. On the other hand, government regulation is criticized

FIGURE 10.1   *Spectrum of Regulation*

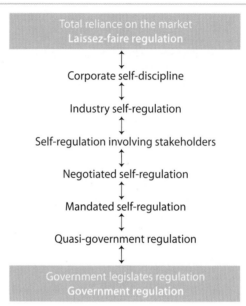

for being oppressive, ineffectual, confused, conflictual, costly, rigid, weakly enforced, and amenable to capture by those it is regulating.

In most forms of capitalism operating in democracies, a mixture of regulation provides a balance among market, self-regulation, and government regulation. The types of regulation discussed will clarify that regulation is not solely a government initiative. Also, regulation varies substantially among industries and even within industries.

What is being sought is a balance between private (business) and public (government), two extremes on the spectrum. The private sector provides for innovation, investment, and risk taking that promotes growth and employment. On the other hand, government provides the institutions, rules, safety nets, education, research, and infrastructure to empower the private sector. There are two possibilities in the relationship: (1) where business directly controls more of the economy than the private sector and (2) where the government controls the economy through a variety of methods. The balance shifts back and forth with different consequences for business and society stakeholders, as will be illustrated in this chapter.

LO 10.2   Types of Regulation

Laissez-Faire Market Regulation

If a rigorous and competitive market exists, there is less need for government-imposed laws or regulations as the corporation is influenced or regulated by market forces. This could also be referred to as a *laissez-faire* approach, where government does not interfere with business. The market disciplines would include competitive rivalry among firms with entry to the market possible and substitutes available. Various stakeholders are involved in influencing the corporation and in effect regulate its behaviours. An example is consumers who can take action to force the corporation to behave in particular ways by refusing to purchase goods or services, or through organized action such as a boycott. Abuses are possible, but are corrected by the market or stakeholder pressures.

Corporate Self-Discipline Regulation

Norms or standards are developed, used, and enforced by the corporation itself. This would be accomplished through mission and values statements, codes of conduct or ethics, or other guidelines. The acceptance and practice of corporate social responsibility (CSR) is the most general form of self-regulation (refer to Chapters 7, 8, and 9). Even though it has received substantial attention recently, CSR is still criticized. It has failed to live up to its promise, and some corporations have been accused of participating only for appearances or on a token basis. The desire for profit maximization still exists, and the corporation's behaviour is a function of market imperatives rather than management's values or corporate structures. There is no assurance that all corporations will participate, and enforcement is a problem. On the other hand, measures of CSR are being increasingly used and pressures are being applied by various stakeholders advocating socially responsible behaviour.

Industry Self-Regulation

Members of an industry can attempt to influence corporate behaviour and even enforce standards. Industry or trade associations often facilitate this type of regulation, and initiatives are undertaken to address industry issues that, if not addressed, may lead to government regulation. Advertising Standards Canada is an industry organization committed to the integrity of advertising through industry self-regulation with the *Canadian Code of Advertising Standards.* The Retail Council of Canada attempts to influence its members' behaviour in various ways, one of which is the *Code Practice: Scanner Price Accuracy Voluntary Code.* One of the most widely recognized industry self-regulation initiatives is Responsible Care by the chemical producing industry, described in Responsibility for Ethics 10.1.

The power to prevent abuses is usually limited as the potential for anti-competitive behaviour limits the effectiveness of this type of regulation. In most industries participation is voluntary, and even when a member violates the standards enforcement and remedial action is limited.

Self-Regulation Involving Stakeholders

With this type of self-regulation, the industry includes non-industry stakeholders by its own volition in the development, application, and enforcement of standards. The stakeholders would include representation from consumers and government, or some independent member of society including non-governmental organizations (NGOs). An example of this type of regulation is the Canadian Standards Association (CSA), a non-profit, membership-based organization serving business, industry, government, and consumers. Its standards committees comprise various stakeholders, and about one-third of its membership is consumers. The problems identified for "industry self-regulation" apply in addition to the fact that appropriate non-industry representatives are sometimes difficult to identify and, when they are, often are co-opted as shown in Responsibility for Ethics 10.2.

Negotiated Self-Regulation

With negotiated self-regulation, some outside body voluntarily negotiates regulatory standards—for example an NGO, a government agency, or a separate entity established by industry. An example of such a self-regulatory organization is the Canadian Motor Vehicle Arbitration Plan (CAMVAP) established to resolve disputes between consumers and vehicle manufacturers relating to defects and warranty programs for new cars. Neutral third parties or arbitrators are used to resolve disputes, and consumer and industry representatives govern the organization. This type of self-regulation is not common, as it is difficult to establish and can be expensive to operate.

The Chemistry Industry's Responsible Care® Ethic and Principles for Sustainability

Launched in 1985 by the Chemistry Industry Association of Canada (CIAC), Responsible Care® is a UN-recognized sustainability initiative that has been adopted in more than 60 countries around the world.

Commitment to Responsible Care inspires CIAC member-companies to continuously improve their health, safety and environmental performance, while delivering products essential to everyday life.

The Responsible Care® Ethic and Principles for Sustainability
We are committed to doing the right thing, and being seen to do the right thing.

We dedicate ourselves, our technology and our business practices to sustainability—the betterment of society, the environment and the economy. The principles of Responsible Care® are key to our business success, and compel us to:

- work for the improvement of people's lives and the environment, while striving to do no harm
- be accountable and responsive to the public, especially our local communities, who have the right to understand the risks and benefits of what we do
- take preventative action to protect health and the environment
- innovate for safer products and processes that conserve resources and provide enhanced value
- engage with our business partners to ensure the stewardship and security of our products, services and raw materials throughout their life cycles
- understand and meet expectations for social responsibility
- work with all stakeholders for public policy and standards that enhance sustainability, act to advance legal requirements and meet or exceed their letter and spirit
- promote awareness of Responsible Care®, and inspire others to commit to these principles

Source: Reprinted with permission from the Chemistry Industry Association of Canada, www.canadianchemistry.ca. 2009 Chemistry Industry Association of Canada. All rights reserved.

Mandated Self-Regulation

Self-regulatory organizations (SROs) Industry groups that are delegated or designated a regulatory function including the development, use, and enforcement of standards.

Government prefers to have industry regulate itself, and grants this under legislation. An example is **self-regulatory organizations (SROs)**, industry groups that are delegated or designated a regulatory function including the development, use, and enforcement of standards. An example is provided by the securities industry in Canada. The provincial securities commissions have delegated some aspects of securities regulation to the Toronto Stock Exchange (TSX), the Investment Industry Regulatory Organization of Canada (IIROC), and the Mutual Fund Dealers Association of Canada (MFDA). The TSX provides a market for trading equity capital and develops and enforces its own rules and regulations relating to corporate listings and the protection of investors. The IIROC regulates the activities of investment dealers in terms of both their capital adequacy and conduct of business, and monitors trading activity on debt and equity markets. The MFDA regulates the sale of mutual funds. The regulation of the investment industry is discussed further in Chapter 11. Professionals such as accountants and lawyers are also regulated by SROs.

RESPONSIBILITY
for Ethics **10.2**

> ## Guide for Environmental Claims
>
> In June 2008, the Competition Bureau Canada and the Canadian Standards Association released *Environmental Claims: A Guide for Industry and Advertisers,* which provided business with guidelines to prevent misleading green marketing. An objective of the *Guide* was to give consumers greater assurance about the accuracy of environmental claims. It provides examples of best practices on how to comply with the false or misleading provisions of laws enforced by the Competition Bureau. Among other practices, the Guide states that:
>
> - The use of vague claims implying general environmental improvement is insufficient and should be avoided.
> - Environmental claims should be clear, specific, accurate, and not misleading.
> - Environmental claims should be verified and substantiated prior to being made.
>
> The *Guide* describes the use of symbols for different environmental claims, and defines selected claims such as degradable, extended life product, recyclable, reduced energy consumption, reusable and refillable, waste reduction, and reduced water consumption.

Sources: Based on Canadian Standards Council media release "What does green really mean? Competition Bureau and Canadian Standards Association seek greater accuracy in environmental claims," http://www.csa.ca/cm/ca/en/search/article/seek-greater-accuracy-in-environmental-claims; and Competition Bureau Canada "Enforcement claims: A guide for industry and advertisers," http://www.competitionbureau.gc.ca/eic/site/cb-bc.nsf/eng/02701.html.

Problems with SROs include potential conflicts of interest between members and customers. SROs may be slow to initiate corrective action, and in some cases unable to enforce standards. In Canada, SROs in the financial services industry have been accused of not taking appropriate action with regard to financial scandals and problems. Stakeholder representation is often token, as with professional associations, and their influence is limited. It is considered a variation on corporatism where government and industry influence dominates that of other stakeholders, in particular consumers or investors.

Quasi-Government Regulation

Rather than regulate an industry directly through a government department, some regulation is delegated to government agencies that operate at arm's length from government. Examples are the Standards Council of Canada (SCC) and the Canadian Radio-television and Telecommunications Commission (CRTC). The SCC operates as a federal Crown corporation mandated to promote efficient and effective standardization and is governed by representatives from governments and the private sector, including NGOs. The CRTC is an independent agency responsible for regulating Canada's broadcasting and telecommunications systems and comprises commissioners appointed by government for limited terms. In some of these agencies staff are political appointments, sometimes former industry employees. Stakeholders are challenged to effectively make presentations before such agencies resulting in some stakeholder interests, in particular consumers not receiving the attention they should. Responsibility for Ethics 10.3 provides an example of an initiative to overcome this lack of representation.

Government Regulation

The government extensively regulates an industry or some aspect of business operations. Standards are developed, applied, and enforced by government or its agents, and the standards apply to everyone. In Canada, government with few exceptions regulates the distribution and

RESPONSIBILITY
for Ethics **(10.3)**

> ## Telecommunications Statement of Consumer Rights
>
> The Canadian Radio-television and Telecommunications Commission (CRTC) was receiving many complaints about the local services provided by incumbent telephone companies (wire-based). Overall, the companies were allegedly not behaving in an acceptable manner toward consumers. As a result, the CRTC developed a "Statement of Consumer Rights." Examples of the rights formulated are:
>
> - Right to local telephone service
> - Right to choose a phone company
> - Rights when service is discontinued
> - Right to block outgoing long-distance calls
> - Right to privacy
> - Rights regarding unsolicited calls
> - Right to detailed monthly billing information
>
> These are not rights in law, or even ones that are generally accepted by the companies. But in order for the regulatory process to be viewed as just, these rights were formulated to represent consumer interests.
>
> The CRTC is going a step further to enhance consumer rights. In October 2012, it decided to seek input from consumers about the need for a "Wireless Code" to address the clarity and content of mobile wireless contracts and related issues.

Sources: Based on Canadian Radio-television and Telecommunications Commission, *Telecom Decision CRTC 2006–52*, "Statement of Consumer Rights," August 2006, http://www.crtc.gc.ca/eng/archive/2006/dt2006-52.htm; and *Telecom Decision CRTC 2012-556*, Wireless Code, October 11, 2012, http://www.crtc.gc.ca/eng/archive/2012/2012-556.htm.

sale of alcohol beverages. The labour collective bargaining process is almost totally regulated directly by government with few aspects delegated to other types of regulation. Governments also are the principal regulators in competition policy, bankruptcy laws, and intellectual property. Governments are always introducing new regulations. In recent years they have regulated online transactions, tattoo artists, organic foods, and ingredients in pet food.

There is no panacea in regulation; the type of regulation should vary to suit the circumstances within an industry. Everyday Ethics 10.1 illustrates the complexity of regulation. Any type of self-regulation, or shared regulation, is likely to occur when there are shared benefits for all stakeholders. It is sometimes difficult to clearly identify the types of regulation used, and in some industries more than one type is implemented. In most industries, it is generally recognized that some degree of regulation is necessary from outside the corporation. The appropriateness and extent of regulation will vary, and generalizations should not be made without considering the types of regulation in practice.

▶ LO 10.3 ◀   Government Regulation of Business

The influence and involvement of government in the business system is substantial and there are ethical implications for businesses. The following discussion presents the scope of government–business relationships.

Government is the architect of economic growth—Government actions affect the economic growth of the economy. Economic growth is impacted by trade, fiscal, monetary,

Everyday Ethics

10.1

Misleading Labels

On March 18, 2012, CBC's *Marketplace* program aired a feature titled "Lousy Labels." It listed ten misleading food product labels that made dubious health and nutrition claims. One drink product manufacturer claimed that two glasses were equivalent to eating 80 oranges, which was not proven. A pizza product manufacturer claimed that its product was healthy even when it contained fat and was high in sodium. A cereal manufacturer claimed that the oats in the product added fibre and nutrition when only the hulls of oats were used.

The product that received much of the publicity associated with the program was Maple Leaf Foods' "Natural Selections" meats. The package stated "No Preservatives Added," and an asterisk referred to a statement in very small print lower on the package that stated "except for those naturally occurring in the ingredients." Nitrite is a preservative that health professionals recommend be avoided as it has been linked to cancer. One of the ingredients, cultured celery extract, contains nitrite. The Maple Leaf Foods Web site disclosed this on a page titled "What you should know about nitrate, nitrite and a healthy balanced diet."

Even though the labelling was accurate and legal, food scientists considered the labelling misleading as it was unlikely that consumers would be aware cultured celery extract contained nitrite. Less than two weeks after the program was broadcast, the Government of Canada announced in its 2012 budget that funding to the Canadian Food Inspection Agency (CFIA), which monitored and enforced non-health and non-safety food labelling, would be cut. Instead the CFIA "will introduce a web-based label verification tool that encourages consumers to bring validated concerns directly to companies and associations for resolution."

Maple Leaf Foods announced that it would be changing the label.

Sources: "Lousy labels," *CBC Marketplace*, episode 224, broadcast March 18, 2012, http://www.cbc.ca/marketplace/2011/lousylabels/, accessed April 3, 2012; "10 misleading food product labels in Canada," *CBC News*, February 3, 2012, http://www.cbc.ca/m/rich/news/story/2012/02/02/marketplace-lousy-labels-full.html, accessed February 7, 2012; "Maple Leaf Foods changes misleading product labels," *CBC News*, February 2, 2012, http://www.cbc.ca/news/canada/story/2012/02/02/marketplace-lousy-labels.html, accessed February 7, 2012; Maple Leaf Foods, "What you should know about nitrate, nitrite and a healthy diet," http://www.mapleleaf.ca/en/market/food-safety/nitrates, accessed February 7, 2012; and Government of Canada, Budget 2012, March 29, 2012, Chapters 5 and Appendix, http://www.budget.gc.ca/2012/plan/toc-tdm-eng.html, accessed April 3, 2012.

taxation, land use, wage, and price controls, and employment policies. Businesspersons play a role in influencing government to follow policies favourable to them. The stimulus spending initiated by governments in 2009 is an example of promoting economic growth during a downturn in the economy.

Government prescribes the rules business is to follow—The government provides the framework legislation enabling businesses to operate. This legislation includes laws relating to competition policy, anti-dumping, bankruptcy, incorporation, intellectual and industrial property, and property rights. These laws provide the "rules of the game"; that is, the conditions under which business will operate.

Government is a major purchaser of goods and services produced by business—The expenditures of all governments—federal, provincial, and municipal—are about 40 percent of GNP. Included in such expenditures are all salaries, the procurement of goods and services, and grants. Business enterprises supply a large portion of the goods and services sought by government. Everyday Ethics 10.2 presents one of the challenges involved with

Everyday Ethics   Preferential Purchasing
10.2

The Toronto Transit Commission (TTC) is purchasing 234 new subway cars and is negotiating a contract with Bombardier Inc. for $499 million. The total cost of the contract with security deposits, spare parts, and tools will be $710 million. No other company was asked to bid on the contract.

The lack of bidding for the contract has some City of Toronto councillors worried as they believe the contract should be test marketed; that is, the bidding for the contract should be open to all suppliers. The mayor says it is preferable to have the cars produced in Bombardier's Thunder Bay plant than somewhere outside of Ontario and Canada. Unions criticized the councillors, saying they should be ashamed of themselves for questioning the creation of jobs in the province.

The contract was evaluated by independent consultants who found that the price of $2.1 million per car was reasonable. But they did not say it was the best price available. The TTC thinks it is doing the right thing. The elected councillors are attempting to represent the interests of taxpayers.

Sources: James Cowan, "Bid for subway cars deemed fair by consultants," *National Post,* August 24, 2006, A11; and James Cowan, "TTC approves controversial train purchase," *National Post,* August 31, 2006, A9.

government procurement, and illustrates the distribution of harms and benefits and the question of whether all stakeholders are being treated fairly by making this exception.

Government is a major promoter and subsidizer of business—Governments promote and subsidize business, including through grants, loans, loan guarantees, and tax credits, in several ways. Only a few will be discussed here.

Governments are suppliers of debt capital to many business enterprises—The federal and all provincial governments operate financial institutions or development agencies that lend to businesses. For example, the federal government operates the Business Development Bank and Export Development, and provincial governments operate development agencies lending to business enterprises. Loan guarantees are also available, and they are a substantial assistance to corporations as they reduce the debt burden.

> **Tax expenditures or tax credits** Potential revenues the government chooses not to collect; any form of incentive or relief granted through the tax system rather than through government expenditures.

Tax expenditures or tax credits are potential revenues the government chooses not to collect and are any form of incentive or relief granted through the tax system rather than through government expenditures. Examples of such tax expenditures are accelerated depreciation, inventory valuation adjustment, capital gains exemptions, and various business deductions. Government influences business through tax expenditures, either by granting or withdrawing them.

> **Chosen instrument** A corporation within a particular industry that receives some form of special attention from government through grants, loans, purchasing policy, or tax incentives.

A **chosen instrument** is a corporation within a particular industry that receives some form of special attention from government through grants, loans, purchasing policy, or tax incentives. The support from government usually goes to a technological leader, an enterprise that is positioned in the industry as a "lead" or "core" company. The intention is to pick a "winner" that will be supported, or preferred, by government for the purposes of developing new technology or penetrating an export market. The corporation is asked to concentrate on a particular technology, product, or process. An example of a chosen instrument corporation is Bombardier Inc., which receives extensive subsidization from the federal and Quebec governments.

Government is a rescuer of failed business—Canadian governments have a long history of coming to the assistance of failing corporations or industries. Bailouts occur to varying degrees and can take different forms. The bailout may involve a one-time capital infusion to overcome a crisis, or the complete takeover of the corporation. Bailouts may involve loans, loan guarantees, and equity positions, or combinations of all. Today, governments are less willing to provide complete bailouts but instead provide assistance to a bailout arrangement that might also include assistance from shareholders, creditors, and employees. An example of this type of government involvement was the automobile vehicle industry, which received assistance to establish and maintain plants in Ontario. The Canadian and Ontario governments took about a 12 percent ownership in General Motors as a result of a bailout in 2009.

Government is the protector of business and producer interests—Examples of protection are tariff and non-tariff barriers that exist to shield Canadian industry from foreign competition. Since 1879, Canadian manufacturing has been protected by tariffs and other barriers such as quotas and regulations. Industries receiving substantial protection in the past have been textiles and shoes, furniture, and appliances. It is argued that this has caused some Canadian industries to be less efficient than they might have been. Freer trade is reducing the influence of these protective measures; for example, through the General Agreement on Tariffs and Trade (GATT) and its successor the World Trade Organization (WTO), the U.S.–Canada Free Trade Agreement, and the North American Free Trade Agreement (NAFTA). Protective measures also exist between provinces, and many businesspersons believe that these barriers are a greater impediment to free trade within Canada than between Canada and other countries.

Government is the owner of business enterprises—Governments at all levels own and operate businesses that provide goods and services that could also be supplied by private-sector corporations. Government-owned enterprises, often referred to as Crown corporations, were formed or acquired for a variety of reasons, including to maintain employment (e.g., the Cape Breton Development Corporation), to fill a gap in the private sector's provision of goods or services (e.g., the Canadian Broadcasting Corporation), to promote economic activity (e.g., the Business Development Bank of Canada), to provide services the public is compelled to purchase (e.g., automobile insurance in B.C., Saskatchewan, and Manitoba), to ensure adequate and stable supplies of important goods and services (e.g., Marine Atlantic), and to control the distribution of goods and services (e.g., liquor corporations or control boards).

Many goods and services are provided to Canadians by government-owned enterprises that operate much like commercial enterprises and, in some cases, that compete with privately owned enterprises. Many government-owned enterprises have been sold or dissolved as governments became disillusioned with their operation or concluded the private sector could operate such corporations more effectively.

Government is a partner with business in some endeavours—Two examples of business and government partnerships are mixed enterprises and public–private partnerships. **Mixed enterprises** are those in which a government owns equity in a private-sector enterprise. Governments have an equity interest in a substantial number of corporations that ranges from small numbers of voting shares, to effective control through a substantial but minority interest, to more than one-half the voting shares. The influence of the government varies from a hands-off approach to explicit direction, which challenges private-sector managers and may adversely affect the performance of the enterprise.

A **public–private partnership (PPP)** is a cooperative venture between the public and private sectors, built on the expertise of each partner, that best meets clearly defined public needs through the appropriate allocation of resources, risks, and rewards.[2] These partnerships increase the involvement of the private sector, for-profit and non-profit, in the provision of government infrastructure and services. The Canadian Council for Public–Private Partnerships identifies several partnership models, including design-build; operation and maintenance; design-build-finance-operate; build-own-operate; build-own-operate-transfer; buy-build-operate; operation licence; and finance only. All models allow for some participation by the private sector.

Advocates for a large role for government in the economy oppose such partnerships, especially public-sector unions, which view them as a type of outsourcing.[3] Everyday Ethics

Mixed enterprises Those in which a government owns equity in a private-sector enterprise.

Public–private partnership (PPP) A cooperative venture between the public and private sectors, built on the expertise of each partner, that best meets clearly defined public needs through the appropriate allocation of resources, risks, and rewards.

10.3 gives illustrations of situations where corporations have assumed greater responsibility in providing services to the public even though many in society oppose it. Corporations have partnered with governments to build the infrastructures listed, usually by building them and then funding through fees or renting back to the government.

Everyday Ethics

10.3

Public–Private Partnerships (PPP)

Each year, the Canadian Council for Public–Private Partnerships gives awards for innovative PPP projects. The following are examples of recent winners:

- *Sea to Sky Highway*—a $600 million project to improve the safety, sightlines, and slope stabilization of the 95-kilometre-long section of Highway 99 from West Vancouver to Whistler, B.C.
- *Ontario Ministry of Government Services Data Centre*—a $352 million new data centre to house increased data storage capacity and security for the government's new online services strategy. Garnered $64.2 million in cost savings.
- *North East Stoney Trail Highway*—a $650.7 million ring road highway around Calgary and Edmonton improved access and safety that was approximately 63 percent of the cost compared to traditional project delivery.
- *Durham Region Courthouse*—a $334 million fully functional and most technologically advanced courthouse in Ontario delivered $49 million in cost savings to the Government of Ontario.
- *Communications Security Establishment Canada*—an $867 million accommodation facility for Canada's national cryptologic agency saved $176 million.

Source: 2011 Award Winners for Innovation and Excellence in PPP Canadian Council for Public–Private Partnerships at http://www.pppcouncil.ca/awards/winners/2011.html, accessed November 9, 2012. Copyright © 2005–2013 The Canadian Council for Public–Private Partnerships.

Government directly manages, through regulation, large areas of private business activity— Theoretically, the regulation of the economy and the business enterprise system should be done by the forces or influences of the marketplace. But in practice this is not the way it works, and a mechanism is required to control monopoly and oligopoly powers, to control the transfer of income from consumers to producers, and to increase efficiency in production. Regulatory organizations do a variety of things, including establishing prices and levels of service, mediating between enterprises, advising governments on policy, controlling expenditures, administering acts or regulations (such as licensing), and operating as quasi-judicial bodies. Table 10.1 contains a listing indicating the extensiveness of government regulation in Canada.

Various governments regulate the operation of business enterprises through commissions, tribunals, agencies, and boards. The following are examples of industries regulated by government-sponsored regulatory agencies: petroleum, insurance, pipelines, some agricultural products including dairy and poultry, utilities (electric, telephone), transportation (trucking, rail, airline, bus, taxi), communications (radio, television), and securities. Government, in one form or another, directly regulates about one-third of the economy through more than 600 organizations. Examples of such regulatory organizations are the Canadian Radio-television and Telecommunications Commission, the Canadian Transportation Commission, the National Energy Board, and public utilities boards in most provinces.

Regulation impacts every business enterprise, and every Canadian. Deregulation has reduced some regulation in selected areas as, for example, with airlines, truck transportation, and telecommunications. Not all regulation is imposed by government; business has

TABLE 10.1	*The Scope of Government Regulation in Canada*

Communications—Broadcasting and telecommunications. To date, the Internet is not regulated.

Consumer Protection/Information—Including false and misleading advertising, packaging and labelling, prohibited transactions (e.g., pyramid sales, referral sales, and rent control)

Cultural/Recreational—Including residency requirements, language (bilingualism), and gambling (lotteries/casinos)

Energy—Nuclear, natural gas, petroleum, hydro-electric, and coal

Environmental Management—Pollution control, resource development, wildlife protection, land use (including zoning), climate change/global warming, and environmentally friendly products

Financial Markets and Institutions—Banking, finance companies, credit unions, pension plans, securities markets, insurance

Food Production and Distribution—Agricultural products marketing, fisheries

Election Laws—Including lobbying and finance contributions to political parties

Health and Safety—Occupational health and safety, product characteristics and use, building codes, health services, animal health, and plant health

Human Rights—Anti-discrimination legislation, protection of privacy, and labour legislation

Professions/Occupational Licensure—Certification, registration, and apprenticeship

Transportation—Airlines, marine, railways, inter-city and urban buses, taxis, pipelines, trucking, and courier services

initiated a lot of it in its own interest, for example seeking protection from the importation of goods from China or other developing countries.

Government is the protector of various interests in society against business exploitation and redistributes resources to meet social ends—Governments have legislated to protect the interests of those with low incomes (for example, rent control) and minorities facing discrimination. Consumers have been protected by extensive legislation as they are often unable to represent themselves or make their voice heard. Corporations are involved in collecting taxes for governments, for example the retail sales tax and the payroll deduction of personal income tax. They also pay taxes on profits, but the total amount they contribute is substantially less than that raised by personal income taxation.

Business cannot leave to chance the relationship that may exist between it and the government. Thus, corporations and business associations make efforts to influence government and to achieve what they consider desirable. The following discussion examines two efforts in this regard, business involvement in politics and lobbying activities. Also discussed is the organizational unit most likely to oversee this influence, the corporate affairs department.

connect Want to learn about **your view of government regulation?** Go to CONNECT.

LO 10.4 ▸ Government Involvement in Corporate Social Responsibility

Governments have become involved in CSR through legislation, regulations, or simply by encouraging CSR or sustainability practices.

Demands to legislate CSR and accountability have occurred at various times. Some morality has been legislated through the legal system. For example, there are laws against dishonest business practices, laws to prevent monopolistic behaviour, laws relating to the health and safety of employees, and laws that prohibit conducting business with corrupt foreign regimes. This type of legislation has provided safeguards to various stakeholders, including investors, consumers, and employees. The demands increase after a corporate scandal. For example, American corporations were held more accountable after the Enron failure, the BP oil disaster in the Gulf of Mexico led to demands for greater regulation in the petroleum industry, and recent Ponzi schemes have prompted calls for more protection of individual investors.

More directly, the federal government has been involved in several initiatives that have influenced the corporate social responsibility of Canadian corporations, including:

- Whitehorse Mining Initiative [1993]—The Mining Association of Canada initiated the process bringing together business, government, environmental NGOs, and Aboriginal groups to ensure social and environmental goals were considered in mining development.

- The Kimberley Process [2000]—The Canadian government was involved in labelling diamonds to prevent the sale of those used to finance conflicts or produced by slave or child labour.

- Voluntary Principles on Security and Human Rights [2000]—These principles provide a broad framework that helps companies operate in ways that provide security to their facilities while respecting human rights and fundamental freedoms. Canada committed to the Principles in 2009.

- Extractive Industries Transparency Initiative [2003]—This initiative was to address corruption in resource-dependent countries. Canada did not join until 2007. Eventually led to *Building the Canadian Advantage: A Corporate Social Responsibility Strategy for the Canadian International Extractive Sector,* which includes a CSR Counsellor and CSR Centre of Excellence [2009].

- National Roundtables on Corporate Social Responsibility and the Canadian Extractive Sector in Developing Countries [2006]—These were established to encourage Canadian corporations operating overseas to conduct their activities in a socially and environmentally responsible manner and in conformity with international human rights standards.

- Several federal government departments have extensive Web sites dealing with CSR, including Industry Canada, Foreign Affairs and International Trade Canada, and Natural Resources Canada.

A recent development has been the federal government's public–private CSR partnership described in Everyday Ethics 10.4. This new initiative is controversial but is also a trend with other governments. It appears that all the government's initiatives are designed to increase the economic success of corporations, particularly those operating in foreign countries, while accepting social and environmental responsibilities for their operations.

LO 10.5   Business Involvement in Politics

Many issues are associated with the involvement of business in politics either as corporations or businesspersons, and there are pros and cons to such involvement. It is a pluralistic right for business to be involved, as corporations are an institution in society and thus have a moral responsibility to take part in the political system. Business influences society and, in addition, corporations pay taxes. Businesspersons are very knowledgeable of economics and finances, and have the information and skills to make a contribution to the political process. Participation by business is necessary to counterbalance the anti-business activity of other groups, for example of unions.

LO 10.6   Business Lobbying

Lobbying All attempts to influence directly or indirectly any government activity; includes any attempt to influence legislators, their staff members, public administrators, and members of regulatory agencies.

Lobbying is defined as all attempts to influence directly or indirectly any government activity, and includes any attempt to influence legislators, their staff members, public administrators, and members of regulatory agencies. Specifically, the act of lobbying government can be defined as including attempts to influence:

1. the making or amending of legislation and regulations;
2. the making or changing of government policies or programs;
3. government decisions in the awarding of grants, contracts, contributions, or any similar benefits; and
4. government appointments to boards, commissions, and any other public office.[4]

There are several types of business lobbyists. The first is business corporations that attempt to influence government through lobbying performed by business interest groups or associations. Examples of business interest groups that act as lobbies include the Canadian Council of Chief Executives (an organization comprising the chief executives of the largest corporations); the Canadian Federation of Independent Business; the Canadian Bankers' Association; the Electrical Association; and the Automobile Parts Manufacturers Association of Canada. Table 10.2 lists the types of business interest groups as identified by Stanbury[5] and provides examples of each. It is estimated that there are hundreds of such associations that regularly lobby government by distributing literature and information; appearing before parliamentary committees, royal commissions, inquiries, and other bodies; and interviewing politicians and civil servants.

TABLE 10.2   *Business Interest Groups*

Type	Examples
Umbrella Associations (also referred to as peak organizations)	Canadian Council of Chief Executives
	Canadian Chamber of Commerce
	Canadian Federation of Independent Business
Sectoral Associations	Food & Consumer Products of Canada
	Canadian Real Estate Association
	Retail Council of Canada
	Fisheries Council of Canada
Activity-Specific Associations	Canadian Marketing Association
	Canadian Manufacturers & Exporters
	Packaging Association of Canada
Industry-Specific Associations	Canadian Bankers' Association
	Forest Products Association of Canada
	The Baking Association of Canada
	Mining Association of Canada
	Canadian Textile Association
Product-Specific Associations	Cement Association of Canada
	Canadian Toy Association
	Soap and Detergent Association of Canada
	Automotive Parts Manufacturers Association
	Canadian Paperboard Packaging Association

The second type of lobbyist is the consultant who specializes in government–business relations and is paid by a corporation, a group of corporations, or a business association to make contact with government, or to tell business how to influence government. Government relations consultants monitor government activities for clients and help them develop strategy and actively lobby for their clients. Independent consultants are often former politicians, civil servants, and political staff, sometimes with industry experience, who operate as individuals or in small partnerships.

A third type of business lobbyist exists where corporations develop lobbying capability "in-house," often referred to as government relations or public affairs staff. Such departments usually report to top management and constantly monitor the political environment for developments that will impact the corporation and industry. They prepare positions for management and may be involved directly in lobbying, or in making presentations to government departments or agencies and civil servants. These departments are discussed in a following section.

There are pros and cons to business lobbying. It is argued that business must lobby to offset the influence of other groups. It should be pointed out that business groups are not the only lobbyists. Consumers, farmers, labour organizations, environmentalists, and religious groups, to name a few, all lobby governments. In fact, such interest group lobbying is part of Canadian society. It is believed that with each group presenting its point of view, government is better prepared to formulate public policies satisfactory to Canadians. Business argues that its opinion or perspective must be made known to governments if informed decisions are to be made about public policies affecting business.

Lobbying is criticized for several reasons. In the past, some of the practices of lobbying groups were unethical, as seen, for example, by the use of bribes, the offering of gifts, the making of improper political contributions, and even blackmail. As a result, many view lobbying as a distasteful, undesirable activity. It is also argued that the business lobby is far too powerful and presents a view that is too one-sided. Other groups in society claim there is unequal access to government and that business is overrepresented while other stakeholders are underrepresented. The cost of business lobbying can be passed on to consumers through the prices paid for goods and services, while other groups, such as consumers and environmentalists, do not have the financial and human resources to lobby effectively.

Business lobbying activities have grown and there is continuing involvement of government in the business system. This has necessitated greater lobbying to ensure that business interests are protected. Also, once one corporation or group starts to lobby, others follow out of necessity. It should be remembered that business groups often lobby against one another in an attempt to influence a government decision. For example, Canadian bicycle manufacturers might lobby for increased tariff protection, but retailers that import bicycles might lobby for lower tariffs. This point illustrates that business lobbying is not just business against other groups in society.

Nevertheless, increasing concern was being expressed about business lobbying, and in 1988 the federal government passed an act respecting the registration of lobbyists. In this act, the definition of lobbyist referred to "paid lobbyists" and included those who lobby on behalf of clients and employees of enterprises and organizations that function as lobbyists. According to the government, the purpose of the legislation is not to regulate lobbying, but to make the lobbying process better understood by identifying who is doing it and on what issues.

The government is a major stakeholder in the business system influencing business operations, and as discussed in this section business influences government policies, legislation, and regulation through involvement in politics and lobbying.

 Want to learn more about **lobbying government**? Go to CONNECT.

> ## LO 10.7 ## Corporate Public Affairs Departments

Corporate public affairs The management function responsible for monitoring and interpreting the governmental environment of the corporation or industry and for managing the responses necessary to protect the interests of the corporation or industry.

Corporate public affairs is the management function responsible for monitoring and interpreting the governmental environment of the corporation or industry and for managing the responses necessary to protect the interests of the corporation or industry. Public affairs or government relations departments have been established in many large corporations and managers of such departments should have knowledge of governmental decision-making processes and have credibility with relevant government officials or departments.

Although public affairs initially focused on the relationship between business and government, its role in some corporations has been expanded to include community relations, media relations, environmental monitoring, issues management, lobbying, and public relations. As a result, the corporate public affairs function is found in corporations under a variety of names. Also, corporate public affairs departments have expanded in response to the growing impact of government involvement in the business system, for example in the areas of diversity, environmental protection, occupational health and safety, and consumer protection. It has also been necessary to counteract the lobbying of other stakeholders in society promoting their interests, for example NGOs.

Corporate public affairs has evolved into an occupational profession represented by the Public Affairs Association of Canada (PAAC), a national, not-for-profit organization founded in 1984. Its principal objective is to help public affairs professionals succeed in their work by providing them with forums for professional development, the exchange of new ideas, and networking.[6] The PAAC has an extensive Statement of Ethical Principles, a portion of which is reproduced in Responsibility for Ethics 10.4.

Public affairs or government relations units continue to play a role when the corporation is attempting to influence government and in interpreting government's influence upon the corporation. Through the three approaches of involvement in politics, lobbying, and public affairs departments, business does influence government policy making and regulation. These approaches raise the issues of corporate agenda and corporate welfare.

Corporate Agenda

Corporate agenda The real or imagined alleged domination of public policy or government programs by corporations or business organizations in their own best interests.

Those individuals and groups in society who question the increasing role of business frequently use the phrase **corporate agenda**, the real or imagined domination of public policy or government programs by corporations or business organizations in their own best interests. The concern is that corporations have too much influence over governments and the lives of individuals. Social activists and union leaders are prominent in their criticism of the alleged corporate agenda.

There is some consensus on the components of such an agenda. The corporate agenda usually includes some or all of the following:

- The reduction of government involvement in the economy through privatization, downsizing, and outsourcing.
- The deregulation of business and industry.
- Reduced corporate taxation and personal income taxation of higher-income earners along with an overall shifting of tax burdens to working individuals.
- Advocacy of deficit and debt reduction.
- Reduction in government expenditures on social services to low- and middle-income individuals.
- The enactment of free trade agreements and support for globalization.

PAAC Statement of Principles

The Public Affairs Association of Canada (PAAC) is a gathering place for the interchange of ideas and ideologies, professional development, and practical networking. As the established national organization of public affairs professionals, the PAAC helps define appropriate conduct.

Public affairs professionals work with corporate, charitable, and political clients to engage various audiences. The public affairs profession is recognized increasingly for its high standard of practice and expertise, as well as the impact practitioners have on the development and debate of issues. It is acknowledged for the value and diversity of its contributions to Canadian society.

Public affairs practitioners will:

1. Avoid acting in such a way as to bring harm or disrepute to the profession, colleague, employer, or client.
2. Respect regulatory statutes and meet in full their obligations for disclosure in particular the Charter of Rights, the federal and provincial Lobbyist Registration Acts, Privacy Legislation, and municipal codes as they apply to the jurisdiction of practice.
3. Provide advice, guidance, and an informed opinion as to the nature of the business, policy, or legislative issue in a manner that is forthright and credibly reasoned.
4. Avoid personal and professional conflicts of interest and inform clients and employers as soon as the potential for conflict arises.
5. Ensure that any new engagement is subject to full disclosure with respect to regulatory requirements, the firm, and the client.
6. Be transparent in the management of financial accounts, contractual matters, obligations, and client/organizational interest.
7. Respect interpersonal confidences and confidential information.

Source: Based on Public Affairs Association of Canada, "Statement of Principles," http://www.publicaffairs.ca/whoweare/ethics.shtml.

- The weakening of unions and workers' right to organize.
- Increasing lobbying and involvement in the political process by business including the formation of partnerships between business and government.

Corporate welfare Any action by municipal, provincial, or federal governments that gives a specific corporation or an entire industry a benefit not offered to others.

Despite this alleged corporate agenda, corporations and industries appear increasingly willing to advocate for and accept government assistance referred to as **corporate welfare**—any action by municipal, provincial, or federal governments that gives a specific corporation or an entire industry a benefit not offered to others.[7] It is a pejorative term attributed to Ralph Nader, who first used the term in 1956 to describe the special treatment received by business. The term "corporate welfare bums" was used by NDP leader David Lewis in the 1972 federal election campaign to emphasize the preferential treatment received by business.

The term contrasts with social welfare and suggests receiving a benefit without doing anything. All forms of government assistance are included, for example grants, loans, loan guarantees, tax breaks, trade barriers, and legislated monopolies. The practice is criticized as it is considered unfair to other corporations and to taxpayers and consumers. The term constantly appears in media stories relating to the subsidies received by business.

The hypocrisy of business lobbying for and accepting government assistance is not lost on many stakeholders. The corporate agenda advocates less government regulation and a reduction in social programs—that is, social welfare—while advocating for benefits to business.

LO 10.8   The Impact of Changing Government Involvement

The influence or impact of government involvement in the economy and society varies over time and is illustrated by the financial crisis of 2008. Although this chapter has outlined the extensiveness of government involvement in the business system, there was a trend toward less government in the years leading up to 2008. Little doubt exists that a change in government involvement constitutes a dynamic element in the Canadian business system. It could be argued that uncertainty may be introduced for business. Some direct benefits (grants, tax incentives) may be lost, as will protection of monopolies by regulation or tariffs. It is predicted that Canadian business will be faced with a more competitive environment both domestically and internationally, and that monopolies, which are almost always formed and sustained by governments, will be fewer. Some consequences of the trend toward less government involvement might be the transfer of jobs from the public to the private sector, the possible widening of share ownership in Canada, and hopefully, increased competition.

The trend was reversed in 2008 when several banks in the United States and the United Kingdom were bailed out with emergency loans or other financial assistance. No Canadian banks received this type of government assistance. However, the bankruptcy of banks elsewhere caused a financial crisis and economic downturn, which did affect the Canadian economy. In particular, the automotive industry was adversely impacted and required government assistance. The U.S. and Canadian governments bailed out General Motors and now own over 70 percent of the company. The Canadian government believed it necessary to stimulate the economy and developed a "stimulus plan" of about $50 billion. The result was a substantial change in the involvement of government in the economy, including acquiring ownership in some corporations.

Two trends are associated with the varying impact of government, deregulation, and privatization. **Deregulation** is the reduction of government influence or impact over the economy allowing for a freer and more efficient marketplace. The reason given for deregulation is that fewer and simpler regulations will lead to a more competitive business environment, resulting in higher productivity, more efficiency, and lower prices. Those opposing deregulation argue that it results in reduced environmental quality standards, greater financial uncertainty as occurred in 2008, and market control by monopolies. Responsibility for Ethics 10.5 provides an example of deregulation from the pipeline industry.

Privatization, one manifestation of lessened government involvement, is discussed as it has substantial implications for business corporations. **Privatization** is the "strengthening of the market at the expense of the state."[8] After reviewing several definitions of privatization, Goodrich concluded that they had four things in common: privatization is defined as the provision of public service by the private sector; there are degrees of privatization, complete or partial; there are many techniques or forms of privatization (for example, divestiture, contracting out); and different terms are used that have overlapping meanings (for example, "contact public agencies," "contracting out service delivery").[9]

The privatization trend provides numerous opportunities for business. Private-sector businesses can provide services formerly delivered by government in several ways, namely participation in conventional markets where buyers and sellers compete for projects or contracts to perform work; monopoly franchises where the private company provides services at specified standards; management contracts; and acquiring ownership of the corporation. The challenges for entrepreneurs and managers are to make sure they are aware of the possibilities by monitoring government initiatives.

The changes in government involvement have implications for the business–government relationship described in the next section.

> **Deregulation** The reduction of government influence or impact over the economy allowing for a freer and more efficient marketplace.

> **Privatization** According to Heald, the "strengthening of the market at the expense of the state."

RESPONSIBILITY
for Ethics **10.5**

Deregulating Pipeline Construction

Pipelines are critical to the development and marketing of Canadian petroleum resources. Corporations are facing increasing challenges when new pipelines are proposed as the issues involved are economic, social, and environmental.

In the past, the economic issues to producers and consumers were the primary focus of any approval or review process. Currently, a process based mainly on economic benefits is not sufficient. Landlords are concerned about rights-of-way and compensation. First Nations groups are concerned about losing their sovereignty, the destruction of sacred sites, and the damage to the natural environment. All aspects of the impact on the environment are assessed including climate change, pollution, and remediation plans. Local employment is viewed as a corporate obligation and concerns are expressed about the exporting of jobs as unrefined petroleum leaves the country. Others are concerned about the security and sustainability of petroleum supply for Canadians.

As a result, it often requires a lengthy review process to get approval for a new pipeline. The Keystone project (Alberta to Texas) review took from July 2008 to March 2010. The Mackenzie Valley project spanned from June 2003 to December 2010. The Northern Gateway project (Alberta to Kitimat, B.C.) review began in November 2005; in January 2012, 217 groups wished to intervene and 4,505 individuals had requested to make oral statements requiring years of hearings. The reviews are complicated by the involvement to two levels of government, and the involvement of various departments and agencies of each government.

Corporations and governments are concerned about the increasing complexity and length of the approval process, referred to as regulatory scope creep. One proposal is to have the regulatory process focus on the issues specific to the pipeline, leaving other issues to be addressed at the government policy level. In other words, social and many environmental issues would not be dealt with when assessing and approving pipeline projects.

In April 2012 the government decided to impose timelines on the approval process, allowing 12 months for a standard review and 24 months requiring an environmental panel review.

Sources: Joseph Doucet, *Unclogging the Pipes: Pipeline Reviews and Energy Policy,* Commentary No. 342, Toronto: C.D. Howe Institute, February 2012; Canada's Economic Action Plan, "Responsible resource development," http://www.actionplan.gc.ca/eng/feature.asp?PAGEId=446, accessed April 18, 2012; and Canada's Economic Action Plan, "What responsible resource development means for environmental protection," http://www.actionplan.gc.ca/eng/media.asp?Id=5285, accessed April 18, 2012.

LO 10.9   Ethical Implications in the Business–Government Relationship

The influence of government on business and of business attempting to influence government results has numerous implications for the ethics and responsibilities of business. The following are examples of these implications.

- The appropriateness of government involvement and interference in the operations of business. Depending upon the business ideology held, the role of government is considered inappropriate and even detrimental to business and some stakeholders.

- The matter of accessibility to government is an issue. Larger corporations and some industries have more access to government than others and are thus receiving more benefits than they should or deserve.
- Doing business with the government is sometimes conducted in an inappropriate manner. For example, the awarding of contracts has been improperly done at times.
- In giving loans, grants, or protection, choices are made that favour some corporations while harming other corporations and stakeholders.
- Businesspersons and organizations are often critical of what they perceive to be costly and inappropriate social programs directed at individuals. On the other hand, they seek some form of government involvement that benefits them. This contributes to the "corporate welfare bums" phenomenon.
- When seeking assistance, corporations will play one government off another in extracting assistance. This is the case where a corporation is seeking a location for a business where employment is to be created.
- Deregulation and privatization trends alter the roles of government and corporations in society. The harms and benefits may not be distributed in an equitable manner.
- The financing of political parties or the leadership campaigns of politicians might be considered inappropriate.
- The endorsement of political candidates or parties by corporations or business organizations might be perceived as expecting favours in the future.
- The lack of transparency in the relationship (that is, influence) between government and business is disadvantageous to other stakeholders.

The purpose in identifying these issues is to recognize that there are ethical implications between the corporation and the government as a stakeholder in the business system just as there are ethical implications between the corporation and its other stakeholders.

LO 10.10 Ethics in Government

The relationship between business and government involves the ethical behaviour of politicians and public administrators. Governments have developed codes and conflict of interest guidelines and generally have implemented the types of ethics programs and leadership outlined in Chapter 6, "Ethics of Business: Management and Leadership." Business codes and guidelines often include clauses identifying appropriate behaviour when dealing with government. Responsibility for Ethics 10.6 lists various initiatives of the federal government to influence the behaviour of politicians and administrators.

Another aspect of ethics in government is the morality of operating some government-owned business corporations. In most provinces governments have a monopoly on the importation, distribution, and retail sale of alcohol, from which they generate significant profits. Governments operate lotteries, which encourage gambling and are profitable. Even worse, government-owned or -controlled video lottery terminal (VLT) machines and gambling casinos collect billions from consumers every year, yet insufficient amounts are spent to prevent gambling and cure gambling addictions.

connect   Want to learn more about **ethics in government**? Go to CONNECT.

Federal Government Initiatives to Influence the Behaviour of Politicians and Public Administrators

The *Federal Accountability Act, 2006* is an initiative to influence the behaviour of politicians and public administrators. The act is extensive; the following provides a summary of the areas that would influence dealings with the federal government:

- Reforming the financing of political parties and banning secret donations to political candidates; imposes a complete ban on contributions by corporations, unions, and organizations.

- Strengthening the role of the Ethics Commissioner including increased descriptions of conflicts of interest.

- Toughening the *Lobbyists Registration Act.* This involves stricter enforcement of the *Act,* requires contacts with senior holders of public office to be recorded, and prohibits ministers, ministerial staffers, and senior public servants from lobbying the Government of Canada for five years after leaving office.

- Cleaning up the procurement and awarding of government contracts. Included would be a review of procurement practices, a statement of principles on procurement to make sure contracts are awarded fairly, and a requirement for an integrity provision in contracts.

- Providing real protection for whistleblowers. Public-sector employees would have direct access to a Public Sector Integrity Commissioner to report wrongdoing.

- Establishing the Office of Values and Ethics (OVE), Treasury Board of Canada Secretariat. OVE is a centre of expertise and leadership that deals with values and ethics within the federal public service.

- Developing the "Principles of the Public Service of Canada," Canadian Centre for Management Development.

- Operating the Public Service Integrity Office, Government of Canada. This office provides public-service employees with an independent and neutral external review of disclosures of wrongdoing in the workplace.

- Establishing the Office of the Ethics Commissioner to guide the behaviour of members of parliament, including the enforcement of a conflict of interest and post-employment code and disclosure requirement guidelines for holders of public office.

Source: Government of Canada, "Turning a new leaf—Federal Accountability Act and Action Plan," http:// www.tbs-sct.gc.ca/faa-lfi/indcx-eng.asp. Reproduced with the permission of the Minister of Public Works and Government Services Canada, 2007.

Your advice to Luke . . .

You advise Luke that you understand he may be somewhat quick in criticizing corporations for receiving government assistance; however, most citizens receive benefits from governments, including students. Hopefully, if loans are involved, they are repaid—unlike the practice with government assistance to business. Everyone should be cautious in accusing others of being social *or* corporate "welfare bums."

SUMMARY

- Business is regulated by market forces, self-regulation by business itself, and government. Many in society believe that only government regulates business. Most economies rely on a combination of the three forms, with only a few communist countries relying on almost complete government oversight. (LO 10.1)

- Eight forms of market, self-regulation, and government regulation exist: *laissez-faire* market regulation, corporate self-discipline regulation, industry self-regulation, self-regulation involving stakeholders, negotiated self-regulation, mandated self-regulation, quasi-government regulation, and complete government regulation. No one form of regulation is preferable to others, and regulation should vary to suit the circumstances within an industry. (LO 10.2)

- The scope of government regulation of business is extensive. Government influences economic growth and lays out the rules that business will follow in conducting its affairs. Government is a major purchaser of the goods and services provided by business. Many subsidies are given to business including tax credits, grants, loans, and loan guarantees, and on occasion government rescues failing corporations or industries. Government protects business and producer interests, a common approach being protection from foreign competitors. Some businesses are owned completely or in part by government, although this is becoming less common. Most industries are regulated to some degree, with the extent of regulation constantly shifting. Lastly, government protects various interests in society against exploitation by business and redistributes resources to meet social ends. (LO 10.3)

- The federal government has recognized the importance of corporate social responsibility and has been involved with several initiatives to ensure Canadian corporations behave in ways that are socially and environmentally responsible. (LO 10.4)

- Business is involved in Canadian politics through financing political parties, supporting particular candidates, expressing views on public issues, allowing employees to participate in the political process, and through businesspersons seeking public office. (LO 10.5)

- Lobbying is any attempt to influence directly or indirectly any government activity, and includes any attempt to influence legislators, their staff, public administrators, and members of regulatory agencies. Corporations or industry organizations can have their own employees as lobbyists or can hire consultants to perform the function. Lobbying is controversial and is being increasingly regulated. Even though business devotes considerable resources to lobbying, its efforts are not always successful. (LO 10.6)

- Corporate public affairs departments perform the management function responsible for monitoring and interpreting the governmental environment of the corporation or industry and for managing the responses necessary to protect the interests of the corporation or industry. (LO 10.7)

- A corporate agenda is the real or imagined domination of public policy or government programs by corporations or industry organizations in their own best interests. While business advocates the deduction of government involvement in the economy, it also seeks government assistance and protection—a practice known as corporate welfare. (LO 10.7)

- There has been an ideological shift away from relying on government to solve society's problems. This decline in government involvement has implications for corporations and their stakeholders. One result of this trend has been the privatization of many government functions; that is, the strengthening of the market at the expense of the state. In 2008, the financial crisis and economic downturn reversed the trend of less government involvement. (LO 10.8)

- The interaction between government and business has numerous ethical implications. (LO 10.9)

- Government itself is aware that society expects a higher standard of ethical behaviour and has instituted various aspects of ethics programs, as corporations have done. The federal government is also legislating an *Accountability Act* and Action Plan to address these expectations. (LO 10.10)

KEY TERMS

Self-regulation
Self-regulatory organizations (SROs)
Tax expenditures or tax credits
Chosen instrument

Mixed enterprises
Public–private partnership (PPP)
Lobbying
Corporate public affairs

Corporate agenda
Corporate welfare
Deregulation
Privatization

CRITICAL THINKING AND DISCUSSION QUESTIONS

1. Why do most Canadians believe that only the government regulates business?

2. Why is it appropriate that various forms of regulation would exist?

3. Why are there continuing demands for more regulation of business activities?

4. Why should government be encouraging corporations to be socially and environmentally responsible?

5. Should corporations and businesspersons be involved in the political process at all?

6. How can business lobbying of government be justified?

7. What are some of the dangers of business lobbying?

8. Why is it necessary for corporations to have a corporate public affairs department? What type of individual should manage it?

9. What evidence is there that governments operate with a corporate agenda?

10. Should corporate welfare be stopped?

11. Is the privatization of government functions always appropriate?

12. Are the ethics of self-government any different from the ethics of business?

CASES

10.1   *Regulating Tips*

Eammon O'Dwyer owned a successful upscale restaurant in Toronto. Many challenges were involved in operating this type of business, including the collection and distribution of tips or gratuities. In the past few years, proposals to regulate tips had been introduced in the Ontario Legislature.

Bill 81, the "Elimination of Automatic Tips Act, 2010," proposed that "No person who owns or operates an eating establishment shall charge any customer an automatic service charge, regardless of whether notice of the service charge is provided in advance." An exception was made for private functions and banquets. Often automatic tips were added to larger parties of six

or more. The proposal raised the issue of whether tips should be given only in recognition of exemplary service, or imposed even if the service was poor. Eammon was of the view that his wait staff had to work harder with larger groups and they deserved a specified tip. Some patrons objected to the automatic aspect.

A second proposed regulation was Bill 107, "Protecting Employees' Tips Act, 2012," which would amend the *Employment Standards Act, 2000* by adding the clause "An employer shall not take any portion of an employee's tips or other gratuities." The regulation was to prevent employers from "tipping out"; that is, taking a cut of the tips received by employees. It was not intended to prevent tip pooling or tip sharing, where all employees, including host and kitchen staff, received a portion of the wait staff gratuities. Eammon knew that some restaurateurs were involved in the "tipping out" practice whereby they took a portion for themselves. He felt that this was not being fair to employees.

The proposed regulations created a lively discussion in the media both for and against regulation. Some staff believed that "tipping out," if properly done, would reduce the income inequity among staff. Many wait staff felt they deserved most of the tips as they worked the hardest. Others said they had no problems with tip pooling and received their share. Unfortunately, some unscrupulous operators took advantage of the "tipping out" practice according to some wait staff. Complaints about these operators had prompted the proposed regulations.

This type of regulation had a substantial impact on the Ontario restaurant industry, which had revenues of $24 billion and employed 30,000 people. The Canadian Restaurant and Foodservices Association (CRFA) stated that tips were a complex issue and that restaurant operators understood their significance to employees and their importance to customer service. The CRFA felt that the regulation was unwarranted and would be difficult to enforce.

Eammon thought that the proposed regulations extended the hand of government too deeply into his business and were not necessary. He felt that there must be better things for government to be doing.

Questions

1. **What are the ethical issues involved with the proposed regulations?**

2. **Who are the stakeholders influenced and/or who can influence the issue?**

3. **Should government regulate business operations to this extent?**

4. **Should the regulations be put in place by the government?**

5. **What would be your view if you were Eammon, a wait staff, or kitchen staff?**

Sources: Government of Ontario, Bill 81, "Elimination of Automatic Tips Act, 2010," http://www.ontla.on.ca/web/bills/bills_detail. do?locale=en&BillID=2375&detailPage=bills_detail_the_bill&Intranet=, accessed July 4, 2012; Government of Ontario, Bill 107, "Protecting Employees' Tips Act, 2012," available http://www.ontla.on.ca/web/bills/bills_detail.do?locale=en&Intranet=&BillID=2657, accessed July 4, 2012; and Canadian Restaurant and Foodservices Association, "CRFA tackles tipping in Ontario," http://www.crfa.ca/news/2012/crfa_tackles_tipping_in_ontario.asp, accessed July 5, 2012.

10.2   *Justifying Local Preference*

In January each year, the City of Easton issues a tender call for horticultural supplies for the following summer season. Most of the supplies are trees, shrubs, and perennials, which are planted in the various parks and landscaped areas throughout the city. The City's Works Department takes pride in its gardening program and the City's efforts have been recognized by several awards despite the very limited budget.

This year six bids were received, three from nurseries in another province and three from local firms. All three out-of-province bids were lower than any of the local nurseries. The successful bid was for $35,000 and the other bids ranged up to $49,000. The lowest local bid was $39,000.

At its meeting on March 16, City Council awarded the contract to the lowest out-of-province bid. One councillor inquired about the fact that the supplier was not local and suggested the City should support local business. The Deputy Mayor stated that she believed the lowest bid had to be accepted according to provincial legislation.

Callers to a local radio call-in program expressed dismay and outrage at this decision. Some referred to the councillors as idiots for not supporting local business.

Others made the point that local nurseries should be awarded the contract because they provide employment in the city. Several pointed out that the difference of $4,000 was insignificant and that the city should be willing to pay this difference.

Mike Manston was the owner of the local nursery that submitted the lowest local bid. He was disappointed, as he considered himself to be a responsible corporate citizen. He employed six persons year-round and dozens more in the summer. He belonged to local service clubs, served on the boards of local charities, and sponsored cultural events and sports teams. Mike was not sure what he should or could do about the situation.

Questions

1. What fundamentals of business (Chapter 2) are involved with this situation?

2. What stakeholders influence the decision and/or are influenced by the decision?

3. Which ethical principles did the city councillors use in making the decision? Which ones did they ignore?

4. What should be done about the city's policy of not giving preferential treatment to local businesses?

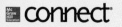

CHAPTER 11
Ownership and Governance of the Corporation

LEARNING OUTCOMES   *After studying this chapter, you will be able to:*

LO 11.1 Appreciate the role of the owner stakeholder and the economic and ethical responsibilities involved.

LO 11.2 List the owners of Canadian business.

LO 11.3 List and explain the ethical and responsibility issues of ownership.

LO 11.4 Describe approaches to protecting owners and investors.

LO 11.5 Define and understand the challenges of responsible investing.

LO 11.6 Define corporate governance.

LO 11.7 Understand the significance of shareholders' rights and list the responsibilities of the board of directors.

LO 11.8 Discuss the issues relating to corporate governance.

LO 11.9 Describe the relationships among ownership, corporate governance, and social responsibility and ethical conduct.

What would you do if . . . ?

Marc Sonsini had reached the point where he could think about becoming an owner or investor in Canadian business. Marc was in his mid-30s and had paid off debts except for the mortgage on the family home. He had contributed to RRSPs and participated in his employer's pension plan. He didn't have a lot of money to spare, but he had accumulated about $10,000 for the purpose of investing in stocks.

Marc's employer had an Employee Share Purchase Plan that allowed him to purchase shares in the company at a reduced rate. He thought this was a good benefit of employment, but there were some restrictions on how many shares could be purchased at a time and how long they must be held. Also, he was reluctant to invest in the company he worked for as he felt he would be "putting all his eggs in one basket," especially if the company failed.

Marc considered investing in companies he viewed as being responsible corporate citizens. He could invest directly through the purchase of common shares traded on a stock exchange, or indirectly with mutual funds.

He was able to find listings of such companies in the *Corporate Knights* Best 50 Corporate Citizens ranking, the *Report on Business Magazine* Corporate Social Responsibility ranking, and the Stratos Inc. *Benchmark Survey of Corporate Sustainability*.

It was also easy to identify dozens of mutual funds that were investing in socially and environmentally friendly corporations. However, he was taken aback by some of the corporations he found in both sources. Syncrude and Suncor were included despite the possible damage their operations may be doing to the environment in Northern Alberta. Other examples of problematic corporations included were Barrick Gold, despite poor stakeholder relations at its Cortez Hills mine site in Nevada; Encana, which had allegedly not respected native property rights in South America; Enbridge, in the news for possibly failing to seek permissions from First Nations groups for pipelines; and Canadian National Railways, which had been accused of a poor safety record.

Marc was puzzled by the results of his research—and he had not even looked at the financial return on the possible investments! Were there no responsible corporations in which to invest? Should he forget becoming a shareholder and invest in bonds or term deposits? Or should he disregard his preoccupation with responsible investing and just base his investment decisions on actual or anticipated financial return?

What is your advice to Marc?

▶LO 11.1◀   Introduction

Owners, also referred to as investors or shareholders, are key stakeholders in a capitalist system as they provide a major portion of the capital to finance corporations. Although many stakeholders influence the corporation, a corporation is for the shareholders; they own it, and should ultimately control it. The ownership patterns of Canadian business are changing, and owners have varying degrees of influence on corporate social responsibility and the moral behaviour of the corporation. In addition, there are integrity issues relating to how some owners are treated by others, and how owners treat other stakeholders. The actions of other stakeholders—for example governments, other corporations, and self-regulatory organizations—influence the owner stakeholder. Knowledge of how owners are influenced and/or influence is important to understanding the implications for corporate citizenship.

This chapter will identify the types of business ownership in Canada. Owners have an economic responsibility if they wish their corporation to survive while at the same time being responsible for the ethical or social impact of the business. Owners have varying influences over the operation of their businesses, including how the corporation responds to its social or ethical environment. Today, many owners are focusing on responsible investing, which is having an impact on how the corporation behaves.

Governing system The processes, structures, and relationships through which decisions are made.

A second section will examine how the corporation is governed. A **governing system** includes the processes, structures, and relationships through which decisions are made. Nations often have formal constitutional documents, and some corporations have mandates similar to constitutions.

Corporate governance is discussed in the business media every day. How corporations are governed became an issue in the early 1990s, when many corporations failed and it appeared that boards of directors were not performing their function well; that is, they were not protecting the interests of shareholders. In the early 2000s, major scandals and bankruptcies reinforced the interest in governance. The board of directors has been the object of many suggestions for reform. The result has been the reform, or reorganization, of the board as the principal body involved with the processes, structures, and relationships through which decisions are made. Corporate governance is defined and many aspects examined. The relationship between governance and performance is discussed along with the relationship to corporate social responsibility and the ethics of business.

LO 11.2 ▸ The Ownership of Canadian Business

Who owns Canadian business? A quick response would be "shareholders," but the answer is not as straightforward as this. The following are the main types of owners of Canadian businesses. Some owners personally own equity in the corporation either as investors, entrepreneurs, employees or managers, customers or consumers, or producers.

Investors Individuals who personally hold equity interests for investment purposes and who are not involved in the corporation as entrepreneurs or managers.

Investors—**Investors** are individuals who personally hold equity interests for investment purposes and who are not involved in the corporation as entrepreneurs or managers. Those individuals who have purchased shares in corporations listed on a stock exchange are an example of this type of owner. Not all Canadians own shares, because share ownership is more risky than other forms of investment and many Canadians lack the knowledge and funds to make this type of investment.

These owners have little influence in making the corporation more socially responsible, but some do attempt it through presenting shareholder resolutions to annual meetings. Examples are provided in Responsibility for Ethics 11.1. Few of these resolutions are successful, but they alert management to social concerns and so do have an influence. Social and environmental responsible investing will be discussed later in the chapter.

RESPONSIBILITY
for Ethics **11.1**

Shareholder Resolutions

The *Canada Business Corporations Act* requires that shareholder proposals or resolutions be circulated to shareholders and voted upon at the corporation's annual meeting. Investor or shareholder resolutions are presented on a variety of topics, including those related to ethical and social responsibility, but are seldom passed. Examples include the following, indicating the corporation targeted:

- Review diversity policies and initiatives (Agrium Inc.)
- Report on climate change (Valener Inc.)
- Prepare a sustainable development report (Alimentation Couche-Tard Inc.)
- Suspend operations of the Marlin mine (Goldcorp Inc.)
- Report on the company's aquatic monitoring progress (Suncor Energy Inc.)
- Close operations in OECD designated tax havens (Bank of Nova Scotia)

Source: Shareholder Resolution Database, Shareholder Association for Research and Education Web site, at http://www.share.ca/en/shareholderdb.

connect Want to learn more about **what shareholders are demanding of corporations?** Go to CONNECT.

Entrepreneurs—Ownership of business by individuals—that is, entrepreneurs—is a common form of ownership and has become increasingly so in recent years. Small businesses, or enterprises with fewer than 100 employees, are an important force in Canada, accounting for nearly 98 percent of all enterprises. Many entrepreneurs are socially responsible, as illustrated in Chapter 8.

Employees and managers—Employees including managers may own all or parts of corporations. Employee ownership can take several forms, including participation in an employee stock purchase plan or employee share ownership plan (ESOP); cooperation with an entrepreneur to refinance a corporation and operate it as a going concern; and establishment of a worker cooperative. Everyday Ethics 11.1 gives an illustration of the latter.

Everyday Ethics

11.1

Just Us! Coffee Roasters Co-op Ltd.

Just Us! Coffee was founded in 1995 as Canada's first Fairtrade coffee roaster, and in 1996 was incorporated as a worker-owned cooperative. Its mission is "People and the Planet Before Profits." It has received numerous awards, including winning the 2005 Maritimes Better Business Bureau's Ethics Award.

It is anticipated that all employees who work at Just Us! Coffee will become worker-owners when they are eligible. Just Us! Coffee's production facility and office are located in Grand Pre, Nova Scotia, with coffee shops in Grand Pre and Wolfville, and two in Halifax. Wholesale sales are made to several food chains and other cafés, restaurants, and small retailers in the Atlantic provinces. In addition to coffee, the co-op sells tea, sugar, and chocolate. All products are organic and obtained through fair-trade practices.

Source: JustUs! Coffee Roasters Co-op Web site at http://www.justuscoffee.com.

Customers or consumers—The most common type of business organization owned by customers is the cooperative, and the most widely recognized among these are retail consumer cooperatives and financial institutions such as credit unions or *caisses populaires*. Cooperatives have been leaders in institutionalizing ethics and responsibilities, as the examples in Everyday Ethics 11.2 illustrate.

Everyday Ethics

11.2

Social Responsibility at Cooperatives and Credit Unions

Mountain Equipment Co-op (MEC) is Canada's largest retailer of quality outdoor equipment and has 3.6 million members, or owners, around the world. One MEC value is to operate ethically and with integrity. It fulfills this value by committing to the ethical sourcing of merchandise, constructing and operating "green" buildings, pursuing energy conservation and waste reduction, and supporting community conservation and outdoor recreation groups. It has 15 stores with total sales of $270 million.

Vancouver City Savings Credit Union (Vancity) is a credit union providing banking, borrowing, lending, and insurance services to its 480,000 customers, or owners, in British Columbia. It has received many awards for its social responsibility and publishes an Accountability Report describing its social responsibility. It focuses on the environment by addressing climate change, practising green banking, indicating ways to grow the social economy, outlining socially responsible investing, and listing community initiatives.

Sources: Based on Mountain Equipment Co-op, http://www.mec.ca; and Vancouver City Savings Credit Union, https://www.vancity.com.

Producers—Producer ownership is through cooperatives of various types. There are more than 150 agricultural marketing cooperatives in dairy, grain, poultry, and other endeavours. In addition there are farm supply, fisheries, and production cooperatives.

Ownership in all cooperatives is based on the principle that one member has one vote, and each member contributes the same amount of equity. Profits are not the purpose of cooperatives, but some do distribute surplus funds equally to members. Employees, customers, and producers most likely become involved in business ownership for social purposes; that is, to preserve jobs, to provide particular goods or services that are socially acceptable, and to establish socially appropriate distribution systems.

With the "direct" individual owners listed above, ownership rights are held by those individuals. With "indirect" individual ownership, the ownership relationship is not as clear and straightforward because an intermediary institution exists between the individual owners and the corporation in which investments are made. The "indirect" owners in this category include mutual and pension funds and union-sponsored investment funds.

Mutual fund A pool of money from many individual investors that is invested on their behalf, usually in a specific kind of investment.

Ownership through mutual funds—A **mutual fund** is a pool of money from many individual investors that is invested on their behalf, usually in a specific kind of investment. Money contributed to equity mutual funds is invested by fund managers in a portfolio of shares in corporations. It is estimated that Canadian common share funds represent 20 percent of all mutual fund assets. Ownership via mutual funds appeals to some investors as it allows them to participate in the stock market without having to make separate decisions about each purchase or sale of stocks. This form of ownership does not include the right to vote as a shareholder, although the mutual fund companies can vote the shares they hold in the fund. Responsible funds can be purchased that are managed with sensitivity to ethical activities and responsibilities.

Ownership interest through pension funds—A substantial portion of pension fund assets are invested in corporate stock. Thus, many Canadians are most likely unaware that they are investing in Canadian business. A federal government report prepared by the National Round Table on the Environment and the Economy (NRTEE), in consultation with the private and public sectors and civil society organizations, concluded that environmental, social, and governance factors should be considered in investment decisions. It recommended that all governments adopt regulations that require pension funds to disclose the extent to which these factors are taken into account when pension fund managers make investment decisions.[1]

Some pension fund managers have endorsed the purchase of ethically and environmentally responsible investments of corporations with a good record of corporate social responsibility. Even the Canada Pension Plan fund now invests in equities and has a responsible investing policy. This policy may satisfy Canadian citizens concerned about social responsibility and alerts managers to criteria used by the CPP when investing in corporations.

Labour-supported investment funds (LSIFs) Funds that provide venture capital primarily to private corporations to create employment.

Union-sponsored investment funds—**Labour-supported investment funds (LSIFs)** are similar to mutual funds that provide venture capital primarily to private corporations to create employment. They are sponsored by labour organizations and usually supported by government through a tax credit to the fund purchaser. Some LSIFs are designed so that investors have a hands-on participation in the fund, while others are involved in social causes such as support to local job creation and assistance to female entrepreneurs. The financial performance of these funds has been poor and they have received modest support from investors.[2]

Corporate ownership—Corporations often own shares in other enterprises. This intercorporate ownership is widespread and is monitored by the government. The purpose of the monitoring is to ascertain whether monopoly behaviour occurs and to identify foreign ownership. Government monitoring does not provide information on corporate social responsibility, but government legislation does influence the relationship of the corporation with society.

Private equity firms Firms that manage large pools of money acquired from wealthy individuals or families and big institutions such as pension and mutual funds.

Private equity firms—**Private equity firms** manage large pools of money acquired from wealthy individuals or families and big institutions such as pension and mutual funds. The firms are private in the sense that they are not listed and traded on a stock exchange.

Private equity firms specialize in corporate buyouts of established companies, sometimes in cooperation with management. Some view them as corporate wreckers, a reputation enhanced by the book and movie *Barbarians at the Gate,* where questionable buyout and takeover tactics are used. There is no research to prove or disprove that this type of owner is more or less socially responsible than others.

Venture capital company A type of private equity firm that usually acquires part ownership of business enterprises for which they provide financial and management assistance.

Venture capital companies—A **venture capital company** is a type of private equity firm that usually acquires part ownership of business enterprises for which they provide financial and management assistance. There are dozens of venture capital companies in Canada, and they invest in new or established enterprises with growth potential that are unable to obtain needed financing from conventional sources. Venture capital investments are made at every stage in business growth, but often are made in speculative and higher-risk ventures. The role a venture capitalist plays varies depending on the success and needs of the enterprise, and is minimized by the successful operation of the firm. It is not known what impact this type of owner has on corporate social responsibility.

Not-for-profit organization ownership—Examples of not-for-profit organizations are churches, non-governmental organizations (NGOs), foundations, and universities, and all are likely to be concerned with the integrity of business. Investment or endowment funds in these organizations sometimes own stock in corporations. The extent of this ownership is not great, and any one organization seldom owns a large portion of a particular enterprise.

However, the influence of these owners may be greater than their small holdings indicate. In particular, church groups or NGOs have achieved a high profile by questioning aspects of a corporation's operations at annual meetings and other public forums. Some of these NGOs, for example Oxfam, may operate commercially oriented social enterprises. The portfolios of universities are carefully scrutinized by students and faculty for investments in corporations involved in unethical activities or irresponsible behaviour. This scrutiny has led to many universities divesting investments in some corporations.

Government ownership—Canadian federal, provincial, and municipal governments all operate a large number of business enterprises, usually referred to as Crown corporations. Government-owned corporations have been used extensively as instruments of public policy implementation, and are considered by some to be part of the Canadian economic culture.[3] Crown corporations have been utilized by all political parties and have played a major role in public policy relating to transportation, financial services, trade, research, communication, agriculture, fisheries, energy, and culture and recreation. They usually operate with some social objective.

Government-owned corporations exemplify ethics and responsibility to various stakeholders as do private corporations. Everyday Ethics 11.3 describes how Hydro One views its responsibilities to society.

Everyday Ethics 11.3   Corporate Responsibility Hydro One

Hydro One, the supplier of electricity in Ontario owned by the government, ranked #7 in the *Corporate Knights* list of "The Best 50 Corporate Citizens in Canada" in 2012. It has several programs to support charities and community groups. It donates to charities, sponsors youth sports teams and festivals, provides grants to community sports facilities, and encourages employees to volunteer in their communities. It is committed to migrating environmental impact, and its environmental policy includes complying with all laws, building more efficient facilities, preventing pollution and continuously improving its environmental management systems. It has a female CEO and four out of 11 on the board of directors are females.

Sources: About Hydro One, Hydro One Web site at http://www.hydroone.com/about/; and Melissa Shin, "Hydro One is number one," *Corporate Knights,* Summer 2009, Issue 28, 20.

The most common ownership types have been identified for two reasons: to emphasize the different categories of owners, and to establish a context in which to examine economic and social challenges relating to ownership. The main objective of owners in the past has been an economic one—that is, a return on their investment. Business was conducted with an emphasis on that objective. There was some logic to this in that owners provided the essential ingredient to the system, capital, and were the principal stakeholder—and the driving force—in the business system. This emphasis is changing with increasing interest in the challenges confronting owners and in the influence of social responsibilities when making investments.

LO 11.3 Ethics and Responsibility Issues of Ownership

Several issues relate to owner influence and to how owners are influenced. These issues involve the sensitivity to corporate social responsibility or corporate citizenship, and the appropriateness of the actions of owners who control the corporation toward other stakeholders, in particular smaller investors. This section explores several of these issues.

Widely Held versus Concentration Ownership

Many corporations that Canadians invest in are controlled by a dominant shareholder, and only a few of Canada's major corporations are widely held. The issue of control is critical to owners in both widely held and concentrated ownership situations.

In the situation when the ownership of the enterprise is widely dispersed among thousands of shareholders, it is argued that management actually controls the enterprise. Individual investors lack the means, and maybe the will, to unite and challenge management's decisions. These investors are often apathetic, or side with the instructions or views of management. Even if shareholders oppose management, they are at a disadvantage in any proxy fight or vote to challenge management.

At the other extreme, investors who are shareholders in corporations dominated by one or a few shareholders who have controlling interests are virtually powerless also. Their few votes make no difference, as sufficient votes are controlled by the dominating shareholder. However, an irony exists in this circumstance. The well-being of the small shareholder is actually dependent on the decisions of the dominant shareholder. This is not necessarily bad, as figures on the performance of such dominated firms have indicated they often outperform composite stock exchange indexes.

Minority versus Majority Shareholders

The widely held versus concentrated ownership issue naturally leads to the treatment of minority shareholders by dominating, or majority, shareholders. This has become an issue with the increase in the number of takeovers where the rights of minority holders were being overlooked. It is required by law that all shareholders be offered the same price, but other problems exist involving new issues and non-voting shares. Some jurisdictions require that a "majority" of the minority shareholders must approve a takeover or management proposal, but it is difficult to mobilize even this scale of opposition. Shareholders are often ill-informed of the implications of the deal or proposal, and usually side with management or the majority shareholders' position out of ignorance. There is some change in this situation in that mutual fund and pension plan managers are beginning to challenge majority shareholders.

Dual-Class Stock

Traditionally, the ownership of one share meant one vote and, at least in principle, the owners of shares directed the affairs of the corporation by evaluating management's performance and deciding upon the acquisition and disposal of assets. In other words, shareholders had certain rights based upon their voting privileges. However, many corporations operate with **dual-class stock,** where more than one type of share or stock with different voting rights and dividend payments is issued by a single corporation.

In 1981, **non-voting shares** or **restricted shares** (sometimes referred to as "uncommon" shares) were allowed on the Toronto Stock Exchange. Non-voting shares are common shares without voting privileges, while restricted shares involve some limit on voting, for example only one vote for every 10 or 100 shares owned. The creation of these types of shares allows management to control the corporation by concentrating voting power in the hands of a few friendly shareholders. Also, existing dominant owners can retain their control while still being able to raise capital. Up to 95 percent of the equity of some corporations is held by non-voting shareholders. The result is ownership (or stake) without control (or influence), and the fundamental tenet that ownership entails control is contradicted. Such a circumstance is believed to represent a threat to economic democracy and might lead to a decay of a central feature of the free market system.

Issues of fairness and rights of other shareholders arise when some shareholders have control through the use of non-voting shares. Often shareholders have no other recourse than to sell their shares if they disagree with the control exercised by the voting shares.

Similar challenges arise with multiple voting shares as with non-voting ones. The class of shares held by a founding family or corporate owner is given more votes than other share classes. Normally one share has one vote, but in some classes of shares each share has 10 or more votes. This arrangement allows a few shareholders to control the corporation and makes takeovers difficult. It also enables the small group of owners to maintain control over managers, and the incumbent board of directors most likely remains. On the other hand, it might allow managers associated with the controlling group to enjoy excessive benefits such as high compensation. A recent illustration of the use of dual class shares is the Facebook initial public offering described in Everyday Ethics 11.4.

Passive versus Active Shareholders

Passive shareholders are those who do not attempt to influence the affairs of the corporation even though they have a legal right to do so. Owners of small share holdings have been passive participants in controlling the activities of the corporation despite having adequate information to do so. Many small shareholders simply cast their votes with management without considering alternatives. There may be a feeling of hopelessness, but nevertheless they have some responsibility for at least being informed about the corporation and exercising their voting privileges.

On the other hand, **active shareholders** are those who participate in the governance to the full extent allowed by the law. This can be an individual shareholder but also the individuals who manage pension and mutual funds. In the past, these managers were "passive"; that is, they did not exercise voting rights or otherwise attempt to influence the affairs of the corporation despite owning substantial numbers of shares. But recently many of these managers have become very active in protecting the interests of the indirect owners and have influenced corporate responses to social issues. This does not mean involvement in the day-to-day decision making but instead examining acquisitions, takeover bids, anti-takeover tactics, and major expenditures that will impact upon the long-term performance of the enterprise. These institutional managers could protect not only their clients' interests, but also the interests of other minority shareholders by, for example, opposing the issuance of non-voting shares. Also, they have the resources to be "active," with research staff to examine proposals and the finances required for soliciting proxies and initiating legal actions.

Dual-class stock More than one type of share or stock with different voting rights and dividend payments is issued by a single corporation.

Non-voting shares Common shares without voting privileges.

Restricted shares Involve some limit on voting, for example only one vote for every 10 or 100 shares owned; sometimes called "uncommon shares."

Passive shareholders Those who do not attempt to influence the affairs of the corporation even though they have a legal right to do so.

Active shareholders Those who participate in the governance to the full extent allowed by the law.

Everyday Ethics
11.4

Facebook's Dual-Class Shares

On February 1, 2012, Facebook, Inc. filed a Prospectus with the United States Securities and Exchange Commission to make an initial public offering (IPO) of shares to the public. Two classes of shares are involved:

- 117,097,143 Class A common stocks will be available to the public and have one vote.
- 1,758,902,390 Class B common stocks will be issued to existing shareholders, including Chief Executive Mark Zuckerberg, and have 10 votes per share.

As a result of this dual-class share structure, Mark Zuckerberg would own about 28 percent of the corporation's equity but would have 57 percent of the voting power. This would enable existing shareholders to retain control of governance issues and the corporation. This type of structure results in a controlled company where one person, group, or corporation can determine who is elected to the board of directors. The argument for this type of structure is that it allows management to focus on the long term. Dual-share corporations are not uncommon, and some studies have shown that returns to Class A shareholders are higher with this type of share structure.

Critics claim that this structure diminishes shareholder rights and board accountability, allowing one or a few shareholders to dictate to the majority of shareholders. Some investors are reluctant to purchase shares in a corporation with dual-class shares.

The share structure did not discourage investors, who on May 18, 2012 purchased all the shares offered at $38 for a total of $16 billion. Facebook shares have since traded as low as one-half of the offering price. The current price can be checked at the symbol FB on the NASDAQ stock market.

Sources: United States Securities and Exchange Commission, Washington, D.C., "Form S-1 Registration Statement under The Securities Act of 1933" (Filed February 1, 2012), Facebook, Inc. accessed at http://www.nasdaq.com/markets/ipos/filing.ashx?filingid=7995138, March 8, 2012; Shayndi Raice, "Advisory service slams Facebook's dual-class share scheme," *Wall Street Journal Online*, February 13, 2012, http://online.wsj.com/article/SB10001424052970204883304577221942476996760.html, accessed March 8, 2012; "Facebook's dual-class share plan jeered," *Edmonton Journal Online*, February 15, 2012, http://www.edmontonjournal.com/business/Facebook+dual+class+share+plan+jeered/6154978/story.html, accessed March 8, 2012; Emily Chasan, "Facebook to join ranks of dual-class listings," *The Wall Street Journal*, February 8, 2012, http://blogs.wsj.com/cfo/2012/02/08/the-big-number-20/, accessed March 8, 2012; and Michael J. de la Merced, "I.S.S. adds to criticism of Facebook's governance," *Wall Street Journal Online*, February 13, 2012, http://dealbook.nytimes.com/2012/02/13/i-s-s-adds-to-criticism-of-facebooks-governance/, accessed March 8, 2012.

connect   Want to learn more about **Facebook Inc.'s governance**? Go to CONNECT.

Arguments can be made for and against the "active" role of professional money managers. The first argument in favour is simply that since they represent owners, they have an obligation to be involved. Also, they have the resources and the means to undertake action and coordinate their actions with other professional managers, a course of action that individual investors do not have. Counterarguments include the idea that the board of directors adequately represents owners; that too much pressure may be placed on corporate managers to produce results that will reflect in fund performance measures; that the personal power of the money managers may distort corporate management decisions; and the fear that money managers, as a group, may have too much power in the financial system.

The Pros and Cons of Employee Ownership

Worker capitalism Describes employee ownership as workers are turned into capitalists through stock ownership.

It is claimed that ownership increases morale and company loyalty, motivating employees to greater effort. Productivity rises, and higher profitability results. **Worker capitalism** is a term used to describe employee ownership as workers are turned into capitalists through stock ownership. If widespread, employee ownership could lead to a deconcentration of wealth. Employee ownership has been shown to be an important variable in reviving the fortunes of corporations that were not profitable enough to satisfy existing owners. Although not bankrupt, these corporations, or branch plants, were often abandoned by their owners and rescued by management, entrepreneurs, and employees. In this manner, jobs were saved.

Employee ownership is not without difficulties. Employees who invest in the corporation for which they work are in effect increasing their stake in the corporation. Their jobs, and often savings and pensions, depend now upon the fate of one corporation. Seldom do employees have majority ownership and control of the corporation. Management may still run the corporation as it wishes, not relinquishing control to employees. By not disclosing financial and operating results, employees are often kept unaware of how well the corporation is doing, and in some cases may be manipulated by management as needed information is not available. If employees own shares their participation in decision making may lead to nothing getting done, with the endless meetings, discussions, and votes being very time consuming. In some cases, only token democracy is practised in the workplace despite the employee involvement in ownership, and the prospects for job security are not enhanced. An example of a very successful employee-owned corporation is given in Everyday Ethics 11.5.

Everyday Ethics
11.5

The PCL Family of Companies

The PCL Family of Companies was founded by Ernest Poole in 1906 and began by constructing schoolhouses in Western Canada. Today, it is the largest general contracting organization in Canada and one of the largest in the United States. Its construction of civil and heavy industrial buildings takes place across North America and is directed out of 31 locations with headquarters in Edmonton. Approximately $6 billion of construction volume is handled annually.

The company converted to employee ownership in 1977 and today it is 100 percent owned by the majority of its 3,500 full-time professional and administrative salaried staff and more than 6,500 hourly tradespeople.

Its guiding principles are "Ownership (we are 100 percent employee owned), Teamwork, Mutual Obligation, Safety, Effective Communication, Diversity, Mobility and Social Responsibility."

Source: PCL Web site at http://www.pcl.com, accessed November 30, 2012.

Accountability of Non-public Corporations

The accountability for economic, social, and environmental responsibilities has become common among publicly traded corporations. Other corporations are less, if at all, accountable, for example privately owned corporations and private equity firms. These corporations avoid much of the government regulation imposed on publicly traded corporations and can often ignore societal pressure. These companies do not have to disclose top management compensation and are not subject to the *Sarbanes-Oxley* legislation. This may change in the future as these corporations use capital provided by pension and mutual funds, which are more publicly accountable, often insisting on corporate social responsibility auditing and reporting.

The Accountability of Government-owned Corporations

The accountability, or control, of the corporations owned by the government has been a major public administration issue. Sexty referred to the control problem being experienced as an "accountability dilemma."[4] The trend to making Crown corporations operate in a more commercial manner has resulted in several accountability problems, including (1) the newly defined, commercially oriented objectives of many government-owned corporations that may be in conflict with social objectives in the national interest; (2) the consequences of evaluating performance based on commercial criteria (that is, profits); (3) the degree of autonomy that should be granted the corporations and their managements; and (4) the techniques for controlling and evaluating the commercial corporations.[5] Just because government owns a corporation does not ensure it will practise appropriate corporate social and environmental responsibility.

This section has identified the issues relating to the ownership and control of Canadian business enterprises. From this discussion, it is recognized that ownership does not necessarily equate with control. Some owners exert considerable control while others have virtually none, and some owners may be disadvantaged.

>LO 11.4<   Protecting Owners and Investors

Shareholder democracy The exercise of power by owners to ensure they are treated fairly and enjoy equally the privileges and duties of ownership.

Protection of owners or investors is a primary issue and several stakeholders are involved, including directors, governments, self-regulatory agencies, financial industry institutions and associations, shareholder activists, and managers. A term used to describe the responsibilities toward owners is **shareholder democracy,** the exercise of power by owners to ensure that they are treated fairly and enjoy equally the privileges and duties of ownership. There is general agreement that shareholders have some rights as owners, namely voting power on major decisions, the transfer of ownership when desired, the entitlement to dividends, and accessibility to accurate and timely financial information. These rights vary with the type of share owned.

Several stakeholders attempt to ensure these rights; many of them are identified in Responsibility for Ethics 11.2. Given the numerous financial scandals, inappropriate market activity, and losses suffered by investors, governments and the financial industry are currently re-examining the adequacy of investor protection. Despite the numerous government initiatives, self-regulatory organizations, and industry associations, investors are still suffering losses due to illegal or unethical behaviour on the part of financial industry managers. Reliance on the government requirements ethic does not appear sufficient to protect shareholders, and it is suggested that no one is guarding the guards—that is, the regulators, whether government or self-regulators.

Responsible investing Screening investments in corporations or mutual and pension funds for their response to social or ethical responsibilities as well as their financial or economic performance.

Although government and other stakeholders are attempting to ensure that owners are treated fairly, the role of boards of directors and managers should not be ignored. Many corporations have investor relations departments. The managers of these departments strive to maintain the confidence of investors and are active in communicating information about the corporation to existing and potential investors.

There are challenges associated with the ownership and control of Canadian business corporations. But, the situation should not be viewed as one of hopelessness. The composition of ownership is always changing, and at the same time there is a shifting influence, or control, by various owners. Given the dynamic nature of the Canadian business system, there will always be owners and other stakeholders who care enough to challenge the existing centres of influence.

>LO 11.5<   Responsible Investing

Responsible investing is the screening of investments in corporations or mutual and pension funds for their response to social or ethical responsibilities as well as their financial or economic performance. These investments are usually stocks of publicly traded corporations, but

RESPONSIBILITY
for Ethics **11.2**

Stakeholders Protecting the Rights of Owners

Governments

- Incorporation and securities laws, for example the *Canada Business Corporations Act,* that protect shareholder rights. Such laws exist at the provincial level also.
- The *Sarbanes-Oxley Act of 2002,* which is U.S. legislation passed to protect investors by improving the accuracy and reliability of corporate disclosures. Canadian corporations are affected if they obtain capital on U.S. markets; this Act established practices later included in Canadian legislation and regulations.
- The RCMP's Integrated Market Enforcement Teams, which are groups of highly specialized investigators dedicated to ensuring that those who commit serious capital market fraud offences will be detected, charged, and prosecuted.

Self-Regulatory Agencies and Organizations

- Stock exchanges—in particular the Toronto Stock Exchange, the largest in Canada—which provide markets for trading equity capital and develop and enforce their own rules and regulations relating to corporate listings and the protection of investors.
- Securities Exchange Commissions in each province and territory, of which the Ontario Securities Commission is the most influential. The 13 securities commissions have formed the Canadian Securities Administrators organization to coordinate and harmonize regulation of the Canadian capital markets.
- Investment Industry Regulatory Organization of Canada (IIROC)—IIROC is the national self-regulatory organization that oversees all investment dealers and trading activity on debt and equity marketplaces in Canada.
- The Canadian Investor Protection Fund, a not-for-profit organization that provides investor protection for investment dealer bankruptcy.
- The Mutual Fund Dealers Association, which oversees the sale of mutual funds. It regulates the activities of members and ensures they adhere to the rules, bylaws, and policies of the MFDA, as well as applicable securities legislation.

Individual and Institutional Activists

- Individuals such as Robert Verdun and Yves Michaud, who for years have attempted to have the small investor's voice heard at bank annual meetings.
- Jarislowsky Fraser Limited, an investment counselling firm, which has for years advocated for the protection of investor interests.
- The Small Investor Protection Association, a volunteer member organization committed to fair practice in the investment industry.
- The Shareholder Association for Research and Education (SHARE), a non-profit organization created by the Canadian labour movement to improve institutional investment practices to protect investors.

---

some funds are comprised of bonds and other investments are "balanced." This is also referred to as "socially responsible investment," "ethical investment," or "social conscience investment," and, in the context of the environment, "green investment" or "environmentally friendly." An example is provided by the Ethical Growth Fund described in Everyday Ethics 11.6.

Everyday Ethics

11.6

Ethical Growth Fund

"The Ethical Growth Fund aims to increase the value of your investment over the long term by investing mostly in common shares of a wide variety of Canadian corporations. It follows a socially responsible approach to investing." Its top holdings include Royal Bank of Canada, Suncor Energy, Barrick Gold Corporation, Goldcorp Inc., Shaw Communications, Scotiabank, and TD Bank.

Awareness is growing surrounding the possibilities of achieving acceptable rates of return and social objectives at the same time. Individual investors have an appreciation of this, but the awareness has most likely been fuelled by the investment decisions of churches and other religious organizations, trade unions, women's organizations, cooperative systems, the environmental movement, universities and colleges, and pensions funds. The Canadian financial community has quickly responded to the growing awareness of and demand for socially responsive investments. Several mutual funds have been established that have "socially responsible" objectives.

These funds are categorized into two types: "do-gooder," with positive screens, or "objectionable," with negative screens. A "do-gooder" fund invests in corporations with good social and environmental records and enlightened industrial and stakeholder relations. The other type, "objectionable" funds, screens out objectionable corporations; those, for example, involved in alcohol, tobacco, weapons, and nuclear power. Examples of investment criteria included in the screens are listed in Table 11.1. Not all funds apply all these criteria.

Responsible investing has sensitized managers to the fact that at least some investors make investment decisions based upon how socially responsible the corporation is. It is not possible to measure the impact on business in any definitive manner, and the total investments in these funds are small in comparison to the total mutual funds market.

TABLE 11.1	*Responsible Investment Criteria*

The criteria or screens used in making responsible investments vary by fund and provide a method by which a prospective investment is judged to be socially acceptable. Activities that might be considered socially irresponsible or unethical include:

- poor employee/labour relations
- failure to promote racial and sexual equality and affirmative programs
- the manufacture of weapons
- involvement in the nuclear industry
- the manufacture of "sin" products such as alcohol or tobacco
- the conducting of business in repressive regimes
- the violation of human rights
- environmentally damaging operations, for example, those that pollute
- unsafe goods and services, questionable marketing practices, and exploitive marketing in Third World countries
- use of animals in product testing
- involvement in gambling and pornography
- factory farm production of animals
- genetically modified products

The motives of the financial community raise compelling thoughts. Does it really believe in socially responsible investing or is this simply a response to a market demand? Are the funds merely shrewd marketing? The motives of investors can also be questioned. For how long would they continue to invest in a socially responsible corporation or fund that lost money?

Several stakeholders monitor or provide sources of information on responsible investing. Also, there are several stock indices of corporate social responsibility performance. Independent organizations have been formed to monitor social investments, one example being the Social Investment Organization (SIO). These stakeholders are listed in Responsibility for Ethics 11.3.

RESPONSIBILITY
for Ethics **11.3**

Stakeholders Monitoring Responsible Investment

Social Investment Organization (SIO)—Established in 1989, the Social Investment Organization is a national non-profit organization dedicated to the advancement of socially responsible investment in Canada. It is funded primarily from membership dues and is accountable to its membership. The SIO has about 400 members across Canada.

Corporate Knights *Magazine*—Publishes an annual responsible investing guide.

Jantzi Social Index (JSI) (Canada)—A stock index of socially screening investments developed to create a benchmark against which investors can measure the performance of their responsible investments.

Domini 400 Social Index (U.S.)—A stock index comprising 400 socially responsible corporations selected on a screen developed by Domini Social Investments.

Dow Jones Sustainability Indexes (U.S.)—Dow Jones has developed indices that reflect the sustainability performance of corporations that create long-term shareholder value by embracing opportunities and managing risks deriving from economic, environmental, and social developments.

FTSE4Good Index Series (U.K.)—These indices provide investors with information on "globally recognized companies that meet globally recognized corporate responsibility standards. The indices are designed to identify and measure the performance of companies that are working towards environmental sustainability, developing positive relationships with stakeholders and up-holding universal human rights."

Sources: Based on Social Investment Organization—The Canadian Association for Socially Responsible Investment, http://www.socialinvestment.ca/AboutSIO.htm; Jantzi Research, "About SJI," http://www.jantzisocialindex.com/; Domini Social Investment, "The Domini 400 Social Index," http://www.domini.com/; Dow Jones Sustainability Indexes, http://www.sustainability-index.com/; "FTSE4Good Index Series: Add Values to Your Investment," http://www.ftse.com/Indices/FTSE4Good_Index_Series/index.jsp.

There are challenges to ascertaining what a socially responsible investment is. In particular, one researcher claimed that social investing was a myth. His critique made the following points:

- The data relied upon are sketchy and the research is highly selective.
- The ratings are not completely objective and misrepresent the complexity of the modern corporation.
- The screenings are tainted by anachronistic, contradictory, idiosyncratic, and ideologically constructed notions of social responsibility.
- Claims of the growing financial impact are questionable.
- No coherent case has been made for why the criteria used for social responsibility are better at effecting social change.
- The researcher concludes that the general approach of social investment advocates is one of vindication of the true believer, not investigation.[6]

It is not always easy to be socially responsible. Also, the financial performance of socially responsible investment funds has been reasonable, not outstanding or weak. Like any other mutual fund, past performance does not guarantee future performance. It is not clear whether mixing profits and principles will actually pay investors over the long term.

connect Want to learn more about **responsible investing**? Go to CONNECT.

Another dynamic of responsible investing is the role of mutual and pension funds. It is possible that the managers of such funds will come under pressure from fund contributors to invest in such a way that reflects their social values. The managers, in turn, might make an investment decision on social criteria that pressures corporation managers to behave in socially responsible ways. Also, some fund managers purchase shares in some corporations in the hopes of changing the corporation's behaviour. The influence of such pressure is not clear at this time. Even so, individuals making direct investments or indirect investments through funds may be prompting decisions that influence managers to improve their corporation's social performance.

Investors or shareholders own the corporation and many efforts are made to ensure they are responsible stakeholders. Their influence includes the corporation's approach to corporate social responsibility, and the most direct way to accomplish this is through responsible investing, a trend that is increasing.

LO 11.6   Defining Corporate Governance

Corporate governance The processes, structures, and relationships through which the shareholders, as represented by a board of directors, oversee the activities of the corporation.

The definition of corporate governance has evolved over time. One definition of **corporate governance** is the processes, structures, and relationships through which the shareholders, as represented by a board of directors, oversee the activities of the corporation. A second frequently used definition is from the literature: Governance is concerned with the intrinsic nature, purpose, integrity, and identity of the institution, with a primary focus on the entity's relevance, continuity, and fiduciary aspects. Governance involves monitoring and overseeing strategic direction, socioeconomic and cultural context, resources, externalities, and constituencies of the institution.[7]

In the first definition the owner and director stakeholders were mentioned, representing a more traditional view. In the second definition, the scope is much greater and the word *constituencies* is used in recognition of the numerous stakeholders that influence the governance of the corporation. A third definition is a more practical or applied one: "Corporate governance" means the process and structure used to direct and manage the business and affairs of the corporation with the objective of enhancing long-term value for shareholders and the financial viability of the business. The process and structure define the division of power and accountability among shareholders, the board of directors, and management, and can have an impact on other stakeholders such as employees, customers, suppliers, and communities.[8]

Stakeholders are identified in this definition, which is a key change in how boards are defined. The definitions illustrate how corporate governance has changed. The changes have involved many issues, some of which will be examined.

LO 11.7   The Rights of Shareholders and the Responsibilities of the Board

The Organisation for Economic Co-operation and Development (OECD) states that corporate governance is important as it deals with the rights and responsibilities of a corporation's management, its board, shareholders, and stakeholders. Good corporate governance is important when corporations are seeking capital on financial markets as governance is one indicator of whether corporations are well run. In particular, the corporate governance process should protect and improve the exercise of shareholders' rights. The OECD has identified these shareholder rights as:

- secure ownership registration
- capability to transfer ownership
- access to relevant corporate information in a timely and regular manner
- participation and voting at shareholder meetings
- election and removal of board members
- share in profits of the corporation
- knowledge of extraordinary transactions or decisions
- disclosure of dual-class shares
- rules and regulations ensuring the efficient and transparent functioning of the capital markets for the corporation's securities
- capability to exercise ownership rights
- ability to consult other shareholders relating to their rights.[9]

Shareholders of Canadian corporations are allowed to present resolutions at the annual shareholders' meeting, and the corporation must circulate information on the resolution. These resolutions often concern management and board integrity, and the corporation's CSR.

Respecting and enhancing these "rights" is a main objective of boards of directors, and this is accomplished through corporate governance practices. The following sections discuss some of these practices.

The Responsibilities of the Board

Board of directors A group of individuals elected by shareholders to govern or oversee the corporation's affairs.

A **board of directors** is a group of individuals elected by shareholders to govern or oversee the corporation's affairs. The role of the board is to monitor and evaluate the corporation's activities and performance. The board has the power to select, evaluate, and terminate the chief executive officer and top management. The directors are required to provide shareholders with financial statements and an auditor's statement, and other financial and operational information required by the articles, by-laws, or a shareholder agreement. This information is usually presented as an annual report.[10] The board should be planning for the longer term by participating in a strategic planning process, and ensuring continuity and succession in the management team. Usually major transactions and ventures are evaluated and approved. The role described includes what are referred to as **fiduciary duties,** obligations owed by directors to shareholders that are prescribed by laws or regulations.

Fiduciary duties Obligations owed by directors to shareholders that are prescribed by laws or regulations.

Today, more is demanded of boards and their members. Corporations listed on Canadian stock exchanges are required to disclose the text of a board's written mandate. Such a mandate would include not only items mentioned above but also the following:

- The board's satisfaction with the integrity of the CEO and other executive members, and that they are creating a culture of integrity throughout the corporation.
- The board's approach to developing governance principles and guidelines specific to the corporation.
- Identification of measures for receiving feedback from stakeholders including the possibility of them contacting independent directors directly.
- Listing expectations and responsibilities of directors to fulfill their duties, for example by attending meetings and reviewing materials prior to meetings.[11]

The OECD promotes good corporate governance practices by issuing the *OECD Principles of Corporate Governance,* which includes some responsibilities in addition to those mentioned in the National Instrument:

- Treating all shareholders fairly where board decisions affect different shareholder groups differently.
- Applying high ethical standards and taking into account the interests of stakeholders.
- Monitoring and managing potential conflicts of interest among management, board members, and shareholders.
- Ensuring the integrity of the corporation's accounting and financial reporting systems.
- Overseeing the process of disclosure and communications.[12]

Many corporations now have charters or constitutions for their boards that contain a description of the board's mandate.

These legal, self-regulatory, and suggested guidelines have enhanced board and director responsibilities, and have led to improvements in corporate accountability. In effect, boards are addressing issues of ethics and responsibilities beyond the immediate interests of shareholders; that is, the corporation's social responsibility to society.

LO 11.8   Corporate Governance Issues

The media cover many corporate governance issues, regulatory bodies are concerned about them, and boards are addressing them. The following are examples of issues confronting boards and stakeholders.

Board Membership

Becoming a board member was once a closed process with corporate executives dominating membership, acquaintances of executives appointed, and the existence of interlocking directorships; that is, directors serving on one another's boards. Corporate governance reform has altered this process in most publicly listed corporations. Director positions have job descriptions outlining what is expected. New members are sought through a nomination process, given an orientation to the corporation, and provided with a continuing education program.

Independent (or unrelated) director "A director who is free from any interest and any business or other relationship which could, or could reasonably be perceived to, materially interfere with the director's ability to act in the best interests of the corporation."

A major issue on board memberships has been their independence from the operations and management of the corporation. A definition of an **independent (or unrelated) director** is "a director who is free from any interest and any business or other relationship which could, or could reasonably be perceived to, materially interfere with the director's ability to act in the best interests of the corporation."[13] Family members, current executives, recently departed members of management, and professional advisers such as lawyers are not considered independent. There must be a majority of independent board members or an appropriate explanation provided. Prospective directors must be interested in the quality and reputation of the existing board, the quality of governance processes, the board's independence, and the corporation's approach for integrity and social responsibility.

The qualifications of a director are varied. Financial acumen and the capability of identifying risk are essential. Operating experience is an asset, and knowledge of governance processes is expected. Knowing the right people is still important in appointment to boards.[14] The recruitment of women and, to a lesser extent, minorities is receiving attention. About 12 percent of the directors of Canada's top 500 corporations are women.[15] Modest progress has been made in increasing the number of women, and Canadian corporations lag behind the proportion of women directors serving on U.S. boards. Many corporations say they want women directors, but few heed the advice and appoint them. It is argued that the pool of qualified applicants is small and that women lack experience as chief financial officers and CEOs.[16] A "critical mass" of three or more female directors is required before they influence the board.[17] Responsibility for Ethics 11.4 describes one initiative by the business community to enhance the diversity of board membership.

RESPONSIBILITY
for Ethics **11.4**

Canadian Board Diversity Council (CBDC)

The Council was set up to promote diversity on Canadian boards of directors by increasing the representation of women, visible minorities, Aboriginal peoples, persons with disabilities, and members of the LGBT (lesbian, gay, bisexual, and transgender) community. One purpose is to conduct research on the progress of the diversity and it publishes an annual report card. It provides an education program in governance to create a greater number of highly skilled diverse board candidates and maintains a database of qualified men and women from across Canada who have the competences to serve on boards. It does not support the use of quotas to achieve diversity representation on boards. CBDC members and business community are made aware of board diversity best practices and principles.

Source: Canadian Board Diversity Council Web site at http://www.boarddiversity.ca, accessed December 3, 2012.

Because more is demanded of directors, including accountability for the corporation's ethics and social responsibilities, it is challenging to find individuals that understand and are willing to accept the risks involved with increasing accountability.

Board Structure

Most boards comprise 10 to 15 members who serve on various committees. The number of committees varies, as does the type. Common committees include audit, finance, human resources, pension, compensation, nominating, governance, and strategic planning. Often these areas are combined, usually resulting in three to six committees. An audit committee is required and should comprise independent members. A recent development has been the formation of social responsibility or environment committees.

The separation of the board chair and CEO positions has been controversial. Corporate governance experts and regulatory bodies recommend that different persons occupy the positions and that an independent director act as chair. The independence of the board is at issue, but many boards have adopted the separation of the positions.

Disclosure and Transparency

Corporate governance reform has focused on disclosure and transparency of the corporation's operations, in particular financial reporting and disclosure, and how the board functions. This became an issue with the failure of many American and Canadian corporations in the 1990s and early 2000s, quite often due to inappropriate behaviour on the part of executives and directors. National Instrument 58-101 contains a clause relating to ethical business conduct that the Canadian Securities Administrators recommends is implemented. This clause is given in Responsibility for Ethics 11.5. Many corporate boards now have a code of ethical business conduct that applies to all, including directors.

A controversial item involving disclosure and transparency is the compensation of executives and directors. Securities regulation requires disclosure of executive compensation

RESPONSIBILITY
for Ethics (11.5)

Disclosure of "Ethical Business Conduct"

National Instrument 58-101 requires that corporations disclose the following in relation to ethical business conduct:

1. (a) "Disclose whether or not the board has adopted a written code for the directors, officers and employees. If the board has adapted a written code:
   (i) disclose how a person or company may obtain a copy of the code;
   (ii) describe how the board monitors compliance with its code, or if the board does not monitor compliance, explain whether and how the board satisfies itself regarding compliance with its code;
   (iii) provide a cross-reference to any material change report filed since the beginning of the issuer's most recently completed financial year that pertains to any conduct of a director or executive officer that constitutes a departure from the code.
2. (b) Describe any steps the board takes to ensure directors exercise independent judgment in considering transactions and agreements in respect of which a director or executive officer has a material interest.
3. (c) Describe any other steps the board takes to encourage and promote a culture of ethical business conduct."

Source: *National Instrument 58–101,* "Disclosure of Corporate Governance Practices, Clause 5," http://www.osc.gov.on.ca/en/14198.htm.

in publicly traded corporations, and many have detailed statements of compensation. The compensation received by executives has several components including salary, bonuses, incentive plans, share grants, and options in addition to various perks such as health and pension plans. Issues exist for all forms of payment and include the criteria used to determine salary, the magnitude of the compensation, the basis for bonus and incentive plans, the inverse relationship that sometimes exists between salary and corporate performance, the amount and pricing of options, and excessive severance and pension payments.

Director compensation has also become an issue recently as it has increased to reflect the demands being placed on directors. Directors can receive an annual retainer, board meeting fee, annual committee retainer, and committee meeting fee. Some directors receive options, considered appropriate because some boards require directors to own shares in the corporation to enhance their stake. A director's compensation for a Canadian corporation can now amount to hundreds of thousands of dollars.

An important contributor to disclosure and transparency is the board's audit committee. An **audit committee** comprises members of the board of directors and oversees the internal and external accounting auditing function to ensure that financial statements accurately and appropriately represent the condition of the corporation and that regulated disclosures are made. The committee makes sure that the corporation is in compliance with all regulations and often oversees the corporation's codes of conduct and/or ethics. Today, corporations are expected to prepare a "charter" for the audit committee that discloses the names of committee members, indicates whether they are independent, and describes the experience and education of each member.

The disclosure requirements of publicly traded Canadian corporations are identified in *Disclosure of Corporate Governance Practices* prepared by the Canadian Securities Administrators, which is summarized in Responsibility for Ethics 11.6. Many Canadian corporations now provide extensive information on their disclosure practices and have statements outlining what is to be done and by whom.

Audit committee Comprises members of the board of directors and oversees the internal and external accounting auditing function to ensure that financial statements accurately and appropriately represent the condition of the corporation and that regulated disclosures are made.

Disclosure of Corporate Governance Practices

The Canadian Securities Administrators require that corporations listed on Canadian stock exchanges provide to shareholders information regarding their governance practices. Examples of the information required are:

- *Board of directors*—Identification of independent directors, other directorships held, and independence status of chair.

- *Board mandate*—Provide the text of the board's mandate.

- *Position descriptions*—For the board and committee chairs, CEO.

- *Orientation and continuing education*—Lists measures to familiarize board members with role of the board, its committees, and its directors, and the nature and operation of the corporation's business.

- *Ethical business conduct*—Disclose whether the board has adopted a written code of its directors, officers, and employees.

- *Nomination of directors*—Describe the process used to identify new candidates for board positions.

- *Compensation*—Describe how the compensation for the corporation's directors and officers is determined.

- *Other board committees*—List and describe functions of committees.

- *Assessments*—Indicate whether the board, its committees, and individual directors are regularly evaluated.

Source: Canadian Securities Administrators, National Instrument 58-101. "Disclosure of Corporate Governance Practices," http://www.osc.gov.on.ca/Regulations/Rulemaking/Current/Part5/rule_20041029_58-101_disc-corpgov-prac.jsp.

The efforts at disclosure and transparency have involved not only financial responsibilities but also ethics and social responsibilities.

Evaluating Board and Director Performance

The evaluation of board performance is one of the most challenging governance reforms to implement. The evaluation of board and director performance has not been common in the past despite the performance appraisal process being widely used in other levels of the corporation. There has been reluctance by many directors who do not believe evaluation is necessary, that the process may expose weaknesses in the governance process and be embarrassing, and that the collegial relationship among board members may be disrupted. Someone must initiate and champion the process, usually the chair or the board's governance committee. The criteria for assessing the board's performance must be established, but are usually based on regulatory requirements. Also, a process must be put in place to deal with the weaknesses uncovered in the evaluation.

Possible criteria for evaluating board performance include:

- *Legal*—Protects interests of shareholders, ensures compliance with all regulations, ensures financial reporting according to standards

- *Strategic and social*—Approves strategic and business plans, participates in strategic decisions such as acquisitions and capital increases, monitors progress toward goals, remains current on external environment developments, monitors stakeholder influences, oversees ethics programs and corporate social responsibility

- *Financial*—Reviews and approves annual capital and operating budgets, monitors financial performance, evaluates risks, and approves procedures to minimize risk

- *Business*—Approves investment guidelines, monitors adherence to corporate governance guidelines, evaluates corporation's performance
- *Human resources*—Selects, evaluates, and monitors CEO performance, determines executive compensation, approves succession plans
- *Governance*—Ensures appropriateness of committees, selects appropriate board members, evaluates member performance, ensures compliance with all governance regulations and legislation.[18]

The evaluation of individual directors is often opposed as many feel uncomfortable with the process. The process requires courage on the part of directors, but is a good way to make performance expectations known and the feedback helps individuals improve performance. Again, who should conduct the evaluation and the criteria to be used is an issue, along with how to deal with poor director performance. Approaches to director evaluation include self-appraisal, peer appraisal, or chair appraisal.[19]

The following is a list of possible criteria for evaluation of directors:

- *Service*—Attends and participates in meetings, prepares for meetings, respects confidentiality, acts as an effective team member, contributes value to discussions and decisions, lends credibility/legitimacy to corporation
- *Control*—Understands and fulfills fiduciary responsibilities, is familiar with by-laws, monitors programs and/or services, is willing to express dissenting opinions, keeps on top of industry issues, gives constructive criticism to senior management
- *Strategy and social*—Participates in and influences strategy and stakeholder management processes, understands corporation's mission and vision, makes knowledgeable and prudent decisions, focuses on major issues, policies, and strategies rather than tactics and operations
- *Shareholder interests*—Represents shareholder interests, gives advice on how to increase shareholder value, challenges management of goals and results.[20]

Many Canadian boards are implementing evaluation schemes, with board performance evaluation being more common than individual director performance. Whether or not boards and directors are evaluating themselves, another stakeholder—the business media—is developing measures to recognize good governance practices, including their efforts at influencing ethics and social responsibilities.

▶LO 11.9◀ The Relationships among Ownership, Corporate Governance, and CSR

Owners are taking more responsibility for the social, ethical, and environmental impacts their corporations have on society. Corporate governance practices have come under increasing scrutiny and owners pressure the corporation's main governing body, the board of directors, to address corporate responsibility and sustainability challenges. Some owners are becoming more active, pressuring the board to implement governance improvements and to account for the corporation's social and environmental performance. In particular, institutional investors—that is, mutual and pension funds—have become more demanding of boards, directors, and management. The trend to responsible investing has also applied pressure to the board and management, but criticism continues.

Criticism of Corporate Governance

Not everyone agrees that the reform of corporate governance has been a good thing. Some businesspersons claim that changes in regulations, such as *Sarbanes-Oxley* and the requirements of the Canadian Securities Administrators, have increased costs and these costs outweigh the benefits. Audit fees have increased substantially, as have the costs incurred to implement new financial systems to provide the information to meet the requirements. Also, the focus on disclosure and transparency has diverted management attention away from the operation of the business. The additional costs imposed by regulation may even make American and Canadian business less competitive in the global market.[21]

It is argued that unless corporate governance reforms result in more choices for generating shareholders' returns, the effort is not worthwhile. Also, it should not be assumed that changing governance structures will reduce the likelihood of investors being taken advantage of.[22] Some argue that separating the CEO and board chair positions and the requirements of independence have not resulted in returns for shareholders. The point is made that definitional independence doesn't guarantee independent-mindedness.[23]

Thus, there may be dangers in too much governance or overregulation as it causes managers to be overly cautious, reduces the business risks they are willing to assume, and suppresses experimentation and innovation in the business. A backlash may develop in opposition to the increasing surveillance of management resulting from governance reform.[24]

Despite the criticism, continuing and increasing attention is being paid to improving governance practices.

Attention to Governance

Some evidence exists that the improvements made in corporate governance in the past 10 years have led to more profitable and better corporations. There is good reason for improving governance. Studies by Foerster have established a clear link between good corporate governance and higher stock prices.[25] Another study in the United States established that good governance policies are associated with good results; that is, total return, profitability, risk, and dividend payout. The study found that "companies with weaker corporate governance perform more poorly, are less profitable and have higher volatility than do firms with stronger corporate governance."[26]

On the other hand, a review of the academic literature concluded that most studies found no link between corporate governance and firm performance. In particular, it was discovered that director independence did not have a positive impact on performance.[27]

The board of directors selects chief executive officers, monitors their behaviour, evaluates their performance, and, if necessary, dismisses them. Some CEOs have not been sufficiently accountable to the board, and thus to the owners of the corporation. It is suggested that there has been an imbalance of power as some managers behaved like absolute monarchs or military dictators. Corporate governance reform has restored power to the board and taken it away from the all-powerful CEO. The board is now more independent; in particular, its audit committee is a much more independent body.

Corporate governance practices have changed substantially in the past few years. In the past, directors may have questioned management's decisions but rarely countermanded them even though they had ultimate authority over key policy decisions. They are now playing a bigger role in determining and assessing strategy, acquisition decisions, succession planning, crisis responses, financial reporting practices, relations with stakeholders, and ethical responsibilities. Boards are meeting more often; seeking more qualified directors, often with particular competencies; meeting without management present; and hiring their own experts on various matters including executive compensation, accounting policies, and legal issues.

In Canada, the regulations of the Canadian Securities Administrators, the stock exchange regulations, and the self-regulatory organizations have had some impact, but not nearly as extensive as in the United States. An example of the influence the securities administrators are attempted to have is outlined in Responsibility for Ethics 11.6, where they argue for the improvement in the disclosure of governance practices. In order to more effectively regulate, it is proposed that a national securities regulator be formed instead of relying on the provincial ones now operating.

Large institutional investors believe that good governance leads to better performance. Many of these investors have formed the Canadian Coalition for Good Governance (described in Responsibility for Ethics 11.7) to develop investor interest and promote changes in governance. David Beatty, the Coalition's managing director, states that, "It's a passionate commitment, a deeply held belief that governance has to be improved if we're going to have efficient capital markets in this country."[28]

RESPONSIBILITY
for Ethics **11.7**

Canadian Coalition for Good Governance (CCGG)

Institutional investors such as pension funds, mutual funds, and third-party money managers have formed CCGG to represent their interests. This is accomplished by encouraging best corporate governance practices in the corporations in which they own shares, mostly corporations that are members of the S&P/TSX Composite Index. CCGG members manage about $2 trillion in assets on behalf of Canadian investors.

CCGG researches and publishes information on governance issues such as executive compensation, majority voting, director compensation, board shareholder engagement, and disclosure of financial and governance information. By making submissions on governance-related matters to stock exchanges, securities commissions, and governments, it attempts to influence the regulation of the securities industry.

Each year, it prepares a Best Practices for Proxy Circular Disclosure report to assist managers and board members. Also, it annually awards Governance Gavel Awards such as the "Best Disclosure of Board Governance Practices and Director Qualifications," recently won by Suncor Energy Inc., and "Best Disclosure of Approach to Executive Compensation," recently won by Canadian National Railway Company.

CCGG members believe that good governance practices result in a greater return to investors who are participating in the financial market through indirect pension and mutual funds ownership.

Source: "About CCGG," Canadian Coalition for Good Governance Web site, http://www.ccgg.ca/index.cfm?pagepath=About_CCGG&id=17564.

At an international level, the inclusion of stakeholders in the definition of corporate governance was an important step and has been endorsed by the OECD. The *OECD Principles of Corporate Governance* included a section on the role of stakeholders. This role includes the following points:

- The rights of stakeholders are respected when established by law or mutual agreements.
- Effective redress should be available to stakeholders when their legally established rights are violated.
- If stakeholders participate in the governance process, they should have access to all the information necessary to carry out their role.
- Stakeholders should be allowed to freely communicate concerns about illegal or unethical practices to the board without fear of retaliation.[29]

Various organizations recognize the best practices of boards or board members; an example is the Canadian Coalition for Corporate Governance's "Governance Gavel Awards." *The Globe and Mail* annually publishes "Board Games: Annual Corporate Governance Rankings." Some of the best governance practices of the five highest ranking corporations are given in Everyday Ethics 11.7.

Everyday Ethics

11.7

Best Corporate Governance Practices

A survey conducted by the Clarkson Centre for Ethics and Board Effectiveness at the University of Toronto for *The Globe and Mail* identified the best-governed corporate boards in Canada. Some features of good governance practices in the five best are listed below.

- *Sun Life Financial Inc.*—independent board; governance, nominations, and investment committee to provide governance guidelines and processes; charter of the board of directors outlining duties, responsibilities, and other operational matters
- *Bank of Nova Scotia*—statement of corporate governance policies, board "corporate governance and pension committee," and mandate statement outlining governance practices
- *Potash Corporation of Saskatchewan Inc.*—statement of governance including board structure, director independence and integrity; board "corporate governance and nominating committee"
- *The Toronto-Dominion Bank*—details of governance structure including corporate governance committee, disclosure statement of governance practices, and board charter
- *TransAlta Corp.*—statement of corporate governance practices, board governance and environment committee; directors' code of conduct

Sources: Listing from "Board games, 11th annual corporate governance rankings," *The Globe and Mail,* November 26, 2012, B9, and at http://www.theglobeandmail.com/report-on-business/careers/management/board-games-2012. Company information from corporate Web sites: Sun Life Financial Inc., http://www.sunlife.com/Global/About+us/Corporate+governance?vgnLocale=en_CA; Bank of Nova Scotia, http://www.scotiabank.com/ca/en/0,,468,00.html; Potash Corp., http://www.potashcorp.com/about/governance/; Toronto-Dominion Bank, http://www.td.com/about-tdbfg/corporate-governance/index.jsp; and TransAlta Corp., http://www.transalta.com/about-us/governance, all accessed December 5, 2012.

Ownership, Governance, and CSR

Directors are the protectors of shareholders' interests and the overseers of strategy and financial responsibility. Recently, directors have also become overseers of CSR and ethical conduct—this is because they are ultimately responsible for everything that happens in the corporation. Pay systems, incentive plans, and performance goals can lead to misconduct on the part of executives and employees. Being responsible for ethical management practices is now another concern in looking after shareholders' interests. Colero recommends that directors ask the following five questions about the corporation's ethics management:

- What is our company's strategy to manage ethics?
- Who is responsible for ethics in our company?
- Are people in our firm equipped to recognize and resolve moral dilemmas?
- Are people in our organization provided with a safe opportunity to discuss ethical issues of concern?
- Do we reward or punish ethical integrity and moral courage if it has a negative impact on the bottom line?[30]

Another perspective on corporate governance, CSR, and ethical conduct relates to an appropriate response to external environment factors, trends, or events. Schacter argues that four factors have to come together requiring boards to pay attention to CSR: globalization, loss of trust, civil society activism, and investor interest in CSR.

Globalization has made it necessary for corporations to consider the economic, social, and environmental impacts on society, including those in developing countries. Corporations are also facing increasing demand to do something about these impacts. Several corporate scandals, excessive executive compensation, outsourcing of jobs, environmental disasters, and stock market declines have resulted in a loss of trust in business and the corporation.

Civil society organizations, including NGOs, are more active and effective in pointing out the mistakes and misdeeds of corporations. Finally, many investors, including mutual and pension funds, have become more interested in responsible investing. Added to this list is the growing pressure for improved corporate governance, more management accountability for the corporation's economic, social, and environmental issues, and increasing regulation.[31]

Directors are still responsible for the creation of wealth for shareholders. There is a reputation risk involved in not responding to CSR and ensuring appropriate ethical conduct. Shareholder wealth may be adversely affected by boards of directors ignoring CSR and ethics management. The long-term interests of owners and stakeholders are interlinked, and through good governance practices boards must set an example for all the corporation's stakeholders and show that they are concerned about CSR and ethics management.

Your advice to Marc. . .

Marc's dilemma is not unusual. Just as it is often challenging to ascertain ethical versus unethical behaviour, responsible investing is often difficult to identify. Not everyone agrees on what is irresponsible corporate economic activity. Also, corporations that can appear responsible may lapse for some reason, sometimes beyond their control. The decision is further complicated by the expected dividends, or return, that the shareholder seeks. Which investment—or investments—to make is a judgment call involving pros and cons. Marc should obtain all the information he can about a particular investment to make an informed decision.

SUMMARY

- Although other stakeholders have an influence on the corporation, it is owned by shareholders or investors. But ownership is not straightforward; there are several types of owners and some owners are not always treated fairly. Direct owners include investors, entrepreneurs, managers, employees, and producers, while indirect owners include mutual, pension, and investment funds. (LO 11.1, LO 11.2)

- Several ethical and responsibility issues are associated with ownership and the actual control of the corporation. These issues include the appropriateness of widely held versus concentrated ownership, the treatment of minority shareholders, non-voting shares, dual-class shares, the pros and cons of employee ownership, the accountability of private corporations, and the accountability of government-owned corporations. (LO 11.3)

- It is necessary to protect the rights of owners through government legislation, self-regulatory agencies, industry association, and individual and institutional activists. Corporations are mindful of owners and often have "investor relations" departments to maintain good relations. (LO 11.4)

- Responsible investing is the screening of investments by corporations or mutual and pension funds for their response to social or ethical responsibilities as well as their financial or economic actions. This process is also referred to as ethical, green, environmental, and social conscience investing. Investments are examined by a screen comprising negative or positive criteria. Several stock market indices identify corporations that qualify for responsible investing. (LO 11.5)

- The definition of corporate governance has changed over the years to reflect developments in the area. Traditionally, the definition referred only to shareholders, but stakeholders are now included. (LO 11.6)

- The rights of shareholders have expanded in recent years and respecting and enhancing these rights is the responsibility of boards of directors in Canadian corporations. The board of directors is elected by the shareholders and is mandated to represent shareholder interests. The board oversees all the affairs of the corporation and today this includes the ethical conduct and social responsibility of the corporation. Many corporations now have charters specifying the board's mandate. (LO 11.7)

- Several issues are related to corporate governance, including the selection process, the need for independence of directors, the qualification of directors, and the size of the board. Corporate governance reform has focused on disclosure and transparency of the corporation's operations; financial reporting and disclosure; social and environment accountability; and executive compensation. (LO 11.8)

- The evaluation of the board's and the individual directors' performance has been a recent reform and one that is resisted. It is felt to be intrusive and difficult to implement. Nevertheless, many corporations are involved with evaluation processes. The implementation of appropriate governance practices is recognized by two Canadian rankings prepared by the business media. (LO 11.8)

- The evidence about the relationship between corporate governance and the corporation's financial performance is mixed. Regulatory agencies and many shareholders, especially the large institutional investors, strongly believe there is a positive relationship between governance practices and performance. (LO 11.8)

- Corporate governance reform has been praised and criticized. The reform has resulted in a change of the relationship between management and the board, with managers losing influence while the board and owners have increased their influence. (LO 11.8)

- A connection exists between corporate governance and stakeholder theory, ethical conduct, and CSR. In fact, governance is now considered one influence on corporations to conduct their affairs appropriately in the interests of shareholders and other stakeholders, and as a part of the corporation's overall corporate social responsibility. (LO 11.9)

KEY TERMS

Governing system	Labour-supported investment	Venture capital company
Investors	funds (LSIFs)	Dual-class stock
Mutual fund	Private equity firms	Non-voting shares

Restricted shares
Passive shareholders
Active shareholders
Worker capitalism

Shareholder democracy
Responsible investing
Corporate governance
Board of directors

Fiduciary duties
Independent (or unrelated)
 director
Audit committee

CRITICAL THINKING AND DISCUSSION QUESTIONS

1. Why are owners an important stakeholder? How does the corporation influence them, and how do owners influence the corporation?

2. What influence do owners such as mutual funds and pension funds have on the corporation?

3. Do owners always control the corporation?

4. What can be done to protect the interests of owners or shareholders?

5. How can owners influence the corporate social responsibility of the corporation?

6. How can an investor identify a responsible investment?

7. Why is it necessary for shareholders to have rights? How are shareholder rights upheld?

8. How have the responsibilities of the board of directors changed?

9. Why is disclosure and transparency important to shareholders and stakeholders?

10. What evidence is there that corporate governance reform has resulted in better performance?

11. Who has gained and who has lost in the redistribution of power in the corporation as a result of regulatory reform?

12. What is the connection between corporate governance and the corporation's ethical conduct and social responsibility?

CASES

11.1   *Aunt Mabel's Experience with Ownership*

Karl Stillings's Aunt Mabel called him on a Saturday morning and wondered if he could drop in to visit her that afternoon. Aunt Mabel was a widow; Uncle Richard had passed away about 18 months ago. She was quite concerned about her investments and would appreciate Karl's advice since he had recently graduated from a business program.

During his visit Karl was not surprised to learn that his aunt had no investment experience—his uncle had looked after all financial matters. She had become a widow at 62 and found she had cash assets of about $200,000 from an insurance policy and savings. She approached a financial institution and was assigned an adviser. The adviser had Aunt Mabel sign an account agreement, which she admitted to Karl she did not read in detail as it was several pages and in small print. Besides, she trusted the financial institution and the young and very personable adviser.

The adviser initially invested the money in low-risk money market funds. A few months later he moved the money into higher risk equity or stock funds with higher fees and commissions. He then arranged a $100,000 loan secured against her existing equity, which he invested in very high-risk equity. Aunt Mabel questioned this, but was told it was allowed in the agreement she'd signed. While visiting the adviser recently, Aunt Mabel was told, after she had insisted, that she had lost $40,000 on her investments. She told the adviser she wanted out, but the adviser said there would be expensive redemption fees. Also, he advised waiting a while as markets turn around, and there was a possibility for making a lot of money. Aunt Mabel became very upset and did not know what to do. She decided to seek someone else's advice and that is why she contacted her nephew.

Over a cup of tea and biscuits, Aunt Mabel asked Karl what she should do now.

Questions

1. **What type of ownership was involved? What can be assumed about this type of ownership? Was it appropriate for Aunt Mabel?**

2. **What stakeholders are involved?**

3. **What are the ethical issues or implications involved?**

4. What ethical responsibilities do the adviser and the financial institution have toward any type of investor, and in particular toward an inexperienced and naïve one?

5. What advice should Karl give?

Sources: Stuart Weinberg, "In advisors we trust, though not always wisely," *The Globe and Mail*, October 21, 2006, B13; Gordon Pape, "Wanted: One impartial financial planner," *CARP Magazine*, June 2007, 52; Jonathan Cheveau, "Giving CFPs more respect," *National Post*, June 10, 2008, FP15; Doug Steiner, "A moral gauge," *Report on Business*, January 2009, 23; and Hugh Anderson, "Investors need better information," *National Post*, October 30, 2007, FP6.

11.2 *Shareholder Democracy at Goldcorp Inc.*

In fall 2006, Goldcorp Inc., a large North American gold producer headquartered in Vancouver, B.C., offered to purchase an American gold producer, Glamis Gold Ltd. In 2005, Goldcorp's revenues were $900 million with assets of $4.1 billion, while Glamis had sales of US$203 million with assets of US$701 million. The takeover was to be paid for by giving 1.69 Goldcorp shares for one share of Glamis. This offer was worth about US$8.6 billion when originally proposed.

Goldcorp's management agreed to the offer, with the exception of one member of the board of directors. One shareholder in particular disagreed; Rob McEwan was the company's founder and chair until 2005 and held 1.5 percent of the company's shares. He believed that the offer diluted or reduced the value of the shares of existing shareholders by 67 percent, which he claimed was too much. McEwan asked for a shareholder vote on the takeover and planned to mount a proxy challenge to the decisions made by management and the board. Ian Telfer, CEO, responded that a shareholder vote was not required under Canadian law and claimed that most of the institutional investors agreed with the proposal. Telfer also stated that requiring a vote would usurp the function and duties of the board and turn it into an advisory body. McEwan argued that a shareholder vote would result in more transparency and would be an example of good disclosure of information to all shareholders. Moreover, he claimed that Ontario corporate business law was being violated.

McEwan was supported by the Ontario Teachers Pension Plan and other shareholders who held more than 5 percent of Goldcorp's shares. It was pointed out that under New York Stock Exchange regulations if a dilution of more than 30 percent occurred a shareholder vote must be held. This regulation did not exist in Canada.

Those opposing the takeover asked the court to order a shareholder vote. Meanwhile, many shareholders were wondering about the future value of their investment in Goldcorp.

Questions

1. Who are the stakeholders involved and what are their roles?

2. What ethical or social issues are involved in this situation?

3. Should the regulations be changed to protect minority shareholders?

Sources: Based on Andy Hoffman, "Goldcorp faces proxy battle," *The Globe and Mail*, September 26, 2006, B1, B29; Andy Hoffman, "Goldcorp's Telfer rejects demand for Glamis vote," *The Globe and Mail*, Drew Hasselback, "Goldcorp founder threatens lawsuit," *National Post*, September 27, 2006, FP4; Andy Hoffman, "McEwan wants court order for Goldcorp vote," *The Globe and Mail*, October 5, 2006, B7; and Lori McLeod, "Ont. teachers back call for Goldcorp vote," *National Post*, October 21, 2006, FP7.

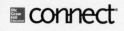

For more information on the resources available from McGraw-Hill Ryerson, go to www.mcgrawhill.ca/he/solutions.

CHAPTER 12
Ethics and Responsibilities in the Workplace and Marketplace

LEARNING OUTCOMES — *After studying this chapter, you will be able to:*

LO 12.1 Explore the ethics and responsibility issues associated with the employee, consumer, competitor, and supplier stakeholders.

LO 12.2 Elaborate on key issues relating to employees and the workplace.

LO 12.3 Learn about the influence the consumer stakeholder has on the marketplace and the influence the marketplace has on the consumer.

LO 12.4 Describe the dynamics and desirability of competition in the marketplace.

LO 12.5 Understand the changing influences on suppliers in a product's supply chain.

LO 12.6 Explain the progression of the supply chain and the influence of factors including sustainability purchasing and fair trade.

What would you do if . . . ?

Phyllis Cramer enjoyed her job as an assistant manager at a large discount department store. It was a demanding job, but she liked the quick pace and the dynamic atmosphere. Among her duties was responsibility for implementing the store's loss prevention, or shoplifting, policy. The policy had recently changed, and Phyllis was concerned about the consequences.

Between 1.5 and 2.5 percent of retail sales are stolen or lost in some way depending on the type of merchandise. About 40 percent of the loss is due to shoplifting by customers, about 35 percent is due to employee theft, about 20 percent is due to administrative and paper errors, and the remaining loss is due to vendor mistakes or theft. Because preventing any loss contributes directly to the store's profitability, the reinforcement of a loss prevention policy is important to the store's financial success.

Of most concern to Phyllis is the loss experienced through customer shoplifting. The store had been very strict about shoplifting and prosecuted everyone regardless of the dollar amount stolen. She realized that this zero-tolerance policy was expensive to enforce. Lawyers' fees and court costs were substantial. Not only was her time involved, but employees had to testify in court on company time. In addition, sometimes the local police force expressed concern at the resources it had to devote to petty thefts.

The new policy would excuse first-time thieves when the value of shoplifted merchandise was less than $25. The store manager said this would allow

Phyllis to focus on the professional shoplifters rather than teenagers, and to devote more time to preventing employee theft. The manager also indicated that the new policy would be less costly to implement.

Phyllis was concerned about the difference in treatment of shoplifters based upon dollar amounts. To her, stealing was stealing no matter how small the amount. She agreed with employees who felt the policy undermined their efforts and might even encourage more shoplifting. She believed the policy really avoided the problem rather than solving it.

Phyllis worried about the ethical implications of such a policy for the store, its employees, and customers who did not steal. Most importantly, she agonized in her own conscience about the policy, in particular letting some thieves get away without any punishment. She did have some sympathy with first-time teenage shoplifters and their parents, but to let them off scot-free was not appropriate either. Phyllis knew that implementing the new policy was not going to be easy.

What is your advice to Phyllis?

LO 12.1   Introduction

The purpose of this chapter is to examine the influence of four stakeholders on the corporation and how the corporation influences them. The four stakeholders to be discussed are employees, consumers, competitors, and suppliers. Employees are stakeholders internal to the corporation and their relationship gives rise to many ethical issues, one of which is illustrated above. Consumers are obviously important, because without them the corporation has no reason to exist. Competitors and suppliers are business-to-business stakeholders primarily involving economic or commercial relationships, but ethical issues also are evident. For most corporations, all four are significant stakeholders in that numerous ethics and responsibilities are associated with them.

Issues relating to the ethics and responsibilities will be identified for each stakeholder and will serve as the basis for discussing them. The purpose of this chapter is not to provide readers with a comprehensive examination of each issue, but instead to provide an appreciation of a wide range, multiplicity, and complexity of issues existing in this area.

LO 12.2   Employees in the Workplace

Employees are almost always identified by corporations as critical or key stakeholders. The relationship with this stakeholder group has always been a challenge, and given the downsizing, retrenchment, and technological changes of the recent past it will be even more so. There are many issues relating to ethics and responsibilities between employees and employers, including those listed in Table 12.1. Note that the "Ethical and Responsibility Issues" column could apply to either the corporation or employees.

Table 12.1 illustrates a range of issues in the relationship between the corporation and the employee stakeholder. Not all of the issues will be examined, but the following sections will focus on the work ethic, employee loyalty, and diversity and discrimination.

connect   Want to learn about **ethical practices in the workplace?** Go to CONNECT.

There are several competitions to identify the best employers in Canada through nomination or survey processes. Corporations that make the list publicize the achievement on letterhead, advertisements, and reports. The presence of these competitions promotes good employee relationships. Responsibility for Ethics 12.1 gives examples of the competitions and winners.

TABLE 12.1	*Examples of Issues Relating to Employees in the Workplace*
Aspect of Employment	**Ethical and Responsibility Issues**
Working Conditions	Provision of safe and healthy workplace
	Taking responsibility for own safety
	Employee's right to know about conditions
	Flexible working hours
	Excessive working hours (overtime without pay)
	Work-life balance
	Wellness programs
	Retirement policies
Workforce Reduction	Shutdown notice
	Severance pay
	Responsibility to retrain or assist in relocation
Workplace Privacy	Health and drug testing
	Monitoring of electronic communications
	Data protection
	Freedom from intrusions
Unions	Anti-union tactics
	Concession bargaining
	Changes in work rules
Fair Compensation	Pay based on performance
	Pay equity
	Availability of fringe benefits
	Pension plans
Employee Loyalty and Duties	Complying with contracts
	Work quality
	Complying with laws
	Respect for working hours, property, and use of resources
	Fair treatment of part-time employees
Diversity Management	Freedom from discrimination and harassment
	Equal opportunities
	Employment equity
	Reverse discrimination
	Physical accessibility to workplace
Right to Due Process	Promotion and dismissal policies
	Discipline policy and procedures
	Access to employment files
Employee Participation	Freedom of conscience, including speech and whistleblowing
	Right to join a union
	Consultation
Right to Work	Fairness in interviews
	Non-discriminatory policies

RESPONSIBILITY
for Ethics **12.1**

Canada's Best Employers

"Best Workplaces in Canada 2012"—A list of best workplaces is compiled by Great Place to Work® Canada and published in *The Globe and Mail*. Recent winner: Intelex Technologies Inc., a Toronto software company, which has brainstorming meetings with employees and top management, has employees vote on core priorities, and offers a comprehensive benefits program.

"Best Employers in Canada 2013"—List prepared by Hewitt Associates, a human resources firm, and published in *Maclean's*. Recent winner: EllisDon Corporation, a Toronto construction and contracting firm, which has profit-sharing and share purchase plans, allows employees to use the company's Windjammer Landing Resort in St. Lucia, and offers extensive in-house training.

"Canada's Top 100 Employers 2013"—Mediacorp and *The Globe and Mail* conduct a study into workplace benefits and identify the 100 best employers by industry but do not rank them. Recent winner: Fairmont Hotels and Resorts, which supports employees' further education by subsidizing tuition, has an academic scholarship program for employees' children, and is committed to environmental stewardship.

"The Best Small and Medium Employers in Canada"—Study conducted by Queen's University's Centre for Business Venturing and published in *The Globe and Mail*. Recent winner: Protegra Inc., an employee-owned Winnipeg corporation where employees are consulted on corporate goals and strategies and encouraged to initiate and join projects in different parts of the business.

Sources: Great Place to Work® Institute, http://www.greatplacetowork.ca/; Best Employers in Canada 2013, https://ceplb03.hewitt.com/bestemployers/canada/pages/currentlist2013.htm and *Maclean's*, October 29, 2012, 39–60; Canada's Top 100 Employers, http://www.canadastop100.com/national/; and The Best Small and Medium Employers in Canada, https://ceplb03.hewitt.com/bestemployers/canada/pages/smallmediumlist2011.htm.

Many employees are seeking greater participation in decisions affecting the work environment. Moreover, many businesspeople are also committed to greater employee involvement as an approach to improving working conditions and performance. Many aspects of how employees are treated are legislated by governments, but the status of employees is influenced by voluntary actions of employers or advocated by employees seeking greater participation. The result might be viewed as employee claims to certain conditions in the workplace, or employee rights.

The concept of the work ethic has been used to establish the different positions employees and employers find themselves in today. Work has changed, and so has the approach to employees. Although employees may be still considered a critical resource, many issues confront human resource management.

The Work Ethic

> **Work ethic** A set of values that holds that work is important to members of society insofar as work influences the qualities or character of individuals; that work is a purposeful activity requiring an expenditure of energy with some sacrifice of leisure; that some gain, usually monetary, is involved; and that through work a person not only contributes to society but also becomes a better individual.

The **work ethic** is a set of values that holds that work is important to members of society insofar as work influences the qualities or character of individuals; that work is a purposeful activity requiring an expenditure of energy with some sacrifice of leisure; that some gain, usually monetary, is involved; and that through work a person not only contributes to society but becomes a better individual. The work ethic as a concept had some origins in religion as labour was believed to be the worthy way to serve God, a calling through which one proved one's worthiness of redemption. Leisure or hedonistic activities were not considered appropriate.

Working hard and accumulating wealth were seen as outward signs of a person's morality. They also provided some assurance of a good life on Earth as well as a good afterlife. The basis for the work ethic is not clear, for while religion is involved so is economics. Although the work ethic was considered as divine dignity, the concept lost some of its piety because the accumulation of wealth countered the religious basis of the ethic, and consumption, much of it conspicuous and made possible by the earnings of work, was inconsistent with saving and investment, or frugality.

Today there are often calls for a return to the work ethic of the past. Arguments can be made for both positions. Many people consider work as only a part of life and instead want time to spend with family, satisfaction from what they do, and a sense of purpose from their job and life. This phenomenon is also described as "backing off the fast track" and focusing more on the quality of life. Work, by itself, is no longer as sufficiently fulfilling as it was in the past. This is manifested in several ways, for example:

- opting out of the labour force; for example, early retirement
- collecting employment insurance or welfare payments rather than accepting low-paying or unattractive jobs
- changing careers
- refusing to perform overtime work
- feeling alienation caused by pressure in the workplace
- questioning traditional authority.

One counterargument for this is that employees are working harder than ever and that more is expected of them in terms of productivity and improved quality, with comparisons made to Japanese workers. Evidence of the work ethic includes the long hours that management and professional persons spend at their jobs or places of business. Work has become an obsession to many, as people have to work harder to keep up with inflation or to make ends meet, and more work is expected from the same or fewer number of employees. Workers fear job loss, and fewer people are available for backup.

Canadians were surveyed about whether or not they still believe in the work ethic. Canadian attitudes toward work ethic include the following, suggesting that the work ethic still exists.

- Canadians are, in principle, committed to work.
- Canadians choose work over most leisure activities when they have to make that kind of choice.
- Canadians would rather work than collect employment insurance.

Other studies have found that Canadians are both strongly motivated to work and that most express overall satisfaction with their jobs.

Table 12.2 lists some issues associated with the work ethic today. It is not known how all these issues affect the work ethic. There is evidence that employees are working longer and harder, yet employers are willing to lay off workers even when skills shortages exist in many occupations.

Many issues exist with employees in the workplace. Only three will be discussed: loyalty of employers to employees and vice-versa, diversity in the workplace, and employee privacy.

Employee Loyalty

Loyalty creates that extra effort and extra drive in employees to perform. It encourages self-motivated behaviour, and reflects employees' confidence in management, their vision, and the corporation's purpose. Loyalty means commitment by employees to the organization they work for. In turn, employers are loyal to employees by providing career-long

TABLE 12.2	*Contemporary Implications on the Work Ethic*

- Workplace stress has increased, according to recent studies. The stress is created by a variety of factors, including many of the items mentioned below.
- Increasing use of part-time or temporary workers has raised concerns about how they are treated.
- Fringe benefits are changing in response to employee demands and efforts by some employers to retain highly qualified workers; for example, elder care, working from home, job sharing, child care, discount programs, and recreational facilities. On the other hand, benefits received from health care and pension plans are declining as employers find them too costly.
- The makeup of compensation is changing, with greater emphasis on pay for performance through cash bonuses, stock purchase, and grant plans.
- Employees are more concerned about being able to balance work and personal life.
- Moonlighting has increased.
- Job insecurity has increased as employers are willing to lay off employees on short notice.
- There is a consensus that Canada is suffering a labour skills shortage and that the shortage will become worse.

employment, good salaries, and other benefits. But has this relationship changed with the new employment environment?

Most managers probably believe that employees should be loyal. Signs of a lack of commitment are easy to detect (turnover, early retirements), but measuring loyalty is much more difficult. Low turnover is not necessarily a sign of loyalty, but instead may mean that employees are tied through benefit plans (particularly pensions), or that no other job opportunities exist. Managers should also be cautious of extreme loyalty; overzealous behaviour by an employee does not necessarily mean that the employee is performing in the best interests of the enterprise. But, given the pressures of change, it may not be possible for management to provide some of the things that in the past encouraged loyalty—for example, job security and good compensation packages.

Employees in today's society often want to be entities unto themselves and are seeking challenging opportunities. Some consider loyalty to self more important than to the corporation. Such employees might be seen to be loyal and dedicated to the job itself, rather than to the corporation they are employed by to do that job. On the other hand, many employees wonder why they should be loyal when corporations may lay them off. It is management's responsibility to provide the environment that engenders loyalty. Intelligent human resource management goes a long way toward doing this. Employees must first be trusted and managers must be loyal to employees. It is critical for managers to give trust and loyalty before expecting it. Managers often assume that they cannot expect loyalty, but loyalty and the commitment it involves can be generated by management initiatives.

In order to improve loyalty, managers must communicate a persuasive corporate image to employees. Employees who demonstrate loyalty must be appropriately rewarded—not only by monetary compensation. In pursuit of loyalty, management should bear in mind the following: loyalty must be a corporate priority and it must start at the top with the CEO; persons at all levels in the organization must be involved; the process takes a long time; and token, one-shot efforts must be avoided. Managers must be careful to distinguish between employee loyalty to individuals and to the corporation. Loyalty to individuals represents personal loyalty and is not as beneficial as loyalty to the organization, which is more enduring.

The blind loyalty of employees that may have existed in the past is unlikely today. On the other hand, managers are finding it more difficult to demonstrate that employees owe them loyalty. Corporate loyalty might need to be redefined in the context of the current situation, where jobs are less secure. It is unreasonable to expect dedicated efforts from employees whose future is insecure. But employees still basically want to think well of the company they work for, as it means thinking well about themselves. Employers will have to honestly explain the need for retrenchment, technological change, and heavier individual workloads. Everyday Ethics 12.1 gives two views on the issue of loyalty during a recession. Another issue related to employee loyalty is whistleblowing, which was described in Chapter 6. Management may view it as an indication of disloyalty, and employees may be reluctant to engage in it for the same reason. Nevertheless, many corporations are establishing whistleblowing policies and procedures.

Everyday Ethics

12.1

Loyalty and a Recession

The recession following the financial crisis in 2008 had an impact on employee loyalty, but the evidence is not clear in which direction. The economic downturn has led to layoffs, salary freezes, cuts in pay, and increased workloads as colleagues are laid off and not replaced. A *Globe and Mail* online poll found that 27 percent of respondents felt less loyal to their employers compared to before the recession. An Ipsos Reid study found that 22 percent of employees surveyed felt less loyal to employers as a result of the recession, 31 percent felt less loyal when salaries were frozen, and 36 percent felt less loyal when colleagues were laid off.

Another study by Kelly Services, a consultant in workforce solutions, found that 30 percent of the 15,000 Canadian employees surveyed felt more engaged and loyal to employers during the economic downturn, 62 percent said it made no difference, and 8 percent said they were less loyal. Forty-five percent felt that they were totally committed to their current employer and the one thing they said contributed to this view was interesting and challenging work.

Sources: "Canadian employee loyalty heightens during economic recession, Kelly workforce survey reveals," Trading Markets.com, March 8, 2010, http://www.tradingmarkets.com/news/stock-alert/kelya_kelyb_canadian-employee-loyalty-heightens-during-economic-recession-kelly-workforce-survey-reveals-830375.html; Marjo Johne, "Workplace loyalty a two-way street," *The Globe and Mail*, August 5, 2009, B13; Jennifer Kruger, "Survey finds employee loyalty rises during recession," PMANewsline, March 10, 2010 http://pmanewsline.com/2010/03/10/survey-finds-employee-loyalty-rises-during-recession/; and Stephanie Findlay, "Employee loyalty takes a nasty fall," *Maclean's*, August 3, 2009, 21.

Managing Employment Diversity

Despite the improvements in labour and human rights legislation, some individuals or groups in the workforce still claim that they are being treated unfairly by employers. **Discrimination** is the preferential (or less than preferential) treatment on bases not directly related to qualifications of the job or performance on the job. The discrimination occurring is often prejudice against certain persons which could be based on such grounds as race (including Aboriginal), gender, nationality, age (young and old), disability, marital status, physical appearance, sexual orientation, and health (for example, HIV/AIDS). Sometimes discrimination is obvious, but it also can be based on habit, custom, and tradition and be barely noticeable.

Most discrimination is addressed by employment equity legislation and corporate policy. **Employment equity** is the fair and equal treatment of employees. Federal and provincial/territorial governments have legislation to implement employment equity. An example of federal government legislation is the *Employment Equity Act*, whose purpose is to:

achieve equality in the workplace so that no person shall be denied employment oppor-tunities or benefits for reasons unrelated to ability and, in the fulfillment of that goal, to

Discrimination The preferential (or less than preferential) treatment on bases not directly related to qualifications of the job or performance on the job.

Employment equity The fair and equal treatment of employees.

correct the conditions of disadvantage in employment experienced by women, aboriginal peoples, persons with disabilities and members of visible minorities by giving effect to the principle that employment equity means more than treating persons in the same way but also requires special measures and the accommodation of differences.[1]

Accompanying legislation is the *Canadian Human Rights Act* (R.S., 1985, c. H-6); its purpose is to:

extend the laws in Canada to give effect . . . to the principle that all individuals should have an opportunity equal with other individuals to make for themselves the lives that they are able and wish to have and to have their needs accommodated, consistent with their duties and obligations as members of society, without being hindered in or prevented from doing so by discriminatory practices based on race, national or ethnic origin, colour, religion, age, sex, sexual orientation, marital status, family status, disability or conviction for an offence for which a pardon has been granted.[2]

The Canadian Human Rights Commission administers the *Canadian Human Rights Act* and is responsible for ensuring compliance with the *Employment Equity Act.* Both laws ensure that the principles of equal opportunity and non-discrimination are followed in all areas of federal jurisdiction.

Provincial governments have passed anti-discrimination laws to ensure fair employment practices. Most provinces prohibit discrimination on the grounds of race, religion, national origin, colour, sex, age, and marital status, and in selected cases the prohibited grounds include political beliefs, ethnic origin, physical handicap, creed, and sexual orientation.

Laws themselves do not prevent discrimination and enforcement is a problem. Some employees are still discriminated against and have little recourse through which to seek remedial action. To a large extent, the individual employer must be relied upon to treat employees and possible employees fairly. The corporation has a major role to play in reducing employment discrimination.

Diversity management A voluntary initiative that goes beyond what is required by law to eliminate workplace discrimination.

Most corporations comply with legislation and many are involved with **diversity management**, a voluntary initiative that goes beyond what is required by law to eliminate workplace discrimination. Responsibility for Ethics 12.2 describes why one corporation has been identified as a best diversity employer. The following section examines feminist ethics as it relates to gender equality and its relationship to business ethics and CSR.

Influence of Feminist Ethics on Business Ethics and CSR

Feminist ethics Diverse, gender-focused approaches to ethical theory and practice.

Feminist ethics is defined as "a diverse set of gender-focused approaches to ethical theory and practice."[3] The objective is to develop non-sexist ethical principles, policies, and practices in society. With regard to business organizations, women have not advanced as owners, managers, professionals, and members of boards of directors relative to men, creating a demand for gender equality and dignity for women. In addition, it is argued that feminist ethics can improve a corporation's overall approach to business ethics and CSR.

It was argued that traditional ethical theories did not consider or value women's moral experience. The theories were more concerned with men's issues, and ignored the nurturing and caring characteristics of women. Masculine traits like independence, autonomy, hierarchy, and domination were overemphasized in comparison to feminine traits of interdependence, community, sharing, joy, and peace. Moral reasoning favoured male ways of thinking based on rules, rights, justice, and universality, which leads to fair, objective, and consistent treatment or outcomes. Female ways emphasized empathy, harmony, responsibilities, care for one another, and healthy relationships.

RESPONSIBILITY
for Ethics **12.2**

Canada's Best Diversity Employers

Mediacorp Inc., with financial assistance from BMO Financial Group and consulting advice from TWI Inc., has developed a list of "Canada's Best Diversity Employers." Description of the program along with a list of winners is available at http://www. canadastop100.com/diversity/. An example of a best diversity employer is Newalta Corporation of Calgary, an operator of waste-processing facilities.

The following are some of the reasons why Newalta Corporation was selected as one of Canada's Best Diversity Employers, 2013:

- established the "Women's Leadership Network" in 2008 to support the advancement of female employees, and recently hosted a national in-house conference, "Women in Leadership," to celebrate and encourage women in the pursuit of their career aspirations
- also created a mentoring program for female employees and partnered with the Calgary Immigrant Women's Association (CIWA) to provide a ten-week work placement opportunity to a CIWA member
- based on the success of the Women's Leadership Network, established a committee to champion diversity
- created a post-secondary scholarship program for Aboriginal students
- partners with community organizations in mentoring programs for students from a local school and new Canadians.

Sources: "Canada's Best Diversity Employers," http://www.canadastop100.com/diversity/; and "Newalta Corporation," http://www.eluta.ca/diversity-at-newalta. © Mediacorp Canada Inc.

There were many gender-centred approaches to ethics, but they can be categorized as either care or power-focused. Care-focused ethics highlight the differences between men and women and the inferior status of women. Women are more likely to consider the views of others and assess situations differently. Also, women have a more nurturing and mentoring approach and place more consideration to relationships through attachment, networks, and connections. The power- or status-focused approach emphasized issues related to domination and subordination of women. Power and how power was used to oppress women was described. Gender equality would be achieved through changes in systems, structures, institutions, and practices that differentiate between the roles and status of men and women in organizations.[4]

Borgerson discussed why feminist ethics should be harmonized with business ethics and CSR. She argued that feminist ethics placed emphasis on three concepts that provided better approaches to recognizing, evaluating, and addressing ethical concerns: relationships, responsibility, and experience. The focus of feminist ethics on these concepts resulted in a superior appreciation of business ethics than that of the traditional theories discussed in Chapter 5.

Greater attention was given to the role of relationships. In traditional theories, individual or group autonomy when considering ethical action and decisions was viewed as appropriate. But more reflection on relationships advocated by feminist ethics increased the stakeholders considered or consulted. A distinction was made between taking and having responsibility. Active willingness was necessary when taking responsibility. There were implications for those not included or chosen in the responsibility taken, and this applied whether women and others were involved. Feminist ethics supported having responsibility, which was beyond the choice of deciding whether or not to take responsibility. Finally, experience involved taking an interest in understanding marginalized individuals or groups. Feminist ethics advocated listening to other voices, which resulted in a broader acknowledgment of human involvement or interaction. Thus, there was a sensitivity to the lives of others that encouraged a more critical reflection on a social or ethical issue or dilemma.[5]

The approaches of feminist ethics allow for deeper insight into decisions relating to business ethics and corporate social responsibility than do traditional ethical theories. Not only is the status of women in business considered, but the status of all stakeholders. The concepts of relationships, responsibility, and experience are critical in stakeholder relationships, assessing ethical issues, and formulating social responsibility programs.

Workplace Privacy

Workplace privacy is a sensitive issue with many legal and ethical challenges, only some of which will be discussed. A fundamental component of privacy is use of an employee's personal information. Employees have the right to control access to personal information, but employers have some rights to obtain information. Privacy of personal information is regulated by the federal government's *Personal Information Protection and Electronic Documents Act (PIPEDA)* and other provincial legislation. PIPEDA requires that organizations hold personal information in a responsible manner, permit individuals to access and correct personal information, and allow individuals to have control over information about themselves. Responsibility for Ethics 12.3 summarizes the Act's "Fair Information Principles."

RESPONSIBILITY
for Ethics **12.3**

Personal Information Protection and Electronic Documents Act (PIPEDA)

The Act requires that businesses and organizations manage personal information according to the following "Fair Information Principles."

- *Accountability*—put systems and people in place to management information
- *Identifying purposes*—understand the uses to which the information will be put
- *Consent*—obtain permission to use personal information
- *Limiting collection*—collect only information that is appropriate and necessary
- *Limiting use, disclosure, and retention*—restrict the use of personal information
- *Accuracy*—minimize the collection of incorrect information
- *Safeguards*—make sure the information is stored and accessed appropriately
- *Openness*—inform stakeholders of the use by personal information
- *Individual access*—allow individuals to see their personal information
- *Provide recourse*—arrange for individuals to have a course of action if they have an issue with their personal information.

Source: Personal Information Protection and Electronic Documents Act—A Guide for Businesses and Organizations, http://www.priv.gc.ca/information/guide_e.pdf, The Office of the Privacy Commissioner of Canada, 2010. Reproduced with the permission of the Minister of Public Works and Government Services Canada, 2013.

Employers have a responsibility for workplace privacy, but they also have a right to some personal information. When hiring, employers need to know the applicant's qualifications and previous work experience. On the other hand, they have no right to personal information such as weight, age, medical records, race, blood type, fingerprints, or marital status.

Employers are challenged to justify what aspects of an employee's personal life are relevant to the job—for example whether that applicant has AIDS/HIV, or uses illegal drugs. Testing for substance abuse is a controversial issue for both employees and employers, especially where a stakeholder's safety may be at risk.

Workplace privacy has been challenged by the emergence of electronic technology and social media. Employees have access to email systems, the Internet, and wireless telephones and other devices that may be used inappropriately. One issue is the appropriate use of electronic technology particularly in relation to social media, discussed in Everyday Ethics 12.2. A related issue is the surveillance or monitoring of email and Internet usage; another is the use of cameras. Employers claim that such monitoring is necessary to avoid liability, to improve productivity and avoid excessive use, and to maintain network security. Employees claim that the employers are violating their personal privacy. As future employees, managers, or entrepreneurs, students will no doubt be exposed to the issues surrounding workplace privacy.

Everyday Ethics
12.2

Ethical Issues and Social Media

The increasing use of social media such as Facebook, Twitter, LinkedIn, and YouTube has raised ethical issues that are not easy for business to resolve.

A prominent issue is how much time employees should spend on social media during working hours. Contributing to a social media site is a time waster and is very visible among many such activities. A related matter is whether the time employees spend on employer computer resources for personal purposes should be monitored. In turn, this raises the matter of the employee's right to privacy.

Another issue involves an employer's use of social media. Employers could, if they wanted, scan social media for employee involvement and comments. If a negative comment is made about the employer, the possibility for discipline or even termination exists. Also, employers could scan social media for information when evaluating potential employees for positions. Applicants might be disqualified based on inaccurate information that appeared on a social media site.

Business is faced with challenges related to social media. Bloggers are free to make comments about the corporation that may or may not be accurate, placing the corporation in a difficult position to respond or counter untruths. Fake blogs might exist that portray corporations negatively. Some social media experts state that corporations have lost control over how they communicate, while bloggers are free to say what they want. On the other hand, corporations can view social media content as a source of feedback on their performance.

In addition to the above issues are several others including risk to computer systems, disclosure of confidential information, harassment by inappropriately discussing others, conflicts of interest between personal interests and duty to the corporation, and usage for espionage or fraud. It is recommended that corporations develop written policies that attempt to prevent or resolve the issues arising from social media.

Sources: Steve James, "Social media ethics: Why you should have a policy," SocialMediaToday, http://socialmediatoday.com/node/481533, accessed April 26, 2012; "Employers should tread carefully in asking for Facebook, other social media passwords," Bloomberg BNA, http://www.infodocket.com/2012/04/03/bna-employers-should-tread-carefully-in-asking-for-facebook-other-social-media-passwords, accessed April 26, 2012; James Hyatt, "The ethics of social media—part I: Adjusting to a 24/7 world," *Business Ethics,* December 10, 2010, http://business-ethics.com/2010/12/14/the-ethics-of-social-media-part-i-adjusting-to-a-24-7-world, accessed April 26, 2012; James Hyatt, "The ethics of social media—part II: Playing by new rules," *Business Ethics,* November 19, 2010, http://business-ethics.com/2010/11/19/the-ethics-of-social-media-part-ii-playing-by-new-rules, accessed April 26, 2012; and Jason Lunday, "Managing the workplace ethics of social media," Corporate Compliance Insights, July 21, 2010, http://www.corporatecomplianceinsights.com/managing-the-workplace-ethics-of-social-media, accessed April 26, 2012.

Employees and CSR

Research has found that a connection exists between corporate social responsibility and sustainability and **employee engagement**, defined as the emotional and intellectual commitment of an individual or group to an organization that supports building and sustaining business performance.[6] A study by Hewitt Associates and CBSR (Canadian Business for Social Responsibility) found a strong correlation between employee engagement and employees' views of the employer's record on CSR. Corporations with a "high employee engagement have a higher degree of readiness to focus on CSR as a strategy to improve overall organizational performance and better meet the needs of employees and external stakeholders." The most frequent CSR activities were community investment, waste reduction, business travel reduction, and responsible purchasing.[7] A later Hewitt Associates study found that when employees had a positive view of their employer's CSR there was greater employee engagement, which corporate managers stated was important to long-term success.[8]

When employees believed that supervisors acted ethically, they also were likely to behave ethically. In other words, a direct correlation exists between the ethical behaviour of supervisors and that of employees.[9] Similarly, it was found that when employees believed their company was adhering to high ethical standards, the employees were more committed to the company.[10] Employers effectively communicating CSR within the corporation are more likely to attract and retain employees. Satisfied employees need to link work to personal life through CSR, feel connected to the corporation, and take opportunities for self-enhancement—all of which increase loyalty, productivity, and commitment.[11] Another study found that employees who gave money or time to social causes felt more committed to their employers. Through helping colleagues, employees considered themselves and their employers to be more caring.[12]

Related to this, research has found that students are searching for meaningful work as demonstrated by a prospective employer's involvement in social issues. Students want their work to align with social and environmental causes such as climate change, renewable energy, and innovative products and processes. In other words, employers are expected to incorporate sustainability and social responsibility into the design of jobs.[13] A Network for Business Sustainability study identified the sustainable practices that are being demanded by future employees. It was found that students wanted employers to promote environmental efficiency through reduced waste and to encourage carbon regulation. Independent evaluation that employers were meeting their social licence was expected along with increased CSR transparency. Students wanted increased involvement in business and increased community engagement by corporations.[14]

LO 12.3   Consumers and Consumption

While employees are internal workplace stakeholders, consumers are external marketplace stakeholders. Their role is critical to corporations: without their participation through purchases, corporations cannot succeed. Fundamental to understanding the consumer stakeholder in the marketplace is knowledge of the consumer sovereignty concept.

Defining Consumer Sovereignty

A review of the literature does not disclose a definitive definition of "consumer sovereignty," but several essential characteristics of a definition are included in the following:

- Consumers, not producers or governments, dictate the type, quality, and quantity of goods and services to be provided.
- Elements of democracy are present, including the idea of voting through purchase decisions and that these decisions are made based upon the preferences of a majority.

- Consumers are free to make their own choices and are not unduly influenced by producers or governments.
- An economic system operates more efficiently when consumers determine production.[15]

As demonstrated the concept is imperfectly defined, as its objective could be considered impossible and its realization in the market far from perfect. Government has become involved and is making many decisions that, in theory, should be made by consumers. Economists say consumers should be protected from those who are convinced they know better than consumers what is best.

The distinction between consumer and producer (any corporation, for example a manufacturer or farmer) is an important one to make. It is argued that consumers have relinquished their sovereignty to producers. Producers and consumers may have conflicting interests and the producers' notions of what satisfies consumers may be influenced by what satisfies them as producers. As a result, consumers become impotent as influencers in the economic system.

The principle of consumer sovereignty is unlikely to be observed unless consumers have freedom of choice and are actually allowed to register their preferences in a market. In this respect, consumer sovereignty is really a front for the individualistic ethic, which holds that freedom is valuable in itself. If this ethic is accepted, one must accept the freedom to offer choices as well as the freedom to choose. Businesspersons often argue the former, but forget the latter. It might be argued that governments forget that consumers should have the freedom to choose.

Consumers and the Marketplace

The conditions of consumer sovereignty are seldom fulfilled in the marketplace, as buyers face high information costs, offensive and often misleading advertising, and shoddy and unsafe goods. Consumers may be manipulated by persuasive, at times misleading, advertising. It is also argued that as a small number of large firms dominate the market for some goods and services, consumers are being forced to purchase what producers provide. Consumer preferences are manipulated by large corporations in which market power has become concentrated. Also, in product development, there may be a difference between what consumers think the alternatives are and what producers think they are, meaning that the actual market choices may not reveal what consumers really want.

On the other hand, consumers do have some influence on the corporation and the marketplace. The most obvious way is of course their decision whether or not to purchase a corporation's products or services, but there are other influences. Consumer sovereignty exerts influence through **consumerism**, a social movement seeking to protect and augment the rights and powers of buyers in relation to sellers. An objective of the consumer movement is to make consumers aware of their place or role in the marketplace. Consumerism is considered necessary because some goods and services supplied by corporations fail to meet acceptable standards relating to product safety, information, performance, and pricing. Consumers may experience poor after-purchase service and might be the victims of retail misbehaviour, such as high-pressure sales tactics and misleading advertisements.

Consumerism A social movement seeking to protect and augment the rights and powers of buyers in relation to sellers.

Consumers have formed organizations to promote their interests. One example is the Consumers' Association of Canada, formed in 1947, which is a voluntary, non-profit organization committed to the improvement of the standard of living in Canadian homes. It studies consumer problems and issues and brings the views of consumers to corporations and governments. The most well-known consumer advocate is the American Ralph Nader. In Canada, Phil Edmonston formed the Nader-style Automobile Protection Association to represent car owners. In addition, dozens of small consumer organizations exist across

Canada. Being informed also enhances the influence of consumers in the marketplace. Print and broadcast information informs consumers, as does access to the Internet. From consumerism, a set of consumer rights have emerged. These rights, with accompanying responsibilities, are presented in Responsibility for Ethics 12.4.

RESPONSIBILITY
for Ethics **12.4**

Consumer Rights and Responsibilities

Rights illustrate a source of influence for consumer stakeholders, but with rights come responsibilities. The first four rights were outlined in a speech in 1962 by U.S. President John Kennedy. U.S. President Gerald Ford added the fifth right in 1970, and over time other rights have been added by consensus.

Consumer Rights	Consumer Responsibilities
To safety	To follow instructions and take precautions
To choose	To make independent, informed consumption choices
To be heard	To make opinions known and to complain in a constructive manner
To be informed	To search out and use available information
To consumer education	To take advantage of education opportunities
To redress	To fight for the quality and service expected
To a healthy environment	To minimize environmental damage by careful choice and use of goods and services

The consumer influence may also be exerted by government. Governments have enacted legislation and regulations to protect the consumer, and one example is the federal government's *Competition Act*. The Act is intended to promote and maintain fair competition so that Canadian consumers can benefit from competitive prices, product choice, and quality services. Responsibility for Ethics 12.5 summarizes legislation to protect consumers in the area of advertising and deceptive market practices.

Consumer sovereignty can be excessive and is reflected in the antagonism toward materialism, selfishness, greed, and the destruction of mankind's natural virtue. It is an expression of individualism as opposed to collectivism. There is no doubt that the concept concentrates on the individual instead of society as a whole, and largely ignores the higher purposes to which the narrow interest of individuals should be subservient. But this is true of any economic system based upon individualism and competitive markets. The assumption is that individual decision making is preferable to centralized, unitary decision making. If individualism and self-interest are acceptable as motivators in a business system, it seems logical that they should also be motivators for consumers. Everyday Ethics 12.3 discusses whether or not this means "the customer is always right."

Consumers and CSR

Consumers are demanding a wide range of ethical or socially responsible products, goods, and services, and business is responding. According to research, about 20 percent of consumers based purchase decisions on ethical or socially responsible considerations. Three factors motivate consumers to make these purchases: CSR information must be available,

RESPONSIBILITY

for Ethics **12.5**

Protecting the Consumer

The Competition Bureau promotes truth in advertising in the marketplace by discouraging deceptive business practices and by encouraging the provision of sufficient information to enable informed consumer choice. The *Competition Act* is a federal law governing most business conduct in Canada. It contains both criminal and civil provisions aimed at preventing anti-competitive practices in the marketplace.

False or misleading ordinary selling price representations—The ordinary selling price provisions of the *Competition Act* are designed to ensure that when products are promoted at sale prices, consumers are not misled by reference to inflated regular prices.

Performance representation not based on adequate and proper tests—Businesses should not make any performance claims unless they can back them up. The *Competition Act* prohibits any representation in the form of a statement, warranty, or guarantee of the performance, efficacy, or length of life of any given product that is not based on adequate and proper testing. The *Competition Act* prohibits:

- the sale or rent of a product at a price higher than its advertised price
- "bait-and-switch" selling, which occurs when a product is advertised at a bargain price but is not available for sale in reasonable quantities
- the supply of a product at a price that exceeds the lowest of two or more prices clearly expressed in respect to the product
- any promotional contest that does not disclose the number and approximate value of prizes and the odds of winning
- misleading warranties and guarantees
- the unauthorized use of tests and testimonials, or the distortion of authorized tests and testimonials.

Pyramid selling—Pyramid selling is illegal in Canada. It is a multi-level marketing plan that includes either compensation for recruitment, required purchases as a condition of participation, inventory loading, or the lack of a buy-back guarantee on reasonable commercial terms.

Source: Competition Bureau of Canada, http://www.competitionbureau.gc.ca/eic/site/cb-bc.nsf/eng/ h_00125.html, Competition Bureau of Canada, 2012. Reproduced with the permission of the Minister of Public Works and Government Services Canada, 2013.

there must be a moral alignment of CSR practices with the consumer on moral values, and the products must be considered affordable.[16]

Table 12.3 lists the types of ethical products available in the marketplace. Many issues are associated with this list. Consumers are often conflicted; for example, they are critical of big-box stores (such as Walmart), but still patronize them. Corporations, in particular retailers, are able to charge higher prices for ethical products and increase profits. Retailers such as Whole Foods Market and The Body Shop have built profitable corporate strategies based upon ethical products. Government policies or non-governmental organization (NGO) pressures may restrict consumer choice, for example banning eggs from caged birds on university campuses.

Corporations promoting socially and environmentally friendly products are accused of greenwashing—that is, making token efforts, or saying one thing and doing another. It is

Everyday Ethics

12.3

"The Customer Is Always Right"

The meaning of consumer sovereignty would suggest that the customer, or consumer, is always right. Although consumers have rights, they also have responsibilities and are expected to behave in an ethical manner.

Sometimes consumers are wrong. Consumers are sometimes ill-informed or overwhelmed by information and thus may not make a decision in their best interests. Some consumers behave badly, for example, requesting a refund for an item not sold by the retailer, making abusive remarks to employees or treating them badly, or returning failed products after misusing them.

There are situations when customer demands involve morals. There may be commercial reasons for accommodating consumers but moral reasons for not, for example, selling pornographic materials, consulting one service provider and then having another perform work, or demanding unjustified returns.

On the other hand, there may be moral reasons for accommodating consumers but stronger commercial reasons for not doing so, for example, overbooking aircraft, or costly product recalls.

The cliché "The customer is always right" illustrates the challenges of attempting to accommodate all stakeholders. There are other stakeholders—for example, employees—and consumers have to be reasonable in their expectations.

Sources: Dawn Iacobucci, Kent Grayson and Amy Ostrom, "Customer Satisfaction Fables," *Sloan Management Review,* Summer 1994, 93–96; Tom Sorell, "The Customer Is Not Always Right," *Journal of Business Ethics,* Volume 13, 1994, 913–914.

questionable that some products are actually ethical. The meaning of organic is not clearly established and the term sometimes is used inappropriately. Certification standards and systems have not been established in some areas, and labelling can be misleading.

In the case of food, the calculation of "food miles" is difficult and misleading. The calculation of benefits must take into account all factor costs in the food production life-cycle and not just transportation miles or costs. Furthermore, consumers in developed countries demand more than can be produced locally and must rely on imported items. Locally produced food is often more expensive and the benefits to the environment are not certain.

connect   Want to learn more about **ethical products and services**? Go to CONNECT.

A major issue with ethical products is whether socially conscious consumers are willing to pay for these types of products. Two researchers undertook a study to review 30 years of literature to ascertain the following: "Are consumers willing to reward firms for their sustainability actions with price premiums or increased purchases?" Many influences, impediments, and enhancements affected three consumer behaviour intentions—willingness to change behaviour, willingness to pay a premium, and willingness to punish. The main finding of the study was that ". . .the average premium for socially conscious products and services is 10%. Some consumers will demand a discount for 'unsustainability', even greater than the premium for sustainability."[17] Figure 12.1 is a model of socially conscious consumerism that summarized the authors' findings. Note the influences, impediments, and enhancements, and how the corporation's CSR actions impact the consumer with the outcome being a willingness to change behaviour, to pay a premium for the corporation's products, or to punish the corporation.

TABLE 12.3	*Examples of Ethical Products*

Food:	**Financial Products:**
• Organic	• Ethical and green mutual funds
• Local	• Ethical and SR stock (sustainability) indices
• Fair trade	• Green mortgages
Housing:	**Travel:**
• Energy efficient	• Eco-travel
Clothing:	• Carbon offsets (e.g., Air Canada)
• Eco-chic—fashionable clothes from organic cotton, hemp, bamboo, flax, soy	• Eco-resorts
• Slow fashion—eco-friendly design	**Jewellery:**
• Recycled (Value Village, etc)	• Gold and diamonds—certification of source
• Fair trade fashions (Fair Indigo, etc)	**Energy:**
• Organic sneakers	• Fluorescent light bulbs
Cosmetics:	• Energy-saving devices
• Natural ingredients	• Clean sources of energy
• No animal testing	• Biofuel (ethanol and bio-diesel)
Green weddings:	**Transportation:**
• Efforts made to use particular clothing, special catering requirements; not using expensive limousines	• "Terror-Free Gas"—gasoline sourced in nations that do not support terrorism
	• Hybrid vehicles
	• Carbon offsets

Other research studied the trade-offs consumers are willing to make when paying more for products with ethical features. Socially conscious features are definitely more important to some consumers and social features will make a difference when functional and price features are satisfied. It was found that some social features were more important than others; for example, avoiding child labour was more important than working conditions and animal testing more important than the use of animal by-products.[18]

There are many issues relating to ethical or sustainable products and services. Some consumers are willing to pay a higher price for these products and corporations are responding, but the ethical claims must be legitimate.

LO 12.4   Competitors and Competition

Competition is necessary, even crucial, for an effective market economy. It encourages innovation, productivity, entrepreneurship, and efficiency. The principal beneficiary when competitive forces exist is the consumer, who is provided with quality products, choice, and the best possible price.

Competition, as one of the fundamentals of the business system, was discussed in Chapter 2. In the context of business, competition is a struggle or rivalry for supremacy, often expressed among corporations as *market share*. Two or more corporations offer the same or similar product or service in many ways—for example, by offering a better product, through use of advertising, or by superior distribution or service. Competition might result in the defeat or destruction of one of the corporations. Business failures do result from

FIGURE 12.1   *A Model of Socially Conscious Consumerism*

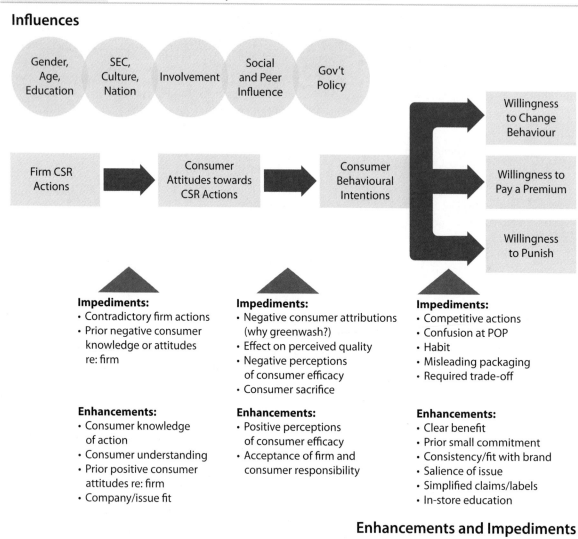

Influences

Gender, Age, Education

SEC, Culture, Nation

Involvement

Social and Peer Influence

Gov't Policy

Firm CSR Actions → Consumer Attitudes towards CSR Actions → Consumer Behavioural Intentions →

Willingness to Change Behaviour

Willingness to Pay a Premium

Willingness to Punish

Impediments:
- Contradictory firm actions
- Prior negative consumer knowledge or attitudes re: firm

Impediments:
- Negative consumer attributions (why greenwash?)
- Effect on perceived quality
- Negative perceptions of consumer efficacy
- Consumer sacrifice

Impediments:
- Competitive actions
- Confusion at POP
- Habit
- Misleading packaging
- Required trade-off

Enhancements:
- Consumer knowledge of action
- Consumer understanding
- Prior positive consumer attitudes re: firm
- Company/issue fit

Enhancements:
- Positive perceptions of consumer efficacy
- Acceptance of firm and consumer responsibility

Enhancements:
- Clear benefit
- Prior small commitment
- Consistency/fit with brand
- Salience of issue
- Simplified claims/labels
- In-store education

Enhancements and Impediments

Source: June Cotte and Remi Trudel, *Socially Conscious Consumerism: Executive Briefing on the Body of Knowledge,* Network for Business Sustainability, Richard Ivey School of Business, University of Western Ontario, 2009, 38, http://www.nbs.net/Docs/NBS_Consumerism_2009.pdf. The authors and the Network for Business Sustainability granted permission to reproduce this diagram.

competition, and if only one corporate structure survives a monopoly situation exists. Although competition does result in the failure of some corporations, the usual result is that some survive and new businesses enter the industry. Thus, competitors are a stakeholder group that most managers must recognize and respond to in some way.

Competition, Ethics, and Responsibilities

Implications for social responsibility are associated with the degree of competitive rivalry existing in a business system. One position is that increased competition and pressure to be competitive has resulted in an increase in unethical or questionable practices. Industrial spying, espionage, and sabotage are now of such concern that industrial or economic security has replaced national security as a major national issue. Practices range from eavesdropping and theft of research and development technology, to hiring the competitor's key employees. It is argued that the practices are much more widespread than reported and that many remain undisclosed either because companies are unaware of them or are too embarrassed to report them.

Several causes of this trend have been identified, including the cutthroat global economy, aggressive competitive tactics, and shorter product cycles necessitating faster responses to competitor initiatives. The copying or counterfeiting of products appears more common and increasingly difficult to control, as there appears to be little reluctance to steal ideas from others.

Society is concerned about the concentration of corporate power in a few corporations or a few groupings of interconnected corporations. There is a concern that a few large corporations may have too much influence over the economy and possibly too much influence over government. Concentration of corporate power can also be measured within a single industry by providing the percentage of sales controlled by the four or eight largest firms.

There are two concerns about industrial concentration—the possibilities for collaboration and higher profitability. In highly concentrated industries, corporations often behave in a similar fashion. For example, packaging changes are copied and prices matched. In less concentrated industries, it is much more difficult to keep track of all competitors and to predict their behaviour. Economists have been concerned that corporations in highly concentrated industries tend to be more profitable.

The high degree of market concentration in some industries plus the high degree of concentrated ownership constitutes a centre of power in society. When this concentration is combined with a capability to influence other stakeholders, especially governments, a controlling power structure is set in place. Many Canadians are fearful of this.

Government Influence to Encourage Competition

Competitive behaviour or the conduct of business in Canada is regulated by the *Competition Act* (R.S.C. 1985, c. C-34). This Act establishes the basic principles for the conduct of business in Canada so that competition is encouraged and maintained. The purpose of the Act is to promote the efficiency and adaptability of the Canadian economy; ensure that small and medium-sized corporations have an equitable opportunity to participate in the Canadian economy; and provide consumers with competitive prices and product choices. If it could be accomplished, this purpose would result in an ideal marketplace. Responsibility for Ethics 12.6 lists clauses in the *Competition Act* that apply to how competitors should behave.

Although the role of government in encouraging competition in the Canadian economy is important, it is only one of several factors determining competitive behaviour. The following is a selected list of such factors:

Entrepreneurship—It should be remembered that the business system involves a life-cycle process in which corporations are formed, grow, and dissolve. There is a constant supply (or birth) of new small businesses, many of which grow in stature and provide competition for large, well-established firms.

Deregulation and privatization—Government initiatives to deregulate some sectors of the economy have influenced the growth of businesses, and efforts to sell off the business corporations it owns have increased opportunities for entrepreneurs (discussed in Chapter 10).

Technology—A multitude of technological developments have encouraged competitive rivalry. New technology has led to new business corporations, for example in electronics and various computer-related industries, and has changed how other industries operate.

Decline of natural monopoly—Utility-type companies often operated as natural monopolies, for example in telephone and cable television. With deregulation and new technologies,

RESPONSIBILITY
for Ethics **12.6**

Regulation of Competitors

The *Competition Act* governs business conduct among competitors. Some of the *Act's* features are as follows:

Conspiracy—This is any agreement, arrangements, or combinations designed to lessen competition unduly in relation to supply, manufacture, or production of a product and includes fixing prices, or preventing competitors from entering the market.

Bid-Rigging—Any arrangement between two or more persons or corporations where one party will refrain from bidding in a call for tenders, or where there was collusion in the submission of bids.

Predatory Pricing—There are two types of predatory pricing: (i) selling products in one region of Canada at prices lower than in another region for the purpose of lessening competition; and (ii) selling products at unreasonably low prices where the intent is to lesson competition.

Review of Mergers—When a merger occurs, the Competition Bureau may decide to examine it and recommend whether or not actions should be taken to preserve competition.

Abuse of Dominant Position—The *Competition Act* provides for remedies where dominant corporations in a market engage in anti-competitive behaviours, such as acquisition of a customer who would otherwise be available to a competitor to impede a competitor's entry into the market; purchase of products to prevent the reduction of existing price levels; and selling articles at a price lower than the acquisition cost to discipline or eliminate a competitor.

Source: Competition Bureau of Canada, http://www.competitionbureau.gc.ca/eic/site/cb-bc.nsf/eng/h_00125.html, Competition Bureau of Canada, 2012. Reproduced with the permission of the Minister of Public Works and Government Services Canada, 2013

neither of these industries can now be considered a natural monopoly. Competition exists in the telephone industry and cable television is under pressure from wireless and new providers.

Global trends in trade—The reduction of some barriers to trade is increasing competition in Canada. World Trade Organization (WTO) agreements encourage international trade, as has the North American Free Trade Agreement (NAFTA). Despite free trade agreements, many barriers to trade exist, especially non-tariff barriers.

Mergers/takeovers—Mergers or takeovers tend to occur in cycles, with the later 1970s and 1980s being two periods of high acquisition activity. Such acquisitions can reduce competition, especially if they are acquisitions in the same industry.

LO 12.5 Suppliers and the Supply Chain

Business-to-business Commercial activity where one corporation sells goods or services to another corporation rather than to consumers.

In **business-to-business** commercial activity, one corporation (a supplier) sells goods or services to another corporation rather than to consumers. Traditionally, the relationship between suppliers and their customers was an adversarial one. Today the relationship is more likely to be one of mutual interdependence based on trust and collaboration. Everyday Ethics 12.4 is an example of a customer attempting to influence the behaviour of suppliers. Purchasers or buyers are recognizing suppliers who cooperate with them and are committed to considering social and environmental responsibilities.

The relationship between customers and suppliers is governed informally by several rights. The supplier expects to have the right to supply goods and services to a customer.

Everyday Ethics

12.4

Influencing Suppliers

An example of how a corporation influences its suppliers is the use of "supplier codes of business conduct." A good example is the *Canadian Tire Principles of Business Conduct,* which includes a section on "Expectations of Suppliers."

- Compliance with laws
- Employment standards
- Wages and benefits
- Working hours
- Child labour
- Forced or slave labour
- Discrimination/human rights
- Disciplinary practices
- Workplace environment
- Environmental protection
- Confidentiality and privacy
- Unlawful payments
- Dealing with the company's employees

Also included are descriptions of supplier certification, supplier assessment and monitoring, enforcement of the code, and reporting and addressing code violations. The reason for selecting this code is that it appears comprehensive. Other retailers and manufacturers have similar codes.

Source: Canadian Tire Corporation, Limited., http://corp.canadiantire.ca/EN/AboutUs/Documents/ CTCSupplierCodeofConduct.aspx July4,2012.pdf. Used with permission 2013.

Preferential treatment is not expected from the customer or received by the supplier. A fair deal is expected, which is negotiated ethically without lies, deception, nondisclosure, or threats. Conflicts of interest are expected to be disclosed. Loyalty by both sides may exist, but not to imply automatic acceptance of terms or conditions offered.

The influence of suppliers varies. Where the customer has several sources of goods and services, the customer will exert more influence over the supplier. If the supplier is the sole source of particular goods or services, the supplier will have greater influence over the transaction.

> **Supply (or value) chain** The route that a product travels from the procurement of raw materials, the transformation into intermediate goods and then final products, and the delivery to consumers through a distribution system to its ultimate disposal by the consumer.

The buyer's purchasing staff and the supplier's sales staff are sometimes confronted with ethical dilemmas when bribes, kickbacks, gifts, and hospitality are offered. Suppliers and their customers have formed professional associations, such as the Purchasing Management Association of Canada (PMAC), to guide the behaviour of these employees. Responsibility for Ethics 12.7 provides an outline of the Code of Ethics formulated by PMAC.

Government legislation governs the relationship between buyers and suppliers. Responsibility for Ethics 12.8 lists clauses in the *Competition Act* that apply to this relationship. As discussed in this section and the one that follows, suppliers are now regulated more by other stakeholders, such as consumers, their business customers, and NGOs.

LO 12.6   The Supply Chain

A **supply chain**, or value chain, is the route that a product travels from the procurement of raw materials, the transformation into intermediate goods and then final products, and the delivery to consumers through a distribution system to its ultimate disposal by the consumer. Figure 12.2 is a basic supply chain applicable to most products.

RESPONSIBILITY
for Ethics 12.7

Purchasing Management Association of Canada (PMAC)

PMAC is a professional association of supply management managers and provides training, education, and professional development. Its professional designation is SCMP—Supply Chain Management Professional.

A condition of membership is adherence to its Code of Ethics. Components of the code include:

- Standards of conduct: Avoidance of conflicts of interest; protection of confidential or sensitive information; maintenance of business relationships; acceptance of gifts, gratuities, and hospitality; and promotion of environmental and social responsibilities.

- Professional principles: Professional competency; professionalism; honesty and integrity, responsible management, serving the public good; and compliance with legal obligations.

Enforcement procedures outlined are compliant process, conduct of investigations, and nature of sanctions.

Source: PMAC Code of Ethics, http://www.pmac.ca/en/join-pmac/code-of-ethics.

RESPONSIBILITY
for Ethics 12.8

Regulation of Suppliers

The *Competition Act* contains the following provisions to ensure suppliers do not take advantage of their customers:

Exclusive dealing, tied selling, and market restrictions—These practices generally occur when a supplier places conditions on the supply of a product that constrain the customer in terms of, for example, what else the customer must buy to obtain supply, where the customer may subsequently market the product, or what other product lines the customer may or may not carry. Although not illegal in themselves, they will be investigated if they are found to have caused, or to be likely to cause, a substantial lessening of competition in a market.

Price discrimination—This exists when a supplier charges different prices to competitors who purchase similar volumes of an article.

Price maintenance—This involves attempts to influence upward or to discourage the reduction of price at which another corporation supplies or advertises a product, or refusing to supply anyone because of that corporation's low pricing policy.

Refusal to deal—Refusal to deal involves situations where a buyer cannot obtain supplies of an available product on usual trade terms and, as a result, is substantially affected in her or his ability to conduct business, resulting in an adverse effect on competition.

Source: Competition Bureau of Canada, http://www.competitionbureau.gc.ca/eic/site/cb-bc.nsf/eng/h_00125.html, Competition Bureau of Canada, 2012. Reproduced with the permission of the Minister of Public Works and Government Services Canada, 2013.

Several aspects of such a supply chain involve ethics and responsibilities. Raw materials may come from several sources and are often from developing countries. Materials such as wood, minerals, and petroleum have many associated environmental issues. Materials from developing countries frequently involve issues such as human rights, child labour, low wages, and dangerous working conditions. Sometimes the raw materials are shipped out of the country for processing, depriving local workers of employment.

FIGURE 12.2	*Stages in a Supply Chain*

Raw Materials
↓
Local Processing
↓
Transportation
↓
Manufacturing or Further Processing
↓
Distribution through Wholesalers or Distributors
↓
Retail Outlets
↓
Consumers and Consumption
↓
Disposal

Not all products follow the same chain; some may involve additional stages and some fewer. Retailers may purchase directly from manufacturers, bypassing wholesalers, or consumers may buy directly from manufacturers. Although a single chain is shown, branches may exist as by-products are produced, or the product at some stage may be sold to another corporation as ingredients for another product. Waste may be produced at different stages, which must be disposed of or sold to be used in other products. Profitability varies along the chain and with the type of product. Different issues impacting different stakeholders exist along the chain. NGOs often play major roles in improving conditions for workers in raw material production facilities. Governments tend to be more influential in downstream sections of the chain.

> **Extended producer responsibility** "An environmental policy approach in which a producer's responsibility, physical and/or financial, for a product is extended to the post-consumer stage of a product's life cycle."

More attention has been focused on product disposal and who is responsible. **Extended producer responsibility** is "an environmental policy approach in which a producer's responsibility, physical and/or financial, for a product is extended to the post-consumer stage of a product's life cycle."[19] "Producer" in this definition refers to manufacturers or distributors. The responsibility for disposal is being shifted upstream to producers and away from consumers and local governments responsible for waste management. The policy is to provide incentives to producers to take environmental considerations into the design of the product.

Supply chains can be extended in another sense; that is, geographically or globally. Global supply chains add another dimension for management and often these chains are more complicated. The Network for Business Sustainability published a study that provided guidance and listed best practices. The first step is to list all stakeholders that influence a corporation's approach to sustainable supply chains. The study found that the following stakeholders want sustainable supply chains: consumers, government, general public, activists (NGOs), media, industry peers, employees, and investors. The key sustainability issues in supply chains included working conditions, the environment, CSR, low wages, human rights, child labour, health and safety, forced labour, and sweatshops. According to the study's authors, there are three steps to developing a sustainable global supply chain:

- Identify Motivators: What is motivating change in the industry? What does the corporation stand to gain and lose? The key motivators were found to be customers, compliance, costs, competitive advantage, and conscience.

- Assess Levers: Seven key levers can facilitate or inhibit efforts to build a sustainable supply chain. Internal levers are purpose—that is, alignment of sustainability with organizational strategy; clear policy statements/codes of conduct; and people—that is, leadership/management support. External levers are industry collaboration; partnerships including trust in supplier engagement; supportive government regulation; and power as represented by organizational size or influence over suppliers.

- Improve Practices: The four most prevalent practices were found to be a code of conduct that set expectations throughout the supply chain, certification as a screening device in selecting suppliers, rigorous selection process to reduce supply risks, and monitoring or auditing to ensure compliance with expectations.[20]

The following section elaborates on sustainability purchasing, whether local or global.

Want to learn more about **sustainable global supply chains**? Go to CONNECT.

Sustainability Purchasing

The focus on ethics and responsibility in purchasing has been referred to as sustainability purchasing. Other terms associated with this approach to purchasing are responsible purchasing, fair trade, ethical sourcing, and ethical trade.

Industry Canada defines **sustainability purchasing** as

> *. . . the acquisition of goods and services ("products") in a way that gives preference to suppliers that generate positive social and environmental outcomes. It integrates sustainability considerations into product selection so that impacts on society and the environment are minimized throughout the full life cycle of the product. Sustainability purchasing entails looking at what products are made of, where they have come from, who has made them, how they will be ultimately disposed—even considering whether the purchase needs to be made at all. It encompasses environmental, social and ethical dimensions and brings benefit to the environment and local and global communities and workers.[21]*

This definition makes it clear that sustainability purchasing applies to the complete product chain, which could also be equated with the life cycle of the product. Sustainability purchasing is a form of regulation imposed on the corporation or industry by stakeholders other than government. Consumers, usually with the help of or prompting by NGOs, apply pressure to change purchasing practices. Retailers often prompt action after being influenced by consumers or NGOs.

Corporations recognize this influence and respond themselves (as illustrated in Everyday Ethics 12.4), through professional or trade associations (as illustrated by PMAC), or by participating in networks promoting sustainable purchasing, an example of which is given in Responsibility for Ethics 12.9. This type of network enables corporations to find suppliers who endorse sustainability practices.

Fair Trade

Another influence on sustainability purchasing is the fair trade movement. **Fair trade** is commonly used to identify products that are involved with sustainability purchasing but usually focuses on the beginning of the product chain. The Fairtrade Foundation's definition is as follows:

> *Fairtrade is about better prices, decent working conditions, local sustainability, and fair terms of trade for farmers and workers in the developing world. By requiring companies to pay*

Sustainability purchasing According to Industry Canada, "the acquisition of goods and services ('products') in a way that gives preference to suppliers that generate positive social and environmental outcomes. It integrates sustainability considerations into product selection so that impacts on society and the environment are minimized throughout the full life cycle of the product."

Fair trade A term commonly used to identify products that are involved with sustainability purchasing; usually focuses on the beginning of the product chain.

RESPONSIBILITY
for Ethics **12.9**

BuySmart Network

The BuySmart Network was established in 2005 in Vancouver as the Sustainability Purchasing Network with the mission "to be the 'go-to' resource centre for green, socially conscious, and ethical supply chains in Canada." It is a non-profit organization supported by partners and sponsors interested in sustainability purchasing.

Some of the features of the site are that it:

- Identifies what sustainability purchasing considers and the range of objectives a sustainability purchasing program may have.

- Explains the services offered, including business case guide, research and tools, best practices, supply chain management and innovation, and stakeholder engagement.

- Includes a "Resources" page that includes lists of purchasing organizations, case studies, topics in sustainability purchasing, and supplier directories.

Source: BuySmart Network, http://web.buysmartbc.com, accessed December 10, 2012.

sustainable prices (which must never fall lower than the market price), Fairtrade addresses the injustices of conventional trade, which traditionally discriminates against the poorest, weakest producers. It enables them to improve their position and have more control over their lives.[22]

The fair trade movement is not anti-capitalist, but instead intends to use the market system to enhance the influence of the supplier stakeholder. The best known fair trade products are coffee, spices, tea, cocoa, and fruit, but today retailers carry many fair trade products including wine, flowers, and beauty products. In Canada, Fairtrade Canada is the coordinator of fair trade initiatives and performs three functions: (1) it is responsible for certifying that Canadian products bearing the Fairtrade certification marks meet international Fairtrade standards; (2) it licenses Canadian companies to use the Fairtrade certification marks and attempts to ensure that licensed companies abide by the standards required of the marks; and (3) it promotes the use of Fairtrade certification marks and certified products. It is a member of Fairtrade International, which is responsible for the international coordination of Fairtrade standards, organizing support for producers around the world, developing fair trade strategy, and promoting global trade justice.[23]

Controversy arose in early 2013 related to the certification of fair trade products in Canada. Competition in labelling has emerged between Fairtrade International and Fair Trade USA. Fairtrade Canada is a branch of Fairtrade International, which uses a circle symbol with the image of a producer against a blue and green roundel with a black background. Fair Trade USA uses a green/white/black label with a farmer holding a bowl. Fair Trade USA has started to certify products in Canada.

Fairtrade International/Fairtrade Canada allows only democratically organized groups of farmers in a cooperative to be certified and does not allow privately operated farms. It signs up farmers who must meet specified labour, environmental, and social standards and secures buyers in developed countries who pay more for the products. Farmers are guaranteed a minimum wage or return. Twenty percent of the product's ingredients must be fair trade to obtain the certification.

Fair Trade USA split from Fairtrade International because it felt that the latter's certification was too strict and not able to provide the volume of products needed in the market. It certifies non-cooperative farms that are privately owned estates or plantations. The certification label is applied to ingredients within a product; that is, the whole product does not have to contain a specified amount of fair trade ingredients. The existence of two fair trade labels in the Canadian market will likely cause some confusion for consumers. This is another illustration of buyer beware, depending upon which specifications a consumer believes are appropriate.[24]

The entrepreneurs promoting fair trade products claim that the local suppliers in developing countries are now receiving a higher price for their product. Initially fair trade was sponsored by NGOs such as Oxfam, Rainforest Alliance, and Traidcraft, but corporations are now developing their own sources in countries where the products are produced; this often occurs in partnership with NGOs. An example of an international organization promoting fair trade is given in Responsibility for Ethics 12.10.

RESPONSIBILITY *for Ethics* **12.10**

The Ethical Trading Initiative (ETI)

The Ethical Trading Initiative (ETI) is an alliance of companies, trade unions, and voluntary organizations that work together to improve the lives of workers in developing countries that make or grow consumer goods. Its vision is ". . . a world where all workers are free from exploitation and discrimination, and work in conditions of freedom, security and equity." The alliance enables ETI to tackle many of the issues that cannot be addressed by individual corporations.

One of ETI's projects focuses on purchasing practices, which involves investigating how the buying practices of corporations can undermine their progress in ethical trading. Practices hindering ethical trading include last-minute changes to orders and shorter lead times, which contribute to excessive overtime, and pressure to reduce prices, which makes it difficult to pay living wages.

Nearly 70 corporations are members, including Gap Inc. and The Body Shop International.

Source: Ethical Trading Initiative, http://www.ethicaltrade.org/about-eti.

Fair trade has been criticized for several reasons. It is claimed that little of the extra paid by consumers for fair trade products actually reaches the producers or farmers, and a positive impact is difficult to prove.[25] Further, a criticism is that not only is the lot of poor farmers not improved, but fair trade also may actually help to impoverish them because problems exist with certification. The poorest farmers may not be able to afford the fees for certification. It is claimed that the certification process is lax and almost impossible to monitor, as farmers and middlemen can get around the system.[26]

Employees, consumers, competitors, and supplier stakeholders are among the most influential for any corporation. The economic, social, and environmental issues are numerous, and this chapter has provided an introduction to them. The following chapter examines other stakeholders that might be influential: non-governmental organizations (NGOs), the media, policy development institutions (think tanks), and religious and educational institutions.

Your advice to Phyllis. . .

You understand that Phyllis faces a dilemma with the contradictions that confront managers. As an employee, she is faced with the task of implementing a policy with which she may not totally agree. What is involved are different approaches to ethical reasoning. A caring ethic would suggest that exceptions should be made. A justice ethic would attempt to treat all so that equitable outcomes occur. A utilitarian ethic would attempt to identify stakeholders and the benefits and harms to each. It appears that Phyllis's concern is that not all shoplifters should be treated the same and maybe they have rights. Her dilemma is not an uncommon occurrence in the retail workplace.

SUMMARY

- Numerous ethics and responsibility issues arise in the relationship between the corporation and employees, consumers, competitors, and suppliers. (LO 12.1)

- Canadian employers and employees face many challenges in their relationship and three topics were discussed. Most Canadians still believe in the work ethic, several factors affect the loyalty of the employee to the employer, and employment diversity is a matter that employers must manage in today's workplace. (LO 12.2)

- According to consumer sovereignty, consumers should be determining what goods and services are available in the marketplace. In reality, this does not occur and consumers must also rely on rights and government legislation and regulation. Corporations are placing numerous "ethical" products in the marketplace. (LO 12.3)

- It is desirable that competitive rivalry exists in the marketplace, but many ethical and responsibility issues arise. Government has enacted legislation to encourage honest, fair, and open competition in the marketplace. Several factors in the economy determine competitive behaviour. (LO 12.4)

- Pressure on suppliers and the supply chain to consider ethics and responsibilities in the marketplace has increased. In general, the relationship between suppliers and their customers has changed from an adversarial one to a cooperative one. (LO 12.5)

- The supply chain identifies the progress of a product from raw material sources through to the consumer and ultimately disposal. Sustainability purchasing takes into consideration ethical, social, and environmental factors in acquiring materials and products. Fair trade is a version of this type of purchasing attempting to improve the economic well-being of people working in the upstream component of the supply chain. (LO 12.6)

KEY TERMS

Work ethic	Feminist ethics	Supply (or value) chain
Discrimination	Employee engagement	Extended producer responsibility
Employment equity	Consumerism	Sustainability purchasing
Diversity management	Business-to-business	Fair trade

CRITICAL THINKING AND DISCUSSION QUESTIONS

1. Is the work ethic concept relevant in today's workplace?

2. Why should employees be loyal to the corporation? How does the corporation express its loyalty to employees?

3. What does the corporation gain from workplace diversity?

4. To what extent does the consumer sovereignty concept apply in today's marketplace?

5. Are consumers adequately protected in the marketplace?

6. What are the pros and cons when competition results in the failure of a business?

7. Can the government encourage competition? If so, how does the government do it?

8. Which stakeholders are influencing the commercial activities along the supply chain?

9. Who should be responsible for the disposal of a product after it is used by the consumer?

10. What are the benefits of sustainability purchasing to corporations?

11. Why are fair trade products popular with consumers?

12.1   The Alleged Kickback Scheme

Karl Langley, CEO of Reliable Auto Supplies Limited, noticed the registered letter on his desk when he returned from a meeting. The envelope was marked "Highly Confidential," so his secretary did not open it as she usually did in preparing his mail. The letter was from one of the company's suppliers and accused Reliable's purchasing agents of demanding kickbacks on orders placed with them. The letter detailed the arrangements to facilitate the kickbacks, which ranged from small gifts to about two percent of the order.

The supplier said that he had stopped most of the kickback scheme in which some of his employees had been involved and had even fired two individuals. The supplier then pointed out that after stopping the kickbacks, his company had received no orders from Reliable.

The letter was very upsetting. Karl did not know the supplier and the supplier had not identified any of the Reliable employees involved. Karl was aware that kickbacks had been a problem in the wholesaling and retailing industries in the past but believed it was mostly under control. Besides, kickbacks were considered to be a corrupt payments offence in the *Criminal Code of Canada*.

Karl had several concerns. He considered the possibility that the supplier may be setting him up to cover up his own employees' actions. From the description in the letter, the kickback scheme would require the cooperation of several Reliable employees. He thought such a conspiracy was unlikely. He also wondered if his managers had been placing too much pressure on the purchasing agents, which led to this type of behaviour. Even more puzzling was the fact that Reliable had developed elaborate codes of conduct for all employees and strict guidelines for purchasing agents regarding the acceptance of gifts.

Karl put down the letter and asked his secretary to get the company's lawyer on the phone.

Questions

1. What stakeholders are involved in this situation?
2. Who else should Karl Langley contact?
3. Why did the code of conduct and gift policy not prevent this situation?
4. What type of ethics program should Reliable put in place?

12.2   Sodium and Ethics

Sodium, a mineral, is found in table salt, which is 40 percent sodium and 60 percent chloride. It is found in meat, fish, poultry, eggs, milk, and cheese, and is highest in processed foods. In addition, consumers season their food with salt. The daily requirement for sodium is 1,500 mg and is supplied by natural, unprocessed foods. Canadians consume about 3,000 mg per day.

High consumption of sodium might cause high blood pressure, from which about 20 percent of Canadians suffer. High blood pressure and related diseases are the world's leading cause of deaths. About 80 percent of salt intake by Canadians is from fast food and processed foods.

The World Action on Salt and Health surveyed food products around the world and gathered statistics on sodium content from food manufacturer Web sites. One of its findings was the high sodium in fast food and processed foods in Canada in comparison to levels in other countries. Some examples include the following:

- Burger King onion rings: In Canada, 0.681 mg sodium per 100 mg compared to 0.159 mg in the U.K.
- Kelloggs All Bran cereal: In Canada, 0.861 mg sodium per 100 mg compared to 0.258 in the U.S.
- KFC Popcorn chicken: In Canada, 0.908 mg sodium per 100 mg compared to 0.560 in Malaysia.
- McDonald's Sausage McMuffin with egg or equivalent: 0.980 mg sodium per 100 mg compared to 0.400 mg in France.

Sodium content was not high or the highest in all the Canadian products surveyed.

Manufacturers point out that ingredients of their products are listed publicly and that they are responding to consumer taste preferences. Yet the Canadian Medical Association is concerned and the issue is receiving considerable media coverage. Salt intake is a serious societal issue and business has some responsibility to address it.

Questions

1. Whose responsibility is it to control salt in Canadian diets?

2. Is it desirable to allow consumers to take personal responsibility for their sodium intake?

3. Should governments regulate? How could this be accomplished?

4. What can/should fast-food and processed-food industries do to address this issue?

Sources: "New research reveals huge differences in salt contents in global foods," World Action on Salt and Health, http://www.worldactiononsalt.com/media/recent_press_releases.htm; Carly Weeks, "The cereal killer: From All-Bran to burgers, study finds food has more salt in Canada," *The Globe and Mail,* July 23, 2009, A1, A5; and Carly Weeks, "Ottawa must act on salt crisis, doctors say," *The Globe and Mail,* September 15, 2009, A1, A11.

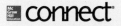 For more information on the resources available from McGraw-Hill Ryerson, go to www.mcgrawhill.ca/he/solutions.

CHAPTER 13
Civil Society Stakeholders

What would you do if . . . ?

Antonio Costello had worked at his family's fast-food restaurant, Tasty Chicken and Ribs, since he was a teenager. His first job was in the kitchen washing dishes, but he gradually assumed better jobs while he worked part time and completed his business degree at a local college. After graduation, his father made him an assistant manager of the restaurant, which included fast-food takeout, a 250-seat restaurant, and a 100-seat banquet room. The menu mainly consisted of chicken and rib dishes, but also offered some vegetarian options.

Antonio was aware of the pressures exerted by animal rights activists on fast-food restaurants serving meat items. The Kentucky Fried Chicken (KFC) outlet down the street had been picketed by six young people carrying posters with messages stating that chickens raised for KFC suffered pain and injuries, lived in crowded conditions, and were cruelly slaughtered. The protesters identified themselves as being from People for the Ethical Treatment of Animals (PETA).

Antonio had read about PETA's support for animal rights and advocacy of vegetarianism. PETA had a history of picketing, boycotting, and violent actions against corporations it considered to be not respecting animal rights. Yum! Brands Inc., KFC's parent company, had circulated information on protests that had been held at various KFC outlets around the world by PETA and other animal rights groups. KFC stated that it was committed to the humane treatment of animals and had developed an animal welfare program, which included several aspects. The company monitored suppliers to determine whether or not they used humane procedures, and it had a policy of dealing only with suppliers who agreed with KFC's commitment and who maintained high standards of animal care. Yum! Brands formed the KFC Animal Welfare Advisory Council, comprising experts in animal husbandry, to advise on the animal welfare program. The Council assisted in the development of animal care guidelines and audit programs for broiler suppliers. Also, KFC participated in restaurant industry efforts to ensure the humane treatment of animals produced for food.

These initiatives did not satisfy PETA and it continued its campaign against KFC by staging protests outside restaurants, promoting anti-KFC Web sites, sponsoring letter writing campaigns, and advertising on television and billboards. The campaign was supported by celebrities such as Pamela Anderson, Dick Gregory, Sir Paul McCartney, and the Dalai Lama. PETA initiated legal action against KFC claiming that statements it made about animal welfare and its policies were lies.

Recently, Antonio read in the newspaper that KFC Canada had yielded to many of PETA's demands. It promised to improve the welfare of chickens at the suppliers from whom it purchased and PETA agreed to end its boycott and its "Kentucky Fried Cruelty" campaign in Canada. The deal included:

- KFC would purchase from suppliers who kill their chickens in the least painful way, by using gas.
- KFC would insist that its suppliers use other animal-friendly measures such as reducing bird crowding, improving lighting, and phasing out non-essential growth hormones and other drugs. KFC's animal welfare audit criteria would be improved to reduce the incidence of broken bones and other injuries to birds.
- A vegan faux-chicken sandwich (similar in taste and texture to chicken) would be made available to KFC customers.
- KFC would form an animal welfare advisory panel to monitor the deal and to make other recommendations.

Antonio wondered if his family's small restaurant would be the next target for PETA activists. Furthermore, he was not sure how his business could address, let alone meet, the demands that may be made.

What is your advice to Antonio?

Sources: Colin Perkel, "KFC bows to PETA demands," *The Globe and Mail*, June 2, 2008, B4; "KFC Canada gives in to PETA's demands," http://getactive.peta.org/campaign/canada_kfc_victory; "KFC's lies stopped: Campaign full speed ahead!" PETA KentuckyFriedCruelty.com, http://www.kentuckyfriedcruelty.com/index.asp; and "Social responsibility: Animal welfare program," http://www.kfc.com/about/animalwelfare.htm.

Civil society The voluntary, community, and social organizations or institutions that contribute to the functioning of society but are usually not related to or supported by government.

Civil society comprises the voluntary, community, and social organizations or institutions that contribute to the functioning of society but are usually not related to or supported by government. Civil society institutions are corporation stakeholders; examples include non-governmental organizations, the media, community-based organizations, civic clubs, trade unions, charities, social and sports clubs, cooperatives, environmental groups, professional associations, policy development institutions, educational institutions, and organized religion.

In this chapter, two civil institutions that have substantial influence on business will be discussed in detail: non-governmental organizations (NGOs) and the media. Corporations and their managers must develop a relationship with these institutions in which managers not only learn about these stakeholders but also recognize their role in society and develop mechanisms for interacting with them. This focus is not one-way but instead is a proactive relationship in which managers understand and respect the roles of these civil society stakeholders. In addition to NGOs and the media, other civil society stakeholders influence business and/or are influenced by business; three are described briefly: policy development institutions (think tanks), religious institutions, and educational organizations.

LO 13.1 Describing Non-Governmental Organizations (NGOs)

The definition of this stakeholder is problematic because different terminology can be used—for example, "public interest," "special interest," or just "interest" groups. Such groups are usually discussed in the context of their influence on public policy formulation, thus the "public interest group" terminology. "Special interest group" is used to describe an association that seeks the advancements of financial interests of its members, for example doctors or lawyers. Although both groups indirectly influence business, the focus of this section is on interest groups that interact with or influence business more directly. Current practice is to refer to these groups as non-governmental organizations (NGOs). A well-known example of such an organization is Mothers Against Drunk Driving (MADD); see Everyday Ethics 13.1.

Everyday Ethics
13.1

Mothers Against Drunk Driving (MADD)

"Mothers Against Drunk Driving (MADD Canada) is a non-profit, grassroots organization that is committed to stopping impaired driving and supporting the victims of this violent crime. At the heart of MADD Canada is our volunteers who include not only mothers, but fathers, friends, business professionals, experts in the anti-impaired driving field and concerned citizens who want to make a difference in the fight against impaired driving.

MADD Canada's aim is to offer support services to victims, heighten awareness about the dangers of drinking and driving, and to save lives and prevent injuries on our roads. Driving while under the influence of alcohol or other drugs is a terrible crime that touches all of our lives and it is an irresponsible, dangerous and intolerable act."

Source: Mothers Against Drunk Driving, "MADD Canada: Learn More," http://www.madd.ca.

Non-governmental organization (NGO) Any group that holds shared values or attitudes about an issue confronting society.

A **non-governmental organization (NGO)** is any group that holds shared values or attitudes about an issue confronting society and advocates for changes relating to the issue. NGOs make claims or demands that business take actions that will be consistent with the group's attitudes or principles. It should be noted that these groups are part of the private sector, not part of government, and are usually but not always non-profit organizations supported by volunteer members and activists. The distinction from government is an important one to make, but there are exceptions. NGOs are able to do things that governments will not or cannot do. NGOs operating in developing countries are sometimes supported by governments, for example those involved with the distribution of foreign aid as contractors acting on behalf of governments unable or unwilling to perform the necessary functions.

NGOs are not new to society; they have existed for hundreds of years. For example, NGOs have opposed slavery in various parts of the world and foot binding in China, advocated for women's voting rights, demanded better working conditions for children, and supported minimum wage laws. In recent times their numbers have proliferated, and they can

TABLE 13.1	*Examples of NGO Societal Issues Relevant to Business*

Numerous societal issues are addressed by NGOs, and this list identifies some of those relevant to business organizations. Some issues may overlap, and particular NGOs may be involved in more than one. The issues are at both the domestic and international or global levels.

Animal rights—Variations in views. Some advocate for the entitlements of animals. Others are concerned about animal welfare, that is, the care given animals. Extreme groups oppose consumption of any meat products and promote vegetarianism.

Technology—Opposed to biotechnology developments; for example, genetic modification of foods. Also concerned about reproduction of life forms.

Economic—Often oppose capitalism and advocate for forms of collectivist enterprise or government ownership. Concerned about concentration of ownership and domination of the economy by the "corporate agenda" or the corporate elite.

Social development—Concerned with the gap between the rich and poor, in Canada but particularly in developing countries. Promote community development, cultural and social activities, and social services such as housing and health care.

Workers'/human rights—Identify the working conditions of labour especially in developing countries. Advocate for union organization and codes of practice. Also concerned with human rights.

Environment—One of the most common causes of NGO activity. Covers all aspects of the environment in Canada and around the world.

Religious activism—Form of activism that is more common recently, especially in the U.S. Local churches and alliances of evangelical churches pressure corporations on their support of social issues such as gay rights and abortion.

be locally based in a community or operate around the world. There are many economic, ethical, and environmental issues that form the basis or belief for an NGO; some of the most common issues that influence business are listed in Table 13.1.

Managers must be aware of the variety of approaches or tactics used in an attempt to influence the corporation or its stakeholders. Understanding the possible tactics is important because of a shift in the focus of influence. At one time, NGOs concentrated their efforts on lobbying or otherwise influencing government policies or regulation toward business. Some NGOs attack or attempt to influence corporations by taking actions directly against them. There has been a shift in recent years to indirectly influencing corporations through other stakeholders, for example shareholders, consumers, or suppliers. Responsibility for Ethics 13.1 lists some commonly used tactics to influence corporations.

connect   Want to learn more about **digital protest movements**? Go to CONNECT.

LO 13.2   The Case For and Against NGOs

Corporations and their managers should not dismiss NGOs as a nuisance or useless stakeholder. Their members are very dedicated to their cause or issue and their existence in society supports structures that allow for a wider cross-section of society to influence events. NGOs facilitated the preparation of the Kyoto Agreement on Global Warming, and they made available lower-cost drugs in developing countries. They generate ideas, knowledge, and solutions, disseminate information on issues, and, of course, pressure for results. Some NGOs have developed product certification systems that corporations have used in their

NGO Tactics

The following are examples of tactics used by NGOs to influence the ethical conduct of corporations:

- Putting pressure on governments and politicians to change policies or regulations
- Generating damaging publicity on the corporation in the media
- Disrupting annual meetings
- Developing shareholder social policy resolutions (after purchasing a few shares)
- Damaging physical property or sabotaging activities
- Occupying corporate premises
- Sponsoring demonstrations or picketing corporate locations
- Picketing managers' homes
- Sponsoring demonstrations or picketing corporate locations
- Organizing boycotts to prevent purchases
- Organizing buycotts (that is, campaigning to buy the products or services of a particular company or country) to recommend purchases from preferred sellers
- Launching letter-writing campaigns, including letters-to-the-editors of newspapers
- Participating in digital protest movements
- Holding public meetings
- Using social media to initiate campaigns on social or environmental issues
- Initiating legal proceedings
- Participating in hacktivism, the non-violent use of the Internet for activist protests
- Developing anti-business or anti-corporate Web sites and "Watch"–type sites—for example Walmart Watch
- Supporting the development of anti-business documentaries and facilitating their distribution
- Providing support for alternative sources of goods and services (e.g., fair trade products, credit unions, employee-owned enterprises)

marketing. NGOs can be agents for change, and can confer legitimacy when governments cannot act alone.

Governments, and business, will listen to NGOs when they operate in a transparent manner, are accountable for their actions, and are accurate in their claims or information.[1] In a report prepared by Canadian Business for Social Responsibility (CBSR), the benefits from partnerships with NGOs include identifying opportunities and risks, influencing public opinion, developing possibilities for innovation, enhancing reputation and trust by the public, creating expertise with in-depth knowledge of specific issues, facilitating employee engagement, and building large networks with other stakeholders.[2]

NGOs may advocate diverse views about the same issue. An example is provided by free trade, to which many NGO groups are opposed. Yet the Global Freedom to Trade campaign advocates for global trade freedom. Other NGOs such as Oxfam Canada support freer trade under certain conditions, and many forms of fair trade practices exist. Managers not only must identify the NGOs related to industry-relevant issues, but also must understand the positions held about these issues because some may be supportive.

Many NGOs do represent a threat to business. Many of the tactics listed in Responsibility for Ethics 13.1 can disrupt business operations. Many are clearly anti-business and anti–free trade or globalization, reducing the support for business in society. Their beliefs in redistribution of wealth and equality of results are inconsistent with business beliefs in economic markets and efficiency measures. Some NGOs are simply "anti" everything associated with business and constantly criticize while offering few if any alternatives.[3]

LO 13.3 Strategies for Relationships with NGOs

NGOs pressure corporations directly and indirectly through other stakeholders. If an indirect approach is the case, Spar and LaMure state that there are three key turning points for the corporation: (1) the NGO must be able to threaten the corporation with significant harm; (2) the corporation must respond to the threat by changing business practice; and (3) the change must serve to advance the NGO's goals. They argue that the corporation becomes the conduit by which outside stakeholders—that is, NGOs—attempt to achieve non-market objectives.[4]

Corporations cannot ignore the influence of NGOs and should not underestimate their power or tenacity. Many corporations do take NGO activism seriously and respond in different ways depending on the corporation's particular position or the type of industry. Spar and LaMure propose that the corporation's response to NGO activism is influenced by three variables: transaction costs, brand impact, and competitive position. There are also three possibilities when corporations are faced with NGO tactics. Resistance is possible, but not recommended in most situations. Capitulation may be the most advantageous in some cases, and preemption in others.

Transaction costs relate to capital and sourcing, and if substantial expenses are involved to meet the NGO's demands the corporation is more likely to resist the demands. This is usually the case in natural resource industries where capital investments are high, or in industries where no other source of supply exists. In consumer goods industries, capitulation to NGO demands is usually less expensive and alternate sources of supply are available.

The greater the value a corporation places on its brand, the more susceptible it is to pressure from the NGO. In this situation, capitulation to the demands is a more logical response. Brand-name footwear and apparel companies can easily switch their sourcing and few, if any, capital costs are involved. By doing so, the corporation is more likely to gain a reputation as a socially responsible citizen.

In very competitive industries, being the first to meet or capitulate to NGO demands might provide a competitive advantage. This is particularly the case where brand recognition is high. Such action would be a preemptive strategy to gain on competitors.[5] Table 13.2 summarizes the strategies and the responses.

Managers do not always reply based on resistance, capitulation, and preemption. They may have personal motives and beliefs that can also motivate their decisions. Managers have values and ethical beliefs as a result of their upbringing or education that provide guidance in moral issues. It should not be assumed that managers always make decisions relating to NGO demands based on cost–benefit analysis or competitive positioning.[6]

A more aggressive response toward NGOs is possible but not recommended. An effort could be made to discredit NGOs with negative attacks, or to launch legal action. Both responses could backfire and complicate the relationship. However, it may be feasible to demand more accountability from NGOs, just as they are demanding the accountability of corporations. Some NGOs do not account appropriately to donors, or they spend funds on questionable activities. It can be pointed out that unrepresentative activists undermine

TABLE 13.2	*Strategies for Relationships With NGOs*		
Three Variables Influencing Response	**Transaction costs**	**Brand impact**	**Competitive position**
	↓	↓	↓
Responses	Resistance (resource industries)	Capitulation (consumer goods)	Preemption (competitive industries)

the effectiveness of credible NGOs, and the corporation can provide evidence of its serious efforts at dialogue with some NGOs.

Some of the anti-business tactics used by NGOs are difficult to tolerate, but at times corporations find that ignoring their extreme positions may be preferable to attempts at countering. Business organizations have countered NGO-sponsored Web sites with NGO-WATCH.org, a site that compiles factual data about NGOs including analysis of relevant issues, treaties, and international organizations where NGOs are active; the site is described in Responsibility for Ethics 13.2. Some industries have supported or formed NGOs that support their position; for example, the tobacco industry has supported smokers' rights organizations. Lastly, business can suggest that NGOs also need a code of ethics and/or conduct to guide their operations.

RESPONSIBILITY
for Ethics **13.2**

NGOWATCH

The Web site NGOWATCH.org is a project of the American Enterprise Institute and the Federalist Society, and has a mission to disclose transparency and accountability issues related to NGOs.

The site maintains that NGOs cannot be ignored for several reasons: governments rely on them to implement aid programs; they address some social and environmental issues more effectively than government; NGO officials are widely quoted in the media and consulted by governments; resisting NGO campaigns can have devastating consequences; and they have been influential in the establishment of globalized standards.

Given the time-honoured role of NGOs in society and their increasing influence, the sponsors of the site believe that NGOs should be monitored and held accountable for their actions.

Source: Based on NGOWATCH, http://www.globalgovernancewatch.org/ngo_watch/.

connect Want to learn more about **"watch" sites**? Go to CONNECT.

Based upon Spar and LaMure's article and from the discussion of NGOs, some observations are possible about their relationship to corporations:

- A preferable strategy is to proactively engage the NGOs and expect to interact with them.
- Do not underestimate the influence of NGOs on the corporation directly or indirectly through other stakeholders.
- Reversing a decision or withdrawing from a project should not be viewed as a defeat.
- Sometimes selective concessions are sufficient to address opposition from NGOs.
- Sometimes it is appropriate to establish a dialogue with "realist" NGOs and ignore the "radical" and "idealist" ones.
- A preemptive strategy may be feasible.

Several questions that managers should pose to learn about an NGO's approach include, Who are they? What do they want? What will they do to achieve their objectives? and What is the best way to deal with them?

LO 13.4   Partnership Relationships with NGOs

A Canadian Business for Social Responsibility (CBSR) report presents another view being advocated regarding relationships with NGOs; that is, one of partnership. The report explores a different type of partnership between business and NGOs: domestic partnerships that build business leadership through social, environmental, and economic success. It is pointed out that philanthropic partnerships have supported and empowered NGOs; for example, Microsoft Canada's partnership with the Royal Canadian Mounted Police and the Toronto Police Service to establish the Child Exploitation Tracking System. However, another form of partnership drives social success and innovation in business by involving all three sectors: business, government, and civil society.[7]

This type of partnership brings together business and NGO resources to address an issue including human, technical, financial, and knowledge interests. The process is not without risks to all involved—damage to reputations, high start-up costs, conflicts of interest, and alienation of stakeholders may be concerns. CBSR identifies four key ingredients to defining the success of a partnership:

- Corporate and NGO leaders must show leadership
- The corporation must be open to change
- There must be a commitment to being committed
- Partners must have a shared goal.[8]

An article at Network for Business Sustainability identified the key lessons for collaboration with NGOs differently. It must be recognized that different perspectives exist which are challenging but also valuable as each partner's knowledge, expertise, and capabilities complement the others'. Secondly, it is important to assign a person responsible for the project and give that person authority and decision-making ability. This champion is necessary to overcome resistance and to indicate to the NGO that the corporation is taking the relationship seriously. Also, the NGO engagement must be part of the corporation's core business; that is, integrated into the operations of business units and not maintained as a separate, standalone operation. Lastly, the relationship must be allowed to evolve over time and accommodate changing circumstances as they arise. Corporate and NGO partnerships are challenging to management, but they can be beneficial to both partners.[9]

Examples of successful partnerships are described in Everyday Ethics 13.2. Another example is the completion of the Canadian Boreal Forest Agreement (CBFA) described in Responsibility for Ethics 13.3; this was a significant accomplishment because of the number of NGOs and corporations involved, and its span across a whole industry. The agreement has been criticized on the grounds that NGOs have no right to determine public policy, especially through the use of intimidations and threats based on unproven claims. Some argue that the boreal forest was not under threat of destruction, and that the agreement would result in higher prices, fewer jobs, zero impact on climate, and reduced profits. CBFA believes that these are only the beginnings of many future innovative partnerships.

This section has described NGOs and some of the relationships that exist between NGOs and business. Although NGOs have been an increasingly influential stakeholder, another civil society stakeholder, the media, plays an important role in influencing the corporation.

Everyday Ethics
....
13.2

Corporate–NGO Partnerships
....

Fairmont Hotels & Resorts and WWF-Canada—In partnership with World Wildlife Fund, Fairmont has made a world-class CO_2 emission reduction commitment that enables CO_2 footprint reductions from operations for both existing and new properties, and includes engaging suppliers, employees, and guests to promote the benefits and need to reduce emissions.

Polaris Minerals and Vancouver Island First Nations—Polaris has developed direct partnerships with the local First Nations in Eagle Rock Quarry Project, which is 70 percent owned by Polaris and 30 percent by local First Nations of which the Hupacasath and Ucluelet First Nations each own 10 percent, with the remaining 10 percent held in trust.

RONA Inc. and David Suzuki Foundation (DSF)—RONA is supporting reforestation programs across Canada by planting almost 50,000 trees a year in partnership with DSF.

PotashCorp and Free the Children—These two organizations have announced a multi-year partnership to help address international food security and encourage youth in Saskatchewan and across Canada to take on this challenge locally and globally.

Sources: "Working with business: Footprint reduction," WWF-Canada, http://www.wwf.ca/about_us/business/; "Corporate social responsibility: Community," Polaris Minerals Corporation, http://www.polarmin.com/operations-projects/eagle-rock-quarry-project/; and RONA Inc., http://www.rona.ca/corporate/In-celebration-of-canadian-athletes-who-competed-in-londonrona-to-plant-close-to-50-000-trees-across-canada.

RESPONSIBILITY
for Ethics **13.3**
....

Canadian Boreal Forest Agreement (CBFA)
....

In May 2010, an agreement was reached among nine environmental non-governmental organizations (ENGOs) and 21 forestry corporations on the management of the Canadian boreal forest. It is a significant agreement illustrating cooperation between ENGOs and the forestry industry. It was considered a historic event and was a model of ENGO/business cooperation.

The ENGOs participating are Canadian Boreal Initiative, Canadian Parks and Wilderness Society, Canopy, David Suzuki Foundation, ForestEthics, Greenpeace, The Nature Conservancy, Pew Environment Group International Boreal Conservation Campaign, and Ivey Foundation. They agreed to stop boycott campaigns against Canadian forest products. Also, they would endorse the purchase of Canadian products if the industry met performance standards specified in the Agreement.

Twenty-one members of the Forest Products Association of Canada (FPAC) are participating in the agreement. The commitments made by the industry included not undertaking any environmentally unfriendly actions; becoming carbon neutral; establishing a caribou habitat; and matching global standards for forest product sustainability.

The "Boreal Business Forum" has been established to audit the progress of the CBFA to protect the boreal forest and to ensure market recognition for sustainable forest products. The forum will meet every six months and comprise 14 members of FPAC and Greenpeace. It can issue "Do Not Buy" notices on corporations with less sustainable standards than under the CBFA.

Sources: Tim Shufelt, "'Globally significant' deal centres on boreal forest," *National Post,* May 18, 2010, A1, A8; Bertrand Marotte, "Keeping tabs on the keepers of the forest," *The Globe and Mail,* April 19, 2010, B6; and Rick Boychuk, "The boreal handshake," *Canadian Geographic,* January/February 2011, 30–45. The Agreement's Web site is http://www.canadianborealforestagreement.com. Details of the Agreement are available at http://www.canadianborealforestagreement.com/index.php/en/the-canadian-boreal-agreement. The companies participating in the agreement are listed at http://www.canadianborealforestagreement.com/index.php/en/whos-involved.

> ## LO 13.5   The Media Stakeholder

This section explores the relationship between business and the media—newspapers, periodicals, television, radio, and the Internet. The media is a stakeholder that can influence the views held by the public about business, and cannot be ignored. In turn, business has some influence over the media. Most media operations are owned by private-sector enterprises, and advertising is a main source of revenue for them. In recent years business has taken on improved respectability in the media and this has led to increased coverage, especially for international business and personal finance.

Managers should realize that dealing with the media is a part of their responsibility and that the media are important in earning and keeping public trust and acceptance. Some managers see the media as intrusive, prying, and prejudicial, an unwelcome and necessary evil. But business needs to communicate with all stakeholders, and the media serve as a vehicle that may reflect owner, employee, consumer, community, and other stakeholder expectations about the ethics of business and its social and environmental responsibilities. The media are entitled to gather, digest, and regurgitate information on business as they do for any other institution in society, and media coverage of business activities can improve economic literacy and attitudes toward business.

Business is a major institution in society, and like any other major institution people have an intrinsic curiosity about it. People have developed the belief that they have a right to know about things that affect them, and this belief has been reinforced by access-to-information law. Thus, over the years, veils of secrecy that sheltered many institutions and organizations have been removed, or at least lifted. People now want to take a closer look at business and are asking tougher, more pointed questions.[10]

The Influence of Popular Media

Books, television, film documentaries, movies, and the Internet portray the operations of business and its relationship to society. Some of the portrayals are positive, but many are negative and receive a lot of attention. The extent to which the popular media influence attitudes toward business is not known for certain.

Many Canadian corporate histories and business biographies have been written, along with general books about the business system. Examples of books with a negative view of business are *Greed, Inc.: Why Corporations Rule Our World and How We Let It Happen,*[11] *The Corporation: The Pathological Pursuit of Profit and Power,*[12] and *Wealth by Stealth: Corporate Crime, Corporate Law, and the Perversion of Democracy.*[13]

Popular television programs also have mixed views of business. Business is often portrayed unfavourably, for example on *The Simpsons.* In addition, television investigative reporting programs uncover corporate wrongdoing or questionable practices. Documentaries made for television and movie theatres have become popular recently, for example *Super Size Me, Roger & Me, Wal-Mart: The High Cost of Low Price,* and *Capitalism: A Love Story.*

Although some crossover occurs between documentaries and movies, movies often focus on the ethics of business and corporate social responsibility. Some movies that have not portrayed capitalism in a good light are *Wall Street, Erin Brockovich, A Civil Action, The Constant Gardener, Blood Diamond, In Good Company,* and *Up in the Air.* Finally, the Internet is a source of information that is critical about business. Many large companies are the subject of "watch" sites, such as *Walmart Watch,* as are industries, such as *MiningWatch.* Some Web sites are critical of business in general, for example *CorporateWatch.*

Numerous newspapers and periodicals cater to business audiences, or those interested in the ethics of business and its responsibilities. Daily newspapers have some business coverage, even if it is simply an abbreviated stock market listing. *The Globe and Mail*

(Toronto) has a "Report on Business" section daily. *National Post* offers daily coverage of finance and business in its *Financial Post* section. *The Globe and Mail* and *National Post* publish monthly business magazines, *Report on Business* and *National Post Business*. Other monthly magazines include *Inside Guide, En Route, Small Business Magazine,* and *Canadian Business*. There also are several regional business magazines, for example *Atlantic Canada Business* and *Alberta Business.*

Coverage of business has changed from domination by print to domination by live television. Television and radio have extensive and immediate coverage of business topics. CBC-TV has a business-related program called *Marketplace,* and the cable television channel *Report on Business* devotes all programming to business and related topics. However, even newspapers respond to events quickly, with lengthy analyses of major business-related events. Their online editions are updated constantly. This trend to instant news has also resulted in the instant expert opinion. If a company produces an unsafe product or pollutes a waterway, experts are available to offer their analysis or comment, although sometimes biased or peripheral.

connect

Want to learn more about **the efforts of OpenMedia.ca to keep the Internet affordable?** Go to CONNECT.

Social media Online technologies and practices that people use to share opinions, insights, experiences, and perspectives.

Finally, the technology of the media stakeholder is changing. The term **social media** describes the online technologies and practices that people use to share opinions, insights, experiences, and perspectives.[14] The ways that information from and about business is received by society are being transformed by new technologies, and discussions of the ethics of business and its responsibilities in these media will occur as well. It is not clear what influence this change will have on the relationships among business, the media, and society.

> **LO 13.6**   **The Interaction Between Business and the Media**

Businesspersons have complained about what they consider to be inappropriate coverage in the media. On the other hand, the media complain about attitudes held by most businesspersons about their reporting practices. Table 13.3 summarizes complaints from both perspectives.

TABLE 13.3   *Business–Media Relations*

Business Complaints about the Media

- Reporters are not sufficiently knowledgeable about business and economics and fail to do their homework.
- The media are interested only in "bad" news that can be sensationalized.
- The media are unable to place the information they are provided into the correct context.
- The media have an inherent bias against business and are dominated by leftist journalists who neither support nor understand a market economy.
- Business reporting is not only biased, but also oversimplified and lacking in insight.
- Reporters do not respect "off-the-record" comments.

Media Complaints about Business

- Businesspersons confuse issues by waffling on details, stonewalling, attempting to hide negative information, or by lying.
- Businesspersons use the excuse that they are accountable only to shareholders, not the media.
- Businesspersons overreact to the process of reporting events and covering issues.

Some managers have attempted to manage the relationship to suit their purposes; press releases are an example. The media are viewed as a tap that can be turned on or off depending on what managers think stakeholders should know. Some corporations fear the damage that can be done by a reporter to a manager's or a corporation's image. But the consequence of not responding to requests from the media is also dangerous. If the media are rebuffed they will turn to more cooperative sources of information—which may not be sympathetic to the business view. For their part, businesspersons and managers have threatened to cancel subscriptions when (or if) negative stories are carried. Advertising has been withdrawn by some businesses as retaliation for an editorial view or certain news coverage.

Another phenomenon influencing media coverage, in particular the publication of books, is "libel chill." **Libel chill** occurs when a business threatens legal action if a particular article or book is published. With this threat present, writers, editors, and publishers impose on themselves a form of self-censorship, holding back on potentially controversial stories. This situation has an impact on the freedom of speech and the public's right to know. Publishers often back down for fear of a long and expensive court case and the possibility that they might lose.

> **Libel chill** Occurs when a business threatens legal action if a particular article or book is published.

Another challenge in business coverage is "media spin." Corporations have access to the services of public relations experts who are frequently able to put a particular "spin," or interpretation, on corporate events or information. This spin is incorporated into corporate press releases supplied to the media, often with supporting materials. Reporters, facing looming deadlines, have been accused of simply repackaging corporate press releases without further input. In turn, reporters may put their own spin on corporate news, particularly news that is not favourable to the corporation. The result is that some business news should be interpreted carefully.[15]

The issue is one of balance. The media should not get away with irresponsible, inaccurate, or scandalous reporting, but neither should businesspersons be allowed to unduly influence reporters and publishers. This discussion of the relationship between business and the media leads to a discussion of unfairness and biased reporting.

Whether media have a left-leaning, anti-business, big-government bias that tends to favour politically correct welfare-state solutions and downplay market realities, or a right-wing, corporate-agenda bias that tends to favour solutions that benefit the wealthy and powerful elite to the exclusion of marginalized and ordinary working people, is difficult to prove. According to Saunders, both positions are strongly supported in Canada; he uses content analysis to prove that reporters and editors are putting a particular ideological spin on the news. He states that although the process appears to be rigorous and to use scientific methods, the results of such analyses are questionable and a waste of time.[16]

A question arising from this discussion of fairness and bias in the media is whether it makes a difference. Corporations certainly think so. Managers worry about the type and tone of information that appears in the media and the influence this has on a company. Research into the relationship between media exposure and change in corporate reputation has for the most part been inconclusive. A study on the relationship between intensive media exposure and changes in corporate reputation concluded that media are a pervasive element in society and appear to be an important influence on the performance of modern companies.[17] Despite some positive findings, the author concluded that much remains to be done before the relationship is fully understood.

Wartick defined media exposure as "the aggregated news reports relating to a specific company within a prescribed period," and for corporate response used the definition "the aggregation of a single stakeholder's perception of how well organizational responses are meeting the demands and expectations of many organizational stakeholders."[18] He based his study on *Fortune*'s "Most Admired Corporations" and related the magnitude, direction, and total movement of change in corporate reputation with the amount, tone, and recency of media exposure.

The tone of media exposure is a key factor associated with both the direction of the change in corporate reputation and the total movement of the change in corporate reputation. Recency is significantly associated with the magnitude of the changes in corporate reputation.[19]

LO 13.7   Media Ownership

Another dimension in the relationship between business and the media comes about because business enterprises own and operate media outlets. Ownership of the broadcast, telecommunications, and print media is now concentrated in multimedia business enterprises such as CTVglobemedia Inc., Postmedia Network Inc., Shaw Communications Inc., Rogers Media, the K.C. Irving Group, Torstar Corp., and Quebecor Media. At one time, the concern was for concentration of ownership within broadcast or print, but today most of these corporations own a variety of media.

Several issues emerge as a result of this ownership, including those surrounding (1) the newspaper monopolies held in some cities by large corporations; (2) the interlocking ownership between print and broadcasting media; (3) the licensing process in broadcasting where some corporations are allegedly favoured over others; and (4) the operation of newspaper chains that are concerned more with financial performance than professional journalism.

The power associated with media ownership is one issue. A related issue is the centralization of the media. This involves the concern that there may be too few voices in the media. Newspapers are suffering declining readership, especially with some age groups, and some have failed. But the availability of magazines has increased, as have alternatives available on television and radio. A problem with control arises when all media are concentrated with one or a few owners; this is not yet the case. However, although the independence of the media is an aspect of free privilege, this is countered by the professionalism of journalists and managers in the media. Some in society do challenge the influence of the media, as illustrated in Responsibility for Ethics 13.4.

RESPONSIBILITY
for Ethics **13.4**

Adbusters and the "Media Carta"

The Adbusters Media Foundation describes itself as a social activist movement dedicated to reforming the media. Based in Vancouver, the Foundation publishes *Adbusters Magazine* (circulation of 120,000), maintains the Adbusters.org Web site, and operates an advocacy advertising agency.

One Adbusters project is focused on the way information flows and the way meaning is produced in society. Adbusters believes that people must launch a movement that enshrines "the Right to Communications in the constitutions of all free nations, and in the Universal Declaration of Human Rights." They are requesting that people sign their *Media Carta*, which states that citizens have:

- lost confidence in the commercial information system as it distorts the view of the world,
- lost faith in the institutions of mass media,
- lost hope in the national media regulators to act in the public interest, and lost patience waiting for reform.

Adbusters imagines a different system—a media democracy.

Sources: Adbusters, "About Adbusters," http://www.adbusters.org/network/about_us.php; and Adbusters, "Sign the *Media Carta*," http://www.adbusters.org/campaigns/mediacarta/sign.

There is increasing specialization and fragmentation in the media. Mindszenthy listed the following types of media: trade journals; specialized consumer publications; all-news networks; cable TV stations; and the dedicated religious, lifestyle, business, weather, and sports networks. In addition, there are household or free-distribution newspapers, call-in and call-out radio and TV programs, and interview programs.[20] At the time same, the circulation of many magazines and most newspapers is declining.[21]

LO 13.8   The Media and CSR

Business topics and issues appear to have gained a new respectability in the media in recent years. In particular, there is increased coverage of the ethics of business and corporate social responsibility (CSR) in the media. Business's ethical, social, and environmental responsibilities are of increasing interest to the public. This seems to have led to increasing coverage of business topics and issues by the media. Businesspersons have responded by complaining less about biased reporting and by preparing themselves better for interacting with media representatives.

The corporations that own the media have recognized the importance of CSR or sustainability, and this is illustrated in the newspaper industry. *The Guardian,* a newspaper published in the United Kingdom, is recognized for its comprehensive annual sustainability report. A recent report is summarized in Everyday Ethics 13.3. Although the media make efforts to be responsible, failings have occurred. The News Corporation in the United Kingdom was accused of hacking telephone services and other corrupt practices. In Canada, a columnist at *The Globe and Mail* was accused of plagiarism. The managers and employees of media corporations must be as sensitive to the ethical implications of their behaviour as would those in other corporations. Two civil society stakeholders—NGOs and the media—have been discussed in detail, but many other institutions can influence business or can be influenced by business. The following discussion briefly describes three others: policy development institutions or think tanks, religious organizations, and educational institutions.

Everyday Ethics   A Newspaper and Sustainability

13.3   Sustainability practice at a media corporation is illustrated by Guardian News and Media, a United Kingdom corporation best known as the publisher of *The Guardian* newspaper. It has been issuing sustainability reports for 15 years, and its 102-page *Living Our Values: Sustainability Report 2012* is the most comprehensive covering economic, social, ethical, and environmental responsibilities. The newpaper's vision is to be a leader in sustainability within the media industry.

Living Our Values outlined the values by which the corporation operated, a theme that provided the report's title. Sections described the newspaper's vision, strategy, carbon reduction programs, and governance. The extent of social responsibility coverage and content, journalism practices, and the results of a readership survey were discussed. The targets and performance 2011–12 were reviewed in several areas: people and community, doing good business, improving digital sustainability, enhancing audience engagement, empowering people and community, low impact operations, and responsible procurement. An Assurance Statement was prepared by independent auditors. Objectives and plans for 2012–13 were presented for each area.

Source: *The Guardian,* "Living our values: *Guardian* news and media sustainability report 2012," http://image.guardian.co.uk/sys-files/Guardian/documents/2012/11/22/Sustainabilityreport2012.pdf.

LO 13.9   Policy Development Institutions (Think Tanks)

Policy development institution (think tank)
An organization that researches and analyzes various important social, economic, and political issues confronting society.

A **policy development institution** or **think tank** is an organization that researches and analyzes various important social, economic, and political issues confronting society. They attempt to influence society's position on various issues, and in particular try to bring fresh thinking to an issue and mould government public policy. Usually they are not connected to government, although government may provide funding. Most funding is provided by business corporations and trade unions. Wealthy individuals, foundations, member contributors, universities, and the sale of services (e.g., consulting, publications, etc.) finance others. Most Canadian think tanks were established in the 1970s and 1980s; they exist in most democracies, with some being international in scope. Responsibility for Ethics 13.5 lists some examples.

Even from the brief descriptions in Responsibility for Ethics 13.5 it is clear that various ideological views are represented. Critics claim that some are merely public relations fronts and advocates for industry or labour sponsors. This appears to be the case in the United States more than in Canada, where think tanks become lobbyists. In such cases the results of research tend to be ideologically driven by member interests, as illustrated in Everyday Ethics 13.4. It is sometimes difficult to distinguish think tanks from lobbyists with vested interests in an issue.

A question for business and managers is whether the think tanks have much influence. Some argue that they have little influence, while others claim they can change the language of public debate. At the least, the think tanks most relevant to a corporation's industry, or that examine an issue of importance to the industry, should be monitored.

LO 13.10   Religious Institutions

Four topics discuss the influence of religion in business: the impact on managerial decision making, the existence of businesses supplying religious goods and services, spirituality in the workplace, and corporate response to religious activism.

The influence of religion on managerial decision making has been discussed extensively. Many argue that religious beliefs or practices have an influence on a manager's perceptions of what is ethical versus unethical, and can play a role in management education. Romar advocates Confucianism as a compelling managerial ethic because it is compatible with accepted managerial practices, it requires individuals and organizations to make a positive contribution to society, it recognizes hierarchy as an important organizational principle and demands managerial moral leadership, and its virtues provide a moral basis for hierarchical and cooperative relationships.[22] The Metanexus Institute is involved in an interdisciplinary social scientific research initiative on the economic and social consequences of religion and spirituality, referred to as "spiritual capital."[23] The Roman Catholic Church has commented on the relationship between business and society over the years. Responsibility for Ethics 13.6 summarizes a recent church publication that addresses business leadership in society and proposes six practical principles for business.

Religion is generating many commercial opportunities in the economy: a religion-based theme park called Holy Land Experience in Florida; Christian literature publishers; retailers, including Walmart, selling religious items, music, and video games; and faith-based mutual funds.[24] A *BusinessWeek* article described how organized religion is even learning to operate like a business. Huge churches are being constructed, seating thousands, with large orchestras and choirs and state-of-the-art electronic communications.[25]

RESPONSIBILITY

for Ethics **13.5**

Policy Development Institutions or "Think Tanks"

Most of these institutions are non-profit, non-partisan, and charitable organizations claiming to be independent.

- *Atlantic Institute for Market Studies*—Provides a distinctive Atlantic comment on public policies at the regional, national, and international levels. It advocates free markets.

- *C.D. Howe Institute*—Aims to improve Canadians' standard of living by fostering sound economic and social policy through independent research and analysis.

- *Caledon Institute of Social Policy*—Does research and analysis; seeks to inform and influence public opinion and to foster public discussion on poverty and social policy; and develops and promotes concrete, practicable proposals for the reform of social programs.

- *Canada West Foundation*—Conducts and communicates non-partisan economic and public policy research of importance to the four western provinces, the territories, and all Canadians.

- *Canadian Centre for Policy Alternatives*—Conducts research and analysis concerned with issues of social and economic justice, and develops workable solutions to the policy questions facing Canadians today.

- *Canadian Labour and Business Centre*—Acts as a centre for business–labour dialogue and consensus building to develop effective public policy in labour market and skills issues.

- *Centre for the Study of Living Standards*—Seeks to contribute to a better understanding of trends in and determinants of productivity, living standards, and economic and social well-being through research.

- *Conference Board of Canada*—Builds leadership capacity for a better Canada by creating and sharing insights on economic trends, public policy, and organizational performance.

- *Fraser Institute*—Has as its objective the redirection of public attention through economic and social research to the role of competitive markets in providing for the well-being of Canadians.

- *Institute for Research on Public Policy*—Conducts research that aims to enhance the quality of the debate on the issues that matter most to Canadians by focusing on the strategic choices they must make to promote economic performance, social progress, and sound democratic governance.

- *Parkland Institute*—Studies economic, social, cultural, and political issues facing Albertans and Canadians using the perspective of political economy, and shares the results of its research widely and promotes discussion of the issues raised.

- *Public Policy Forum*—Provides a neutral venue where the private sector and the public sector can meet to learn from one another, and promotes excellence in government by encouraging reform in public-sector management.

Sources: Canajun Guide, "Think tanks and policy research," http://canajun.com/canada/politics/think.htm; and Hillwatch.com, "Think tanks: A directory of Canadian and international think tanks," http://www.hillwatch.com/PPRC/Think_Tanks.aspx.

Everyday Ethics

13.4

Think Tank Views on Business and Society Issues

The following are examples of recent reports or studies produced by various think tanks. Note the variety of topics. The think tanks are good sources of views on many business and society issues.

- Fraser Institute: *Measuring Income Mobility in Canada* argues that the debate on income inequality fails to account for income mobility, where four out of five low-income Canadians move up the income ladder over 10 years.
- Canadian Centre for Policy Alternatives: *BC's Legislated Greenhouse Gas Targets vs Natural Gas Development: The Good, The Bad and the Ugly* claims that B.C. government–legislated targets for reducing greenhouse gas emissions will not be met in 2020.
- Conference Board of Canada: *The Sky's the Limit: The Viability of Canada's Food Economy* explores the viability of Canada's food economy. It considers the industry, company, plant, and farm viability that, while achieving commercial success, address the nutritional needs of Canadians.
- Public Policy Forum: *Building Authentic Partnerships: Aboriginal Participation in Major Resource Development Opportunity* discusses building authentic partnerships by developing human capital, enhancing community control over decision making, promoting entrepreneurship and business development, and increasing access to financial participation.

Sources: Fraser Institute report at http://www.fraserinstitute.org/researchandpublications/publications/6981. aspx; Canadian Centre for Policy Alternatives report at http://www.policyalternatives.ca/reports/2009/10/ article2319/?pa=BB736455; Conference Board of Canada report at http://www.conferenceboard.ca/ documents.aspx?did=3234; and Public Policy Forum report at http://www.ppforum.ca/publications/ rebooting-economy-what-role-government-transforming-economy.

Effort by some businesses to integrate religion into the workplace is also discussed extensively in the literature.[26] The types of activities carried out in the workplace include spiritual, faith-based, and Bible study sessions; devotional prayer services; and the hiring of corporate chaplains to counsel employees. The introduction of religion into the secular corporation makes some feel uneasy. Although most activities are voluntary, employees may still feel pressure from religious employers. Customers have been subjected to open evangelizing by Christian-dominated corporations. Such activities are not necessarily associated with organized religion. Instead, they are referred to as **spirituality**, an individual's sense of peace or purpose with him/herself and the connection to others and even nature that provides meaning to life and a sense of one's self. Responsibility for Ethics 13.7 describes two initiatives relating to spirituality in the workplace. Even if discussed only briefly, it is possible to recognize that the relationship between business and religious institution stakeholders gives rise to many issues.

Spirituality An individual's sense of peace or purpose with him/herself and the connection to others and even nature that provides meaning to life and a sense of one's self.

Business must be careful in responding to religious activism or it might get caught in crossfire, particularly with conservative groups. *BusinessWeek* referred to this possibility as "culture wars" and posed the question, "When should companies take public positions on social issues?" Some of the social issues of concern identified in the article included support for gay rights, advertising on unacceptable television programs, and the pursuit of embryonic stem-cell research. The article concluded that the only way for a company to respond is to return to its core values. Companies should consider themselves the ultimate judge of what is socially acceptable and not be driven by the dogma of particular religious activism.[27]

RESPONSIBILITY

for Ethics **13.6**

The Church's Reflection on Business Leadership

The Roman Catholic Pontifical Council for Justice and Peace studied the role of business in society and concluded that the vocation of the businessperson was a genuine human and Christian calling. But, in dealing with the complex issues facing society and business, a need existed for businesspersons to base decisions on the foundational principles of human dignity and the common good. These principles should provide direction for business in organizing the labour and capital employed in a market system, and the processes of innovation.

The following summarizes a portion of the findings:

SIX PRACTICAL PRINCIPLES FOR BUSINESS

The principles of respect for human dignity and pursuit of the common good are the foundations of the Church's social teaching. Joined with the six practical principles of business, they can offer more specific guidance on the three broad business objectives.

Meeting the Needs of the World through the Creation and Development of Goods and Services

1. Businesses that produce goods which are truly good and services which truly serve *contribute to the common good.*
2. Businesses maintain *solidarity* with the poor by being alert for opportunities to serve deprived and underserved populations and people in need.

Organising Good and Productive Work

3. Businesses make a contribution to the community by fostering the special *dignity of human work.*
4. Businesses provide, through *subsidiarity,* opportunities for employees to exercise appropriate authority as they contribute to the mission of the organisation.

Creating Sustainable Wealth and Distributing It Justly

5. Businesses model *stewardship* of the resources—whether capital, human, or environmental—they have received.
6. Businesses are *just* in the allocation of resources to all stakeholders: employees, customers, investors, suppliers, and the community. [page 17]

The study also recommended that the Reflection be discussed by faculty and students to: "see the Challenges and opportunities in the world of work; judge them according to the social principles of the Church; and act as leaders who serve God." The study provided a checklist for following the six principles.

Source: "Vocation of the business leader: A reflection," Pontifical Council for Justice and Peace, The Vatican, March 30, 2012, available http://www.ipade.mx/prensa/Documents/vocation_eng.pdf or http://www.stthomas.edu/cathstudies/cst/VocationBusinessLead/VocationTurksonRemar/SecondeditionsextonF.pdf.

▶LO 13.11◀   Educational Institutions

The appropriateness of business involvement in the education system has been controversial. The issue has become more prominent recently as various educational institutions seek assistance from business after government support has declined. Business is now involved in education from the kindergarten to post-secondary levels. The extent of involvement can be illustrated at the university level, where the following are of concern: the establishment

RESPONSIBILITY
for Ethics **13.7**

> ## Spirituality in the Workplace
>
> Two organizations that are promoting and facilitating spirituality in the workplace are described below.
>
> - Outreach Canada formed Corporate Chaplains Canada (CCC) in 2003 to minister to employees, management, and company owners in manufacturing plants, showrooms, hotels, restaurants, service facilities, offices, and stores focusing on non-religious counselling services. Today, CCC cares for over 700 employees at corporations in B.C., Alberta, and Ontario. They promote the overall relational health of employees, stress caring for extended family needs, and provide moral and spiritual support when requested. The intended result is a work environment that is a better, more profitable place for employees and employer alike. One of the goals is for owners to experience an increase in their effectiveness in managing their workforce.
>
> - The mission of the Workplace Centre for Spiritual and Ethical Development is "to serve the business community by advancing spirituality and ethics in the workplace." It "promotes the benefits of individual spiritual well-being; supports the study and practice of business ethics; and organizes programs and events which advance the understanding of spiritual values and ethical standards at work." Its values are listed as spiritual wholeness, cultural diversity, ethical business practices, wisdom of all communities of faith, individual dignity, and environmental sensitivity. The Centre is located in Vancouver, B.C.

Sources: Outreach Canada, "Corporate chaplains," http://en.outreach.ca/ServingYou/CorporateChaplains. aspx; and "About Workplace Centre," Workplace Centre for Spiritual and Ethical Development, http://www. workplacecentre.org/page140.htm.

of private, for-profit colleges; funding for buildings or centres from private sources with some conditions attached; conflicts of interest in the funding of research; the commercialization of research; and exclusivity agreements to provide goods and services.[28]

There are two views regarding the issue. The modern, pragmatic view looks at education and corporate money, or involvement in any form, as a mutually beneficial partnership. An example occurs when a business donates money to a school's athletic program and is allowed to advertise on team uniforms. The other view is that educational institutions should be places of unencumbered thought and considered a custodian of rights of the liberated human spirit. This view is strongly held in universities by many students and faculty. There are many variations between these extreme views, and the circumstances vary depending on the type of institution.

Many businesspeople sincerely believe in the partnership and that it helps the economy. The demands of the global marketplace and information age require skills that are best provided in the educational system. Thus, business has a role in improving the quality of education, and it is in its self-interest to become involved. Partnerships have appeal for educators, from kindergarten teachers to university presidents, as resources formerly provided by governments have been reduced. As educators are financially squeezed, they overlook the ethical implications that might accompany the acceptance of assistance from business.

Many students and faculty oppose partnerships as they fear "market-driven" learning, leading to students being taught only topics of interest to them, universities dropping areas that are not currently popular, job "relevance" being the main criterion for what is taught, and efficiency being emphasized at the expense of social concerns. It is believed that the results would be greater social and economic disparities and loss of competitiveness in technology. There would be negative effects from this narrow focus as it alters the way society invests in higher education as a fundamental social institution. The economic needs of business are met, while the broader and more basic social and cultural needs are ignored.

There is a fear of losing control over what is taught and that the traditional role of the university would be changed. The university was traditionally viewed as a community of free and independent scholars, as an open forum for ideas, and as an institution that could be critical in its assessment of other societal institutions. Many fear that this traditional, and desirable, role would be reduced and possibly eliminated.[29]

Another perspective relates to the social responsibility and sustainability of colleges and universities. In other words, they have economic, social, and environmental responsibilities to society in a way similar to that of business corporations. The University of Guelph's recent fundraising campaign where it raised funds from individuals and corporations focused on social responsibility, as described in Everyday Ethics 13.5.

Everyday Ethics

13.5

The University of Guelph and Social Responsibility

The University of Guelph's recent fundraising campaign, The Better Planet Project, focused on what the university could do to make the planet better by addressing the world's challenges. A quotation from the Project's Web site states:

> *Leading the way in environmental and social responsibility, our exceptionally talented people blend caring and collaboration, turning scientific discoveries into meaningful change that will improve the quality of life for people around the world.*

Although fundraising was involved, the University wanted to emphasize its responsibility to the sustainability of the community and society. The University stated it had the expertise and leadership to work on the changes necessary to improve life on the planet. It planned to raise $200 million by 2014 to fund faculty and staff activities that would lead to breakthroughs in four essential areas of life: food, environment, health, and community.

Source: The Better Planet Project, University of Guelph, http://www.thebetterplanetproject.ca/index2.html, accessed May 14, 2012.

Educational institutions are addressing environmental issues through a variety of initiatives including supply management sustainability. An example of one university's program is provided in Everyday Ethics 13.6. The Association for the Advancement of Sustainability in Higher Education's (AASHE) mission is to empower higher education to lead the sustainability transformation. Sixty Canadian universities and colleges are members.[30] These examples are illustrations of how seriously education institutions take their responsibility to the environment.

Educational institutions are under pressure to seek a balance between the opportunities and challenges of accepting funding from corporations. At the same time, they are expected to be involved in sustainability practices as a responsibility to society.

Everyday Ethics
....

13.6

University of British Columbia's Sustainable Supply Management

The University of British Columbia (UBC) has a comprehensive sustainable supply management program. It contains information on supply management plus practical examples to illustrate sustainable purchasing. The overall benefits of sustainable purchasing for society are listed; a table summarizing the business case for sustainable purchasing is presented; a description of extended producer responsibility (EPR) is given; and a link to UBC's Supplier Code of Conduct is provided.

UBC's Web site outlines its supply management sustainability initiatives, lists the Principles of Sustainability for Supply Management, defines responsible sourcing, and identifies its partners—that is, suppliers in sustainability. Access is also given to *Buying into the Future: The UBC Sustainable Purchasing Guide,* which defines sustainable purchasing and extended producer responsibility, lists UBC's Sustainable Purchasing Guidelines, and discusses why UBC is involved with sustainable purchasing and the costs/savings. Information is provided on implementing the guidelines for a variety of goods and services.

Sources: University of British Columbia, "Principles of sustainability," http://www.supplymanagement. ubc.ca/about-us/principles-sustainability-supply-management; "Sustainable purchasing," http://www. supplymanagement.ubc.ca/about-us/principles-sustainability-supply-management; "Sustainability," http://www. sustain.ubc.ca; and "Buying into the Future: The UBC Sustainable Purchasing Guide," http://www.sustain.ubc.ca/ campus-initiatives/purchasing/sustainable-purchasing-guide.

NGOS, the media, policy development institutions, religious organizations, and educational institution stakeholders all influence business, and business influences them in return. Today's managers require the skills and talents to engage all these stakeholders.

Your Advice to Antonio. . .
....

Small businesses have not been the target of NGO activism, because examples are made of large corporations and attempts are made to get them to change policies. Antonio is faced with the possibility of having actions imposed upon his business by NGOs; in effect, this is another type of regulation beyond government. Also, he might be forced to follow the policies agreed to by his larger competitors. Meanwhile, Antonio's customers may not be concerned about the issue, and if he makes the changes his customers will be denied choices. Small businesses must also address social, ethical, and environmental issues and are not immune to NGO influences.

SUMMARY

- Civil society stakeholders are voluntary, community, and social organizations that represent society's views on business and society issues and through advocacy can influence the behaviour of corporations. There are many types of these stakeholders, but in this chapter only five are discussed: non-governmental organizations (NGOs), media, policy development institutions (think tanks), religious organizations, and educational institutions. (LO 13.1)

- Non-governmental organizations are numerous, use a variety of tactics, and are varied in their positions on issues and influence on business. NGOs serve a beneficial role in society and their views should be identified and analyzed by corporations. A variety of strategies are possible in responding to NGO initiatives and the strategy selected depends on the issue involved and the influence of the NGO. (LO 13.2)

- NGOs do not always oppose business actions and some are consistent with business views. (LO 13.3)

- Recently, there have been many partnership initiatives between corporations and NGOs. (LO 13.4)

- The media stakeholder is one that can influence society's attitudes toward business and one that business can influence. The establishment of an appropriate relationship with the media is important to most

corporations, and many have public relations or media departments to facilitate the relationship. Today, business enjoys extensive and largely favourable coverage in the media. (LO 13.5, LO 13.6, LO 13.7, LO 13.8)

- Policy development institutions or think tanks are numerous and advocate various points of view on business and society issues. They influence government's—and society in general's—attitudes toward business. Many of these think tanks are supported by corporations and views consistent with capitalism are promoted. (LO 13.9)

- Some businesspersons are influenced by organized religions or by spirituality. Here, corporate values are determined by religious beliefs and this is reflected in business operations. (LO 13.10)

- Considerable controversy surrounds the relationship between business and the educational institution stakeholder. Businesses are increasing their presence on campus by supporting research, financing buildings and programs, and operating services. Some students and faculty members believe that the presence of business has an adverse influence on the educational institution, in particular reducing its academic independence. (LO 13.11)

KEY TERMS

Civil society
Non-governmental organization
   (NGO)

Social media
Libel chill

Policy development institution
   (think tank)
Spirituality

CRITICAL THINKING AND DISCUSSION QUESTIONS

1. What roles do NGO stakeholders play in business and society?

2. Are all the tactics used by NGOs appropriate—that is, ethical?

3. What strategies should corporations use in dealing with NGOs?

4. What are the benefits and dangers of forming partnerships with NGOs?

5. What influence does the media stakeholder have on business and what influence does business have on the media?

6. Does business manipulate the media?

7. What challenges do the new forms of participatory media present to business?

8. What roles do the policy development institutions (think tanks) play in business and society?

9. Should religion—organized or spiritual—be associated with business? How can you integrate your faith into your work?

10. What are the benefits and dangers of business's involvement with the educational institutions stakeholder?

CASES

13.1   *The American Red Cross vs. Johnson & Johnson: Who Is Being Double Crossed?*

In August 2007, a dispute broke out between the American Red Cross and Johnson & Johnson, a large U.S. healthcare products company, over the use of the Red Cross emblem.

The American Red Cross was founded in 1881 by Carla Booth and officially chartered by the U.S. Congress in 1905. It provides humanitarian care to victims of wars and natural disasters, and operates various programs to prevent and relieve human suffering. Its programs include services to the needy, support and comfort to military personnel and their families, promotion of health and safety through education, and international relief and development. It also collects, processes, and distributes blood and blood products. It has nearly one million volunteers and 35,000 employees. Its annual revenues are about US$6 billion, of which about 91 percent is spent on humanitarian services and programs.

Johnson & Johnson is a publicly traded American corporation with annual revenues of about US$53 billion and net earnings of US$11 billion. Its businesses include over-the-counter pharmaceuticals and nutritionals, adult skin and hair care, baby care, first aid, personal care, and consumer sanitary protection products. In addition, it produces and markets a wide range of prescription therapeutic products and medical devices and diagnostics. The corporation was formed in New Jersey in 1887 and today employs approximately 120,000 persons in operations around the world.

On August 8, 2007, Johnson & Johnson filed a civil lawsuit against the American Red Cross to restore the legal boundaries surrounding the use of the Red Cross emblem. Since an agreement reached in 1895, both held separate and distinct rights to use the Red Cross emblem. Johnson & Johnson used the trademark on commercial consumer products and the American Red Cross had rights to use the trademark in connection with its non-profit relief services. The two had cooperated with these legal rights until Johnson & Johnson objected to the American Red Cross's use of the trademark on a variety of products sold commercially in competition to similar Johnson & Johnson products.

An American Red Cross press release stated, "For a multi-billion dollar drug company to claim that the Red Cross violated a criminal statute that was created to protect the humanitarian mission of the Red Cross—simply so that J&J can make more money—is obscene," and, "I hope that the courts and Congress will not allow Johnson & Johnson to bully the American Red Cross." The American Red Cross said that funds generated from sale of the products were reinvested in humanitarian programs and services. It also suggested that use of the emblem encouraged consumers to purchase preparedness products for use in case of natural or other disasters.

A Johnson & Johnson press release stated its respect for the American Red Cross, and that the company had supported the organization with $5 million in donations and products in the previous three years and would remain committed to supporting the philanthropic efforts. Johnson & Johnson also offered to submit the disagreement to third-party mediation but the American Red Cross declined.

Questions

1. **What are the economic and ethical issues involved?**

2. **Are the American Red Cross's actions justifiable and its comments appropriate?**

3. **Is Johnson & Johnson being unreasonable in its action? What are the risks for the corporation?**

4. **Review Johnson & Johnson's "Social Responsibility" Web site at http://www.jnj.com/community/index.htm, in particular its "Our Credo" at http://www.jnj.com/our_company/our_credo/index.htm. Do these Web pages influence your view of Johnson & Johnson?**

5. **Who do you think is right and why?**

Sources: American Red Cross Web site, http://www.redcross.org/index.html; American Red Cross press room release, "J&J (NYSE: JNJ) sues Red Cross over use of Red Cross emblem," http://www.redcross.org/pressrelease/0,1077,0_314_6907,00.html; Johnson & Johnson, "Investor relations," http://www.investor.jnj.com; Johnson & Johnson press release, "Johnson & Johnson statement on civil complaint against the American National Red Cross and commercial licensees," http://www.redcross.org/pressrelease/0,1077,0_314_6907,00.html; David Crary, "J&J sues Red Cross over trademark," *The Globe and Mail,* August 10, 2007, B6; and Stephanie Saul, "J&J claims doublecross," *National Post,* August 10, 2007, FP11.

13.2   *SLAPPing CRASH*

SLAPP is an acronym for Strategic Lawsuits Against Public Participation. "SLAPPs are legal actions (usually defamation actions such as libel and slander) launched for the primary purpose of shutting down criticism, and without a strong cause of action. The plaintiff's goal in a SLAPP is not to win the lawsuit, but is rather to silence a critic by instilling fear of large legal costs and the spectre of large damage awards." Despite their right to free speech, critics or defendants may be frightened into silence. They may be required to take down Web sites, remove comments made online, remove printed materials, withdraw statements, and issue apologies.

CRASH (Canadians for Responsible and Safe Highways) is a non-governmental organization "dedicated to making sure that the concerns of the general public and taxpayers are heard about the safety, environmental, and financial impacts of big truck operations on public roads." CRASH is the only national, voluntary organization addressing the issue of truck safety. It claims that about 600 Canadians are killed annually in collisions with big trucks.

In May 2003, CRASH submitted a report to Transport Canada based on its research of the issue. Highlights of the report include the following:

- Concern for driver fatigue from working the longest hours in any regulated jurisdiction.

- Concern that the trucking industry's lobby group, the Canadian Trucking Alliance (CTA), appeared to be able to influence government policy too much.

- Concern regarding questions of a possible conflict of interest when the CTA hired an employee of an NGO that supported its position.

- Concern surrounding allegations of secret dealings between the CTA and the union representing some drivers.

The CTA threatened legal action for defamation with respect to the CTA official named in the report and the damage to CTA's reputation. CTA demanded that the defamatory statements be removed from CRASH's Web site and an apology be made. CRASH complied with all the demands as it could not afford the legal costs required to defend itself.

Questions

1. **Should SLAPPs be used against NGOs or even individuals who criticize a corporation or industry?**

2. **What stakeholders are involved in this issue?**

3. **What are the ethical implications of the use of SLAPPs?**

Sources: Based on CRASH (Canadians for Responsible and Safe Highways), http://www.web.ca/`crash/about.html; SLAPP definition from "Defamation and SLAPPs," Canadian Internet Policy and Public Interest Clinic, University of Ottawa, http://www.cippic.ca/en/faqs-resources/defamation/#faq_slapps; and example from Susan Lott, Corporate Retaliation Against Consumers: The Status of Strategic Lawsuits Against Public Participation (SLAPPs) in Canada, Ottawa: Public Interest Advocacy Centre, September 2004, 26-28 available at http://www.piac.ca/consumers/corporate_retaliation_against_consumers/.

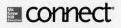 For more information on the resources available from McGraw-Hill Ryerson, go to www.mcgrawhill.ca/he/solutions.

For additional study tools and interactive ways to learn about ethics, visit **www.mcgrawhillconnect.ca**

CHAPTER 14
The Environment and Business Responsibilities

What would you do if . . . ?

Vivian Duveen was standing by the fish counter in her local supermarket. She planned to purchase salmon for her family's dinner but hesitated. Fresh salmon had become very popular; it was a healthy meal, and her family enjoyed it. Today she noted that she could choose between fresh wild or farmed salmon, which was a little less expensive.

Vivian had been researching salmon as a food and the pros and cons of wild versus farmed sources. She found that it was a complicated issue with contradictions in articles and lots of unsubstantiated claims on both sides. There were numerous issues including nutritional value, the operation of farms, and the impact on the environment.

Many sources claimed that wild salmon was nutritionally superior to farmed salmon. Wild salmon was firmer, 20 percent less fatty, and contained 20 percent more protein. Other sources disagreed with these figures. Because it was fattier, farmed salmon contained more omega-3 acids, a desirable characteristic. Dietitians recommended eating two servings of salmon a week whether it was wild or farmed as it was one of the healthiest foods.

Farmed salmon were confined to crowded pens where they were fed daily to saturation, resulting in their growing faster and producing an oilier product. The fish were fed pellets of concentrated nutrients that included plant-based proteins, fish meal, and antibiotics as necessary. It was alleged that the farms produced excessive waste from uneaten food and that some fish escaped to interbreed with wild stocks threatening to weaken the wild salmon's gene pool. Critics of farms claimed that toxins, including PCBs and pesticides, in the fish produced were up to ten times greater than in wild stocks. The farm operators denied these claims.

In contrast, wild salmon lived in natural surroundings, but were subject to many stressors as they did not feed regularly and had many predators. They were carriers of furunculosis, a devastating bacterial disease that farmed salmon were vaccinated against. Sea lice were a problem with salmon but an antibiotic could be included in the food for farms to eliminate them. Some toxins were found in wild salmon depending on their habitat.

In Canada, fish farming was regulated by government to prevent abusive practices. The harvesting of farmed salmon followed strict regulations. The fish were starved for seven days to clear the alimentary tract to ensure a quality product. The harvesting process was monitored, while it is not clear what happens with the harvesting of wild fish. The farm economies of scale resulted in lower prices for consumers, but it was alleged that these lower prices threatened small wild fishing operations.

Fish farms supplied about 50 percent of the fish consumed worldwide. The existence of farms for popular fish such as salmon has taken the pressure off wild stocks and prevented their deletion. The industry has been talking with ENGOs about ways to improve their practices. The farm operators argued that farming was more sustainable and socially responsible than wild catches. The industry claimed that wild fish cannot supply the world's demand for fish.

Vivian reached into the refrigerated display case and picked up a package of salmon.

What is your advice to Vivian?

Sources: Lisa Gosselin, "Which salmon should I buy?" http://ca.shine.yahoo,com/which-salmon-should-i-buy-.html, accessed March 3, 2012; "Farmed vs. wild salmon—Which is better?" ctvbc.ca, March 4, 2010, http://www.ctvbc.ctv.ca/servlet/an/local/CTVNews/20100219/ bc_ctv_investigates_food_fish_100219/20100304, accessed March 21, 2012; David Cox, "Farmed vs wild salmon? A comparison," Fish Vet Group, http://www.thefishsite.com/articles/107/farmed-vs-wild-salmon-a-comparison, accessed March 30, 2012; Wild salmon vs. farmed raised: Which is better?" Pays to Live Green, http://www.paystolivegreen.com/2009/02/wild-salmon-vs-farmed-raised-which-is-better, accessed March 30, 2012; Joseph Schwartz, "Wild versus farmed salmon: The pros and cons," *Medical News Today*, December 26, 2005, http://www.medicalnewstoday.com/releases/35370.php, accessed March 30, 2012; and "Is there any nutritional difference between wild-caught and farm raised fish? Is one type better for me than the other?" The World's Healthiest Foods, http://www.whfoods.com/genpage .php?tname=george&dbid=96, accessed March 30, 2012.

There is increasing concern for the natural environment in Canada and around the world. The need to preserve and protect the environment is now so compelling that there is no question of its relevance for business—the natural environment is an issue that must be addressed. In other words, business has responsibilities toward achieving a sustainable environment.

Concern for the environment has been intensified by disasters such as Chernobyl and Three Mile Island (nuclear plant meltdowns), the Love Canal (pollution in New York), the *Exxon Valdez* (oil spill in Alaska), the BP oil disaster in the Gulf of Mexico, and the tsunami in Japan (and resulting nuclear power plant disaster). In addition, the depletion of the ozone layer, the greenhouse effect, acid rain, deforestation, pollution, energy depletion, and waste management are steadfast reminders of how compelling an issue our natural environment is.

This chapter describes how environmental concerns affect corporations and the many issues that arise with stakeholders. All stakeholders have an obligation to the environment and the key stakeholders influencing it are identified. The various ways that business is responding to its obligation to the environment are identified, as are the challenges involved for management.

LO 14.1   Business, Its Stakeholders, and the Natural Environment

Environmental issues confront virtually all aspects of the corporation, from the input of resources to the manufacturing process, and from workplace conditions through to the way products are packaged and sold. Managers must cope with planning, organizing, leading, and controlling all the aspects of the environmental issue. The ethical and responsibility issues identified in Table 14.1 are diverse; thus, a comprehensive environmental management approach is necessary. The following sections identify how corporations deal with the environment.

Although most business and society scholars do not consider the natural environment to be a stakeholder of business, there is agreement that it is influenced by stakeholders and/or has an influence on stakeholders. As a result, the natural environment can be viewed as a **commons,** or a resource used as though it belongs to all. Business has been able to use shared resources such as the environment simply because it wanted or needed to. In the past, for example, pollution was put into the environment without thinking about the damage and little regulation existed to prevent it. Through uncontrolled use, many in society believed that the environment as a commons was being destroyed. Often this destruction was occurring even though it was not the intent of the user—that is, business—and ownership was not an issue.

Commons
Any resource used as though it belongs to all.

The concept of the commons was popularized by an article published in 1968 by Garrett Hardin.[1] Hardin described what would happen to a commons as illustrated by an unregulated pasture where all sheep herders added more sheep at no cost to them but their actions might lead to the destruction of the pasture for everyone. This behaviour can be explained, in part, by the individualism and economic freedom fundamental of capitalism described in Chapter 2 and the self-interest ethic described in Chapter 5.

connect   Want to learn more about **the "tragedy of the commons"**? Go to CONNECT.

Fortunately, most corporations and their stakeholders have recognized the real and potential damage to the environment of their actions. The remainder of the chapter examines this issue from various perspectives.

LO 14.2   Defining the Environmental Ethic and Sustainable Development

Business's responsibilities to the environment are exemplified by the environmental ethic corporations achieve and by management's understanding of sustainable development.

An **environmental ethic** is the set of values or principles that govern a corporation's practices relating to the environment. Concern for the environment has existed for some time, and an environmental ethic is evolving from this focus on ecology. Society and many businesspersons now have some sense of obligation or moral responsibility to the environment that is expressed in different ways. For a business enterprise, the values or principles include the idea that new business development needs to take account of

Environmental ethic
The set of values or principles that govern a corporation's practices relating to the environment.

TABLE 14.1	*Principal Stakeholders and Issues Involved in Business's Response to the Environment*
Stakeholder	**Ethical Issues and Responsibilities for Managers**
Shareholders	Investment decisions influenced by the handling of the environment
	Risk associated with environment problems or disasters
	Establishment of "green" investment criteria
Directors	Getting environment issues on the board agenda
	Liability for environmental contamination
	Challenge of motivating management to address the issue
Employees	Workplace exposures to environmental problems (e.g., indoor air pollution)
	Refusal to perform tasks causing environmental problems
	Whistleblowing on employer
Customers/Consumers	Inconsistencies between concerns expressed about the environment and the consumption of environmentally unfriendly products
	Unwillingness to pay higher prices for environmentally friendly products/services if necessary
	The viability of "green" products
Lenders/Creditors	Need to assess increased financial risk
Suppliers	Must respond to demands for more environmentally friendly products
	Reassessing most appropriate transportation and packaging of supplies
Service Professionals	Familiarity with laws and regulations
	Design of appropriate audits
	Identification of full environmental cost accounting methods
Competitors	Consequence of competitive edge being obtained by making products more environmentally friendly
NGOs	How to respond to groups based upon environmental concerns
Media	How to respond to media coverage of environmental problems
Government	Complying with laws and regulations
	Influencing public policy

the environment from the design stage through to ultimate disposal; that environmental management should be the responsibility of staff at all levels as an integral part of their job; that environmental performance should be built into the reward structure of the organization; that product and process responsibility should occur from cradle to grave; and that agreed-upon values and beliefs should be used as the guiding principles for conducting all business.[2]

The concept of "sustainable development" has received attention from governments, international agencies, and some business quarters. **Sustainable development** is defined as development ensuring that the use of resources and the impact on the environment today does not damage prospects for the use of resources or the environment by future generations. This was a theme in the report of the United Nations World Commission

Sustainable development
Development ensuring that the use of resources and the impact on the environment today does not damage prospects for the use of resources or the environment by future generations.

on Environment and Development (1987), which concluded that continued economic growth not only is possible, but also is necessary to reduce poverty and to sustain future generations.[3] Sustainable development has been endorsed by many businesspersons as an approach that allows environmental and economic concerns to coincide and makes economic progress possible.

Business sustainable development means "adopting business strategies and activities that meet the needs of the enterprise and its stakeholders today while protecting, sustaining, and enhancing the human and natural resources that will be needed in the future."[4] This definition was developed by the International Institute for Sustainable Development (IISD), a non-profit private corporation established and supported by the governments of Canada and Manitoba to promote sustainable development in government, business, and individual decision making. This definition captures the sense of the concept as presented in the World Commission's report, but focuses on areas of specific interest and concern to business. It recognizes that economic development must meet the needs of the corporation and its stakeholders. The definition also highlights the dependence of the corporation's economic activities on human and natural resources as well as to physical and financial capital.

> **Business sustainable development** According to the IISD, "adopting business strategies and activities that meet the needs of the enterprise and its stakeholders today while protecting, sustaining, and enhancing the human and natural resources that will be needed in the future."

LO 14.3 ◄ Environmental Concerns in Business and Society

In order to illustrate the extensiveness of the environment issue in society and the challenges that confront business, the following discussion lists the major concerns. Some terms overlap or are interrelated, but all are frequently used and should be understood.

- *Acid rain*—**Acid rain** is a generic term used for precipitation that contains an abnormally high concentration of sulphuric and nitric acid. Industrial activities create general gas emissions that combine with water to form the acids.[5]

> **Acid rain** A generic term used for precipitation that contains an abnormally high concentration of sulphuric and nitric acid.

- *Air pollution*—Air quality is affected by various pollutants caused from the burning of fuels, emissions from industrial sites, and emissions from transportation vehicles. Smog is one form of air pollution.

- *Ecosystems*—An **ecosystem** is a biological community of interacting organisms and their physical environment. It is recommended that industry take an ecosystem approach to the environment; that is, recognizing the interrelationships among land, air, water, wildlife, and human activities.[6]

> **Ecosystem** A biological community of interacting organisms and their physical environment.

- *Energy production and consumption*—The generation of energy is usually damaging to the environment, as are the pollutants released when the energy fuel is used. Industry is responsible for many of the problems created, but so are consumers. Business has been emphasizing the efficient use of energy through the development of new technologies for itself and consumers.

- *Nature and wildlife*—There is concern for the harm caused to birds, mammals, fish, and plants by the operations of business. Endangered species are of particular concern.

- *Ozone*—**Ozone** is a naturally occurring gas, formed from normal oxygen, that protects Earth by filtering out ultraviolet (UV) radiation from the Sun. The thinning of the ozone layer in the upper atmosphere has resulted in increased UV radiation.[7]

> **Ozone** Naturally occurring gas, formed from normal oxygen, that protects Earth by filtering out ultraviolet (UV) radiation from the Sun.

- *Pollution*—Pollution involves any form of contamination in the environment. Business is under pressure to reduce its polluting of the environment.

Waste management "Disposal, processing, controlling, recycling and reusing the solid, liquid, and gaseous wastes of plants, animals, humans and other organisms."

- *Waste management*—**Waste management** is "disposal, processing, controlling, recycling and reusing the solid, liquid, and gaseous wastes of plants, animals, humans and other organisms."[8] Wastes often are hazardous, making the process more challenging. Recycling is described by the four Rs: reduce, reuse, recycle, and recover.

- *Water quality*—Water quality is determined by the presence of contaminants affecting its chemical and bacterial composition. Supply of safe drinking water is a concern in Canada. Corporations take on different environmental projects, as illustrated by the Royal Bank's decision to focus on water as described in Everyday Ethics 14.1.

Everyday Ethics 14.1   The RBC Blue Water Project

RBC considers water to be "the lifeblood of our planet and lack of access to clean fresh water is one of the most significant humanitarian, environmental and economic issues facing the world today." The main focus is a ten-year donations program supporting projects that help protect and preserve water. As of 2012, RBC had pledged over $36 million to over 500 charitable organizations for projects to protect watersheds and improve access to clean drinking water; $6 million has been pledged to universities for water programs. RBC's Blue Water Project will focus on supporting initiatives that help protect and preserve water in urban areas between 2013 and 2014.

RBC also seeks partnerships to promote responsible water use and will consider financing business solutions to water issues.

RBC is involved with other environmental initiatives including reduction of its footprint, use of green products and services, and the promotion of environmental sustainability. It issues an Environment Blueprint Report Card and an Environmental Footprint Report.

Source: RBC Blue Water Project™, Royal Bank of Canada, http://www.rbc.com/community-sustainability/environment/rbc-blue-water/index.html.

Climate change (global warming) "The result of human activities altering the chemical composition of the atmosphere through the build-up of greenhouse gases that trap heat and reflect it back to the Earth's surface."

A term that captures the effects of the concerns listed above and that is frequently used today is *climate change*. **Climate change,** also referred to as **global warming,** is "the result of human activities altering the chemical composition of the atmosphere through the build-up of greenhouse gases that trap heat and reflect it back to the Earth's surface." This process has resulted in an increase in global temperatures and more frequent weather events. Note that greenhouse gases are "those that absorb and trap heat in the atmosphere," and that the greenhouse effect is "the phenomenon whereby certain gases that absorb and trap heat in the atmosphere cause a warming effect on the Earth."[9] Climate change is a major issue for society, as highlighted in Responsibility for Ethics 14.1.

connect   Want to learn about **calculating your carbon footprint**? Go to CONNECT.

LO 14.4   Government's Influence

Extensive government involvement exists through public policy formulation and the regulation of all aspects of the natural environment. The federal and provincial governments have passed environmental legislation, and are considering further legislation. Governments have announced various programs to create cleaner air, land, and water; to encourage sustainable resources; to develop parks and wildlife areas; to protect the Arctic regions; and

Al Gore and An Inconvenient Truth

Al Gore is a former U.S. vice-president, and *An Inconvenient Truth* is a documentary film about climate change, or global warming, in which he starred. Gore tells about his interest in the environment since college, reviews scientific evidence about climate change, and identifies the consequences of not taking action. He views the threat of climate change as the biggest moral challenge facing our global civilization, but he also states that there is time to do something about it. The film was released in May 2006 and did very well at the box office. It was widely reviewed and received a "two thumbs up" rating from film critics Roger Ebert and Richard Roeper. Gore has also authored a book by the same name.

There has been substantial criticism of Gore's thesis. Critics have pointed out several perceived inaccuracies, for example the suggestion that the melting of snow on Mount Kilimanjaro, Hurricane Katrina, the drying up of Lake Chad in Africa, and the drowning of polar bears were due to global warming. Critics claim that many sources have proven these claims incorrect. Others point out that the film is one-sided and ignores studies and facts.

Sources: Based on "About the film *An Inconvenient Truth*," http://www.climatecrisis.net/an-inconvenient-truth .php; Marlo Lewis, Jr., "Al Gore's *An Inconvenient Truth* one-sided, misleading, exaggerated, speculative, wrong," Competitive Enterprise Institute, *CEInPoint* No. 108, September 28, 2006, http://cei.org/pdf/5539.pdf, accessed February 5, 2013; "Criticisms of Al Gore's *An Inconvenient Truth*," ClimateSanity, http://climatesanity.wordpress .com/criticisms-or-al-gores-an-inconvenient-truth/, accessed February 5, 2013; and Jan Lundberg, "The inconvenient truth about *An Inconvenient Truth*: Why Al Gore is part dangerous politician," Culture Change Letter #138, August 3, 2006, http://www.culturechange.org/cms/content/view/66/1/, accessed February 5, 2013.

to reduce global warming, ozone depletion, and acid rain. This section does not examine government initiatives in detail, but instead discusses the coordination of public and corporate policies on environment and identifies a range of policies that will impact on business.

Corporations should engage in a dialogue with government agencies so that their interests are protected and to contribute to the resolution of environmental problems. Governments may directly regulate activities of the corporation or introduce policy changes through taxation rates, the elimination or establishment of subsidies, international trade agreements, or the creation of markets in tradeable pollution permits. Business enterprises must establish mechanisms so that they can "listen" to what government is considering, and mechanisms so that they can "talk" to government.

Government departments and agencies have been established not only to regulate the activities of corporations, but also to assist them in meeting environmental performance targets. Responsibility for Ethics 14.2 gives some examples of such organizations in the federal government, but others exist in the provinces and territories.

Governments have passed legislation to protect the environment that places obligations and responsibilities on business. An example of such legislation is the federal government's *Canadian Environmental Protection Act*.[10] It is not uncommon for the legislation to require that an environmental audit be undertaken by corporations or governments involved in environmentally sensitive projects.

Government legislation often stipulates that an environmental assessment document, or report, be submitted to relevant departments of the environment for review and approval. Although legislation varies among the federal and provincial governments, the report usually has to contain a description of the project, a list of reasons for the project, alternatives to the project, an outline of how the project and its alternatives will affect the environment

RESPONSIBILITY
for Ethics **14.2**

Government Departments and Agencies

Some government departments and agencies that are influencing the environmental performance of Canadian corporations include the following:

- *Environment Canada*—This is the federal department responsible for the environment. The department operates various programs, tracks and reports on environmental issues, and administers environmental legislation and regulations. Similar departments exist in most provinces and territories.

- *Canadian Council of Ministers of the Environment (CCME)*—CCME comprises environment ministers from the federal, provincial, and territorial governments and meets at least once a year to discuss national environmental priorities and determine work to be carried out under the auspices of CCME.

- *Canadian Environmental Assessment Agency (CEAA)*—This agency was formed to provide high-quality environmental assessments that contribute to informed decision making relating to sustainable development.

Sources: Based on Environment Canada, "About us," http://www.ec.gc.ca/default .asp?lang=En&n=BD3CE17D-1; Canadian Council of Ministers of the Environment, "What is CCME?" http://www.ccme.ca/about/; and Canadian Environmental Assessment Agency, http://www.ceaa-acee.gc.ca/ default.asp?Lang=En&n=D75FB358-1.

directly or indirectly, an identification of the actions necessary to prevent those effects, and an evaluation of the advantages and disadvantages of the project to the environment and alternative ways to carry it out. The report is submitted for evaluation to an environmental assessment agency and often is followed by public hearings. Most corporations are now familiar with the environmental process and incorporate it into their decision making. Corporations also conduct audits and assessments even when not required by governments. Such audits often are of the whole organization and not restricted to particular projects or plants, and are designed to provide a "total picture" of the environmental circumstances of the corporation.

Another government initiative has implications for business and how it performs environmentally. The **Kyoto Protocol** is an agreement formulated by the United Nations Framework Convention on Climate Change where countries agreed to reduce emissions of carbon dioxide and other greenhouse gases to 6 percent below 1990 levels by 2012. The Protocol was signed by more than 160 countries and covers more than 55 percent of global greenhouse emissions. Canada ratified the Protocol in 2002. If the targets are to be met, corporations must cooperate with government and a commitment from stakeholders is necessary.

Kyoto Protocol An agreement formulated by the United Nations Framework Convention on Climate Change where countries agreed to reduce emissions of carbon dioxide and other greenhouse gases to 6 percent below 1990 levels by 2012.

In late 2009, an international meeting was held to formulate a new protocol, the Copenhagen Accord, but there was a lack of consensus and no agreement on reduction of CO_2 emissions, mitigation compensation to developing countries impacted by global warming, or a blueprint for a global market in emission credits. However, the Canadian government agreed to reducing greenhouse gases by 17 percent below its 2005 levels by 2020. To accomplish this target, Canada must reduce emissions by 178 million tonnes.

Recent developments with the federal government have raised concerns about its commitment to the environment. It withdrew from the Kyoto Protocol in December 2012. The reason given was the prohibitive estimated $14 billion cost to the economy. In April 2012, there were changes to the federal government's approach to environmental assessment. It announced a new plan, Responsible Resource Development, that would continue to have the highest standards to protect the environment, but also would encourage business to go ahead with projects to create jobs and economic growth. The plan would simplify the environmental assessment process by moving toward one review for a project. This would be accomplished by delegating some reviews to the provinces, and consolidating the reviews required by federal agencies. In addition, timelines would be set for reviews—12 months for a standard review and 24 months requiring an environmental public panel review—and there would be enhanced consultation with Aboriginal peoples.[11] The process would be strengthened in several ways, including higher monetary penalties for violations of federal legislation, increased numbers of inspectors with greater authority to check on whether conditions of a decision statement were met, and increased funding for the Canadian Environmental Assessment Agency.[12] Environmentalists claimed that this would reduce environmental protection, while business groups spoke in favour of the plan.

Finally, the *Report of the Commissioner of the Environment and Sustainable Development to the House of Commons* stated that expected reductions in emissions are nowhere near those projected goals and forecasts indicate that the government's targets under various plans will not be met.[13] Overall, it appears that the federal government is less committed to influencing through regulation the impact business has on the environment.

LO 14.5 ▸ Environmental NGO Influence

Environmental non-governmental organizations (ENGOs) Groups that hold shared values or attitudes about the challenges confronting the natural environment and advocate for changes to improve the condition of the environment.

Environmental non-governmental organizations (ENGOs) are groups that hold shared values or attitudes about the challenges confronting the natural environment and advocate for changes to improve the condition of the environment. Dozens of these groups exist in Canada; some are described in Responsibility for Ethics 14.3. The activities, policies, and initiatives of these groups should be monitored to assess the potential impact on the corporation. This monitoring function may be performed by the environmental affairs department, by the managers responsible for environmental matters, or by consultants.

The list in Responsibility for Ethics 14.3 illustrates the ENGOs' diversity of interests covering the concerns listed above. Environment groups are not always easy to deal with and use a variety of tactics. They can be involved in protests, blockades, boycotts, and sometimes make use of annual shareholders' meetings as platforms for protest. Canadian environmental groups are also often part of a global network of organizations. Protests about logging the Clayoquot Sound forests in British Columbia, as an example, are an alliance effort and have received impressive international attention.

A study identified the factors that lead ENGOs to target particular corporations. Hendry reviewed existing research on the environmental movement, stakeholder theory, and corporate social performance from which he formulated eight propositions that might explain how target corporations are selected. Five case studies of ENGOs were used to examine the validity of the propositions. Hendry found that the factors ranked as follows, from most influential to least:

- The greater the certainty among ENGOs that the firm is the source of an environmental impact, the more likely ENGOs are to target the firm.
- The more consequential the firm's actions are for the natural environment, the more likely ENGOs are to target the firm.
- The denser the relationships among the firm's ENGO stakeholders, the better able those ENGOs are to monitor the firm and share information about the firm, and the more likely those ENGOs are to target the firm collectively.
- The larger the firm, the more likely ENGOs will target the firm.

RESPONSIBILITY

for Ethics **14.3**

Examples of Environmental Non-Governmental Organizations (ENGOs)

- *Greenpeace Canada*—"Greenpeace is an independently funded organization that works to protect the environment. We challenge government and industry to halt harmful practices by negotiating solutions, conducting scientific research, introducing clean alternatives, carrying out peaceful acts of civil disobedience and educating and engaging the public." Recent campaigns have involved saving the boreal forest, stopping climate change, and opposing genetic engineering.

- *Energy Probe*—"Energy Probe is a consumer and environmental research team, active in the fight against nuclear power, and dedicated to resource conservation, economic efficiency, and effective utility regulation." Current priorities include restoring strong regulation of energy markets, promoting renewable energy sources, and stopping nuclear energy.

- *Friends of the Earth Canada*—"Friends of the Earth (FOE) Canada is a charitable, non-profit environmental organization. Our mission is to serve as a national voice for the environment, working with others to inspire the renewal of our communities and the earth, through research, education and advocacy." Campaigns include opposition to the use of genetically modified organisms (GMOs), enforcement of pollution regulations, and safety of water supplies.

- *Pollution Probe*—"Pollution Probe is a Canadian environmental organization that defines environmental problems through research, promotes understanding through education, and presses for practical solutions through advocacy." Its main program areas are air, water, climate change, and energy.

- *World Wildlife Fund Canada (WWF-Canada)*—WWF-Canada is a conservation organization supported by more than 50,000 Canadians. Its mission is to "stop the degradation of the planet's natural environment and to build a future in which humans live in harmony with nature." It main focus is to protect Canadian wilderness areas from damage.

Sources: Based on Greenpeace Canada, "About Greenpeace," http://www.greenpeace.org/canada/en/; Energy Probe, http://ep.probeinternational.org; Friends of the Earth Canada, http://www.foecanada.org/; Pollution Probe, "Who are we?" http://www.pollutionprobe.org; and WWF-Canada "About WWF," http://www.wwf.ca/about_us/.

- To maximize the effects of mimetic isomorphism, ENGOs target corporations that are influential in their organizational fields and therefore likely to be imitated.

- The more previous interactions between the firm and a particular ENGO, the more likely the ENGO will target the firm.

- The closer the firm is to consumers in the supply chain, the more likely ENGOs will target the firm.

- The more well-known the firm's brands are, the more likely ENGOs will target the firm.[14]

Although this discussion has focused on ENGOs targeting corporations, an increasing amount of cooperation or partnership is occurring between business and ENGOs. Many corporations recognize the contributions of individuals and organizations in their efforts to protect the environment, and examples have been used throughout the book. Nonetheless, some ENGOs are reluctant to cooperate with corporations as they do not trust them and view such cooperation as a "sell-out" to business.

>LO 14.6<   Market-Driven Environmentalism

In addition to environmental initiatives being driven by government or pressures from ENGOs, there is a market-driven response to the environment. **Standard environmentalism** occurs when government regulation is a necessary remedy for the market's failure to provide enough environmental amenities. On the other hand, **market environmentalism** exists where economic incentives created by the market are more effective at protecting the environment than is government intervention.[15] Not everyone agrees with the market approach and argues that regulation and new technologies are more effective.[16] Nevertheless, market approaches are being considered and to some extent implemented.

The market factors influencing environmentalism are economic growth, free trade, and property rights. The differences among these approaches are summarized in Table 14.2, and highlight why free-market environmentalism is a possible approach.

The debate on a market orientation to environmentalism is only beginning, and standard environmentalism dominates at this time. However, some examples of market-driven environmentalism exist in emissions trading (also referred to as carbon trading and carbon offsets).

Emissions trading is a system whereby corporations set targets for greenhouse gas reduction; if one corporation cannot meet its target it purchases carbon credits from those corporations that have met their targets (also referred to as cap and trade). The target is calculated in tons of carbon or equivalents emitted. The objective is to reduce overall emissions and is similar to a process proposed under the Kyoto Protocol among nations. Exchanges exist in some countries where the credits are traded, but no such exchange exists in Canada; the Montreal Exchange is considering one, to be called the Montreal Climate Exchange.[17] Canadian corporations are reluctant to become involved until the government decides on its policy toward the Kyoto Protocol.[18] The government has not endorsed the Kyoto targets and does not appear to have a policy to do so.

A variation on emissions trading is the system of offsets. Carbon emissions can be offset, or made neutral, through clean-energy projects—for example, wind generation, solar installations, geothermal plants, or biomass energy generation—that replace emissions

TABLE 14.2	*Differences between Standard and Market Environmentalism*	
Factors	**Standard**	**Free-Market**
Economic Growth	Viewed as destructive, because producing more creates more environmental harm	World is dynamic and two forces counteract harm: (1) increased income drives a demand for more environmental quality, and (2) stimulation of innovation that improves environmental quality
Free Trade	Considered part of the problem: prevents countries from following own higher levels of protection; and belief that rich countries exploit poor	Forces industries to be more competitive, accelerating adoption of newer, cleaner technologies; trade restrictions possible to protect environment under WTO; countries open to trade grow faster
Property Rights versus Regulation	Faith in government to solve problem for the public good	Powerful tool for protecting because ownership incentive creates stewardship incentive and gives individuals power to protect the environment.

Source: Summarized from Laura Jones, "A Different Kind of Environmentalist," *Fraser Forum,* April 2001, 4–6.

Offsets (emissions-reduction credits)
Credits purchased from other corporations or organizations to mitigate greenhouse gases released into the environment.

from polluting sources. Another possibility is to finance carbon removal activities, for example reforestation. **Offsets,** or **emissions-reduction credits,** are credits purchased from other corporations or organizations to mitigate greenhouse gases released into the environment. The funds generated are used to finance undertakings that will result in the reduction of emissions. Everyday Ethics 14.2 describes two corporations involved in the provision of offsets.

Everyday Ethics
14.2

Offset Providers

There are many offset providers operating and two examples are:
- *Zerofootprint*—Zerofootprint holds a diverse portfolio of Canadian-based, ISO-compliant offsets and offers access to carbon offsets in accordance with the world's leading carbon standards, including ISO 14064, UNFCCC Clean Development Mechanism, The Gold Standard, and Voluntary Carbon Registry. Offsetting is an interim measure used to deal with the ecological impact that is difficult to avoid. For example, if a business requires travel and travel is not yet "green," it can offset the impact with real, tangible, additional benefits to the environment. Using offsets in this way sets a price for the services the environment provides and that our economy doesn't reward.
- *Bullfrog Power*—By purchasing from wind and low-impact hydro generators, Bullfrog Power considers itself a completely green electricity retailer. These sources are viewed as producing clean, renewable electricity that is non-polluting and non–CO_2 emitting. Corporations or consumers access their electricity supply from Ontario's electricity grid but are actually purchasing it from Bullfrog.

Sources: Zerofootprint, "Zerofootprint Offsets," http://www.zerofootprint.net/products/offsets/; and Bullfrog Power, "About us," http://www.bullfrogpower.com.

Carbon capture and storage (CCS) Carbon emissions are captured and injected into underground formations.

Corporations are examining the possibility of storing their carbon emissions through **carbon capture and storage (CCS).** With CCS, carbon dioxide emissions are captured and injected into underground formations. The practice is sometimes referred to as carbon sequestration or geosequestration. Downsides are that it is expensive, because the infrastructures do not exist, the underground storage may weaken, it requires a large amount of energy to implement, and it needs a 1,000-year monitoring program. Alberta's Energy Resources and Conservation Board has approved Shell Canada Limited's CSS carbon capture and storage project north of Edmonton, but imposed 23 conditions regarding additional data collection, analysis, and reporting.[19]

Controversy surrounds market-driven environmentalism. Its effectiveness is questioned; that is, whether there is an actual reduction of emissions. It is viewed as image polishing with no real commitment to the environment. Corporations are able to continue damaging the environment by avoiding addressing their environmental problems. Effective trading systems have not yet been developed, and some countries' governments are not committed to emissions reduction.

LO 14.7   Managing Responses to Environmental Concerns

Whether corporations are forced by governments, pressured by environmental non-governmental organizations, or involved in market-environmentalism, managers must adapt the corporation by making changes to its organizational structure and by identifying its strategic approach.

Management positions and committees should be created to deal with the environment issue. Structural arrangements are put in place to ensure environmental matters are addressed starting at the top with the board of directors; some boards have environmental committees. It is key to have top management commitment so that there are practical principles to guide the corporation's environmental efforts, to integrate environmental affairs with operations, and to encourage environmental professionals to meet mounting environmental requirements.

Some business enterprises are hiring senior managers and other staff to focus on environmental matters. Senior managers' positions carry titles such as vice-president, environment; environmental director; corporate manager of environmental affairs; and environmental coordinator. In addition to senior managers there are numerous titles for staff with various specialties in the environment, for example vegetation management biologist, hydrogeologist, and site remediation engineer. One of the challenges is to find individuals with the appropriate environmental expertise and knowledge and adequate managerial capabilities, as a combination of managerial and technical expertise is necessary.

The issue of centralization versus decentralization of authority is also a challenge. In large, diversified corporations it is necessary to have top management commitment, but at the same time environmental matters are usually addressed at the unit or divisional levels. Often committees are formed to provide interlocks between the top and bottom of the organization, and to coordinate efforts across functions or divisions. Such a coordinating environmental group forms policies, establishes standards, and carries out planning strategies.

From a strategic perspective, corporations can choose among the following strategies in their approach to environmental concerns:

Greenwashing Occurs when the corporation does not seriously address environmental issues but merely talks about how it does, or takes token actions rather than really solving the problem.

- *Token response*—The focus here is on damage control as problems arise and attempts are made to fix them. This is a reactive strategy still adopted by some corporations, but given the increased attention to the environment by many stakeholders it is not recommended. Another token response is **greenwashing,** where the corporation does not seriously address environmental issues but merely talks about how it does, or takes token actions rather than really solving the problem. According to an environmental marketing agency, there are seven sins of greenwashing: hidden trade-offs, no proof, vagueness, worshipping false labels, irrelevance, lesser of two evils, and fibbing.[20] Today, greenwashing is usually disclosed quickly by consumers, regulators, or competitors.

- *Compliance with laws and regulations*—Concern about exposure to lawsuits and prosecution has motivated many directors and senior executives to adopt strategies of compliance. Some enterprises continue to ignore legislative and regulatory requirements, but those companies that do follow policies of compliance establish programs and organizational structures to implement and monitor their compliance with the legislation and regulations. Legal requirements or the government requirements ethic are the bases for the corporation's strategy.

- *Comprehensive environmental management*—Under this strategy, management seeks to gain a competitive advantage by taking an active stance on environmental issues. Simple compliance with legislation and regulation is not sufficient. In these companies, everyone becomes involved in environmental management. Environmental issues are integrated into all aspects of corporate management. Environmental objectives are set for key operating activities; they are not left to just the "environmental services department." There is internal and external corporate reporting and the development of environmental policies and codes of conduct.

This strategy has been widely adopted within certain industries in some industrialized countries.

- *Sustainable development*—Businesses that follow this strategy integrate the concepts of sustainable development into their business strategies and environmental policies. Sustainable development is a natural extension of many corporate environmental policies. It requires that management consider the effect of its activities on the environment and on the long-term interests and needs of stakeholders. These enterprises engage in a different type of dialogue and consultation with their stakeholders. Their business strategies and activities are designed to balance the need for financial returns with the needs of the environment and various stakeholder groups. Mechanisms such as advisory panels and committees are established to facilitate communication with stakeholders. Corporate reporting expands in relation to the needs of stakeholders. They may also engage independent auditors to attest to their report's accuracy and reliability.[21]

Corporations need comprehensive environmental policies and programs, referred to as environmental management systems (EMS). These plans ensure that environmental practices become an important component of the corporation's overall strategy. While an EMS has an internal focus, green supply chain management (GSCM) focuses on making sure suppliers share the same commitment to the environment (supply chains are discussed in Chapter 12). EMS and GSCM allow for instilling a culture of continuous improvement inside and beyond the corporation. It also is important to plan strategically for the long term by establishing long-term goals, identifying opportunities to further reduce the impact on the environment, and taking advantage of these opportunities.[22]

The National Round Table on the Environment and the Economy (NRT) developed a strategy for success for corporations in designing programs in changing climate. The three phases of the strategy are presented in Figure 14.1. The NRT points out that the dashboard

FIGURE 14.1   *NRT Dashboard for Business Success in a Changing Climate*

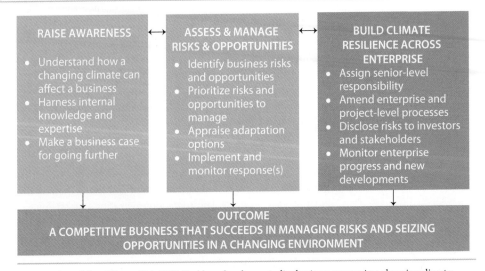

Source: Adapted from Figure 14.1, NRT Dashboard and case studies business success in a changing climate, *Facing the Elements: Building Business Resilience in a Changing Environment/Case Studies*, Ottawa: National Round Table on the Environment and the Economy, Cat. No. En133-40/5-2012E-PDF, p. 13. Used with permission.

is not prescriptive, as the appropriate strategy will depend on the corporation's risk exposure, capabilities, and current knowledge of problems and solutions.

No matter which approach or management system is used, corporations must understand and plan for the impact they are having on the environment. Research suggests that environmental practices and performance are key elements to corporate success, including achieving market leadership and keeping ahead of competitors. A study found that environmental activities enabled corporations to stay ahead of competition.[23] In conclusion, according to research by the Network for Business Sustainability, a corporation should consider environmental impacts and develop policies for reasons that include reducing costs, responding to investor demands, facilitating regulatory approaches and mitigating operational risk, hiring the best employees, and meeting consumer demand for "green" products and services.[24] These are convincing reasons for responding to environmental concerns.

LO 14.8 The "Greening" of Business Functions

Another approach to viewing a corporation's response to environmental concerns is by functional areas; that is, finance, marketing, human resources, and production. Although this approach does not cover all areas of a corporation's activities, it does address the main ones.

Financial Management

Financial management now includes consideration of environmental factors and involves many aspects, for example:

- Accounting guidelines require companies to unequivocally state on their balance sheets the estimated liability for restoring capital assets to environmentally sound conditions.
- "Eco-insurance" products are now available in response to the liability associated with environmental problems.
- The banking industry has also been affected by the environmental issue. Environmental assessments are necessary to determine the influence on financial performance and liability.
- Investments are being screened for environmental performance. Individual investors usually seek out environmentally friendly mutual funds. To obtain information on this aspect of performance, institutional investors use sustainability indices described in Responsibility for Ethics 14.4. An example of how seriously institutional investors are viewing climate change is given in Everyday Ethics 14.3.
- Shareholders unhappy with a corporation's environmental policy may hurt its financial performance, maybe more than the actions of ENGOs. A concerned shareholder can submit a resolution at the annual meeting arguing that the corporation is increasing its environmental risk and thus the financial risk to shareholders. Investment analysts are more influenced by such resolutions than by the actions of ENGOs such as boycotts, protests, lawsuits, demonstrations, or sit-ins to raise awareness of a corporation's poor environmental record.[25]

Financial regulators also recommend greater disclosure of environmental information. The Ontario Securities Commission (OSC) issued National Instrument 51–102, *Continuous Disclosure Obligations,* which requires public corporations to disclose information about environmental matters. The following summarizes the OSC's findings:

1. *Environmental liabilities*—Corporations should quantify the accounting estimate where quantitative information is reasonably available and would provide useful information

RESPONSIBILITY
for Ethics 14.4

Sustainability Indices

Corporations are being evaluated on their environmental sustainability activities by several indices, including the Citigroup Global Markets Sustainability Mining Index, the Dow Jones Sustainability Index, and the Innovest Strategic Value Advisors Global 100 Ranking. These indices are finding that a positive relationship exists between a corporation's environmental practices and profitability. Canadian corporations that have ranked high on these indices include the major banks and insurance companies; base metal producers such as Alcan and Inco; petroleum producers such as Suncor, Nexen, Shell Canada, and Encana; and pipeline companies Enbridge and Trans Canada Corporation.

In March 2010, the Toronto Stock Exchange announced the first Canadian sustainability index, the S&P/TSX Clean Technology Index. The index is designed to measure the performance of corporations listed on the TSX whose core business is in the development and deployment of green technologies. Corporations were selected for inclusion based on their commitment to five environmental themes: production and distribution of renewable energy; specialized suppliers of renewable energy; energy efficiency; waste reduction and water management; and low-impact materials and products. Examples of corporations included are Westport Innovations Inc., Cascades Inc., and Ballard Power Systems Inc.

Sources: Citibank, "The environment," http://www.citigroup.com/citi/environment/; Dow Jones Sustainability Indexes, http://www.sustainability-index.com/; "Innovest identifies the 100 most sustainable companies in the world," http://www.csrwire.com/press_releases/22978-Innovest-Identifies-the-100-Most-Sustainable-Companies-in-the-World; and "S&P/TSX clean technology index," http://www.tmx.com/en/news_events/news/news_releases/2010/3-25-2010_TSX-CleanTechnologyIndex.html.

Everyday Ethics
14.3

The Carbon Disclosure Project (CDP)

Several Canadian financial institutions are among the 665 institutional investors who collaborate in the Carbon Disclosure Project (CDP), an independent not-for-profit organization holding the largest database of primary corporate climate change information in the world. Its goals are to tackle climate change through the reduction of greenhouse emissions, to promote sustainable water use by business and cities, and to mitigate environmental risk in corporate supply chains. The largest corporations in the world are sent questionnaires requesting disclosure of information on their greenhouse gas emissions. The investors view the information as critical in helping them decide how to allocate capital. The data are also made available to corporations, public-sector organizations, government bodies, academics, and the public.

Two hundred of Canada's largest corporations were surveyed each year and a separate report prepared, *The Carbon Disclosure Project Canada 200 Report*. Results indicate that Canada's largest corporations in both the low- and high-carbon-impact sectors have implemented significant initiatives to prepare for successfully operating in a carbon-constrained world. The highest-ranking Canadian corporations by quality and comprehensiveness of CDP included Suncor Energy Inc., Newmont Mining Corporation, and the Bank of Montreal.

Sources: Carbon Disclosure Project, https://www.cdproject.net/en-US/Pages/HomePage.aspx; and *CDP Canada 200 Climate Change Report 2012*, https://www.cdproject.net/en-us/whatwedo/pages/canada.aspx.

to investors. Corporations should also disclose potential environmental liabilities not reflected in financial statements.

2. *Asset retirement obligations*—Corporations are required to identify asset retirement obligations in their financial statements. Environmental examples would be the remediation costs for a mining operation or the disposal of hazardous waste.

3. *Financial and operational effects of environmental protection requirements*—The costs of these requirements should be quantified and the impact of these costs on financial statements identified.

4. *Environmental policies fundamental to operations*—Corporations are required to describe the policies and the steps taken to implement them.

5. *Environmental risks*—These must be identified so that investors can assess the impact on operational and financial performance.

The OSC concluded that a meaningful discussion of material environmental matters is important to achieve fair presentation of the corporation's financial condition. The risks and liabilities associated with the environment must now receive more attention by boards of directors and audit committees. Critics point out that quantifying the risks will be difficult as there are no agreed-upon standards of measurement.[26]

Marketing

Green seems to be the most popular colour with business today, since it expresses society's concern for the environment. **Green marketing** involves selling environmentally friendly goods and services to consumers. Providing such products is necessary for many corporations if they are to survive, and doing so can provide a new opportunity to make money. Responsibility for Ethics 14.5 describes how Canadians can be "green" consumers.

RESPONSIBILITY
for Ethics (14.5)

The "Green" Consumer

Canadian consumers are expressing an interest in being green; that is, making purchasing decisions that will reduce harm to the environment. A Harris/Decima poll released in August 2009 found that over 70 percent of respondents said environmental consciousness has become more important to them in the past few years. The same survey found that 73 percent said they were making more of an effort to be environmentally conscious in 2009 than in the previous year. There is an issue around how this is done—through rewards or costs. *The Globe and Mail* asked readers, "What's more likely to make you environmentally responsible, penalties for non-green actions or rewards for eco-friendly choices?" Twenty-four percent indicated penalties would impact choices, while 76 percent chose rewards.

Canadians are able to practise what they believe in. The Energy Star label identifies the most energy efficient products, and the Ecologo label identifies products or services that improve energy efficiency, reduce hazardous by-products, and use recycled materials. Green consumer guides are provided by several Web sites, including that of *Corporate Knights* magazine. Organic foods are available in supermarkets, green electricity can be purchased in some areas, and energy-efficient hybrid cars are on the market. Consumers are asking for environmentally friendly products, and businesses are responding.

Sources: Kate Lunau, "The eco-sell," *Maclean's,* October 12, 2009, 50–51; Thomas Homer-Dixon, "The enticements of green carrots," *The Globe and Mail,* August 8, 2009, A13; and *Corporate Knights,* "Green consumer guide," http://www.corporateknights.ca/special-reports/71-green-consumer-guide.html.

Dozens of so-called "green" products are on the market: liquid soap products that offer plastic refill pouches to reduce packaging waste; coffee filters made without bleach; recyclable or degradable trash bags; dishwasher detergent that is phosphate-free; and foam plates and cups without chlorofluorocarbons. Packaging is an obvious area where the four Rs—reduce, reuse, recycle, and recover—can be practised, and is getting considerable attention.

The federal government has an Environment Choice program certifying products that are environmentally friendly, examples of which are re-refined oil, insulation material made from recycled paper, and types of household and office products made from recycled plastic. Consumers have access to substantial information on the environmental friendliness of products.

The issue remains as to whether consumers are willing to pay the increased prices often necessary for many green products. Research has found that the attributes of the sustainable products influence these purchase decisions. Attributes like safe and gentle were valued for products like baby shampoo; attributes like strong and tough were preferred when purchasing car shampoo. Also, consumers were more likely to use green products when being watched.[27] The latter point was found to also be the case in other studies. Although consumers expected corporations to address environmental issues, they liked to give the impression that they are environmentally conscious when this may not be so. Consumers responded more positivity to advertisements informing them how they can save money than to those advertisements promoting the benefits to the environment.[28] It is difficult for business to anticipate how consumers will respond to environmentally friendly products.

Human Resources

Eco-friendly policies and practices are influencing the recruitment and retention of employees. Such policies are emphasized in recruitment when prospective employees ask recruiters about the employer's environmental practices.[29] Students in particular are searching for environmentally friendly workplaces.

A green workplace is even more important in retention of employees especially in tight employment markets. Employees satisfied with their employer's environment policies are proud of working for the company. Those employees not satisfied are likely to leave if they can find a green workplace.[30] Some of the practices that create an environmentally friendly workplace are listed in Table 14.3.

The benefits to employers of a green workplace include improved employee morale, a stronger public image, increased consumer confidence, a positive bottom line, and healthier employees. Barriers to a green workplace are implementation and maintenance costs, lack of top management support, lack of employee commitment, and concern for lower employee productivity. One study found that one-half of corporations surveyed had environmentally friendly workplace policies and believed that they benefited from them.[31] Another study found that when employees believe their employer is committed to the environment, they are more likely to become involved in eco-initiatives such as recycling and saving energy. In order to encourage such initiatives, management should develop environmental policies and communicate them to employees.[32] There appears to be a trend toward green workplace policies and practices.

There is increasing coverage in the media about environmentally friendly employment and Aon-Hewitt, a human resources consulting firm, annually identifies "Canada's Greenest Employers."[33] Of interest to students is the high demand for individuals with skills and experience in the green or environmental sectors.[34] An indication of the interest in "green" jobs is a job site that specializes in environment-related employment.[35]

 Want to learn more about **environmental jobs**? Go to CONNECT.

TABLE 14.3	*Practices and Policies to Create the Green Workplace*

- Offering a recycling program for office products, including donating and discounting used office furniture to employees or charities, and banning disposables such as plastic utensils and paper cups and plates.

- Conserving energy by using energy efficient lighting systems and equipment, and installing automatic shutoffs of idle equipment.

- Reducing consumption of paper, packaging, and other office supplies, including not printing electronic documents.

- Encouraging employees to be more environmentally friendly by promoting walking, biking, and using public transport to work or car-pooling. Providing bike stands, showers, and fare subsidies.

- Creating a pesticide-free green landscape with trees, lawns, and gardens.

- Reducing emissions through less travel and climate control, and striving for carbon neutrality.

- Purchasing renewable energy credits.

- Conducting virtual meetings through video and teleconferencing thus reducing travel.

- Using natural lighting, with windows and skylights.

- Investing in community environmental initiatives.

- Requiring suppliers to be green.

- Publically disclosing sustainability initiatives through reports that identify objectives and detail the progress made in achieving them.

- Convincing employees of program benefits and top management support.

- Providing incentives for environmentally friendly behaviour.

- Organizing employee committees to provide advice on practices.

Operations

Business is trying to implement environmentally friendly processes and technologies into all aspects of operations or the production function. Environmental issues have added complexity to supply chains, with pressure coming from consumers, competitors, employees, NGOs, and governments. Three areas of activity have been briefly mentioned: pollution reduction, waste management and recycling, and energy conservation. Everyday Ethics 14.4 describes one standard of certification for environmentally friendly practices in the construction industry.

All Canadians pollute the environment, and the volume of garbage is growing faster than the Canadian population. Pollution comes from many sources, including aerosols, hydrocarbons, automobile exhaust, untreated sewage, and pesticides. Even packaging is a form of pollution; for example, many convenience goods are packaged in throwaway containers. Often pollution is attributed to large business enterprises that dump wastes into the water, air, or landfills. But consumers also create pollution. Thus, corporations are concerned with reducing not only their own pollution activities but also those of consumers.

Waste management is the handling and disposal of unwanted materials left after industrial production or individual consumption. The traditional method of getting rid of our garbage has been to bury it in landfills. These are easy to operate and are relatively inexpensive. But the problem exists of finding locations for new landfill sites: no one wants to live near a dump. As a result, many governments and businesses are developing methods to reuse or manage waste. Research and development and design take the impact of particular materials on the environment into account. Waste from the manufacturing process can be recycled as an input in the production of another product. The reduction of waste is sought,

Everyday Ethics

14.4

"Green" Construction

The Canada Green Building Council's (CaGBC) mission is to lead and accelerate the transformation to high-performing, healthy green buildings, homes, and communities throughout Canada. It works to change industry standards, develop best design practices and guidelines, and advocate for green buildings.

CaGBC's mission is accomplished through the Leadership in Energy and Environmental Design (LEED) Green Building Rating System™. This system encourages and accelerates global adoption of sustainable green building and development practices through the creation and implementation of universally understood and accepted tools and performance criteria. A whole-building approach to sustainability is promoted in five key areas of human and environmental health: sustainable site development; water efficiency; energy efficiency; materials selection; and indoor environmental quality.

LEED is a third-party certification program and an internationally accepted benchmark for the design, construction, and operation of high-performance green buildings. It provides building owners and operators the tools they need to have an immediate and measurable impact on their building's performance.

Source: Canada Green Building Council, http://www.cagbc.org.

but there is also emphasis on recycling, the retrieval and reuse of suitable waste material such as paper, glass, metal, and plastics. An example of effective waste disposal is given in Everyday Ethics 14.5.

Everyday Ethics

14.5

Turning Waste into Profitable Products

Ensyn Corporation is involved in two activities: developing industrial applications for technology and applying them to the biomass sector. One example of Ensyn's activities is a biomass refinery in Renfrew, Ontario. It converts green tons of wood daily into natural resin products, co-polymers, other chemicals, liquid fuel, and green electricity. Biomass refers to plant and animal wastes, which have traditionally been burned for energy but now are being transformed into products. Another Ensyn plant converts wood sawdust into liquid fuel and chemicals such as resins for plywood, emulsifiers for asphalt, and natural food colourings.

Source: Ensyn Corporation, http://www.ensyn.com/about.htm.

Once a good has been used by the consumer, it can be disposed of as waste in a landfill or it can become a recyclable product. As a recyclable product, two alternative means of disposal exist: incineration or reuse. Incineration can be used to generate energy, which in turn can be utilized by consumers or manufacturers, although the process discharges some pollution to the environment.

Reuse involves collecting and sorting items, and is often performed by corporations. New technology for processing recycled materials and the availability of markets for recycled materials are making recycling businesses more viable. But problems still exist. The public has been so enthusiastic about recycling materials that the capacity of recycling facilities has been overtaxed. Markets for recycled materials have not grown fast enough to keep pace with the collection of recyclable materials. Once processing of the materials has occurred, they are recycled as raw materials in the manufacturing process.

Canadians are great users and abusers of energy, and growth in energy consumption has been levelling off only recently. As consumption rises, additional sources of energy must be found, placing demands on the environment. Hydro sites and petroleum production areas must be established. Furthermore, preserving the environment adds costs to energy that consumers may not be aware of.

Business is taking many actions to conserve energy. Companies are reducing their consumption in producing and marketing goods and services as well as in the construction of energy-efficient buildings. Also, corporations are introducing products that will enable consumers to conserve energy.

LO 14.9 Measuring and Reporting on Environmental Sustainability

Business can use several measures of sustainability to audit, monitor, and evaluate its environmental performance. These measures have been developed by business organizations, non-governmental organizations, and government agencies; some of these are described in Responsibility for Ethics 14.6.

RESPONSIBILITY
for Ethics **14.6**

Environmental Sustainability Measures and Standards

- *Coalition for Environmentally Responsible Economies (Ceres)*—Ceres is an organization comprising investors and environmental organizations who work with corporations to address sustainability challenges such as climate change. It was involved with the launch of the Global Reporting Initiative (GRI), publishes research reports, and assists in sustainability reporting. (As a matter of interest, Ceres is the Roman goddess of fertility and agriculture.)

- *International Organization for Standardization ISO 14000*—ISO is an international non-governmental organization comprising standards institutions in 157 countries. The ISO 14000 standard evaluates environmental management—that is, the efforts by a corporation to minimize the harmful effects of its activities on the environment—and stresses the need for continual improvement in its environmental performance.

- *International Institute for Sustainable Development (IISD)*—IISD is a Canadian-based, not-for-profit organization promoting change toward sustainable development. It is working to develop, enhance, and apply measurement and assessment tools to assist business in better managing environmental issues.

- *Canadian Sustainability Indicators Network (CSIN)*—The purpose of this organization is to enhance the progress toward sustainability development by encouraging the development and use of sustainability indicators. CSIN is supported by various governments and foundations.

- *Environmental and Sustainable Development Indicators Initiative (ESDI), National Round Table on the Environment and the Economy*—ESDI was a three-year multi-stakeholder program aimed at developing a small set of credible and understandable indicators to track whether Canada's current economic activities threaten the way of life for future generations.

Sources: Based on Ceres, "About us," http://www.ceres.org/about-us; International Organization for Standardization, "About ISO," http://www.iso.org/iso/about.htm; International Institute for Sustainable Development, "About IISD," http://www.iisd.org/about/; Canadian Sustainability Indicators Network (CSIN), "Welcome to CSIN," http://www.csin-rcid.ca/about.aspx; and National Round Table on the Environment and the Economy, "About," http://www.nrtee-trnee.com/eng/.

The indicators used to evaluate environmental performance are extensive. Examples include the following:

- Type and amount of materials used to provide the good or service, and cooperation with suppliers
- Source of energy and efficiency of use
- Source and quality of water
- Impact on biodiversity; that is, impact on location of operations, land use, nature, and species
- Reduction of emissions, effluents, and waste including hazardous materials
- Design of products and services to minimize impact on the environment
- Compliance with environmental regulations
- Use of efficient transportation mode[36]

Chapter 9 discussed the approaches to measuring and reporting corporate social responsibility and sustainability. Most of the measures discussed there apply to environmental sustainability reporting. An example is the Network for Business Sustainability's guide for measuring environmental impacts. The guide comprises four steps: step 1 defines success by identifying pressures and establishing goals for addressing them; step 2 decides what to measure for materials, energy, water, biodiversity, emissions, products and services, compliance, and transport; and step 3 determines how to measure impacts, for example through life cycle analysis or environmental footprint, and to value them through ecosystem service valuation, or environmental input–output modelling. Finally, in step 4 the environmental measures must be incorporated into management decision making.[37]

Many corporations have prepared environmental policy statements or codes. The purpose of environmental codes is much the same as it is for codes of ethics: to increase awareness of the issue throughout the organization and to signal to other stakeholders that the enterprise is active in this area. Corporations are being recognized for their efforts at minimizing their impact on the environment. Responsibility for Ethics 14.7 describes one such Canadian award; several international ones also exist.

RESPONSIBILITY
for Ethics **14.7**

Awards for Environmental Practices and Reporting

GLOBE Foundation of Canada is a private, non-profit organization created to help environmental firms, corporate environmental managers, and financial institutions capitalize on investment opportunities in the business of the environment. It gives awards for environmental excellence in several categories; the 2012 winners are listed below.

- The Corporate Award for Environmental Excellence—Unilever Canada
- The Award for Excellence in Emerging Technology—Terragon Environmental Technologies Inc.
- The Award for Technology Innovation and Application—Pulse Energy
- The Award for Excellence in Urban Sustainability—Waterfront Toronto/Halsall Associates
- The Award for Sustainability in Finance—Royal Bank of Canada
- The Award for Best Green Retailing Practices—Canadian Tire Corp.
- The Next Gen Entrepreneur Award—Eden Full, Roseicollis Technologies

Sources: GLOBE Foundation of Canada, http://www.globe.ca; and "GLOBE awards," http://www.theglobeawards .ca/ and http://www.theglobeawards.ca/winners.

Many corporations are assisted in practising environmental ethics and sustainability using standards or codes established by industry associations.

LO 14.10   Dissenting Views on the Environment

Not everyone agrees that business should be playing a leading role in protecting the environment. Some business journalists are particularly critical of sustainability for a variety of reasons:

- The concept is difficult to define and understand.

- It means stopping, or constraining, economic development.

- It implies that capitalism is unsustainable and morally lacking.

- It lacks understanding of markets and the moralistic system of markets.

- Executives are being misled into responding to it as a social issue, and the interest many have is merely as a public relations exercise.[38]

Many researchers have challenged environmentalism and sustainability; a prominent critic's view is described in Responsibility for Ethics 14.8.

RESPONSIBILITY
for Ethics **14.8**

Bjørn Lomborg and The Skeptical Environmentalist

Dissenting views on the state of the environment exist. A controversial one was presented by Bjørn Lomborg, a Danish statistician, in his book *The Skeptical Environmentalist: Measuring the Real State of the World*. He challenged widely held beliefs that the global climate was getting worse, and even claimed that it was actually improving. The main points of his argument were that green activists and the media are overstating the environmental problems, technology that can reduce the damage is improving, Western lifestyles are environmentally sustainable, and the Kyoto Protocol was bad policy and too costly. He used statistics to support his position and was accused of misleading research; these charges were later dismissed. In 2004, he and others organized the Copenhagen Consensus Center, a think tank that increases awareness of the best ways to spend development money on addressing the major challenges facing the planet. In 2012, these challenges were as follows: armed conflict, biodiversity, chronic disease, climate change, education, hunger and malnutrition, infectious diseases, natural disasters, population growth, and water and sanitation. A second book, *Cool It: The Skeptical Environmentalist's Guide to Global Warming*, is also a film documentary and makes the case that many of the expensive and elaborate solutions to climate change will have little impact on the environment. Lomborg believes most solutions are based on emotional rather than strictly scientific assumptions.

Source: Bjørn Lomborg Web site, http://lomborg.com, and Copenhagen Consensus Center Web site, http://www.copenhagenconsensus.com/Default.aspx?ID=1626.

Adding to these dissenting views are the mixed reactions received from consumers. It is not easy to interpret public opinion, as illustrated by consumption patterns, concern for jobs, and the reluctance to pay for improvements.

- Despite polls that confirm the concern Canadians have for the environment, consumers still purchase environmentally unfriendly products. Canadians still lead the world in energy consumption and generate the most household garbage.

- Canadians express strong views about conserving forests, reducing pollution, and halting hydroelectric projects. But if job losses result, their concerns about the environment are reduced.

- As most actions to improve environmental quality cost money, the issue becomes one of who will pay—that is, government, business, or consumers. Ultimately, the consumer and/or taxpayer pays, and many are unwilling to assume the costs. Most direct charges to consumers are resented.

Public opinion may express concern for the environment, but this concern is not always reflected in consumption patterns, the desire for jobs at the expense of the environment, and the reluctance to pay. These dissenting views leave corporations and managers uncertain about the course of action to follow.

A poll of Canadian business leaders also indicated that they are not serious about the environment. Only 12 percent had a policy for auditing the impact of greenhouse gases from their operations. While 83 percent thought a corporation's responsibility was to earn a return for shareholders, 56 percent did indicate that corporations had an obligation to adopt low-emission environmental practices. Many of the respondents doubted the reliability of the science behind climate change, and some thought Kyoto was a scam.[39]

The contradictions are illustrated further by what appears to be a paradox. Everyday Ethics 14.6 gives some common inconsistencies in various initiatives that are promoted as being good for the environment but also have unintended consequences. Some researchers have argued that a greater environmental paradox exists. The Millennium Ecosystem Assessment concluded that the capacity of ecosystems to provide services is low, which should mean that

Everyday Ethics
14.6

Paradoxical Environmentalism

Various stakeholders, governments, NGOs, or consumers often advocate for initiatives they claim will reduce damage to the environment. Many of these initiatives have unintended consequences that do not lead to the results expected. In some, there are trade-offs that reduce the benefits alleged to be gained. These contradictions challenge the course of action for business. The following are some examples that may be labelled "showcase environmentalism" in that they do not result in the environmental benefits claimed:

- *Fluorescent (CF) versus incandescent light bulbs*—Incandescent bulbs may use less energy but they contain mercury and the disposal of these bulbs has not yet been resolved.
- *Electric versus gasoline cars*—Electric cars reduce petroleum emissions but require a lot of energy to make the necessary batteries, not to mention the copper and aluminum needed to build them.
- *Plastic versus other bags*—Single-use plastic bags are environmentally unfriendly. However, decomposable plastic is available. Reusable cloth bags can become contaminated with repeated use.
- *Organic versus regular milk*—Fewer hormones and antibiotics are used in organic milk production but the low yields results in more cows being needed, which requires more feed and produces more methane.
- *Local versus global food*—It is claimed that local food is safer and reduces transportation costs. However, consumer choice is reduced and prices are higher with less competition.

human well-being is declining. The Human Development Index, which measures literacy, life expectancy, and income, is improving in both rich and poor countries. The researchers are questioning why this is the case and what the implications are for society.[40]

> **LO 14.11**   ## The Environment: Corporate Opportunities and Challenges

Corporations face many challenges as they attempt to develop an environmental ethic and practise sustainable development. These challenges are both opportunities and threats.

The reputations of corporations that make an effort to address the environmental issue are most likely enhanced, and they gain greater prominence in the marketplace. Customers are attracted, as investors might be, after a positive investment screening for environmental matters. Costs are reduced through recycling of materials, better control of pollution, energy conservation, and lower insurance. More competent staff might be attracted, and the enterprise becomes better integrated with the local community.

Business opportunities emerge from the development of new technologies or expertise to address environmental concerns. More efficient ways of producing products are found and better products are marketed. There is increasing evidence that responding to environmental concerns need not be costly, and that profitability can even be improved. The environment itself is an opportunity for some who provide the technology or expertise to address the concerns. Environmental product manufacturers include those that provide equipment for water pollution control, air pollution control, solid waste management, measuring instruments, chemicals for pollution control, and noise control. Examples of environmental services include waste handling, consultation services, assessment and control functions, laboratory services, and environmental research.

Several challenges for corporations exist if the environment is ignored. The corporate image deteriorates, and revenues may suffer as customers prefer products and services less damaging to the environment. Investors become more difficult to attract as the enterprises cannot meet the criteria for environmental and ethical screening. Material and production costs may increase faster than for corporations practising reduction and recycling. The financial penalties are becoming higher and directors and managers are being held legally responsible for pollution. Insurance premiums are high for corporations that do not reduce their pollution risk. Alienation may occur from the local community, and failure to act may provoke stricter legislation and regulation.

The management of the natural environment is a challenge for managers. Business must take on some of the responsibility for the environment, and many have already. For others, it is a matter of what type of response is appropriate and when. As an ideal, corporations should be evolving an environmental ethic to enhance sustainable development in society.

Your advice to Vivian . . .

This vignette illustrated how an everyday purchase decision can involve several economic, social, and environmental issues. The decision also illustrates a dilemma, and is a paradox for a consumer facing complex and contradictory information. It is difficult for consumers to be aware of all the issues, much less to research them extensively; this is but one decision among many on any given trip to the grocery store. The ultimate decision is up to the consumer because there is no authority to provide a definitive answer.

SUMMARY

- Concern for the natural environment is widespread in society and business has a responsibility to respond. Responding to this concern is challenging as many stakeholders and issues influence corporations. (LO 14.1)

- Corporations must develop an environmental ethic or set of values relating to their practices toward sustainable development in the economy. Each corporation must develop strategies and practices to meet its own and its stakeholders' needs today while ensuring that future resources will be available. (LO 14.2)

- Environmental concerns are summarized in the descriptions of several topics: acid rain, air pollution, ecosystems, energy production and consumption, nature and wildlife, ozone, pollution, waste management, and water quality. Together these topics influence climate change or global warming. (LO 14.3)

- Governments have implemented environmental policies through legislation and regulations and the establishment of various agencies. Environmental assessments are now commonplace. However, the federal government is reducing its regulation of environmental impacts. (LO 14.4)

- Influence of a different type comes from environmental non-governmental organizations (ENGOs). Hundreds of such organizations exist and corporations are learning how to respond to or cooperate with them. (LO 14.5)

- Another possibility is to leave solutions to environmental concerns to market-driven initiatives. Instead of being required by governments to respond, it is argued that relying on market forces is more effective. Emissions trading and offsets are two examples. (LO 14.6)

- When corporations act on environmental concerns, the responses must be managed with appropriate organizational structures, environment management systems, and corporate strategies. (LO 14.7)

- As corporations attempt to respond to environmental concerns, there are implications for all the major functions of business: financial management, marketing, human resources, and production. (LO 14.8)

- Many sustainability measures and standards have been developed by ENGOs, business organizations, and industry associations. Indicators that measure a corporation's environmental performance are used. Many corporations issue elaborate environmental reports. (LO 14.9)

- Dissenting views on the environment are held in the business community and by other stakeholders. Not all businesspersons believe that climate change is a problem. Even public attitudes are mixed in that surveys indicate consumers are concerned, but this concern is not always reflected in purchasing decisions. This inconsistency complicates business decision making. (LO 14.10)

- The environment presents corporations with opportunities and threats. But, many corporations are developing an environmental ethic that achieves sustainable development. (LO 14.11)

KEY TERMS

Commons
Environmental ethic
Sustainable development
Business sustainable development
Acid rain
Ecosystem
Ozone

Waste management
Climate change (global warming)
Kyoto Protocol
Environmental non-governmental organizations (ENGOs)
Standard environmentalism
Market environmentalism

Emissions trading
Offsets (emissions-reduction credits)
Carbon capture and storage (CCS)
Greenwashing
Green marketing

CRITICAL THINKING AND DISCUSSION QUESTIONS

1. Why is business's approach to environmental concerns so challenging for managers?

2. Is the concept of the commons applicable today? Give examples.

3. What is the relationship between sustainable development and climate change?

4. What should be government's role in influencing business's response to environmental concerns?

5. What should be the relationship between corporations and ENGOs?

6. How can market forces help achieve sustainable development?

7. What strategic approach should a corporation implement regarding society's concerns about the environment?

8. How does the environment impact business functions, financial management, marketing, human resources, and production?

9. What purposes do sustainability measures and standards serve?

10. Why do dissenting views exist on the seriousness of the danger of business activities to the environment?

11. Do the opportunities presented by sustainable development outweigh the threats?

CASES

14.1   *Challenging a Conventional Wisdom*

Beverley Hendler graduated from university ten years ago with a bachelor of business administration, with a major in accounting. She went to work with an accounting firm and later obtained her chartered accountancy designation. Through her work as an auditor she met and married Ross, and they now have two children, aged four and two years old. When their second child was born, Beverley decided to stay home to care for the children. The firm suggested she work from home approximately half-time, especially during the busy January to April auditing period. This arrangement worked well and she was able to attend to family and work obligations.

After having children, Beverley took more interest in the food consumed by the family. She researched the desirability of consuming organic foods. There are many definitions of organic food, but it involves using little, or no, synthetic pesticides and fertilizers in food production, and opposes genetic modification. There were several reasons for her interest in organic foods, but in particular she thought that they were more environmentally friendly.

She received a shock one day when reading one of her business magazines. Even though many consumers stated that the main reason for purchasing organic foods was to protect the environment, two articles challenged this conventional wisdom. Intensive farming on a large scale and using fertilizers was much more productive. To produce the same amount of food organically would require much more land because crop yields are lower. The more land required would result in deforestation of large areas.

According to the articles, it was questionable whether organic farming was more energy efficient. More energy was necessary because of the lower yields and the necessity to plow fields to control weeds. Even the purchase of local foods was not always more environmentally friendly. Consumers driving to local farmers' markets used more energy than obtaining the food at centrally located food supermarkets. Furthermore, it is more environmentally friendly and energy efficient to produce some food in other countries than to attempt to grow it locally.

The articles got Beverley wondering about the appropriateness of consuming organic food. A friend suggested that she should not believe anything from business magazines as they were conservative, business-oriented news magazines. The articles did not dismiss the significance of consumers' interest in organic foods, and stated that it was appropriate for consumers to vote with dollars for the types of food they wished to purchase and from where. It was even suggested that consumer purchase decisions were resulting in changes in the way food was produced and distributed.

Questions

1. **What are the issue(s) and stakeholders involved?**

2. **A conventional wisdom is a widely accepted belief or view with regard to some matter that is usually not questioned. The view that locally produced food is more environmentally friendly is widely held. How do conventional wisdoms form? How is business affected? What can business do about a conventional wisdom?**

3. **What should Beverley do?**

14.2   *Is Dr. Seuss Misleading Children?*

For generations, books by Dr. Seuss have been read to and by children. His books were often commentaries on social and political issues; for example, *Yertle the Turtle* had a theme based on totalitarianism, *The Sneetches* dealt with discrimination, and *How The Grinch Stole Christmas* criticized the commercialization of holidays. *The Lorax* discusses the threat to the environment.

The principal character in *The Lorax* is the Once-ler, who represents business. He cuts down the beautiful Truffula Trees to make a Thneed, which could be used for many things including shirts, hats, or gloves. The Lorax, a small, "mossy" creature who spoke for the trees and animals in the forest, asked the Once-ler to stop cutting down the Truffula Trees. But the Once-ler recognized the market potential of the Thneed and he set up a factory to manufacture even more of them.

The business grew bigger and the Once-ler cut down more and more trees to meet the demand. Animals that depended on the Truffula Trees lost their source of food. Smog and water pollution were created by the factories. The Once-ler said he had rights and was going to continue his business expansion. Eventually the last Truffula Tree was down, ending the production of Thneeds. The Once-ler realized his mistake and asked the readers to take the last Truffula Tree seed and plant it, take care of it, and protect it from those who want to chop it down.

Dr. Seuss wanted to make several points: the planet faces environmental problems such as pollution and the depletion of resources; these problems have serious implications for society; and there is some urgency necessary to address them. The story delivers a message that business is rapidly destroying the environment and that things will not change until people start to care and do something to stop the destruction.

In March 2012 the animated movie *The Lorax* was released to theatres in 2-D and 3-D. Most reviewers felt that it followed the book's pro-environmentalism and anti-capitalism themes. The movie stressed the dangers of overconsumption and corporate greed, and the virtue of conservation. There was a consensus that the movie was very colourful, the musical numbers were mediocre, and the voices of the characters were excellent. Many reviewers felt that young audiences might be influenced by the warnings against rampant capitalism which led to deforestation.

The story both in print and on-screen is very pessimistic and treats the business system harshly, and may be giving children an overly negative view of business. The positive aspects of the business system are not discussed; for example, explaining how business is essential to ensuring a high standard of living, how it creates employment, and how it provides innovative products and services. The story does not suggest that the environment and business activity can coexist.

Questions

1. **Is it appropriate that children's stories contain anti-business messages? What are the ethical implications of this practice?**
2. **Today, who performs the role of the Lorax?**
3. **How would Dr. Seuss view sustainable development?**
4. **What other media contain messages that are critical of business?**
5. **Will you read *The Lorax* to children (including your own)?**

Sources: MovieReviewIntelligence, "Dr. Seuss's *The Lorax* Movie Reviews," http://moviereviewintelligence.com/movie-reviews/dr_seuss_the_lorax/, accessed December 12, 2012; and Rotten Tomatoes, "*The Lorax* Movie Reviews," http://rottentomatoes.com/m/the_lorax/reviews, accessed December 12, 2012.

connect® For more information on the resources available from McGraw-Hill Ryerson, go to www.mcgrawhill.ca/he/solutions.

For additional study tools and interactive ways to learn about ethics, visit **www.mcgrawhillconnect.ca**

CHAPTER 15
Globalization and Business Responsibilities

LO 15.1 Recognize that global business brings new business responsibilities.

LO 15.2 Define globalization, identify related issues, and list the pros and cons.

LO 15.3 Describe the role international non-governmental organizations play in influencing business.

LO 15.4 Name the main supranational institutions influencing globalization.

LO 15.5 Understand the connection between globalization and Canadian business and society.

LO 15.6 Become familiar with the international standards that are guiding and influencing the behaviour of multinational corporations.

LO 15.7 Appreciate the special challenges confronting business as a result of globalization.

LO 15.8 Link the reduction of poverty in developing countries to aspects of capitalism.

What would you do if . . . ?

Claudia Merchant was viewing a Web site that offered for sale an Hermès Birkin handbag that was exactly what she had been looking for. She had always wanted a bag of this type and this one was being sold for a fraction of the price. Claudia began filling out the order form, and then paused.

Her Business Law professor had devoted a whole class lecture to discuss the counterfeiting and pirating of intellectual property, which was a major issue in the globalization of business. Claudia recalled her referring to an intellectual property crime statistics report by the RCMP. The main types of products involved were footwear, clothing and accessories,

copyrighted works, consumer electronics, and pharmaceuticals. In one year, the RCMP had seized more than $67 million in counterfeit and pirated goods, 80 percent of which originated in China.

The professor emphasized the seriousness of the problem, explaining why it even threatened Canada's economic integrity. Local merchants were unable to compete and sometimes failed as a result. Because the products were produced overseas, jobs in Canada were lost. These products were not produced to Canadian standards and often threatened the health and safety of consumers. Real dangers were associated with purchasing counterfeit medications, electrical and electronic devices, alcohol and food products, toys, cosmetics, condoms, and sporting equipment. In a report, the Canadian Anti-Counterfeiting Network stated there were some troubling ethics about the culture of piracy in Canada and that more had to be done to change the view that it was ethically acceptable to purchase these goods.

According to Claudia's professor, counterfeiting and piracy were big business globally and were very profitable for those involved. Another aspect of the problem, according to the RCMP report, was that organized crime, criminal gangs, and even terrorist organizations increasingly were involved. Consumers were often attracted to luxury products such as the Hermès handbag by prices that saved them a lot of money. Many of these street vendors and Internet sites appeared quite legitimate and induced consumers to make innocent purchases.

The picture of the handbag was very clear and there were close-ups of the stitching and finish. The handbag looked legitimate, but the price was very low. Claudia started wondering about the Web site, and realized she did not recognize the name of the corporation. She wondered whether or not she should go ahead and purchase. The handbag would really go well with several of her outfits.

What is your advice to Claudia?

Sources: Royal Canadian Mounted Police, "2011 intellectual property (IP) crime statistics," http://www.rcmp-grc.gc.ca/fep-pelf/ipr-dpi/report-rapport-eng.htm, accessed May 1, 2012; and Canadian Anti-Counterfeiting Network, *Report on Counterfeiting and Piracy in Canada: A Road Map for Change,* http://www.cacn.ca/publications/Roadmap_for_Change.pdf, accessed May 1, 2012.

>LO 15.1<   Global Business Responsibilities

Globalization is placing challenges on Canadian business, including new economic, ethical, and environmental responsibilities. Canadian corporations have no choice but to face the challenges presented by the more complex world economy that is evolving. Many believe that international business activities have the potential for distributing goods and services more equitably and for improving the standard of living for all people. Corporations subject to market forces and managed by private rather than government employees are believed to be more efficient at supplying the goods and services needed by the citizens of any country.

Globalization is not a new phenomenon. Historians have recorded trade in goods between regions since ancient times. Civilizations around the Mediterranean Sea traded among each other over land and by sea. As transportation and communications technologies improved traders ventured farther, to the Far East and the Americas. At times freer trade flourished, but over the centuries there have been periods of protectionism when countries believed it was in their best interests to restrict international commerce. The most recent occurrence of this was in the twentieth century until about 1980; after two World Wars and the Great Depression of the 1930s, governments became very protectionist and began to perform more of the economic functions in society. Gradually this view changed, and in the last two decades of the century attitudes toward trade and market systems evolved. Today, this new view toward trade and markets is referred to as *globalization*.

This chapter describes globalization, its impact on corporations, the challenges associated with it, the standards of conduct that are influencing it, and the emergence of capitalism as the predominant economic system in the world. Throughout the chapter, the increasing complexity of the corporation's economic, ethical, social, and environmental responsibilities in the global marketplace is identified.

LO 15.2 Defining Globalization and the Implications for Business

Globalization
A process of decreasing constraints on the interactions among the nations and peoples of the world.

A general definition of **globalization** is a process of decreasing constraints on the interactions among the nations and peoples of the world. There are several dimensions to globalization; three important ones for business are economic, political, and social or cultural.

Economic globalization involves the integration of fragmented markets into a global economy. The markets for goods and services, information, capital, and labour become worldwide, leading to free trade among nations; although progress has been made, the world has a long way to go before this is fully implemented. Barriers still exist to free trade among nations even through developing nations are now the producers of many goods and services consumed in industrialized economies (refer to Everyday Ethics 15.1). This could eventually mean worldwide standards or practices for product quality, pricing, service, and design. This is the type of globalization that is most commonly being referred to when the term is used.[1]

Economic globalization
The integration of fragmented markets into a global economy.

Everyday Ethics

15.1

Benefits and Harms at the World Trade Organization (WTO)

The WTO is the only global international organization dealing with the rules of trade between nations with the purpose of increasing the movement of goods and services; that is, enhancing free trade.

Many NGOs argue that this will harm people living in developing countries. Others argue that it will have the opposite effect. An example is provided in the production of agricultural products. Developed areas, the United States, and the European Union are protecting their farmers with high tariffs or by giving high subsidies. This prevents some agricultural products from being produced in developing countries. Quite often consumers pay higher prices than they would if freer trade existed.

Nevertheless, the WTO is an organization attempting to promote economic globalization.

Political globalization
The process by which world power relationships change and there is a loss of sovereignty by the state.

Political globalization is the process by which world power relationships change and there is a loss of sovereignty by the state. The reduced role of the state is replaced by power being assumed by multinational corporations, religious organizations, non-governmental organizations, social movements, and transnational terrorism. New forms of governance emerge, for example United Nations organizations (such as the Global Compact described in Responsibility for Ethics 15.1), the Organisation for Economic Co-operation and Development (OECD), the European Union (EU), and the World Trade Organization (WTO). Thus, economic activity is less hindered by political boundaries.[2]

Social or cultural globalization The emergence of a worldwide cultural system.

Social or cultural globalization is the emergence of a worldwide cultural system. This system emerges due to a variety of social and cultural activities, including common patterns of consumption (such as demand for American entertainment and brand-name clothing), worldwide sporting events such as football competitions and the Olympic Games, increasing tourism travel, movements common around the world such as environmentalism and the trend toward holding business accountable for social and environmental responsibilities, and health problems affecting most of the world such as AIDS and flu pandemics. As a result, the world is thought of more as a single place.[3] There are some challenges to cultural globalization, as described in Everyday Ethics 15.2.

RESPONSIBILITY
for Ethics (15.1)

The United Nations Global Compact

The Global Compact asks corporations to embrace, support, and enact, within their sphere of influence, a set of core values in the areas of human rights, labour standards, the environment, and anti-corruption. More than 6,000 corporations have signed on to the Compact, but only 62 are Canadian. The following are the Compact's "Principles of Responsible Investing."

Human Rights

- *Principle 1:* businesses should support and respect the protection of internationally proclaimed human rights; and
- *Principle 2:* make sure that they are not complicit in human rights abuses.

Labour Standards

- *Principle 3:* businesses should uphold the freedom of association and the effective recognition of the right to collective bargaining;
- *Principle 4:* the elimination of all forms of forced and compulsory labour;
- *Principle 5:* the effective abolition of child labour; and
- *Principle 6:* the elimination of discrimination in respect of employment and occupation.

Environment

- *Principle 7:* businesses should support a precautionary approach to environmental challenges;
- *Principle 8:* undertake initiatives to promote greater environmental responsibility; and
- *Principle 9:* encourage the development and diffusion of environmentally friendly technologies

Anti-Corruption

- *Principle 10:* businesses should work against all forms of corruption, including extortion and bribery.

Source: The United Nations Global Compact, "The ten principles," http://www.unglobalcompact.org/AboutTheGC/TheTenPrinciples/index.html.

Globalization increases business's economic, social, and environmental responsibilities, including issues arising from the following:

- Damage to the environment occurring as a result of using natural resources, including pollution and depletion.
- Business's alleged support for oppressive governments.
- Criticism of the marketing practices of many industries and corporations, for example tobacco, pharmaceutical, and baby formula products.
- Businesses associated with the arms trade are blamed for facilitating violence and warfare in various parts of the world.
- The treatment of employees in developing countries, the existence of sweatshops in industrialized as well as developing countries, and the attempts to prevent union formation.

Everyday Ethics
15.2

American Cultural Imperialism

American cultural imperialism is promoted by the worldwide presence of McDonald's and other fast-food chains, brand-name clothing, and popular entertainment. Many consider this presence undesirable as it dominates foreign lifestyles and values. The influence is subtle, and less obvious than a military presence. It may result in the discarding of local traditions for everything that is Western. American culture may be destabilizing, for example through movies and television that glorify violence and rebellion.

On the other hand, brand names such as Coke, McDonald's, and Nike are cultural ambassadors representing American lifestyles and ideas that can be liberating and uplifting. American culture does bring desirable changes; for example, queuing versus a scrum in retail outlets, service with a smile, good service at low prices, safe food, and cleanliness.

Sources: Based on Jeffrey E. Garten, "'Cultural Imperialism' is no joke," *BusinessWeek,* November 30, 1998, 26; and John Gapper, "Brands triumph over anti-U.S. feeling," *National Post,* January 22, 2004, FP13.

- In many parts of the world, including Canada, indigenous peoples are attempting to regain control over ancestral lands.
- Genetic modification of plants and animals has aroused concern, as has the patenting of life forms in the production of food.
- Corruption, bribery, and questionable payments are involved with doing business in some countries.

As a result of these issues and others, the desirability of globalization is open to debate.

Globalization has generated considerable controversy. The pros and cons of globalization have been discussed extensively and the main arguments on each side are summarized in Table 15.1. **Globalists,** individuals and organizations that support globalization, make the arguments for globalization; **anti-globalists** are individuals and organizations that oppose globalization or are critical of it.

It is unlikely that globalization can be halted, but its pace might be slowed. Businesspersons, as well as governments, should devise approaches to overcoming some of the downsides of globalization so that even more stakeholders benefit from the process. The existence of international non-governmental organizations, many of which oppose globalization, must be recognized and appropriate responses formulated.

Globalists Individuals and organizations that support globalization.

Anti-globalists Individuals and organizations that oppose globalization or are critical of it.

LO 15.3 ## Globalization and International Non-governmental Organizations (INGOs)

International non-governmental organizations (INGOs) Groups that hold shared values and attitudes about the issues relating to globalization and advocate for changes to improve the conditions in developing countries.

Business is being made aware of its responsibilities arising from globalization. **International non-governmental organizations (INGOs)** are groups that hold shared values and attitudes about the issues relating to globalization and advocate for changes to improve the conditions in developing countries. Many issues arise in addition to those listed, and INGOs are putting pressure on corporations and governments. Many INGOs are opposed to globalization and attempt to counterbalance what they consider the excessive influence of multinational corporations. Some address all issues of globalization, while others focus on human rights or the environment. Sometimes INGOs are referred to as transnational non-government actors (TNGOs), or transnational social movement organizations (TSMOs). Responsibility for Ethics 15.2 gives examples of INGOs.

TABLE 15.1	*The Pros and Cons of Globalization*

Globalists' Arguments	Anti-globalists' Arguments
• Trade is encouraged as it leads to the most efficient production of goods and services from which all gain.	• The expansion of global corporations is undesirable as decisions are based on profit making or greed.
• Private corporations and open markets provide better goods and services to society.	• Conspiracies exist between corporations and governments resulting in any benefits being received by a few.
• Opportunities for employment and higher incomes are enhanced in developing countries.	• Unemployment is created in developed economies.
• The standard of living has increased in most developing countries.	• Poverty and inequality increases in the developing economies.
• The transfer of capital, technology, intellectual property, and even skilled labour occurs.	• Periodic financial crises are caused disrupting the economies of many countries.
• Several stakeholders benefit, including owners, consumers, suppliers, and employees.	• There is destruction of local environments as standards are lowered to attract developments.
	• The cultures of societies are lost or changed.
	• Human rights are violated, in particular in relation to sweatshops.
	• Questionable payments are made to governments or their officials to facilitate business.
	• Intellectual property is not respected.
	• The sovereignty of nations is undermined.
	• Worldwide organizations such as the World Bank, the International Monetary Fund, and the World Trade Organization have too much influence.

RESPONSIBILITY
for Ethics **15.2**

Examples of INGOs

- *Corporate Watch*—This is an INGO whose purpose is to hold corporations accountable for their actions. It investigates and exposes corporate violations of human rights, environmental crimes, and fraud and corruption around the world. It works to foster global justice, to promote independent media activism, and to gain democratic control over corporations.

- *Oxfam International*—"Oxfam International is a confederation of 13 organizations working together with over 3,000 partners in more than 100 countries to find lasting solutions to poverty, suffering and injustice."

- *Amnesty International*—Amnesty International (AI) is a worldwide organization with 1.8 million members, supporters, and subscribers in 150 countries and territories. It campaigns for internationally recognized human rights; one current campaign is "Economic Globalization and Human Rights." In this campaign, AI maintains that corporations have a responsibility to observe international human rights standards.

- *Greenpeace International*—Greenpeace is a global organization focusing on worldwide threats to the planet's biodiversity and environment. Issues include opposition of genetic engineering, the elimination of toxic chemicals, and encouragement of sustainable trade.

Sources: Based on CorpWatch: Holding Corporations Accountable, "About CorpWatch," http://www.corpwatch .org/article.php?id=11314; Oxfam International, "About us," http://www.oxfam.org/en/about/; Amnesty International, "About Amnesty International," http://web.amnesty.org/en/who-we-are/about-amnesty-international; and Greenpeace International, "About Greenpeace," http://www.greenpeace.org/international/about.

Such organizations have received considerable attention, particularly with demonstrations at world economic gatherings. A coalition of civil society and environmental INGOs plus labour organizations disrupted the WTO meetings in Seattle in fall 1999, World Bank meetings in spring and fall 2000, the G8 Summit in Genoa, Italy, in 2001, and the G8 and G20 Summits in Ontario in 2010. In addition, their publications, media events, and Web sites are influential.

INGOs believe that they have a role to play in globalization by representing those with the least voice, including the poor, sick, and uneducated; the victims of civil wars; and indigenous peoples. This role is an important contribution in civil society and cannot be ignored by governments or corporations. Not all INGOs are alike or hold the same views, and not all are opposed to globalization. However, they do believe that poverty and inequality must be addressed. They are concerned that rich countries are becoming better off and that rich persons within countries are becoming richer at the expense of the poor. It is believed that corporate influence is dominating government decision making and that corporate ownership of the media prevents alternative views from being aired.

On the other hand there is increasing cooperation between corporations and INGOs, as described in Chapter 13 where the pros and cons of partnerships with NGOs are discussed. Everyday Ethics 15.3 describes a partnership between an INGO and a corporation in Kenya.

Everyday Ethics
15.3

"Sustainable Tea," Unilever, and the Rainforest Alliance

Unilever, a manufacturer of food, home care, and personal care products, is working toward sustainability in the production of its products. It is the world's largest producer of tea and it has announced plans to source its entire tea supply sustainably. Unilever developed its own sustainable agricultural principles concerning such things as working conditions, higher rewards for farmers/workers, and agricultural practices to protect the environment and increase productivity.

Unilever cooperated with the Rainforest Alliance, an INGO promoting economically viable, environmentally sound, and socially equitable agriculture. Unilever sought Rainforest Alliance certification of its tea and started the process at the Lipton Estate in Kericho, Kenya. The Estate covers 13,000 hectares, and employs 13,000 people with 80,000 dependants. Because Unilever had its own sustainable agriculture program, certification of this estate took only a year. By 2015, all Lipton tea bags will be certified. Fortunately, tea does not require a lot of chemicals and through careful pruning it was possible to reduce pests. Use of compost reduced the need for fertilizer. Unilever did not go fully organic as it believed that sustainable production was preferable because it combines environmental care, worker welfare, and economic viability of the industry. As Unilever was a major producer of tea, the Rainforest Alliance believes other corporations will follow to remain competitive.

Sources: "Unilever, the world's largest tea company, commits to rainforest alliance certification," http://www.rainforest-alliance.org/news.cfm?id=unilever, May 25, 2007; "Profiles in sustainable agriculture: Unilever Tea Kenya redefines 'green' tea," Rainforest Alliance, http://www.rainforest-alliance.org/profiles/documents/kericho_profile.pdf; Unilever, "Sharing the journey—Lipton and National Geographic," http://www.unilever.com/brands/nutrition/cookingandeating/articles/sharingthejourney.aspx; and Uniliver, "Sustainable tea," http://www.unilever.com/sustainable-living/sustainablesourcing/tea/, accessed September 5, 2012.

> **LO 15.4**   ## Institutions of Globalization

Supranational institution
An international organization that transcends national boundaries, where the member states share in decision making on particular issues pertaining to the members.

No one global governance institution exists as such, but several organizations have an influence on the global economy beyond that of a particular nation. This type of organization is known as a **supranational institution,** an international organization that transcends national boundaries where the member states share in decision making on particular issues pertaining to the members. They are usually viewed as economic agencies, but they can also have an impact on the ethical, social, and environmental responsibilities of the corporation. INGOs are often critical of such institutions as they promote globalization. Four supranational institutions are described: the World Bank, the International Monetary Fund, the International Labour Organization, and the World Trade Organization.

The World Bank was established with the objective of providing financing to enhance the economic development of countries after the Second World War. Today it focuses its financial and technical assistance to developing countries in Africa, Asia, Latin America, and the Middle East. The bank is owned by the 184 member countries and aims to reduce poverty and improve living conditions in developing countries. Low-interest loans, interest-free credit, and grants are given for education, health, infrastructure, communications, and other purposes.[4] An example of a World Bank project is outlined in Everyday Ethics 15.4.

Everyday Ethics
15.4

The World Bank and Mozambique's Mozal Project

The World Bank helped to finance an aluminum smelter in Mozambique that has had a major economic impact on the country. The plant's production contributes substantially to the growth in the country's GDP, brings in new technical skills, creates thousands of jobs, and contributes to infrastructure development.

In addition, the project is adhering to good social and environmental practices. A partnership has been formed with government, NGOs, and the local community to provide 17,000 local residents with education and training and health care services that aim to fight AIDS and malaria. World-class environmental practices are being followed.

Source: International Development Association, The World Bank, "Encouraging investments and growth in Mozambique," http://web.worldbank.org/WBSITE/EXTERNAL/COUNTRIES/AFRICAEXT/MOZAMBIQUEEXTN/0,,contentMDK:21321646~menuPK:3950068~pagePK:1497618~piPK:217854~theSitePK:382131,00.html, accessed September 5, 2012.

The International Monetary Fund (IMF) is "an organization of 188 countries, working to foster global monetary cooperation, secure financial stability, facilitate international trade, promote high employment and sustainable economic growth, and reduce poverty."[5] Although monetary and financial policies are a focus for the organization, it is also concerned with the social impacts of these policies. The Fund's efforts in the area of reducing poverty are described in Everyday Ethics 15.5.

The International Labour Organization (ILO) is the United Nations agency that "seeks the promotion of social justice and internationally recognized human and labour rights." It formulates standards of basic labour rights including the freedom of association, the right to organize, collective bargaining, abolition of forced labour, and equality of opportunity and treatment. This organization has been influential in the area of accountability for sweatshops in developing countries. It also established the World Commission on the Social Dimension of Globalization to assist people coping with changes brought about by globalization. The Commission is searching for innovative ways to combine economic, social, and environmental objectives.[6]

Everyday Ethics   The IMF's Poverty Reduction and Growth Facility

15.5   The Poverty Reduction and Growth Facility (PRGF) was established to emphasize the IMF's objectives of poverty reduction and growth. Seventy-eight countries are eligible for the low-interest-rate lending, which supports poverty reduction strategies designed by the individual country. The program emphasizes broad public participation in program development and greater attention to poverty and social impacts of key macroeconomic policies.

Source: Based on International Monetary Fund, "The Poverty Reduction and Growth Facility (PRGF)," http://www.imf.org/external/np/exr/facts/prgf.htm.

The World Trade Organization (WTO), which came into force on January 1, 1995, is an international body that oversees and coordinates agreements reducing trade barriers. There have been many NGO demonstrations at WTO meetings, mostly opposing the liberalization of trade. The issues identified include the unfairness to developing nations, the abuse of workers, the low prices received by producers, the arbitrary practices of multinational corporations, and the loss of jobs.

These institutions are viewed as being focused on economic matters, but as outlined above they are also influential in social, ethical, and environmental issues confronting the countries they are attempting to assist.

LO 15.5   Globalization and Canadian Business and Society

Canadian business is influenced by globalization and must respond; there are several implications. With global markets emerging, Canadian business is under pressure to forge international links as there will be less distinction between domestic and foreign enterprises. Ownership and control of business will be less important than performance at supplying goods and services. Canada, and Canadian business, has no choice but to meet the challenges of global market restructuring as new trading agreements are completed by governments. Several developing nations are becoming major economies—for example India, Brazil, Russia, and China—and Canadian business must prepare for the opportunities and threats that are emerging.

Canada must attract more investment in plants that further process our natural resources. Such investment will lead to productivity growth, increased competitiveness, and greater employment opportunities. On the other hand, Canadian direct investment abroad is a critical element in globalization. Businesspeople must be willing to invest money in operations outside of Canada. Governments must "think globally" when developing programs and policies, and be aware of the trend to globalization and encourage business to react appropriately.

In this global economy, Canadian corporations must be competitive with those from other countries in order to also behave as responsible corporate citizens. One measure of this ability to compete is the "Competitiveness Scoreboard" published annually by the International Institute for Management Development, which surveys the competitiveness of most national economies. Four factors are measured: economic performance, government efficiency, business efficiency, and infrastructure. Canada ranked 6th, behind the United States, Hong Kong, Switzerland, Singapore, and Sweden.[7]

A second measure of competitiveness is provided by the "Global Competitiveness Report" published by the World Economic Forum, an independent international organization committed to improving the state of the world by engaging leaders in partnerships to shape global, regional, and industry agendas. A Global Competitiveness Index provides an overview of a country's productivity and competitiveness based on nine factors. On this Index, Canada ranked 14th and has been improving because of its highly efficient goods, labour, and financial markets, transparent institutions, and excellent infrastructure. Canada's score is being dragged down by inadequate research institutions and government purchasing policies.[8]

How well Canadian business is able to compete in the global market influences how well Canadian corporations can respond to social, ethical, and environmental responsibilities associated with globalization. Many Canadian corporations with global operations willingly accept, or are being pressured to accept, these additional responsibilities. The International Code of Ethics for Canadian Business provides assistance in this area. This Code was developed especially for Canadian businesses by a joint effort among an academic institution, business leaders, and public administrators. It comprises four parts: a vision statement, a list of beliefs, a list of values, and a set of principles. The Code includes a vision statement:

> *Canadian business has a global presence that is recognized by all stakeholders as economically rewarding to all parties, acknowledged as being ethically, socially, and environmentally responsible, welcomed by the communities in which we operate, and that facilitates economic, human resource, and community development within a stable operating environment.*[9]

The principles of the Code are given in Responsibility for Ethics 15.3.

Many Canadian corporations are attempting to behave as responsible corporate citizens in the countries where they operate. Everyday Ethics 15.6 gives an example of a Canadian corporation that was faced with challenging circumstances when undertaking a mining project in Africa.

All Canadians have been affected by globalization. The two most common ways are through the availability of lower-priced goods in greater variety and the employment adjustments that occur from outsourcing goods and services. The well-being of Canadian society is increasingly influenced by the performance of Canada's corporations in the global environment both within and outside Canada. As well, societies and stakeholders in developing countries are being affected; some benefit, while others are harmed. The following section reviews the standards of conduct and accountability of corporations involved in global business.

LO 15.6 ▶ Standards of Conduct and Accountability for Global Business

Numerous codes, guidelines, or principles provide direction to corporations operating in the global economy. These measures are developed by various INGOs, some in cooperation with business, supranational institutions, business associations, or other civil society organizations. Corporations can use the standards to assess their response to social and environmental responsibilities relating to international business.

Standards of conduct apply to the worldwide operations of a multinational corporation (MNC) and are applicable to all, although compliance is voluntary. Responsibility for Ethics 15.4 lists some of the common standards, but many others exist. The following topics are covered in standards of conduct, but vary from one standard to another.

- *Political factors*—MNCs must respect national sovereignty and observe domestic laws, regulations, and administrative procedures. Corporations must not interfere (illegally) in the internal affairs of the countries in which they operate and adhere to taxation policies.

The International Code of Ethics for Canadian Business Principles

The Code is based on the following principles:

A. Concerning Community Participation and Environmental Protection, we will:

- strive within our sphere of influence to ensure a fair share of benefits to stakeholders impacted by our activities
- ensure meaningful and transparent consultation with all stakeholders and attempt to integrate our corporate activities with local communities as good corporate citizens
- ensure our activities are consistent with sound environmental management and conservation practices
- provide meaningful opportunities for technology, training and capacity building within the host nation

B. Concerning Human Rights, we will:

- support and promote the protection of international human rights within our sphere of influence
- not be complicit in human rights abuses

C. Concerning Business Conduct, we will:

- not make illegal and improper payments and bribes and will refrain from participating in any corrupt business practices
- comply with all application laws and conduct business activities in a transparent fashion
- ensure contractor's, supplier's and agent's activities are consistent with these principles

D. Concerning Employees Rights and Health & Safety, we will:

- ensure health and safety of workers is protected
- strive for social justice and promote freedom of association and expression in the workplace
- ensure consistency with universally accepted labour standards, including those related to exploitation of child labour

Source: Schulich School of Business, *Compendium of Ethics Codes and Instruments of Corporate Responsibility,* York University, Toronto, http://www.schulich.yorku.ca/SSB-Extra/businessethics.nsf/Lookup/Codes Compendium_Aug_2003/$file/Codes_Compendium Aug_2003.pdf. Used with permission.

- *Sociocultural objectives and values*—MNCs should respect the social and cultural objectives, values, and traditions of the countries in which they operate.
- *Disclosure of information*—Information about operations should be available, but not to the extent that business confidentiality is violated. MNCs will issue CSR and environmental reports.
- *Competition*—Activities should not be undertaken that adversely affect competition by abusing a dominant position of market power.
- *Financing*—Corporate financing should be arranged to consider the impact on national balances of payments and credit policies.

RESPONSIBILITY

for Ethics 15.4

Global Standards of Conduct Developed by International Organizations

- *Caux Round Table: Caux Principles*—The "Caux Principles of Business" were developed by a network of senior business leaders from both industrialized and developing nations. The principles cover responsibilities to all stakeholders, economic and social impact of business, business behaviour, respect for rules, support for multilateral trade, respect for the environment, and avoidance of illicit operations.

- *OECD "Guidelines for Multinational Enterprises"*—This is one of the oldest guidelines and has influenced corporate behaviour around the world. Clauses include disclosure, employment and industrial relations, environment, combating bribery, consumer interests, science and technology, competition, and taxation.

- *Principles for Global Corporate Responsibility: Benchmarks for Measuring Business Performance*—This is a comprehensive set of more than 100 principles, 129 criteria, and 118 benchmarks to measure business's social and environmental performance. It was developed by interfaith organizations from several countries including the Taskforce on the Churches and Corporate Responsibility of Canada (TCCR, now KAIROS-Canada).

- *United Nations Global Compact Network*—In 1999, the World Economic Forum developed a set of principles referred to as the Global Compact, covering human rights, labour, and environment.

- *Global Reporting Initiative (GRI)*—GRI guidelines cover all aspects of economic, social, and environmental reporting and apply to multinational corporations. Refer to Chapter 9 for a description.

Sources: Caux Round Table, "Principles of business," http://www.cauxroundtable.org/index.cfm?&menuid=8; Organisation for Economic Co-operation and Development, "The OECD guidelines for multinational enterprises," Policy Brief, http://www.oecd.org/dataoecd/12/21/1903291.pdf; and "Principles for global corporate responsibility: Benchmarks for measuring business performance," http://www.bench-marks.org/.

- *Employment and human resources*—MNCs should respect the right of their employees to join trade unions, observe standards of employment and industrial relations, train persons from the local labour force, and be sensitive to the impacts of layoffs and closures. MNCs should respect human rights, not be involved in child or forced labour, and provide safe and healthy workplaces.

- *Science and technology*—MNCs must cooperate with the scientific and technological policies of the countries in which they operate and grant licences for the use of industrial property rights under reasonable terms.

- *Corrupt practices*—MNCs shall refrain from offering, promising, or giving any payment, gift, or other advantage to the benefit of a public official or politician.

- *Environmental protection*—MNCs shall carry out their activities in accordance with national laws, regulations, administrative practices, and policies relating to the preservation of the environment of the countries in which they operate and with due regard to international standards of sustainability.

- *Stakeholder consideration*—MNCs shall consider the interests of all stakeholders. Consumers must be dealt with fairly, marketing and advertising practices must be honest, privacy must be respected, and products sold must be safe and of good

Everyday Ethics

15.6

Barrick Gold's CSR Programs and Reputation

Canadian Barrick Gold Corporation, with the largest gold production, gold reserves, and market capitalization, has 26 mining operations around the world. Having won many rewards for its CSR initiatives, it is considered a model of corporate responsibility. It has a Corporate Social Charter, a CSR Advisory Board, and publishes extensive reports on its performance, including a comprehensive Responsibility Report and performance tables on environment, community, and safety and health initiatives. It reports using the Global Reporting Initiative framework and the UN Global Compact.

Barrick is facing challenges in several of its mining projects, in particular the North Mara gold mine in Tanzania. African Barrick Gold plc (ABG), a corporation 73.9 percent owned by Barrick Gold, has been accused of ignoring human rights abuses. Several villagers have been shot and killed when stealing waste rock from which they pick out small flakes of gold. The Legal and Human Rights Centre in Tanzania claims that 19 villagers were killed in 2009–10 by ABG security personnel and local police. In addition, the corporation has been accused of allowing several assaults on women by its security guards and local police. Barrick's reputation has been tarnished by these events.

Barrick and ABG have been involved in several CSR activities in the community, for example by joining with NGOs and others to implement HIV/AIDs, tuberculosis, and malaria health programs. In addition, ABG has initiated a program to win back the trust of the local communities by spending US$8.5 million on school, water, road, and health projects in seven villages. It has also joined the Voluntary Principles on Security and Human Rights, a multi-stakeholder organization engaged in a dialogue on security and human rights issues. Even corporations with superior CSR programs can encounter social and ethical difficulties that challenge them.

Sources: Barrick Gold Corporation, "Corporate responsibility," http://www.barrick.com/CorporateResponsibility/default.aspx; African Barrick Gold, "Voluntary principles on security and human rights," www.africanbarrickgold.com, http://www.voluntaryprinciples.org; and Business & Human Rights Resource Centre, http://www.businesshumanrights.org/Categories/Individualcompanies/A/AfricanBarrickGold.

quality. The views of INGOs should be taken into consideration. Local supplier capacity should be developed.

- *Corporate governance*—The MNC shall follow appropriate governance practices.

Most of the standards cover a range of economic, ethical, and environmental measures. Human rights are included in most, but corporate governance practices in only some. They are a valuable resource for corporations and can be modified by industry. They provide a basis for reporting and guidelines for establishing policies. If used, there is need for annual auditing of compliance, preferably by an independent body or consultant. If not used or followed, any benefits from the standards will be lost.

connect   Want to learn about **the international Principles of Responsible Investment?** Go to CONNECT.

LO 15.7   **Special Challenges of Global Business**

Some special challenges confront Canadian business as it participates increasingly in the global economy: the presence of corruption, respect for human rights, the use of sweatshop production, and the reduction of poverty.

When operating in a global economy, Canadian corporations must be aware of the legal and ethical circumstances existing in various countries. Transparency International (TI) has developed an index of corruption, the Corruption Perception Index (CPI), to assist corporations in coping with particular countries. TI defines **corruption** as "the abuse of entrusted power for private gain."[10] Table 15.2 lists the CPI scores for the five least corrupt countries and the five most corrupt according to TI. Out of the 183 countries surveyed, Canada ranks 10th with a score of 8.7, and the United States 24th with a score of 7.6.

Corruption According to Transparency International, "the abuse of entrusted power for private gain."

TABLE 15.2	*Corruption Perceptions Index Scores 2011 (score out of 10)*		
Least Corrupt Countries	**CPI Score**	**Most Corrupt Countries**	**CPI Score**
New Zealand	9.5	Uzbekistan	1.6
Denmark	9.4	Afghanistan	1.5
Finland	9.4	Myanmar	1.5
Sweden	9.3	North Korea	1.0
Singapore	9.2	Somalia	1.0

Source: Compiled from Corruption Perceptions Index 2011. Copyright 2011 Transparency International: The Global Coalition against Corruption. For more information, visit http://www.transparency.org.

 Want to learn more about **Transparency International**? Go to CONNECT.

Bribery is a type of corruption that is widespread and insidious in some parts of the world. When managers of Canadian corporations operating overseas are confronted with this practice, ethical dilemmas arise. **Bribery** involves making questionable payments, or bribes, to government officials to influence their decisions. Sometimes bribes are referred to as *facilitation payments,* and involve smaller payments to expedite something an official should be doing by encouraging him or her to do it faster and more efficiently. Such payments may be justified as necessary to do business in a particular country and often are rationalized since everyone does it; bribery is an accepted practice and considered akin to a commission, tax, or compensation. On the other hand, there are numerous arguments against making such payments: it is viewed as being simply wrong, unacceptable, and illegal. The practice compromises a manager's ethical standards when honesty and fairness should be practised all the time. Some corporations simply refuse to deal with corrupt governments, because in the long term limited benefits exist and once started the practice is unlikely to stop. Bribery illustrates *ethical relativism,* described in Chapter 5. In some cultures and national environments bribery is an acceptable practice, and it is argued that foreigners accept it. Thus, managers can justify acting according to the circumstances in which they find themselves.

Bribery Making questionable payments, or bribes, to government officials to influence their decisions.

Several organizations monitor and measure bribery practices. TI conducts a Bribe Payers Survey, which allows it to evaluate foreign bribery by corporations in more than 20 countries by exploring the frequency of different types of foreign bribery. The three types of bribery assessed included:

- "bribery of high-ranking politicians or political parties
- bribery of low-level public officials to 'speed things up'
- the use of personal or familiar relationships to win public contracts."

In the survey, Switzerland and the Netherlands practised the least bribery, with a score of 8.8 out of 10. Canada was sixth, with a score of 8.5. U.S. corporations placed tenth, with a score of 8.1. At the other end of the spectrum, Russia ranked last with a score of 6.1, just below China (6.5), Mexico (7.0), and Indonesia (7.1).[11] Another effort at disclosing bribery, "Publish What You Pay," has been undertaken by a coalition of more than 680 NGOs and calls for the mandatory disclosure of all payments to governments made by companies in extractive industries such as oil, gas, and mining.[12]

Canadian corporations and managers must adhere to the *Corruption of Foreign Public Officials Act* when doing business globally. This act features three offences: bribing of a foreign public official; laundering of property and proceeds; and possession of property and proceeds. In addition to this act, the federal government is participating in anti-corruption initiatives through organizations such as the Organisation for Economic Co-operation and Development (OECD), the Organization of American States, the Council of Europe, the Commonwealth of Nations, and the United Nations.[13]

In March 2011, the OECD released a report pointing out that Canada is doing a poor job at enforcing bribery practices. Canada has prosecuted and convicted only one case, in 2005, and has one ongoing prosecution and more than 20 cases under investigation. The report made the following recommendations to the Canadian government:

- Provide more resources to its lawyers to prosecute more cases.
- Clarify the Act to apply to all conduct, not just "for profit" business.
- Make sanctions more effective.
- Make sure to prosecute Canadian businesspersons for bribery.
- Eliminate factors such as national economic interests and relations with a foreign state from consideration in making a decision to prosecute.[14]

In early 2013, OECD's concern appeared to be confirmed when several Canadian corporations were highlighted in the media for their corrupt behaviour. Several allegations of corruption were facing SNC-Lavalin Inc., a Montreal engineering firm, including alleged ties with the deposed regime of Moammar Gadhafi in Libya and alleged bribery involving a bridge project in Bangladesh. Griffiths Energy International Inc., a Calgary oil and gas company, was fined $10.5 million for bribing government officials in Chad. The federal government stated that it would be cracking down on the corrupt practices of Canadian corporations.[15]

Corporations operating in the global economy are increasingly disclosing information or being transparent about their activities and behaviour in the countries where they do business. Responsibility for Ethics 15.5 describes one organization's efforts to increase disclosure

---

RESPONSIBILITY
for Ethics (15.5)

Extractive Industries Transparency Initiative (EITI)

The Extractive Industries Transparency Initiative (EITI) is a global standard that promotes revenue transparency by monitoring and reconciling corporation payments and government revenues at the country level. It believes that in countries that are rich in oil, gas, and minerals, the revenues received from the extraction of these resources should be used to foster economic growth and reduce poverty. When the government systems are inadequate, the revenues may be lost through corruption or used to finance conflicts. EITI aims to strengthen governance by improving transparency and accountability in the extractives sector. The process is overseen by participants from the government, corporations, industry associations, INGOs, institutional investors, and supranational institutions. More than 50 of the world's largest oil, gas, and mining corporations support and actively participate in the EITI process including the Canadian corporations Barrick Gold, Talisman Energy, and Teck Resources.

Source: Extractive Industries Transparency Initiative www.eiti.org; and EITI Fact Sheet 26, November 2009 at http://www.eiti.org/files/2009-11-26%20EITI%20Fact%20Sheet.pdf. Used with permission.

in the petroleum and mining industries. As Canadian corporations in resource industries operate around the world, Canadian managers are aware of the efforts to avoid corruption.

connect

Want to learn more about **defining the Canadian mining industry's social licence?** Go to CONNECT.

Human rights The fundamental rights and freedoms to which all individuals, groups, and societies are entitled.

Human rights are the fundamental rights and freedoms to which all individuals, groups, and societies are entitled. The list of rights involved is large and has been expanded over the years, but one reference point is the United Nations' *Universal Declaration of Human Rights,* adopted in 1948.[16] Canadian corporations operating on a global scale need proactive human rights policies and practices both globally and within Canada. Financing and human talent may be harder to obtain without attention being given to human rights. Respect for human rights is a key to establishing market footholds in developing countries—which is import-ant as they are the largest untapped market, estimated at 3 billion.

The sourcing of products from sweatshops in developing countries and to a lesser extent within Canada is an issue with most retailers. Goods are supplied at low costs, but the plants where they are produced violate many human rights through the abuse of workers. The abuses include child labour, low pay, poor working conditions, poor health and safety, and overall mistreatment of workers. This has become a major issue to which retailers have responded; one example is given in Everyday Ethics 15.7.

Everyday Ethics
15.7

Reitmans (Canada) Limited's Code of Conduct for Suppliers

Most retailers relying upon global sources for merchandise now have supplier codes and require suppliers to follow them. Reitmans, a Canadian clothing retailer, provides an example of such a code. The components of their Code of Conduct for Suppliers are:
- *Child labour*—Workers must be at least 15 years of age. The only exceptions are where 14 years old is allowed by law in a country, or younger if the compulsory school requirement is completed.
- *Forced labour*—Not allowed.
- *Discrimination*—Workers must be hired on the basis of ability and not subjected to discrimination in any aspect of employment.
- *Environment*—Suppliers must comply with all applicable environmental laws and regulations in the country in which they are located.
- *Working conditions*—Workers are to be treated with respect and dignity, and must work in a safe and healthy environment. They must not be subject to corporal punishment or any form of harassment. The required working conditions are listed, as are standards for dormitories if applicable.

Reitmans specifies a monitoring program for all suppliers, and their representa-tives must be allowed to inspect plants. To enforce the Code, Reitmans has the right to terminate its contract with the supplier if the Code is violated.

Source: Compiled from Reitmans (Canada) Limited, "Code of conduct for suppliers," http://content.reitmans.ca/ethical/code_of_conduct.pdf.

In addition to corporations developing policies and codes, many industries also have done so. Many INGOs monitor production facilities, often on behalf of the corporations. Consultants have specialized in the area of verifying the conditions and practices of these plants. Despite all these efforts, some suppliers in developing countries are avoiding labour rules and inspections.[17] Others argue that sweatshops are a stage in the industrial development of a country; they provide employment where there would be little or none and the developing economy is better off, which eventually leads to further economic development.[18]

Human rights and sweatshop labour abuses are related to the reduction of global poverty. This issue has been receiving more attention in part because of the United Nations' Millennium Development Goals (listed in Responsibility for Ethics 15.6), which identify the needs of the world's poorest. The private corporation will have to be involved if the goals are to be met, and some Canadian corporations have initiated projects to address various goals. Although governments shoulder much of the responsibility for human development, it is in business's interests to participate. An opportunity exists to capture future markets, corporations benefit from the stability of enhanced human development, and the risks of doing business are reduced. Business brings inherent skills to meet the goals, including providing leadership through partnerships and cooperative undertakings.[19]

Globalization has increased the reliance on markets and corporations to provide goods and services around the world. The accomplishment of the Millennium Goals requires use of these features of a capitalist economic system.

RESPONSIBILITY
for Ethics **15.6**

The UN Millennium Development Goals

1. Eradicate extreme poverty and hunger
2. Achieve universal primary education
3. Promote gender equality and empower women
4. Reduce child mortality
5. Improve maternal health
6. Combat HIV/AIDS, malaria, and other diseases
7. Ensure environmental sustainability
8. Develop a global partnership for development

Information on how well the Millennium Development Goals are being accomplished is available at the official United Nations MDG Indicators Web site at http://mdgs.un.org/unsd/mdg/Default.aspx and the MDG Monitor Web site at http://www.mdgmonitor.org. The goals are to be accomplished by 2015.

LO 15.8   ### The Acceptance of Global Capitalism

The emergence of globalization has occurred with the increasing acceptance of capitalism around the world. The trend to greater reliance on market systems rather than government initiatives is illustrated by some recent initiatives: the "Bottom of the Pyramid" concept, fair trade, microfinance, and increasing entrepreneurship in developing countries.

Business corporations may appropriately play a greater role in alleviating poverty in the world by applying the concept of the Bottom of the Pyramid (BOP). This concept was popularized by an article by C.K. Prahalad and Stuart L. Hart in 2002,[20] and by a book Prahalad wrote on the concept in 2005.[21]

The concept is that corporations should not ignore—as potential customers—the segment of the world's population living in poverty. An estimated 4 billion persons are in this segment, living on less than $2 per day. Individually they do not have much purchasing power, but collectively they do. The market potential for these people is often overlooked as corporations focus on the few wealthy customers or the emerging middle-income people in a developing economy.

If corporations are innovative enough, they can profitably market goods and services to those living in poverty. If corporations succeed in this, they will experience growth and profits while at the same time improving the living conditions of those persons and aiding regional development. This approach empowers those at the bottom by providing new options for improving their state. It allows corporations to make money and at the same time be socially responsible. Thus, the concept appeals to businesses that are pressured by various stakeholders to be more socially responsible.

Prahalad and Hart outlined the commercial infrastructure necessary at the bottom of the pyramid:

- Creating Buying Power: Giving persons in poverty access to credit that can be used to establish economic activity to generate income.

- Shaping Aspirations: This can be accomplished through consumer education and sustainable development of developing countries' resources.

- Tailoring Local Solutions: The solutions include targeted product development appropriate to developing economies and bottom-up innovation.

- Improving Access: Developing distribution systems and communication links within countries to facilitate economic activity and trade.

For success at the bottom of the pyramid, all aspects of this infrastructure must be put together in an appropriate way to facilitate the commercial efforts.

In June 2007, the Aspen Institute's Business and Society Program issued a bulletin on the Bottom of the Pyramid concept. It identified how the concept is being incorporated into the curricula for business programs and the university centres interested in the concept. Teaching materials were also identified. The bulletin asked some interesting questions about the BOP concept:

- Is the concept merely an academic fad, or will the trends of increasing curricular exposure to the topic continue?

- Why is a discussion of the concept noticeably absent from most top academic journals?

- Will corporations address the felt needs of the poor when providing goods and services or rather exploit marketing tactics to promote any potentially profitable product?[22]

Another example of a business approach to addressing the globalization issue relating to the low prices received by producers in developing countries has been fair trade. The Fairtrade Foundation, Oxfam, and Traidcraft have agreed on the following common definition of fair trade: "an alternative approach to conventional international trade. It is a trading partnership which aims at sustainable development for excluded and disadvantaged producers. It seeks to do this by providing better trading conditions, by awareness raising and by campaigning."[23] The fair trade movement is not anti-capitalist, but instead intends to use the market system to enhance the influence of the supplier stakeholder. The best known fair trade product is coffee, and today most retailers carry a fair trade product. Other fair trade products are flowers, spices, and cocoa. The entrepreneurs promoting fair trade products claim that the local suppliers in developing countries are now receiving a higher price for their product. Fair trade was also discussed in Chapter 12.

Microfinance is the provision of financial products, such as micro-credit, micro-insurance, and savings accounts, to persons living in areas of poverty without access to banking services. Organizations providing these services are often referred to as micro-financial institutions (MFIS). Micro-credit has received the most attention and involves making small loans to poor persons to start or expand small businesses. Women are often the entrepreneurs who borrow money. The practice started about 30 years ago; the pioneer

Microfinance
The provision of financial products, such as micro-credit, micro-insurance, and savings accounts, to persons living in areas of poverty without access to banking services.

in this approach was Muhammad Yunus and the Grameen Bank in Bangladesh (see Every-day Ethics 15.8). Today, as many as 10,000 other institutions are involved in the practice, including government, business foundations, and aid agencies as well as commercial banks.[24]

Everyday Ethics

15.8

Muhammad Yunus and the Nobel Peace Prize

The 2006 Nobel Peace Prize was won by Muhammad Yunus and the Grameen Bank for initiating the microfinance approach with the poor in Bangladesh. Small loans are made mainly to women to start or expand businesses, with no collateral but with significant interest rates. The loans are for business activity, not for consumption purposes. Yunus formed the Grameen Bank, which is more than 90 percent owned cooperatively by its customers.

Sources: "Face Value: Macro Credit," *The Economist,* October 21, 2006, 78; Nobel Prize.org, "The Nobel Peace Prize 2006," http://nobelprize.org/nobel_prizes/peace/laureates/2006/index.html; and Grameen Bank, http://www.grameen-info.org.

Although promoted as an approach to alleviating poverty, microfinancial institutions have been criticized. The primary criticism is the high rates of interest charged, at 20 to 30 percent. The rates are justified on the higher costs of administering, making, and collecting the loans and administering small savings accounts. Some MFIS have been accused of pursuing growth by ignoring the ability to pay and using coercive collection tactics. Overlending is another problem, where multiple loans are made to the same person. There has been consideration of regulating the MFIS, for example by limiting the interest rates, but this may discourage lenders and force borrowers to less scrupulous lenders. Other initiatives to improve the industry include the establishment of credit bureaus, requirement of more transparency, and stronger ethical and regulatory framework. These actions are similar to the regulation of the payday loan industry in Canada. Finally, an issue is the morality of profiting by providing services that are intended to alleviate poverty.

The role of small business in improving the circumstances in developing countries has increased. This is illustrated by the Grameen Bank, which is a commercial, profit-making operation. One view of reducing poverty is to rely more on business models and less on aid or charity, which have failed in many cases to reduce poverty. The assumption is that the poor are assisted more by unleashing their energy, creativity, and entrepreneurial spirit. Corporations must realize that doing business with the poor benefits the poor and themselves. It will be necessary for some governments to eliminate the barriers to private enterprise or capitalism. Challenges are involved, including poor infrastructure, illiteracy, religious/racial/tribal tensions, crime, corruption, and excessive government regulation.

The trends and drivers behind implementing this new thinking and creating a favour-able environment to start engaging the poor include the following:

- Many corporations see a need to break out of mature market sectors.
- Framework conditions in many developing countries are improving.
- Communications are faster and cheaper, making the world a smaller place.
- Public expectations of corporations are changing.
- New and better partners are available.
- Aid and investment are beginning to reinforce one another.[25]

Thousands of examples exist where corporations are cooperating with governments and INGOs in programs to enhance entrepreneurial capability as an approach to reducing poverty. One such program is described in Everyday Ethics 15.9. Note how society bene-fited from more employment and the corporation increased its distribution.

Everyday Ethics

15.9

Coca-Cola and Entrepreneur Development in Africa

Coca-Cola created an Entrepreneur Development Program to help new entrepre-neurs enter the corporation's supply chain and profit from new sustainable business ventures. Micro-entrepreneurs are targeted in undeveloped markets, and taught basic business skills. Manual distribution centres (MDCs) are created to handle Coca-Cola's products in hard-to-reach urban and semi-urban areas in Africa. Those who set up MDCs employ others in the area, who then sell and distribute beverage products to retailers, often by bicycle or pushcart. The MDCs account for more than 80 percent of Coca-Cola's sales in East Africa. There are over 2,500 MDCs in Africa, generating over 12,000 jobs and more than US$500 million in annual revenues. The progress of the entrepreneurs is monitored to evaluate the success of each new business.

Sources: World Business Council for Sustainable Development, Advancing New Solutions for Economic Development: Coca-Cola, http://www.wbcsd.ch/templates/TemplateWBCSD5/layout .asp?type=p&MenuId=ODY&doOpen=1&ClickMenu=RightMenu.

One approach that Canadian business can use to assess the economic and political cir-cumstances in a country is the Index of Economic Freedom; the measures of economic freedoms are prime conditions for capitalism. (The economic freedoms measured by this index are described in Chapter 2.) Many economies have improved their standing in the index as government regulations and restrictions have been reduced and markets allowed to operate.[26]

Globalization has resulted in a reduction of government involvement in most economies and an increase in the reliance on markets and capitalism to provide society's goods and services. This trend reinforces the definition of globalization stated at the beginning of the chapter. It involves more than economic activities and is interwoven with the social and environmental responsibilities of business. Some question exists as to whether globalization will be influenced by the economic downturn and financial crisis in 2008–09 and the eco-nomic recession since. It appears that the trend may be slowing, but there is little evidence that it is being reversed.

Your advice to Claudia . . .

Many Canadians do not realize that globalization is impacting them in many ways every day. The ethics involved with selling counterfeit and pirated products is one example. Persons purchasing these products will benefit by allowing self-interest to influence their purchase decision. But other stakeholders are harmed, for example Canadian busi-ness retailers and their employees. It could be argued that the workers in China benefit, but they are likely working for low wages and in poor working conditions. You advise Claudia that you know her personal ethics and responsibilities are being challenged in this situation and it is important that she is aware of the ethical issues. Globalization impacts everyone in society, often in unexpected ways.

SUMMARY

- The globalization of business has brought numerous issues relating to business's economic, social, and environmental responsibilities. The impact of globalization on the Canadian corporation has been, and will continue to be, extensive. (LO 15.1)

- A general definition of globalization is a process of decreasing constraints on the interactions among the nations and peoples of the world. The three global dimensions important to business are economic, political, and social. Those in favour of globalization (globalists) and those opposed (anti-globalists) continue to debate the pros and cons. (LO 15.2)

- Many non-governmental organizations focus on globalization. They have exerted considerable influence on international corporations and in some cases are partnering with business on projects to reduce poverty in developing countries. (LO 15.3)

- Supranational institutions are influencing globalization economically, socially, and environmentally. Four prominent supranational institutions described are the World Bank, the International Monetary Fund, the International Labour Organization, and the World Trade Organization. (LO 15.4)

- Globalization affects Canadian business and society in several ways. Canadian business must remain competitive with corporations from other countries. The International Code of Ethics for Canadian Business provides guidelines for corporate behaviour. Many Canadian corporations are setting an example for corporate citizenship in developing countries. (LO 15.5)

- Several international standards of conduct have been developed that provide guidelines for corporate activities in developing countries. These standards can also be used as frameworks for reporting of their global responsibilities. (LO 15.6)

- Along with globalization comes the trend to rely on market systems and corporations more than requesting government involvement. This trend presents some special challenges for business, including responding to corruption, accommodating human rights in all operations and in particular in sweatshops, and contributing to the accomplishment of the UN's Millennium Development Goals. (LO 15.7)

- Globalization has embraced capitalism. Today, corporations are more likely to be privatized than nationalized. Microfinance and fair trade are examples of initiatives based more on business models than government ones. Entrepreneurship is increasingly taking hold in developing countries. (LO 15.8)

KEY TERMS

Globalization
Economic globalization
Political globalization
Social or cultural globalization
Globalists

Anti-globalists
International non-governmental
    organizations (INGOs)
Supranational institution
Corruption

Bribery
Human rights
Microfinance

CRITICAL THINKING AND DISCUSSION QUESTIONS

1. Why has globalization occurred at this time?

2. Why is globalization so difficult to define?

3. Do the benefits of globalization offset the drawbacks?

4. Do INGOs play a significant role in business's response to globalization?

5. How do supranational institutions influence globalization?

6. Why is the competitiveness of Canadian business important?

7. What function do the various standards of conduct have?

8. What happens when corporations do not adhere to the standards or guidelines of conduct?

9. How do corporations deal with corruption?

10. Why should business support the UN's Millennium Development Goals?

11. What is the relationship between capitalism and globalization?

CASES

15.1   *The Ethics of Bioprospecting*

Bioprospecting, or biodiversity prospecting, is the "examination of biological resources for features that may be of value for commercial development." It involves collecting and testing plants, animals, and microorganisms to find the features as well as collecting knowledge of the resource from indigenous peoples. Bioprospecting results in the development of drugs, improvements to crop yields and features, and various industrial products.

Companies, in particular pharmaceutical firms, search the globe for biological resources that can be commercially exploited. Many of the products developed are beneficial; for example, more than 60 percent of all cancer drugs have been created from bioprospecting discoveries. However, there are few regulations governing the use of the biological resources, and indigenous peoples in developing countries seldom benefit financially from the discoveries.

An attempt to correct this situation was the Convention of Biological Diversity, produced in 1992 and ratified by 188 countries—but not the United States, which argues that it stifles innovation and undermines the patent system. Peru and Brazil have attempted to challenge the American position but they have been unsuccessful in overturning U.S. patents on several bioprospecting-discovered products.

The maca plant, grown by the Quechua Indians of Peru for hundreds of years, illustrates the issue. A concoction is made from its tuber roots that is said to boost stamina and sex drive. The Indians believe that the plant is a part of nature's bounty and belongs to no one in particular.

In 2001, an American company, PureWorld Botanicals, received a U.S. patent for "MacaPure," an extract of the maca's active libido-enhancing compounds. The Peruvians view this as "biopiracy" and plan to make it a test case. The companies that develop products from biological resources argue that it takes millions of dollars and extensive research to develop them. Several maca-based products—from powders and pills to jams and jellies—are in existence and the export of the plant helps Peru's economy.

Questions

1. **Who owns the maca plant?**
2. **What stakeholders are involved?**
3. **What are the ethical, social, and environmental issues?**
4. **What can, or should, be done to resolve the controversy surrounding bioprospecting and, in particular, the maca plant?**

Sources: Based on Government of New Zealand, Ministry of Economic Development, "What is bioprospecting?" http://www.med.govt.nz/; and Rick Vecchio, "Who owns the maca plant?" *The Telegram* (St. John's, NL), January 8, 2007, B1.

15.2   *Food Retailing in India: Revolution or Evolution?*

Modern retailing approaches are evolving in India, especially in the food sector. It is common practice to shop for groceries in *kirana* stores, small neighbourhood shops and produce markets operated by entrepreneurs. In these retail outlets, the fruits and vegetables often are not good quality or in good condition, and the shops are not attractive or comfortable for shoppers. The owners are known for being wasteful, buying in small quantities, selling at high prices, lacking storage capability, and having no expertise in inventory control. There are about 12 million of these small family-operated outlets. In addition, there are 200 million pushcart vendors and hawkers who depend on the highly fragmented retail market for their livelihood.

Large Indian corporations have entered the market, such as Reliance Retail Ltd., with 300 stores in 30 cities across India. Some are opening modern North American–style supermarkets and hypermarkets while others are operating chains of produce shops. These stores are air-conditioned, brightly lit and clean, with trained workers. A greater variety of higher quality fruits and vegetables are available. Goods are neatly packaged, accurately weighed, and refrigerated. Most importantly, prices are lower. Modern retailing supply chain practices are being introduced, including distribution efficiency, high technology farming, and waste reduction. Some suggest that the farmers will receive more for their products as middlemen will be eliminated from the supply chain.

Another dimension of this issue is the restriction on foreign retailers' entry into the Indian market. Foreign retailers cannot sell directly to consumers. To circumvent this regulation, foreign corporations are entering at the wholesale level or in joint ventures or partnerships with Indian corporations. For example, Walmart has a joint venture with Bharti Enterprises, an Indian conglomerate. Other foreign retailers are attempting to enter the Indian market, including the U.K.'s Tesco PLC, and France's Carrefour SA.

The operators of the smaller stores have protested this trend and have called upon government to stop the large corporations from entering the market. They feel that they cannot compete with the new retailers and would become unemployed with no other form of work available to them. The Indian government is monitoring this retail revolution closely and is under political pressure from the small shopkeepers, opposition parties, and socialist groups. There is concern that the arrival of modern retailing reduces the opportunities for self-employment, especially among the poor. The state of Uttar Pradesh even ordered the closing of ten Reliance supermarkets to placate protestors.

Economists argue that the retail market, estimated at US$328 billion, is large enough for both traditional and modern retailers. The liberalization of retail trade in India is not yet a revolution, and barely an evolutionary trend. In November 2012, the Indian government announced that it would allow foreign investments in supermarkets and department stores.

Questions

1. Who are the stakeholders involved and what are their positions?

2. What are the issues relating to business and society? What dilemmas arise for Indian business and society?

3. How are the harms and benefits of the retail trade liberalization distributed?

4. Should foreign corporations be allowed to operate freely in India?

Sources: Steve Hamm and Nandini Lakshman, "Widening aisles for Indian shoppers," *BusinessWeek,* April 30, 2007, 44; Rajesh Mahapatra, "Wal-Mart taps into booming Indian market," *The Globe and Mail,* August 7, 2007, B8; Anuj Choppa, "Retail giants push India's shopkeepers to the brink," *The Globe and Mail,* October 30, 2007, B17, and "India retreats on retail reform," *The Globe and Mail,* December 8, 2011, p. B8.

connect   For more information on the resources available from McGraw-Hill Ryerson, go to www.mcgrawhill.ca/he/solutions.

CHAPTER 16
Sustainability Strategy

LEARNING OUTCOMES — *After studying this chapter, you will be able to:*

LO 16.1 Understand the link between corporate strategic management and sustainability strategy, and why corporations have different types of sustainability strategies.

LO 16.2 Relate sustainability strategy to a corporation's purpose as represented by its vision, mission, and values statements.

LO 16.3 Understand the importance of strategy formulation, including an assessment of the environment for social and environmental issues, the evaluation of the corporation's internal resources and capabilities, the development of objectives to a sustainability strategy, and the generation of sustainability options.

LO 16.4 Elaborate on the implementation and evaluation of a sustainability strategy.

LO 16.5 Appreciate that there are different approaches to achieving a sustainability strategy and that challenges are involved in the process.

LO 16.6 Acknowledge the role of business programs in increasing student understanding of corporate ethics, responsibilities, and sustainability.

What would you do if . . . ?

Industries go through life cycles, with some—such as high-technology products—in an emerging or growth phase, others—such as brewing—in a maturity or no-growth phase, and still others—like some manufacturing sectors—in decline. As industries go through these phases, there are different implications for how companies are managed and different consequences for various individuals and organizations in society as well as government. Many challenges face companies in declining industries as they attempt to meet their economic and social responsibilities.

An example of a resource manufacturing sector in decline is forest products, including lumber and pulp and paper. Many challenges have faced the forest products industry. The sector directly employed more than 235,000 Canadians; this number rose to 600,500 if indirect employment was included. The $57 billion industry contributed about 2 percent of Canada's gross national product, and exported products worth about $26 billion. The sector operated hundreds of plants across the country, with about 200 forestry-dependent communities. Since 2006, 86,000 jobs have been lost.

Many of the plants were inefficient, but government policies prevented a consolidation of companies and plant operations. Government ownership of timber supply had complicated the initiatives the companies could undertake to become more efficient. Government assistance often propped up obsolete and inefficient plants. The increased value of the Canadian dollar had increased the prices of its products on world markets, and energy costs had increased. The industry was facing increasing global competition from, for example, more productive plants in Finland, fast-growing tree farms in Chile, and the accessing of unexploited forests in Russia.

David King had joined a large Canadian pulp and paper corporation immediately after his graduation with a business degree. During the past 15 years he had enjoyed a successful and rewarding career, eventually becoming the manager of a pulp and paper plant in Northern Ontario. David was impressed by the corporate social responsibility program that had evolved in the corporation over the years. The corporation viewed its social responsibilities seriously and donated to national and local charities, cooperated with Aboriginal peoples to provide employment, supported employees participating in volunteer activities, practised many progressive human relations policies, and developed and implemented codes of conduct and ethics. Also, the corporation had been forward thinking in its regard for the environment. Pollution was reduced, more efficient forest management was implemented, and water and energy use were reduced.

Recycled materials were used in their products, and new environmentally friendly products had been developed. The corporation's practices toward its social and environmental responsibilities had been recognized by several awards. There was an elaborate 75-page booklet and a Web site that reported on all the social and environmental responsibilities. The corporation viewed itself as practising sustainability in its operations.

However, economic responsibilities were becoming a challenge and plant closures were being considered. David's plant employed 300 well-paid individuals and was the main industry in the town of 3,000. The plant was one of several owned by the company that was losing money and was included in a strategic planning exercise to address the economic situation. Despite David's best efforts, the plant's profitability was declining and it would lose money this year. He has not been informed of anything yet, but he fears his plant will be closed.

Many thoughts occurred to David. How would he disclose the news? How could the plant be closed in a socially responsible manner? How could he explain the inconsistency between the sustainability strategy and the social and economic consequences that the closure will have on the community? What responsibilities does the corporation have to the community? Of course, there was a self-interest aspect too—David wondered what would happen to him.

What is your advice to David?

Source: Data from the Forest Products Association of Canada, http://www.fpac.ca.

LO 16.1 Sustainability Strategy Continuum

Social, ethical, and environmental responsibilities are increasingly being integrated into the strategic management process. This widely practised planning approach has traditionally focused on the economic responsibilities and the financial performance of the corporation, but this approach is changing. The result is a **sustainability strategy,** a plan that views economic, ethical, social, and environmental responsibilities more intensively and integrates corporate social responsibility (CSR) into all facets of the corporation's operations. A sustainability strategy is also referred to as a CSR strategy by some corporations.

> **Sustainability strategy**
> A plan that views economic, ethical, social, and environmental responsibilities more intensively and integrates corporate social responsibility (CSR) into all facets of the corporation's operations.

There is no one approach to developing a sustainability or CSR strategy, and the strategies developed vary with management preferences, how well managers understand CSR, and industry environments. In order to understand the different variations of a sustainability strategy, a corporation's approach can be assessed using a four-stage continuum:

Amoral sustainability strategy
↓
Compliance-based sustainability strategy
↓
Emerging sustainability strategy
↓
Comprehensive sustainability strategy

The purpose of this continuum is to assess the extent of a corporation's sustainability strategy. It also provides guidance to the development of plans and to make improvements in an existing strategy. Although four stages are identified, it is unlikely corporations will fit perfectly in one stage. Table 16.1 identifies some of the characteristics of each strategy. This chapter provides illustrations of CSR being practised by Canadian corporations in many different ways.

TABLE 16.1   *Main Characteristics of Sustainability Strategies*

	Amoral	Compliance-based	Emerging	Comprehensive
Awareness	Little or none; avoids sustainability practices	Motivated by legal requirements and public disapproval; some written policies	Beyond legal requirements; voluntarily accepts 3E responsibilities	Full acceptance and understanding; key element in economic strategy
Stakeholder focus	Owners	Most likely customers, lenders, employees, suppliers, and government	All identified and consciously considered	Stakeholder engagement
Management/staff involvement	No training or rewards	Negative sanctions; some rewards Enforcement by HR and legal departments	Responsibility of senior manager or compliance officer Support resources provided Stronger focus on rewards and recognition	High-level management responsibility Integrated with compensation and performance appraisal systems
Board involvement	Unlikely	Restricted to that legally required and to maintain corporate reputation; no committee	Receive regular reports; possibility of CSR committee	Board committee oversees
Ethics program	None explicit Reflects management views	Rules-based Possible code of conduct	Codes of conduct and ethics Deliberate program	Complete, explicit program
CSR program	Ad hoc donations	Donations, sponsorships, voluntarism Public relations focus	More comprehensive, with community investment	Complete, explicit program
Reporting	None	Possible mention in annual reports	More extensive; possible separate report	Separate report with evaluation such as Global Reporting Initiative (GRI)

With an amoral sustainability strategy, the corporation ignores sustainability but cannot be viewed necessarily as deliberately doing so. It simply does not address economic, social, and environmental issues in a deliberate or explicit manner. Also, some corporations may consciously avoid or resist the consideration of sustainability practices. Corporations adopting this strategy are vulnerable to sustainable issues as their lack of attention to them reduces their preparedness if problems or issues arise.

Some consideration is given to sustainability in a compliance-based strategy, but it is motivated by legal requirements and the possibility of public backlash or disapproval of corporate behaviour. Thus, sustainability is accepted because of the possible economic consequences of doing nothing and the fear of negative publicity. The strategy is legalistic, focusing on what should not be done, what is within the law, and what is required by government.

Strategy extends beyond what is legally required and the corporation voluntarily considers its economic, ethical, and environmental responsibilities in an emerging sustainability strategy. Many more aspects of ethics and corporate social responsibility are taken into account.

The comprehensive sustainability strategy becomes a key component of the corporate strategy in corporations that fully understand and embrace their economic, social, and environmental responsibilities. Implementation requires integration with all aspects of the corporation's planning and operations. This process needs managers who understand sustainability, and corporations are establishing management positions to oversee sustainability or corporate social responsibility. The positions have a variety of names, and can be as high-level as a vice-president. The Network for Business Sustainability identified "10 Things New Sustainability Managers Need to Know":

1. Whether there is pay back, for example in cost savings or customer loyalty
2. How to make sustainability a part of corporate culture
3. How to make the supply chain competitive and sustainable
4. Whether customers will pay more for sustainable products or services
5. How to best engage stakeholders
6. How to identify the best measurements of a corporation's environmental impact
7. Whether corporate sustainability attracts and retains employees
8. How a corporation can mitigate and adapt to climate change
9. The meaning of business sustainability
10. How to identify resources, including research, about sustainability and related issues[1]

Strategic management
The process through which a corporation establishes its mission and objectives, analyzes the environment and resource capabilities in order to formulate strategy, creates the organizational systems and processes needed to implement the strategy, and devises mechanisms for evaluating performance.

An approach to achieving a comprehensive sustainability strategy is through the use of **strategic management,** the process through which a corporation establishes its mission and objectives, analyzes the environment and resource capabilities in order to formulate strategy, creates the organizational systems and processes needed to implement the strategy, and devises mechanisms for evaluating performance. Managers are increasingly recognizing the potentially positive relationship between sustainability and financial return. Many corporations are consciously using the strategic management model to improve their performance economically, ethically, and environmentally. Some managers are using sustainability concepts as rhetoric to maximize profits, or appear to be formulating and implementing a sustainability strategy when in reality it is superficial or done without commitment. However, many corporations today are taking sustainability seriously, viewing it as critical to their success or longevity.

Want to learn more about **Canadian corporations with comprehensive sustainability strategies?** Go to CONNECT.

The following section describes how the components of strategic management relate to a corporation's sustainability strategy.

LO 16.2   Sustainability Strategy and Purpose

The purpose component of strategic management includes the development of vision, mission, and values statements. These statements represent the goals and core values important to the corporation as well as where the corporation wishes to be in the future. Corporations with strong vision, mission, and values have an advantage in achieving goals.

A **vision** is a statement of what the corporation wants to become or where it wants to be at some date in the future. A vision provides an overall goal or objective for the corporation and gives a sense of direction for the next five years or more.

A **mission** is an enduring statement that specifies in broad, even philosophical, terms the organization's "reason for being" and what distinguishes it from similar organizations. This is usually a short statement of not more than a paragraph. If a sustainability strategy is to receive attention, there is some reference to social and environmental responsibility. The mission statement becomes a critical document in communicating to and influencing the corporation's stakeholders.

Many corporations identify their core values and disclose them to stakeholders. There is no definitive set of values, but instead the values selected vary by corporation and industry. The identification of values is important as it influences how managers and employees behave.

Values are the basic assumptions about which ideals are considered desirable or worth striving for. Values are derived from personal experience including family backgrounds, religious training, and educational systems. Most business corporations are concerned to some extent about ethical behaviour and integrity in the operation of the corporation, for example in relation to employee health and safety, the environment, and product quality and service.

Corporations do not necessarily have all three of these statements, but they usually have two. Everyday Ethics 16.1 gives the vision, mission, and values statements for Domtar Corporation.

Vision A statement of what the corporation wants to become or where it wants to be at some date in the future.

Mission An enduring statement that specifies in broad, even philosophical, terms the organization's "reason for being" and what distinguishes it from similar organizations.

Values The basic assumptions about which ideals are considered desirable or worth striving for.

Everyday Ethics   Domtar's Vision, Mission, and Values

16.1

Domtar Corporation is a major Canadian producer of pulp and paper headquartered in Montreal. It refers to itself as "The Sustainable Paper Company" and states that "sustainability is in our fiber." The use of the word fiber refers to the textural component of Domtar's products, and the nature or characteristic upon which the corporation conducts business.

Our Vision
To be the leader in innovating fiber-based products, technologies, and services; committed to a sustainable and better future.

Our Mission
As a world-class industry leader we deliver the highest value to our customers, empower our employees to excel, and positively impact our communities.

Our Values
It's in our fiber to be agile.
It's in our fiber to be caring.
It's in our fiber to be innovative.

Source: Domtar Corporation Web site, accessed May 16, 2013, at http://www.domtar.com/en/corporate/index.asp.

›LO 16.3‹ **Sustainability Strategy Formulation**

CSR strategy formulation includes assessment of the external and internal environments, establishment of objectives, and the process of selection from among alternatives.

Assessment of the External Environment

A corporation must develop the capability to assess the external environment in which it operates and to understand when and how this environment influences it. The environmental factors considered include the structure of the industry, social trends, developments in technology, government policies, the behaviour of competition, and demographic changes. Key to forming a sustainability strategy is an assessment of stakeholder expectations and influence, and the identification of the social/ethical and environmental issues of concern to them.

An assessment of the environment should provide the corporation with insights into significant social and environmental responsibilities, which will vary by industry. For example, pharmaceutical manufacturers are concerned about the treatment of animals in drug testing. Fat content in its products may be the current strategic issue for McDonald's restaurants.

It is easy for managers to concentrate on economic responsibilities and overlook social responsibilities when examining the environment using well-known approaches such as competitive analysis, strategic groups, portfolio analysis, and shareholder value theory. These approaches see industry or market structure as the primary determinant of firm and industry profitability. Today, it is expected that managers will be aware of the social, ethical, and environmental issues that impact their corporation and industry. The challenge is to correctly identify the stakeholders involved and to correctly interpret the issues. Furthermore, managers must be familiar with CSR best practices or benchmarks in their industry.

Assessment of Resources and Capabilities

Management evaluates the corporation's internal resources and capabilities to ascertain its ability to take advantage of opportunities in the environment and to overcome any threats. An audit is performed of resources, for example an audit of financial, production, marketing, and human competencies. An assessment is also made of how well these resources integrate or interact with each other to determine resource capability.

An assessment of the corporation's resources and capabilities should also ascertain how effectively it can respond to social and environmental issues. In the past this was not usually done but some corporations are now explicitly identifying social/ethical and environmental resources and capabilities, which allows them to identify strengths and weaknesses in these areas.

Establishment of Objectives

Objectives are the ends the corporation seeks to achieve through its existence and operations. Most corporations have more than one objective, and many have objectives other than economic goals such as profitability, rate of growth, and market share. Socially oriented objectives are often included by a corporation, and when this occurs it reflects the strategists' preferences, their personal values and beliefs, and the corporation's culture. It indicates that the corporation recognizes its social responsibilities and wants to do something about them.

The setting of objectives is critical to strategic management from the outset since the mission statement is an objective stated in general terms. However, not all objectives can be established at the beginning of the process. After assessing the environment and corporate resources, managers or strategists are in a position to set specific objectives and priorities that are consistent with the corporation's purpose. Managers now have a better understanding of what the corporation is capable of achieving and the issues it has to, or wishes to, address. These objectives become the corporation's priority and establish key performance measures when strategies are evaluated. Everyday Ethics 16.2 illustrates the non-financial objectives for the Canadian Imperial Bank of Commerce's CSR strategy. These objectives reflect the ethical, social, and environmental performance of the bank.

Everyday Ethics

16.2

Non-Financial Objectives at CIBC

In its 2011 Corporate Responsibility Report and Public Accountability Statement, the Canadian Imperial Bank of Commerce (CIBC) identified the following non-financial objectives:

- Clients: Help our clients achieve what matters to them
- Employees: Create an environment where employees can excel
- Community: Make a real difference in our communities
- Environment: Demonstrate environmental responsibility in all activities
- Governance: Be a leader in governance practices

The report listed how these objectives were accomplished during the year. Financial objectives and their accomplishments were also listed.

Source: "What matters gets measured," CIBC 2011 Corporate Responsibility Report and Public Accountability Statement, https://www.cibc.com/ca/corporate-report/what-matters-gets-measured.html, accessed October 5, 2012. Used with permission.

CSR Strategy Options and Selection

The next step is to identify the strategic options available to the corporation. More than one usually exists, and they are described by terminology such as cost leadership, differentiation, internal growth, vertical integration, diversification, and strategic alliances. From the strategic options, or alternatives through which the objectives can be achieved, one is selected as the most appropriate given the corporation's circumstances.

Similarly for the sustainability strategy, there is more than one way to close the gap between a corporation's current social and environmental performance and where it desires to be. Awareness of social and environmental responsibilities will influence the number of options to be considered. The strategic management process to this point should have increased the awareness.

Several factors influence the strategist's preferences. First is the influence of the strategist's **beliefs**, the basic assumptions about the world in which an individual operates and how it works. Personal experience also plays a major role in determining beliefs. Experiences from the past lead to particular beliefs about business practices, or how much the judgment and expertise of others is trusted. An individual also has beliefs about his or her own competencies or capabilities.

Corporate culture is the complex set of values, beliefs, assumptions, and symbols that define the way in which an organization conducts its business. Often this culture is not stated explicitly and instead is reflected in structures, behaviours, processes, rites and rituals, myths, traditions, symbols, language systems and metaphors, and value systems (the values generally held by employees of the organization). Well-run organizations have a distinctive culture that promotes the creation, implementation, and maintenance of successful strategies. A study by Waterhouse Human Capital identified "Canada's 10 Most Admired Corporate Cultures": the 2011 winners were Agrium Inc., CIBC, Coast Capital Savings Credit Union, ING Direct Canada, Kinross Gold Corporation, Ledcor Group of Companies, Loblaw Companies Limited, RBC, Shoppers Drug Mart, and WestJet Airlines.[2]

Another influence is the basic need of all individuals (to some degree) for achievement, power, security, and recognition. The drive to fulfill these needs influences the degree of

Beliefs The basic assumptions about the world in which an individual operates and how it works.

Corporate culture The complex set of values, beliefs, assumptions, and symbols that define the way in which an organization conducts its business.

success or failure of the strategist in pursuing particular strategies. The circumstances in which a strategist operates also influence preferences, for example the size of the corporation, the hierarchical structure, the type of technology used, and the practices of the industry. The dynamics of group leadership and the interactions of group members influence the preferences for particular strategies. Strategists often must convince others, and in some cases strategic decisions are made by groups.

connect

Want to learn more about **organizational culture and sustainability**? Go to CONNECT.

These factors mould a strategist's preferences, including the values they hold, their beliefs about society, the personal needs that motivate them, the circumstances of their workplace or industry, and the influence of peer groups. These factors shape the attitudes of strategists about risk, ethics, social issues, profits, and short- versus long-term planning either positively or negatively. They can create the force that drives the initiation and maintenance of strategic management process, or they may act as filters that prevent the identification of all viable strategic options, or even the social and ethical implications of corporate decisions. Although this view is broader than the financial view, it is still too narrow in scope and unlikely to include diverse views from outside the corporation.

After the options have been identified and analyzed, a strategy can be selected that management considers the most effective in addressing the priority issues and the objectives established. For some companies, the approach to obtaining a sustainability strategy is to purchase an existing corporation with an established and recognized strategy. Everyday Ethics 16.3 provides illustrations.

Everyday Ethics
16.3

Buying Corporations with CSR Strategies

Companies that are recognized for their progressive approach to CSR strategies are being purchased by large, multinational corporations. The founders of the CSR-aware companies, who usually are the majority shareholders, accept offers from the larger corporations. This acquisition-type strategy suggests that larger companies recognize value in businesses that have a successful CSR strategy. Some examples of these takeovers are:

- *Body Shop*—Anita Roddick, who founded the cosmetics chain in 1976, sold the company in 2006 to L'Oréal, a French beauty company.
- *Ben and Jerry's Ice Cream*—The company produced socially and environmentally friendly ice cream and was sold to Unilever in 2000.
- *Tom's of Maine*—The company, which produced natural oral and personal care products, was sold to Colgate-Palmolive Co. in 2006.
- *Zenon Environment Inc.*—Zenon, based in Oakville, Ontario, is a leader in water purification by means of osmotic filtration technology. The company was sold to General Electric Co. in 2006.
- *Jenny Craig Inc.*—Jenny Craig, a major weight-loss company, was purchased by Nestlé for $600 million in 2006.
- *Burt's Bees*—This producer of beeswax lip balm and other all-natural personal care products was sold to Clorox Co. for US$925 million in 2007.

Sources: Based on David Teather, "Roddick nets £130M from Body Shop Sale," *Guardian Unlimited,* http://business.guardian.co.uk/story/0,,1733641,00.html; Ben and Jerry's press release, http://www.benjerry.com/company/media-center/press/join-forces.html; Shawn McCarthy, "'Earth-friendly' firm sells control to giant Colgate," *The Globe and Mail,* March 22, 2006, B3; Leonard Zehr, "Water treatment player Zenon goes to GE," *The Globe and Mail,* March 15, 2006, B1; and Melissa Shin, "Green targets: What happens when a big company swallows a little green pill," *Corporate Knights,* Vol. 6.3, 14–17.

> **LO 16.4**   **Sustainability Strategy Implementation and Evaluation**

Sustainability implementation includes designing the corporation's structure, allocating resources, developing information and decision-making processes, and managing human resources, including such areas as the reward system, approaches to leadership, and staffing. In other words, the corporation must focus on "how" the strategy will be executed.

Aspects of implementing a sustainability strategy have been covered in various chapters of this book:

- The development of stakeholder relationships in Chapter 4
- Ethical management and leadership in Chapter 6
- The practice of corporate social responsibility in Chapter 8
- The reporting and communicating of social responsibility achievements in Chapter 9

Management systems for delegation, communications, accountability, and rewards, in addition to structures or organizational arrangements (e.g., departments, task forces or committees, and staffing), must be in place to integrate CSR strategy with overall corporate strategic management. Support for the sustainability strategy must be established with the board of directors and management at all levels.

The structures or organizational arrangements component is involved with actually putting social policies in place and making them work, and with establishing operational objectives throughout the organization to make sure implementation occurs. The policies are guides for helping operational managers carry out the macro view to social policy. Examples of such policies include starting social response in the immediate area of the corporation's operations prior to addressing more distant regions; concentrating social action in areas strategically related to the economic activities of the enterprise (e.g., pharmaceutical companies might support hospital fundraising campaigns); and limiting social actions to a particular area (e.g., support of literacy programs or art museums).

Operational objectives are a further specification of general objectives established at the macro-view level. For example, a general objective would be to minimize dysfunctional economic impacts on communities in which corporate operations are terminated. An operational objective would be to donate $20,000 to a community industrial development organization to aid in attracting new industry to the community.

A discussion of implementation cannot avoid the mention of rewards in the process, especially those received by top management. They are paid well—even too well, according to some stakeholders. It could be argued that managers are paid to be socially responsible; that is, to see that their corporation is a satisfactory corporate social performer as well as a satisfactory economic one. One reason for high executive salaries is that executives are responsible for social and ethical matters relating to the corporation and they are expected to avoid moral, along with financial, risks. Lastly, executives are in positions to educate and influence others in the corporation to ensure satisfactory social and ethical performance. Executives should send messages that emphasize ethical business practices, and they should ensure that codes of ethics are developed, discussed, and enforced. Some executives have failed at this function because they were inadequately prepared for it, or chose to ignore it.

CSR Strategy Evaluation

Any planning process needs some form of control, or evaluation, through monitoring and review to see whether it is accomplishing what was intended—that is, to confirm that the strategy is followed and the objectives met. This is also true for sustainability strategy where continuous monitoring and reviewing of actions and initiatives is undertaken to address social environmental responsibilities. Evaluation of sustainability is also undertaken by the media, NGOs, and consultations as described in Chapter 9. The external auditing of sustainability reports is another type of evaluation and control.

There are several reasons why it has become important for strategists to incorporate social policies into the strategic management process. Professional managers today realize that business legitimacy depends on corporations being responsible for social issues. Secondly, there is still a threat that governments will increase regulation if business does not undertake some initiatives in the social area. Lastly, a business's success and continued existence are interrelated with how well it responds to social and environmental issues.

Reporting on the corporation's sustainability strategy performance is now common with larger, publicly traded corporations. Verification of the performance is being made by independent, neutral organizations such as NGOs and consulting firms. Note that the measures present those issues of most importance to the corporation given the industry in which it operates.

Monitoring and evaluation of sustainability is also being performed by NGOs and by Web sites such as CorpWatch and McSpotlight. Finally, a variety of awards and recognition activities influence the corporation. Many corporations list these in their sustainability reports. Corporations are also affiliating themselves with various organizations that research or advise on sustainability strategies.

LO 16.5   Achieving a Sustainability Strategy

What will influence capitalism and what will the corporation look like in the future? Accountability for social, ethical, and environmental responsibilities has resulted in profound changes to how business operates. The following are two approaches to conceptualizing corporate sustainability.

Corporate Social Responsibility to Corporate Social Integration

Porter and Kramer argue that corporations have not analyzed CSR initiatives using the same frameworks that guide their core business choices. CSR should not be thought of as a cost, constraint, or charitable deed, but instead of as an opportunity, innovation, and competitive advantage. The authors viewed most CSR initiatives as being reactive and many as being merely cosmetic; that is, public relations, media campaigns, and glossy reports. According to Porter and Kramer, reports seldom offer a coherent framework for CSR activities.[3]

The authors identified the prevailing justifications for CSR and their limitations, which are summarized in Table 16.2. They concluded that these prevailing justifications focused on tensions between business and society, and that to improve CSR there must be a better understanding of the interrelationship between the corporation and society.[4]

The authors proposed that the CSR model should become a corporate social integration model approach, which would integrate social perspective with business strategy. This would be accomplished by identifying the points of intersection between business and society, choosing which social issues to address, creating a corporate social agenda, and integrating inside-out and outside-in linkages.

The interdependence between business and society takes two forms: inside-out linkages, which represent the corporation's positive and negative influence on society through its operations, and outside-in linkages, which represent society's positive and negative influences on the corporation.[5]

Social issues must be prioritized into three types: generic, value chain, and social dimensions of competitive context. Generic social issues are those that do not significantly affect

TABLE 16.2	*Prevailing Justifications for CSR*	
Justification or Motivation for CSR	**Description**	**Limitations**
Moral Obligation	Corporations have an obligation or duty to be good citizens and to "do the right thing." Corporations are to be economically successful, but to be so in a way that honours ethical values and respects people, communities, and the environment.	Moral principles do not always provide direction where corporate choices involve balancing values, interests, and costs.
Sustainability	Environmental and community stewardship is to be emphasized. This involves consideration of the long-term consequences of activity.	Sustainability tends to be enlightened self-interest; that is, doing what is best in the long term. Questions are raised about the trade-offs between long-term objectives and short-term costs.
Licence to Operate	Corporations require the tacit permission of society to do business.	Control over social agenda is determined by outside stakeholders, (e.g. government, NGOs).
Reputation	CSR initiatives are justified as they improve the corporation's image, strengthen its brand, enliven morale, and increase its stock price.	Focus on external stakeholders and risk of confusing public relations with business results.

Source: Compiled from Porter, Michael E., and Mark R. Kramer, "Strategy and society: The link between competitive advantage and corporate social responsibility," *Harvard Business Review*, Vol. 84, Issue 12, December 2006, 81–83.

the corporation but are important to society. Value chain social issues are significantly affected by the corporation as it carries out business. Lastly, social dimensions of competitive context are "factors in the external environment that significantly affect the underlying drivers of competitiveness in those places where the company operates."[6]

Porter and Kramer categorize a corporation's involvement in society into two approaches, responsive and strategic. Responsive CSR includes the generic social impacts and efforts to mitigate harm from value chain activities. More importantly, strategic CSR includes transforming "value-chain activities to benefit society while reinforcing strategy," and "strategic philanthropy that leverages capabilities to improve salient areas of competitive context."[7]

Strategic CSR is beyond best practices and will identify a competitive position advantageous to the corporation. Inside-out and outside-in dimensions must work together to produce shared value opportunities. In this way the social dimension is enhanced while at the same time reducing the constraints on the corporation's value chain. Several examples are given, including Marriott's training program for hospitality industry employees, Nestlé's efforts to purchase from small producers in developing countries, and Whole Foods's value proposition of selling organic, natural, and healthy food products.[8]

Porter and Kramer conclude that CSR should be viewed more appropriately as corporate social integration. Instead of thinking in the short term, viewing CSR as correcting something business has done wrong or merely corporate giving, think of it as creating shared value for all stakeholders involved, in particular governments, NGOs, and corporations themselves.[9]

The Ceres Roadmap for Sustainability

Ceres (an acronym for Coalition for Environmentally Responsible Economies) is an advocate for sustainability leadership accomplished through the mobilization of a powerful network of investors, corporations, and public interest groups to accelerate and expand the adoption of sustainable business practices and solutions to build a healthy global economy.[10] It considers the integration of economic, ethical, social, and environmental considerations into the corporate strategy and capital markets key for long-term success. One aspect of their description of sustainability is a roadmap to guide managers through the setting of new standards and expectations for business leadership. A condensed version of the roadmap is presented in Table 16.3 and the contents reflect the topics covered in this book.

The continuum described at the beginning of this chapter identified various degrees of sustainability strategy acceptance or practice. An article in the *Ivey Business Journal* identified and explained the top ten hurdles for business sustainability[11]:

1. There are too many metrics that claim to measure sustainability—and they're too confusing.
2. Government policies need to incent outcomes and be more clearly connected to sustainability.
3. Consumers do not consistently factor sustainability into their purchase decisions.
4. Companies do not know how best to motivate employees to undertake sustainability initiatives.
5. Sustainability still does not fit neatly into the business case.
6. Companies have difficulty discriminating between the most important opportunities and threats on the horizon.

TABLE 16.3   *The Ceres Roadmap for Sustainability*

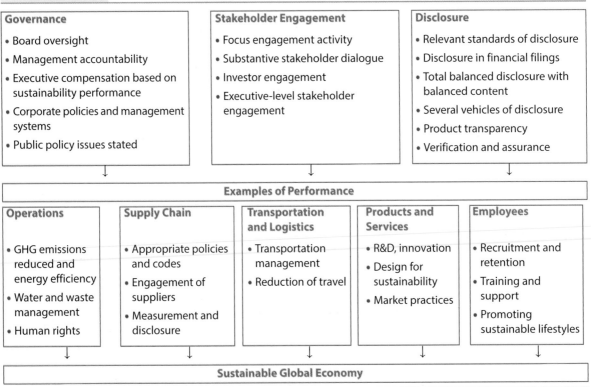

Governance
- Board oversight
- Management accountability
- Executive compensation based on sustainability performance
- Corporate policies and management systems
- Public policy issues stated

Stakeholder Engagement
- Focus engagement activity
- Substantive stakeholder dialogue
- Investor engagement
- Executive-level stakeholder engagement

Disclosure
- Relevant standards of disclosure
- Disclosure in financial filings
- Total balanced disclosure with balanced content
- Several vehicles of disclosure
- Product transparency
- Verification and assurance

Examples of Performance

Operations
- GHG emissions reduced and energy efficiency
- Water and waste management
- Human rights

Supply Chain
- Appropriate policies and codes
- Engagement of suppliers
- Measurement and disclosure

Transportation and Logistics
- Transportation management
- Reduction of travel

Products and Services
- R&D, innovation
- Design for sustainability
- Market practices

Employees
- Recruitment and retention
- Training and support
- Promoting sustainable lifestyles

Sustainable Global Economy

Source: Compiled from *The 21st Century Corporation: The Ceres Roadmap for Sustainability,* http://www.ceres.org/resources/reports/ceres-roadmap-to-sustainability-2010, accessed October 3, 2012.

7. Organizations have trouble communicating their good deeds credibly, and avoid being perceived as greenwashing.

8. Better guidelines are needed for engaging key stakeholders, such as aboriginal communities.

9. There is no common set of rules for sourcing sustainably.

10. Those companies that try leading the sustainability frontier often end up losing.

Many examples have been described in this book in which corporations have accepted and practise corporate social responsibility or sustainability strategies; this should be expected in many pluralist market systems. But, overall, strong evidence exists that sustainability strategies are being increasingly considered by Canadian business corporations.

Mc Graw Hill Education **connect**   Want to learn more about **sustainability and strategy**? Go to CONNECT.

The programs in Canada's business schools must incorporate sustainability concepts, frameworks, and theories into course work and research. The schools themselves might have sustainability reports, and students can be involved in sustainability initiatives.

LO 16.6   Business Programs and Sustainability

Business programs in colleges and universities are responding to the increasing awareness of the ethics of business and corporate social responsibilities. The response takes various forms and business education programs are feeling the impact. More important is the benefit for students. When they enter the workplace, they will be confronted by ethical dilemmas. When they become managers they will encounter various aspects of ethical business practice and be confronted by numerous business and society issues that will affect their corporations.

This section highlights some of the responses by discussing the pros and cons of teaching ethics, outlining ethics programs in business schools, and describing student voluntarism and pledges/oaths.

Teaching Ethics in Business Schools

The following points summarize the principal arguments in favour of teaching ethics at a post-secondary level.

- There are so many immoral or unethical events taking place that it is essential to teach ethics in an attempt to increase awareness.

- Teaching ethics sends a powerful message to students; that is, "this school feels it is a priority for students to follow generally accepted rules of business when they graduate."

- Businesspersons, as well as students, suffer from ethical naïveté. A course in business ethics alerts students to the existence of ethical conflicts and dilemmas. It is important to increase awareness of actual and potential ethical issues.

- From an ethical perspective, the business environment is changing radically and students must be made aware of this. Old principles or standards do not work today, and what is acceptable today may not be in the future.

- Only a separate course in business ethics focuses on the long-term perspective and asks "what if" questions. Most courses emphasize short-term objectives and management of the "bottom line"; that is, making profits. Longer-term perspectives are largely neglected in corporate planning, and courses in ethics may assist in changing this emphasis.

- Ethics courses can provide students with some tools or techniques of analysis, or with a conceptual framework for analyzing ethical issues. It is possible to teach the essential tools of moral reasoning, deliberation, and justification that should be helpful to future businesspersons in explaining corporate behaviour.

- Ethics courses legitimize the consideration of ethical components as an integral part of managerial decision making.

The principal arguments against post-secondary ethics education are as follows.

- There is little need for it. Business ethics are not a major problem. In particular, Canada has not experienced the major problems with insider trading and stock fraud found in the United States.

- There is little likelihood that university or college professors or instructors can meaningfully alter the ethical behaviour of students. Students' underlying moral convictions are obtained throughout life—from family, peers, grade school, religious instruction, and the community—and are not likely to be altered much.

- There are few qualified teachers of ethics in business and management departments. If anything, students should be sent to philosophy departments to learn about ethics in general.

- Specific business ethics courses are unlikely to be of much help in 20 or more years when students are in positions with executive responsibility. This is particularly the case given the rapid change in the business environment.

- Many business problems involve ethical considerations that are not resolvable: managers lack any influence over many factors in the business environment.

- Offering a separate ethics course suggests to managers that ethics are a "separate" consideration in decision making. In fact, ethics are fundamental to all decision making.

- There are few formulas or techniques that can be taught to solve the ethical problems confronting business.[12]

Ethics Programs for Business Schools

Corporations have ethics or social responsibilities programs and there is increasing discussion of ethics programs at business schools. Such programs might have several components:

- There could be a statement of values or philosophy.

- The curriculum could include core and elective courses on ethics and related areas such as social enterprise and environment. Degree programs could be offered that focus on ethics and corporate responsibilities.

- The faculty could follow codes of ethics or conduct relating to teaching and research. Teaching materials, such as cases, could be developed in addition to publications in academic journals.

- Students could have their own code of ethics or conduct, and form and support organizations related to social responsibility. Students could be involved in volunteer activities and take pledges or oaths committing themselves to ethical and socially responsible behaviour (see Responsibility for Ethics 16.1).

The Association to Advance Collegiate Schools of Business (AACSB) has joined the Aspen Institute's Business and Society Program, the European Foundation for Management Development (EFMD), and several other leading associations as co-conveners of the United Nations Global Compact to craft the first iteration of a global set of principles that acknowledge business schools' critical role in advancing socially responsible business leadership. These principles are listed in Responsibility for Ethics 16.1.

RESPONSIBILITY
for Ethics **16.1**

The Six Principles of Responsible Management Education

Principle 1

Purpose: We will develop the capabilities of students to be future generators of sustainable value for business and society at large and to work for an inclusive and sustainable global economy.

Principle 2

Values: We will incorporate into our academic activities and curricula the values of global social responsibility as portrayed in international initiatives such as the United Nations Global Compact.

Principle 3

Method: We will create educational frameworks, materials, processes and environments that enable effective learning experiences for responsible leadership.

Principle 4

Research: We will engage in conceptual and empirical research that advances our understanding about the role, dynamics, and impact of corporations in the creation of sustainable social, environmental and economic value.

Principle 5

Partnership: We will interact with managers of business corporations to extend our knowledge of their challenges in meeting social and environmental responsibilities and to explore jointly effective approaches to meeting these challenges.

Principle 6

Dialogue: We will facilitate and support dialogue and debate among educators, business, government, consumers, media, civil society organizations and other interested groups and stakeholders on critical issues related to global social responsibility and sustainability.

We understand that our own organizational practices should serve as examples of the values and attitudes we convey to our students.

Source: Principles for Responsible Management Education (PRME), http://www.unprme.org/.

Students and Sustainability

Stakeholders in society expect business to adopt and practise sustainability. It must be remembered that sustainability is the responsibility of all stakeholders, including students. Students support sustainability in several ways; examples of ways students can become involved with sustainability initiatives are given in Everyday Ethics 16.4.

Everyday Ethics

16.4

Examples of Students and Sustainability

Office of Community-Based Research, University of Victoria—Its mission is "to create and support inter-disciplinary and multi-sectoral engagement and research to create vibrant, sustainable and inclusive communities."

The Community Experience Initiative (CEI), Sauder Business School, University of British Columbia—This is a "summer internship program focusing on placing MBAs in social enterprises, and leveraging their business skills to strengthen the capacity of Canada's community sector."

Ivey Connects, Richard Ivey School of Business, Western University—Ivey Connects is a student-led organization working to inspire students to contribute in the societies in which they operate.

Students Without Borders (SWB), World University Service of Canada—SWB is a partner-driven program where qualified students spend a semester or more in Africa, Asia, or Latin America.

The Graduation Pledge of Social and Environmental Responsibility—"I pledge to explore and take into account the social and environmental consequences of any job I consider and will try to improve these aspects of any organizations for which I work." This pledge is widely used in the United States.

The Canadian MBA Oath, Telfer School of Management, University of Ottawa—In 2009, the graduating MBA class developed the Oath, and planned to have other universities in Canada participate.

Sources: Office of Community-Based Research, University of Victoria, http://web.uvic.ca/ocbr/; The Community Experience Initiative (CEI), Sauder Business School, University of British Columbia, http://www.sauder.ubc .ca/Faculty/Research_Centres/ISIS/Research/Social_Economy; Ivey Connects, Richard Ivey School of Business, Western University, http://www.ivey.uwo.ca/iveyconnects/; Students Without Borders (SWB), World University Service of Canada, http://wusc.ca/en/swb; Graduation Pledge Alliance, http://www.graduationpledge.org/; and The Canadian MBA Oath, Telfer School of Management, University of Ottawa, http://sites.telfer.uottawa,ca/ mbaoath/node/39, accessed October 3, 2012.

Students should check out their college or university's sustainability policy or strategy. Some have comprehensive policies, for example the University of British Columbia and University of Northern British Columbia.[13] At some colleges, the Student Union will also have a sustainability program. Many universities have investments in endowment funds used to support scholarships or research. Students can lobby officials to follow socially responsible investing as described in Chapter 11. Some universities already belong to the Coalition of Universities for Responsible Investing (CURI), a forum for dialogue, collaborative action, and education on socially and environmentally responsible investing among Canadian universities.[14]

Students can also become directly involved in sustainability initiatives. Volunteering for campus or community projects and in support of social causes is possible, or local issues could be studied. Community-Based Research Canada (CBRC) is a network of people and organizations engaged in research to meet the needs of people and communities. Several Canadian universities are involved with CBRC.[15]

International volunteer service in a developing country is another possibility. This could involve travel with the purpose of studying an issue or aspect of life in a particular country. There is the possibility of living in a country for some time by seeking out a semester internship or a volunteer position. Some well-known organizations involved in this type of learning are Engineers Without Borders, Students Without Borders, Cuso International, and Projects Abroad.

Service-learning is a method of teaching, learning, and reflecting combining classroom learning with service to the community either locally or in developing countries. It can be done for credit and involves a service activity to fulfill a community need and provides a way to gain further understanding of course content. More can be learned about service-learning at the Canadian Alliance for Community Service-Learning (CSL) Web site.[16]

Pledges or oaths to engage in ethical behaviour have been formulated. A pledge is proposed for first-year students that will increase their awareness of ethics and responsibilities, as described in Chapter 1. Another is taken upon graduation to emphasize consideration of the social and environmental consequences of the jobs students may accept. Finally, in recent years, students in MBA programs are taking oaths similar to the one described. Considerable controversy surrounds these pledges and oaths, with critics pointing out that they are window dressing or greenwashing and that they cannot be enforced.

> **Service-learning** A method of teaching, learning, and reflecting, combining classroom learning with service to the community either locally or in developing countries.

Concluding Comment

Evidence exists that many corporations do the things mentioned throughout the book, in particular those in this chapter. This book has outlined the paradigm shift that has occurred in the relationship between business and society during the most recent couple of decades. The business system is constantly changing along with the relationship between business and society.

The characteristics of the business system or capitalism are influenced by the fundamentals described in Chapter 2. The fundamentals are the same, but vary in influence over time. In turn, this impacts the ethics in Canadian business and society. Stakeholder influence changes over time, as do the issues that have an impact on the corporation. This leads to changes in the ethics of business and how corporate social responsibility is defined, practised, and reported.

Some stakeholders are more influential than others, and/or are influenced more by the corporation. The regulation of business is always present but it varies, as illustrated by the increase in self-regulatory mechanisms. Recently, the role of owners has changed and corporate governance has been reformed. Civil society stakeholders, in particular nongovernmental organizations, are increasing their influence, but corporations also are making their efforts to influence them. Two areas of focus today are the natural environment and globalization. Managers cannot ignore these areas and must attempt to understand the consequences for their corporations.

Lastly, an ethics of business, corporate social responsibility, or corporate sustainability now represents a strategic competence of management. This trend is unlikely to change in the near future.

Your advice to David . . .

David's employer says that it is implementing a sustainability strategy. However, David realizes that the economic responsibilities and realities are dominating decisions. Strategic sustainability should be applicable at all times, including when a corporation is facing downsizing through plant closures. You advise David that practising sustainability during these periods is particularly challenging, but the strategy should not be ignored or dropped during hard times.

SUMMARY

- Corporate sustainability is a more comprehensive form of corporate social responsibility (CSR) that integrates social/ethical, environmental, and governance issues into the corporation's planning through strategic management. Corporations are at different stages on the sustainability continuum: amoral, compliance-based, emerging, and sustainability. There is no definitive description of a sustainable corporation. (LO 16.1)

- Vision, mission, and values statements identify the corporation's purpose. These statements should also contain some indication of the corporation's approach to a sustainability strategy. (LO 16.2)

- Strategy formulation includes several components. A thorough assessment of the corporation's external environment will include identification of the key social and environmental issues. Internal resources and capabilities should be ascertained to understand how the corporation can respond to social and environmental issues. Objectives are established for the corporation's strategy so that actual performance can be evaluated. Alternatives to what the sustainability strategy should be always exist. The selection will be based on the corporation's purpose, the circumstances in the environment, and the resources and capabilities available. (LO 16.3)

- Following through with implementation is key to a successful sustainability strategy. Previous chapters contain many concepts, methodologies, and techniques applicable to implementation. There is no standard approach to implementation, and corporations will use different ones. The sustainability strategy will be evaluated internally by management, but also externally by NGOs and CSR-related organizations. Various award programs recognize successful strategies. (LO 16.4)

- It is argued that business should be thinking in terms of corporate social integration instead of corporate social responsibility, and seriously considering the redesign of the corporation so that it can respond more appropriately to the demands of ethics and responsibilities. The Ceres Roadmap for Sustainability is an example of a process through which a corporation can achieve sustainability; such a process involves many hurdles or challenges. (LO 16.5)

- Business school programs are emphasizing the ethics of business and sustainability. Students are being prepared for confronting ethical dilemmas in the workplace and for understanding corporate responsibilities to society. Students can contribute to sustainability while attending colleges or universities. (LO 16.6)

KEY TERMS

Sustainability strategy	Mission	Corporate culture
Strategic management	Values	Service-learning
Vision	Beliefs	

CRITICAL THINKING AND DISCUSSION QUESTIONS

1. Why are there different stages of sustainability strategies?

2. What is the relationship between strategic management and sustainability strategy?

3. Why are vision, mission, and values statements important to CSR strategy?

4. Why is it important to establish objectives in a sustainability strategy?

5. What influences the selection of the most appropriate sustainability strategy from among various options?

6. What advice would you give to managers when implementing a sustainability strategy?

7. What approaches to evaluating a sustainability strategy are there?

8. What is different about Porter and Kramer's approach to CSR?

9. How do roadmaps such as the one developed by Ceres help corporations?

10. What approach should business programs take toward ethics, social responsibility, and sustainability?

11. How can students contribute to sustainability?

CASES

16.1   *Learning Ethics from a White-Collar Fraudster*

The federal government's sponsorship program in the second half of the 1990s and into the twenty-first century resulted in millions of dollars being misspent or stolen. The fraud became known as the Adscam scandal because it involved advertising contracts.

One businessman who benefited from the program was Paul Coffin, who owned an advertising firm in Montreal. Between 1997 and 2002 it is alleged that his firm made about $5 million, some of it obtained by billing for work never performed. Mr. Coffin was charged with 18 counts of fraud. He later pleaded guilty to 15 counts and admitted to helping to defraud the government of $1.6 million.

In September 2005, an out-of-court settlement was reached and Mr. Coffin agreed to repay $1 million. He was also sentenced to a jail term of two years less one day. This was waived and one of the conditions attached to the sentence was that he would give public addresses on ethics in the business world. The judge commented that Mr. Coffin had been a law-abiding citizen for decades, and had an unblemished reputation with a high standing in society.

Later in the month, Mr. Coffin addressed an Introduction to Organizational Behaviour class of 180 students at McGill University. The lecture was not open to the public, but reports by some who attended said he admitted losing perspective and yielding to temptation after a career of 30 years. Students had mixed views on the lecture. One stated that he did not learn anything about ethics, but did learn about the consequences of a lapse in ethics. Others thought the talk was a great experience and related to their course material. There were a few protesters outside the classroom, who felt it was an affront to the university to have a convicted felon lecture on ethics.

Questions

1. **What are the issues in this incident?**

2. **From whom should students learn about the ethics of Canadian business and society?**

3. **Is it appropriate for individuals convicted of white-collar crime to teach business students ethics?**

4. **Would you attend a lecture of this type? Why or why not?**

Sources: Erika Meere, "Convicted Adscam Thief Lectures McGill Management Students on Business Ethics," *McGill Daily,* September 29, 2005, http://www.mcgildaily.com/view.phpaid=4194; Ingrid Peritz, "Coffin Avoids Prison for Ad Fraud," *The Globe and Mail,* September 20, 2005, http://www.theglobeandmail.com/servlet/story/RTGAM.20050920.wxcoffin20/BNStory/National/; and "Protesters Greet Paul Coffin at McGill," CBC News, September 28, 2005, http://www.ctv.ca/servlet/ArticleNews/story/CTVNews/20050327/paulcoffin_mcgillspeech_20050927/20050927?hub=Canada

16.2   *CSR and the Closure of a Neighbourhood Supermarket*

On January 14, 2012, Loblaws Inc. closed its SaveEasy supermarket in the Churchill Square shopping centre in St. John's, NL. There had been a supermarket on the site for 55 years, originally operated by a local business but later acquired by Loblaws Inc. The Churchill Park residential area was developed after World War II and included a small-scale mixed retail square and open spaces.

The Square was located on the edge of the Memorial University of Newfoundland campus, which had about 20,000 students, faculty, and staff. By 2012, there was a predominance of retired persons living in apartment buildings and individual homes in and around the Square. The SaveEasy supermarket closure left a gap in the retail makeup of the Square. As one resident pointed out, the Square had a lot to offer including medical and dental offices, restaurants, clothing stores, and a pharmacy, post office, bank, hairdresser, coffee shop, pub, sports outfitter, and dry cleaner—but now no food store.

Most of the students did not own cars and many retirees either did not own cars or were unable to drive. As the nearest supermarkets were now a distance of about two kilometres away, both these groups were inconvenienced by the closure of the neighbourhood supermarket. The closure was consistent with the trend in food stores. The Churchill Square SaveEasy was a small-scale supermarket that, when built, replaced smaller local grocery stores. Recently, the model for supermarket stores used by Loblaws and other food retailers was to centralized full-service stores as they followed the big-box store trend. Loblaws' centralization of its stores resulted in the closure of several other stores in St. John's.

Residents objected to the closure and contacted Loblaws. The information they received was that the store was not very profitable and the building was deteriorating, requiring expensive repairs. The Deputy Mayor expressed concern over the closure of SaveEasy grocery store in Churchill Square and asked that the Mayor write Loblaws expressing concern. In addition, the Deputy Mayor suggested that Council meet with Loblaws on the matter. A petition with hundreds of signatures was tabled at a City Council meeting, which read:

> We the undersigned deplore the closure of SaveEasy in Churchill Square. We urge City Council not to approve any other kinds of uses of the location. A food store is absolutely essential to the neghbourhood, particularly for seniors and students.

A copy of the petition was forwarded to Loblaws. These initiatives had no impact.

Many residents and students felt that Loblaws was not being a good corporate citizen and referred to a quotation from the corporation's *2011 Corporate Responsibility Report:* "We embrace our role as a leading corporate citizen." The report described Loblaws' CSR commitment that included respecting the environment, sourcing with integrity, making a difference in communities, reflecting the nation's diversity, and being a good place to work. In 2011, Loblaws was one of *Maclean's* magazine's Top 50 Socially Responsible Corporations. Those opposing the closure felt that Loblaws was focusing more on its bottom line than on good corporate citizenship.

As the months passed, another issue arose relating to the closure. Loblaws would not allow another grocery store to rent or purchase the building, in effect keeping competition out. Considerable discussion took place in the local media about Loblaws' unwillingness to give up the space, creating what was referred to as "economic black holes." Some people argued that City Council should have a vacant building policy requiring the owners to allow the structure to be occupied if some business were willing to rent or acquire the space. It was pointed out that Loblaws was not breaking any laws and was paying the taxes on the building. Others pointed out that Loblaws could not be expected to help its competitors. Meanwhile, the vacant store was a constant reminder of the inconvenience imposed on several stakeholders.

Questions

1. Who were the stakeholders and what was their influence?

2. Is it socially responsible to prevent the former store from being rented or sold to another business?

3. Should City Council take any action in this situation?

4. Was Loblaws being socially responsible? Does it have a moral obligation to keep the store open?

Sources: John Furlong, "Assigning blame for lost jobs helps no one," *CBC News,* Jan. 1, 2012, http://www.cbc.ca/news/canada/newfoundland-labrador/story/2011/12/30/nl-john-furlong-supermarket-fishery-101.html, accessed February 5, 2013; Morgan Murray, "Not in the market," *The Scope,* Feb. 29, 2012, http://thescope.ca/storefront/not-in-the-market, accessed February 5, 2013; John Gushue, "St. John's, old supermarkets and economic black holes," *CBC News,* May 27, 2012, http://www.cbc.ca/news/canada/newfoundland-labrador/story/2012/05/25/nl-john-gushue-dominion-vacant-527.html, accessed February 5, 2013; Susan Flanagan, "All I want for Christmas is a supermarket," *The Telegram* (St. John's, NL), December 11, 2012, http://www.thetelegram.com/Arts%20-%20Life/2012-12-11/article-3137642/All-I-want-for-Christmas-is-a-supermarket/1, accessed February 5, 2013; and Susan Flanagan, "Place-holder policies," *The Telegram* (St. John's, NL), January 22, 2013, B1; City of St. John's Council Minutes for January 9, 2012 and May 14, 2012; and Loblaws Inc., "Responsibility," http://www.loblaw.ca/English/responsibility/default.aspx.

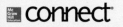

Ethics, Responsibilities, and Sustainability Cases

ZAPPING SALES AND TAXES[1]

Julia Hoben had graduated from a college business program with a major in accounting. She designed her program so that it enabled her to obtain a Certified General Accountant (CGA) designation within two years. She was employed as an accountant with a regional school board and she was enjoying the work.

Recently, her uncle asked if she was interested in doing some accounting for his restaurant. Julia first thought about this as moonlighting, of which her employer might not approve. She checked her employer's policy handbook and did not find any mention of moonlighting.

Julia had learned in a Human Resources course about moonlighting and the issues involved. Moonlighting, or outside employment, is defined as paid work in which an employee engages outside of the normal working hours of his or her primary job. The most common reason for engaging in such activity is to earn extra money to pay expenses, reduce debt, or save. Individuals also do it to gain experience, improve their skills, start small businesses, and simply because they enjoy it.

Employers are concerned about the possible interference with job performance and conflicts of interest. Moonlighting may result in employees being stressed or fatigued, reducing productivity. It could involve the inappropriate use of company resources, for example communications, computers, and copying facilities. Conflicts of interest can arise, especially if the work being performed is the same and in the same industry. Conflicts also occur when personal interests resulting from moonlighting clash with the interests of the employer who expects employee loyalty. As a result, employers often require that employees disclose outside employment. From a societal perspective, moonlighting is perceived as taking jobs that could be filled by unemployed persons, and governments are concerned about tax evasion.

Her uncle assured her that he needed Julia's services for a maximum of three hours a week and would pay her an hourly rate. Julia would not be performing bookkeeping tasks, because her aunt looked after that aspect. Her uncle wanted Julia to look after the various tax filings for the provincial government and the Canadian Revenue Agency (CRA) as the filings would be considered more reliable if prepared by someone with a professional accounting designation. Julia concluded that there was no conflict between working for a school board and in the restaurant industry, and agreed to the offer. She did not feel it necessary to inform her employer.

During the first months, Julia experienced several complications in this part-time employment. Her first concern was prompted when her uncle paid her in cash for the first two weeks of work. At first, Julia did not think much about this, but upon further reflection she acknowledged that cash payments to employees or suppliers in the restaurant industry was a possible approach to avoiding taxes.

Things got more complicated in the following weeks. The restaurant used a POS (point of sale) computerized system to record sales according to whether they were credit card or cash, and summarized sales by menu items and waiter. Julia reviewed the reports from this system in preparing taxation returns. She noticed that daily cash versus credit sales fluctuated greatly and more than would be expected. Also, she found two POS reports for the same day with differing totals.

Julia had read newspaper articles about tax avoidance in the restaurant industry. In fact, CRA had conducted an extensive investigation into tax fraud in the industry. One practice involved the use of "zapper" computer software to delete specific data, for example cash sales or employee hours. This practice was difficult to detect because a stand-alone software application was used that was contained on a CD or memory stick.

This situation placed Julia in a difficult position. First of all, family was involved and it would harm family relationships if she reported the practice to the taxation agencies, or if she even mentioned it to her uncle. Besides the personal dilemma, there was also a professional one. As a CGA she was subject to CGA Canada's 27-page Code of Ethical Principles and Rules of Conduct. Two items in the CGA's Code of Ethical Practices were applicable, Responsibilities to Society and Deceptive Information.

Under the Responsibilities to Society principle, unlawful activity was described as:

R102 Unlawful Activity
A member shall not permit the member's firm name or the member's name to be used with, participate in, or provide services to any activity which the

member knows, or which a reasonable and informed third party would believe, to be unlawful. (page 5)

Two clauses under the Deceptive Information principle also concerned Julia:

R401 Communication Issued in Connection with Financial Information
A member shall not issue a communication on any financial information, whether for publication or not, when the information is prepared in a manner which might tend to be misleading.

R402 Association with Financial Information
A member shall not be associated with any letter, report, statement, representation, financial statement, or tax filing, whether written or oral, which the member knows, or should know, is false or misleading, regardless of any disclaimer of responsibility. (page 13)

These principles seemed very clear to Julia. Her conscience would not allow her to sign a taxation return when she suspected fraud. Julia felt very alone as she was not sure with whom she could discuss this matter, and more importantly, what she should do.

Source: This is a fabricated situation with background information obtained from the following. Certified General Accountants of Canada, CGA-Canada Code of Ethical Principles and Rules of Conduct, Version 2.12, June 2011, http://www.cga-canada.org/en-ca/StandardsLib/ca_ceproc.pdf.

CORPORATE SOCIAL RESPONSIBILITY TO FOOD BANKS[2]

Phillip Veldhuis was president of Savalot Enterprises, a small, family-owned wholesale food business. The company operated in a medium Canadian city and its customers included health and educational institutions, restaurants, catering groups, and service clubs. Savalot's main social responsibility initiative was supporting the local food banks. Surplus edible food items were forwarded weekly to the food banks and the company made a substantial monetary donation each year.

Phillip fully understood the need for the food banks as outlined by Food Banks Canada, a national charitable organization of Canadian food banks. Located in Toronto, its mission was "to reduce hunger in Canada by enabling an effective food bank community that addresses both the short-term need for food and longer-term solutions." Its vision was "to be the voice for the hungry in Canada," and it embraced the values of Teamwork, Transparency, and Integrity.

Every year Food Banks Canada published statistics on hunger and the usage of the food banks, and recommended solutions to hunger. Statistical highlights from a recent publication were the following:

- 349,842 households comprising 851,014 Canadians received food from a food bank in March 2011
- The number using food banks was 26 percent higher than in 2008, and was the second highest level on record
- Food banks assisted 2.5 percent of the Canadian population with 93,085 using assistance for the first time
- Post-secondary students made up 4 percent of those receiving assistance
- There are about 900 food bank facilities across Canada

Corporations contribute about 6,400,000 kilograms of food a year, and about 80 percent of Food Bank Canada's revenues come from corporate donors. It acts as a clearing house mostly for food, sending it out to food banks across the country. Community food banks have their own local sources of food and funding.

The economy had taken a downturn in the area where Savalot operated, and Phillip believed that this might be part of the reason why food bank usage had also increased in his community. It seemed that each year the local food bank was faced with an increasing demand for food.

Despite the frequency of usage and the apparent need for food banks, Phillip had been reading about the problems associated with them. Some critics argued that food banks may provide some relief but they did not really address the problems causing hunger. Even Food Banks Canada indicated that high rents and lack of affordable housing, the high rates for early learning and child care, and an inadequate Employment Insurance system forced Canadians to use food banks.

Phillip also noticed that there had been considerable criticism of the food bank approach to alleviating hunger. Letters to the editor of various newspapers claimed that some users abused the food banks and that many were too lazy to find work. Other critics claimed that hunger will never be eliminated, and to suggest that it could be if more were donated was misleading. Many experiencing hunger did not use the food banks as they were reluctant or too embarrassed to accept charity. Those who do use food banks often felt that the experience was stigmatizing, humiliating, and degrading.

Furthermore, food banks alone were not providing all the food needed and some users were still hungry. Most food banks had to ration food offerings to once a week or month, and the best that could be done was to ensure that users experienced less hunger. Food banks were criticized for not giving out the most nutritious food given the focus on canned fruits and vegetables, staples such as flour and coffee, and boxed dried food like instant soups, macaroni and cheese dinners, and dry cereals. These foods contained salt and trans-fats or other ingredients not desirable in the diets of some people.

Others pointed out that food banks had been operating for over 30 years, having been established during the recession in the 1980s in Alberta. They suggested that the problem of hunger was too big for charities alone to solve and governments would have to help out. In fact, it was suggested that the operation of food banks by charities was enabling governments to avoid their responsibility to this social issue.

Phillip was shocked when he read the comments by Elaine Power, associate professor in the School of Kinesiology and Health Studies at Queen's University about food banks and the role of corporations. In reality, food banks are somewhere to dispose of their surplus edible food they cannot sell. Furthermore, corporate sponsored food drives are good for employee morale but do not result in alleviating hunger as much as claimed. Power emphasizes that the problem of hunger is a complicated one not addressed solely by food banks, and that all are complicit in ignoring the problem. This includes corporations that benefit from their donations by displaying to society that they are good corporate citizens, and by not having to pay to dispose of the food in a landfill.

Phillip felt a little guilty, because in effect his business was using food banks to dispose of food products it could not sell for one reason or another. He wondered if, despite his company's best intentions, it may not be contributing much to address the underlying causes of the problem and to providing sufficient assistance to those in need.[3]

Sources: Information on Food Banks Canada was from its web site at http://www.foodbankscanada.ca/. Views attributed to Elaine Power were contained in personal correspondence and permission was granted to use. Other information was obtained from: Dietitians of Canada, "Food Banks," Practice: Exploring Members' Practice Issues," Monday, January 18, 2010 accessed at http://www.practiceblog.dietitians.ca/2010/01/food-banks.html on February 29, 2012; Jeff Nield, "Will Closing Food Banks Help End Hunger?," Tree Hugger web site July 29, 2011 accessed at http://www.treehugger.com/green-food/will-closing-food-banks-help-end-hunger.html on February 29, 2012; Elaine Power, "Canadian food banks: Obscuring the reality of hunger and poverty," Food Ethics, Winter 2011, Volume 6, Issue 4, 18–20; Elaine Power, "Time to close our food banks," *The Globe and Mail*, July 25, 2011, A11; and "Food banks a 'smoke screen' for other poverty issues," accessed at CTV.ca web site at http://www.ctv.ca/CTVNews/Canada/20110731/food-banks-canada-long-term-solution-110731/ on February 29, 2012.

CATERPILLAR SHUTS DOWN ITS CANADIAN LOCOMOTIVE PLANT[4]

The headline read "Caterpillar closes Electro-Motive plant in London."[5] On February 3, 2102, Caterpillar Inc. announced the closing of its subsidiary Electro-Motive Diesel (EMD) located in London, Ontario. With globalization, the closing of manufacturing plants in Canada by foreign corporations had become more frequent as exemplified in the closing of plants by Navistar International and Ford Motor. The EMD plant had operated in London for over 60 years and employed about 700 persons producing several products, in particular railway locomotives. The plant's history and its closing illustrated several economic, political, and social issues associated with plant closures.

History of Electro-Motive Diesel Inc.

The Electro-Motive Engineering Company was founded in 1922 by two Americans in Cleveland, Ohio, with the name later shortened to Electro-Motive Company. General Motors purchased the company in 1930 and operated it as a part of its Diesel Division. In 1950, a branch plant was opened in London, Ontario. The plant was established to avoid tariffs on manufactured goods and to become eligible for Government of Canada contracts. General Motors sold the division in 2005 to a private equity fund which operated the business as Electro-Motive Diesel Inc. In 2010, Caterpillar Inc., a large U.S. manufacturer of construction and mining equipment, bought the company and operated it under its wholly owned subsidiary Progress Rail Services Corp. Throughout its existence, the London plant was always American owned.

EMD used the London plant for the assembly, painting, and testing of locomotives. Over the years, the London plant also produced a variety of other products including transit buses and military vehicles, and manufactured locomotive underframes, traction motors, truck assemblies, and locomotive equipment racks. The plant was on a 100-acre site and included two main and several ancillary buildings totalling over 500,000 square feet. There was also a locomotive test track. The plant was ISO 9001 Certified for Quality and ISO 14001 Certified for Environmental Management.

In 2011, the plant had about 700 employees, of which 465 were members of the Canadian Auto Workers Union (CAW) who earned up to $34 per hour. Businesses dependent on the plant were estimated to employ about 1,000 more persons. The company and CAW began negotiating a new collective agreement the same year.

The Negotiations, Lockout, and Shutdown

During late 2011, a new labour contract was being negotiated and the union was faced with several demands by the company. The company sought pay cuts of 50 percent in many job categories, the elimination of the defined benefit pension plan, reductions in dental and other benefits, and the end of the cost of living adjustment to wages. The negotiations were difficult for the union, but it had been assured that the plant would not be closed during negotiations.

On January 1, 2012, EMD employees were locked out after their union refused to accept a 50 percent reduction in wages for most workers and the union immediately set up picket lines. EMD had recently announced that it would refurnish an old plant to manufacture locomotives at Muncie, Indiana, where employees received about one-half the wages of the London plant employees. This opening put subtle pressure on the London union and its members to accept the wage reduction if they wished to keep their jobs.

Caterpillar's Progress Rail Services announced the closure of the London plant on February 3, 2012.[6] The announcement stated that it was regrettable, but the cost structure of the London plant was not sustainable and it had not been possible to negotiate a new, competitive collective agreement. The high Canadian dollar made manufacturing in Ontario more costly, and the weak U.S. labour market made labour available. There were weaker labour laws in several states, and the union agreement at London imposed antiquated work rules causing quality problems.

Issues Surrounding the Closing

Several interrelated economic, social, and political issues were evident in the closing of the Electro-Motive plant: the impact of globalization, role of governments, the decline of union influence, and corporate strategies.

Challenges of Globalization

Changes were occurring in the global economy that influenced corporate decision makers. Multinational corporations shifted manufacturing to areas with cost advantages, in particular lower-wage areas. In the past, this involved outsourcing production or building plants in Asia, for example. Recently there had been a change in direction for some American multinationals that were now moving production back to the United States. There were several reasons for this. Unemployment levels in the United States were higher than in the past and labour was available. Some re-established production in the United States to take advantage of the government's "Buy America" purchase policies introduced to counter the 2008 economic downturn. Exchange rates had an influence as the value of the U.S. dollar had declined, a factor particularly affecting Canadian plants. There were more favourable labour laws in several states that reduced the influence of unions. In addition, many states were offering comprehensive assistance programs to entice investment.

Influence of Governments

Governments played a role in the establishment or closure of manufacturing plants. The Canadian government's high tariff policy contributed to the original establishment of the plant in London. If foreign corporations wanted to compete in Canada, it was necessary for them to build a plant in the country. These tariffs were reduced or eliminated with the free trade agreement between the United States and Canada. Similarity, the U.S. government's "Buy America" was a contributing factor in its closure in that products had to be produced in the country to take advantage of that government policy.

Canadian politicians had attempted to influence the London plant. In 2008, Prime Minister Harper visited the plant and promised $5 million in tax credit breaks to the purchasers of locomotives produced at the plant. The 2008 Budget allowed purchasers to double the cost allowance deduction on locomotive purchases. No direct government assistance was proposed for Electro-Motive Diesel Inc. itself.

On February 6, 2012, Ontario Premier Dalton McGuinty claimed that the federal government's foreign investment laws were outdated as they allowed a Canadian plant to be purchased and stripped within 18 months after the approval to take it over was given. The federal government responded, stating that what was happening fell under the province's industrial relations laws.[7]

Programs of some American states were also a factor; an example was those of Indiana. In order to attract the plant to Muncie, the Indiana state government provided $3.5 million in performance-based tax credits, $1 million in cash for employee training, and $1 million in infrastructure assistance. The state also agreed to assist the company in applying for U.S. federal government grants. Tax abatements of $22.5 million were obtained and some financing was available from the local county government.

Union's Influence

Globalization led to more volatile economic times and there had been an adverse impact on Canadian unions. Canadian private-sector union members were largely based in manufacturing industries and had been adversely impacted as manufacturing jobs disappeared. Also, automation in manufacturing had increased productivity and reduced the numbers of workers necessary. Overall, there were strong industrial relations laws in Canada but this did not prevent a decline in union membership. Only about 15 percent of the private-sector work force was unionized as newer service-type industries are more difficult to organize.

In addition, there were those in Canada who were critical of organized labour. Union leadership were accused of being more interested in their personal well-being than the interests of members. Restrictive work rules negotiated over years made improving productivity and product quality more difficult. It was alleged that unions fomented mistrust between workers and management. Critics stated that unions should be more transparent and accountable to members, for example by disclosing financial information which under Canadian law they were not required to do.

A trend in the United States toward right to work laws had been enacted in several U.S. states to encourage corporate investment and create jobs. Such laws allowed for a unionized workplace but gave workers an option of whether or not to join the union. As a result, many workers freeloaded off of those who agreed to join and pay the voluntary dues. This trend led to underfunded unions with less clout when negotiating contracts. As a result, some plants employing CAW members were attracted to the United States.

Nevertheless, the CAW attempted to protect the interests of its members at EMD. As early as December 21, 2011, Ken Lewenza, CAW president, sensed that EMD may leave. He called upon the federal government to conduct a review of Caterpillar's takeover of Canada's only locomotive manufacturer.[8] The federal government had not formally reviewed the takeover under the foreign investment regulations as the takeover was not large enough to be considered.[9] In a press release and letter to Industry Minister Christian Paradis on February 10, 2012, the CAW president demanded that the federal government provide details of the purchase of EMD by Caterpillar's Progress Rail Services in 2010. He requested that the government strengthen the regulations over foreign investment by:

- Improving transparency of the ultra-secretive Investment Canada process
- Allowing broader stakeholder input to reviews

- Closing loopholes that exempt most takeovers from scrutiny (including takeovers that are "too small" or reflect "indirect purchases" of companies)
- Strengthening and more clearly defining the "net benefit" test
- Ensuring that government can enforce commitments attached to approved takeovers[10]

With regard to the EMD closure, Lewenza stated that Caterpillar was exhibiting a "greedy, and frankly immoral, behaviour coming from a profitable company."[11] A large rally was held in London in support of the laid-off workers. Information picketing of Caterpillar outlets in various cities was organized and radio ads were broadcast.

Support from unions in Caterpillar plants in Belgium, France, and Italy stated that the EMD workers were "victims of a revolting blackmail."[12] The unions gave their full support to the London workers and stated that they would intervene before the local works councils in Europe. These initiatives had little impact on the decision.

Corporate Behaviour

Caterpillar was impacted by globalization and adjusted its corporate strategies. Instead of establishing plants overseas or outsourcing, new plants were being built in the United States. An example was its recent building of a new plant in Georgia where production was shifted from Japan as the market for some products had changed to North and South America. Also, several U.S. states had become friendlier to investment with less restrictive industrial-relations legislation, lower taxation, and their willingness to provide infrastructure and other incentives. Caterpillar was taking advantage of initiatives by some states that were becoming more aggressive in attracting investment and jobs.[13]

A factor in closing the London plant related to Caterpillar's strategy to become a major competitor in the train locomotive business. It recognized the increasing demand for freight and passenger train locomotives. New technologies had made the operation of locomotives more cost-effective, especially with regard to fuel consumption. Caterpillar was positioning itself in the locomotive business, and it needed to become efficient to compete with General Electric Co., its major competitor. As a part of this strategy, Caterpillar was refurnishing a plant in Muncie and thus closing the older, less efficient plant in London.

The profits of Caterpillar Inc. were an issue with the closure. The company achieved a profit of $4.9 billion in 2010, an 83 percent increase over the previous year, on sales of $60.1 billion.[14] A related issue was CEO Douglas Oberhelman's 2011 compensation of $10,550,300.[15] CAW's President Ken Lewenza said that the wage concessions were not necessary given Caterpillar's profits. He said: "What we're experiencing in London is a total injustice. It's shameful. It's completely hypocritical."[16]

Trends in the global economy presented challenges for Canadian stakeholders influenced by, or who could influence, the shutdown of the EMD plant. The union and governments appeared to have little influence on the decision. The corporation was implementing a global strategy in the best interests of its shareholders. As a result, another several hundred Canadians lost their jobs and many jobs were created in the United States.

The social responsibility toward workers after the closure of any plant was complicated. A component of social responsibility was the corporation's concern to employees and their well-being, present and past. The social obligation or legal requirement Caterpillar had to the displaced workers was an issue that still had to be addressed.

500 BIRDS ON A POND[17]

The Alberta Oil Sands

Early explorers were aware of oil type substances, or bitumen, for over 200 years in areas now known as northern Alberta. It is believed that First Nations peoples repaired and sealed canoes with the oily materials. It was not until the twentieth century that research and development of these oily materials occurred. The first development in the early part of the century was the drilling of wells north of Fort McMurray, but no oil, in a liquid form, was discovered. Other ventures attempted to find commercially viable extraction methods, but failed technically and commercially. It was not until the 1960s that serious development occurred. Alberta government publications stated that oil production from the oil sands was commercially feasible and announced an oil sands policy designed to encourage the orderly development of the oil sands in an area known as the Athabasca Oil Sands Region. The first two major commercial developments were by Great Canadian Oil Sands (GCOS) Project (later Suncor Energy), which produced oil in 1967, and the Syncrude consortium formed in 1964, which started building a facility in 1973 and producing oil in 1978.

The production of oil from the sands was controversial from the beginning. Petroleum companies, industry organizations, and governments favoured developing the sands and producing oil while environmentalists, NGOs, some First Nations groups, and some think tanks opposed it. The media coverage of the controversy was extensive and attempted balance, although negative news stories dominated at times. Society at large, or the general public, had a mixed opinion of the development. Many agreed with the development for the economic growth and employment generated, while others became increasingly concerned over the environmental impact of other major projects being built to extract the oil.

Many of the arguments supporting oil production from the oil sands and those critical are summarized in Table 1.

Syncrude Canada Ltd.

Syncrude Canada is a joint venture owned by Canadian Oil Sands Limited (36.74%), ConocoPhillips Oil Sands Partnership II (9.03%), Imperial Oil Resources (25%), Mocal Energy Limited (5%), Murphy Oil Company Ltd. (5%), Nexen Inc. (7.23%), and Petro-Canada (12%). It is the largest producer of crude oil from the oil sands with a production capacity equivalent to over 15 percent of Canada's crude oil requirements. It employs more than 5,000 persons and is the largest industrial employer of Aboriginal peoples in Canada.

Syncrude's 2007 Sustainability Report described its economic, social, and environmental obligations and achievements. The corporation's contribution to the economy included employment, materials purchasing, and royalty payments of $1.6 billion. It produced 111.3 million barrels of oil, and contributed $4.9 billion to the Canadian economy.

Social sustainability included Syncrude's stakeholder engagement approach to Aboriginal communities, advocacy groups, contractors, educators, governments, industry groups, local community groups, NGOs, suppliers, and employees. The company supported various community investment initiatives by contributing $4.2 million. Its safety record improved substantially over previous years.

Syncrude was involved in several environmental initiatives: air quality, involving reducing odours and emissions; reclaiming mined land; resource conservation through energy use reduction and recycling waste water; projects addressing climate change; and waste management.

Ducks Land on a Pond

Some of the oil production facilities required large quantities of water in their processes. After use, the water was recycled if feasible but some was mixed with other materials and stored in large constructed ponds estimated to cover 50 square kilometres. The

TABLE 1	*Arguments Supporting and Critical of Oil Sands*
Arguments in Support of Production from the Oil Sands	**Arguments Critical of Production from the Oil Sands**
• Government policy allows for responsible development enabling economic growth and protection of the environment. Oil sands development is regulated.	• Oil sands development is out of control with new projects starting. NGOs are concerned about carbon dioxide emissions, destruction of the boreal forest, and tailing ponds that might contaminate local rivers. Government cannot monitor all aspects of developments.
• Only 4 percent of Canada's GHG emissions and less than one-tenth of one percent of global emissions are from oil sands production.	• Total emissions are up over 37 percent since 1990. The oil sands are the fastest growing source of Canada's emissions increase.
• Carbon dioxide emissions have decreased by 45 percent per barrel since 1990.	• Intensity targets reduce per barrel emissions but let overall emissions increase.
• By 2050, emissions will be 14 percent below 2005 levels.	• The new technology to capture carbon is not available until 2018.
• Ninety percent of water is recycled.	• Two to four barrels of water are required to produce each barrel of oil, and the Athabasca River flow is reduced in the winter.
• Disturbed lands are restored as required by law.	• The landscape is difficult to restore and it takes 50 years.
• Regulators inspect ponds for seepage, and there are rules requiring that birds be kept away.	• Fifty square kilometres of ponds exist with no plan for remediation.
• The Alberta government requires waterfowl protection plans to deter birds from ponds.	• Society cannot trust companies to report spills and harms to animals.
• Testing has found no downstream risks to communities.	• First Nations at Fort Chipewyan are worried about wildlife, water supply, and health, in particular bile-duct cancer.
• Only 20 percent of oil is from mined sands. Most of it is from "in-situ" process; that is, injecting steam into the ground and heating the heavy oil so it can be pumped to the surface.	• "In-situ" is a better way of extracting but it is still disruptive to the environment and requires a lot of energy.
• The Alberta oil industry is the most environmentally conscious in the world with higher standards.	• This may be so, but the industry can do better.
• Corporations operating in the oil sands are the most socially responsible.	• There is the possibility of greenwashing.
• Supporting publication: *Alberta's Oil Sands: Opportunity. Balance,* Government of Alberta, March 2008, http://www.environment.alberta.ca/documents/oil_sands_opportunity_balance.pdf.	• Supporting publication: *The Most Destructive Project on Earth,* Environmental Defence, February 2008, http://www.environmentaldefence.ca/reports/tarsands.htm.

Sources: Compiled from numerous government and industry publications and media coverage.

For additional study tools and interactive ways to learn about ethics, visit **www.mcgrawhillconnect.ca**

ponds—referred to as tailings, waste, toxic or tar ponds—were a mixture of clay, water, sand, hydrocarbons, and heavy metals. Syncrude's Aurora North mine north of Fort McMurray contained such a pond.

The oil sands are on the migratory routes of several bird species and the oil companies are required to have plans to keep the birds off the ponds. The ponds do not freeze over as quickly as fresh water and may thaw sooner in the spring. One method used to frighten the birds from landing is using propane-fired cannons. On April 28, 2008 at 9:30 a.m., an estimated 500 ducks, including mallards, buffleheads, and goldeneyes, were discovered on the Aurora North pond by a Syncrude employee. The birds were heavily soaked from the residual oil on the pond's surface and could not fly. Although regulations required immediate notification, the Alberta Government's Fish and Wildlife Office was not called until noon.[18]

Sources: "Oil Sands History," Syncrude Canada Ltd. Web site, http://www.syncrude.ca/users/folder.asp?FolderID=5657; "Sustainability Report 2007," Syncrude Canada Ltd., http://www.syncrude.ca/users/folder.asp?FolderID=5713; "Hundreds of ducks trapped on toxic Alberta oilsands pond," CBC News online, April 29, 2008, http://www.cbc.ca/canada/edmonton/story/2008/04/29/oilsands-birds.html; Hanneke Brooymans and Jim Farrell, "Syncrude faces scrutiny after ducks land on toxic pond," *National Post* online edition, April 30, 2008, http://www.nationalpost.com/news/canada/story.html?id=482931; and Jason Markusoff, "Ducks the new symbol of oil sands activism," *The Edmonton Journal* online edition, May 4, 2008, http://www.canada.com/edmontonjournal/news/story.html?id=dc6561fd-eb68-4b36-96ba-77960387a911

ALBERTA ENERGY COMPANY AND THE ETHICS OF OPERATION KABRIOLE[19]

It is September 1998. Gwyn Morgan, President and CEO of the Alberta Energy Company (AEC), has a difficult decision to make that could affect his company immensely. He was approached by the Alberta RCMP with a proposal that may finally put an end to the industrial sabotage that had plagued not only his company, but also the entire oil and gas industry. The terrorism had been costly and had intimidated company staff.

AEC's operations were focused on two aspects of the petroleum business: four upstream operations in natural gas and oil exploration and production, and two midstream operations in natural gas storage, pipelines, and natural gas liquids processing. Its 1997 revenues were over $1.2 billion, with net earnings of $21.7 million.

The production and processing of natural gas and oil involved substantial risk for the environment. The potential for adverse impact of their operations on the environment was a major challenge for the company. One challenge was the use of flare stacks at well sites. Flaring was routinely used in the energy industry worldwide. A typical use was when oil was being produced and the solution gas (gas that bubbles out of the oil as it is brought to surface pressure) was uneconomical to recover and is flared (burned) near the well site. In 1996, Alberta alone had more than 5,200 solution gas flares operating. The theory was that through flaring, substances in the gas were converted to their safest form possible even though it released some 250 compounds. Referred to as sour gas, farmers believed it was these toxins that caused health problems in their families, livestock, and crops.

Farmers were increasingly vocal and active regarding the effects of pollution on their families and farms. Health problems alleged to be associated with flaring included asthma, coughing, headaches, aching muscles, shortness of breath, and memory loss. Illness in cattle and poor crops were also attributed to the pollution. There was a growing perception among farmers that their concerns were not being taken seriously. Many reports of these problems appeared in newspapers and other media. The stories claimed that farmers could not get help from government or through the legal channels such as the Alberta Energy and Utilities Board's Environmental Appeals Board set up to deal with farmers' concerns.

The situation became volatile, with acts of terrorism occurring against the oil and gas industry. In February 1998, a particularly violent event occurred near Bowden, Alberta, when a beef farmer shot and killed an oil and gas company vice-president supervising the cleanup of a well site on his farm. Another petroleum company that had operated the site had caused the pollution. The farmer had been trying to get the well cleaned up for two and a half years and apparently broke down over all the frustrations at getting the cleanup done.

The eco-terrorism took place in AEC's operations in northwest Alberta, especially in the Peace River area. In the mid 1990s, the vandalism of petroleum installations began and continued during 1997 and into 1998. Over 100 acts of terrorism had occurred since mid-1996; the major acts are listed in Table 1. Property damage was running into the millions of dollars, and there was

TABLE 1	*Chronology of Selected Terrorist Activities*
Date	**Event**
1996	Nails are thrown on remote roads on land leased by oil companies. Power lines are cut down. Shots are fired through offices of two gas plants near Hythe, AB.
December, 1997	A fire occurs at a Norcen Energy well site south of Hythe, AB and cement studded with shotgun shells is found.
April 25, 1998	Three shots are fired at AEC well site building.
June 16, 1998	An AEC pipeline is hit with homemade projectile bomb.
July 31, 1998	An AEC sweet gas well at Goodfare, AB is bombed.
Aug. 2, 1998	A sour gas well near Demmitt, AB is bombed.
Aug. 24, 1998	A Suncor Energy oil well south of Hinton, AB is bombed.

concern for the safety of field workers and neighbours. Some employees received threats of harm, but the RMCP had not charged anyone with responsibility for the acts. The police force was experiencing a staff shortage and had limited resources to devote to the terrorism. The petroleum industry's concern for its property and for employees and neighbours, plus the inability of the police to address the problem, resulted in cooperative efforts between the industry and the police.

Operation "Kabriole" and the Sting

The petroleum industry, the police, and the communities in the area were increasingly concerned about the vandalism. In late summer 1998, the RCMP put together a special initiative labelled "Operation Kabriole"[20] to focus on the petroleum vandalism problem, and asked the industry for assistance. The operation was targeted at Wiebo Ludwig, leader of the Church of the Shepherd King sect of the Christian Reform Church who, along with his friend, Richard Boonstra, felt strongly that flaring was responsible for a range of human and animal birth deformities and still-births. Ludwig was widely known as an outspoken critic of the petroleum industry and flaring in particular, and he and his supporters were to be under 24-hour ground and airplane surveillance. The operation's budget was $354,750, but before it was over the operation would cost $750,000.

Ed McGillivary, AEC's director of environment, health, and safety, received a call from Robert Wraight, a friend of Ludwig's. Wraight offered his services as an undercover agent if AEC purchased his land for $109,000. AEC flew Wraight, at their expense, to Calgary and set up a meeting with the RCMP.

After discussions with the RCMP, Wraight agreed to become a paid agent and attempted to gather evidence for a case against Ludwig. The evidence gathering included wearing a concealed tape recorder while visiting the Ludwig farm. As an informant, Wraight was given a $10,000 signing bonus and placed on the payroll at $475 per week. Later the police picked up $14,000 in other expenses that he incurred. AEC did not purchase Wraight's farm.

The RCMP approached AEC for their cooperation and the company agreed to provide resources if it would help solve the vandalism problem. The company offered to supply high-tech night vision equipment from its private security firm. This offer was refused, as it was not consistent with RCMP policy. The security firm was to provide tips to the RCMP on Ludwig's movements, something that many other organizations and individuals were doing.

In order to enhance Wraight's credibility, the RCMP proposed that a petroleum installation be deliberately vandalized. The RCMP proposed blowing up an old vehicle that they were willing to purchase from AEC for $8,000. Gwyn Morgan objected to this as he felt that it would cause stress among employees who feared that their vehicles might be vandalized. Instead, it was agreed that an abandoned, remote petroleum site building would be bombed. No date was set for the bombing but all agreed—the sooner the better.

Gwyn Morgan's Moral Dilemma

Gwyn Morgan was being asked to approve an act of vandalism and the company would not be able to disclose its involvement in the near future. All through the planning of the sting, he expressed that he wanted a complete disclosure of the context for AEC's cooperation. He knew that this might be difficult, given the process through which charges are laid and the timing of court proceedings.

Morgan was concerned that the vandalism was escalating into life-threatening sabotage. The direct and indirect costs to AEC were now over two million dollars, but there were more serious concerns. Placing explosive devices on wellheads, pipelines, and gas production facilities was dangerous to employees, and potentially dangerous to surrounding residents. Employees had received anonymous death threats, creating stress for them and their families.

Morgan had much to think about as he considered the decision. He was concerned about how the public would react to being deceived. Although the RCMP had assured him that the explosion would be safely discharged, he still worried about the success of the clandestine operation. He agonized over the level of cooperation between AEC and the RCMP, even though the RCMP assured him that such cooperation would be helpful in preventing extremely serious crimes. Only four others at AEC knew of the operation, and he wondered how shareholders, directors, and other employees would react when the event was disclosed.

He was aware that injury or death could be avoided and thought that to do nothing by being a bystander was the easy way out. Furthermore, the company was cooperating with an organization that society relies upon for law and order. Despite this, he anticipated that it might be viewed differently in the future as the media and the public questioned the close relationship between the company and the RCMP. The public might perceive that the line between corporate interests of the oil industry and law enforcement had become blurred. Moreover, they may not appreciate the company having been less than forthcoming about the staged bombing.

He knew that he and the company would be held accountable in any judicial process if the eco-terrorists were caught and charged. The public may not consider it appropriate for business to supply money and other resources to a police force. Thinking back over the events of the preceding months, he wondered if cooperating with the RCMP had been wise or appropriate. He, AEC's security firm, and Ed McGillivary had been in contact with the police force.

The dilemma for Morgan meant agonizing over compliance with the RCMP sting or be a bystander resisting any further involvement with police attempts to catch those responsible. He had to balance the protection of individuals from harm and the inclination to cooperate with the police against the consequence to be less than forthcoming in corporate announcements. How would he explain his actions to the company's directors and shareholders after the fact? How would they react? How would the industry react? How would the media respond? How would the nearby residents and communities feel? He wondered how things had reached this point. He was President and CEO, and it was his decision to make.

THE ETHICS OF EXPORTING ASBESTOS[21]

Canadians were aware of the dangers of asbestos and it had been removed from many public buildings, including the Parliament Buildings in Ottawa. Exposure to asbestos endangered health through asbestosis, lung cancer, and a more serious cancer referred to as mesothelioma, cancer of the lung's protective lining. Most countries had banned all forms of asbestos as it was considered a health risk. Chrysotile, or "white" asbestos, was the only form that continued to be produced. It was mined in Canada, Russia, China, Kazakhstan, Brazil, and Zimbabwe, and about $100 million worth was exported annually by Canadian producers, primarily to India, Indonesia, Sri Lanka, and Brazil.[22]

The Canadian Industry

Chrysotile was first mined in Quebec in 1879, and in 2010 there remained two active mines that employed fewer than 1,000 persons, down from 7,000 when asbestos was more widely used. The two remaining producers were LAB Chrysotile Inc. of Telford Mines and JM Asbestos Inc. of Asbestos, both in Quebec. Ninety-five percent of the production was exported to developing countries where it was used in asbestos cement building products. The Governments of Canada and Quebec allowed these exports and had spent over $20 million since 1984 in promoting the product's use abroad.

The use of chrysotile was promoted by an industry organization, the Chrysotile Institute, headquartered in Montreal. Its objectives were to promote the safe use of chrysotile, provide information to chrysotile producers and users, gather and disseminate medical, scientific, and technical data about chrysotile, and inform and advise all stakeholders of the potential risks related to breathable fibres.[23] The Institute stated that some people mistakenly claimed chrysotile killed thousands and they did not distinguish between chrysotile and amphiboles asbestos. According to the Institute, the fibre from chrysotile was harmless even if inhaled or ingested. On the other hand, amphibole asbestos fibres had a different chemical composition that threatened health. It was pointed out that the industry only markets chrysotile when encapsulated in a cement or resin and there was minimal risk of danger to the user's health.[24]

In Canada, the production of chrysotile was politically sensitive. Political parties did not wish to alienate voters in the regions where the industry provides employment.[25] Thus, governments supported the industry and contributed financially to the operation of the Chrysotile Institute. On the other hand, the federal government limited the use of any asbestos in Canada. Health Canada posted a consumer product safety notice about asbestos.[26] In 2007, Health Canada concluded that chrysotile showed a "strong relationship of exposure to cancer."[27] Canada has been called hypocritical because it promoted the sale of asbestos to developing countries while banning its use within the country.[28]

Opposition to Asbestos

The opposition to the use of chrysotile was widespread, including from the Canadian and Quebec Medical Associations, Canadian Cancer Society, and Canadian Lung Association. The World Health Organization (WHO) stated "all types of asbestos cause cancer in humans."[29] It was concerned about the continuing use of asbestos cement in the construction industry, as there was a large workforce and it was difficult to control exposure to asbestos fibres. The International Labour Organization (ILO) adopted a resolution at the 95th Session of the International Labour Conference, June 2006, stating, "the elimination of the future use of asbestos and the identification and proper management of asbestos currently in place are the most effective means to protect workers from asbestos exposure and to prevent future asbestos-related diseases and deaths."[30] The Office of the Auditor General of Canada, in a statement on "Canada's Policies on Chrysotile Asbestos Exports," pointed out concerns about air quality, human health/environmental health, international cooperation, natural resources, and toxic substances.[31]

An editorial in the *Canadian Medical Association Journal* (CMAJ) in October 2008 was very critical of Canada's "asbestos mortality." According to the editorial, Canada was "the only Western democracy to consistently oppose international efforts to regulate the global trade in asbestos." Furthermore, the Canadian government had done so with political manipulation of science and in alliance with countries such as Russia and Zimbabwe. Canada's position was that chrysotile was safer and less carcinogenic, thus posing less of a risk to health.[32] Another medical publication, *The Lancet,* the world's leading general medical journal, and specialty journals in oncology, neurology, and infectious diseases also criticized Canada for producing and exporting asbestos.[33]

The Canadian Auto Workers (CAW) had a "Ban Asbestos Campaign" that refuted the argument that asbestos was safe. Sample letters were provided that could be forwarded to politicians. The union published a 172-page report, *Pure White: Asbestos—A Canadian Scrapbook,* to provide useful information about the dangers of asbestos in workplaces and communities. A CAW "Health and Safety Fact Sheet" also described asbestos and its dangers.[34]

Use in Developing Countries: The Customers

Asbestos products had appealing properties in developing countries. They were cheaper than alternatives, did not corrode, and were virtually indestructible. Roofing tiles made from chrysotile and cement, for example, were far superior to alternatives available in these countries as they were fireproof, easily and securely installed, and reduced noise from rainfall. However, there was concern about the workers in plants producing or fabricating the products, as dust created could be dangerous to their health.[35]

There were some initiatives undertaken by nongovernmental organizations (NGOs) opposing the sale of chrysotile in developing countries. An International Ban Asbestos Secretariat (IBAS) was formed in 2000 to coordinate opposition to asbestos and was working to achieve a global asbestos ban. It pointed out that although asbestos was seldom used in developed countries it continued to be used in developing nations.[36] At a conference in Hong Kong in April 2009, the Asian Ban Asbestos Network (A-BAN) was launched. It was a network of "organizations and individuals from countries and regions in Asia and the Pacific, which agreed to work together on activities towards achieving common objectives."[37]

Canada's production and marketing of chrysotile received considerable media coverage. NGOs and world health organizations were opposed to trade in asbestos, yet Canada continued support production and encourage exports.

Death and Possible Revitalization of the Industry

By 2011, the Canadian asbestos industry appeared to be on its last legs. LAB Chrysotile ceased production in December 2011 but still sold from inventory. In early January 2012 the company declared bankruptcy, but hoped to reform.[38] The Jeffrey mine had reduced production and employed only 25 workers in July 2011. It requested a $58 million loan guarantee from governments to relaunch the mine. The mine had been an open pit operation but the accessibility to ore had run out and it was necessary to develop an underground mine.[39]

There were continued warnings that the export of asbestos was ethically problematic, that it was harming Canada's reputation, and that it was hypocritical. Editorials in Canada's two national newspapers criticized the export of asbestos: "Subsidizing Shame" in *The Globe and Mail*[40] and "Saying No to Canada's Asbestos" in the *National Post.*[41] On July 24, 2012, the Joint Policy Committee Societies of Epidemiology issued a statement calling for a global ban on the mining, use, and export of all forms of asbestos. The statement had been endorsed by 150 public health and civil society organizations, and individual scientists from 20 countries.[42]

In June 2011, the United Nations' Rotterdam Convention[43] met to compile a list of hazardous chemicals. Canada single-handedly blocked the inclusion of chrysotile asbestos on the list even though the major customers for the materials, Vietnam, Kazakhstan, Kyrgyzstan, and India, agreed to the listing. The list did not ban asbestos but would merely warn customers of the health hazards. Canada's Health Department had recommended that asbestos be added to the list.

The Canadian government supported asbestos exports. During the 2011 election campaign, Prime Minister Harper had defended asbestos exports despite the health risks.[44] The Opposition parties in Parliament supported a motion to ban exports of asbestos:

That, in the opinion of the House, the government should: (a) ban the use and export of asbestos; (b) support international efforts to add chrysotile asbestos to the list of hazardous chemical products under the Rotterdam Convention; (c) assist affected workers by developing a Just Transition Plan with measures to accommodate their re-entry into the workforce; (d) introduce measures dedicated to affected older workers, through the employment insurance program, to assure them of a decent standard of living until retirement; and (e) support communities and municipalities in asbestos producing regions through an investment fund for regional economic diversification.[45]

On November 11, 2011, the House of Commons defeated the motion 152–123 with the Conservative and Bloc Quebecois parties voting against and the New Democratic, Liberal, and Green parties voting for the motion. Despite all the criticism and warnings, the governments of Canada and Quebec were still supporting the export of asbestos. In July 2012, it was only a matter of time before further support for the industry would be announced. Many in Canada and around the world questioned this support, and wondered why Canada was exporting asbestos and death for some users.

CRISIS AT MAPLE LEAF FOODS INC.[46]

In the summer of 2008, Canada experienced a serious outbreak of listeriosis, which resulted in 57 persons becoming seriously ill and caused the deaths of 22 individuals. Listeriosis is one of about 250 food-borne illnesses that include *salmonella, E. coli,* and the Norwalk virus. It results from consuming food contaminated with a bacterium called *Listeria monocytogenes* and any form of disease or invasive infection that results is given the name listeriosis. Older persons, those with compromised immune systems, and some pregnant women have a higher risk of being affected. A significant characteristic of listeriosis is the time between eating contaminated food and the onset of illness, which can range from three to 70 days. In comparison, *salmonella* causes illness within 12 to 72 hours. The most common forms of listeriosis are sepsis (bloodstream infection), infection of the central nervous system (usually meningitis), and miscarriage, stillbirth, or premature birth. It usually is not identified until blood samples are diagnosed in a laboratory.[47]

A Chronology of Events

The *Report of the Independent Investigator into the 2008 Listeriosis Outbreak* gave a detailed chronology of the chain of events related to the outbreak from July through September 2008. The report covered all sectors of Canada's health and safety systems, but the following chronology lists only some of the events, and in particular those relating to the source of the contamination, Maple Leaf Foods.

TABLE 1	*Chronology of Selected Crisis Events*
July 10:	First listeriosis cases diagnosed in a Toronto-area long-term care home.
July 16:	Toronto Public Health begins investigating the two cases.
July 18:	Match confirmed on DNA fingerprinting from first two human samples.
July 21:	Food samples picked up by Toronto Public Health from long-term care home.
July 23:	Long-term care home removes high-risk foods such as cold cuts, cheeses, and ice cream.
July 25:	More cases show up on provincial surveillance system.
August 4:	Some of the samples from the long-term care home test positive for *Listeria monocytogenes.*
August 6:	The Toronto-area long-term care home suspects Maple Leaf Foods (MLF) products as the cause of the listeriosis.
August 7:	The Canadian Food Inspection Agency (CFIA) initiates a food safety investigation.
August 8:	The CFIA requests deli meats distribution records from MLF Sales Office but it is closed for the weekend.
August 11:	Distribution records are received from MLF. Sure Slice brand products sold to hospitals, long-term care homes, prisons, restaurants, and hotels are suspected. Search begins for unopened food packages to verify the source.
August 12:	National outbreak indicated. Unopened packaged meat products located and sent for testing. Two other possible cases identified.
August 13:	MLF advises distributers not to sell Sure Slice roast beef, corned beef, and Black Forest ham. Possible link to MLF's Bartor Road plant identified.
August 14:	Confirmation of first listeriosis death in mid-June linked to deli meats.
August 15:	Ontario institutions advised to stop serving Sure Slice products.
August 16:	CFIA confirms *Listeria monocytogenes* in unopened Sure Slice package.
August 17:	Consumers warned not to eat two Sure Slice products and MLF voluntarily recalls two products.
August 19:	Consumers warned not to eat 23 additional MLF deli meat products and company announces second recall.
August 20:	MLF suspends all production at the Bartor Road plant and announces that it is voluntarily recalling 23 products.
August 21:	It is confirmed that 18 products from the Bartor Road plant are contaminated.
August 23:	The link between human illness and contaminated deli meats is confirmed and MLF issues third recall of products—recalling all products made at the Bartor Road plant.[48]

Source: Listeriosis Report, Chapter 6, "How did events unfold," 47–60.

Maple Leaf Foods Inc.

The history of Maple Leaf Foods can be traced for over 100 years. It is the result of amalgamations and mergers of companies in the food industry, making it Canada's major food processing corporation. In 2008, the controlling shareholders were the McCain Capital Corporation and the Ontario Teachers' Pension Plan Board, and the company was publicly traded on the Toronto Stock Exchange. Headquartered in Toronto, it employed 23,000 people in Canada, the United States, the United

Kingdom, and Asia. Maple Leaf Foods comprised three major groups: Meat Products—fresh and packaged meat; Bakery Products—fresh, frozen, and specialty bakery foods; and Agribusiness Products—including hog, rendering, and biodiesel production. Its main product brands were *Maple Leaf*®, *Schneiders*®, and *Dempster's*®. The company's 2007 sales were over $5 billion with 76 percent in Canada, 12 percent in the United States, and 12 percent in the rest of the world. Its net earnings for 2007 were $195 million.[49]

In August 2008, Michael McCain, president and CEO, and other senior management were wondering what public action to take other than recalling products. The company's lawyers and public relations staff were advising caution, in particular about accepting responsibility because of the legal implications, which could lead to future legal expenses and costly settlements. Some managers were concerned about the cost of recalling products not proven to be contaminated, potentially in the tens of millions. Still others pointed out that the company met all government standards and regulations and that its food safety policies and procedures were as high as any other company in the food industry. Some felt that the company could wait for government agencies to take initiative, with Maple Leaf Foods reacting as necessary. Others argued that the company should be open, admit its mistakes, and take responsibility for what happened. On August 23, it was decided that Michael McCain, the CEO, should make a national statement about the crisis.

JUST DUMP IT IN THE LAKE[50]

On February 21, 2009, a "Notice of a Proclamation Exempting the Waters of Sandy Pond from Section 22 of the Navigable Waters Protection Act" appeared in the *Canada Gazette,* the official newspaper of the Government of Canada.[51] The Notice stated that "interested parties may make representations concerning the proposed proclamation within 30 days after the date of publication of this notice."[52] Those opposing the project had until March 21 to respond.

The Environment and Mining

Mining has several impacts on the environment; a major one relates to disposing or storing of waste materials or tailings after a processing or refining process. In the past, the tailings were simply put in piles, dumped in bodies of water, including the ocean, or contained in human-made holding areas or ponds. All of these approaches threatened the environment and possibly the health of surrounding residents. As a result, the industry sought better ways to dispose of the waste materials. Research suggested an approach whereby waste materials would be deposited in natural lakes, which would contain the harmful chemicals. Ideal lakes for this approach would be near the plant, have limited watershed, and be deep. This approach was preferable to constructing open holding ponds that might leak and were expensive to build and maintain.

In order to do this, some way had to be found to get around existing legislation, in particular, the Fisheries Act, which made it illegal to pollute fish-bearing waters.[53] However, the "Metal Mining Effluent Regulations" of the Act allowed federal bureaucrats to redefine a lake as a tailing impoundment area. To date, 16 sites have been applied for and listed in Schedule 2 of the regulations.[54]

In order for a lake to be listed, a notice must be issued exempting the lake from Section 22 (see Table 1) of the Navigable Waters Protection Act. An Order in Council[55] is necessary under Section 23 (see Table 1) to place the lake on Schedule 2 and allow for the dumping of waste into the body of water.

Vale's Sandy Pond Proposal

Vale planned construction of a hydromet nickel processing plant at Long Harbour, Newfoundland and Labrador, 100 kilometres west of St. John's. Plant construction was to begin in 2009, and completed by 2012 at an estimated cost of $2.17 billion. It would employ 1,600–2,000 persons in the construction stage and about 400–450 full-time employees when in operation. The plant is intended to process 50,000 tonnes of nickel, 3,270 tonnes of copper, and 2,460 tonnes of cobalt annually from ore mined at the company's Voisey Bay mine in NL.

The facility required a disposal of tailings plan and the company decided to use Sandy Pond. About 400,000 tonnes of effluent would be dumped in the lake annually. The pond was about 6 kilometres from the plant and covered about 38 hectares. Dams would be constructed to enlarge the holding area to about 78 hectares. Vale was a signatory to the Mining Association of Canada's "Towards Sustainable Mining (TSM)" initiative.[56] The company stated that it accepted responsibility for the environment and acted responsibly.[57]

TABLE 1	*Sections 22 and 23 of the Navigable Waters Protection Act*

22. No person shall throw or deposit or cause, suffer or permit to be thrown or deposited any stone, gravel, earth, cinders, ashes or other material or rubbish that is liable to sink to the bottom in any water, any part of which is navigable or that flows into any navigable water, where there are not at least twenty fathoms of water at all times, but nothing in this section shall be construed so as to permit the throwing or depositing of any substance in any part of a navigable water where that throwing or depositing is prohibited by or under any other Act.
R.S., c. N-19, s. 20.
23. The Governor in Council, when it is shown to the satisfaction of the Governor in Council that the public interest would not be injuriously affected thereby, may, by proclamation, declare any rivers, streams or waters in respect of which sections 21 and 22 apply, or any parts thereof, exempt in whole or in part from the operation of those sections, and may revoke the proclamation.
R.S., c. N-19, s. 21.

Source: Department of Justice, Government of Canada, Navigable Waters Protection Act, Chapter N-22, R.S., C. N19, s.1, http://laws.justice. gc.ca/PDF/Statute/N/N-22.pdf. Reproduced with the permission of the Minister of Public Works and Government Services Canada, 2010.

Arguments Supporting the Use of Sandy Pond

Vale said that it had seriously studied the alternatives and their environmental impact. It claimed that using Sandy Pond was the most environmentally friendly approach and stated that the Department of Fisheries and Oceans agreed. Submerging the waste prevents oxidization, which releases toxic substances. Ponds do not leak and human-made holding ponds would be much larger, requiring 180 hectares. Economically the pond made sense as costs of using the pond were $62 million versus $490 million for a human-made holding pond. Overall, using Sandy Pond was the least threat to the environment and the health of the community. Furthermore, the economic development was needed in the area of high unemployment after a phosphorus plant closed about 20 years prior.

Arguments Opposing the Use of Sandy Pond

Using lakes as dumps is an emotional issue. Environmentalists stated that Sandy Pond was a pristine lake with trout, eels, and smelt and used for local recreation. Mining Watch complained that the government was making it too easy to use lakes as industrial waste dumps and disposal sites. Moreover, there was a "hidden subsidy" to the mining industry when it managed to get around the *Fisheries Act* enabling it to reduce costs.

The controversy over Sandy Pond generated substantial public comment. Opposition to the dumping of wastes came from stakeholders such as Centre for Long Term Environmental Action NL (CLEANf/Ld), the Sierra Club of Canada, the Council of Canadians, the New Democratic Party, the Canadian Union of Public Employees, the David Suzuki Foundation, and Maude Barlow, a senior adviser on water to the United Nations.

PROFESSOR MURRAY'S ETHICAL DILEMMAS[58]

Everyone in their workplace, personal life, or society is confronted with ethical dilemmas from time to time. College instructors are no exception. Much has been written on teaching ethics, but little about the ethics of teaching. Yet all instructors have their personal integrity to consider and a responsibility to teach in an ethical manner. Also, they should consider the ethical implications of actions taken by colleagues, students, and themselves.

Below are incidents that present ethical dilemmas for college or university instructors. For each incident, identify what the dilemma is, the stakeholders involved,

what the instructor should do, and who is harmed by or benefits from the decision. In addition, identify the ethical principle that formed the basis for the decision.

Incident #1

Professor Wayne Murray answered a knock at his door to find a young man whom he did not recognize. The young man explained that he represented a used-book company that gathered textbooks and then sold them to bookstores. These stores then resold them at prices lower than new copies, thus saving students money. He offered to purchase any "sample" or "inspection" copies of textbooks that Professor Murray had received from publishers that he did not need.

Professor Murray often received free textbooks from the publishers and had not recommended most of them for use in his courses. Such textbooks sat on his book shelves for years, were thrown out, or sometimes sent to educational institutions in developing countries. The young man was a student at the university for whom this part-time job would help him finance his education. Professor Murray was not sure what he should do.

Incident #2

Professor Murray had taught general management courses, such as strategy management, at a Canadian university for over 15 years. Despite his experience, he was still uneasy when students requested extensions to assignments or examination deferrals.

The assignments were described in detail on course outlines distributed at the first class. This was a requirement for all courses and all instructors complied with the policy. As a result, all students were aware of all assignment due dates and the dates of mid-term examinations well in advance.

Each semester, Professor Murray received several requests for extensions or deferrals. The reasons for the requests could be categorized into three types: (1) those based upon student illness or an illness or death in the student's family or close friends; (2) those based on work overload resulting from several assignments or examinations occurring at the same time; and (3) those based on the student's claim that he or she was busy with work and/or extracurricular activities.

The first category presented no difficulty for Professor Murray. He granted the request for extension usually without requiring documentation. But, the second and third reasons concerned him.

Professor Murray was particularly concerned about the ethical implications of the requests and of the actual granting of extensions. He was concerned about fairness and justice to students who worked to meet the deadlines. He worried about consistency in dealing with the requests and their legitimacy. He did not believe that students fully appreciated the awkward position in which these requests placed him.

Incident #3

As a professor of management, Professor Murray attempted to keep up-to-date on his area of specialization by reading selected academic journals. He felt this improved his teaching as students would be presented with recent research discoveries. He also tried to keep track of research developments so that he could use them to enhance his own research activity.

A colleague's research was in a related area and Professor Murray always read these articles out of interest and so that he could discuss the findings with his colleague. Last year, his colleague published an excellent article that tested a management theory. The article included a comprehensive six-page review of relevant literature and Professor Murray had used this review himself to prepare lecture materials. This year his colleague published another article in a different journal testing a similar theory. However, the literature review for this article included five pages from the previous article without any alterations. Furthermore, his colleague did not state that the review had been previously published.

Plagiarism was a serious problem with student assignments. Students had been warned of the seriousness of the practice and three students had been expelled for copying the writings of others without referencing them. Professor Murray was taken aback by the fact that his colleague had plagiarized, even if it was his own work.

Incident #4

Students were frequently used as subjects for professors' research projects. Such a practice was convenient for the professors as it reduced the need to recruit participants. Furthermore, students were contributing to the advancement of knowledge, which they may or may not have appreciated. Although less frequently, the practice still occurred. There were college policies relating to the practice and agencies that funded research had strict policies about obtaining consent and making participation voluntary.

Professor Murray had colleagues who used students as research subjects. He had heard that some of his colleagues secretly conducted surveys in their classes without advising the administration. He thought that students should not be asked to participate in a study by their professor under any circumstances. It was difficult, if not impossible, to eliminate the real or perceived influence or power that the professor had with students. He was thinking of proposing a college policy that disallowed soliciting survey participation in the classroom setting. If faculty wanted to use students in their studies, they should advertise for them and perhaps offer incentives. The important point would be that the studies would not be associated with a particular course and classroom setting. Some of Professor Murray's colleagues felt that he was being too strict and limiting their ability to conduct research.

Incident #5

Professor Murray and his colleagues were alarmed at the reports of student cheating at colleges and universities. *Maclean's* magazine carried several stories on the subject with titles such as, "The great university cheating scandal" (Feb. 12, 2007, 32–36), "Cheating? Who us?" (Feb. 26, 2007, 41), and "Cheating on your exam? It's no big deal" (June 25, 2007, 25). There was considerable discussion of the issue and some codes of conduct were developed at his college. Students were advised of the college's policy regarding cheating and the fact that students could be expelled. From his experience and according to his colleagues, cheating continued.

One of the *Maclean's* articles stated that 44 percent of professors said that they didn't report students caught cheating. This statistic became more relevant when Professor Murray suspected a student of cheating in an examination. First of all, Professor Murray saw the student leaning over and reading the papers of students beside him. Secondly, the same student was seen removing a piece of paper from his shirt sleeve.

Professor Murray found it awkward to do anything at the time, as approaching the student would have disrupted the examination. He thought that it was not fair to other students that this student should get away with cheating. But, he concluded that it would be difficult to prove that the cheating occurred; it would be his word against the student's. Furthermore, he did not look forward to the numerous meetings and hearings that would be involved if he accused the student of cheating.

Incident #6

In one of his courses, Professor Murray assigned several case studies which the students could purchase online from the Harvard Business School. On the day when the first case was to be discussed, he asked how many had purchased the case. About half of the students held up their hands. He then asked if the others had the case and had read it. They informed him that they had obtained the case for free from an Internet site. He was able to access the Harvard site, which provided a count of the number of sales along with the names of the students who had bought the case. About half of the students had purchased the cases. Given this situation, Professor Murray discussed in class the appropriateness of obtaining the cases and that copyright issues were involved. However, he did not mention that he had access to sales data.

Before the next class, when another case was to be discussed, Professor Murray searched the Internet and could not find the case available. He then checked the Harvard site again. The number of sales had not changed. He wondered how he should deal with this in the class. Should he tell the students he could see who had purchased the case? Then again, he was unsure of whether he should have told the students upfront that he had access to this information. He wondered what to do, and whether he should do anything at all.

FORTIS AND THE CHALILLO DAM: BALANCING ECONOMIC DEVELOPMENT AND ENVIRONMENTAL IMPACT[59]

Fortis Corporation

Fortis Inc. is a diversified electric utility holding company headquartered in St. John's, NL. *Fortis* is a Latin word meaning strong, powerful, and firm. [Fortis Inc. is not associated with the Fortis international banking and insurance financial firm headquartered in The Netherlands and Belgium.]

In 2001, Fortis wholly owned Newfoundland Power Inc., the principal distributor of power in Newfoundland and Labrador, Maritime Electric Company Limited, the main distributor in Prince Edward Island, and Fortis Properties, a non-utility subsidiary with investments in commercial properties in Atlantic Canada. Other financial interests included electric utilities in Ontario, New York State, the Cayman Islands, and Belize. The Belizean interests were 67 percent of Belize Electricity Limited (BEL), the only distributor of electricity in Belize, and 100 percent of Belize Electric Company Limited (BECOL), which owned a hydroelectric plant on the Macal River at Mollejon, Belize.

The Fortis operations in Belize embroiled the company in an environmental responsibility issue that consumed substantial costs, time, and energy. BEL had been owned by the Government of Belize and was the main supplier of electricity in the country. In October and November 1999, Fortis Inc. acquired 67 percent of the company for $36 million in cash. It later acquired BECOL and a proposal by this company to develop a hydroelectric project in Belize received international attention and became a sensitive issue for management.[60]

The Chalillo Project

Fortis, through BECOL, proposed construction of a dam on the Macal River in the Cayo District of western Belize at cost of about US$27.3 million. The site was located in an unpopulated wilderness area, part of which was in the Mountain Pine Ridge Forest Reserve and Chaquibul National Park. These areas covered most of the southern half of Cayo district. It would produce 7.3 MW of electricity for the Belize network and regulate the river's flow. The control over the water flow would increase the productivity and reliably of the Mollejon hydro power station downstream.

The Chalillo project included:

- a 49.5 m high by 340 m wide dam on the river,
- a reservoir with a total surface area of 9.5 km²,
- a powerhouse at the foot of the dam,
- an 18 km transmission line from the powerhouse to the Mollejon plant, and
- ancillary requirements including an access road and construction camp.[61]

There were benefits to the Belizean citizens and the country's economy. Most importantly, the project would increase electrical output and raise energy self-sufficiency. The second dam on the Macal River would increase the productivity of the existing electrical plant at Mollejon. The output from the two plants would reduce reliance on petroleum generation as diesel-fuelled generators could be closed. This would reduce greenhouse gas emissions and the possibility of oil spills.

A large portion of Belizean electrical energy was imported from Mexico under a contract that was to expire in 2008. The Mexican system experienced difficulties and it was not a stable source, resulting in power outages in Belize. The completion of the Chalillo project meant that Belize would have a more reliable and secure supply of electricity, stabilizing and possibly reducing prices. Alternative sources of energy were examined by the government and BEL including thermal options (diesel and gas turbines), biomass, Battery Energy Storage Systems, and solar and wind power. Studies by BEL determined that power generated from the hydro source was less expensive than any other. However, BEL was committed to purchasing power from a bagasse-fuelled generation facility planned by Belize Sugar Industries Limited (BSI). The facility would produce energy by burning crushed sugarcane and wood wastes from nearby sawmills.

There were other benefits to the project. The dam and reservoir would control flooding on the Macal River with significant economic, health, and safety benefits to downstream residents, many of whom lived in the river's floodplain. Also, there would be a steadier supply of water for residents especially during the dry season. Employment would be created during construction and there would be economic benefits from supplying goods and services to the project.[62]

Opposition to the Project

During 2001, criticisms and opposition were voluminous. Several Canadian print and broadcast media carried stories, there were letters to the editor in newspapers, and protest Web sites were established.

Numerous environmental non-governmental organizations (ENGOs) campaigned against the project, including:

- Probe International (PI)
- Natural Resources Defense Council (NRDC)
- Sierra Club of Canada
- Belize Alliance of Conservation Non-Governmental Organizations (BACONGO)
- Humber Environmental Action Group
- Humber Natural History Society
- Petitcodiac Riverkeeper
- Action Environment
- Defenders of Wildlife
- Environment Coalition of Prince Edward Island
- Falls Brook Centre

In particular, PI carried out an aggressive campaign and coordinated the protests of other ENGOs.[63] PI is an environmental advocacy group that fights to stop ill-conceived aid, trade projects, and foreign investments. It works to give citizens the tools they need to stop such projects using the rule of law, democratic processes, and honest and transparent accounting. It is a division of the Energy Probe Research Foundation, a well-known Canadian environmental and energy policy ENGO created in 1980. Its tactics include writing letters to public officials, preparing and publishing reports and articles, media releases, speech presentations, and public demonstrations.

The other main opposition came from NRDC, an environmental action group founded in 1970. Its mission is to safeguard the Earth: its people, plants, and animals, and the natural systems on which all life depends. It has offices in seven U.S. cities, staff of about 300 lawyers, scientists, and policy experts, and about 1 million

EXHIBIT 1	*Main Criticisms of the Chalillo Project*

- The threat to wildlife and plant life, especially endangered species.
- The dam would exacerbate the water quality problems downstream.
- The dam may flood Maya ruins destroying the cultural landscape.
- Limestone caves may drain the reservoir.
- The claim that the project was uneconomic and not the cheapest option. The only reason the project was viable was because BEL had a monopoly and could recover costs from captive customers.
- Fortis's unwillingness to consider alternative sources, denying consumers the right to better and cheaper electricity.
- The allegation that Fortis asked the Canadian government, through CIDA, to pay for a study justifying the project. It was claimed that the study was biased, involved too much secrecy, and failed to promote and ensure effective stakeholder consultation.
- According to environmental groups, Fortis denied them access to pertinent information and failed to consult them.
- Fortis wouldn't make its own geology studies and engineering plans public or agree to an independent panel review.
- There was insufficient information on the impact of the project.

Source: Used with permission of Probe International.

members. Robert F. Kennedy, Jr., a lawyer, was the main spokesperson for NRDC on the Chalillo project.[64]

PI maintained an elaborate Web site in opposition to the project. Another Web site devoted exclusively to the Chalillo project was Stop Fortis! (www.stopfortis.org), which contained extensive information on the project including photographs. Several environmental groups placed advertisements in Canadian newspapers.

The criticisms of Fortis's practices and the dam's construction are summarized in Exhibit 1. Fortis, and Stanley Marshall, President and CEO, responded to this criticism. A news release was issued on November 1, 2001, "Decision to Build Hydroelectric Dam in Belize Should Reside with Belizeans." The main points made in the release were:

- Belizeans should decide on the construction of the dam.
- Contrary to information from ENGOs, the dam is economically feasible and will ensure a more stable energy supply.

- Information presented by ENGOs is misleading the media about the environmental impact of the project.
- Fortis is willing to review its business activities with stakeholders.[65]

In a story in *The Telegram* on November 2, Marshall stated to a reporter, "This bombardment in the media of misleading information is putting enormous pressure on me, attacking me personally and inundating the media with lies." He also said, "Whatever we do as an electric company will impact the environment, but it's a question of how well we can manage our activities. On balance, this project is a good one. If I felt personally that we were going to threaten an endangered species and wipe it out—no. I would not propose going ahead with it."[66]

The project had consumed a lot of time, energy, and resources, and Fortis management wondered whether or not it was worth it. There might be less demanding projects that would add as much value to the company.

Endnotes

Preface

1. These environments are similar to those identified by the domain statement of the Social Issues in Management Division, Academy of Management, and listed on the Academy's Web site at http://www.aomonline.org.

2. Mark S. Schwartz and Archie B. Carroll, "Integrating and Unifying Competing and Complementary Frameworks: The Search for a Common Core in the Business and Society Field," *Business and Society* 47, no. 2 (June 2008): 148–186.

Chapter 1

1. Richard T. De George, *Competing with Integrity in International Business* (Oxford: Oxford University Press, 1993).

2. Ibid.

3. Tyler Hamilton, "Clean Capitalism Superheroes Lead Evolution of Free Enterprise," *Corporate Knights: The Magazine for Clean Capitalism,* Winter 2013, Vol. 11, Issue 4, 8.

4. John H. Tory, "Integrity Tops the List for Essential Qualities of Good CEO," *The Globe and Mail,* September 2, 2002, B5.

5. Eric Beauchesne, "Canadians Reward Responsible Businesses: Poll," *The Telegram* (St. John's, NL), April 21, 2005, D3.

6. Janet McFarland, "Survey Finds Business View Does Not Match Public's," *The Globe and Mail,* October 31, 2006, B12.

7. Charlie Arnot, "Stop Play Not to Lose and Start Playing to Win: Redefining Today's Dairy to Build Consumer Trust," The Centre for Food Integrity at http://www.foodintegrity.org.

8. "What Is the Social License?" On Common Ground Consultants Inc. and Robert Boutilier and Associates Web site, at http://socialicense.com/definition.html, accessed October 9, 2012.

9. Harvey McLeod and Howard Plewes, "Can Tailing Dams Be Socially Acceptable?" ICOLD Symposium on Major Challenges in Tailings Pools, June 15, 2003, 1–6.

10. "What Is the Social License?"

11. Martin Patriquin, "The Great University Cheating Scandal," *Maclean's,* February 12, 2007, 32–36.

12. Michael E. Porter and Mark R. Kramer, "Strategy and Society: The Link Between Competitive Advantage and Corporate Social Responsibility," *Harvard Business Review,* Vol. 84, Issue 12, December 2006: 83–84.

Chapter 2

1. Charlie Gillis and Chris Sorensen, "The New Underclass: Why an Entire Generation of Ambitious, Smart and Well-Educated Young Canadians Have No Future," *Maclean's,* January 21, 2013, 38–41.

2. Portions of this chapter are a revised and expanded version from Robert W. Sexty, "The Fundamentals of Canadian Capitalism: Theoretical and Practical Perspectives," in *Canadian Business and Society: Understanding Social and Ethical Challenges* (Scarborough, ON: Prentice-Hall Canada Inc., 1995), 37–46.

3. The forms are adapted from Christopher Farrell, "Faces of Capitalism," *BusinessWeek* (Special 1994 Bonus Issue), November 18, 1994, 19.

4. More information at the Conscious Capitalism Web site, at http://consciouscapitalism.org and the Conscious Capitalism Alliance Web site, at http://consciouscapitalismalliance.onefireplace.com. A recent book on the approach is John Mackey, Rajendra Sisodia, and Bill George, *Conscious Capitalism: Liberating the Heroic Spirit of Business* (Boston: Harvard Business Review Press, 2013).

5. Bill Gates, "Making Capitalism More Creative," *Time* (online edition), July 31, 2008, http://www.time.com/time/printout/0,8816,1828069,00.html.

6. Ian Bremmer, "State Capitalism and the Crisis," *McKinsey Quarterly* (online), July 9, 2009, http://www.mckinseyquarterly.com/home.aspx; and Pete Engardio, "State Capitalism," *BusinessWeek,* February 9, 2009, 39–43.

7. *2009 Edelman Trust Barometer,* Edelman, http://www.edelman.com/trust/2009/docs/Trust_Book_Final_2.pdf, pp. 2, 4, 13.

8. Michael E. Porter and Mark R. Kramer, "Creating Shared Value: How to Reinvent Capitalism—And Unleash a Wave of Innovation and Growth," *Harvard Business Review,* January–February 2011, 63–77.

9. Ibid, 64–65.

10. Ibid, 66.

11. Ibid, 67–72.

12. Ibid, 74–75.

13. Ibid, 76. A table comparing CSR to CSV is provided.

14. Ibid, 77.

15. "Oh, Mr. Porter: The New Big Idea from Business's Greatest Living Guru Seems a Bit Undercooked," *The Economist,* March 12, 2011, 78.

Chapter 3

1. This definition is based on the work of R. Edward Freeman in *Strategic Management: A Stakeholder Approach* (Boston: Pitman, 1984), 53.

2. Freeman, *Strategic Management,* 45.

3. Ibid, 45.

4. Jack Kapica, "Pope Warns of Profitability over People," *The Globe and Mail,* May 2, 1991, A6; and George Bragues, "The Capitalist Pope," *National Post,* April 5, 2005, FP23.

5. William C. Frederick, Keith Davis, and James E. Post, *Business and Society: Corporate Strategy, Public Policy, Ethics* (New York: McGraw-Hill, 1988), chapter 4.

6. Henry Mintzberg, *Power In and Around Organizations* (Englewood Cliffs, NJ: Prentice-Hall, Inc., 1983), chapters 4 and 9.

7. Robert Phillips, "Some Key Questions about Stakeholder Theory," *Ivey Business Journal* (online), March/April 2004.

8. John Argenti, "Stakeholders: The Case Against," *Long Range Planning* 30 (1997): 442–445.

9. Andrew Campbell, "Stakeholders: The Case in Favour," *Long Range Planning* 30 (1997): 446–49.

10. Steven L. Wartick and John F. Mahon, "Toward a Substance Definition of the Corporate Issue Construct," *Business and Society,* Vol. 33, No. 3, December 1994, 308.

11. This definition is based upon one formulated by Jon Johnson, "Issues Management—What Are the Issues?" *Business Quarterly* 48 (Fall 1983): 1.

12. Steven L. Wartick and Robert E. Rude, "Issues Management: Corporate Fad or Corporate Function?" *California Management Review* 29 (1986): 132–36; and Joseph F. Coates et al., *Issues Management: How You Can Plan, Organize and Manage the Future* (Mt. Airy, MD: Lomond Publishers, Inc., 1986), 15–16.

13. Coates, *Issues Management,* 19–20.

14. Archie B. Carroll, *Business and Society: Ethics and Stakeholder Management* (Cincinnati, OH: South-Western Publishing, 1989), 479–489; and John M. Bryson, *Strategic Planning for Public and Nonprofit Organizations* (San Francisco: Jossey-Bass Publishers, 1988).

15. Steven Fink, *Crisis Management: Planning for the Inevitable* (New York: AMACOM, 1986).

16. Ibid, 15–16.

17. Ibid, 20–28.

18. Norman R. Augustine, "Managing the Crisis You Tried to Prevent,"

Harvard Business Review, November–December 1995, 147–158.

19. Ibid, 149–157

20. Jonathan L. Bernstein, "The Ten Steps of Crisis Communications," *Crisisnavigator,* Vol. 11, Issue 4 (April 2010), available at http://www.crisisnavigator.org/The-Ten-Steps-of-Crisis-Communications.490.0.html; and Daniel F. Muzyka, "Communicating in a Crisis: Act with Honesty and Empathy," *The Globe and Mail,* June 9, 2008, B8.

Chapter 4

1. Archie B. Carroll, *Business and Society: Ethics and Stakeholder Management* (Cincinnati, OH: South-Western Publishing, 1989), 62.

2. Edward R. Freeman, *Strategic Management: A Stakeholder Approach* (Boston: Pitman, 1984).

3. Ibid, 53.

4. Ibid, 54–64.

5. Ibid, 64–69.

6. Ibid, 69–73.

7. John M. Bryson, *Strategic Planning for Public and Nonprofit Organizations: A Guide to Strengthening and Sustaining Organizational Achievement,* revised edition (San Francisco: Jossey-Bass Publishers, 1995), 284–286.

8. Paul C. Nutt and Robert W. Backoff, *Strategic Management of Public and Third Sector Organizations: A Handbook for Leaders* (San Francisco: Jossey-Bass Publishers, 1992), 196–98; and Bryson, *Strategic Planning for Public and Nonprofit Organizations,* 285–286.

9. Grant T. Savage, Timothy W. Nix, Carlton J. Whitehead, and John D. Blair, "Strategies for Assessing and Managing Organizational Stakeholders," *Academy of Management Executive* 5(2) (1991): 61–75.

10. Freeman, *Strategic Management,* 142–144.

11. Ronald K. Mitchell, Bradley R. Agle, and Donna J. Wood, "Toward a Theory of Stakeholder Identification and Salience: Defining the Principle of Who and What Really Counts," *Academy*

of Management Review, Vol. 22, No. 4 (1997): 853–86.

12. Ibid, 289–293.

13. Jeff Frooman. "Stakeholder Influence Strategies," *Academy of Management Review,* Vol. 24, No. 2 (1999): 191–205.

14. Ibid, 196–197.

15. Ibid, 198.

16. Jeanne Liedtka, "Collaborating across Lines of Business for Competitive Advantage," *Academy of Management Executive Journal,* Volume 10, No. 2 (1996): 20–37.

17. Ann Svendsen, *The Stakeholder Strategy: Profiting from Collaborative Business Relationships* (San Francisco: Berrett-Koehler Publishers, 1998), 2–5.

18. Ibid, 71–184.

19. Paul Adler and Seok-Woo Kwon, "Social Capital: Prospects for a New Concept," *Academy of Management Review,* Vol. 27, No. 1 (2002): 17–40.

20. Scott E. Seibert, Maria L. Kraimer, and Robert C. Linden, "A Social Capital Theory of Career Success," *Academy of Management Journal,* Vol. 44, No. 2 (2001): 220.

21. Ann Svendsen, Robert G. Boutilier, and David Wheeler, *Stakeholder Relationships, Social Capital and Business Value Creation* (Toronto: The Canadian Institute of Chartered Accountants, 2003).

22. Ibid, 4.

23. Ibid, 18.

24. Ibid, 19–20.

Chapter 5

1. Philip V. Lewis, "Defining Business Ethics: Like Nailing Jello to a Wall," *Journal of Business Ethics* 4 (1985): 381.

2. Larue Tone Hosmer, "Strategic Planning As If Ethics Mattered," *Strategic Management Journal* 15 (1994): 23.

3. Larue Tone Hosmer, *The Ethics of Management* (Homewood, IL: Irwin, 1987), 96.

4. *An Inquiry into the Nature and Causes of the Wealth of Nations,* published in 1776. Online edition available at the Adam Smith Institute Web site, http://www.adamsmith.org.

5. Larue Tone Hosmer, *Moral Leadership in Business* (Burr Ridge, IL: Irwin, 1994).

6. Ian Maitland, "The Human Face of Self-Interest," *Journal of Business Ethics* 38 (2002): 3–17.

7. John Kaler, "Reasons to Be Ethical: Self-Interest and Ethical Business," *Journal of Business Ethics* 27 (2000): 161–173.

8. Ibid.

9. Anthony M. Pagano, "Criteria for Ethical Decision Making in Managerial Situations," *Proceedings* (New Orleans: National Academy of Management, 1987): 1–12.

10. Hosmer, "Strategic Planning As If Ethics Mattered."

11. Lawrence Kohlberg, "The Claim of Moral Adequacy of a Highest Stage of Moral Judgment," *The Journal of Philosophy* LXX (1973): 630–646; Lawrence Kohlberg, *Essays on Moral Development, Vol. 1: The Philosophy of Moral Development* (New York: Harper and Row, 1981); and Lawrence Kohlberg, "Stage and Sequence: The Cognitive Development Approach to Socialization," in *Handbook of Socialization Theory and Research,* D.A. Goslin, ed. (Chicago: Rand McNally, 1969), 347–480.

12. L. Kohlberg and R. Ryncarz, "Beyond Justice Reasoning: Moral Development and Consideration of a Seventh Stage," in C. Alexander and E. Langer, eds., *Higher Stages of Human Development: Perspectives on Adult Growth* (New York: Oxford University Press, 1990).

13. Linda Klebe Treviño and Michael E. Brown, "Managing to Be Ethical: Debunking Five Business Myths," *Academy of Management Executive,* Vol. 18, No. 2 (2004): 69–72, 77.

14. Mahzarin R. Banaji, Max H. Bazerman, and Dolly Chugh, "How (Un)ethical Are You?" *Harvard Business Review,* Vol. 81, Issue 12, December 2003, 56–64.

Chapter 6

1. Michel Dion, "Corporate Citizenship as an Ethic of Care: Corporate Values, Codes of Ethics, and Global Governance," in Jorg Andriof and Malcolm McIntosh, *Perspectives on Corporate Citizenship* (London: Greenleaf Publishing, 2002), 118–137.

2. Jack Kooten, *Strategic Management in the Public and Nonprofit Organization* (New York: Praeger, 1989), 125.

3. Lee Ginsberg and Neil Millier, "Value-Driven Management," *Business Horizons,* May/June (1992): 23–27.

4. Errol P. Mendes and Jeffrey A. Clark, "The Five Generations of Corporate Codes of Conduct and Their Impact on Corporate Social Responsibility," Human Rights Research Centre, University of Ottawa, http://www.cdp-hrc.uottawa.ca/publicat/five.html, accessed January 23, 2003.

5. Laura L. Nash, "Ethics without the Sermon," *Harvard Business Review,* November–December 1981, 79–89.

6. Ibid, 89.

7. Anthony M. Pagano, "Criteria for Ethical Decision Making in Managerial Situations," *Proceedings,* National Academy of Management, New Orleans (1987): 1–12.

8. This is a variation of a definition by Michael McDonald, "Ethics and Conflict of Interest," the W. Maurice Young Centre of Applied Ethics, University of British Columbia, http://www.ethics.ubc.ca/people/mcdonald/conflict.htm.

9. Kenneth Kernaghan and John W. Langford, "Conflict of Interest," chapter 6 in *The Responsible Public Servant* (Halifax: The Institute for Research on Public Policy and The Institute of Public Administration of Canada, 1990), 133–155.

10. Competition Bureau Canada, "Whistleblowing Study—Models of Whistleblowing Protection," http://www.competitionbureau.gc.ca/internet/index.cfm?itemid=1276&lg=e.

11. Stephen M. Kohn, "The Sarbanes-Oxley Act ('Sox'): Legal Protections for Corporate Whistleblowers," National Whistleblowing Center, http://www.whistleblowers.org/html/sarbanes-oxley.htm.

12. Steven Bavaria, "Corporate Ethics Should Start in the Boardroom," *Business Horizons,* January–February (1991): 9–19.

13. James Gillies, *Boardroom Renaissance: Power, Morality and Performance in the Modern Corporation* (Toronto: McGraw-Hill Ryerson, 1992), chapter 8.

14. Archie B. Carroll, "The Moral Leader: Essential for Successful Corporate Citizenship," in Jorg Andriof and Malcolm McIntosh, *Perspectives on Corporate Citizenship* (London: Greenleaf Publishing, 2002), 145–150.

15. André Nijhof, Olaf Fisscher, and Jan Kees Looise, "Coercion, Guidance and Mercifulness: The Different Influences of Ethics Programs on Decision Making," *Journal of Business Ethics* 27, 1–2 (September 2000): 33–42.

16. Ibid, 35.

17. Ibid, 38.

18. Ibid, 39.

19. *Management Ethics,* Summer 2008, 66–67.

20. Max B.E. Clarkson, "Ethics and Profit: The Changing Values of Business in Society." Unpublished presentation to the Faculty of Business Administration, Memorial University of Newfoundland, St. John's (March 3, 1993).

21. Ibid.

22. Gene Laczniak, "Business Ethics: A Manager's Primer," *Business* (Georgia State University, 1983): 23–29.

23. Free Management Library, *Business Ethics: Managing Ethics in the Workplace and Social Responsibility,* http://www.managementhelp.org/ethics/ethxgde.htm#anchor33077.

24. Linda Klebe Treviño and Michael E. Brown, "Managing to Be Ethical: Debunking Five Business Myths," *Academy of Management Executive* 18, no. 2 (May 2004): 69–81.

25. Literature reviewed for this section: Trevor Cole, "Why Good People Do Bad Things," *University of Toronto*

Magazine, Winter 2005, 1927; Charles D. Kerns, "Why Good Leaders Do Bad Things," *Graziadio Business Review,* Vol. 6, Issue 4 (2003), available at http://gbr.pepperdine.edu/2010/08/why-good-leaders-do-bad-things; N. Craig Smith et al., "Why Managers Fail to Do the Right Thing: An Empirical Study of Unethical and Illegal Conduct," *Business Ethics Quarterly,* Vol. 17, Issue 4 (2007): 633–667; Sunday Samson Babalola, "Determinants of Unethical Business Behaviour among Owner–Managers," *Journal of Human Values,* Vol. 15, No. 1 (January/June 2009): 61–75; and Yuri Mishima, "Why Pressure Makes Good People Do Bad Things," Network for Business Sustainability, posted May 6, 2011, available at http://www.nbs.net/csr/8536/.

Chapter 7

1. *Guidance on Social Responsibility,* International Organization for Standardization, 2009, Section 2.1.18, available at http://isotc.iso.org/livelink/livelink/fetch/-8929321/8929339/8929348/3935837/3974907/ISO_DIS_26000_Guidance_on_Social_Responsibility.pdf?nodeid=8385026&vernum=-2, pp. 3–4. Additional information on ISO 26000 available at http://www.iso.org/iso/catalogue_detail?csnumber=42546.

2. Roger A. Buchholz, "Corporate Responsibility and the Good Society: From Economics to Ecology," *Business Horizons* (July/August 1991): 19.

3. Alexander Dahlsrud, "How Corporate Social Responsibility Is Defined: An Analysis of 37 Definitions," *Corporate Social Responsibility and Environmental Management* 15 (2008): 1–13.

4. Donna J. Wood, "Corporate Social Performance Revisited," *The Academy of Management Review,* Vol. 16, No. 4 (1991): 695.

5. Ibid, 695–700.

6. "The Good Company: A Survey of Corporate Responsibility," *The Economist,* 24-page special section and editorial, January 22, 2005: Special Section and 11.

7. "The World According to CSR: Good Corporate Citizens Believe That Capitalism Is Wicked But Redeemable," The Good Company: A Survey Of Corporate Social Responsibility, *The Economist,* January 22, 2005, 10–14.

8. "The Ethics of Business: Good Corporate Citizens, and Wise Governments, Should Be Wary of CSR," The Good Company: A Survey of Corporate Social Responsibility, *The Economist,* January 22, 2005, 20–22.

9. Ian Davis, "The Biggest Contract: By Building Social Issues into Strategy, Big Business Can Recast the Debate about Its Role," *The Economist,* May 28, 2005, 69–71.

10. "Analyze This! An Analysis of *The Economist*'s Analysis of CSR," *Corporate Knights,* Spring 2005, 30–33.

11. "Just Good Business: A Special Report on Corporate Social Responsibility," *The Economist,* January 19, 2008.

12. Ibid, 12–13.

13. Richard J. Klonoski, "Foundational Considerations in the Corporate Social Responsibility Debate," *Business Horizons* (1991, July/August): 16.

14. Ibid, 16.

15. Archie Carroll, "The Pyramid of Corporate Social Responsibility: Toward the Moral Management of Organizational Stakeholders," *Business Horizons* (July/August 1991): 39–48.

16. Ibid, 39–43.

17. Marcel van Marrewijk, "Concepts and Definitions of CSR and Corporate Sustainability: Between Agency and Communion," *Journal of Business Ethics* 44, No. 2 (2003): 102–103.

18. Peter W. Roberts and Grahame R. Dowling, "Corporate Reputation and Sustained Superior Financial Performance," *Strategic Management Journal* 23 (2002): 1077–1093.

19. The Aspen Institute, "Social Impact Management: A Definition," http://www.aspeninstitute.org/site/c.huLWJeMRKpH/b.729881/k.5FC2/Social_Impact_Management_A_Definition.htm.

20. Ibid.

21. Wayne Norman and Chris MacDonald, "Getting to the Bottom of 'Triple Bottom Line,'" *Business Ethics Quarterly,* Vol. 14, Issue 2 (2004): 243–262.

22. World Economic Forum—The Business Case for Corporate Citizenship, "Global Corporate Citizenship," http://www.weforum.org/site/homepublic.nsf/Content/Global+Corporate+Citizenship+Initiative.

23. Donna J. Wood and Jeanne M. Logsdon, "Theorising Business Citizenship," in Jörg Andriof and Malcolm McIntosh, *Perspectives on Corporate Citizenship* (London: Greenleaf Publishing, 2002), 87.

24. Dirk Matten and Andrew Crane, "Corporate Citizenship: Towards an Extended Theoretical Conceptualization," *Academy of Management Review* 30, No. 1 (2005): 166–179.

25. Ibid, 172–173.

26. Ibid, 174.

27. Ibid, 175.

28. Wood and Logsdon, 83–103.

29. Ibid, 87.

30. Ibid.

31. Mark S. Schwartz and Archie B. Carroll, "Integrating and Unifying Competing and Complementary Frameworks: The Search for a Common Core in the Business and Society Field," *Business and Society,* Vol. 47, No. 2 (June 2008): 148–186.

32. Ibid, 168.

33. Ibid, 169.

34. Ibid, 171.

35. Ibid, 173.

Chapter 8

1. Christian Aid, "Behind the Mask: The Real Face of Corporate Social Responsibility (2004)," http://www.christianaid.org.uk/indepth/0401csr/index.htm.

2. "Corporate Citizenship," Imagine Canada Web site, http://www.imaginecanada.ca/node/33, accessed November 2, 2012.

3. Minda Zetlin, "Companies Find Profit in Corporate Giving," *Management Review* (December 1990): 10.

4. Elizabeth Bihl, "Sponsorship Makes Good Business Sense," *Canada Export,* Vol. 10, No. 11 (1992): 2.

5. Ibid, 2, 7.

6. John Pepin, "Venture Capitalists and Entrepreneurs Become Venture Philanthropists," http://www.evpa. eu.com/downloads/PepinArticle_ VenturePhilanthropy_revised0404_pdf. pdf.

7. "Benefits of Caring and Sharing," *The Times* (London), Public Agenda Section, May 24, 2005, 11.

8. Randy Ray, "A Social Conscience, and Skills in Demand," *The Globe and Mail,* May 25, 2006, C1.

9. "The New Powers of Giving," *The Economist,* July 1, 2006, 64.

10. Heerad Sabeti, "The For-Benefit Enterprise," *Harvard Business Review,* November 2011, 99–104.

11. Certified B Corporation (B Corp) Hub, MaRS Centre for Impact Investing Web site, http://impactinvesting. marsdd.com/strategic-initiatives/ benefit-corporation-b-corp-hub/, accessed November 1, 2012.

12. "What Are B Corps?" Certified B Corporation Web site, http://www. bcorporation.net/, accessed November 1, 2012.

13. Lisa Princic et al., *Engaging Small Business in Corporate Social Responsibility* (Vancouver: Canadian Business for Social Responsibility, October 2003), 13.

14. Ibid, 16.

15. This list was generated from a student assignment, "Corporate Social Responsibility and Small Business," Business 7010—Business and Society, Faculty of Business Administration, Memorial University of Newfoundland, Winter 2006.

16. Heledd Jenkins, "A Critique of Conventional CSR Theory: An SME Perspective," *Journal of General Management,* Vol. 29, No 4 (Summer 2004): 37–57.

17. "Working with Community Groups: A Guide for Small Business," Network for Business Sustainability, November 5, 2012. Available at http://nbs.net/ wp-content/uploads/SME-Resource-Community-Engagement.pdf.

18. Robert Sexty, "Small Business/ Entrepreneurship Biography of Social Responsibility & Ethics," April 2006. Available from the author at rsexty@ mun.ca.

19. "The Business of Giving: A Survey of Wealth and Philanthropy," *The Economist,* February 25, 2006, 1–8.

20. Business for Social Responsibility, "Community Involvement," http://www. bsr.org/AdvisoryServices/CI.cfm.

21. Grace Yogaretnam, "Community Bonds and the Rise of Local Power," *Corporate Knights,* Vol. 10.4, Winter 2012, 27–28.

22. "Budget 2012: Summary of Items Affecting the Charitable and Nonprofit Sector," Imagine Canada Web site, http://www.imaginecanada.ca/files/ www/en/publicpolicy/budget_2012_ analysis.pdf, accessed June 2013.

23. Terry Macalister, "Corporate Social Responsibility: A Change in the Climate: Credit Crunch Makes the Bottom Line the Top Issue," *The Guardian,* March 6, 2008, 28.

Chapter 9

1. The last three points are from the "Quality, Credibility and Communications" assessment criteria used in *Corporate Sustainability Reporting in Canada,* Ottawa: Stratos Inc., December 2005, 39, http://www. stratos-sts.com/insights/sustainability-reporting-and-communication.html.

2. C. J. Fombrun, *Reputation: Realizing Value from the Corporate Image* (Boston: Harvard Business School Press, 1996), 72.

3. Steven L. Wartick, "Measuring Reputation: Definition and Data," *Business and Society* 41, 4 (December 2002): 371–392.

4. Mary Choquette and Peri Turnbull, "How Corporate Social Responsibility Can Affect Your Reputation," Members'

Briefing 302, Ottawa: The Conference Board of Canada, November 2000, 1–2.

5. John F. Mahon, "Corporate Reputation: A Research Agenda Using Strategy and Stakeholder Literature," *Business and Society* 41, 4 (December 2002): 428.

6. Dylan Minor and John Morgan, "CSR as Reputation Insurance: *Primum Non Nocere,*" *California Management Review,* Vol. 53, Issue 2 (Spring 2011): 40–59.

7. Jay Janney and Steve Gove, "Reputation and Corporate Responsibility Aberrations, Trends, and Hypocrisy: Reactions to Firm Choices in the Stock Option Backdating Scandal," *Journal of Management Studies,* Vol. 48, No. 7 (2011): 1562–1585.

8. Andrea Stanaland and Patrick Murray, "Consumer Perceptions of the Antecedents and Consequences of Corporate Social Responsibility," *Journal of Business Ethics,* Vol. 102 (2011): 47–55.

9. Jantzi Social Index, "About the JSI," http://www.jantzisocialindex.com/.

10. Dow Jones Sustainability Indexes, "Welcome to the Dow Jones Sustainability Indexes," http://www. sustainability-index.com/.

11. Sandra E. Martin, "Staff Stay at Companies with Heart," *National Post,* August 16, 2004, FP10.

12. Arthur B. Laffer, Andrew Coors, and Wayne Winegarden, "Does Corporate Social Responsibility Enhance Business Profitability?" CSRWatch™/SRIWatch, http://www.csrwatch.com/Sub/ Resources/csr_profitability.htm.

13. H.E. Bowman and W. Haire, "A Strategic Posture Towards Corporate Social Responsibility," *California Management Review* 18 (1975): 49–58.

14. Marc Orlitzky, Frank L. Schmidt, and Sara L. Rynes, "Corporate Social and Financial Performance: A Meta-Analysis," *Organizational Studies* 24 (2003): 403–441.

15. Joshua D. Margolis and James P. Walsh, "Misery Loves Companies: Rethinking Social Initiatives by Business," *Administrative Science Quarterly* 48 (2003): 273–278.

16. John Peloza, "Primer: Valuing Sustainability," Network for Business Sustainability Web site, http://nbs.net/knowledge/business-case/valuing-sustainability/primer, accessed November 6, 2012; and "Metrics for Valuing Business Sustainability: A Framework for Executives," Network for Business Sustainability, 2011, http://nbs.net/wp-content/uploads/NBS-Executive-Report-Valuing.pdf, accessed November 6, 2012.

17. *GoodCompany: Guidelines for Corporate Social Performance* (Vancouver: Canadian Business for Social Responsibility, 2002), http://www.cbsr.ca/sites/default/files/GoodCompany-SummaryDocument.pdf.

18. Conference Board of Canada, "Corporate Responsibility Assessment Tool," http://www.conferenceboard.ca/GCSR/CR_AT/.

19. Canadian Centre for Ethics and Corporate Policy, "About Us," http://www.ethicscentre.ca/EN/about/.

20. The Accountability Project, "Welcome," http://www.theaccountabilityproject.ca.

21. "About GRI," Global Reporting Initiative Web site, https://www.globalreporting.org/information/about-gri/Pages/default.aspx, accessed November 6, 2012.

22. GRI 3.1 Guidelines at https://www.globalreporting.org/reporting/latest-guidelines/g3-1-guidelines/Pages/default.aspx, accessed November 6, 2012.

23. Sustainability Reporting Guidelines, 2000–2011, Version 3.1; https://www.globalreporting.org/resourcelibrary/G3.1-Sustainability-Reporting-Guidelines.pdf, accessed November 6, 2012, 1.

24. Ibid, 3.

25. Aaron Chatterji and David Levine, "Breaking Down the Wall of Codes: Evaluating Non-Financial Performance Measurement," *California Management Review,* Vol. 48, No. 2 (2006): 29–30.

26. Ibid, 44–48.

27. Compiled from Diana McLaren, " Measuring the Good Global Citizen," *The Globe and Mail,* November 26, 2008, B18; and *CSR Trends: A Comprehensive Survey of Corporate Social Responsibility Report Trends, Benchmarks and Best Practices,* Craib Design & Communications and PricewaterhouseCoopers LLP study, http://www.craib.com/craib_public/pdf/ARTrends/CSR_TRENDS_3_LR.pdf.

28. Mary Choquette and Peri Turnbull, "How Corporate Social Responsibility Can Affect Your Reputation," Members' Briefing 302 (Ottawa: Conference Board of Canada, November 2000), 3–4.

29. AACSB International—The Association to Advance Collegiate Schools of Business is a global, nonprofit membership organization of educational institutions, businesses, and other entities devoted to the advancement of management education.

30. *Eligibility Procedures and Standards for Business Accreditation* (St. Louis, MO: AACSB International, 2003), 14–15.

31. Coro Strandberg, *The Future of Corporate Social Responsibility* (Vancouver: VanCity Credit Union, 2002).

32. Ibid, 5.

33. Ibid, 7–16.

34. Ibid, 17.

35. White, Allen L. *Fade, Integrate or Transform? The Future of CSR* (San Francisco: Business for Social Responsibility, 2005).

Chapter 10

1. This spectrum borrows from that developed by J.J. Boddewyn, "Advertising Self-Regulation: Private Government and Agent of Public Policy," *Journal of Public Policy and Marketing,* Vol. 4, No. 1 (1985): 129–41.

2. The Canadian Council for Public–Private Partnerships, "About PPP—Definitions," http://www.pppcouncil.ca/resources/about-ppp/definitions.html.

3. Ibid.

4. Bruce Carson, Registration of Lobbyists, *Library of Parliament Current Issue Review* (Ottawa: Supply and Services Canada. Cat. No. YM32-1/86-18-1988-05E 1988), 8.

5. W.T. Stanbury, *Business–Government Relations in Canada* (Toronto: Methuen, 1986), 308–310.

6. Public Affairs Association of Canada, "Profile," http://www.publicaffairs.ca/whoweare/profile.shtml.

7. Based upon a definition in Donald L. Barlett and James B. Steele, "Corporate Welfare," *Time Canadian Edition,* November 9, 1998, 32.

8. David Heald, "Privatization, Analysing Its Appeal and Limitations," *Fiscal Studies* 5.1 (1984): 36.

9. Jonathan N. Goodrich, "Privatization in America," *Business Horizons* (January–February 1988): 11–17.

Chapter 11

1. *Capital Markets and Sustainability: Investing in a Sustainable Future* (Ottawa: National Round Table on the Environment and the Economy, February 2007), http://www.nrtee-trnee.com/eng/publications/capital-markets/NRTEE-capital-markets.pdf.

2. Shirley Won, "Labour Funds Fall from Favour," *The Globe and Mail,* May 13, 2009, B12; and Douglas Cumming, "Labour-Sponsored Funds Didn't Work," *National Post,* February 10, 2009, FP12.

3. Herschel Hardin, *A Nation Unaware: The Canadian Economic Culture* (Vancouver: J. J. Douglas, 2004).

4. Robert W. Sexty, "The Accountability Dilemma in Canadian Public Enterprises: Social versus Commercial Responsiveness," *Annals of Public and Co-operative Economy* 54, No. 1 (January–March, 1983): 19–33.

5. Robert W. Sexty, "Summary of the Issues Involved in the Commercialization and Privatization of Public Enterprise, Parts 1 & 2," St. John's, Canada: Faculty of Business Administration, Memorial University of Newfoundland, 1986, Working Papers 86-14 & 86-15.

6. Jon Entine, "The Myth of Social Investing: A Critique of Its Practices and Consequences for Corporate Social Performance Research," *Organization and Environment,* Vol. 16, No. 3 (September 2003): 352–368.

7. Robert K. Mueller, "Changes in the Wind in Corporate Governance," *Journal of Business Strategy* 1(4) (1981): 9.

8. Report of the Toronto Stock Exchange, *Committee on Corporate Governance in Canada* (Toronto: The Toronto Stock Exchange, 1994), 7.

9. *OECD Principles of Corporate Governance* (Paris: OECD Publications, 2004): 18–19, 32–39, http://www.oecd.org/topic/0,2686,en_2649_34813_1_1_1_1_37439,00.html.

10. *Canada Business Corporations Act,* Government of Canada, R.S., 1985, c. C44, Sections 97(1), 116, and 149(1).

11. National Instrument 58–201, "Disclosure of Corporate Governance Practices," http://www.osc.gov.on.ca/documents/en/Securities-Category5/rule_20050415_58-201_gov-practices.pdf.

12. *OECD Principles of Corporate Governance*: 24–25.

13. *Where Were the Directors: Guidelines for Improving Corporate Governance in Canada* (Toronto: Toronto Stock Exchange Committee on Corporate Governance in Canada, May 1994), 24. There are many definitions of independence and this one was not adopted in National Instrument 58–201.

14. Virginia Galt, "Want to Be a Director? Here's How to Get on Board," *The Globe and Mail,* March 4, 2006, B12.

15. Ibid.

16. Janet McFarland, "Female Directors Need Apply," *The Globe and Mail,* October 10, 2006, B1, B4.

17. Janet McFarland, "For Female Directors, Three's a Charm," *The Globe and Mail,* November 18, 2006, B9.

18. Adapted from Monica Belcourt and Holger Kluge, "Measuring Board Performance: How Effective Is Your Board?" *Ivey Business Journal* (March/April 1999): 28–29.

19. Jay A. Conger and Edward Lawlor III, "Individual Director Evaluations: The Next Step in Boardroom Effectiveness," *Ivey Business Journal* (September/October 2003): 1–5.

20. Adapted from Belcourt and Kluge, "Measuring Board Performance": 30–31.

21. Peter Fitzpatrick, "Is Good Governance Too Costly?" *National Post,* December 3, 2003, FP1, FP8.

22. Poschmann, "Good (for Nothing) Corporate Governance," *National Post,* November 20, 2003, FP11.

23. Janet McFarland, "Mr. Dey's About Face," *The Globe and Mail,* July 7, 2006, B1, B5; and Finn Poschmann, "Keeping It In the Family," *National Post,* February 3, 2004, FP11.

24. Janet McFarland, "Strides in Governance Threatened by Backlash, Ex-SEC Boss Warns," *The Globe and Mail,* April 13, 2006, B5; and Bengt Holmstrom and Steven N. Kaplan, "The Dangers of Too Much Governance," *National Post,* February 23, 2004, FP4.

25. Steve Foerster, "Taking the High Road: Steve Foerster's Research Shows That Good Governance Pays," *Ivey Impact,* Vol. 9, No.12 (December 1, 2003).

26. Neal Lipschutz, "Good Governance, Good Results Go Together," *The Globe and Mail,* February 6, 2004, IN1.

27. Beth Young, "Corporate Governance and Firm Performance: Is There a Relationship?" *Ivey Business Journal* (September/October 2003): 1–3.

28. Keith Kalawsky, "Teachers' Bertram No Market Preacher," *National Post,* March 10, 2004, FP1, FP7.

29. *OECD Principles of Corporate Governance*: 21, 46–48.

30. Larry Colero, Crossroads Programs, Inc., "Five Questions That Directors Should Ask," University of British Columbia, The W. Maurice Young Centre for Applied Ethics, at http://www.ethics.ubc.ca/papers/invited/5questions.html accessed on 11/7/2006.

31. Mark Schacter, *What Directors Need to Know about Corporate Social Responsibility* (Ottawa: Mark Schacter Consulting, 2004), 4–5, 10.

Chapter 12

1. *Employment Equity Act,* 1995, C.44, s. 2.

2. *Canadian Human Rights Act,* 1986. c. 14, s. 1.

3. Rosemarie Tong, "Feminist Ethics," *Encyclopedia of Business Ethics and Society,* Robert W. Kolb, Ed., Thousand Islands, CA: Sage Publications Inc. Online Edition 2007.

4. "Feminist Ethics: An Alternative Voice," Villanova University, MPA 8300 Leadership Ethics at http://www83.homepage.villanova.edu/richard.jacobs/MPA%208300/theories/feminist.html, accessed February 20, 2013; and Rosemarie Tong and Nancy Williams, "Feminist Ethics," *The Stanford Encyclopedia of Philosophy (Summer 2011 Edition),* Edward N. Zalta (ed.), at http://plato.stanford.edu/entries/feminism-ethics, accessed January 21, 2013.

5. Janet L. Borgerson, "On the Harmony of Feminist Ethics and Business Ethics," *Business and Society Review,* Vol. 112, No. 4 (December 2007): 477–509.

6. Hewitt & Associates, "CSR as a Driver of Employee Engagement," Canadian Business for Social Responsibility Web site, at http://cbsr.ca/blog/csr-driver-employee-engagement, accessed December 7, 2012.

7. "Hewitt and CBSR Data Establishes Strong Relationship between Employee Engagement and Views on CSR," Press Release, Hewitt Associates, January 25, 2010.

8. Maria José Ramos, "CSR as a Driver of Employee Engagement," Canadian Business for Social Responsibility Web site, at http://cbsr.ca/blog/csr-driver-employee-engagement, accessed December 7, 2012.

9. D.M. Mayer et al., "Who Displays Ethical Leadership and Why Does It Matter? An Examination of Antecedents and Consequences of Ethical Leadership," *Academy of Management Journal,* Vol. 55, Issue 1 (February 2012): 151–171.

10. Jindeck Chun, et al., "How Does Corporate Ethics Contribute to Firm Performance? The Mediating Role of Collective Organizational Commitment and Organizational Citizenship Behavior," *Journal of Management,* Vol. 20 (January 2011): 1–15.

11. C.B. Bhattacharya et al., "Listing Corporate Social Responsibility to Win the Way for Talent," *M.I.T Sloan*

Management Review, Vol. 48, No. 2 (2008): 37–44.

12. Adam Grant et al., "Giving Commitment: Employee Support Programs and the Prosocial Sensemaking Process," *Academy of Management Journal* 51 (2008): 898–918.

13. Janice Obuchowski, "Searching for Meaningful Work," *National Post,* March 23, 2010, FP10.

14. "The New Normal: Sustainable Practices Your Future Employees Will Demand," Network for Business Sustainability, January 11, 2010, at http://nbs.net/knowledge/perspectives-from-students-on-how-organizations-can-be-more-sustainable, accessed December 7, 2012.

15. Robert W. Sexty, "Defining Consumer Sovereignty," *Canadian Business and Society: Understanding Social and Ethical Challenges* (Scarborough, ON: Prentice-Hall Canada, 1995), 352–354.

16. Magdaiena Öberseder et al., "Why Don't Consumers Care About CSR? A Qualitative Study Exploring the Role of CSR in Consumption Decisions," *Journal of Business Ethics,* Vol. 104, No. 4 (2011): 449–460.

17. June Cotte and Remi Trudel, *Socially Conscious Consumerism: Executive Briefing on the Body of Knowledge,* Network for Business Sustainability, Richard Ivey School of Business, University of Western Ontario, 2009, http://www.nbs.net/Docs/NBS_Consumerism_2009.pdf.

18. Pat Augar et al., "Do Social Product Features Have Value to Consumers?" *International Journal of Research in Marketing,* Vol. 25, No. 3 (2008): 183–91.

19. Environment Canada, "Extended Producer Responsibility," http://www.ec.gc.ca/epr/default.asp?lang=En&n=EEBCC813-1.

20. Stephen Brammer et al., "Managing Sustainable Global Supply Chains: Frameworks and Practices," May 25, 2011, Network for Business Sustainability Web site, at http://nbs.net/wp-content/uploads/NBS-Executive-Report-Supply-Chains.pdf.

21. "Sustainability Development— Top 10 Sustainability Shopping List," Industry Canada, http://www.buysmartbc.com/UserFiles/File/SPN-IC-ShoppingTipsFinalDec07.pdf.

22. Fairtrade Foundation, FAQs, "What Is Fairtrade?" http://www.fairtrade.org.uk/what_is_fairtrade/faqs.aspx.

23. "About Fairtrade," Fairtrade Canada Web site, at http://fairtrade.ca/en/about-fairtrade/what-fair-trade.

24. Fairtrade International Web site, at http://www.fairtrade.net; Fairtrade Canada Web site, at http://www.fairtrade.ca; and Fair Trade U.S.A. Web site, at http://www.fairtradeusa.org, all accessed on February 10, 2013.

25. Peter Griffiths, "Ethical Objections to Freetrade," *Journal of Business Ethics,* Vol. 105, No. 3 (2012): 357–373.

26. Tina D. Beuchelt and Manifred Zeller, "Profits and Poverty: Certification's Troubled Link for Nicaragua's Organic and Fair-Trade Coffee Producers," *Ecological Economics* 70 (2011): 1316–1324.

Chapter 13

1. Michael Edwards, "Part 1: The Case for NGOs—The Mouse That Roared," *The Globe and Mail,* January 3, 2002, A15.

2. *Partnering for Innovation: Driving Change Through Business/NGO Partnerships* (Vancouver: Canadian Business for Social Responsibility, 2005), 7–8. Also available at http://www.cbsr.ca.

3. Alan Rugman and Karl Moore, "Part 2: Are NGOs a Threat? Biting the Hand That Feeds Us," *The Globe and Mail,* January 4, 2002, A13.

4. Debora L. Spar and Lane I. LaMure, "The Power of Activism: Assessing the Impact of NGOs on Global Business," *California Management Review,* Vol. 45, No. 3 (Spring 2003): 81.

5. Ibid, 84–85.

6. Ibid, 85.

7. *Partnering for Innovation: Driving Change Through Business/NGO Partnerships* (Vancouver: Canadian Business for Social Responsibility, 2005), 3–4. Also available at http://www.cbsr.ca.

8. Ibid, 10–12.

9. Jonathan Doh, "Partnering with NGOs: The 4 Keys to Success," Network for Business Sustainability, July 19, 2012, available at http://nbs.net/partnering-with-ngos-the-4-keys-to-success/, accessed December 10, 2012.

10. Bart J. Mindszenthy, "Issues and Media Relations," *Business Quarterly* (March 1987): 76–83.

11. Wade Rowland, *Greed, Inc.: Why Corporations Rule Our World and How We Let It Happen* (Toronto: Thomas Allen Publishers, 2005).

12. Joel Bakan, *The Corporation: The Pathological Pursuit of Profit and Power* (Toronto: Viking Canada, 2002).

13. Harry Glasbeek, *Wealth by Stealth: Corporate Crime, Corporate Law, and the Perversion of Democracy* (Toronto: Between the Lines, 2002).

14. "Social Media," Wikipedia, http://en.wikipedia.org/wiki/Social_media.

15. Bruce Livesey, "Rough Handling," *Financial Post,* May 10, 1987, 26–27; and Leisa Stangret, "Media Accept 'Spin' on So-Called News," *National Post,* December 9, 2000, 8.

16. Doug Saunders, "Manufacturing Media Bias," *The Globe and Mail,* March 22, 1997, D2.

17. Steven Wartick, "The Relationship Between Intense Media Exposure and Change in Corporate Reputation," *Business and Society* (Roosevelt University), Vol. 3, No. 1 (1992): 33–49.

18. Ibid, 34.

19. Ibid, 43.

20. Bart J. Mindszenthy, "Issues and Media Relations," *Business Quarterly* (March 1987): 76–83.

21. Grant Robertson, "Internet Takes Bite out of Canadian Magazine Readership," *The Globe and Mail,* March 30, 2007, B2.

22. Edward J. Romar, "Virtue Is Good Business: Confucianism as a Practical Business Ethic," *Journal of Business Ethics,* Vol. 38 (2002): 119–131.

23. "Spiritual Capital Research Program," Metanexus Institute, http://www.metanexus.net/spiritual%5Fcapital/.

24. Peter Goodspeed, "Faith in the Marketplace," *National Post,* June 17, 2005, A1, A12.

25. William C. Symonds, "Earthly Empires: How Evangelical Churches Are Borrowing from the Business Playbook," *BusinessWeek,* May 23, 2005, 78–88.

26. Michelle Conlin, "Religion in the Workplace: The Growing Presence of Spirituality in Corporate America," *BusinessWeek,* November 1, 1999, 151–158; Ian I. Mitroff and Elizabeth A. Denton, *A Spiritual Audit of Corporate America: A Hard Look at Spirituality, Religion and Values in the Workplace* (San Francisco: Jossey-Bass Publishers, 1999); Robert A. Giacalone and Carole L. Jurkiezicz, "Right from Wrong: The Influence of Spirituality on Perceptions of Unethical Business Activities," *Journal of Business Ethics* 46 (2003): 85–97.

27. Symonds, "Earthly Empires."

28. Robert W. Sexty, Business and Education. Working Paper #02–05. Faculty of Business Administration, Memorial University of Newfoundland, St. John's, NL, 2002.

29. Ibid.

30. The Association for the Advancement of Sustainability in Higher Education (AASHE) Web site, at http://www.aashe.org/.

Chapter 14

1. Garrett Hardin, "The Tragedy of the Commons," *Science,* Vol. 162, December 13, 1968, 1243–1248.

2. Colin Hutchison, "Environmental Issues: The Challenge for the Chief Executive," *Long Range Planning* 25(3) (1992): 58.

3. United Nations, *The World Commission on Environment and Development: Our Common Future* (New York: Oxford University Press, 1987).

4. *Business Strategy for Sustainable Development: Leadership and Accountability for the '90s* (Winnipeg: International Institute for Sustainable Development, 1992), 11.

5. Environment Canada, "Glossary of Terms," http://www.ec.gc.ca/default. asp?lang=En&n=7EBE5C5A-1; and Environment Canada, "What Is Acid Rain?" http://www.msc.ec.gc.ca/cd/factsheets/acidrain/index_e.cfm.

6. Environment Canada, "Glossary of Terms."

7. Environment Canada, "Stratospheric Ozone," http://www.ec.gc.ca/indicateurs-indicators/.

8. Environment Canada, "Glossary of Terms."

9. Environment Canada, "Glossary of Terms."

10. *Canadian Environmental Protection Act, 1999.* Available at http://laws-lois. justice.gc.ca/eng/acts/c-15.31/.

11. "Responsible Resource Development," Canada's Economic Action Plan, April 2012, http://www.actionplan.gc.ca/eng/feature.asp?PAGEId=446, accessed April 18, 2012.

12. "What Responsible Resource Development Means for Environmental Protection," Canada's Economic Action Plan, April 2012, http://www.actionplan.gc.ca/eng/media.asp?Id=5285, accessed April 18, 2012.

13. *Report of the Commissioner of the Environment and Sustainable Development to the House of Commons,* Office of the Auditor General of Canada, Ottawa. Cat. No. FA1-2/2012-1-OE-PDF.

14. Jamie R. Hendry, "Taking Aim at Business: What Factors Lead Environmental Non-Government Organizations to Target Particular Firms?" *Business and Society,* Vol. 45, No. 1 (March 2006): 47–86.

15. Laura Jones, "A Different Kind of Environmentalist," *Fraser Forum,* April 2001, 4.

16. "When Regulation Beats Market Mechanisms," *National Post,* March 27, 2007, FP15.

17. Bertrand Marotte, "Exchange to Trade Emission Credits," *The Globe and Mail,* July 13, 2006, B3; and Tavia Grant, "Climate Right for Emissions Exchange," *The Globe and Mail,* September 29, 2006, B13.

18. Tavia Grant, "Caron Cutters in the Grips of Uncertainty: Firms Struggle with Environmental Plans as Government Waffles on Climate Policy," *The Globe and Mail,* July 10, 2006, B4.

19. "Shell Quest CSS Project Approved with Conditions," News Release, Energy Resources and Conservation Board, Calgary, July 10, 2012.

20. "The Seven Sins of Greenwashing," TerraChoice Environmental Marketing at http://sinsofgreenwashing.org/findings/the-seven-sins/.

21. *Business Strategy for Sustainable Development: Leadership and Accountability for the '90s* (Winnipeg: International Institute for Sustainable Development, 1992), 21–24.

22. Nicole Darrnall et al., "Environmental Management Systems and Green Supply Chain Management: Complements for Sustainability," *Business Strategy and the Environment,* Vol. 17 (2008): 30–45

23. Bruce Hofer et al., "The Competitive Determinants of a Firm's Environmental Management Activities: Evidence from US Manufacturing Industries," *Journal of Operations Management,* Vol. 30 (2012): 9–84.

24. "Measuring and Valuing Environmental Impacts: An Introductory Guide," Network for Business Sustainability, http://nbs.net/wp-content/uploads/NBS-Executive-Report-Impacts.pdf.

25. I.B. Vasi and B. King, "Social Movements, Risk Perceptions, and Economic Outcomes: The Effect of Primary and Secondary Stakeholder Activism on Firm's Perceived Environmental Risk and Financial Performance," *American Sociological Review,* Vol. 77, No. 4 (2012): 1–24.

26. OSC Staff Notice 51–716– Environmental Reporting, Ontario Securities Commission, February 29, 2008; Janet McFarland, "Clean Up Environmental Disclosure: OSC," *The Globe and Mail,* February 28, 2008, B4; and Sandra Rubin, "When OSC Goes Green, Lawyers See Red," *The Globe and Mail,* March 19, 2008, B7.

27. Michael Lucins et al., "The Sustainability Liability: Potential Negative Effects of Ethicality on Product Acceptance," *Journal of Marketing,* Vol. 74 (2010): 15–31.

28. John Peloza, "What Makes Your Consumers Go Green? It Depends on Who's Around," April 16, 2012, Network for Business Sustainability at http://nbs.net/what-makes-your-consumers-go-green-it-depends-on-whos-around/.

29. "Going Green Can Attract and Keep Employees," *The Globe and Mail,* January 19, 2008, B16.

30. Marjo Johne, "Show Us the Green, Workers Say," *The Globe and Mail,* October 10, 2007, C1, C6.

31. "SHRM Survey Asks How 'Green' Is the American Workplace," Society for Human Resource Management, Press Release, January 16, 2008.

32. Catherine Ramus and Ulrich Steger, "The Roles of Supervisory Support Behaviours and Environmental Policy in Employee 'Ecoinitiatives' at Leading-Edge European Companies," *Academy of Management Journal,* Vol. 43, No. 4 (2000): 605–626.

33. "Employees Identify Aon Hewitt's 'Green 30' Organizations Based on Eco-Friendly Programs and Practices," April 26, 2012, available at http://www.newswire.ca/en/story/962169/employees-identify-aon-hewitt-s-green-30-organizations-based-on-eco-friendly-programs-and-practices. Also published by *Maclean's;* a recent example is "Canada's Green 30 Companies for 2012: Employees grade employers on Environmentally Positive Practices," *Macleans.ca* on Friday, April 27, 2012, accessed at http://www2.macleans.ca/2012/04/27/canadas-green-30-for-2012/.

34. Rebecca Walberg, "Green Careers Are Growing," *National Post,* March 23, 2010, FP9.

35. GoodWork Canada at http://www.goodworkcanada.ca/.

36. "Sustainability Reporting Guidelines—G3 Version for Public Comment," Global Reporting Initiative, Amsterdam, The Netherlands, 2006, 18–18; "Sustainability Reporting Guidelines," Global Reporting Initiative, Amsterdam, The Netherlands, 2002, 47–50.

37. "Measuring and Valuing Environmental Impacts: An Introductory Guide," Network for Business Sustainability Web site, at http://nbs.net/wp-content/uploads/NBS-Executive-Report-Impacts.pdf.

38. Mark Steyn, "'Sustainable' Development? There's No Such Thing," *National Post,* September 3, 2002, A12; and Peter Foster, "Sustainability Scam," *National Post,* April 8, 2006, FP19.

39. Peter Nowak, "Few Taking Leadership Role on Environment," *National Post,* September 25, 2006, FP2.

40. Anantha K. Duraiappsah, "Ecosystem Services and Human Well-Being: Do Global Findings Make Any Sense?" *BioScience,* Vol. 61, No. 1 (January 2011): 7–8, and Clara Raudsepp-Hearne et al., "The Paradox Persists: How to Resolve It," *BioScience,* Vol. 61, No. 1 (January 2011): 11–12.

Chapter 15

1. John Black, "Globalization," *A Dictionary of Economics* (Oxford University Press, 2002). Oxford Reference Online, Oxford University Press, Memorial University of Newfoundland, http://www.oxfordreference.com/views/ENTRY.html?subview=Main&entry=t19.e1359.

2. Andrew Hurrell, "Globalization," *The Concise Oxford Dictionary of Politics.* Ed. Iain McLean and Alistair McMillan (Oxford University Press, 2003). Oxford Reference Online, Oxford University Press, Memorial University of Newfoundland, http://www.oxfordreference.com/views/ENTRY.html?subview=Main&entry=t86.e554.

3. John Scott and Gordon Marshall, "Globalization," *A Dictionary of Sociology* (Oxford University Press, 2005). Oxford Reference Online, Oxford University Press, Memorial University of Newfoundland, http://www.oxfordreference.com/views/ENTRY.html?subview=Main&entry=t88.e937.

4. World Bank, http://www.worldbank.org/.

5. International Monetary Fund, http://www.imf.org/.

6. International Labour Organization, "About the ILO," http://www.ilo.org/public/english/about/index.htm.

7. Institute for Management Development, "World Competitiveness Year Book," http://www.imd.org/research/publications/wcy/index.cfm.

8. World Economic Forum, "Global Competitiveness Report," http://www.weforum.org/issues/global-competitiveness

9. *Compendium of Ethics Codes and Instruments of Corporate Responsibility,* Schulich School of Business, York University, Toronto, http://www.schulich.yorku.ca/SSB-Extra/businessethics.nsf/Lookup/Codes_Compendium_Aug_2003/$file/Codes_Compendium_Aug_2003.pdf.

10. Transparency International, "About Transparency International," http://www.transparency.org/about_us.

11. Transparency International, "2011 Bribe Payers Index Report," http://www.transparency.org /bpi2011/results.

12. Publish What You Pay, http://www.publishwhatyoupay.org/.

13. *The Corruption of Foreign Public Officials Act: A Guide,* May 1999, Department of Justice, http://www.justice.gc.ca/eng/dept-min/pub/cfpoa-lcape/index.html.

14. "Canada's Enforcement of the Foreign Bribery Offence Is Lagging; Must Urgently Boost Efforts to Prosecute," OECD Newsroom at http://www.oecd.org/document/31/0,3746,en_21571361_44315115_47443999_1_1_1_1,00.html; and "Canada: Phase 3—Report on the Application of the Convention on Combating Bribery of Foreign Public Officials in International Business Transactions and the 2009 Revised Recommendation on Combating Bribery in International Business Transactions," Directorate for Financial and Enterprise Affairs, OECD accessed at http://www.oecd.org/dataoecd/55/25/47438413.pdf.

15. Theresa Tedesco, "Boards Must Step Up on Corporate Crime," *National Post,* January 24, 2013, FP2; and Terence Corcoran, "Rooted in Government," *National Post,* February 6, 2013, FP1, 3.

16. United Nations, "Universal Declaration of Human Rights," http://www.un.org/Overview/rights.html.

17. Dexter Roberts and Pete Engardio, "Secrets, Lies, and Sweatshops," *BusinessWeek,* November 27, 2006, 50–58.

18. Nicholas D. Kristof, "Fight Poverty: Build Sweatshops," *National Post,* June 7, 2006, A20; and Michael Walker, "Why the World Needs More Sweatshops," *Fraser Forum,* March 2006, 3–4.

19. *Canadian Business and the Millennium Development Goals* (Vancouver: Canadian Business for Social Responsibility, 2005).

20. C.K. Prahalad and Stuart L. Hart, "The Fortune at the Bottom of the Pyramid," *Strategy+Business,* Issue 26, 2002.

21. C.K. Prahalad, *The Fortune at the Bottom of the Pyramid: Eradicating Poverty Through Profits,* (Upper Saddle River, NJ: Pearson Education Inc. Wharton School Publishing 2005).

22. "Bottom of the Pyramid," Aspen Institute, www.CasePlace.org.

23. Fairtrade Foundation, "A Common Definition of Fair Trade," http://www.fairtrade.org.uk/.

24. Tavia Grant, "Major World Banks Join Microfinance Revolution," *The Globe and Mail,* November 23, 2006, B11.

25. *Doing Business with the Poor: A Field Guide* (Conches-Geneva: World Business Council for Sustainable Development, 2004), 10–14.

26. Index of Economic Freedom, http://www.heritage.org/index.

Chapter 16

1. "10 Things New Sustainability Managers Need to Know," Network for Business Sustainability, at http://nbs.net/wp-content/uploads/10-Things-for-Managers1.pdf.

2. Canada's Most Admired Corporate Cultures, Waterhouse Human Capital Web site, at http://www.waterstonehc.com/cmac/about-canadas-10/2011-national-and-regional-winners, accessed October 5, 2012.

3. Michael E. Porter and Mark R. Kramer, "Strategy and Society: The Link Between Competitive Advantage and Corporate

Social Responsibility," *Harvard Business Review,* Vol. 84, Issue 12, December 2006, 78–92. Note that Porter and Kramer use the term CSR instead of sustainability.

4. Ibid, 83.

5. Ibid, 84.

6. Ibid, 85.

7. Ibid, 85.

8. Ibid, 89–91.

9. Ibid, 92.

10. Ceres, "About Us," http://www.ceres.org/, accessed on October 3, 2012.

11. Pamela Laughland and Tima Bansal, "The Top Ten Reasons Why Businesses Aren't More Sustainable," *Ivey Business Journal* (online), January/February 2011. The article is available at http://www.iveybusinessjournal.com/the-top-ten-reasons-why-businesses-aren%e2%80%99t-more-sustainable.

12. Robert W. Sexty, *Canadian Business and Society: Understanding Social and Ethical Challenges* (Scarborough, ON: Prentice Hall Canada, 1995), 145–146.

13. UBC Sustainability at http://www.sustain.ubc.ca; Canada's Green University at http://www.unbc.ca/green.

14. Coalition of Universities for Responsible Investing Web site, at http://www.curi.ca/.

15. Community Based Research Canada (CBRC) Web site, at http://communityresearchcanada.ca.

16. Canadian Alliance for Community Service-Learning Web site, at http://www.communityservicelearning.ca/en/index.htm.

Ethics, Responsibilities, and Sustainability Cases

1. This is a fabricated situation with background information obtained from the following: Certified General Accountants of Canada, CGA-Canada Code of Ethical Principles and Rules of Conduct, Version 2.12, June 2011, http://www.cga-canada.org/en-ca/StandardsLib/ca_ceproc.pdf.

2. This case was prepared from public sources to provide material for classroom discussion, and it is not intended to illustrate either effective or

ineffective response to a business and society managerial situation. This is a fabricated case, and the names Phillip Veldhuis and Savalot Enterprises are fictitious.

3. Information on Food Banks Canada was from its Web site, at http://www.foodbankscanada.ca/. Views attributed to Elaine Power were contained in personal correspondence and permission was granted to use. Other information was obtained from the following: Dietitians of Canada, "Food Banks," *Practice: Exploring Members' Practice Issues,* January 18, 2010, http://www.practiceblog.dietitians.ca/2010/01/food-banks.html, accessed February 29, 2012; Jeff Nield, "Will Closing Food Banks Help End Hunger?" Tree Hugger Web site, July 29, 2011, http://www.treehugger.com/green-food/will-closing-food-banks-help-end-hunger.html, accessed February 29, 2012; Elaine Power, "Canadian Food Banks: Obscuring the Reality of Hunger and Poverty," *Food Ethics,* Winter 2011, Vol. 6, Issue 4, 18–20; Elaine Power, "Time to Close Our Food Banks," *The Globe and Mail,* July 25, 2011, A11; and "Food Banks a 'Smoke Screen' for Other Poverty Issues," CTV.ca, http://www.ctv.ca/CTVNews/Canada/20110731/food-banks-canada-long-term-solution-110731/, accessed February 29, 2012.

4. This case was prepared from public sources to provide material for classroom discussion, and it is not intended to illustrate either effective or ineffective response to a business and society managerial situation.

5. Rob Ferguson, Robert Benzie, and Tanya Talaga, thestar.com, http://www.thestar.com/printarticle/1125718, accessed July 18, 2012.

6. "Progress Rail to Close London (ON) Locomotive Production," Canada News Wire, February 3, 2012, http://www.newswire.ca/en/story/915677/progress-rail-to-close-london-on-locomotive-production, accessed July 18, 2012.

7. "McGuinty Blames Ottawa for Electro-Motive Closing," CTV News, February 6, 2012, http://toronto.ctv.ca/servlet/an/local/CTVNews/20120206/

mcguinty-blames-ottawa-electro-motive-120206/20120206?hub=Toronto NewHome, accessed July 20, 2012.

8. "CAW Urges Harper to Review Caterpillar Purchase of London Locomotive Plant," CAW Press Release, December 21, 2012, http://www.caw.ca/en/10812.htm, accessed July 18, 2012.

9. Takeovers of less than $300 million did not require a formal review.

10. "CAW President Demands Ottawa Release Details of Caterpillar Purchase, Close Loopholes in Investment Canada Act," CAW Press Release, February 10, 2012, http://www.caw.ca/en/10952.htm, accessed July 19, 2012.

11. "Caterpillar Picketed Today in a Dozen Canadian Cities," CAW Press Release, January 26, 2012, http://www.caw.ca/en/10889.htm, accessed July 18, 2012.

12. "Caterpillar, Incorrigibly Antisocial!" released February 10, 2012, http://www.caw.ca/assets/images/0216-lock_out_EMDC_(EN).pdf, accessed July 19, 2012.

13. "Why Caterpillar Is Bringing Jobs Home," CCN Money video, http://money.cnn.com/video/news/2012/02/17/n_caterpillar_ceo_georgia_plant.cnnmoney/, accessed July 23, 2012.

14. "Caterpillar Reports Record Sales and Profit for the Fourth Quarter and Full-Year 2011; 2011 Profit up 83 Percent from 2010," Caterpillar Inc. press release, January 26, 2012, http://www.caterpillar.com/cda/files/3276340/7/Caterpillar+Inc.+4Q2011+Final.pdf, accessed July 18, 2012.

15. Proxy materials to shareholders, April 29, 2011, http://www.caterpillar.com/cda/files/2729956/7/2011_proxy.PDF, accessed July 18, 2012.

16. "Caterpillar Demands for Cuts Prove Groundless in Wake of Record Profit Announcement, CAW President Says," CAW Press Release, January 25, 2102, http://www.caw.ca/en/10890.htm, accessed July 19, 2012.

17. This case was prepared from public sources to provide material for classroom discussion, and it is not intended to illustrate either effective or ineffective response to a business and society managerial situation.

18. Sources for this case are "Oil Sands History," Syncrude Canada Ltd. Web site, http://www.syncrude.ca/users/folder.asp?FolderID=5657; "Sustainability Report 2007," Syncrude Canada Ltd., http://www.syncrude.ca/users/folder.asp?FolderID=5713; "Hundreds of Ducks Trapped on Toxic Alberta Oilsands Pond," CBC News online, April 29, 2008, http://www.cbc.ca/canada/edmonton/story/2008/04/29/oilsands-birds.html; Hanneke Brooymans and Jim Farrell, "Syncrude Faces Scrutiny after Ducks Land on Toxic Pond," *National Post* online edition, April 30, 2008, http://www.nationalpost.com/news/canada/story.html?id=482931; and Jason Markusoff, "Ducks the New Symbol of Oil Sands Activism," *Edmonton Journal* online edition, May 4, 2008, http://www.canada.com/edmontonjournal/news/story.html?id=dc6561fd-eb68-4b36-96ba-77960387a911.

19. This case was prepared from public sources to provide material for classroom discussion, and it is not intended to illustrate either effective or ineffective response to a business and society managerial situation.

20. Note about Kabriole: If spelled with a "c" instead of a "k," the word refers to a curved, tapered leg, often with a decorative foot, characteristic of Chippendale and Queen Anne furniture and named after its resemblance to the leg of a leaping animal.

21. This case was prepared from public sources to provide material for classroom discussion, and it is not intended to illustrate either effective or ineffective response to a business and society managerial situation.

22. Juliet O'Neil and Andrew Mayeda, "Two Tories Defy Party's Asbestos Support," *National Post,* August 28, 2009, A4.

23. "About the Institute" at http://www.chrysotile.com/en/about.aspx.

24. "Chrysotile and Asbestos Amphiboles: Two Different Fibre Types," http://www.chrysotile.com/en/chrysotile/overview/default.aspx.

25. O'Neil and Mayeda.

26. Health Canada, "Consumer Product Safety—Asbestos," at http://www.hc-sc.gc.ca/cps-spc/house-domes/decor/construct_asbestos-amiante-eng.php.

27. Martin Mittelstaedt, "Motive Questioned in Failure to Disclose Asbestos Study, *The Globe and Mail,* April 22, 2009, A11.

28. "Asbestos Mortality: A Canadian Export," Editorial, *Canadian Medical Association Journal (CMAJ),* October 21, 2008, 886–887, and "Hazardous Hypocrisy," *The Economist,* October 15, 2008, 49.

29. World Health Organization, "Elimination of Asbestos-Related Diseases," at http://www.who.int/occupational_health/publications/asbestosrelateddiseases.pdf.

30. International Labour Organization, "Resolution Concerning Asbestos, 2006," at http://www.ilo.org/safework/normative/lang--en/WCMS_108556/index.htm.

31. "Canada's Policies on Chrysotile Asbestos Exports." Office of the Auditor General of Canada, 2006, available at http://www.oag-bvg.gc.ca/internet/English/pet_179_e_28915.html.

32. "Asbestos Mortality."

33. Tony Kirby, "Canada Accused of Hypocrisy over Asbestos Exports," *The Lancet,* Vol. 376, Issue 9757, December 2010, 1973–1974.

34. Canadian Auto Workers, "Ban Asbestos Campaign," at http://www.caw.ca/en/2184.htm.

35. Jennifer Wells, "Canada's Booming Asbestos Market," *The Star.com,* December 20, 2009, at http://www.thestar.com/news/world/india/article/741085--canada-s-booming-asbestos-market.

36. The International Ban Asbestos Secretariat (IBAS) at http://ibasecretariat.org/about.htm.

37. Asian Ban Asbestos Network (A-BAN), at http://www.anroav.org/

index2.php?option=com_content&do_pdf=1&id=83.

38. "Asbestos Mine in Bankruptcy But Hopes for Turnaround," *National Post,* January 5, 2012, FP2.

39. "Canadian Asbestos Production Grinds to Halt," *The Globe and Mail,* November 25, 2011, B7.

40. "Subsidizing Shame," *The Globe and Mail,* July 5, 2012, A12.

41. "Saying No to Canada's Asbestos," *National Post,* July 27, 2012, A14.

42. "Position Statement from the Joint Policy Committee Societies of Epidemiology," June 4, 2012, available at http://www.jpc-se.org/documents/01. JPC-SE-Position_Statement_on_Asbestos-June_4_2012-Summary_and_Appendix_A_English.pdf.

43. Steve Rennie, "Canada Keeps Asbestos Off UN Hazard List," *The Globe and Mail,* June 23, 2011, A8.

44. Robert Benzie, "Harper Defends Asbestos Exports Despite Cancer Risks," *Thestar.com,* http://www.thestar.com/news/canada/politics/article/980449--harper-defends-asbestos-exports-despite-cancer-risks, accessed August 10, 2012.

45. Parliament of Canada, Edited Hansard, October 31, 2011, http://www.parl.gc.ca/HousePublications/Publication.aspx?DocId=5214918&Language=E&Mode=1#OOB-4524285.

46. This case was prepared from public sources to provide material for classroom discussion, and it is not intended to illustrate either effective or ineffective response to a business and society managerial situation.

47. "What Is Listeriosis?" *Report of the Independent Investigator into the 2008 Listeriosis Outbreak,* Government of Canada, July 2009, 5–6. The report

will be referred to as the *Listeriosis Report* and is available at http://www.listeriosis-listeriose.investigation-enquete.gc.ca/lirs_rpt_e.pdf.

48. *Listeriosis Report,* Chapter 6, "How Did Events Unfold," 47–60.

49. "Corporate Information," Maple Leaf Foods Inc. Web site, http://www.mapleleaf.com/en/corporate/company-info/overview/.

50. This case was prepared from public sources to provide material for classroom discussion, and it is not intended to illustrate either effective or ineffective response to a business and society managerial situation.

51. "About Us," *Canada Gazette,* Government of Canada, http://www.gazette.gc.ca/cg-gc/about-sujet-eng.html.

52. *Canada Gazette,* Vol. 143, No. 8, February 21, 2009, http://www.gazette.gc.ca/rp-pr/p1/2009/2009-02-21/html/reg2-eng.html.

53. *Fisheries Act.* Government of Canada. R.S., c. F-14, s. 1, http://laws.justice.gc.ca/en/F-14/index.html.

54. "Metal Mining Effluent Regulations," Environment Canada, Government of Canada, http://gazette.gc.ca/rp-pr/p1/2010/2010-05-15/html/reg1-eng.html#REF10.

55. An order in council is a notice of an administrative decision originating with the Canadian federal cabinet and is approved by the Governor General. Orders in council can be notices of appointments or regulations or legislative orders in relation to and authorized by an existing act of parliament. Orders in council are published in the *Canada Gazette.*

56. "Towards Sustainable Mining Guiding Principles," Mining Association of Canada, http://www.

mining.ca/www/media_lib/TSM_Documents/principleseng.pdf.

57. "Sustainability Management: Environment," Vale, http://nickel.vale.com/sustainability/.

58. This case was prepared from public sources to provide material for classroom discussion, and it is not intended to illustrate either effective or ineffective response to a business and society managerial situation. Professor Wayne Murray is a fictional character.

59. This case was prepared from public sources to provide material for classroom discussion, and it is not intended to illustrate either effective or ineffective response to a business and society managerial situation.

60. *Generating Growth 2001 Annual Report,* Fortis Inc., 10–24.

61. Information for this section was obtained from "Chalillo Hydropower Project Summary," a brochure published by Fortis Inc., Belize Electric Company Ltd., and Belize Electricity Limited, October 2001, 10.

62. Ibid, 7, 10, 15–17.

63. Probe International, http://www.probeinternational.org/category/campaigns/dam-watch/fortis-belize.

64. Natural Resources Defense Council, http://www.nrdc.org/about/.

65. Fortis Inc. Web Site, News Article, November 1, 2002, http://www.fortisinc.com/News/Article.aspx?id=134.

66. Will Hilliard, "Dam Opponents Misled: Fortis," *The Telegram* (St. John's, NL), November 2, 2001, A3.

Glossary

A

Acid rain A generic term used for precipitation that contains an abnormally high concentration of sulphuric and nitric acid.

Active shareholders Those who participate in the governance to the full extent allowed by the law.

Anti-globalists Individuals and organizations that oppose globalization or are critical of it.

Audit committee Comprises members of the board of directors and oversees the internal and external accounting auditing function to ensure that financial statements accurately and appropriately represent the condition of the corporation and that regulated disclosures are made.

B

Beliefs The basic assumptions about the world in which an individual operates and how it works.

Board of directors A group of individuals elected by shareholders to govern or oversee the corporation's affairs.

Bribery Making questionable payments, or bribes, to government officials to influence their decisions.

Business citizenship Includes the responsibilities of corporate citizenship on a local and national basis and extends it to a global or universal scope.

Business ethics The rules, standards, codes, or principles that provide guidelines for morally right behaviour and truthfulness in specific situations.

Business sustainable development According to the IISD, "adopting business strategies and activities that meet the needs of the enterprise and its stakeholders today while protecting, sustaining, and enhancing the human and natural resources that will be needed in the future."

Business-to-business Commercial activity where one corporation sells goods or services to another corporation rather than to consumers.

C

Capitalism An economic system that allows for private ownership of the means of production (land, labour, and capital) and assumes that economic decision making is in the hands of individuals or enterprises who make decisions expecting to earn a profit.

Carbon capture and storage (CCS) Carbon emissions are captured and injected into underground formations.

Cause-related marketing The purchase of a particular product results in a donation being made by a corporation to a non-profit organization's program.

Charitable foundation A corporation or trust that is constituted and operated exclusively for charitable purposes.

Chosen instrument A corporation within a particular industry that receives some form of special attention from government through grants, loans, purchasing policy, or tax incentives.

Civil society The voluntary, community, and social organizations or institutions that contribute to the functioning of society but are usually not related to or supported by government.

Clean capitalism Defined by *Corporate Knights* magazine as "an economic system that incorporates the social, economic and ecological costs (and benefits) into our marketplace activities and the prices we pay."

Climate change (global warming) "The result of human activities altering the chemical composition of the atmosphere through the build-up of greenhouse gases that trap heat and reflect it back to the Earth's surface."

Code of conduct Explicitly states what appropriate behaviour is by identifying what is acceptable and unacceptable.

Code of ethics A statement of principles or values that guide behaviour by describing the general value system within which a corporation attempts to operate in a given environment.

Collaboration A meta-capability to establish and maintain relationships that allows the organization to tap into a powerful source of creative energy, a large pool of innovative ideas, and a wider network.

Commons Any resource used as though it belongs to all.

Community bond A debt instrument issued by a social enterprise to a network of supporters and used to finance or advance a specific proposal.

Community investment The efforts of a corporation to help develop a community and create economic opportunities through a variety of means, from donations to direct involvement in commercial undertakings.

Competition The condition in a market system in which many rival sellers seek to provide goods and services to many buyers.

Conflict of interest A situation in which an individual has a private or personal interest that is sufficient to appear to influence the objective exercise of that individual's duties.

Conscious capitalism The reorientation of business from a single focus on profits to emphasis being placed on integrity, higher standards of corporate behaviour, and inclusion of all stakeholders.

Consumer sovereignty The assumption existing in an economy that consumers have and exercise power over producers through the decisions they make in purchasing the goods and services provided by corporations.

Consumerism A social movement seeking to protect and augment the rights and powers of buyers in relation to sellers.

Corporate agenda The real or imagined alleged domination of public policy or government programs by corporations or business organizations in their own best interests.

Corporate citizenship Occurs when a corporation demonstrates that it takes into account its complete impact on society and the environment as well as its economic influence.

Corporate culture The complex set of values, beliefs, assumptions, and symbols that define the way in which an organization conducts its business.

Corporate ethics programs Some combination of a statement of values, code of conduct and/or ethics, ethics training, ethics audits and consulting services, ethics officers and committees, and ethics reporting systems.

Corporate governance The processes, structures, and relationships through which the shareholders, as represented by a board of directors, oversee the activities of the corporation.

Corporate philanthropy The effort of business to contribute to society socially; manifested by donations of money or goods and services in kind, voluntarism (where corporate employees work for social causes), and sponsorship of events that contribute to society.

Corporate public affairs The management function responsible for monitoring and interpreting the governmental environment of the corporation or industry and for managing the responses necessary to protect the interests of the corporation or industry.

Corporate reputation As defined by Fombrun, "a perceptual representation of a corporation's past actions and future prospects that describes the corporation's overall appeal to all of its

key constituents [stakeholders] when compared with other leading rivals."

Corporate social responsibility (CSR) The way a corporation achieves a balance among its economic, social, and environmental responsibilities in its operations so as to address shareholder and other stakeholder expectations.

Corporate social responsibility (CSR) reporting (sustainability reporting) A management function that documents the corporation's economic, ethical/social, and environmental responsibilities and initiatives, and communicates this information to relevant stakeholders.

Corporate sponsorship A partnership between a business sponsor and an event or a non-profit organization that is established for mutual benefit.

Corporate sustainability (CS) Corporate activities demonstrating the inclusion of social and environmental as well as economic responsibilities in business operations as they impact all stakeholders to ensure the long-term survival of the corporation.

Corporate voluntarism The time and talent employees commit to community organizations with support and/or consent from employers who recognize the value of such efforts to society.

Corporate welfare Any action by municipal, provincial, or federal governments that gives a specific corporation or an entire industry a benefit not offered to others.

Corruption According to Transparency International, "the abuse of entrusted power for private gain."

Creative capitalism Places the resolution of social needs as primary, instead of secondary to economic activity and performance.

Crisis A turning point, a crucial time, and a situation that has reached a critical point.

Crisis management An approach involving planning and removing much of the risk and uncertainty,

allowing the corporation to achieve more control over events.

D

Deontological ethics An approach to ethics that determines goodness or rightness from examining the acts, rather than from the consequences of the acts.

Deregulation The reduction of government influence or impact over the economy allowing for a freer and more efficient marketplace.

Discrimination The preferential (or less than preferential) treatment on bases not directly related to qualifications of the job or performance on the job.

Diversity management A voluntary initiative that goes beyond what is required by law to eliminate workplace discrimination.

Dual-class stock More than one type of share or stock with different voting rights and dividend payments is issued by a single corporation.

E

Economic freedoms Exist when the business system operates with few restrictions on its activities.

Economic globalization The integration of fragmented markets into a global economy.

Economic system An arrangement using land, labour, and capital to produce, distribute, and exchange goods and services to meet the needs and wants of people in society.

Ecosystem A biological community of interacting organisms and their physical environment.

Emissions trading A system whereby corporations set targets for greenhouse gas reduction; if one corporation cannot meet the target it purchases credits from those corporations that have met their targets.

Employee engagement The emotional and intellectual commitment of an individual or group to an

organization that supports building and sustaining business performance.

Employment equity The fair and equal treatment of employees.

Environmental ethic The set of values or principles that govern a corporation's practices relating to the environment.

Environmental non-governmental organizations (ENGOs) Groups that hold shared values or attitudes about the challenges confronting the natural environment and advocate for changes to improve the condition of the environment.

Equality of opportunity The assumption that all individuals or groups have an even chance at responding to some condition in society.

Ethic of caring Gives attention to specific individuals or stakeholders harmed or disadvantaged and their particular circumstances.

Ethic of justice Considers that moral decisions are based on the primacy of a single value: justice.

Ethical relativism The belief that ethical answers depend on the situation and no universal standards or rules exist to guide or evaluate morality.

Ethics audit A systematic effort to discover actual or potential unethical behaviour in an organization.

Ethics committee A group, comprising directors, managers, or staff, formed to monitor ethical standards and behaviour.

Ethics of business The rules, standards, codes, or principles that provide guidance for morally appropriate behaviour in managerial decision making relating to the operation of the business enterprise's and business's relationship with society.

Ethics officer An independent manager, reporting to the board of directors or CEO, who reviews complaints or information from anyone in the organization or any stakeholder, studies the situation, and recommends action if necessary.

Extended producer responsibility "An environmental policy approach in which a producer's responsibility, physical and/or financial, for a product is extended to the post-consumer stage of a product's life cycle."

F

Fair trade A term commonly used to identify products that are involved with sustainability purchasing; usually focuses on the beginning of the product chain.

Feminist ethics Diverse, gender-focused approaches to ethical theory and practice.

Fiduciary duties Obligations owed by directors to shareholders that are prescribed by laws or regulations.

For-benefit corporation Operates to make profits but also has a strong commitment to addressing social and environmental problems.

Free enterprise system An economic system characterized by ownership of private property by individuals and enterprises, the profit motive, a competitive market system, and a limited involvement by government. Also referred to as the *private enterprise system*.

G

Global Reporting Initiative (GRI) A non-profit organization that works toward a sustainable global economy by providing guidance in sustainability reporting.

Globalists Individuals and organizations that support globalization.

Globalization A process of decreasing constraints on the interactions among the nations and peoples of the world.

Governing system The processes, structures, and relationships through which decisions are made.

Greed The excessive desire to acquire or possess more, especially more material wealth, than one needs or deserves.

Green marketing Selling environmentally friendly goods and services to consumers.

Greenwashing Occurs when the corporation does not seriously address environmental issues but merely talks about how it does, or takes token actions rather than really solving the problem.

H

Human rights The fundamental rights and freedoms to which all individuals, groups, and societies are entitled.

I

Independent (or unrelated) director "A director who is free from any interest and any business or other relationship which could, or could reasonably be perceived to, materially interfere with the director's ability to act in the best interests of the corporation."

Individual rights ethic Relies on a list of agreed-upon rights for everyone that will be upheld by everyone and that becomes the basis for deciding what is right, just, or fair.

Individualism The view that the individual, and not society or a collective, is the paramount decision maker in society; assumes that the individual is inherently decent and rational.

Influence pathway Occurs where withholding and usage strategies could be performed by an ally of the stakeholder with whom the organization has a resource dependence.

Integrity The appropriateness of a corporation's behaviour and its adherence to moral guidelines acceptable to society such as honesty, fairness, and justice.

Integrity management An ethics program that combines a compliance-based and a values-based approach.

Intellectual property Umbrella term for patents, copyrights, trademarks, industrial designs, integrated circuit topographies, and plant breeders' rights.

International non-governmental organizations (INGOs) Groups that hold shared values and attitudes about the issues relating to globalization and advocate for changes to improve the conditions in developing countries.

Investors Individuals who personally hold equity interests for

investment purposes and who are not involved in the corporation as entrepreneurs or managers.

Issue A point in question or a matter that is in dispute where different views are held of what is or what ought to be corporate performance–based management or stakeholder expectations.

Issues management A systematic process by which the corporation can identify, evaluate, and respond to those economic, social, and environmental issues that may impact significantly upon it.

K

Kyoto Protocol An agreement formulated by the United Nations Framework Convention on Climate Change where countries agreed to reduce emissions of carbon dioxide and other greenhouse gases to 6 percent below 1990 levels by 2012.

L

Labour-supported investment funds (LSIFs) Funds that provide venture capital primarily to private corporations to create employment.

Laissez-faire capitalism An economic system operating with absolute minimum interference by the government in the affairs of business; government involvement is strictly limited to providing essential services such as police and fire protection.

Legitimacy A generalized perception or assumption that the actions of an entity are desirable, proper, or appropriate within some socially constructed system of norms, values, beliefs, and definition that is based on the individual, the organization, or society.

Libel chill Occurs when a business threatens legal action if a particular article or book is published.

Lobbying All attempts to influence directly or indirectly any government activity; includes any attempt to influence legislators, their staff members, public administrators, and members of regulatory agencies.

M

Market environmentalism Exists where economic incentives created by the market are more effective at protecting the environment than is government intervention.

Matrix mapping A technique of categorizing an organization's stakeholders by their influence according to two variables; usually involves plotting them on a two-by-two matrix.

Microfinance The provision of financial products, such as micro-credit, micro-insurance, and savings accounts, to persons living in areas of poverty without access to banking services.

Mission An enduring statement that specifies in broad, even philosophical, terms the organization's "reason for being" and what distinguishes it from similar organizations.

Mixed enterprises Those in which a government owns equity in a private-sector enterprise.

Moral reasoning A systematic approach to thinking or reasoning through the implications of a moral problem or issue.

Moral standards The means by which individuals judge their actions and the actions of others based upon accepted behaviour in society.

Mutual fund A pool of money from many individual investors that is invested on their behalf, usually in a specific kind of investment.

N

Non-governmental organization (NGO) Any group outside of the public and private sectors that holds shared values or attitudes about an issue confronting society.

Non-voting shares Common shares without voting privileges.

O

Offsets (emissions-reduction credits) Credits purchased from other corporations or organizations to mitigate greenhouse gases released into the environment.

Oligopoly A type of competition where the few sellers in an industry behave similarly.

Owners Those individuals or groups who have invested in a corporation in the form of equity or shares; usually referred to as shareholders.

Ozone Naturally occurring gas, formed from normal oxygen, that protects Earth by filtering out ultraviolet (UV) radiation from the Sun.

P

Passive shareholders Those who do not attempt to influence the affairs of the corporation even though they have a legal right to do so.

Personal virtues ethic An individual's or corporation's behaviour is based upon being a good person or corporate citizen with traits such as courage, honesty, wisdom, temperance, courage, fidelity, integrity, and generosity.

Philanthrocapitalism Draws upon modern business practices and an entrepreneurial spirit to get more from corporate social responsibility.

Pluralistic society One where influence or power is decentralized by dispersing it among a variety of institutions.

Policy development institution (think tank) An organization that researches and analyzes various important social, economic, and political issues confronting society.

Political globalization The process by which world power relationships change and there is a loss of sovereignty by the state.

Power A relationship among social actors in which one social actor, A, can get another social actor, B, to do something that B would not otherwise do.

Private equity firms Firms that manage large pools of money acquired from wealthy individuals or families and big institutions such as pension and mutual funds.

Privatization According to Heald, the "strengthening of the market at the expense of the state."

Profits The excess of revenues over expenses; closely associated with competition.

Public–private partnership (PPP) A cooperative venture between the public and private sectors, built on the expertise of each partner, that best meets clearly defined public needs through the appropriate allocation of resources, risks, and rewards.

R

Reputation management Any effort to enhance the corporation's image and good name; in the past, the focus of these efforts was on media and public relations and, to some extent, crisis management.

Resource dependence Exists when a stakeholder is supplying a resource and can exert some form of control over it.

Responsible corporation A business undertaking that responds to social, ethical, and environmental responsibilities in addition to its economic obligations.

Responsible enterprise system An economic system operating as a free enterprise system but incorporating the element of accountability.

Responsible investing Screening investments in corporations or mutual and pension funds for their response to social or ethical responsibilities as well as their financial or economic performance.

Restricted shares Involve some limit on voting, for example only one vote for every 10 or 100 shares owned; sometimes called "uncommon shares."

Right of private property The legal right to own and use economic goods, for example land and buildings.

S

Salience The degree to which managers give priority to competing stakeholder claims.

Self-interest ethic Individuals or corporations set their own standards for judging the ethical implications of their actions; only the individual's values and standards are the basis for actions.

Self-regulation Regulation imposed by the corporation or industry and not by the government or market forces.

Self-regulatory organizations (SROs) Industry groups that are delegated or designated a regulatory function including the development, use, and enforcement of standards.

Service-learning A method of teaching, learning, and reflecting, combining classroom learning with service to the community either locally or in developing countries.

Shared value The idea that economic value to companies can be obtained by creating social value.

Shareholder democracy The exercise of power by owners to ensure they are treated fairly and enjoy equally the privileges and duties of ownership.

Social auditing A systematic assessment that identifies, measures, evaluates, reports, and monitors the effects an enterprise has on society that are not covered in the traditional financial reports.

Social capital Any aspect of a corporation's organizational arrangements that creates value and facilitates the actions of stakeholders within and external to the corporation.

Social enterprise A model of business operation where some or all profits are deliberately used to further social aims.

Social entrepreneur An innovative, visionary leader of a non-profit or for-profit business with real-world problem-solving creativity and a high awareness for ethical, social, and environmental considerations.

Social entrepreneurship The activities undertaken to enhance social wealth in some innovative way.

Social impact management Defined by the Aspen Institute as "the field of inquiry at the intersection of business needs and wider societal concerns that reflects and respects the complex interdependency between the two."

Social licence The privilege of operating in society with minimal formalized restrictions—that is, legislation, regulation, or market requirements—based on maintaining public trust by doing what is acceptable to stakeholders in the business and society relationship.

Social media Online technologies and practices that people use to share opinions, insights, experiences, and perspectives.

Social or cultural globalization The emergence of a worldwide cultural system.

Social venture philanthropy The investment of human and financial resources by corporations in non-profit community development agencies to generate a social return instead of only a financial one.

Spirituality An individual's sense of peace or purpose with him/herself and the connection to others and even nature that provides meaning to life and a sense of one's self.

Stakeholder An individual or group who can influence and/or is influenced by the achievement of an organization's purpose.

Stakeholder capitalism An economic system in which corporations accept broader obligations beyond financial ones for shareholders. Corporations are expected to balance the interests of shareholders with those of other stakeholders in the business system and to behave with greater social responsibility and be sensitive to the ethical consequences of their actions.

Stakeholder engagement Efforts by a corporation to understand and involve relevant individuals, groups, or organizations by considering their moral concerns in strategic and operational initiatives.

Stakeholder management capability The ability of managers to identify stakeholders and their influence, to develop the organizational practices to understand stakeholders, and to undertake direct contact with stakeholders.

Standard environmentalism Occurs when government regulation is a necessary remedy for the market's failure to provide enough environmental amenities.

State capitalism An economic system in which governments manipulate market outcomes for political and social purposes.

Statement of values A description of the beliefs, principles, and basic assumptions about what is desirable or worth striving for in an organization.

Strategic giving An attempt to rationalize the shareholder interest with corporate philanthropy where the corporation benefits directly from the funds given.

Strategic management The process through which a corporation establishes its mission and objectives, analyzes the environment and resource capabilities in order to formulate strategy, creates the organizational systems and processes needed to implement the strategy, and devises mechanisms for evaluating performance.

Supply (or value) chain The route that a product travels from the procurement of raw materials, the transformation into intermediate goods and then final products, and the delivery to consumers through a distribution system to its ultimate disposal by the consumer.

Supranational institution An international organization that transcends national boundaries, where the member states share in decision making on particular issues pertaining to the members.

Sustainability purchasing According to Industry Canada, "the acquisition of goods and services ('products') in a way that gives preference to suppliers that generate positive social and environmental outcomes. It integrates sustainability considerations into product selection so that impacts on society and the environment are minimized throughout the full life cycle of the product."

Sustainability strategy A plan that views economic, ethical, social, and environmental responsibilities more intensively and integrates corporate social responsibility (CSR) into all facets of the corporation's operations.

Sustainable development Development ensuring that the use of resources and the impact on the environment today does not damage prospects for the use of resources or the environment by future generations.

T

Tax expenditures or tax credits Potential revenues the government chooses not to collect; any form of incentive or relief granted through the tax system rather than through government expenditures.

Teleological ethics An approach to ethics that focuses on outcomes, or results of actions.

Triple bottom line The evaluation of a corporation's performance according to a summary of the economic, social or ethical, and environmental value the corporation adds or destroys.

Triple-E (economic, ethical, and environmental) bottom line Evaluates a corporation's performance according to a summary of the economic, social, and environmental value the corporation adds or destroys.

U

Universal rules ethic Ensures that managers or corporations have the same moral obligations in morally similar situations.

Urgency The degree to which the stakeholder's claim or relationship calls for immediate attention; exists when a claim or relationship is of a time-sensitive nature and when that claim or relationship is important or critical to the stakeholder.

Usage strategies The approach when the stakeholder continues to supply a resource but specifies how it will be used.

Utilitarian ethic Focuses on the distribution of benefits and harms to all stakeholders with the view to maximizing benefits.

V

Value judgments Subjective evaluations of what is considered important; based on how managers intuitively feel about the goodness or rightness of various goals.

Values The basic assumptions about which ideals are considered desirable or worth striving for.

Venture capital company A type of private equity firm that usually acquires part ownership of business enterprises for which they provide financial and management assistance.

Virtue ethics An approach to ethics that emphasizes the individual's character or identity, and focuses on being instead of doing.

Vision A statement of what the corporation wants to become or where it wants to be at some date in the future.

W

Waste management "Disposal, processing, controlling, recycling and reusing the solid, liquid, and gaseous wastes of plants, animals, humans and other organisms."

Whistleblowing An act of voluntary disclosure of inappropriate behaviour or decisions to persons in positions of authority in an organization.

Withholding strategies The approach when the stakeholder discontinues providing a resource to an organization with the intention of changing a certain behaviour.

Work ethic A set of values that holds that work is important to members of society insofar as work influences the qualities or character of individuals; that work is a purposeful activity requiring an expenditure of energy with some sacrifice of leisure; that some gain, usually monetary, is involved; and that through work a person not only contributes to society but also becomes a better individual.

Worker capitalism Describes employee ownership as workers are turned into capitalists through stock ownership.

Index